Lecture Notes in Computer Science 11634

Commenced Publication in 1973
Founding and Former Series Editors:
Gerhard Goos, Juris Hartmanis, and Jan van Leeuwen

More information about this series at http://www.springer.com/series/7410

Xingming Sun · Zhaoqing Pan ·
Elisa Bertino (Eds.)

Artificial Intelligence and Security

5th International Conference, ICAIS 2019
New York, NY, USA, July 26–28, 2019
Proceedings, Part III

 Springer

Editors
Xingming Sun (iD)
Nanjing University of Information
Science and Technology
Nanjing, China

Zhaoqing Pan (iD)
Nanjing University of Information
Science and Technology
Nanjing, China

Elisa Bertino (iD)
Purdue University
West Lafayette, IN, USA

ISSN 0302-9743   ISSN 1611-3349 (electronic)
Lecture Notes in Computer Science
ISBN 978-3-030-24270-1   ISBN 978-3-030-24271-8 (eBook)
https://doi.org/10.1007/978-3-030-24271-8

LNCS Sublibrary: SL4 – Security and Cryptology

This Springer imprint is published by the registered company Springer Nature Switzerland AG
The registered company address is: Gewerbestrasse 11, 6330 Cham, Switzerland

Preface

The 5th International Conference on Artificial Intelligence and Security (ICAIS 2019), formerly called the International Conference on Cloud Computing and Security (ICCCS), was held during July 26–28, 2019, at New York University, New York, USA. Over the past four years, ICAIS has become a leading conference for researchers and engineers to share their latest results from research, development, and applications in the fields of artificial intelligence and information security.

We used the Microsoft Conference Management Toolkits (CMT) system to manage the submission and review processes of ICAIS 2019. We received 1529 submissions from 20 countries and regions, including USA, Canada, UK, Italy, Ireland, Japan, Russia, France, Australia, South Korea, South Africa, India, Iraq, Kazakhstan, Indonesia, Vietnam, Ghana, China, Taiwan, and Macao, etc. The submissions cover the areas of artificial intelligence, big data, cloud computing and security, information hiding, IoT security, multimedia forensics, encryption and cybersecurity, and so on. We thank our Technical Program Committee members and external reviewers for their efforts in reviewing papers and providing valuable comments to the authors. From the total of 1,529 submissions, and based on at least three reviews per submission, the Program Chairs decided to accept 230 papers, yielding an acceptance rate of 15%. The volume of the conference proceedings contains all the regular, poster, and workshop papers.

The conference program was enriched by a series of keynote presentations, and the keynote speakers included: Nasir Memon, New York University, USA; Edward Colbert, Virginia Tech Hume Center for National Security and Technology, USA; Quanyan Zhu, New York University, USA; Zhihua Xia, Nanjing University of Information Science and Technology, China; Tom Masino, TradeWeb, USA; etc. We thank them for their wonderful speeches.

There were 45 workshops organized at ICAIS 2019, covering all the hot topics in artificial intelligence and security. We would like to take this moment to express our sincere appreciation for the contribution of all the workshop chairs and their participants. We would like to extend our sincere thanks to all authors who submitted papers to ICAIS 2019 and to all Program Committee members. It was a truly great experience to work with such talented and hard-working researchers. We also appreciate the external reviewers for assisting the Program Committee members in their particular areas of expertise. Moreover, we want to thank our sponsors: Nanjing University of Information Science and Technology, Springer, New York University, IEEE Broadcast Technology Society (BTS) Nanjing Chapter, ACM China, Michigan State University, Taiwan Cheng Kung University, Taiwan Dong Hwa University, Taiwan Providence University, Nanjing University of Aeronautics and Astronautics, State Key Laboratory of Integrated Services Networks, and the National Nature Science Foundation of China.

May 2019

Xingming Sun
Zhaoqing Pan
Elisa Bertino

Organization

General Chairs

Yun Q. Shi   New Jersey Institute of Technology, USA
Mauro Barni   University of Siena, Italy
Xingang You   China Information Technology Security Evaluation
     Center, China
Elisa Bertino   Purdue University, USA
Quanyan Zhu   New York University, USA
Xingming Sun   Nanjing University of Information Science
     and Technology, China

Technical Program Chairs

Aniello Castiglione   University of Salerno, Italy
Yunbiao Guo   China Information Technology Security Evaluation
     Center, China
Suzanne K. McIntosh   New York University, USA
Zhihua Xia   Nanjing University of Information Science
     and Technology, China
Victor S. Sheng   University of Central Arkansas, USA

Publication Chair

Zhaoqing Pan   Nanjing University of Information Science
     and Technology, China

Workshop Chair

Baowei Wang   Nanjing University of Information Science
     and Technology, China

Organization Chairs

Edward Wong   New York University, USA
Zhangjie Fu   Nanjing University of Information Science
     and Technology, China

Technical Program Committee

Saeed Arif   University of Algeria, Algeria
Anthony Ayodele   University of Maryland University College, USA

Zhifeng Bao	Royal Melbourne Institute of Technology University, Australia
Zhiping Cai	National University of Defense Technology, China
Ning Cao	Qingdao Binhai University, China
Paolina Centonze	Iona College, USA
Chin-chen Chang	Feng Chia University, Taiwan, China
Han-Chieh Chao	Taiwan Dong Hwa University, Taiwan, China
Bing Chen	Nanjing University of Aeronautics and Astronautics, China
Hanhua Chen	Huazhong University of Science and Technology, China
Xiaofeng Chen	Xidian University, China
Jieren Cheng	Hainan University, China
Lianhua Chi	IBM Research Center, Australia
Kim-Kwang Raymond Choo	University of Texas at San Antonio, USA
Ilyong Chung	Chosun University, South Korea
Robert H. Deng	Singapore Management University, Singapore
Jintai Ding	University of Cincinnati, USA
Xinwen Fu	University of Central Florida, USA
Zhangjie Fu	Nanjing University of Information Science and Technology, China
Moncef Gabbouj	Tampere University of Technology, Finland
Ruili Geng	Spectral MD, USA
Song Guo	Hong Kong Polytechnic University, SAR China
Jinsong Han	Xi'an Jiaotong University, China
Mohammad Mehedi Hassan	King Saud University, Saudi Arabia
Debiao He	Wuhan University, China
Russell Higgs	University College Dublin, Ireland
Dinh Thai Hoang	University Technology Sydney, Australia
Wien Hong	Nanfang College of Sun Yat-Sen University, China
Chih-Hsien Hsia	National Ilan University, Taiwan, China
Robert Hsu	Chung Hua University, Taiwan, China
Yongjian Hu	South China University of Technology, China
Qiong Huang	South China Agricultural University, China
Xinyi Huang	Fujian Normal University, China
Yongfeng Huang	Tsinghua University, China
Zhiqiu Huang	Nanjing University of Aeronautics and Astronautics, China
Patrick C. K. Hung	University of Ontario Institute of Technology, Canada
Farookh Hussain	University of Technology Sydney, Australia
Hai Jin	Huazhong University of Science and Technology, China
Sam Tak Wu Kwong	City University of Hong Kong, SAR China
Chin-Feng Lai	Taiwan Cheng Kung University, Taiwan, China
Loukas Lazos	University of Arizona, USA

Sungyoung Lee	Kyung Hee University, South Korea
Bin Li	Shenzhen University, China
Chengcheng Li	University of Cincinnati, USA
Feifei Li	Utah State University, USA
Jiguo Li	Hohai University, China
Jin Li	Guangzhou University, China
Jing Li	Rutgers University, USA
Kuan-Ching Li	Providence University, Taiwan, China
Peng Li	University of Aizu, Japan
Xiaolong Li	Beijing Jiaotong University, China
Yangming Li	University of Washington, USA
Luming Liang	Uber Technology, USA
Haixiang Lin	Leiden University, The Netherlands
Xiaodong Lin	University of Ontario Institute of Technology, Canada
Zhenyi Lin	Verizon Wireless, USA
Alex Liu	Michigan State University, USA
Guangchi Liu	Stratifyd Inc., USA
Guohua Liu	Donghua University, China
Joseph Liu	Monash University, Australia
Mingzhe Liu	Chengdu University of Technology, China
Pingzeng Liu	Shandong Agricultural University, China
Quansheng Liu	University of South Brittany, France
Xiaodong Liu	Edinburgh Napier University, UK
Yuling Liu	Hunan University, China
Zhe Liu	University of Waterloo, Canada
Wei Lu	Sun Yat-sen University, China
Daniel Xiapu Luo	Hong Kong Polytechnic University, SAR China
Junzhou Luo	Southeast University, China
Xiangyang Luo	Zhengzhou Science and Technology Institute, China
Suzanne K. McIntosh	New York University, USA
Nasir Memon	New York University, USA
Sangman Moh	Chosun University, South Korea
Yi Mu	University of Wollongong, Australia
Jiangqun Ni	Sun Yat-sen University, China
Rongrong Ni	Beijing Jiao Tong University, China
Rafal Niemiec	University of Information Technology and Management, Poland
Zemin Ning	Wellcome Trust Sanger Institute, UK
Shaozhang Niu	Beijing University of Posts and Telecommunications, China
Srikant Ojha	Sharda University, India
Jeff Z. Pan	University of Aberdeen, UK
Wei Pang	University of Aberdeen, UK
Rong Peng	Wuhan University, China
Chen Qian	University of California Santa Cruz, USA
Zhenxing Qian	Fudan University, China

Chuan Qin	University of Shanghai for Science and Technology, China
Jiaohua Qin	Central South University of Forestry and Technology, China
Yanzhen Qu	Colorado Technical University, USA
Zhiguo Qu	Nanjing University of Information Science and Technology, China
Kui Ren	State University of New York, USA
Arun Kumar Sangaiah	VIT University, India
Zheng-guo Sheng	University of Sussex, UK
Robert Simon Sherratt	University of Reading, UK
Yun Q. Shi	New Jersey Institute of Technology, USA
Frank Y. Shih	New Jersey Institute of Technology, USA
Biao Song	King Saud University, Saudi Arabia
Guang Sun	Hunan University of Finance and Economics, China
Jiande Sun	Shandong Normal University, China
Jianguo Sun	Harbin University of Engineering, China
Jianyong Sun	Xi'an Jiaotong University, China
Krzysztof Szczypiorski	Warsaw University of Technology, Poland
Tsuyoshi Takagi	Kyushu University, Japan
Shanyu Tang	University of West London, UK
Xianping Tao	Nanjing University, China
Jing Tian	National University of Singapore, Singapore
Yoshito Tobe	Aoyang University, Japan
Cezhong Tong	Washington University in St. Louis, USA
Pengjun Wan	Illinois Institute of Technology, USA
Cai-Zhuang Wang	Ames Laboratory, USA
Ding Wang	Peking University, China
Guiling Wang	New Jersey Institute of Technology, USA
Honggang Wang	University of Massachusetts-Dartmouth, USA
Jian Wang	Nanjing University of Aeronautics and Astronautics, China
Jie Wang	University of Massachusetts Lowell, USA
Jing Wang	Changsha University of Science and Technology, China
Jinwei Wang	Nanjing University of Information Science and Technology, China
Liangmin Wang	Jiangsu University, China
Ruili Wang	Massey University, New Zealand
Xiaojun Wang	Dublin City University, Ireland
Xiaokang Wang	St. Francis Xavier University, Canada
Zhaoxia Wang	A-Star, Singapore
Sheng Wen	Swinburne University of Technology, Australia
Jian Weng	Jinan University, China
Edward Wong	New York University, USA
Eric Wong	University of Texas at Dallas, USA

Q. M. Jonathan Wu	University of Windsor, Canada
Shaoen Wu	Ball State University, USA
Shuangkui Xia	Beijing Institute of Electronics Technology and Application, China
Lingyun Xiang	Changsha University of Science and Technology, China
Shijun Xiang	Jinan University, China
Yang Xiang	Deakin University, Australia
Yang Xiao	The University of Alabama, USA
Haoran Xie	The Education University of Hong Kong, SAR China
Naixue Xiong	Northeastern State University, USA
Xin Xu	Wuhan University of Science and Technology, China
Wei Qi Yan	Auckland University of Technology, New Zealand
Aimin Yang	Guangdong University of Foreign Studies, China
Ching-Nung Yang	Taiwan Dong Hwa University, Taiwan, China
Chunfang Yang	Zhengzhou Science and Technology Institute, China
Fan Yang	University of Maryland, USA
Guomin Yang	University of Wollongong, Australia
Ming Yang	Southeast University, China
Qing Yang	University of North Texas, USA
Yuqiang Yang	Bohai University, USA
Ming Yin	Purdue University, USA
Xinchun Yin	Yangzhou University, China
Shaodi You	Australian National University, Australia
Kun-Ming Yu	Chung Hua University, Taiwan, China
Yong Yu	University of Electronic Science and Technology of China, China
Gonglin Yuan	Guangxi University, China
Mingwu Zhang	Hubei University of Technology, China
Wei Zhang	Nanjing University of Posts and Telecommunications, China
Weiming Zhang	University of Science and Technology of China, China
Xinpeng Zhang	Fudan University, China
Yan Zhang	Simula Research Laboratory, Norway
Yanchun Zhang	Victoria University, Australia
Yao Zhao	Beijing Jiaotong University, China
Linna Zhou	University of International Relations, China

Organizing Committee

Xianyi Chen	Nanjing University of Information Science and Technology, China
Yadang Chen	Nanjing University of Information Science and Technology, China
Beijing Chen	Nanjing University of Information Science and Technology, China

Huajun Huang	Central South University of Forestry and Technology, China
Jielin Jiang	Nanjing University of Information Science and Technology, China
Zilong Jin	Nanjing University of Information Science and Technology, China
Yan Kong	Nanjing University of Information Science and Technology, China
Yiwei Li	Columbia University, USA
Yuling Liu	Hunan University, China
Lirui Qiu	Nanjing University of Information Science and Technology, China
Zhiguo Qu	Nanjing University of Information Science and Technology, China
Guang Sun	Hunan University of Finance and Economics, China
Huiyu Sun	New York University, USA
Le Sun	Nanjing University of Information Science and Technology, China
Jian Su	Nanjing University of Information Science and Technology, China
Lina Tan	Hunan University of Commerce, China
Qing Tian	Nanjing University of Information Science and Technology, China
Yuan Tian	King Saud University, Saudi Arabia
Zuwei Tian	Hunan First Normal University, China
Xiaoliang Wang	Hunan University of Science and Technology, China
Lingyun Xiang	Changsha University of Science and Technology, China
Lizhi Xiong	Nanjing University of Information Science and Technology, China
Leiming Yan	Nanjing University of Information Science and Technology, China
Hengfu Yang	Hunan First Normal University, China
Li Yu	Nanjing University of Information Science and Technology, China
Zhili Zhou	Nanjing University of Information Science and Technology, China

Contents – Part III

Information Hiding

IoT Security

Multimedia Forensics

Encryption and Cybersecurity

Cloud Computing and Security

Evaluation and Testing of PCI Express 8-Gbps Re-timer in Storage Server

Yinghua Zhang[1,2]([✉]) [iD], Lei Wang[1] [iD], Jian Liu[1], Yunfeng Peng[1], Jiapeng Pu[2], and Guozhong Sun[3]

[1] School of Computer and Communication Engineering,
University of Science and Technology Beijing,
Beijing 100083, People's Republic of China
82774807@qq.com, zhangyh@sugon.com, ustb_wl16@163.com,
{liujian,pengyf}@ustb.edu.cn
[2] Dawning Information Industry Co., Ltd.,
Beijing 100193, People's Republic of China
pujp@sugon.com
[3] Dawning Information Industry Chengdu Co., Ltd.,
Chengdu 610213, People's Republic of China
sungzh@sugon.com

Abstract. A long channel backplane PCI Express (PCI-E) 8-Gbps transmission technology for next-generation high-speed I/O applications is adopted in a scale-out x86 CPU based server. Traditional Red river technology has the disadvantage of severe random jitter, crosstalk, power supply noise and high Bit Error Ratio. High speed signal simulation technology is applied here and Re-timer chip is selected for the long distance transmission of 8-Gbps PCI-E Gen3 signals. The signal transmission model is built, based on which the simulation tool is used to optimize design of connector via, cascade connection S parameter model of all sub-links and connectors. The whole S parameter model of PCI-E link is built, followed by which the PCB boards of the system are designed. CTLE and DFE parameters of Re-timer can be tuned to achieve desirable Bit Error Ratio and Contour Eye Diagram. The electrical properties of the whole PCI-E physical link are measured using High-Speed Digital Oscilloscope and BERT (Bit Error Ratio Tester) Scope. Prospective results are achieved and robustness of the server system is evaluated.

Keywords: PCI-E · Re-timer · Insertion loss · Equalization · Bit Error Ratio · Eye-diagram

1 Introduction

According to IDC report, in 2018H1, the capacity of storage market worldwide reached 111.8EB, representing 70.7% YOY growth. Meanwhile the factory revenue of storage market reached 13.2 billion, representing 21.3% YOY growth.

This work is supported by Sugon Program of Intelligent Manufacturing Standardization of Ministry of Industry and Information Technology (No. 2016ZXFB01001).

IDC forecasts the storage market will continue to show health growth (CAGR growth is 9.8%) in the next five years, and the capacity may reach around 90EB in total [1]. Challenges also exists, Telecom will grow slowly because of the carriers begin to use scale-out x86 server to replace traditional external disk storage in related applications. Interconnect speeds in data storage systems based on the Serial Attached SCSI (SAS) point-to-point bus protocol has increased to 24-Gbps by 2016 [2]. InfiniBand protocol is used predominantly for rack-to-rack communication in enterprise data centres and high-performance computers (HPC) is already moving to 25-Gbps per lane in 2016 [3]. Following this trend, server and storage suppliers in Chinese mainland have designed 4U server with 24 or 36 HDDs based on Intel x86 platform (known as x86 storage server). These x86 storage servers are similar in form and function. The density and performance cannot fulfil the increasing demands of the market and the customers. So much higher density x86 storage server with PB or EB capacity in one single chassis is to be designed. The Re-timer solution of 8-Gbps PCI-E Gen3 signal is discussed in this paper, and a kind of scale-out x86 server with PB capacity is designed.

2   Challenges and Problems

In this scale-out x86 server system, up to 80 3.5-in. HDDs and 8 2.5-in. HDDs are integrated in 5U space. The high speed signal topology of the system is shown in Fig. 1. There are four black slots in the topology, which support standard 8-Gbps PCI-E Gen3 devices.

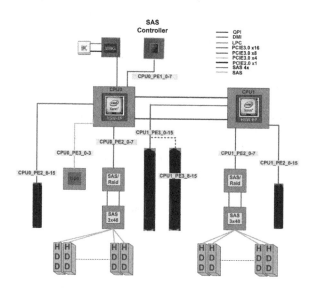

Fig. 1. High speed signal topology of the storage server.

PCI-E signals are transmitted from Intel Haswell-EP CPU to edge of motherboard, and then connected to I/O expander module through backplane. At last the signals are connected to standard PCI-E slots, as shown in the Fig. 2. Standard PCI-E devices can be plugged into these slots to achieve particular applications. Just as the whole physical signal transmission link depicts, the PCI-E trace length of motherboard is 12.8 in., and the backplane is about 8 in., and the I/O expander module is 10.9 in. So the total length of transmission is 31.7 in., which exceeds PCI-E specification with standard FR4 substance. Meanwhile, signals transmit through high speed connectors for three times, which also causes attenuation.

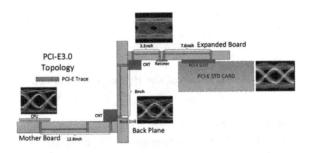

Fig. 2. PCI-E Gen3 signal transmission model.

According to the PCI Express Base Specifications R3.1, the whole attenuation of PCI-E link insertion loss, known as SDD21, is limited to -20 ± 2 dB@4 GHz [4,5], as shown in Fig. 3. This brings great challenge to the system design.

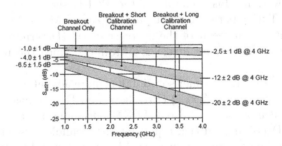

Fig. 3. Insertion loss guideline for calibration/breakout channels.

In scale of system design, manufacturing processes, cost optimization and several other conditions, N4000-13SI (DK = 3.4, Df = 0.010) is chosen as the PCB material based on adequate simulation and feasibility demonstration.

During the phase of PCB layout design, ANSYS HFSS and Designer are used to optimise design of connector via, cascade connection S parameter models of all sub-links and connectors. Finally, the whole S parameter model of PCI-E link is

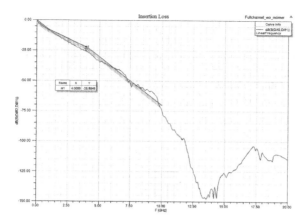

Fig. 4. Insertion loss of the PCI express channel.

established. The insertion loss curve (the SDD21 parameter) of the longest PCI-E link is shown in Fig. 4. The SDD21 reaches up to -25.8546 dB@4 GHz. Obviously, traditional method of increasing system performance by selecting ultra low loss materials with lower dielectric constant (dk) and dissipation factors (Df) cannot reach the goal of below -20 ± 2 dB@4 GHz. A new effective solution is essential to be researched.

3 Simulation and Re-timer Solutions

Signal Redriver technology is always used in traditional solutions of signal compensation. However, in this technology, the PCI-E signals are amplified linearly by tuning TxEQ parameters in physical layer. Meanwhile, the physical link is compensated as a result of the decrease of DJ (Deterministic Jitter) [6]. Inevitably, more RJ (Random Jitter) is introduced since the use of Redriver chip.

In comparison, PCI-E Re-timer solution has more advantages. The FIR filter is used in Tx link to achieve TxEQ (Pre-shoot and De-emphasis) function and implement linear compensation. Also, CTLE (Continuous Time Linear Equalization) and DFE (Decision Feedback Equalization) technology is integrated in Rx link to revise non-linear attenuation caused by impedance discontinuity factors such as via, connectors, and PCB trace. Re-timer circuit can provide reference clock and CDR (Clock Data Recovery) module, which receives analog signal and retransmit it after digital conversion. This process not only reduces DJ of PCI-E signal but also reset RJ [7,8]. Besides, Re-timer has the advantage of protocol aware feature. During the process of PCI-E training, the optimal TxEQ and Rx CTLE parameter can be searched through self-adaptive method to achieve the optimal BER [5].

According to the above description, to solve the complex problem of excessive attenuation for the SDD21 parameter, IDT T0816P 8-Lane(16 Channels)

Re-timer is creatively introduced to the I/O expander backplane during the phase of prototype design, as shown in Fig. 2. TxEQ and CTLE/DFE parameters of signal channel are tuned to compensate high frequency distortion caused by link attenuation, which can avoid Eye-diagram closure in Rx end and improve design margin of the system [9].

During the phase of prototype design, channel equalization module is inserted into the link to simulate the actual system. In Fig. 5, the results of simulation indicate that the link with Re-timer could comply with the requirement of PCI-SIG PCI-E Gen3 specification. In front of the Re-timer chip, the loss is -19.4324 dB@4 GHz for the 24.1-in. link circuit, as shown in Fig. 5(a). The downstream of the Re-timer chip, the loss is -9.4383 dB@4 GHz for the 7.6-in. link circuit, as shown in Fig. 5(b). Both the loss values are below -20 ± 2 dB@4 GHz acknowledged by the PCI-SIG organization [10].

(a) The insertion loss of 24.1-inch trace

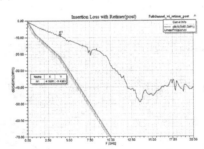

(b) The insertion loss of 7.6-inch trace

Fig. 5. The insertion loss with equalization technology.

TxEQ Coefficient Space Triangular Matrix is adopted during the process of system debug, as shown in Fig. 6. Horizontal axis stands for C-1 of 3 tap FIR filter, which is to adjust Pre-shoot parameter. Vertical axis stands for C+1, which is to adjust De-emphasis parameter. BER is abbreviation of Bit Error Ratio. Green squares indicate that the BER is below 10–12. The optimal TxEQ equalization pair can be quickly located through traversal of different area of Pre-shoot and De-emphasis [5,11].

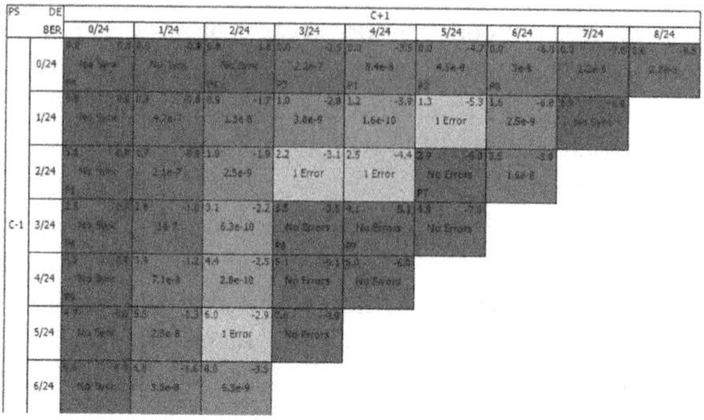

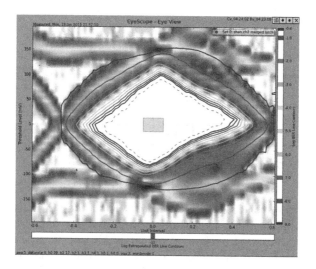

Fig. 6. TxEQ coefficient space triangular matrix. (Color figure online)

In the process of adjusting Rx CTLE and DFE parameter, Rx equalization parameter gained through simulation as shown in Fig. 5 is used as the reference setup of RxEQ parameter of the T0816P Re-timer [8]. The parameter can be slightly adjusted by integrated On-chip diagnostics function in On-die oscilloscope. The 4 Point Eye can be gained through process of odd lane (1, 3, 5, 7) or even lane (2, 4, 6, 8) link signal, and the parameter of Eye Height and Eye Width can be read by I2C or JTAG, based on which the Eye Contour is drawn. Figure 7 shows the actual Bit Error Ratio Contour Eye of the PCI-E signal through 31.7 in. transmission and tuned by the Re-timer chip. It is obvious that the physical link equalized by Re-timer can fulfil the requirement of PCI-E Eye Opening parameter.

Fig. 7. Bit Error Ratio contour eye diagram.

4   Results and Validation

To evaluate the robustness of the server system before new production introduction, it is essential to validate the electrical properties of the whole PCI-E
physical link.

(a) Tektronix DSA72004C (20 GHz, 100GS/s) Oscilloscope associated with ver-
    sion 3.0 CLB (Compliance Load Board) provided by PCI-SIG organization is
    used to perform compliance measurement to the PCI-E slot of I/O expander
    backplane.
(b) Tektronix BSA175C BERTScope associated with DPP125C and CLB is used
    to perform Stressed Eye Calibration and Receiver Testing by cascade the
    PCI-E link of the server system into the BERT Scope [5].

Compliance measurement of Tx port shows that the Tx link electrical properties of PCI-E slot of I/O expander backplane have been greatly improved.
The measured value complies with PCI-E Gen3 CEM3.0 Specification [12]. Eye
Height exceeds 35 mv, Eye Width exceeds 37.5 ps, and ample margin is reserved
as shown in Fig. 8.

Since both the Re-timer chip and Intel Haswell CPU support PCI-E Loop-
back Compliance Mode, the actual working condition of PCI-E link can be
simulated through injecting Random Jitter and Deterministic Jitter into the
Data+/Data-signal and stressed voltage testing can be performed. As shown in
Table 1, the whole PCI-E link complies with BER requirement of PCI-E specification [13–15].

Table 1. Test settings and patterns.

Item	Setting
PG	RJ 3.4 pS-RMS, SJ 12.5 pS, DMSI 10.5 mV
SSC	SSC Disabled
DPP	Ampl Setting: 512.0
ED	UserGrabNGo
CR	Not Present
PG pattern	Empty A-Modified Compliance B_lane0.ram
Det pattern	UserGrabNGo

Two storage server systems based on Intel E5-2600 series processors are used
to evaluate the performance and efficiency of the transmission of PCI-E bus. Each
server is equipped with an InfiniBand card, and the two servers are connected
with Fibre optic cable. The protocol used in the transmission is FDR (4 lane of
14.0625 Gbps Date Rate) with a theoretical rate of 56-Gbps. The transmission
bandwidths with different block sizes are shown in Fig. 9. A Rapid Direct Memory Access (RDMA) bidirectional Write test is accomplished and the biggest

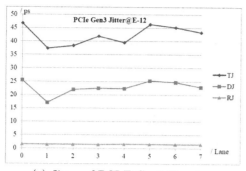

(a) Jitter of PCI-E Gen3 Signal

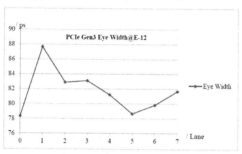

(b) Eye Width of PCI-E Gen3 Signal

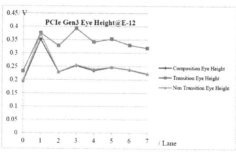

(c) Eye Height of PCI-E Gen3 Signal

Fig. 8. The measured value of PCI-E Gen3 signal.

Table 2. Stressed eye calibration and receiver testing results.

Item	Value	Unit
Amplitude	800	mV
DMSI	10.5	mV
Eye height	50	mV
Eye width	45	ps
RJ	3.4	ps
SJ	12.5	ps

achieved bandwidth with block size of 1024 bytes is 9293.05 MB/s. The actual efficiency ratio can reach up to 90%, which completely fulfil the requirement in the field of engineering applications (Table 2).

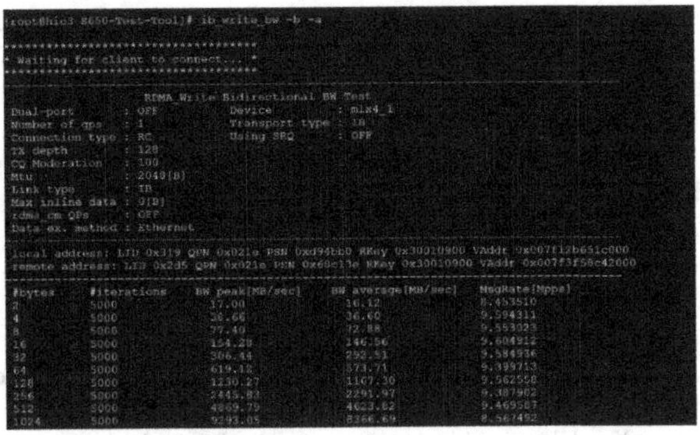

Fig. 9. Point to point RDMA bidirectional writing test between two server systems.

5 Conclusions

The paper describes a novel PCI-E Re-timer solution for insertion loss reduction, in which the transmission channel is designed using linear compensation technique and jitter is reduced by selecting the most suitable equalization technique. The insertion loss of each trace is simulated firstly, then the Re-timer is creatively introduced to the I/O expander backplane during the phase of prototype design. Through the tuning of Re-timer equalization parameters, the insertion loss of Re-timer PCI-E upstream and downstream link can be limited to -20 ± 2 dB@4 GHz. And the actual Bit Error Ratio Contour Eye of the PCI-E signal through 31.7 in. transmission conforms with the PCI-E Base 3.1 Spec. and The stressed voltage and stressed jitter Rx tests are conducted to simulate the PCI-E real link working condition with the help of BERT Scope, through injecting Random Jitter and Deterministic Jitter into the Data+/Data- signal. Performance experiments were also carried out using two scale-out x86 CPU based servers, and competitive performance was achieved.

References

1. IDC's Worldwide Quarterly Enterprise Storage Systems Tracker (2018). http://www.idc.com/tracker
2. Storage Bridge Bay (SBB) Specification. Storage Bridge Bay Working Group Inc. (2008)
3. InfiniBand Roadmap. InfiniBand Trade Association (IBTA) (2016)
4. Angus, M.: Advanced Equalization Techniques for PCIe 8GT/s. PCI-SIG (2011)
5. PCI Express Base Specification, Rev. 3.1. PCI-SIG, December 2013

6. Liu, H., Wang, Y.: A 5-Gb/s serial-link redriver with adaptive equalizer and transmitter swing enhancement. IEEE Trans. Circuits Syst. **61**, 1001–1011 (2013)
7. Yuuki, F., Kogo, K.: Transmission design technique for 25-Gbps retime. In: IEEE CPMT Symposium Japan (ICSJ) (2016)
8. Chen, Z.: Behavioural circuit models of data clocked and reference clock driven retimers for signal integrity transient simulation. In: IEEE 66th Electronic Components and Technology Conference (ECTC) (2016)
9. T0816P 8-Lane (16 Channel) PCI-E Re-timer User Manual. Integrated Device Technology, Inc., July 2014
10. PCI Express Simulation and Validation. Intel Corporation Data Centre Platform Application Engineering, December 2013
11. PCI-E 3.0 Re-timer and Switch SERDES Settings for Gen 3 Auto Negotiation. Integrated Device Technology, July 2012
12. PCI Express Card Electromechanical Specification Revision 3.0. PCI-SIG, July 2013
13. Sha, C., Ren, X.: High-speed channel design and simulation of high density storage server. J. Natl. Univ. Defense Technol. **37**(5), 39–46 (2015)
14. Yin, W., Zhang, X.: Electronic structure and physical characteristics of dioxin under external electric field. CMC: Comput. Mater. Continua **55**(1), 165–176 (2018)
15. Sha, C., Ren, X.: On the privacy-preserving outsourcing scheme of reversible data hiding over encrypted image data in cloud computing. CMC: Comput. Mater. Continua **55**(3), 523–539 (2018)

Virtualization of 5G Cellular Networks: A Combinatorial Share-Averse Auction Approach

Yuanyuan Xu[1(✉)] and Shan Li[2]

[1] Hohai University, Nanjing, China
yuanyuan_xu@hhu.edu.cn
[2] Nanjing University of Aeronautics and Astronautics, Nanjing, China
shanli@nuaa.edu.cn

Abstract. Wireless virtualization can enable resources (e.g., subchannels) owned by an infrastructure providers (InP) shared by multiple MVNOs. Naturally, the problem of resource allocation between an InP and multiple mobile virtual network operators (MVNOs) appear. Several existing works only considered how to assign the resources to one MVNO without sharing with other MVNOs. However, shareness plays an important role in maximizing utilization of resources. In this paper, a combinatorial share-averse auction model is proposed, based on which a truthful and efficient resource allocation framework is provided. Specifically, for maximizing the payment, a winner determination problem (WDP) is formulated considering different requirements of users, and a computationally tractable algorithm is proposed to solve the WDP. Also, a pricing scheme is designed. Simulation results show that the proposed system model with share-averse bidders can perform better than traditional allocation system model with the same allocation algorithm and pricing scheme.

Keywords: 5G · Wireless virtualization ·
Combinatorial share-averse auction · Winner determination problem

1 Introduction

The forthcoming fifth generation (5G) cellular networks are envisioned to provide higher data rates, lower end-to-end latency, enhanced end-user quality-of-experience (QoE), and improved energy efficiency. To achieve these goals, several emerging technologies, such as full-duplex, cloud-based radio access network (C-RAN), and wireless virtualization have been developed [1]. In this paper, we will focus on the technology of wireless virtualization which has received widespread

This work was partially supported by National Natural Science Foundation of China under Grant No. 61801167 and Natural Science Foundation of Jiangsu Province of China under Grant No. BK20160874.

X. Sun et al. (Eds.): ICAIS 2019, LNCS 11634, pp. 13–24, 2019.
https://doi.org/10.1007/978-3-030-24271-8_2

attention from some areas [2,3]. Wireless virtualization is a technology that abstracts wireless resources into virtual resources. Accordingly, the role of infrastructure provider (InP) can allocate virtual resources to multiple mobile virtual network operators (MVNOs). In this case, a main challenge for wireless virtualization is resource allocation. The issue of how to efficiently allocate the virtual resources of MVNOs to maximize payment and the utilization of resources arises.

Several existing works have been done for the resource allocation in wireless virtualization considering different scenarios. Specifically, in [4], the InP allocates the resources to MVNOs using their proposed opportunistic sharing based resource allocation scheme. A game theory approach was proposed for dynamic wireless resource allocation among multiple operators in [5]. Auction can be used in resource allocation [6]. In [7], a hierarchical combinatorial auction mechanism was proposed to jointly address the two-level resource allocation problem for virtualization of massive MIMO-based 5G cellular networks. However, these existing works do not consider the shareness among MVNOs which may lead to plenty of resources waste and lower the utilization of resources.

To track above problem, we propose a combinatorial share-averse auction approach in which items can in principle be allocated to arbitrarily many bidders, but the valuation of each individual bidder decreases as the items get allocated to more bidders. For example, let us consider the problem of selling a valuable piece of information or dataset. In principle, the information or dataset can be sold to all bidders by the seller. In this case, the information or dataset can be shared by multiple bidders instead of using by one bidder. Like information or dataset referred above, in wireless virtualization, the resources can also be shared which can be used at the same time by MVNOs. We call it as resources allocation with share-averse bidders [8]. In [9,10], share-averseness is considered in the scenario of auctions to maximize the utilization of resources. In these paper, we can see share-averseness is a negative allocation externality among the winners, and utility depends not only on the valuation of bidders, but also on the number of bidders sharing the same resources. Besides resource allocation among multiple bidders, the InP needs a proper pricing scheme to figure out prices of allocated resources, despite of a fixed pricing scheme whose resulting prices can be predicted using collected past data [11].

Specifically, for applying combinatorial share-averse auction for the virtual resource allocation between an InP and multiple MVNOs, the following three issues need to be addressed. Firstly, how to design the combinatorial auction model with share-averse model and how to design the share-averseness method among bidders; Secondly, how to solve the winner determination problem (WDP) in a computational efficient way when the resources are shared by bidders; Lastly, how to design an incentive compatible pricing scheme. In this work, we address all the above questions. And the main novelty and contributions of this paper can be summarized as follows:

- A combinatorial share-averse auction based resource allocation mechanism is designed considering one-sided auction among one service provider and multiple bidders. Also, the share-averseness method is designed.

- A computationally tractable algorithm for solving the WDP and pricing with share-averse bidders is proposed.
- Simulations are conducted and show that high resource utilization can be achieved which show the good performance of the proposed scheme.

The rest of this paper is organized as follows: Sect. 2 describes the system model, assumptions, and presents the proposed combinatorial share-averse auction model. In Sect. 3, WDP formulation is given and the corresponding solution algorithms and pricing schemes are presented. Also, theoretical analysis of auction properties is provided. Numerical results are analyzed in Sect. 4. Section 5 concludes the paper.

2 System Model and Assumptions

2.1 System Model

For the system model shown in Fig. 1, we consider the uplink transmission of a cellular system in which an InP dynamically allocates resources to multiple MVNOs with different requirements. Specially, MVNOs can make requests for these physical resources, known as virtual network requests (VNRs). VNRs have different priorities which based on the service level that the MVNO wants to provide to its services or users. In exchange for providing the resources, the InP obtains revenue from the MVNOs. The revenue depends on the number of resources used, the valuations and so on.

Without loss of generality, we consider an InP providing infrastructure services (including base stations and wireless resources) to a set of $N = \{1, 2, \cdots, N\}$ MVNOs. Each MVNO i then provides services to K_i subscribed users in the considered cell. In order to explain the problem model proposed by us in a clear way, we only consider the subchannel allocation in the design of this system model. We set that the InP owns a set of $C = \{1, 2, \cdots, c\}$ subchannels each with bandwidth W. Also, we make the assumption that other physical resources (e.g., power and antennas) are large enough to meet the requirements for MVNOs to provide to their services or users.

2.2 Proposed Combinatorial Share-Averse Auction Model

We propose a combinatorial share-averse auction model. The InP acts as the seller to maximize her own profit while satisfying the resources requirements of MVNOs who act as the buyers. Also, the InP acts as the auctioneer in responsibility for collecting bids, deciding allocation lists and final prices. In general, an auction involves the following procedures:

- Bidding procedure: according to his own valuation v_i of the resources bundle, every bidder i places a bid b_i. The valuation is the evaluation of the resources bundle which bidder i want to bid, and it is the personal information which can be private or public. Different bidders may have different valuations for the same bundle.

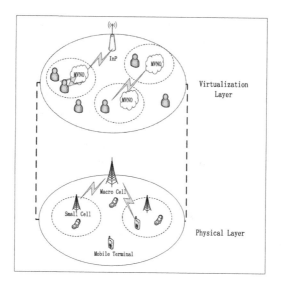

Fig. 1. System model of a cellular system

- Allocation procedure: after collecting bids from all the bidders, the auctioneer needs to decide how to allocate the resources among the bidders and how to share resources between winners and losers. The bidder who is allocated the required resources is winner.
- Pricing procedure: after deciding the allocation of the resources, the auctioneer needs to decide the price p_i which is the charge to each winning bidder i.

In this paper, the proposed combinatorial auction is singe-seller multiple-buyer auction model. We model the allocation of subchannels with share-averse bidders by an auction. The valuations of all bidders for subchannel resources with share-averse bidders are denoted by the vector $\mathbf{v} = (v_1, v_2, \cdots, v_n)$. v_i is the valuation of bidder i as the a winner and v_i is drawn from continuous distribution G_i. $g(\cdot)$ is denoted to be the corresponding probability density function of $G = G_i$. Each bidder i has a private valuation v_i, if she is allocated the item exclusively. If she shares the item with k other bidders, her valuation decreases to $v_i \cdot f(k_i)$. f_i is denoted as the share-averse function which is a decreasing function such that $0 \leq f(\cdot) \leq 1$. $\mathbf{v}_{i-1} = (v_1, v_2, \cdots, v_{i-1}, v_{i+1}, \cdots, v_n)$ represents the valuation vector after removing bidder $i's$ valuation. Similarly, G_{-i} represents the joint distribution function without bidder i. We make the assumption that the distribution has the monotone rate property, i.e., $h(\cdot) = \frac{g(\cdot)}{1-G(\cdot)}$ is increasing. We denote the virtual value as follows:

$$\phi(\cdot) = v_i - \frac{1 - G(\cdot)}{g(\cdot)} \tag{1}$$

We denote the conditional allocation to bidder i by which we model the incentive constraint in the Bayesian setting as:

$$Q_i(v_i) = \int_{\mathbf{v}_{-i}} x_i(\mathbf{v}) f(\sum_j x_j(\mathbf{v})) dG_{-i}(\mathbf{v}_{-i}), \tag{2}$$

where Q_i is interim allocation of bidder i and x_i is a binary variable which is defined as follows:

$$x_i = \begin{cases} 1, & \text{if bidder } i \text{ wins,} \\ 0, & \text{otherwise.} \end{cases} \tag{3}$$

And also x_j is a binary variable and is defined as follows:

$$x_j = \begin{cases} 1, & \text{if bidder } i \text{ can share resources with bidder } j, \\ 0, & \text{otherwise.} \end{cases} \tag{4}$$

In this auction, the buyers place bids for their required resources bundles, and bidders can acquire resources from a single seller or be shared by other bidders who are win. In order to describe briefly, we define b_i as the users' bids.

2.3   Utility Functions and Social Welfare

(1) Utility Functions: In this proposed combinatorial auction model, we consider the bidders to be self-interested which carefully chooses the bidding strategy to maximize his own utility under the given designed auction mechanism (including allocation and pricing procedures). Specifically, the utility of bidder i is defined as follows:

$$u_i(\mathbf{v}, k_i) = x_i(\mathbf{v}) \cdot v_i \cdot f(k) - p_i(\mathbf{v}), \tag{5}$$

where $u_i(\mathbf{v}, k_i)$ represents the utility of bidder i and p_i represents the price paid by bidder i. Besides, x_i is a binary variable and is defined as:

$$x_i = \begin{cases} 1, & \text{if bidder } i \text{ wins,} \\ 0, & \text{otherwise.} \end{cases} \tag{6}$$

(2) Social Welfare: In this paper, we adopt combinatorial auction which allows the bidders to express their preferences over bundles or combinations of resources (e.g., bundles of subchannels). In the case that there are possible substitutions and complementarity properties among the channels, the value of a bundle of channels may not be equal to the sum of individual value of each service in the bundle. So, the combinatorial auction can build more efficient allocations compared with the case where a traditional single-item auction is repeated for each item in the bundle. A bidder i is a winning bidder and he is allocated the required bundle, so that he can receive the value v_i. Different from single-item auction and ordinary combinatorial auction, our designed combinatorial

share-averse auction can share resources with other bidders who lose the auction when some constraints are satisfied. So there could be more winning bidders in a combinatorial share-averse auction. The social welfare is the sum of all the valuations of winning bidders. Specially, it could be obtained as:

$$V = \sum v_i \cdot f(k_i), \tag{7}$$

where V represents the social welfare. In our scheme, the user of combinatorial auction can achieve social efficiency if all bidders bid truthfully. Note that when designing an auction, the following properties must be satisfied: (1) individual rationality; (2) incentive compatibility; (3) allocation efficiency.

3   Resources Allocation as a Single-Seller Multiple-Buyer Combinatorial Auction

In this section, we will show how the proposed combinatorial auction model can be applied for resource allocation among seller and bidders. Specifically, we will address the following issues: (1) how do the bidders place their bids? (2) how to determine the winning bids and winners list? (3) how to compute allocation and payments?

3.1   Bidding Expressions

Bids for users: We consider that the users convey their resources demands in a explicit way when applying auction schemes for resources allocation. We suppose that each user is single-minded and only submits a bundle in each round. In this case, the bid $\mathbf{B}_i$ of user i can be expressed as follows:

$$\mathbf{B}_i = \{C_i, b_i\}, \tag{8}$$

where we use a vector $\mathbf{B}_i$ to represent the bid of bidder i and C_i represents bidder i's required resources bundle. Assume that bidder i can share the resources with bidder j, C_j must be a subset of C_i. Besides, b_i is the user i's bid to his required bundle, and C_i can be expressed as follows:

$$C_i = \{x_1^i, x_2^i, \cdots, x_c^i\}, \forall i \in [0, N], \tag{9}$$

where $x_j^i \in \{0, 1\}$ represents whether the c_j is required by user i.

3.2   Problem Formulation

We consider resources provider to be self-interested who wish to maximize his profit. We consider the following lemma [12] to simplify the WDP problem.

Lemma 1 (Myerson's lemma). For every truthful mechanism $(\mathbf{x}, \mathbf{p})$, the expected payment of bidder i with valuation distribution G satisfies $\mathbb{E}_{\mathbf{v}}[p_i(\mathbf{v})] = \mathbb{E}_{\mathbf{v}}\left[\phi(v_i)x_i(\mathbf{v})f(\sum_j x_j(\mathbf{v}))\right]$.

According to these above analytic, the WDP for services allocation with clear user resource requirement can be formulated as:

$$\text{maximize} \quad \sum_{i=1}^{N} \mathbb{E}_{\mathbf{v}} \left[\phi(v_i) x_i(\mathbf{v}) f(\sum_{j} x_j(\mathbf{v})) \right]$$

$$\text{subject to} \quad C1 : \sum_{i=1}^{N} x_i(v) C_i(v) \leq C$$

$$C2 : u_i(v, k) \geq 0, \forall i, v, k$$

$$C3 : Q_i(v) \geq 0, \forall i, v$$

$$C4 : C_j \subseteq C_i$$

$$C5 : x_i \in \{0, 1\}, \forall i \in N$$

$$C6 : x_j \in \{0, 1\}, \forall j \in N,$$

$$(10)$$

where C is the total number of subchannels which the seller have. The objective function in this problem is the total payment from all bidders. It is well known that for a monotone allocation there exists a payment scheme that maintains the incentive constraint in a single-parameter Bayesian setting. Hence incentive constraint requires monotonicity of Q which has defined above. In above formulation, constraint C1 ensures that all allocated subchannels are smaller than all the subchannels which the seller have. Constraints C2 and C3 are standard non-negativity requirements. The last two constraints represents whether the subchannels are allocated or shared. 1 represents that it is allocated or shared and 0 is opposite. Besides, we denote by $\phi(v_i)$ the ordered virtual values, i.e., $\phi(v_i) \geq \phi(v_{i+1})$ for $i = 1, 2, \cdots, n - 1$.

3.3 Mechanism Design

After formulating the WDP problem, the next step is to solve it to determine the winning bidders and price of each bidder. It can be easily seen that above problem is an NP-hard problem [13]. Generally, there are two methods to solve the above problem. The first is the methods (e.g., branch-and-bound) for achieving exact optimal solutions. However, the first method can only be used when the scale of problem is sufficiently small. The second is to design methods for achieving approximate optimal solutions. Considering the scale of the problem, a heuristic mechanism is proposed which takes k_i into consideration, motivated by [14].

In this section, we study this optimal mechanism that mainly involves computing k_i, the optimal number of winners and the payments. We further show that the pricing scheme analysis designed in this mechanism.

Computing Allocation and Pricing. To derive an approximate optimal mechanism, we first relax the incentive constraint and solve the non-game theoretic optimization problem. We then show that the resulting mechanism is also incentive compatible. The proposed mechanism is shown in Algorithm 1:

Algorithm 1. The mechanism designed in this model.

1: **Phase I - Collect Bids:**
2: **for** $i = 1 \cdots N$ **do**
3:     Solicit and accept sealed bids $\mathbf{b} = (b_1, \cdots, b_n)$
4: **end for**
5: **Phase II - Winner Determination:**
6: Initialize each of $x_i = 0, x_j = 0, k_i = 0, C' = 0$;
7: **for** $i = 1$ to N **do**
8:     **for** $j = 1$ to N **do**
9:         **if** $(C_j \subseteq C_i)$ **then**
10:             $x_j = 1$;
11:             $k_i = k_i + 1$;
12:         **end if**
13:     **end for**
14: **end for**
15: For each $i = 1$ to N, calculate each user i's virtual bid $\phi_i = b_i - \frac{1-G(i)}{g(i)}$;
16: For each $i = 1$ to N, calculate $\mathbb{E}[\phi_i f(k_i)]$;
17: Reorder the B by $\mathbb{E}[\phi_i f(k_i)]$ such that:

$$\mathbb{E}[\phi_1 f(k_1)] \geq \mathbb{E}[\phi_2 f(k_2)] \geq \cdots \geq \mathbb{E}[\phi_n f(k_n)];$$

18: **for** $i = 1$ to N **do**
19:     **if** $(C' \leq C)$ **then**
20:             $x_i = 1$;
21:             $C' = C' + C_i$;
22:     **end if**
23: **end for**
24: **Phase II - Pricing:**
25: For each $i = 1$ to N, calculate each winners' prices:
26: **for** $i = 1$ to N **do**
27:     $p_i(\phi) = f(C(\mathbf{b}_{-i})) \sum_{j \in C(\mathbf{b}_{-i})} \phi(j) - f(k_i) \sum_{j \in C(\mathbf{b})} \phi(j)$;
28: **end for**

Each ϕ_i is computed at b_i. In step 7–14, we should compute the optimal k_i by solving the following problem:

$$k_i = \arg\max_{k_i} f(k_i) \sum_{i=1}^{k_i} \phi(i). \tag{11}$$

Analysis of the Pricing Scheme. We now analyze the pricing scheme of the proposed approximate optimal auction mechanism which have been shown in the previous section.

The algorithm calculates the profit maximizing set of allocations x that are related to the top k_i virtual values. The virtual payments p_i are calculated by the following:

$$p_i(\phi) = f(C(\mathbf{b}_{-i})) \sum_{j \in C(\mathbf{b}_{-i})} \phi(j) - f(k_i) \sum_{j \in C(\mathbf{b})} \phi(j). \tag{12}$$

The VCG-like virtual payment p is not the same as the Vickrey payment in the standard auction. It may be infeasible that the optimal allocation vector x combined with the standard Vickrey payment that is restricted to k units. Suppose for bidder i with true valuation v_i his allocation associated with reporting v_i is winning together with total k bidders. It implies that his payoff $u_i(v_i, v'_i)$ of reporting the true valuation is shown as follows:

$$u_i(v_i, v'_i) = f(k'_i) \left[v_i - \max\left\{ r, v_{k'_i+1} \right\} \right], \tag{13}$$

where $u_i(v_i, v'_i)$ corresponding to a new allocation with total k'_i winners. r is the value of the reserve price $r = \phi_1$. We already discussed the allocation of the auction mechanism corresponding to increasing bids. Suppose that the new allocation has the number of winner $k'_i < k_i$. We might have $u_i(v_i, v'_i) > u_i(v_i, v_i)$. In other words, when bidder i increases his reported valuation he improves his interim allocation. At the same time, this might eventually improve his payoff.

4 Performance Evaluation

By means of a numerical study we validate the performance of the proposed approximation algorithm in various settings. Each setting consists of a prior distribution of the valuation distribution G, size of the number of MVNO N and decreasing function f. f which we set is shown as follows:

$$f(k) = 1 - \frac{k-1}{N}, \tag{14}$$

where N is selected from $\{10, 50, 100\}$. We consider three distributions with increasing hazard rate functions. The first distribution is the continuous uniform distribution between 0 and 1. The second one is the gamma distribution with parameters $(\lambda, \alpha) = (1, 2)$ and the density function is shown as follows:

$$g(t, \lambda, \alpha) = \frac{\lambda_\alpha t_{\alpha-1} e_{-\lambda t}}{\tau(\alpha)}. \tag{15}$$

The third distribution is the truncated normal distribution between 0 and 1 with parameters of mean and standard deviation $(\mu, \sigma) = (1/2, 1/2)$, which we denote by T-normal. The three distributions are chosen in the numerical analysis because they are commonly used in practice and parameters are further configured to make the hazard rate functions monotone increasing. We make the assumption that the expected values for the three distributions are the same.

For numerical analysis, we mainly consider one performance aspect for resource allocation: total utility (i.e., the sum value of all accepted valuations). Also, for comparison purpose, we implement two algorithms, including the proposed approximate heuristic algorithm with share-averse bidders which is termed as "Heuristic" and the ordinary algorithm using Greedy method without share-averse bidders which is termed as "Greedy" for which winners can be share items with losers. The total utilities achieved by these two algorithms which uses the continuous uniform distribution are shown in Fig. 2. We can see that the proposed "Heuristic" algorithm can achieve a better total utility than another algorithm. Note that the total utility under "Heuristic" increases faster and faster as there are more and more bidders. The reason to this phenomenon is that when the number of bidders increases, the rise of the number of winners leads to the increase in the average utility of the users. Besides, when the number of users passes a certain point, there are more users becoming losers. At that time, winners can share items with some losers so that there are more winners leading to the faster increasing in total utility. For "Greedy", when the number of users passes a certain point, there are more users becoming losers, resulting in the decline of the utility.

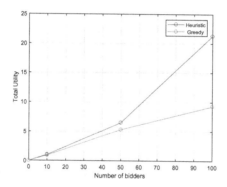

Fig. 2. Total utility with increasing number of bidders in Uniform distribution.

The same performance evaluations with the gamma distribution and the truncated normal distribution are shown in Figs. 3 and 4. The performances between "Heuristic" and "Greedy" with these two distributions are similar to which shown with the continuous uniform distribution above, so the reason why the performances perform like this will not be repeated. From these three figures, it can be seen that whatever the distribution methods we used, performance of algorithm with share-averseness does better than the other one without share-averseness.

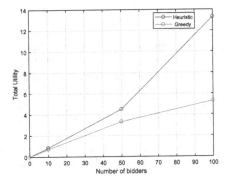

Fig. 3. Total utility with increasing number of bidders in Gamma distribution.

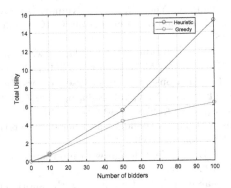

Fig. 4. Total utility with increasing number of bidders in T-normal distribution.

5   Conclusions

In this paper, we have proposed a combinatorial share-averse auction framework for efficient resource allocation to maximize payment. Specifically, we have considered a single-seller multiple-buyer auction model and the users are considered to be single-minded. With the bids as well as the valuations of users, a winner determination problem (WDP) is formulated concerning computing share-averseness number and determining winners. A heuristic algorithm has been proposed to solve the WDP and to determine the winners in this one-side auction. Moreover, a VCG-like pricing scheme has been designed to determine the final prices. Finally, simulations and comparisons have been done which show the effectiveness of the proposed scheme.

References

1. Hossain, E., Hasan, M.: 5G cellular: key enabling technologies and research challenges. IEEE Instrum. Meas. Mag. **18**(3), 11–21 (2015)
2. Liang, C., Yu, F.R.: Wireless network virtualization: a survey, some research issues and challenges. IEEE Commun. Surv. Tuts. **17**(1), 358–380 (2014)
3. Costa-Perez, X., Guo, T., Mahindra, R., Rangarajan, S.: Radio access network virtualization for future mobile carrier networks. IEEE Wirel. Commun. Mag. **51**(7), 27–35 (2013)
4. Yang, M., Li, Y., Jin, D., Yuan, J., Su, L., Zeng, L.: Opportunistic spectrum sharing based resource allocation for wireless virtualization. In: Proceedings of IEEE VTC (2014)
5. Liu, B., Tian, H.: A bankruptcy game-based resource allocation approach among virtual mobile operators. IEEE Commun. Lett. **17**(7), 1420–1423 (2013)
6. Zhang, J., Xie, N., Zhang, X., Yue, K., Li, W., Kumar, D.: Machine learning based resource allocation of cloud computing in auction. CMC: Comput. Mater. Continua **56**(1), 123–135 (2018)
7. Zhu, K., Hossain, E.: Virtualization of 5G cellular networks as a hierarchical combinatorial auction. IEEE Trans. Mob. Comput. **15**(10), 2640–2654 (2016)
8. Salek, M., Kempe, D.: Auctions for share-averse bidders. In: Papadimitriou, C., Zhang, S. (eds.) WINE 2008. LNCS, vol. 5385, pp. 609–620. Springer, Heidelberg (2008). https://doi.org/10.1007/978-3-540-92185-1_67
9. Brocas, I.: Auctions with type-dependent and negative externalities: the optimal mechanism. SSRN Electron. J. (2007)
10. Jehiel, P., Moldovanu, B.: Efficient design with interdependent valuations. Econometrica **69**(5), 1237–1259 (2001)
11. Wang, B., et al.: Research on hybrid model of garlic short-term price forecasting based on big data. CMC: Comput. Mater. Continua **57**(2), 283–296 (2018)
12. Pei, J., Klabjan, D., Xie, W.: Approximations to auctions of digital goods with share-averse bidders. Electron. Commer. Res. Appl. **13**, 128–138 (2014)
13. Jehiel, P., Moldovanu, B., Stacchetti, E.: Multidimensional mechanism design for auctions with externalities. Sonderforschungsbereich Publ. **85**(2), 258–293 (1994)
14. Sandholm, T.: Approaches to winner determination in combinatorial auctions. J. Ind. Eng. Eng. Manag. **28**(1), 165–176 (2004)

Equipment Fault Detection Based on SENCForest

Shanting Su[1(✉)], Xiangmao Chang[1], Yuan Qiu[1], Jing Li[1], and Tong Li[2]

[1] Nanjing University of Aeronautics and Astronautics, Nanjing, China
sushanting10@126.com, xiangmaoch@nuaa.edu.cn
[2] State Grid Liaoning Electric Power Research Institute, Shenyang, China

Abstract. Fault detection is a key element to ensure continuous operation of equipment. It is important to detect new emerging fault types of equipment in time and classify it. Existing fault detection methods are only suitable for detecting and classifying known faults, and cannot detect and classify new emerging unknown faults efficiently. By using the anomaly detection principle of the iForest, this paper proposes an effective classification method for both known and unknown faults. By extracting features from raw data, constructing a completely random forest, we achieve the classification for known faults. Then by setting reasonable partition boundaries according to the distribution characteristics of known anomaly data, we achieve the classification for unknown faults. Real data based simulations show the feasibility and effectiveness of our proposed classification method.

Keywords: Fault detection · Classification · Isolate forest · Feature extraction

1 Introduction

In modern industries, machines have become more automatic, precise, and efficient than ever before [1–3], which makes their health condition monitoring more difficult. Equipment failures, if not handled in a timely manner, often result in larger failures or significant economic losses. A well-established and accurate fault detection and classification system is very necessary for safety production management. It can help the staff to efficiently monitor the running status of the equipment and timely find faults for maintenance.

Fault diagnosis techniques can be divided into two broad categories based on the technology applied: model-based diagnostic methods [3–5] and data-driven diagnostic methods [6–12]. The model-based diagnostic method predicts the fault by establishing a model, and uses the difference between the model-simulated signal and the actually measured signal for fault detection. This technique typically requires a complete set of system parameters to reduce uncertainty and to ensure high accuracy in troubleshooting. However, due to the complexity of actual engineering, the establishment of models is often very difficult to implement. The data-driven diagnostic method has a greater advantage because it does not need to establish any physical model. Most data-driven diagnostic methods require machine learning techniques [13, 14].

© Springer Nature Switzerland AG 2019
X. Sun et al. (Eds.): ICAIS 2019, LNCS 11634, pp. 25–34, 2019.
https://doi.org/10.1007/978-3-030-24271-8_3

The technology trains the existing fault data to the classifier to achieve the classification purpose of the fault type. However, as the device usage time increases, a new type of failure will follow, and the new fault data will be directly assigned to the classifier for classification, which will lead to erroneous diagnosis. Therefore, it is necessary to develop a fault diagnosis model that automatically detects new faults and classifies them. The model enables accurate classification of known faults, detects new faults in real time and automatically updates the model.

In 2017, Xin Mu, etc. proposed the SENCForest [15], which achieves good performance on classification under streaming emerging new classes. Enlightened by the SENCForest, we attempt to achieve fault detection and classification in device fault detection problems by using iForest in this paper. We first segment the original data and extract the features of each segment, then use principal component analysis to select features that can significantly express fault data. Then we use iForest to construct a completely random forest and classify normal data and known abnormal data. According to the distribution characteristics of known anomaly data, a reasonable division boundary is set to classify unknown faults. The method proposed in this paper can be applied to the detection of equipment faults, achieve the efficient detection of known faults and the newly emerging unknown faults.

The rest of this paper is organized as follows. Section 2 introduces related technologies SENCForest. Section 3 presents the data processing method. We analyze the problem and design the fault detection algorithm in Sect. 4 and evaluate the performance of the algorithm in Sect. 5. Section 6 concludes the paper.

2   A Brief Introduction of SENCForest

SENCForest [13] is an incremental learning model based on iForest, which can detect new classes and classify known classes with high precision.

Define data set $A = \{(x_i, y_i)\}_{i=1}^m$, where x_i is a randomly extracted sample point, m is the number of data sets and $y_i = \{1, 2, \ldots K\}$ is its corresponding label. There are four main steps to building a SENCForest:

a. Construct iForest: obtain the threshold η of the data classification, According to the threshold η, the area where the normal data is located can be divided into other areas.
b. Build the ball C: construct a ball C based from the data on each leaf node to divide the abnormal region into a known anomaly region and an unknown anomaly region, the ball center $c = \frac{1}{p}\sum_{x_i \in O'} x_i$, where p is the number of data in O', radius $r = \max(\text{dist}(c, x_i))$, where $x_i \in O'$, the label of the ball is the majority data class label which contained in the ball.
c. Verification test: the test data traverses each tree to get the corresponding label for each tree, and the type with the largest proportion of labels is set as the label type of the data.
d. Update the model.

Schematic diagram of the SENCForest model based on the SENCTree structure is shown in Fig. 1. The normal data area is distinguished according to threshold η, and the abnormal data area is divided by the sphere. The data falling outside the sphere is called the abnormal "remote" data.

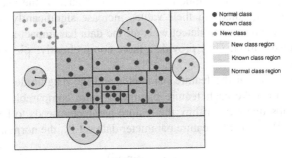

Fig. 1. Schematic diagram of data set classification based on SENCTree.

3   Data Preprocessing

Since the signal generated by the fault is a timing signal, in order to effectively mine the correlation between different fault data, we use sliding window to analyze and extract the signals over a period of time. As shown in Fig. 2, the window length s is moved every t data points, the time sequence signal of the previous time period in the window is removed, a new time sequence signal is added at the end of the window, and feature extraction is performed on the window data after each movement.

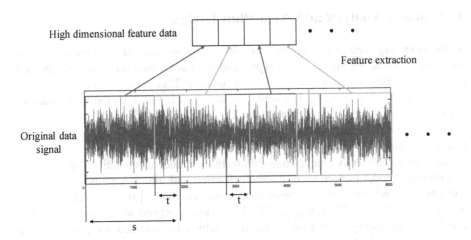

Fig. 2. Signal feature extraction method based on sliding window.

When the equipment fails, the waveform characteristics, energy size and frequency distribution of the vibration signal may change, and the characteristic parameters of the changes caused by the signals of different fault types are also different. The time domain signal provides a global feature of the device health state and has a clear physical meaning. Therefore, it is decided to extract the mean, standard deviation, peak, kurtosis, pulse index and skewness from the time domain signal. The standard deviation reflects the dynamic component of the signal energy, the peak and kurtosis values are sensitive to faults and their values increase significantly with respect to normal data, the pulse index can detect whether the data has impact and the skewness reflects the data distribution. They provide a more comprehensive picture of the health of the equipment.

Since the dimension of the feature parameter and the magnitude of the value are different, in order to make each feature parameter more comparable and ensure the accuracy of the subsequent algorithm, the feature parameter needs to be standardized. For each data $x_i \in P_n$ in the nth feature parameter data set P_n, the normalized data $\hat{x}_i$ is:

$$\hat{x}_i = \frac{x_i - \min(x_i)}{\max(x_i) - \min(x_i)}$$

Due to the high dimensionality of the data set obtained by the above feature extraction, the model has a large amount of computation, and there is a certain relationship between the feature parameters, resulting in redundancy of the data set. In order to ensure that the original feature information is not lost, the data is characterized by less features. This paper uses the principal component analysis method to analyze the data set extracted by the above features. Under normal circumstances, the first several components with a cumulative contribution rate exceeding 85% can be used to characterize the fault data well.

4 Problem Analysis and Algorithm Design

As the operating time of the device increases, the probability of an unknown failure increases. Assume we know n fault types, and we have a data set X_i for the ith fault type. We also have a data set X_{normal} for normal data. Then we can get a training data set $X = \{X_1, X_2, \ldots, X_n, X_{normal}\}$, where $normal = n + 1$. For any monitoring data set X', it may contain new unknown faults X'_{new}. Let $X' = \{X'_1, \ldots, X'_n, X'_{normal}, X'_{new}\}$, where $new = n + 2$. The problem studied in this paper is to classify $X'_1, \ldots, X'_n, X'_{normal}$ and X'_{new} from X'.

In order to efficiently characterize data features, reduce computational complexity, and improve model performance, feature extraction and dimensionality reduction for datasets X, X' are required. The resulting feature sets $SD = \{SD_1, \ldots, SD_n, SD_{normal}\}$ and $SD' = \{SD'_1, \ldots, SD'_n, SD'_{normal}, SD'_{new}\}$ are closely related to the waveform characteristics and energy magnitude of the data, which is important for improving the accuracy of later fault detection. Randomly extract m data points from SD to build a training set $A = \{(x_i, y_i)\}_{i=1}^{m}$, where $y_i = \{1, 2, \ldots, normal\}$ is the corresponding label. Randomly extract b data from SD' to form a test set $B = (x_i)_{(i=1)}^{b}$, it is worth noting that x_i in test set B has no corresponding label.

Based on the iForest principle, SENCForest obtains the path length threshold by constructing multiple isolated trees, classifies the normal data and the known abnormal data, The boundary is then divided according to the known anomaly data distribution characteristics, the data falling within the boundary is identified as a known fault and classified reasonably, and the data falling outside the boundary is considered to be an unknown fault type. The model is sensitive to new unknown classes, has high precision for known classes, and can dynamically update models. Since the attributes of SENCForest are in line with our problem, we have fine-tuned SENCForest here to adapt to fault data, thus solving the problem of equipment fault detection classification.

In this paper, the feature extraction is performed on the original dataset X, X' based on a sliding window of size s and moving step size t: mean, standard deviation, peak, kurtosis, pulse index and skewness calculation were performed to obtain six-dimensional data sets. The six-dimensional data sets is subjected to principal component analysis, and the first several components with cumulative contribution rate exceeding 85% are extracted to achieve the feature set SD, SD'. Randomly select b data points from SD' as the training set A for constructing the SNECForest. Randomly select b data points from SD' for model test classification. If a new fault type is detected, we apply it to the model update. The model pseudo code is shown as Algorithm 1.

Algorithm 1 Detection classification model.

Input: Original fault data set X,X'; Interval data point, t; Size of window, s; Feature dimension, f; Number of training set m; Number of tree r;

Output: Data corresponding label, y;

1:    initial $y \leftarrow \{\}$;
2:    $D,D' \leftarrow$ extraction feature from sliding window $(X, s, t), (X', s, t)$;
3:    $SD,SD' \leftarrow$ pincipal component analysis of data set D,D';
4   **for** $i = 1$; $i <= r$; $i++$ **do**
5        $A \leftarrow$ sample(X, m);
6        $SENCForest \leftarrow SENCForest \cup SENCTree(A)$
7   **end for**
8    $y \leftarrow SNECForest(B)$;
9   **if** $y = new$ **then**
10   Update SENCForest;
11   **end if**
12   **return** $y \in \{1, ..., n, normal, new\}$;

In the data preprocessing stage, the time complexity of the algorithm is $\frac{(l-s)}{t}$. Where l is the original data length. In the training phase, the time complexity of constructing SENCForest is $O(rm \log m + rcm)$; in the test phase, the time complexity is $O(r(\log m + c))$, and the update phase time complexity is $O(rb \log b + rcb)$. The space complexity is $O(b + rcm)$.

5   Performance Evaluation

This paper uses the fan end bearing vibration data released by the Case Western Reserve University (CWRU) Bearing Data Center as the original experiments data for fault detection model verification. Figure 3 shows the axle assembly consisting of a three-phase induction motor on the left, a load motor on the right and a torque sensor in the middle. The motor shaft is supported by the test bearing. By using EDM to cause bearing failure, the accelerometer is placed on the side of the bearing device for measuring vibration signals. The speed was set to 1797 rpm, the fault diameter was set to 0.007 mm, and the motor load was 0 hp. The test data sampling frequency is 12 kHz, and the data includes six types of types: the normal state, the inner ring fault, the rolling element fault, the central fault of the outer ring corresponding to the load zone, the central orthogonal fault of the outer ring corresponding load zone, and the center opposite fault of the outer ring corresponding load zone.

Fig. 3. Relationship between model parameter changes and fault classification accuracy.

Intercept every 100 data points for each equipment status type, using a window size of 1024. Correspondingly, the number of six types of fault data respectively obtained is 4082, 1197, 1203, 1205, 1954, and 1102. The mean value, standard deviation, peak value, skewness, wave factor, crest factor and pulse factor of the bearing vibration signal are extracted and principal component analysis is performed from the six types of equipment status data. The final results obtained are reported in Table 1.

From the results in Table 1, it is known that the cumulative contribution rate of the first three principal components is 0.8569%. Therefore, the first three principal components are selected in this paper to characterize the high-dimensional dataset, which achieves the goal of reducing the dimension and eliminating redundancy.

Table 1. Results of principal component analysis

Principal component	Contribution rate	Cumulative contribution rate
1	0.678%	0.678%
2	0.1585%	0.8365%
3	0.0204%	0.8569%
4	0.0619%	0.9188%
5	0.0356%	0.9544%
6	0.0443%	0.9987%

In order to verify the validity of the fault detection classification model, The sampling frequency $Sf = t/s$ is defined, and the influence on the fault classification detection accuracy under the parameters of changing the number of trees, the amount of data in the single tree training set, and the frequency of use is observed. Set other parameters unchanged, the experimental results are shown in Fig. 4.

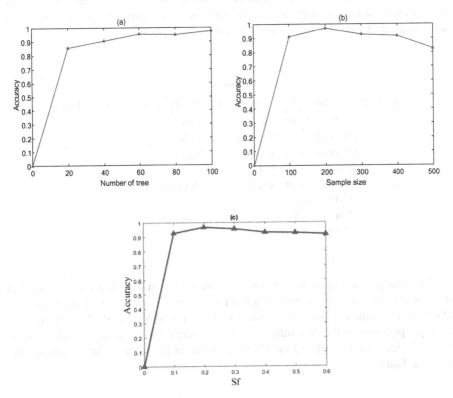

Fig. 4. Relationship between model parameter changes and fault classification accuracy.

It can be concluded from Fig. 4 that the accuracy of the fault detection classification model is greatly affected by the number of trees and the single tree training set data volume. It can be seen from Fig. 4(a) that the accuracy of the fault detection classification increases with the increase of the number of trees. When the number of trees exceeds 20, the accuracy of the fault detection classification increases slowly. It can be inferred from Fig. 4(b) that when the single tree training set data volume does not reach 200, the accuracy of the fault detection classification increases with the training set data volume. When the single tree training set data volume exceeds 200, the fault detection classification the accuracy decreases slowly as the number of nodes increases. It can be inferred from Fig. 4(c) that the accuracy of the fault detection classification tends to be stable, and the accuracy is the highest at $Sf = 0.2$.

After many changes to the model parameter test, it is concluded that the number of trees is 100, the single tree training set data volume is 200 and $Sf = 0.2$, and the accuracy of the fault detection classification model reaches the maximum of 97.6%.

To verify the performance of the model algorithm in this paper, the detection classification algorithm is compared with the CAE algorithm [17] and SVM algorithm [16]. Five different data sets were selected as the abscissa, and the effects of the five data sets on the accuracy of the above algorithm were observed. The equipment status data contained in the data set is shown in Table 2:

Table 2.

Data set	Number of known fault types	Number of unknown fault types
1	Normal, Inner race	Null
2	Normal, Inner race, Ball	Null
3	Normal, Inner race, Ball, Outer race centered	Null
4	Normal, Inner race, Ball, Outer race centered	Outer race opposite
5	Normal, Inner race, Ball, Outer race centered	Outer race opposite, Outer race orthogonal

The corresponding accuracy rate changes are shown in Fig. 5: It can be seen that when the data set has only known equipment status, its accuracy rate has reached more than 85%. When the data set has an unknown fault, the SENCForest algorithm used in this paper performs well, while other algorithms decrease significantly. This is because the SVM algorithm in [16] and the CAE algorithm in [17] cannot detect and identify unknown faults.

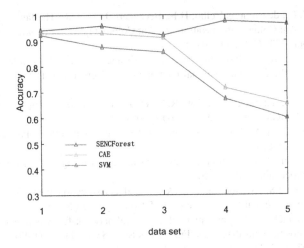

Fig. 5. Accuracy comparison test of three fault detection classification algorithms.

6   Conclusion

Based on the anomaly detection principle of iForest, this paper proposes a classification model for equipment fault intelligent detection. The mechanical bearing fault data and multiple fault detection classification algorithms are compared and tested to verify the feasibility and effectiveness of the model. Considering that the model can only detect and identify a new type of fault at a time, it is necessary to improve the model to achieve a fault detection classification to identify multiple unknown fault types.

Acknowledgement. This work is supported by the National Natural Science Foundation of China (Grant No. 61672282), the Basic Research Program of Jiangsu Province (Grant No. BK20161491) and the State Grid Corporation Science and Technology Project (Contract No.: SGLNXT00YJJS1800110).

References

1. Kolokas, N., et al.: Forecasting faults of industrial equipment using machine learning classifiers. In: IEEE International Conference on Innovations in Intelligent Systems and Applications. IEEE (2018)
2. Zou, M., Zhu, H., Gao, L.: Application of the fuzzy mathematics in fault diagnosis for hydraulic equipment. Metall. Equip. **06** (1995)
3. Rigatos, G., Siano, P.: Power transformers' condition monitoring using neural modeling and the local statistical approach to fault diagnosis. Int. J. Electr. Power Energy Syst. **80**, 150–159 (2016)
4. Echevarría, L.C., et al.: A variant of the particle swarm optimization for the improvement of fault diagnosis in industrial systems via faults estimation. Eng. Appl. Artif. Intell. **28**, 36–51 (2014)

5. Echevarría, L.C., de Campos Velho, H.F., Becceneri, J.C., et al.: The fault diagnosis inverse problem with Ant Colony Optimization and Ant Colony Optimization with dispersion. Appl. Math. Comput. **227**, 687–700 (2014)
6. Knorr, E.M., Ng, R.T.: Algorithms for mining distance based outliers in large data sets. In: Proceedings of the 24th International Conference on Very Large Databases, pp. 392–403 (1998)
7. Breuning, M.M., Kriegel, H.P., Ng, R.T., et al.: LoF: indentifying density-based local outliers. ACM SIGMOD Rec. **29**, 93–104 (2000)
8. He, Z., Xu, X., Deng, S.: LoF: discovering cluster-based local outliers. Pattern Recogn. Lett. **24**, 1641–1650 (2003)
9. Karimi, M., et al.: Classification of power system faults using ANN classifiers. In: IPEC Conference Proceedings. IEEE (2011)
10. Jan, S.U., Koo, I.S.: Sensor faults detection and classification using SVM with diverse features. In: International Conference on ICT Convergence (2017)
11. Ozyurt, B., Kandel, A.: A hybrid hierarchical neural network-fuzzy expert system approach to chemical process fault diagnosis. Fuzzy Sets Syst. **83**(1), 11–25 (1996)
12. Liu, F.T., Ting, K.M., Zhou, Z.-H.: Isolation forest. In: Proceedings of 8th IEEE International Conference Data Mining, pp. 413–422 (2008)
13. Zhang, Y., Wang, Q., Li, Y., Wu, X.: Sentiment Classification based on piecewise pooling convolutional neural network. Comput. Mater. Continua **56**, 285–297 (2018)
14. Fang, W., Zhang, F., Sheng, V.S., Ding, Y.: A method for improving CNN-based image recognition using DCGAN. Comput. Mater. Continua **57**(1), 167–178 (2018)
15. Yu, K., et al.: Classification with streaming features: an emerging-pattern mining approach. ACM Trans. Knowl. Discov. Data **9**(4), 1–31 (2015)
16. Jan, S.U., Koo, I.S.: Sensor faults detection and classification using SVM with diverse features. In: International Conference on Information and Communication Technology Convergence (ICTC), pp. 576–578 (2018)
17. Yang, J., Lee, Y., Koo, I.: Convolutional auto encoder-based sensor fault classification. In: Tenth International Conference on Ubiquitous and Future Networks (ICUFN), pp. 865–867 (2018)

Research on Telemedical Monitoring System Based on Homomorphic Encryption

Fei Xiao[⊠], Shaofeng Lin, Wei Tan, Fengchen Qian,
and Xiaopeng Li

College of Information and Communication, National University
of Defense Technology, Xi'an, China
Phoebe.xixi@163.com

Abstract. Social trends such as the accelerating aging of the population and the prevalence of chronic non-communicable diseases have made high-quality and long-term medical care gradually become the focus of attention of the whole society. Telemedical monitoring technology can greatly reduce the demand of hospital-centered medical resources, but increase the risk of data disclosure of personal privacy at the same time. How to ensure the privacy data security of patient in the course of telemedicine is an urgent problem to be solved in the development of new medical system. Based on the technology of homomorphic encryption, this paper studies the feasibility and specific encryption implementation of the telemedical surveillance system, after obtaining the patient indicators, and creates a prototype of a real-time early warning system for hospital, family and individual patients. At last a simulation test is designed on the Windows platform. The results and conclusion provide some reference for the future research of "cloud medicine" technology and give some advise on the application of homomorphic encryption technology.

Keywords: Telemedicine · Homomorphic encryption ·
Medical privacy security

1 Background and Introduction

1.1 Telemedical Surveillance and Medical Privacy Security

With the acceleration of the ageing of the world population and the prevalence of chronic non-communicable diseases, medical resources become scarce in traditional medical systems. While the annual related medical expense increases, it become one of the great challenge of modern economic and social development.

The establishment of a telemedicine system with quality and long-term medical care is helpful to the real-time exchange of information between doctors and patients without time and space restrictions, especially for elder people who are unable to take care of themselves and persons with disabilities, which enhance the quality of life of patients and save medical resources at the same time.

Meanwhile, with the gathering of more and more personal information, the sharing of regional network database of electronic medical records, and the connection of major databases, it poses new challenges to the protection of medical privacy. In order to

X. Sun et al. (Eds.): ICAIS 2019, LNCS 11634, pp. 35–46, 2019.
https://doi.org/10.1007/978-3-030-24271-8_4

personalize the medical scheme, telemedical services need to collect a large amount of information from each patient more comprehensively, and develop a unique and optimal treatment and prevention plan for each patient on the basis of information sharing [1]. But "big data itself means sharing, and it is also the beginning of privacy runaway [2, 3]". The risk of medical privacy leak increases when people's medical information and other related health information can be shared in different medical, health, insurance, scientific research institutions and pharmaceutical companies. In March 2014, the medical websites of Korean such as the *Korean Medical Association* were hacked and about 156,000 users' personal information was stolen. In June 2014, the *Community Health* company, which operates more than 200 hospitals in the United States, was attacked by hacker and the personal information of 4.5 million patients was leaked. In February 2015, the system vulnerability of US medical insurance company was hacked, which results in the disclosure of more than 2 million personal medical information. New statistics show that only in 2017 there were more than 15 major medical information leaks in the United States in one year. According to conservative estimates, the information of more than 3 million patients were leaked. In my country, the problem is no less serious. The domestic situation is also not optimistic. In September 2017, it is reported by the "Legal Daily" paper that the service information system of one hospital was hacked. In this process, as many as 700 million patients' information was leaked and more than 80 million information was sold, including some important and privacy information such as patients' names, ages, addresses, telephone numbers, medical history, and bank accounts.

The risk of disclosure of medical privacy has caused people's anxiety on privacy security 4, and more patient are unwilling to provide true information, which bring adverse affect on the effectiveness of health services. If there is no good strategy to solve the problem of personal information protecting, it will have a negative impact on the development of medical informatization and the integration and utilization of medical data.

1.2   Outline

The study on the telemedical monitoring system based on homomorphic encryption is put forward to solve the shortcomings of the traditional telemedical surveillance system, and reducing the above disclosure risk of medical privacy. The paper is divided into five parts. First, the research background is introduced and the definition of homomorphic encryption is given. Then the telemedicine monitoring system is designed, which security module is designed based on homomorphic encryption method. In Sect. 3, the overall architecture of the system is shown and illustrated, as well as the main functional components. In Sect. 4, the basic functions of the system are verified through some experimental tests. At last, in Sect. 5, there are the conclusions and suggestions for the future work.

1.3   Our Contribution

A telemedical monitoring system is built in this paper. The system uses homomorphic encryption to make the telemedicine health monitoring more convenient and safer.

According to some function tests, the performance of the system is proved. The conclusions in this research also provide important reference for the future development of cloud medicine.

2 Preliminaries

Homomorphic encryption, also known as privacy homomorphism, is a cryptographic technique based on the complexity theory of mathematical problems, which is first proposed by Rivest [5] et al. in 1978. The basic idea of Homomorphic encryption is to process some calculation on the data that has been homomorphic encrypted and obtain an output. When decrypting this output, the result is the same as the output result obtained from the original unencrypted data in the same calculation.

After this concept was been proposed, cryptographers designed many encryption schemes with homomorphic properties, such as the implementation of electronic voting systems [6], confidential information retrieval protocols, etc., and has been widely used in cloud computing [7], cloud security privacy protection [8], signature protection [9] and other fields.

The current homomorphic encryption scheme can be divided into three types [10]: Partial homomorphic encryption, shallow homomorphic encryption and full homomorphic encryption. The partial homomorphism can only implement a certain kind of algebraic operation(Add/Or, Multiplication and Addition) [11, 12]. The shallow homomorphism can simultaneously implement the finite addition and multiplication operations. The full homomorphism can achieve any times of algebraic operation.

2.1 Homomorphism

Assume that the encryption function and decryption function of an encryption system are $E : P_\varepsilon \to C$ and $D : C \to P_\varepsilon$, respectively, P_ε and C are plain-text space and cipher-text space. The operator $\oplus$ and $\otimes$ sum are defined as algebraic or arithmetic operations in plain-text space and cipher-text space, respectively. The homomorphism of the encryption scheme is defined as: given any $p_1, p_2 \in P_\varepsilon$, if the encryption function of an encryption system satisfies the algebraic relationship with the decryption function as,

$$p_1 \oplus p_2 = D(E(p_1) \otimes E(p_2)) \ (\text{or } E(p_1 \oplus p_2) = E(p_1) \otimes E(p_2)) \tag{1}$$

It is said that the encryption system is homomorphic.

2.2 Partial Homomorphic Encryption (PHE)

For encryption algorithms ε and operations $(\oplus, \otimes)$ on plain-text domains P_ε, $\forall p_1, p_2, \ldots, p_n \in P_\varepsilon$, if only the addition or multiplication operation is established in Eq. (1), the encryption algorithm ε is called an partial homomorphic encryption algorithm.

2.3   Full Homomorphic Encryption (FHE)

For encryption algorithms ε and operations $(\oplus, \otimes)$ on plaint-ext domains P_ε, $\forall p_1, p_2, \ldots, p_n \in P_\varepsilon$, if any times of addition or multiplication operation is established in Eq. (1), the encryption algorithm is called a full homomorphism encryption algorithm.

As shown in Fig. 1, m is the user's data, P_k is the encryption key, S_k is the decryption key, where the full homomorphism encryption allows the user to submit his data to the server in cipher-text form $C = Enc_{P_k}(m)$. The server calculates the user's cipher-text data according to the user's computational needs f, and the results $c^* = Eval(f, c)$ are fed back to user, then the user can obtain the calculation results of the data m, which is $f(m) = Dec_{S_k}(c^*)$, by decrypt the feedback results of the server.

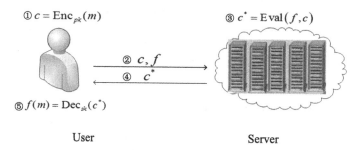

Fig. 1. Diagram of full homomorphic encryption process

3   Telemedical Monitoring System Based on Homomorphic Encryption

3.1   System Top-Level Architecture

The telemedicine system based on homomorphic encryption consists two part of client and server. The intelligent monitoring client connects to the telemedicine monitoring system via cable or wireless network, and the physiological parameters collected such as pulse and blood pressure are homomorphic encrypted locally and uploaded to the server. On the server side, threshold judgment is made on the uploaded encrypted information, and multiple judgment information is synthesized. If several physiological parameters exceed the threshold at the same time, the system will consider that the patient's health value exceeds the normal range, and the system will automatically alarms both the doctor and the patient. The system structure is shown in Fig. 2:

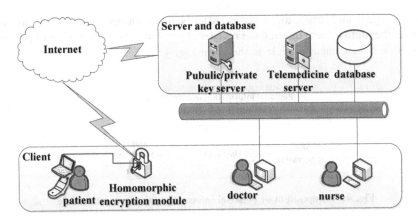

Fig. 2. Top-level structure of the telemedicine monitoring system

According to the function of the system, the telemedicine monitoring system based on homomorphic encryption can be divided into four modules, data acquisition module, personal information management module, encryption module, and alarming module.

3.2 Data Acquisition Module

The data acquisition is designed as an interface between intelligent monitoring terminal and the system, as shown in Fig. 3. The intelligent monitoring terminal can gather the human body's multi-physiological signal acquisition, and complete the previous analysis and processing. The original data being pre-processed is send to the encryption module by data acquisition module.

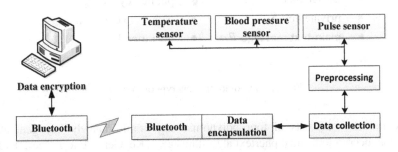

Fig. 3. Data acquisition module

3.3 Personal Information Management Module

The personal information management module includes three sub-functions, as user registration, user login and user information deletion and modification. When users first use the monitoring system, they need to fill in personal information through the registration page and send it to the server. After being confirmed by the server, the user can enter the login system through the registered account. The composition of personal information management module is shown in Fig. 4.

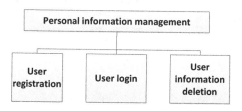

Fig. 4. Composition of personal information management module

3.4 Encryption Module

The system in this paper uses a homomorphic encryption system based on the fault tolerant learning problem in the loop proposed by Brakerski [13] et al. The homomorphic encryption model is shown in Fig. 5.

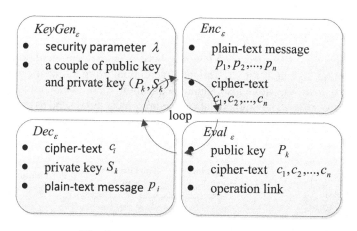

Fig. 5. Homomorphic encryption model

The model is consists of four polynomial algorithms, namely key generation, encryption, decryption, and ciphertext algorithms $\varepsilon = \{KeyGen_\varepsilon, Enc_\varepsilon, Dec_\varepsilon, Eval_\varepsilon\}$. Compared with the traditional public key encryption system, the algorithm $Eval_\varepsilon$ is increased.

In $KeyGen_\varepsilon$, the security parameter λ is entered in and a couple of public key and private key (P_k, S_k) is putted out.

In Enc_ε, the plain-text message $p_1, p_2, \ldots, p_n$ is entered in, and the ciphertext $c_1, c_2, \ldots, c_n$ is output by encryption algorithm.

In Dec_ε, the ciphertext message c_i is entered in, and the plaintext p_i is output by decryption algorithm using a private key S_k.

In $Eval_\varepsilon$, the public key P_k and a group of ciphertext $c_1, c_2, \ldots, c_n$ are entered in, and the operation link is created, where ciphertext $c^* = Eval_\varepsilon(\bullet)$ satisfied that $C(p_1, p_2, \ldots, p_n) = Dec_\varepsilon(S_k, c^*)$.

The algorithm is implemented in C++ language, and part of the code are shown in Fig. 6, as follows.

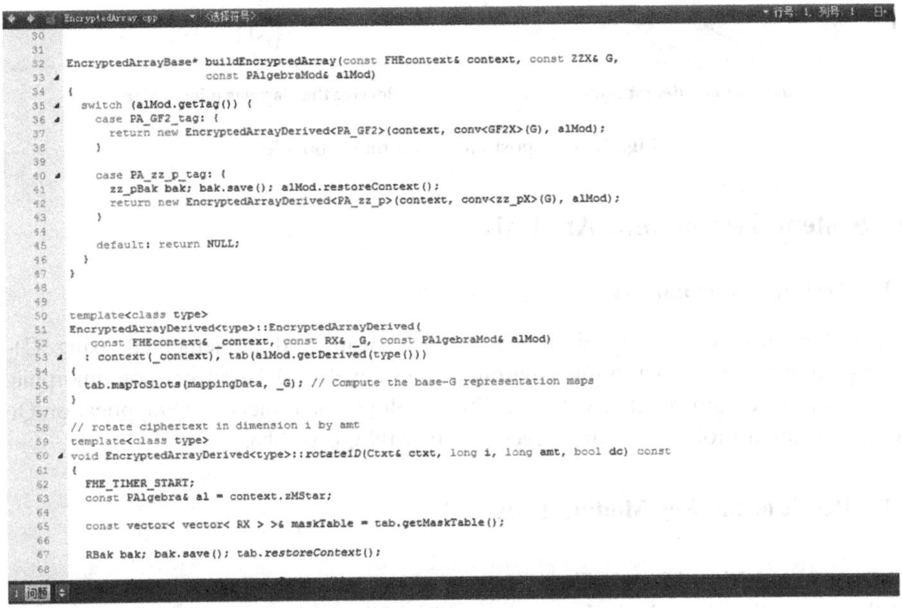

Fig. 6. Part of the homomorphic encryption code

3.5 Alarming Module

The alarming module is mainly based on the doctor's opinion to set up the operation rules of the remote intelligent monitoring center server. First, the normal value range of each body parameter is given. If the data transmitted by the intelligent monitoring terminal is not within this normal range, the server sends out an alert message to the user. The form of early warning is to display the parameter information in a color different from other parameters within the normal range, by vibration of the mobile phone and calling the designated number alert, and sending the abnormal parameter to the hospital expert system. The expert system will provide users with medical advice and guidance online. The composition of alarming module is shown in Fig. 7.

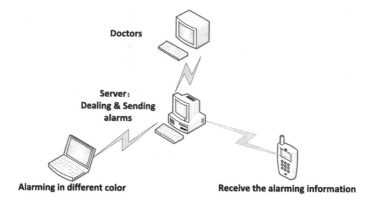

Fig. 7. Composition of alarming module

4 System Testing and Analysis

4.1 Testing Environment

The test environment is based on *Qt 5.1.0* software and implemented using C++ programming. The encryption environment is developed based on homomorphic encryption development library *Helib*. The development project is Qt/application/Qt GUI application project, and the server installs MySQL database.

4.2 Result of the Key Module Tests

A. Data Acquisition Module Test

At this stage, the physiological parameters of intelligent patients were collected. The wearable medical device on the patient is connected to computer by Bluetooth. When the system is logged in, the system can automatically acquire the physiological parameters collected in real time on the wearable medical device and display it on the patient's client. And it is uploaded to the server after being encrypted.

We compared the obtained parameters from data acquisition module and actual physiological parameters. Test results are as follows Table 1.

Table 1. Function test of data acquisition module.

Test serial number	Collected data/actual data				Test result
	Temperature(° C)	Weight (kg)	Blood pressure (mmhg)	Heart rate (bpm)	
1	36.8/36.9	74.4/74.5	119-75/119-76	78/77	Good
2	37.0/37.0	69.9/70.0	117-74/116-74	76/76	Good
3	36.6/36.7	65.5/65.5	116-76/117-75	75/74	Good
4	38/37.9	71.2/71.0	115-73/115-73	72/74	Good
5	37.5/37.7	69.8/69.6	120-77/121-78	73/72	Good

B. Encryption Module Test

This stage mainly tests the encryption function of the system. After the user client obtains the patient's real-time physiological parameters, homomorphic encryption is performed on the parameters. When the server processes the ciphertext, it also returns an another ciphertext. This feedback ciphertext contains the information of the result of system processing. Through the test program and the encrypted file saved in the database, we can clearly see the encrypted ciphertext and the return result. Because the homomorphic encrypted ciphertext data is large, part pf the ciphertext is shown in following Fig. 8.

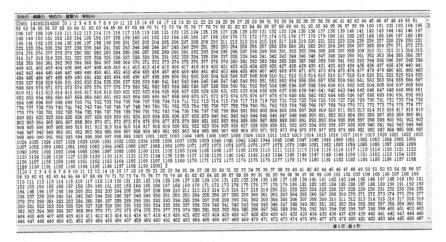

Fig. 8. Part of the cipher-text

C. Alarming Module Test

At this stage, the system alarm function is tested. When the server judges that a patient's physiological parameter exceeds the threshold, the server will send an alarm to the doctor and the family client. If the physiological parameter is normal, the alarm will not be issued. Test method is: taking a patient as an example, selecting patient data at different time points to test whether the system will alert the potential danger. Test results as shown in Table 2.

Table 2. Function test of alarming module.

Temperature(℃)	Blood pressure(mmhg)	Heart rate (bpm)	Alarm
38.0	**144-91**	87	**Yes**
37.8	**140-92**	**103**	**Yes**
36.5	130-85	88	No
37.1	130-85	**105**	**Yes**
36.6	127-81	97	No
36.8	**142-90**	**104**	**Yes**
36.9	138-88	93	No
36.6	127-80	**103**	**Yes**
36.7	131-82	97	No

According to testing, the alarming success rate > 99.5%.

4.3   Analysis

In general, for the privacy of information in medical institutions, the following methods are usually applied:

- Encrypted storage of the key data such as patient information;
- Isolation of medical data from unrelated user;
- Record and statistical database access behaviour in order to identify problems;
- Use vulnerability detection tools to regularly scan the system and detect problems;
- Implementation of authority subdivision, unrelated user can not see specific customers' health records, electronic medical records and other personal information.

The system in this paper is designed according to the encrypted storage method. It applies the homomorphic encryption algorithm on the safety module. The performance of the system are mainly about the security performance, convenience performance and practicality performance.

A. Security Performance

The communication between patients and doctors is encrypted throughout the whole process. And the information both on network and in database are in the state of ciphertext. If the remote server located in hospitals or information service centers are attacked, the patient's personal privacy data will not be used for leaks without decryption key.

B. Convenience Performance

The system is not limited by time and space. It allows doctors and patients to exchange information in real time. Patients can receive expert medical services timely in the local area, which saves patients' time and avoid long-distance move. At the same time it reduces both the patient's economic pressure and the hospital's resource pressure.

C. Practicality Performance

The system can be used as an assistant method on traditional hospital centered diagnosis and medical care. By applying the telemedicine mode to the social medical care system, the medical care services can be optimized, and thus the process of the construction of medical information infrastructure in China will be accelerated.

5 Conclusions and Perspectives

5.1 Conclusion

The development of "Internet + Medical" can not be separated from the support of telemedicine services. The telemedicine service can be helpful to individual prevention, health diagnosis and accurate medical treatment. During this process, the support of medical teams and network equipment is needed, and it is also necessary to face up to the data security and privacy protection issues, such as the security risks of the equipment itself, the data protection mechanisms lacking in the process of data acquisition and transmission, the lack of national supervision of data security and privacy protection, and the lack of clear regulations on the scope of privacy data. By adding encryption module to the traditional telemedicine surveillance system, the paper realizes the secure encryption of patient's privacy data, and the prototype system supports remote access, which provides great convenience for both doctors and patients. According to the rests, the practicability of the system has been verified. The system can be used as an auxiliary way of traditional medicine which centered on hospitals. Applying telemedicine to the social medical care system will optimize the medical care services, and accelerating the process of medical information in China.

5.2 Further Work

The prototype system developed in this paper can already encrypt the data uploaded by user, and the server can process the ciphertext, and at the same time feedback the processed ciphertext to the user. After decrypting the feedback ciphertext, user can get information about his own medical diagnosis. Totally, the test system is running steadily and performing well. However, when the number of users increases, the number of data uploaded to the server will multiply, and more efficient storage services will needed. In further work, the system will be implemented in the cloud platform, and provide greater reference value for the information security transmission and processing of telemedicine systems.

Acknowledgments. Thanks for the valuable suggestion from ICAIS/ICCCS2019 paper viewers. And particularly grateful to ICAIS/ICCCS2019 committee for their works on the publish of paper. The study is supported by Research Project of National University of Defense Technology (ZK18-03-46), and part of the research results participated in the 2016 National College Students Information Security Competition, to whom we also owe many thanks.

References

1. Li, J., Gu, J.: Challenges and opportunities of medicine in the age of big data and personalized medicine. Med. Philos. **35**(1A), 5–10 (2014)
2. Xue, F., Chen, H.-B.: Analysis of privacy ethics of big data. Stud. Dialectics Nat. **2**, 44–48 (2015)
3. Schwab, K: The Fourth Industrial Revolution. http://www.foreignaffairs.com/articles/2015-12-12/fourth-industrial-revolution. Accessed 26 Mar 2016
4. Wang, Q.-F.: Rational thinking on hierarchical control of medical privacy in the era of big data. Med. Philos. (A) **37**(5A), 5–8 (2016)
5. Rivest, R., Adleman, L., Dertouzos, M.: On Data Banks and Privacy Homorphisms. Foundations of Secure Computation. Academic Press, New York (1978)
6. Cohen, J., Fischer, M.: A robust and verifiable cryptographically secure election scheme. In: Proceedings of the 26th Annual Symposium on Foundation of Computer Science, pp. 372–382. IEEE, Piscataway (1985)
7. Li, S., Dou, J., Wang, D.: Survey on homomorphic encryption and its applications to cloud security. J. Comput. Res. Dev. **52**(6), 1378–1388 (2015)
8. Li, Z.-Y., Gui, X.-L., Gu, Y.-J., LI, X.-S., Dai, H.-J., Zhang, X.-J.: Survey on homomorphic encryption algorithm and its application in the privacy-preserving for cloud computing. J. Softw. **29**(7), 1830–1851 (2018)
9. Peng, C.-H., Tian, Y.-L., Zhang, B., Xu, Z.-P.: General transitive signature scheme based on homomorphic encryption. J. Commun. **34**(11), 18–25 (2013)
10. Gong, L., Li, S., Guo, Y.: the development and applications of homomorphic encryption. ZTE Technol. J. **22**(1), 26–29 (2016)
11. Meng, R., Rice, S.G., Wang, J., Sun, X.: A fusion steganographic algorithm based on faster R-CNN. CMC: Comput. Mater. Continua **55**(1), 001–016 (2018)
12. Liu, Y., Peng, H., Wang, J.: Verifiable diversity ranking search over encrypted outsourced data. CMC Comput. Mater. Continua **55**(1), 037–057 (2018)
13. Brakersk, Z., Vaikuntanathan, V., Wee, H., Wichs, D.: Obfuscating conjunctions under entropic ring LWE. In: Proceedings of the 2016 ACM Conference on Innovations in Theoretical Computer Science, Massachusetts, USA, pp. 14–17 (2016)

Phase Retrieval via Accelerated Gradient Descent

Yi Qin[✉]

School of Information Science and Technology, ShanghaiTech University,
Shanghai 201210, China
qinyi1@shanghaitech.edu.cn

Abstract. Phase retrieval, as a non-convex optimization problem arises in many areas of signal processing, is to recover the missed signal phase. Based on the Truncated Wirtinger Flow (TWF), where the updating can be regarded as stochastic gradient descent, we present the Accelerated Wirtinger Flow (AWF), which updates the iterative process with accelerated steepest descent. WF algorithm solves the problem by two steps: (a) initialization signal with truncated spectral initialization method provided in TWF and (b) a series of updates this initial estimate by iteratively applying a novel update rule, AWF. Meanwhile, according to the Amplitude Flow objective, the proximal gradient method is suggested.

Keywords: Phase retrieval · Accelerated gradient descent · Wirtinger Flow

1 Introduction

Non-convex optimization can be widely used in a great number of areas [17,18], within which the phase retrieval problem is a non-convex optimization problem with applications in several domains. For example, in studying X-ray crystallography, it can be used to find the molecule structure by revealing the interior composition of both inorganic and organic compounds through imaging specimens [10]. In Phase retrieval can also be used in Transmission Electron Microscopy, which uses a focused beam of electrons to image the object of study [9]. Coherent Diffraction Imaging is to study nanostructures such as nanotubes and nanocrystals by recovering the structure from a diffraction pattern produced by the diffracted rays [13].

These application may be considered as phase retrieval, which is equivalent to discovering a complex signal using observations that reveal the magnitudes of that signal, with only the linear measurements but not the phases of the measurements. The recovery of the signal in such situations, where the phase of a signal being measured is irrevocably lost or unreliably obtained, becomes our concern.

Although quadratic equations are computationally difficult to solve exactly, typical phase retrieval systems usually require solving quadratic systems that

© Springer Nature Switzerland AG 2019
X. Sun et al. (Eds.): ICAIS 2019, LNCS 11634, pp. 47–55, 2019.
https://doi.org/10.1007/978-3-030-24271-8_5

have nice randomized structures in the coefficients of the quadratic equations. These structures can be exploited to efficiently, solving these systems as below:

$$y_r = | < \mathbf{a}_r, \mathbf{z} > |^2, \tag{1}$$

where $\mathbf{z} \in \mathcal{C}^n$ is the decision variable, $\mathbf{a}_r \in \mathcal{C}^n$ are known sampling vectors, and $y_r \in \mathcal{R}$ are observed measurements. The problem is broadly studied in the following two settings [12]:

- The n measurements in (1) accord with the Fourier transform and the signal has apriori information.
- The set of measurements $\mathbf{y}$ are overcomplete, while some apriori information about the signal may or may not be available.

In order to recover a signal from data of such form (1), the community has developed a number of methods. The pioneering research of the algorithm were from Gerchberg and Saxton [8]. In their original work, Gerchberg and Saxton proposed to use a random vector for initialization and to proceed by iteratively applying a pair of projections. The most empirically successful approach has been to directly optimize various naturally formulated nonconvex loss functions [9,14], the most notable of which are displayed below:

- Wirtinger Flow objective [3]:

$$f(\mathbf{z}) := \frac{1}{m} \sum_{r=1}^{m} (| < \mathbf{a}_r, \mathbf{z} > |^2 - y_r)^2, \tag{2}$$

- Amplitude Flow objective [16]:

$$f(\mathbf{z}) := \frac{1}{m} \sum_{r=1}^{m} (| < \mathbf{a}_r, \mathbf{z} > | - y_r)^2, \tag{3}$$

- Robust Wirtinger Flow objective [1]:

$$f(\mathbf{z}) := \frac{1}{m} \sum_{r=1}^{m} (| < \mathbf{a}_r, \mathbf{z} > |^2 - y_r^2)^2, \tag{4}$$

These loss functions have good properties making them amenable to different kinds of optimization schemes [7,15]. Various gradient descent methods as linear and nonlinear programming [11], including proximal gradient decent algorithm, as first-order methods in optimization can be used to solve the quadratic programming. Some of these methods also involve adaptive measurement pruning to enhance performance. Candès et al. describe the algorithm via matrix completion [2], and give its exact and stable signal recovery via convex programming and solving quadratic equations [5]. The author also proposes the theory and algorithms of phase retrieval via Wirtinger Flow (WF) [3] and Truncated Wirtinger Flow (TWF) [4].

The paper's contribution includes what based on Phase Retrieval via Wirtinger Flow, the accelerated steepest gradient method applied to this problem, and some discussion about the algorithm of Amplitude Flow objective is also presented. The remainder of this paper is structured as follows: Sect. 2 introduces related work on Phase Retrieval, and Sect. 3 introduces the Phase Retrieval via Accelerated Steepest Decent and presents numerical experiments and discusses the results; Proximal Gradient Method is discussed in Sect. 4, and make the summary in the last section.

2   Related Work

2.1   Phase Retrieval via Alternating Minimization

One of the most popular approaches for solving the phase retrieval problem is known as the Gerchberg-Saxton Alternating Minimization (GSAM) [8], which is based on the routine - there exist two parameters of interest in the problem - the phase of the data points i.e., $y_r/|y_r|$, and the true signal $\mathbf{z}^*$.

Algorithm 1. Alternating Minimization

Input: Observations $\{y_r\}_{r=1}^m$ and sampling vectors $\{\mathbf{a}_r\}_{r=1}^m$, and desired accuracy ϵ.

Set $T = log1/\epsilon$.

Partition m data points into $T+1$ sets $S_0, S_1, \cdots, S_T$.

Initialize $\mathbf{z}_0$ as the leading eigenvector:

$$\mathbf{z}_0 = eig(\frac{1}{|S_0|} \sum_{r \in S_0} |y_r|^2 \cdot \mathbf{a}_r \mathbf{a}_r^T, 1).$$

for $t = 1$ to T **do**

   Phase Estimation:

$$\Phi_r = \frac{\mathbf{a}_r^T \mathbf{z}_{t-1}}{|\mathbf{a}_r^T \mathbf{z}_{t-1}|}, \ \forall r \in S_t.$$

   Signal Estimation:

$$\mathbf{z}_t = arg \min_{\mathbf{z} \in \mathcal{C}^n} \sum_{r \in S_t} |\Phi_r \cdot |y_r| - \mathbf{a}_r^T \mathbf{z}|^2.$$

end for

Output: $\mathbf{z}_T$

Algorithm 1 is a simple application of the gAM approach to alternately estimate Φ_r and $\mathbf{z}^*$. Given the true phase values of the points $\Phi_r = y_r/|y_r|$, the signal can be recovered simply by solving a system of linear equations: $\Phi_r \cdot |y_r| - \mathbf{a}_r^T \mathbf{z}$, $r = 1, \cdots, m$. On the other hand, given $\mathbf{z}^*$, estimating the phase of the points is straightforward as $\Phi_r = \mathbf{a}_r^T \mathbf{z}/|\mathbf{a}_r^T \mathbf{z}|$.

2.2 Wirtinger Flow Algorithm

Wirtinger Flow Algorithm (WF) [3] lets loss function be the simple quadratic loss $l(x, y) = (x - y)^2$, which measures the differences between both of its scalar arguments. The loss function is non-negative and comes to zero only when $x = y$. Then any solution to minimize $f(\mathbf{z})$, $\mathbf{z} \in \mathcal{C}^n$ is a solution to the generalized phase retrieval problem (1). Although (2) doesn't simplify the problem since the function $f(\mathbf{z})$ is non-convex. Minimizing non-convex objectives is NP-hard in general, since it may have a lot of stationary points. WF algorithm solve the problem by two step:

– initialize estimation by a spectral method, and
– update by a novel rule similar to gradient descent scheme iteratively.

The algorithm of initialization of $\mathbf{z}_0$ was described as Algorithm 2. The update step find the decision variable $\mathbf{z}$, where the iterative procedure inductively is defined as below for $t = 0, 1, 2, \cdots$:

$$
\begin{aligned}
\mathbf{z}_{t+1} := \mathbf{z}_t &- \frac{\mu_{t+1}}{\|\mathbf{z}_0\|^2} [\frac{1}{m} \sum_{r=1}^{m} (|\mathbf{a}_r^* \mathbf{z}_t|^2 - y_r)(\mathbf{a}_r \mathbf{a}_r^*)\mathbf{z}_t] \\
&= \mathbf{z}_t - \frac{\mu_{t+1}}{\|\mathbf{z}_0\|^2} \nabla f(\mathbf{z}_t)
\end{aligned}
\tag{5}
$$

This term can still be viewed as a gradient based on Wirtinger derivatives. (5) is a form of steepest descent and the parameter μ_{t+1} can be viewed as step size and is inversely proportional to the magnitude of the initial estimation.

Algorithm 2. Wirtinger Flow

Input: Observations $\{y_r\}_{r=1}^m$, sampling vectors $\{\mathbf{a}_r\}_{r=1}^m$, and step size μ_t.
  Initialize $\mathbf{z}_0$ as the leading eigenvector:

$$
\mathbf{z}_0 = eig(\frac{1}{n} \sum_{r=1}^{n} |y_r|^2 \cdot \mathbf{a}_r \mathbf{a}_r^*, 1).
$$

for $t = 1$ to T **do**

$$
\mathbf{z}_t = \mathbf{z}_{t-1} - \frac{\mu_t}{\|\mathbf{z}_0\|^2} [\frac{1}{m} \sum_{r=1}^{m} (|\mathbf{a}_r^* \mathbf{z}_{t-1}|^2 - y_r)(\mathbf{a}_r \mathbf{a}_r^*)\mathbf{z}_{t-1}]
$$

end for
Output: $\mathbf{z}_T$.

For a certain random model, if the initialization $\mathbf{z}_0$ is accurate enough, then the sequence $\{\mathbf{z}_t\}$ will converge toward a solution to the generalized phase problem (1). The paper [3] proposes computing the initial guess $\mathbf{z}_0$ via a spectral method, and then use gradient descent to update, the Algorithm 2 describes it as above. Here z_0, the leading eigenvector of $\mathbf{Y} = \frac{1}{m} \sum_{r=1}^{m} y_r \mathbf{a}_r \mathbf{a}_r^*$, can be computed by the Power Method (Algorithm 3).

Algorithm 3. The Power Method

Input: Matrix $\mathbf{Y}$.
   Initialize ν_0 as a random vector on the unit sphere of $\mathcal{C}^n$.
   for $\tau = 1$ to T **do**
      $\nu_\tau = \frac{\mathbf{Y}\nu_{\tau-1}}{\|\mathbf{Y}\nu_{\tau-1}\|}$
   end for
Output: $\tilde{\mathbf{z}}_0 = \nu_T$.

2.3 Truncated Wirtinger Flow

Following the spirit of WF, Chen and Candès propose a novel procedure called Truncated Wirtinger Flow (TWF) [6] adopting a more adaptive gradient flow. It computes an initial guess $\mathbf{z}_0$ by means of a spectral method applied to a subset S_0 of the observations $\{y_r\}$; and then loops by

$$\mathbf{z}_{t+1} = \mathbf{z}_t + \frac{\mu_{t+1}}{m} \sum_{r \in S_{t+1}} \nabla l(\mathbf{z}_t, y_r)$$

for some index subset $S_{t+1} \subseteq \{1, \cdots, m\}$ determined by $\mathbf{z}_t$.

Algorithm 4. Truncated Wirtinger Flow (TWF)

Input: Observations $\{y_r\}_{r=1}^m$ and sampling vectors $\{\mathbf{a}_r\}_{r=1}^m$; trimming thresholds α_z^{lower}, α_z^{upper}, α_h, α_y.
Initialize $\mathbf{z}_0$ as the leading vector of the truncated sum

$$\mathbf{Y} = \frac{1}{m} \sum_{r=1}^m y_r \mathbf{a}_r \mathbf{a}_r^* \mathbf{1}_{\{|y_i| \leq \alpha_y^2 \lambda^2\}}.$$

for $t = 0$ to T **do**

$$\mathbf{z}_{t+1} = \mathbf{z}_t + \frac{2\mu_{t+1}}{m} \sum_{r=1}^m \frac{y_r - |\mathbf{a}_r^* \mathbf{z}_t|^2}{\mathbf{z}_t^* \mathbf{a}_r} \mathbf{a}_r \mathbf{1}_{\xi_1^r \cap \xi_2^r},$$

where

$$\xi_1^r := \{\alpha_z^{lower} \leq \frac{\sqrt{n}}{\|\mathbf{a}_r\|} \frac{|\mathbf{a}_r^* \mathbf{z}_t|}{\|\mathbf{z}_t\|} \leq \alpha_z^{upper}\},$$

$$\xi_2^r := |y_r - |\mathbf{a}_r^* \mathbf{z}_t|^2| \leq \alpha_h \cdot \frac{1}{m} \sum_{i=1}^m |y_i - |\mathbf{a}_i^* \mathbf{z}_t|^2| \cdot \frac{\sqrt{n}}{\|\mathbf{a}_r\|} \frac{|\mathbf{a}_r^* \mathbf{z}_t|}{\|\mathbf{z}_t\|}.$$

end for
Output: $\mathbf{z}_T$

---

3   Accelerated Steepest Decent

3.1   Accelerated Steepest Decent

This paper uses a careful initialization obtained by truncated spectral initialization (get $\mathbf{z}_0$ as Algorithm 4) firstly, then applies a series of updates refining this initial estimate by iteratively applying an accelerated steepest decent (Algorithm 5) [11], since (2) is differentiable everywhere and satisfies $\beta - Lipschitz$ condition. Note that $(\gamma_t)^2 = \gamma_{t+1}(\gamma_{t+1} - 1)$, $\gamma_t > t/2$ and $\alpha_t < 0$.

Algorithm 5. Accelerated Steepest Decent

Input: $\mathbf{z}_0$ as truncated WF Algorithm 4, and β.
    Initialize $\gamma_0 = 0$, $\tilde{\mathbf{z}}_0 = \mathbf{z}_0$.

$$\gamma_{t+1} = \frac{1 + \sqrt{1 + 4(\gamma_t)^2}}{2}, \ \alpha_t = \frac{1 - \gamma_t}{\gamma_{t+1}},$$

$$\tilde{\mathbf{z}}_{t+1} = \mathbf{z}_t - \frac{1}{\beta}\nabla l(\mathbf{z}_t),$$

$$\mathbf{z}_{t+1} = (1 - \alpha_t)\tilde{\mathbf{z}}_{t+1} + \alpha_t\tilde{\mathbf{z}}_t$$

3.2   Numerical Experiments

Coded Diffraction Model. Consider an acquisition model as [4] says, where to collect data of the form

$$y_r = |\sum_{t=0}^{n-1} x[t]\bar{d}(t)e^{-i2\pi\omega_k t}|^2, \ \omega_k \in \Omega, \tag{6}$$

where the coded diffraction patterns (CDP) gives the information about the spectrum of the signal $\{x(t)\}$ modulated by the code $\{d(t)\}$. In this paper, we collect the magnitude of the discrete Fourier transform (DFT) of L modulations of the signal $\mathbf{x}$. We study a model with i.i.d. $d_l(t)$'s (where $1 \leq l \leq L$), each having $i.i.d.$ entries sampled from a distribution d. Assume d to be symmetric, admissible and obey $|d| \leq M$.

    Since the photo is RGB image, we run the algorithm on $n_1 \times n_2 \times 3$ arrays with i.i.d. CDP masks following a uniform distribution over $\{1, -1, j, -j\}$ (sample phase) on each color band. Let $\mathbf{x}$ denote original image and $\hat{\mathbf{x}}$ the recovered image, then the relative error is $\|\hat{\mathbf{x}} - \mathbf{x}\|/\|\mathbf{x}\|$.

    After initialize with 50 iterations of the power method, the result images are shown in Fig. 1 and the mean running times and relative error are shown in Fig. 2. We may find that the error converges less than 10^{-15} after about 200 iteration. The computational time we report is the computational time averaged over the RGB images.

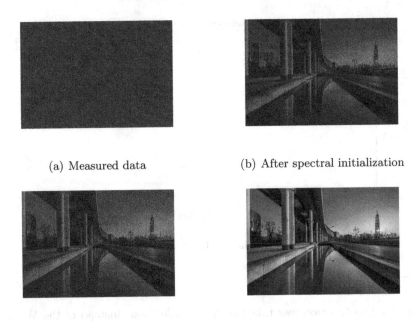

(a) Measured data

(b) After spectral initialization

(c) Regularized spectral initialization

(d) Recovered Image

Fig. 1. Example image size is 400 * 600 pixels. There are 12 patterns×2 (FFT&IFFT) ×(300 gradient steps + 50 power iterations) = 8400 FFTs in this example.

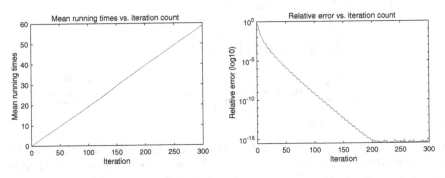

Fig. 2. 2D CDP: Mean running times & Relative error v.s. iteration count

Gaussian Model. The algorithm is applied to complex-valued data by generating $\mathbf{a}_r \sim \mathcal{N}(\mathbf{0}, \frac{1}{2}\mathbf{I}) + j\mathcal{N}(\mathbf{0}, \frac{1}{2}\mathbf{I})$ and real-valued independent Gaussian $\mathbf{a}_r \sim \mathcal{N}(\mathbf{0}, \mathbf{I})$ respectively.

As showed in Fig. 3, for 1-dimension Gaussian phaseless measurements, the signal can be recovered as well. Even though the exact recovery for complex-valued mask takes more time and slightly higher error than real-valued, the overall performance makes the relative error less than 10^{-15} as expected.

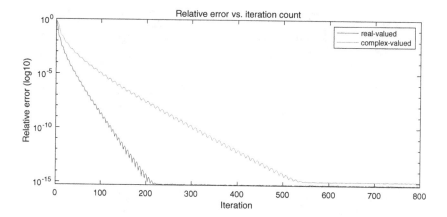

Fig. 3. 1D Gaussian simulation: Relative error v.s. iteration count

4   Discussion

When the loss function was take the Amplitude Flow, instead of the Wirtinger Flow to solve the phase retrieval problem, we can present the loss function with a sum of three function:

$$
\begin{aligned}
f(\mathbf{z}) &= \frac{1}{2m} \sum_{r=1}^{m} l(y_r, |\mathbf{a}_r^* \mathbf{z}|), \ \mathbf{z} \in \mathcal{C}^n \\
&= \frac{1}{2m} \sum_{r=1}^{m} (y_r^2 + |\mathbf{a}_r^* \mathbf{z}|^2 - 2y_r |\mathbf{a}_r^* \mathbf{z}|) \\
&= \frac{1}{2m} \sum_{r=1}^{m} | <\mathbf{a}_r, \mathbf{z}> |^2 - \frac{1}{m} \sum_{r=1}^{m} y_r | <\mathbf{a}_r, \mathbf{z}> | + \frac{1}{2m} \sum_{r=1}^{m} y_r^2 \\
&= h(\mathbf{z}) + g(\mathbf{z}) + c,
\end{aligned}
\tag{7}
$$

where h is smooth, g is nonsmooth, and c is constant. We may then use the proximal gradient and its relative method. This make the origin quartic equation into a quadratic function. It can be expected that the lower degree, the lower complexity of the problem.

5   Conclusion

Accelerated Wirtinger Flow to solve the phase retrieval problem is an effective algorithm. The loss functions have many choice, some of them are nonconvex and nonsmooth. There are more other algorithm including projected subgradient methods, block proximal gradient method and alternating direction method of multipliers, etc. On the other hand, we can let the loss function to be activation function, then construct neural networks such as convolutional neural networks to regularize phase retrieval problems and improve recovery performance.

References

1. Duchi, J.C., Ruan, F.: Solving (most) of a set of quadratic equalities: composite optimization for robust phase retrieval. Inf. Infer.: A J. IMA (2017). https://doi.org/10.1093/imaiai/iay015
2. Candès, E.J., Eldar, Y.C., Strohmer, T., Voroninski, V.: Phase retrieval via matrix completion. CoRR abs/1109.0573 (2011). http://arxiv.org/abs/1109.0573
3. Candès, E.J., Li, X., Soltanolkotabi, M.: Phase retrieval via wirtinger flow: theory and algorithms. IEEE Trans. Inf. Theory $61(4)$, 1985–2007 (2015). https://doi.org/10.1109/TIT.2015.2399924
4. Candès, E.J., Li, X., Soltanolkotabi, M.: Phase retrieval from coded diffraction patterns. Appl. Comput. Harmonic Anal. 39 (2013). https://doi.org/10.1016/j.acha.2014.09.004
5. Candès, E.J., Strohmer, T., Voroninski, V.: Phaselift: exact and stable signal recovery from magnitude measurements via convex programming. CoRR abs/1109.4499 (2011). http://arxiv.org/abs/1109.4499
6. Chen, Y., Candès, E.J.: Solving random quadratic systems of equations is nearly as easy as solving linear systems. CoRR abs/1505.05114 (2015). http://arxiv.org/abs/1505.05114
7. Eldar, Y.C., Mendelson, S.: Phase retrieval: stability and recovery guarantees. Appl. Comput. Harmonic Anal. $36(3)$, 473–494 (2014). https://doi.org/10.1016/j.acha.2013.08.003. http://www.sciencedirect.com/science/article/pii/S106352031 3000717
8. Gerchberg, R., Saxton, W.O.A.: A practical algorithm for the determination of phase from image and diffraction plane pictures. Optik 35, 237–250 (1971)
9. Jain, P., Kar, P.: Non-convex optimization for machine learning. Found. Trends® Mach. Learn. 10, 142–336 (2017). https://doi.org/10.1561/2200000058
10. Lucas, A.: A-DNA and B-DNA: comparing their historical x-ray fiber diffraction images. J. Chem. Educ. 85 (2008). https://doi.org/10.1021/ed085p737
11. Luenberger, D., Ye, Y.: Linear and nonlinear programming (2008). https://doi.org/10.1007/978-0-387-74503-9
12. Netrapalli, P., Jain, P., Sanghavi, S.: Phase retrieval using alternating minimization. IEEE Trans. Signal Process. $63(18)$, 4814–4826 (2015). https://doi.org/10.1109/TSP.2015.2448516
13. Shechtman, Y., Eldar, Y.C., Cohen, O., Chapman, H.N., Miao, J., Segev, M.: Phase retrieval with application to optical imaging. CoRR abs/1402.7350 (2014). http://arxiv.org/abs/1402.7350
14. Shuo Tan, Y., Vershynin, R.: Phase retrieval via randomized kaczmarz: theoretical guarantees. Inf. Infer.: A J. IMA (2017). https://doi.org/10.1093/imaiai/iay005
15. Sun, J., Qu, Q., Wright, J.: A geometric analysis of phase retrieval. CoRR abs/1602.06664 (2016). http://arxiv.org/abs/1602.06664
16. Wang, G., Zhang, L., Giannakis, G.B., Akçakaya, M., Chen, J.: Sparse phase retrieval via truncated amplitude flow. CoRR abs/1611.07641 (2016). http://arxiv.org/abs/1611.07641
17. Xiong, Z., Shen, Q., Wang, Y., Zhu, C.: Paragraph vector representation based on word to vector and CNN learning. CMC: Comput. Mater. Continua $055(2)$, 213–227 (2018)
18. Zhang, J., Xie, N., Zhang, X., Yue, K., Li, W., Kumar, D.: Machine learning based resource allocation of cloud computing in auction. CMC: Comput. Mater. Continua $056(1)$, 123–135 (2018)

Anti-noise Quantum Network Coding Protocol Based on Bell States and Butterfly Network Model

Zhiguo Qu[1]([⊠]), Zhexi Zhang[2], and Zhenwen Cheng[3]

[1] Jiangsu Collaborative Innovation Center of Atmospheric Environment and Equipment Technology (CICAEET), Nanjing University of Information Science and Technology, Nanjing 210044, People's Republic of China
qzghhh@126.com
[2] School of Computer and Software, Nanjing University of Information Science and Technology, Nanjing 210044, People's Republic of China
[3] School of Electronic and Information Engineering, Nanjing University of Information Science and Technology, Nanjing 210044
People's Republic of China

Abstract. How to establish a secure and efficient quantum network coding algorithm is one of important research topics of quantum secure communications. Based on the butterfly network model and the characteristics of easy preparation of Bell states, a novel anti-noise quantum network coding protocol is proposed in this paper. The new protocol encodes and transmits classical information by virtue of Bell states. It can guarantee the transparency of the intermediate nodes during information, so that the eavesdropper Eve disables to get any information even if he intercepts the transmitted quantum states. In view of the inevitability of quantum noise in quantum channel used, this paper analyzes the influence of four kinds of noises on the new protocol in detail further, and verifies the efficiency of the protocol under different noise by mathematical calculation and analysis. In addition, based on the detailed mathematical analysis, the protocol has functioned well not only on improving the efficiency of information transmission, throughput and link utilization in the quantum network, but also on enhancing reliability and anti-eavesdropping attacks.

Keywords: Network coding · Quantum network coding · Bell states · Butterfly network model · Quantum communication · Eavesdropping detection

1 Introduction

In recent years, quantum secure communication has become one of important research hotspots in the field of information security due to its absolute security compared with classical communication [1–3]. So far, the development of quantum secure communication mainly focuses on quantum key distribution (QKD) [4], quantum secret sharing (QSS), quantum secure direct communication (QSDC) [5] and quantum identity verification (QIV). The intermediate nodes of the traditional classical network

© Springer Nature Switzerland AG 2019
X. Sun et al. (Eds.): ICAIS 2019, LNCS 11634, pp. 56–67, 2019.
https://doi.org/10.1007/978-3-030-24271-8_6

are only responsible for routing, but do not process the data, which will do nothing to improve the efficiency of information transmission in the network. Instead, network coding is an information exchange technology that integrates routing and coding, which is of great significance for improving network transmission efficiency. There are abundant research achievements in quantum communication technology and quantum network encoding technology [6–8], and the specific achievements are described as follows.

In terms of quantum secure communication, the relevant research [9–12] also indicated that large-scale network communication is an inevitable trend in the development of quantum communication. And the complexity of the large-scale structure of the network itself will lead to transmission congestion, which may contribute to problems such as low communication efficiency. Hayashi et al. [7] used the butterfly network model to achieve two arbitrary quantum states probabilistic cross transmission in 2006, which made the quantum network coding possible. They also proposed the famous XQQ protocol. In 2009, Akter et al. [13] implemented quantum network coding for various network models. In 2010, based on the results of Hayashi's research, Ma et al. [14] proposed an effective implementation of m-qubit cross transfer protocol through senders sharing non-maximum entangled states. In 2012, Yan et al. [15] proposed a quantum network coding protocol to transmit 2-level quantum entanglements through two pairs of non-maximized GHZ entangled states shared between two senders as the transmission channel, which make the transmission in the butterfly network more efficiency. In 2013, Nishimura [16] defined the limits of the reachable rate in quantum network coding based on butterfly network.

From the quantum network coding achievements given, it's easy to know that quantum network coding technology has a great development prospect. Additionally, some new researches on resisting quantum noise has emerged in recent years. In 2010, Korotkov et al. [17] proposed a protocol to overcome decoherence by using quantum non-collapse measurements. In 2014, Guan et al. [18] analyzed the remote preparation of two arbitrary quantum bits in the noise environment and calculated the effect of quantum noise on protocol efficiency. In 2015, Fortes et al. [19] made a detailed analysis of the effect of noise on the quantum teleportation and concluded that the interaction between the two kinds of noises has some symmetry. In 2017, Wang et al. [20–22] conducted quantum noise analysis on quantum remote preparation of single particles, two particles and multiple particles, and gave the efficiency of some protocols in the noise environment respectively.

In this paper, a novel quantum network coding protocol based on butterfly network model and Bell states is proposed. The protocol takes Bell states as the carrier, codes and hides classical information by virtue of Pauli operators. The transparency of the intermediate nodes to the specific information transmitted, and the detection and eavesdropping in the transmission process also guarantee the reliability of the protocol and the ability to prevent attacks. In addition, we also analyze the efficiency of the protocol under noise, and find that the amplitude damping noise has the least impact on the channel, while the depolarizing noise has the greatest impact.

The arrangement of this paper is described below. Section 2 introduces the preliminary knowledge related to the new protocol, including butterfly network model, Bell states and Pauli operators. Section 3 introduces the main steps of the new quantum network coding protocol in detail. Section 4 analyses the effect of noise on the fidelity of communication. Section 5 provides security and resource consumption analysis. Finally, the conclusion is given in Sect. 6.

2 Preliminary

2.1 Butterfly Network Model

Butterfly network model [23] (Fig. 1) is a typical example of implementing maximum flow transmission, which can clearly indicate the advantages of network coding. As shown in Fig. 1, the source nodes S_1 and S_2 send 1 bit information a and b to the target nodes T_1 and T_2 respectively. All channels in the figure are set up to transmit 1 bit information.

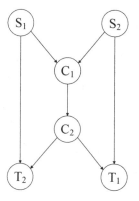

Fig. 1. Butterfly network model.

According to the max-flow min-cut theorem [24], the maximum transmission rate from the source node $S_1(S_2)$ to the target node $T_1(T_2)$ should be less than or equal to 2.

In the traditional network transmission, the average transmission efficiency is 1.5 bit/unit time. Through the network coding transmission, the node C_1 encodes information received from S_1 and S_2. The coding results $a \oplus b$ will be sent to the node C_2, and then node C_2 sent it to T_1 and T_2. The target node $T_1(T_2)$ obtains information b and $a \oplus b$ (a and $a \oplus b$), $T_1(T_2)$ can obtain the information $a(b)$ from $S_1(S_2)$ by decoding $b \oplus (a \oplus b) = a$ ($a \oplus (a \oplus b) = b$). In this case, the average transmission rate is 2 bit/unit time, which achieves the network maximum flow value.

2.2 Bell States and Pauli Matrices

Bell states are entangled states consisting of two particles. In a Bell state, the two particles are correlated, that is, the change of one particle will affect another particle. The four Bell states in the protocol are defined as follows.

$$|\Phi^+\rangle = \frac{|00\rangle + |11\rangle}{\sqrt{2}} = \frac{|++\rangle + |--\rangle}{\sqrt{2}} \tag{1}$$

$$|\Phi^-\rangle = \frac{|00\rangle - |11\rangle}{\sqrt{2}} = \frac{|+-\rangle + |-+\rangle}{\sqrt{2}} \tag{2}$$

$$|\Psi^+\rangle = \frac{|01\rangle + |10\rangle}{\sqrt{2}} = \frac{|++\rangle - |--\rangle}{\sqrt{2}} \tag{3}$$

$$|\Psi^-\rangle = \frac{|01\rangle - |10\rangle}{\sqrt{2}} = \frac{|+-\rangle - |-+\rangle}{\sqrt{2}} \tag{4}$$

In this paper, four Pauli operators are used to encode classical information. The four Pauli operators are given as follows.

$$I = \begin{pmatrix} 1 & 0 \\ 0 & 1 \end{pmatrix} = |0\rangle\langle0| + |1\rangle\langle1| = U_0 \tag{5}$$

$$\sigma_Z = \begin{pmatrix} 1 & 0 \\ 0 & -1 \end{pmatrix} = |0\rangle\langle0| - |1\rangle\langle1| = U_1 \tag{6}$$

$$\sigma_X = \begin{pmatrix} 0 & 1 \\ 1 & 0 \end{pmatrix} = |0\rangle\langle1| + |1\rangle\langle0| = U_2 \tag{7}$$

$$i\sigma_Y = \begin{pmatrix} 0 & 1 \\ -1 & 0 \end{pmatrix} = |0\rangle\langle1| - |1\rangle\langle0| = U_3 \tag{8}$$

3 Quantum Network Coding Protocol

As shown in Fig. 2, two senders S_1 and S_2 are required to send 2 bits of classic information to T_1 and T_2 respectively. Let suppose that $S_1(S_2)$ transmit the classical information $m_1(m_2)$, corresponding to the Pauli operator $U_{m1}(U_{m2})$. Among them, the channels $C_1 \rightarrow C_2$, $C_2 \rightarrow T_1$ and $C_2 \rightarrow T_2$ transmit two quantum bits, and other channels transmit single quantum bit.

Only the senders and receivers know the corresponding relations between four Pauli operators and 2-bit classical information. This paper defines four coding schemes as follows:

$$\begin{aligned}
&Scheme\ 1: I \leftrightarrow 00, \sigma_Z \leftrightarrow 01, \sigma_X \leftrightarrow 10, i\sigma_Y \leftrightarrow 11 \\
&Scheme\ 2: I \leftrightarrow 00, \sigma_Z \leftrightarrow 10, \sigma_X \leftrightarrow 01, i\sigma_Y \leftrightarrow 11 \\
&Scheme\ 3: I \leftrightarrow 11, \sigma_Z \leftrightarrow 01, \sigma_X \leftrightarrow 10, i\sigma_Y \leftrightarrow 00 \\
&Scheme\ 4: I \leftrightarrow 11, \sigma_Z \leftrightarrow 10, \sigma_X \leftrightarrow 01, i\sigma_Y \leftrightarrow 00
\end{aligned} \tag{9}$$

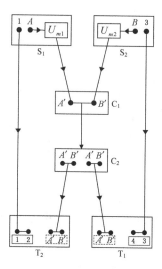

Fig. 2. Diagram of anti-noise quantum network coding protocol, where dotted lines rectangles represent Bell base measurements and solid rectangles represent joint measurements.

Pauli operators coding scheme and Bell states vector $|\varphi\rangle$ are determined randomly between S_1, S_2, T_1 and T_2 in advance, and they also share a set of secret keys. Two senders S_1 and S_2 share a pair of Bell states $|\varphi\rangle_{A,B}$, where S_1 has the particle A and S_2 has the particle B. S_1 and T_2, S_2 and T_1 share a pair of Bell states $|\varphi\rangle_{1,2}$ and $|\varphi\rangle_{3,4}$, respectively, where S_1 has the particle 1, T_2 has the particle 2, S_2 has the particle 3 and T_1 has the particle 4.

The protocol process can be described as follows:

Step (1) S_1 and S_2 determine the location of the particles in the message mode or control mode according to the key.

Step (2) (a) In the control mode, $S_1(S_2)$ sends the particle $A(B)$ on hand directly to C_1, and then C_1 gets $|\varphi\rangle_{A,B}$. (b) In the message mode, $S_1(S_2)$ applies U_{m1} (U_{m2}) on the particle $A(B)$ and sends it $(|\varphi\rangle_{A',B'})$ to $C_1(C_1)$, at the same time, $S_1(S_2)$ applies U_{m1} (U_{m2}) on the particle 1(3) and sends it to $T_2(T_1)$.

Step (3) C_1 sends the particles $|\varphi\rangle_{A,B}$(or $|\varphi\rangle_{A',B'}$) to C_2.

Step (4) C_2 prepares the particles $|\varphi\rangle_{A,B}$(or $|\varphi\rangle_{A',B'}$) and sends them to T_1 and T_2 respectively.

Step (5) For particles in the control mode, T_1 and T_2 measured the obtained particles $|\varphi\rangle_{A,B}$ and compared with the initially determined Bell state carrier $|\varphi\rangle$. If the error rate is higher than a certain threshold, the communication will be abandoned. Otherwise, it turns to the step (6).

Step (6) Let decode the information at node T_1 and T_2 respectively to obtain the classical information.

Where, at node T_2, we can get U_{m1} by perform the joint measurement on the particles 1 and 2. Then $U_{m1}U_{m2}$ can be obtained by measuring the Bell state $|\varphi\rangle_{A',B'}$ transmitted by C_2. Finally, we can get U_{m2} by comparing U_{m1} and $U_{m1}U_{m2}$, so that we can restore m_2. In the same way, we can decode m_1 at the node T_1, the whole process is shown as Fig. 3.

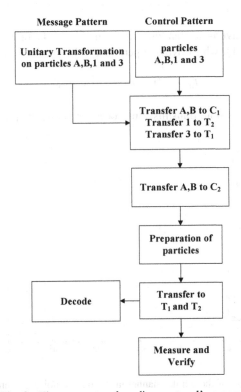

Fig. 3. The new network coding protocol's process.

For clarity, an example to illustrate the process of the message mode is given as follow. Let suppose the scheme 1 in Eq. (9) is adopted as the coding method, and the Bell state carrier is the quantum state as Eq. (1). S_1 wants to transmit 00 to T_1, which is corresponding to the operation U_0, and S_2 wants to transmit 01 to T_2, which is corresponding to the operation U_1. S_1 and S_2 apply the unitary operations on the particle they have. As a result, C_1 gets $|\Phi^-\rangle_{A,B}=\frac{|00\rangle-|11\rangle}{\sqrt{2}}$. S_1 applies U_{m1} on the particle 1 and sends it to T_2, T_2 gets $|\Phi^+\rangle_{1,2}=\frac{|00\rangle+|11\rangle}{\sqrt{2}}$. In the same way, T_1 gets $|\Phi^-\rangle_{3,4}=\frac{|00\rangle-|11\rangle}{\sqrt{2}}$. Finally, T_1 gets $|\Phi^-\rangle_{3,4}$ and $|Phi^-\rangle_{A,B}$, and T_2 gets $|\Phi^+\rangle_{1,2}$ and $|\Phi^-\rangle_{A,B}$. Finally, T_2 compares the results measured by $|\Phi^-\rangle_{A,B}$ and $|\Phi^+\rangle_{1,2}$ to obtain $U_{m1}=\sigma_Z$ and gets the information **01**. By using the same method, T_1 can get the information **00**.

4 Analysis of Noise and Fidelity

In this section, four noise environments in quantum channel will be illustrated, as well as the fidelity of the channels under the influence of four classical quantum noises, the bit-flip, phase-flip, amplitude damping and depolarizing noises.

4.1 Bit-Flip Noise

The bit-flip noise converts a quantum bit from $|0\rangle$ to $|1\rangle$ or from $|1\rangle$ to $|0\rangle$ with probability $p(0 \leq p \leq 1)$, whose Kraus operator can be expressed as follow

$$E_0 = \sqrt{1 - P}I, E_1 = \sqrt{P}\sigma_X \tag{10}$$

The fidelity of the whole transmission process is shown as Fig. 4.

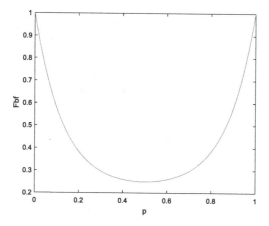

Fig. 4. The fidelity of the whole channel in the bit-flip noise and phase-flip noise.

$$F_{BF} = 16p^6 - 48p^5 + 64p^4 - 48p^3 + 22p^2 - 6p + 1. \tag{11}$$

According to the analysis results above, the effect of bit-flip noise has symmetry. When the noise probability $p = 0.5$, the channel has the lowest fidelity. When $0 \leq p \leq 0.5$, the channel fidelity decreases as the probability increases. When $0.5 \leq p \leq 1$, the fidelity of channel increases with the decrease of p.

4.2 Phase-Flip Noise or Phase Damping

The phase-flip noise turns a quantum bit from $|1\rangle$ to $-|1\rangle$ with probability $p(0 \leq p \leq 1)$, the Kraus operator can be expressed as follows

$$E_0 = \sqrt{1 - P}I, E_1 = \sqrt{P}\sigma_Z. \tag{12}$$

The fidelity of the whole transmission process is shown as Fig. 5.

$$F_{PF} = 16p^6 - 48p^5 + 64p^4 - 48p^3 + 22p^2 - 6p + 1. \tag{13}$$

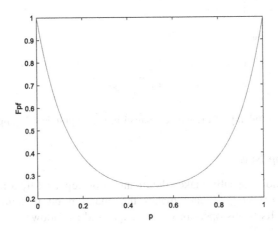

Fig. 5. The fidelity of the whole channel in the phase-flip noise.

According to the analysis results above, It is not difficult to find that the effect of bit-flip noise and the effect of phase-flip noise on the channel is the same. When the noise probability exceeds 0.5, the fidelity is enhanced instead, indicating that this channel has good resistance to strong bit-flip noise and strong phase-flip noise, which is very suitable to use in such an environment.

4.3 Bit-Flip Noise

The amplitude damping noise denotes the loss of information due to energy decay, whose probability of a recession is $p(0 \leq p \leq 1)$. The Kraus operator can be expressed as follow

$$E_0 = \begin{pmatrix} 1 & 0 \\ 0 & \sqrt{1-P} \end{pmatrix}, E_1 = \begin{pmatrix} 0 & \sqrt{P} \\ 0 & 0 \end{pmatrix} \tag{14}$$

The fidelity of the whole transmission process is shown as Fig. 6.

$$F_{AD} = \frac{1}{8}p^6 - p^5 + \frac{13}{4}p^4 - \frac{11}{2}p^3 + \frac{21}{4}p^2 - 3p + 1 \tag{15}$$

According to the analysis results above, the channel fidelity decreases as the probability decreases.

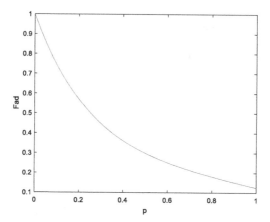

Fig. 6. The fidelity of the whole channel in the amplitude damping noise.

4.4 Depolarizing Noise

The depolarizing noise usually makes the quantum bit replaced by a fully mixed state with probability $p(0 \leq p \leq 1)$, and makes the quantum bit remain the same with probability $1 - p$. Its Kraus operator can be expressed as follow

$$E_0 = \sqrt{1 - p}I, E_1 = \sqrt{\frac{p}{3}}\sigma_X, E_2 = \sqrt{\frac{p}{3}}\sigma_Z, E_3 = \sqrt{\frac{p}{3}}\sigma_Y \qquad (16)$$

The fidelity of the whole transmission process is shown as Fig. 7.

$$F_D = \frac{256}{81}p^6 - \frac{128}{9}p^5 + \frac{736}{27}p^4 - \frac{256}{9}p^3 + \frac{52}{3}p^2 - 6p + 1 \qquad (17)$$

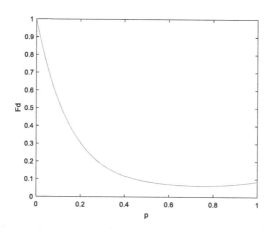

Fig. 7. The fidelity of the whole channel in the depolarizing noise.

According to the analysis results above, channel fidelity increases with probability. If $0 \leq p \leq 0.3$, the channel fidelity decreases sharply with the decreasing probability. If $0.3 \leq p \leq 0.8$, the fidelity decreases slowly with the decreasing probability. If $p > 0.8$, the fidelity of the channel is steepened again as the probability decreases.

4.5 Comparison of Four Noise Effects

Comparison of channel fidelity under the influence of four kinds of noise is shown in Fig. 8.

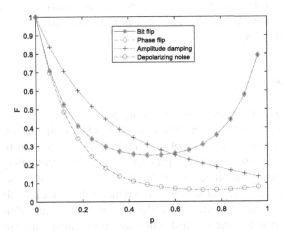

Fig. 8. The comparison of four noise effects.

It can be seen from Fig. 8 that, when the noise probability $p \leq 0.6$, the comparison of four kinds of noise's fidelity of the channel indicate that the amplitude damping has the least impact, the depolarizing noise has the largest impact, and the bit-flip noise and phase-flip noise have the same impact on the channel between that of the amplitude damping and that of the depolarizing noise. In the case of the probability of noise $p > 0.6$, the fidelity of bit-flip and phase-flip increases with the increase of noise probability. It means that they have good resistance to strong noise, and is very suitable to use in this noise environment.

5   Analysis of Security and Resource Consumption

The analytical results present following show that the novel protocol a good performance on security. The encoding agreement of U_x and option of Bell states can be viewed as the key for message transmission, which is only visible to the senders and the receivers. Assuming that the attacker Eve carries out the intercept attack, he can eavesdrop to obtain all the information received by T_2. However, the only thing he get is the unitary operator, for the reason that he does not know the corresponding relationship between the four Pauli operators and the classical information, the attacker cannot get the message m_2 which is send to T_2 by S_2. In addition, the attacker cannot get the information sent by S_1 based on the information obtained by T_2, because he does not know which Bell state the sender uses as carrier and which Bell state the unitary operator is acted on. If Eve carries out the interception-retransmission attack, then he can make a Bell state randomly and send it to the destination node. In this case, the false Bell state obtained by the receiver can be detected with a certain probability. As a result, this communication will be abandoned to ensure the authenticity of the information received by the receiver.

In this protocol, the shared Bell entangled states between S_1 and T_2, S_2 and T_1 only plays an auxiliary role. So that, the new protocol accounts for a large part of the resource consumption. However, in the main transfer part, the consumption of resources is not very large.

6   Conclusions

In this paper, a novel quantum network coding protocol is proposed, which uses Bell states as the carrier to encode and transmit classical information by applying Pauli operators. The new algorithm can not only realize the information transmission with better efficiency, but also effectively prevent potential eavesdropping attackers from obtaining information transmitted. By analyzing the influence of four kinds of noises on the quantum channel in this protocol, it is found that if the noise probability $p \leq 0.6$, the amplitude damping noise has the least influence on the quantum channel, meanwhile the depolarizing noise has the greatest influence on the quantum channel. If the noise probability $p > 0.6$, the quantum channel has better resistance on bit flip and phase flip noises. Moreover, the protocol is possible to be combined with QSDC protocol or identity authentication mechanism to improve on the security performance of quantum network coding further.

Based on the detailed mathematical analysis to the efficiency and security, it can be concluded that the proposed protocol not only perform well on improving the efficiency of information transmission, throughput and link utilization in quantum network, but also on enhancing reliability and preventing eavesdropping attacks.

Acknowledgments. This work was supported by the National Natural Science Foundation of China (No. 61373131, 61303039, 61772281, 61232016, 61501247), Natural Science Foundation of Jiangsu Province (Grant No. BK20171458), Sichuan Youth Science and Technique Foundation (No. 2017JQ0048), NUIST Research Foundation for Talented Scholars (2015r014), PAPD and CICAEET funds.

References

1. Yu, S.L., Pan, J.W.: I have a quantum dream in mind. The People's Daily, 04 June 2014
2. Qu, Z.G., Zhu, T.C., Wang, J.W., Wang, X.J.: A novel quantum stegonagraphy based on brown states. Comput. Mater. Continua **56**(1), 47–59 (2018)

3. Liu, W.J., Chen, Z.Y., Liu, J.S., Su, Z.F., Chi, L.H.: Full-blind delegating private quantum computation. Comput. Mater. Continua **56**(2), 211–223 (2018)
4. Bennett, C.H.: Quantum cryptography using any two nonorthogonal states. Phys. Rev. Lett. **68**(21), 3121 (1992)
5. Bennett, C.H., Brassard, G.: Quantum cryptography: public key distribution and coin tossing. In: Proceedings of IEEE International Conference on Computers Systems and Signal Processing, vol. 175, pp. 175–179 (1984)
6. Hayashi, M.: Prior entanglement between senders enables perfect quantum network coding with modification. Phys. Rev. A **76**(4), 538 (2007)
7. Hayashi, M., Iwama, K., Nishimura, H., Raymond, R., Yamashita, S.: Quantum network coding. In: Thomas, W., Weil, P. (eds.) STACS 2007. LNCS, vol. 4393, pp. 610–621. Springer, Heidelberg (2007). https://doi.org/10.1007/978-3-540-70918-3_52
8. Shang, T., Zhao, X.J., Wang, C., et al.: Controlled quantum network coding scheme based on single controller. Acta Electronica Sinica **42**(10), 1913–1917 (2014)
9. Bennett, C.H., Brassard, G., Crepeau, C.: Teleporting an unknown quantum state via dual classical and Einstein-Podolsky-Rosen channels. Phys. Rev. Lett. **70**(13), 1895–1899 (1993)
10. Moroder, T., Kleinmann, M., Schindler, P., Monz, T., Gühne, O., Blatt, R.: Certifying systematic errors in quantum experiments. Phys. Rev. Lett. **110**(18), 180401 (2012)
11. Peng, C.Z., Yang, T., Bao, X.H., et al.: Experimental free-space distribution of entangled photon pairs over 13 km: towards satellite-based global quantum communication. Phys. Rev. Lett. **94**(15), 150501 (2005)
12. Yin, J., Ren, J.G., Lu, H., et al.: Quantum teleportation and entanglement distribution over 100-kilometre free-space channels. Nature **488**(7410), 185–188 (2013)
13. Akter, L., Natarajan, B.: QoS constrained resource allocation to secondary users in cognitive radio networks. Comput. Commun. **32**(18), 1923–1930 (2009)
14. Ma, S.Y., Chen, X.B., Luo, M.X.: Probabilistic quantum network coding of M-qudit states over the butterfly network. Opt. Commun. **283**(3), 497–501 (2009)
15. Yan, S.S., Kuang, H.M., Guo, Y.: Quantum coding of butterfly network based on controlled quantum teleportation. National Sci. Paper Online Excellent Paper **5**(20), 1996–2001 (2012)
16. Nishimura, H.: Quantum network coding — How can network coding be applied to quantum information. In: International Symposium on Network Coding, pp. 1–5. IEEE (2013)
17. Korotkov, A.N., Keane, K.: Decoherence suppression by quantum measurement reversal. Phys. Rev. A **81**(81), 1334–1342 (2010)
18. Guan, X.W., Chen, X.B., Wang, L.C.: Joint remote preparation of an arbitrary two-qubit state in noisy environments. Int. J. Theor. Phys. **53**(7), 2236–2245 (2014)
19. Fortes, R., Rigolin, G.: Fighting noise with noise in realistic quantum teleportation. Phys. Rev. A **92**(1), 012338 (2015)
20. Wang, M.M., Qu, Z.G.: Effect of quantum noise on deterministic joint remote state preparation of a qubit state via a GHZ channel. Quantum Inf. Process. **15**(11), 4805–4818 (2016)
21. Wang, M.M., Qu, Z.G., Wang, W.: Effect of noise on deterministic joint remote preparation of an arbitrary two-qubit state. Quantum Inf. Process. **16**(5), 140 (2017). UNSP
22. Wang, M.M., Qu, Z.G., Wang, W., Chen, J.G.: Effect of noise on joint remote preparation of multi-qubit state. Int. J. Quantum Inf. **15**(02), 175–179 (2017)
23. Yu, W., Cioffi, J.M.: FDMA capacity of Gaussian multiple-access channels with ISI. In: IEEE International Conference on Communications, vol. 50, no. 1, pp. 102–111 (2002)
24. Iri, M.: On an extension of the maximum flow minimum cut theorem to multicommodity flows. J. Oper. Res. Soc. Japan **13**, 129–135 (1971)

A Privacy-Preserving Multi-keyword Ranked Search over Encrypted Data in Hybrid Clouds

Hua Dai[1,2]([⊠]), Yan Ji[1], Liang Liu[3], Geng Yang[1,2], and Xun Yi[4]

[1] Nanjing University of Post and Telecommunication, Nanjing 210023, China
{daihua,yangg}@njupt.edu.cn, jiyan199504@163.com
[2] Jiangsu Security and Intelligent Processing Lab of Big Data, Nanjing 210023, China
[3] Nanjing University of Aeronautics and Astronautics, Nanjing 210016, China
liangliu@nuaa.edu.cn
[4] Royal Melbourne Institute of Technology University, Melbourne 3001, Australia
xun.yi@rmit.edu.au

Abstract. Due to the convenience, economy and high scalability of cloud computing, more and more individuals and enterprises are motivated to outsource their data or computing to clouds. In this paper, we propose a privacy-preserving multi-keyword ranked search over encrypted data in hybrid cloud, which is denoted as MRSE-HC. The keyword partition vector model is presented. The keyword dictionary of documents is clustered into balanced partitions by a bisecting k-means clustering based keyword partition algorithm. In accordance with the partitions, the keyword partition based bit vectors are defined for documents and queries which are utilized as the index of searches. The private cloud filters out the candidate documents by the keyword partition based bit vectors, and then the public cloud uses the trapdoor to determine the result in the candidates. The security analysis and performance evaluation show that MRSE-HC is a privacy-preserving multi-keyword ranked search scheme for hybrid clouds and outperforms the existing scheme FMRS in terms of search efficiency.

Keywords: Hybrid cloud · Privacy-preserving ·
Multi-keyword ranked search · Searchable encryption

1 Introduction

Nowadays, the cloud computing is well developed and becoming more and more popular in business, government, et al. Resources such as storage and computing

This research was supported by the National Natural Science Foundation of China under the grant Nos. 61872197, 61572263, 61772285, 61672297 and 61872193; the Postdoctoral Science Foundation of China under the Grant No. 2019M651919; the Natural Science Foundation of Anhui Province under grant No. 1608085MF127; the Natural Research Foundation of Nanjing University of Posts and Telecommunications under the grand No. NY217119.

© Springer Nature Switzerland AG 2019
X. Sun et al. (Eds.): ICAIS 2019, LNCS 11634, pp. 68–80, 2019.
https://doi.org/10.1007/978-3-030-24271-8_7

are treated as the on-demand services in clouds. Attracted by the convenience, economy and high scalability features, data owners (such as individuals, enterprises, et al.) are motivated to outsource their data to the cloud. However, once the data are stored in the remote cloud servers, data owners are unable to control and manage their data directly, and they could be worried about whether their data are well kept in protection and utilized by the authorized users. The cloud service providers, having the root privilege, could abuse or analyze their data, especially the sensitive data, such as medical records, government documents and emails. Such misconduct leads to the breaches of data privacy. Doubts about the security and privacy of outsourced data that are still the major obstacles to the development of cloud computing [1].

A native approach to keep the outsourced data in privacy is to encrypt it before outsourcing. Traditional information retrieval techniques are mainly focused on the plaintext data and cannot be directly adopted to the encrypted data. Obviously, downloading all the encrypted data from the cloud and then decrypting the ciphertext locally to get the result is wasteful and impractical. It is a challenge to research and give searchable encryption schemes that support privacy-preserving multi-keyword ranked search over encrypted cloud data.

To support the multi-keyword search over the outsourced encrypted cloud data, researchers have proposed many Searchable Encryption (SE) schemes [2,3, 6–12,15]. Song et al. [2] proposed the first symmetric searchable encryption (SSE) scheme. Cao et al. [3] realized the first multi-keyword ranked search scheme which adopts Vector Space Model (VSM) [4] and secure KNN [5]. Li et al. [6] proposed a fine-grained multi-keyword search scheme over encrypted cloud data, which supports boolean queries. Xia et al. [7] proposed a secure and dynamic multi-keyword ranked search scheme on the basis of a special tree-based index structure. Zhu et al. [8] and Chen et al. [9] proposed efficient privacy-preserving ranked keyword search schemes, which utilize clustering algorithm to improve search efficiency. Wang et al. [10] and Fu et al. [11] presented multi-keyword fuzzy search schemes, which is able to handle spelling mistakes in queried keyword. All the above works focus on the public clouds, and only Yang et al. [15] have proposed an efficient search scheme for the hybrid clouds which consists of the public cloud (Pub-Cloud) and the private cloud (Pri-Cloud). In this scheme, Pub-Cloud is honest-but-curious while Pri-Cloud is trust. They cooperate to accomplish a ranked search where Pri-Cloud is on charge of finding the candidate documents and then Pub-Cloud calculates the final result during the candidates.

In this paper, we propose a privacy-preserving multi-keyword ranked search over encrypted data in hybrid clouds (MRSE-HC). First, the keyword partition vector model is given. In this model, the keyword dictionary of documents is clustered into balanced partitions by the keyword partition algorithm on the basis of the bisecting k-means clustering. The document filtering bit vector (DFB-vectors) and the query filtering bit vector (QFB-vector) are defined for documents and queries respectively. The former is utilized as the index of achieving efficient searches. Second, stages of the proposed scheme are introduced. In the setup stage, DFB-vectors are generated and deployed in Pri-Cloud while the encrypted documents and the corresponding encrypted vectors are generated and outsourced to Pub-Cloud. In the search stage, once a query with multi-keywords is started, the corresponding QFB-vector and trapdoor are generated and submitted to Pri-Cloud and Pub-Cloud respectively. Pri-Cloud uses the QFB-vector and DFB-vectors to filter out the candidate documents. Then Pub-Cloud uses the trapdoor to determine the result in the candidates. Because keywords in a partition are in high relevance with each other and the keywords of a query are usually relevant to each other in practice, the number of target partitions is small and the candidate documents are less correspondingly. Therefore, the proposed search scheme is more efficient than the existing scheme, which is also indicated in the performance evaluation result.

2 Notations and Preliminaries

2.1 Notations

For the sake of clarity of this paper, we give the main notations as follows.

- d_i — A plaintext document.
- D — A plaintext document collection, $D = \{d_1, d_2, ..., d_m\}$.
- V_{d_i} — The n-dimensional document vector of d_i.
- V_D — The set of document vectors of documents in D, $V_D = \{V_{d_1}, V_{d_2}, ..., V_{d_m}\}$.
- $\widetilde{d_i}$ — The encrypted document of d_i.
- $\widetilde{D}$ — The encrypted document collection of D, $\widetilde{D} = \{\widetilde{d_1}, \widetilde{d_2}, ..., \widetilde{d_m}\}$.
- $\widetilde{V}_{d_i}$ — The encrypted n-dimensional document vector of $\widetilde{d_i}$.
- $\widetilde{V}_D$ — The set of encrypted documents vectors, $\widetilde{V}_D = \{\widetilde{V}_{d_1}, \widetilde{V}_{d_2}, ..., \widetilde{V}_{d_m}\}$.
- W — A keyword dictionary having n keywords, $W = \{w_1, w_2, ..., w_n\}$.
- PL — A list of keyword partitions, $PL = \{P_1, P_2, ..., P_\tau\}$.
- VF_{d_i} — The τ-dimensional DFB-vector of d_i.
- VF_D — The set of DFB-vectors of the documents, $VF_D = \{VF_{d_1}, VF_{d_2}, ..., VF_{d_m}\}$.
- Q — A query request with multi-keywords.
- V_Q — The n-dimensional query vector of Q.
- $\widetilde{V}_Q$ — The trapdoor of Q which is the encrypted n-dimensional query vector.
- VF_Q — The τ-dimensional QFB-vector of Q.
- CID — A set of candidate document IDs for the query Q.

2.2 Preliminaries

We introduce three key preliminaries of our work, the vector space model, the relevance score measurement and the secure inner product operation.

Vector Space Model. The vector space model [4] along with TF-IDF [17] is widely used in the secure multi-keyword search. We adopt the classic definitions of term frequency (TF) and inverse document frequency (IDF). Each document

d_i is represented as a n-dimensional vector which equals the capacity of the keyword dictionary. $V_{d_i}[j]$ stores the normalized TF value of the keyword w_j. Additionally, the queried keywords in Q are also transformed into a n-dimensional vector V_Q which stores the normalized IDF values of the keywords in Q.

Relevance Score Measurement. In this paper, we use the same measurements in [20] to calculate the relevance score between a document and a search. Given a document d_i and a query Q with multiple queried keywords, the relevance score between d_i and Q is represented by the inner product between the corresponding document vector V_{d_i} and the corresponding query vector V_Q, i.e. $V_{d_i} \cdot V_Q$.

Secure Inner Product Operation. We adopt the secure inner product operation in our scheme which is proposed in [5]. The operation is able to calculate the inner product of two encrypted vectors without knowing the plaintext value of them. The basic idea of this is as follows. Assuming that p and q are two n-dimensional vectors and M is a random $n \times n$ invertible matrix. M is treated as the secure key. The encrypted form of p and q are denoted as $\widetilde{p}$ and $\widetilde{q}$ respectively, where $\widetilde{p} = pM^{-1}$ and $\widetilde{q} = qM^T$. Then we have $\widetilde{p} \cdot \widetilde{q} = (pM^{-1}) \cdot (qM^T) = pM^{-1}(qM^T)^T = pM^{-1}Mq = p \cdot q$, i.e. $\widetilde{p} \cdot \widetilde{q} = p \cdot q$. Therefore, we have that the inner product of two encrypted vectors equals the inner product of the corresponding two plaintext vectors.

3   Problem Description

The system considered in this paper is the same as [15] which has four entities: the data owner (DO), the data user (DU), the private cloud (Pri-Cloud) and the public cloud (Pub-Cloud). DO is on charge of outsourcing its data to Pub-Cloud and storing the index in Pri-Cloud. DU is the user authorized by DO which is on charge of starting a query and receiving the search result. Pri-Cloud is on charge of storeing the index and filtering out the candidate document IDs. Pub-Cloud is on charge of storing the outsourced data and performing ranked searches. The cooperation of them is shown in Fig. 1.

We consider the same threat model as [15], which assumes that DO, DU and Pri-Cloud are trusted [13], but Pub-Cloud is considered as "honest-but-curious". It means that Pub-Cloud honestly performs the established algorithms and returns search results correctly, but it is curious of the outsourced plaintext data and could breach the private information from them. We assume that Pub-Cloud knows not only ciphertext but also the encryption and decryption algorithms, but it does not know the keys. According to the background information that Pub-Cloud has, we adopted the known ciphertext threat model and known background threat model which are also adopted in many related works [3,7–9,11].

In this paper, we focus on the multi-keyword ranked search scheme over encrypted data in the hybrid clouds. The goal is to achieve the following functions and security guarantees:

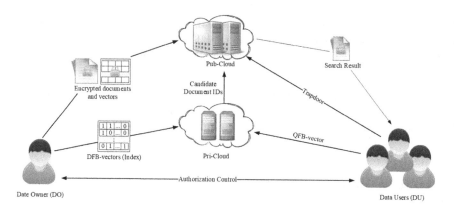

Fig. 1. System model

(1) **Multi-keywords ranked search.** The proposed scheme is designed that Pub-Cloud is able to return most relevant and ranked k documents in the form of ciphertext through the cooperation of Pri-Cloud.

(2) **Search efficiency.** The proposed scheme aims to achieve efficient ranked searches by adopting a novel keyword partition vector model based index. It helps to filter out candidate documents and prune numerous irrelevant documents.

(3) **Privacy-preserving.** The proposed scheme aims to protect the private information from the curious Pub-Cloud. Specifically, the privacy of documents, index, queried keywords and trapdoor unlinkability [3,7,8] should be preserved.

4   Keyword Partition Vector Model

To describe the keyword partition vector model (KPVM), the clustering based keyword partition algorithm is first introduced in this section. Then the keyword partition based bit vectors are defined formally, which are the index of the proposed search scheme.

4.1   Clustering Based Keyword Partition

We design the algorithm *GenPartitions* to partition the keyword dictionary W which is on the basis of the bisecting k-means clustering [14] and shown in Algorithm 1. The Normalized Google-Distance [16] is adopted to measure the distance between keywords. A partition list, denoted as $PL = \{P_1, P_2,..., P_\tau\}$, is the output of this algorithm where τ is a threshold to control the number of partitions.

Algorithm 1: *GenPartitions(W,τ)*

Input: The keyword dictionary W.
Output: The keyword partition list PL.

1 Initialize $PL=\emptyset$;
2 Add W to PL where W is treated as a keyword partition;
3 **while** $|PL| < \tau$ **do**
4 $\quad P_{max} = max(PL)$;
5 $\quad$ Apply the bisecting k-means clustering algorithm to the partition P_{max} by using the Normalized Google-Distance of keywords, and then append the generated two keyword clusters as two partitions in PL;
6 **end**
7 **Return** PL

In Algorithm 1, $max(PL)$ is the function to get the biggest partition of PL which has the most documents. In each round of bisecting k-means clustering, the biggest partition of PL is divided into two smaller partitions. Therefore, Algorithm 1 is a balanced keyword partition algorithm which tends to balance the number of keywords of generated partitions. Meanwhile, keywords with high relevance are clustered into partitions because of the adoption of the bisecting k-means clustering and the Normalized Google-Distance.

Definition 1. *Involved Partitions.* *Given a document $d_i \in D$, the involved partitions of d_i are the partitions that have at least a keyword of d_i. We denote the set of involved partitions of d_i as IPS(d_i), then we have*

$$IPS(d_i) = \{p_j | p_j \cap d_i \neq \emptyset \land P_j \in PL\} \tag{1}$$

Definition 2. *Covered Documents.* *Given a keyword partition $P_i \in PL$, the covered documents of Pi are the documents that have at least a keyword of P_i. We denote the set of covered documents of P_i as CDS(P_i), then we have*

$$CDS(P_i) = \{d_j | d_j \cap P_i \neq \emptyset \land d_j \in D\} \tag{2}$$

Definition 3. *Target Partitions.* *Given a query Q with multi-keyword, the target partitions of Q is the keyword partitions that have at least one queried keywords of Q. We denote the set of target partitions of Q as TPS(Q), then we have*

$$TPS(Q) = \{P_i | Q \cap P_i \neq \emptyset \land P_i \in PL\} \tag{3}$$

Definition 4. *Candidate Documents.* *Given a query Q, the candidate documents of Q are the covered documents of the target partitions of Q. We denote the candidate documents of Q as CDocs(Q), then we have*

$$CDocs(Q) = \bigcup_{P_i \in TPS(Q)} CDS(P_i) \tag{4}$$

4.2   Keyword Partition Based Bit Vectors

Definition 5. *Document Filtering Bit Vector (DFB-Vector).* *Given a document $d_i \in D$, the DFB-vector of d_i is a τ-dimensional bit vector which is denoted as VF_{d_i}. If there is a keyword in d_i belongs to a partition $P_j \in PL$, then $VF_{d_i}[j] = 1$ otherwise $VF_{d_i}[j] = 0$, i.e.*

$$VF_{d_i}[j] = \begin{cases} 1, \exists w_P \in d_i (w_P \in P_j) \\ 0, Else \end{cases} \quad where \quad j \in \{1, 2, ..., \tau\} \qquad (5)$$

Definition 6. *Query Filtering Bit Vector (QFB-Vector).* *Given a query Q with multiple keywords, the QFB-vector of Q is τ-dimensional bit vector which is denoted as VF_Q. If there is a keyword in Q belongs to a partition $P_i \in PL$, then $VF_Q[i] = 1$ otherwise $VF_Q[i] = 0$, i.e.*

$$VF_Q[i] = \begin{cases} 1, \exists w_P \in Q (w_P \in P_i) \\ 0, Else \end{cases} \quad where \quad i \in \{1, 2, ..., \tau\} \qquad (6)$$

According to Definitions 5 and 6, we have that the DFB-vector indicates the involved partitions of the corresponding document while the QFB-Vector indicates the target partitions of a query. For example, if $VF_{d_i}[j] = 1$, then P_j is a involved partition of d_i, which means that d_i is a covered document of P_j. And if $VF_Q[j] = 1$, then P_j is the target partition of the query Q and di is a candidate document of Q. Therefore, we can deduce Observation 1 as follows.

Observation 1. Given a query Q, we have

$$CDocs(Q) = \{d_i | VF_{d_i} \& VF_Q \neq \{0\}^\tau \wedge d_i \in D\} \qquad (7)$$

where "&" is the bitwise AND operator and $\{0\}^\tau$ represents a τ-dimensional zero bit vector.

Observation 1 indicates that, given a document d_i, if the bitwise AND operation result between the DFB-vector of d_i and the QFB-vector of Q is not a zero bit vector, then d_i is a candidate document of Q. Therefore, the DFB-vectors and QFB-vector are the index for filtering out the candidate documents and speeding up the searches.

5   MRSE-HC Scheme

On the basis of the keyword partition vector model, we give the detail of our scheme which consists of two stages which are setup stage and search stage. The former is to set up the system while the latter is to perform the search.

5.1   Algorithms in Setup Stage

(1) $SK \leftarrow GenKey(1^{l(n)})$

DO generates the secure key $SK = \{S, M_1, M_2, g\}$ where S is a random n-dimensional bit vector, M_1 and M_2 are random $n \times n$-dimensional invertible matrix, and g is the key for document encryption. SK is shared by DO and DU.

(2) $PL \leftarrow GenPartitions(W, \tau)$

This algorithm is given in Algorithm 1 in detail. It is on the basis of the bisecting k-means clustering and the Normalized Google-Distance measurement. After performing the algorithm, keywords with high relevance in the keyword dictionary are clustered into partitions and the partition list $PL = \{P_1, P_2, ..., P_\tau\}$ is generated where τ is a threshold to control the number of output partitions.

(3) $\{V_D, VF_D\} \leftarrow GenVectors(D, PL)$

For each $d_i \in D$, DO generates the corresponding document vector V_{d_i}, and then generates the corresponding DFB-vector VF_{d_i} according to Definition 5. The sets of generated document vectors and DFB-vectors are $V_D = \{V_{d_1}, V_{d_2}, ..., V_{d_m}\}$ and $VF_D = \{VF_{d_1}, VF_{d_2}, ..., VF_{d_m}\}$ respectively. Here, the generated DFB-vectors will be utilized as the index in our scheme to filter out the candidate documents and speed the ranked searches.

(4) $\{\widetilde{D}, \widetilde{V}_D\} \leftarrow EncData(D, V_D, SK)$

For each $d_i \in D$ and the corresponding document vector $V_{d_i} \in V_D$, DO first encrypts d_i into $\widetilde{d_i}$ by a symmetric encryption (such as DES, AES, et al.) with the secret key g in SK. Second, DO generates two random n-dimensional vectors $\{V_{d_i}^1, V_{d_i}^2\}$ according to the random bit vector S in SK. Specifically, if $S[j] = 0$, then $V_{d_i}^1[j] = V_{d_i}^2[j] = V_{d_i}[j]$; otherwise $V_{d_i}^1[j] = GenRand()$ and $V_{d_i}^2[j] = V_{d_i}[j] - V_{d_i}^1[j]$ where $GenRand()$ is a random value generator. Then, the encrypted document vector $\widetilde{V}_{d_i}$ is calculated, $\widetilde{V}_{d_i} = \{V_{d_i}^1 M_1^T, V_{d_i}^2 M_2^T\}$. Through the above operations, the encrypted documents $\widetilde{D} = \{\widetilde{d_1}, \widetilde{d_2}, ..., \widetilde{d_m}\}$ and the corresponding encrypted document vectors $\widetilde{V}_D = \{\widetilde{V}_{d_1}, \widetilde{V}_{d_2}, ..., \widetilde{V}_{d_m}\}$ are generated.

After the above steps, DO outsources the encrypted documents $\widetilde{D}$ and the corresponding encrypted document vectors $\widetilde{V}_D$ to Pub-Cloud. And then DO uploads the DFB-vectors VF_D to Pri-Cloud. It is noticeable that the corresponding document IDs are both stored in Pub-Cloud and Pri-Cloud. At this time, the setup stage is finished and the system is prepared for the multi-keyword search over encrypted documents.

5.2 Algorithms in Search Stage

(1) $\widetilde{V}_Q \leftarrow GenTrapdoor(Q, SK)$

Once a query Q with multi-keywords is applied, DU generates the query vector V_Q and two random n-dimensional vectors $\{V_Q^1, V_Q^2\}$ according to the random bit vector S in SK. Specifically, if $S[i] = 0$, then $V_Q^1[i] = V_Q^2[i] = V_Q[i]$; otherwise $V_Q^1[i] = GenRand()$ and $V_Q^2[i] = V_Q[i] - V_Q^1[i]$. Then, the encrypted query vector $\widetilde{V}_Q$ is calculated, $\widetilde{V}_Q = \{V_Q^1 M_1^{-1}, V_Q^2 M_2^{-1}\}$, which is the trapdoor of Q and submitted to Pub-Cloud.

(2) $VF_Q \leftarrow GenQFBVector(Q, PL)$

According to Definition 6, DU generates the QFB-vector of Q, VF_Q, which indicates the target partitions of Q. And then DU transmits VF_Q to Pri-Cloud.

(3) $CID \leftarrow Filtering(VF_Q, VF_D)$

Pri-Cloud utilizes the DFB-vectors as the index to filter out the candidate documents for the query. It performs the bitwise AND operation between each DFB-vector and the received QFB-vector and then find out the corresponding IDs of the candidate documents for the query Q according to Observation 1. Specifically, for each $VF_{d_i} \in VF_D$, if $VF_{d_i} \& VF_Q$ is not a zero-vector, then $Identity(d_i)$ is added in the ID set CID. Here, $Identity(d_i)$ is the ID of d_i. After processing all the DFB-vectors of VF_D, Pri-Cloud transmits CID to Pub-Cloud. The complexity of this algorithm is $O(m * \tau)$ since there are $m * \tau$ bitwise AND operations.

(4) $\Re \leftarrow Searching(\widetilde{D}, \widetilde{V}_D, \widetilde{V}_Q, CID, k)$

Pub-Cloud computes the inner products between the trapdoor $\widetilde{V}_Q$ and the encrypted document vectors $\{\widetilde{V}_{d_i} | \widetilde{V}_{d_i} \in \widetilde{V}_D \wedge Identity(d_i) \in CID\}$. According to the secure inner production, the inner products between the trapdoor and the encrypted document vectors equal to the inner products between the corresponding plaintext query vector and document vectors respectively, and the inner products represent the relevance scores between the queried keywords and the documents according to the relevance score measurement in the Preliminaries Section. The ranked k encrypted documents with the highest k inner products are the result encrypted documents $\Re$ which is returned to DU. The complexity of this algorithm is $O(|CID| * n + k * |CID|) \approx O(|CID| * n)$ since $k \ll n$ holds generally. $|X|$ represents the item number of the set X.

At last, when DU receives the result encrypted documents $\Re$ from Pub-Cloud, it uses the shared secure key to decrypts the encrypted documents and get the plaintext result documents.

5.3 Security Analysis

In this section, we analyze the MRSE-HC scheme according to the three predefined privacy demands in the problem description.

As shown in the stages of our scheme, the outsourced data in Pub-Cloud are all ciphertext. Specifically, all documents vectors are encrypted by random invertible matrixes and all documents are encrypted by symmetric encryption. According to [3], it is computation-infeasible for Pub-Cloud to deduce the concrete random matrixes on the basis of grasping its stored data, including the encrypted documents, the encrypted vectors and the trapdoor of queries. So the keys for vector encryption are secure. The other security keys in SK are only shared between DO and DU but private to Pub-Cloud. Besides, the DFB-vectors which are the index of the proposed scheme, are stored in Pri-Cloud and Pri-Cloud is trust. Thus, the confidentiality of documents, index and queries are protected from Pub-Cloud. In addition, by adding phantom terms into document vectors, query vectors and partition based bit vectors in the proposed scheme, the keyword privacy and trapdoor unlinkability are well preserved according to the conclusions of [3,7,8]. As a result, we have that MRSE-HC is a privacy-preserving multi-keyword ranked search scheme over encrypted data in hybrid clouds.

6   Performance Evaluation

In this section, we evaluate the performance of our proposed scheme MRSE-HC and compare it with the scheme presented in [15] which is denoted as FMRS. We implement MRSE-HC and FMRS and perform the evaluations on the search time cost on the real data set of NSF Research Award Abstracts provided by UCI [18]. The dataset includes about 129000 abstracts. We use IK Analyzer [19] to extract the keywords from randomly selected abstracts. In detail, we measure the impacts of the parameters m, τ, t and k on the time cost which are the number of documents, keywords in the dictionary, clustered partitions, queried keywords and request documents respectively.

In the following experiments, we evaluate the time cost of searches where one of the above parameters changes and the other parameters adopt the default values. The results are shown in Figs. 2, 3, 4 and 5.

Figures 2, 3, 4 and 5 all show that the proposed MRSE-HC outperforms FMRS in the time cost of ranked searches and the former saves about 70% of the time cost than the latter on average. The reason is that the target partitions of MRSE-HC are usually less than FMRS when a query is applied because the partitions generated in the former is clustered according to the relevance between keywords and the queried keywords are usually relevant to each other. The less are the target partitions, the less are the candidate documents determined, which improves the search efficiency. However, the change of parameters have impacts to the search time cost of both schemes independently. Figure 2 indicates that, as τ grows up, the time cost of MRSE-HC and FRMS both decrease. Figure 3 shows that the increase of the number of request documents k have little impact

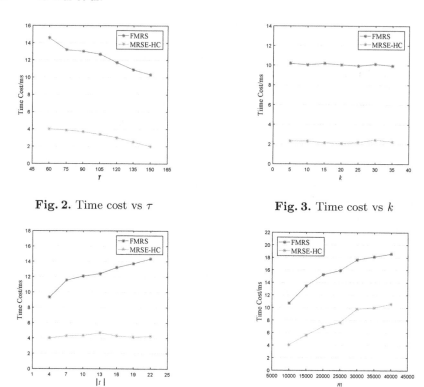

Fig. 2. Time cost vs τ **Fig. 3.** Time cost vs k

Fig. 4. Time cost vs t **Fig. 5.** Time cost vs m

on the time cost of MRSE-HC and FMRS. Figure 4 indicates that as the number of queried keywords t grows up, the time cost of FMRS increases while the time cost of MRSE-HC just has random oscillations. Figure 5 indicates that the time cost of MRSE-HC and FMRS both increase as m grows up.

7   Conclusions

The multi-keyword ranked search over encrypted cloud data is a problem in clouds which provide storage and computing outsourcing services. In this paper, we propose a privacy-preserving multi-keyword ranked search over encrypted data in hybrid cloud. The keyword partition vector model is proposed to define partition based bit vectors as the index. Such partitions are generated by a bisecting k-means clustering based keywords partition algorithm. The partition based bit vectors are deployed in the private cloud while the encrypted documents and the corresponding encrypted vectors are outsourced to the public cloud. When a query is started, the private cloud filters out the candidate documents by using its stored partition based bit vectors, and then the public cloud uses the trapdoor to determine the result in the candidates. Besides, we utilize secure inner product operation to against two threat models. The experimental results show that the scheme proposed in this paper has better performance in terms of search efficiency compared with the existing method.

References

1. Grzonkowski, S., Corcoran, P.M., Coughlin, T.: Security analysis of authentication protocols for next-generation mobile and CE cloud services. In: Proceedings of the IEEE International Conference on Consumer Electronics, Berlin, Germany, pp. 83–87 (2011)
2. Song, D.X., Wagner, D., Perrig, A.: Practical techniques for searches on encrypted data. In: Proceedings of the IEEE Symposium on Security and Privacy, pp. 44–55. IEEE, Oakland (2000)
3. Cao, N., Wang, C., Li, M., Ren, K., Lou, J.: Privacy-preserving multi-keyword ranked search over encrypted cloud data. IEEE Trans. Parallel Distrib. Syst. **25**(1), 222–223 (2014)
4. Witten, I.H., Moffat, A., Bell, T.C.: Managing gigabytes: compressing and indexing documents and images. IEEE Trans. Inf. Theory **41**(6), 79–80 (1995)
5. Wong, W.K., Cheung, D.W., Kao, B., Mamoulis, N.: Secure kNN computation on encrypted databases. In: Proceedings of the 2009 ACM SIGMOD International (2009)
6. Li, H., Yang, Y., Luan, T., et al.: Enabling fine-grained multi-keyword search supporting classified sub-dictionaries over encrypted cloud data. IEEE Trans. Dependable Secur. Comput. **13**(3), 312–325 (2016)
7. Xia, Z., Wang, X., Sun, X., et al.: A secure and dynamic multi-keyword ranked search scheme over encrypted cloud data. IEEE Trans. Parallel Distrib. Syst. **27**(2), 340–352 (2016)
8. Zhu, X., Dai, H., Yi, X., Yang, G., Li, X.: MUSE: an efficient and accurate verifiable privacy-preserving multikeyword text search over encrypted cloud data. Secur. Commun. Netw. **2017**, 1–17 (2017)
9. Chen, C., et al.: An efficient privacy-preserving ranked keyword search method. IEEE Trans. Parallel Distrib. Syst. **27**(4), 951–963 (2016)
10. Wang, B., Yu, S., Lou, W., et al.: Privacy-preserving multi-keyword fuzzy search over encrypted data in the cloud. In: IEEE INFOCOM 2014 - IEEE Conference on Computer Communications, pp. 2112–2120. IEEE, Piscataway (2014)
11. Fu, Z., Wu, X., Guan, C., et al.: Toward efficient multi-keyword fuzzy search over encrypted outsourced data with accuracy improvement. IEEE Trans. Inf. Forensics Secur. **11**(12), 2706–2716 (2016)
12. Liu, Y., Peng, H., Wang, J.: Verifiable diversity ranking search over encrypted outsourced data. CMC: Comput. Mater. Continua **55**(1), 37–57 (2018)
13. Xie, X., Yuan, T., Zhou, X., Cheng, X.: Research on trust model in container-based cloud service. CMC: Comput. Mater. Continua **56**(2), 273–283 (2018)
14. Yu, Z.: Symmetric repositioning of bisecting K-means centers for increased reduction of distance calculations for big data clustering. In: 2016 IEEE International Conference on Big Data, Washington, DC, USA, pp. 2709–2715 (2016)
15. Yang , Y., Liu, J., Cai, S., Yang, S.: Fast multi-keyword semantic ranked search in cloud computing, vol. 40 (2017)
16. Cilibrasi, R., Vitanyi, P.M.B.: The google similarity distance. IEEE Trans. Knowl. Data Eng. **19**(3), 370–383 (2007)

17. Manning, C.D., Raghavan, P., Schutze, H.: Introduction to Information Retrieval. Cambridge University Press, Cambridge (2008)
18. Lichman, M.: UCI Machine Learning Repository. University of California, School of Information and Computer Science, Irvine, Calif, USA (2013)
19. Wang, Z., Meng, B.: A comparison of approaches to chinese word segmentation in hadoop. In: 2014 IEEE International Conference on Data Mining Workshop, Shenzhen, China, pp. 844–850 (2014)
20. Chen, C., Zhu, X., Shen, P., et al.: An efficient privacy-preserving ranked keyword search method. IEEE Trans. Parallel Distrib. Syst. **27**(4), 951–963 (2016)

Application of Blockchain Technology in Agricultural Product Traceability System

Zhihua Wang[1,2] and Pingzeng Liu[1,2(✉)]

[1] Shandong Agricultural University, Tai'an 271018, China
lpz8565@126.com
[2] Shandong Provincial Agricultural Information Center, Ji'nan 250013, China

Abstract. Agricultural products are the foundation of the people's survival, and the quality of agricultural products has always been the focus of attention of society and the government; the original agricultural product traceability system is too difficult to tamper with data due to the excessive concentration of data storage, it faces the challenge of fraudulent data tracing, and it is difficult for consumers to trust such traceability results. Moreover, the centralized storage method is not conducive to the centralized management of traceable data from many enterprises, and there will be problems of low traceability and difficulty in government supervision. The emergence of blockchain technology provides a new solution for data security problems of food traceability, its decentralization, anti-tampering and other characteristics and data encryption technology improve the difficulty of data fraud and ensure data security. If the blockchain is combined with the traceability of agricultural products, the safety of traceable data and the tampering of data can be guaranteed to the greatest extent, the producer's production behavior can be regulated, and consumers' confidence in food quality can be improved. This paper mainly proposes a framework of agricultural product traceability system based on Hyperledger technology, it uses blockchain to store the traceability data of agricultural products safely, and proposes a traceability model of agricultural products, which can cover the entire industrial chain of agricultural products, and consumers can query the authentic source of traceability of agricultural products [1].

Keywords: Blockchain · Traceability of agricultural products · Hyperledger · Trusted traceability

1 Introduction

In recent years, with the improvement of living standards, people's requirements for food quality are getting higher and higher, no longer satisfied with not being hungry, but also requiring healthy eating and eating nutrition. The quality and safety of agricultural products has become the focus of the whole society.

Nowadays, the quality of agricultural products on the market is now uneven, and people cannot always buy quality agricultural products. Although the traditional agricultural product traceability system can guarantee the quality of agricultural products to a certain extent, its centralized data storage method cannot guarantee the security of data, it cannot guarantee that the traceability information of agricultural

© Springer Nature Switzerland AG 2019
X. Sun et al. (Eds.): ICAIS 2019, LNCS 11634, pp. 81–90, 2019.
https://doi.org/10.1007/978-3-030-24271-8_8

products that consumers have inquired is authentic and reliable, this is a blow to consumers' confidence in the quality of agricultural products [2].

As bitcoin is popular all over the world, blockchain is known as the underlying technology and is being understood by more and more people. The decentralization and tamper resistance of the blockchain have pointed out a new direction for the upgrading and optimization of the traceability system of agricultural products, if the traditional agricultural product traceability system is combined with the blockchain, the problem of data fraud can be solved to a large extent, and it will enhance consumer confidence in the traceability of agricultural products.

2   Blockchain Technology

2.1   Research Background

At the earliest, blockchain existed as the underlying technology of bitcoin.

On October 31, 2008, a person named Satoshi Nakamoto presented the bitcoin project white paper "Bitcoin: A Peer-to-Peer Electronic Cash System".

The first bitcoin was generated on January 3, 2009. Bitcoin combines the achievements of many disciplines such as economics, probability theory, and cryptography, and it has been running steadily for nine years without unattended management without major system failures, and blockchain, as its core technical support, is recognized by more and more people.

Now, blockchain technology has been used independently of the Bitcoin system and is used in many fields such as finance, logistics, credit reporting, and trade.

2.2   Core Technology

Blockchain technology based on Hyperledger, is a chain structure consisting of blocks connected in series, every block in the chain holds data. Blockchain contains three elements: data, block, chain. blockchain structure (see Fig. 1) [3].

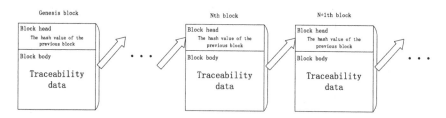

Fig. 1. Blockchain structure diagram

Data: Traceable data is information generated during the production, processing, transportation, etc. of agricultural products, for product traceability; in the Bitcoin system, the transaction data is stored.

Block: Is a data structure, divided into block headers and block entities, the block header stores information such as the hash value of the previous block, and the above data is stored in the block body. In the Bitcoin system, block body stores transaction data, in this traceability system, block body stores traceable data.

Chain: Sorting the chained structure in tandem according to the time sequence of block generation.

Each block contains the hash value of all the data in the previous block, and traceability data. Due to this mechanism, once you modify any of these blocks, it will lead to a series of chain reactions, So the blocks that have been added to the chain cannot be changed. Blockchain keeps track of and protects data security, is the basis for realizing credible traceability of agricultural products.

2.3 Key Technology

Key technologies for blockchain include consensus algorithms and smart contracts.

Consensus algorithm: The consensus algorithm is an algorithm that determines how each node chooses when facing multiple data to be added to the block, this algorithm keeps the consistency of the data stored in each node to the greatest extent possible. The most widely used consensus algorithm is the Byzantine algorithm.

Smart contract: Smart contracts exist in blockchain systems based on Hyperledger technology, it is a piece of code contract, a logic for processing transactions, it can be understood as an electronic contract [4]. Nodes in the blockchain can negotiate to write smart contracts, methods for processing transactions is defined in a smart contract, When a condition is triggered, the blockchain system can automatically execute the corresponding processing flow according to the pre-agreed transaction processing method in the smart contract. The execution of smart contracts has the characteristics of enforcement [5].

2.4 Blockchain Characteristics

Blockchain has the characteristics of decentralization and tamper resistance.

Decentralization: The physical storage of the blockchain is distributed, block node system contains multiple nodes, all nodes are maintaining the same blockchain, these nodes can store information or publish information, each node maintains a full backup of the blockchain, any message can only be saved by all nodes through the consensus algorithm, if the data of a node is missing, data can be re-imported based on backups from other nodes, the more nodes, the more secure the data.

Tamper protection: Due to the above decentralization, once the data is added to the blockchain through the consensus algorithm, it cannot be deleted. To modify the data in the blockchain, you need to modify the data in all nodes, the cost is often huge, which makes the data counterfeiters worth the loss [6].

2.5 Blockchain System Research Example

In recent years, research on blockchain traceability systems has been underway in all parts of the world.

First attempt to add blockchain technology to logistics systems in the field of cross-border logistics. Maersk Line is the world's largest container logistics company, in 2016, together with the blockchain experts at the University of Information Technology in Copenhagen, it is demonstrated whether the application of blockchain technology to the logistics system is feasible, and they developed a batch of floral logistics systems. In March 2017, Maersk Group and IBM collaborated to develop a logistics system based on blockchain technology, and completed the test, it turns out that blockchain technology has greatly improved the efficiency of logistics and greatly reduced the number of paper documents in the logistics process [7].

Large department stores are also quickly combining blockchain technology with their product traceability systems. In July 2017, in order to improve the transparency of the commodity supply chain, Wal-Mart and IBM form a blockchain alliance with Jingdong Company and Tsinghua University in China. Prior to this, Wal-Mart worked with IBM, Food traceability systems based on blockchain technology have been released in China and the United States, for tracing the Chinese pork and the American mango, it can track a range of information of products from feeding or planting, to processing or picking, To logistics sales, etc. [8].

3 Traditional Agricultural Product Traceability System

3.1 Architecture

The traditional agricultural product traceability system is divided into user layer, system layer, data storage layer, data transmission layer and physical layer (see Fig. 2) [9].

User layer: Is the interface between the user and the system, users can operate the agricultural product traceability system through this interface. The user layer mainly includes interactive methods such as web application, mobile APP, and WeChat applet.

System layer: Agricultural product traceability system, Is the main body of the traceability system of agricultural products. The system is mainly divided into three modules: enterprise operation management module, government supervision module, user service module. enterprise operations management module for enterprise management production activities, including management of employees, control of production process, supervision of financial details of enterprises, management of product sales process, management of storage situation, inquiry of product logistics and transportation, monitoring of environmental information of factory, real-time image monitoring And other functions; the government supervision module is used by the government to supervise the production activities of enterprises, including real-time monitoring of the production environment of the enterprise, displaying the test results of the products, querying the warehousing information, and displaying the traceability information of the products; The customer service module is used for customer inquiry and understanding of the company and its products, including traceability information of the product, company and product introduction, online store, suggestions or complaints.

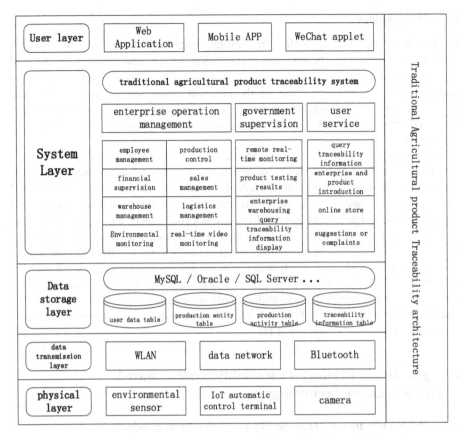

Fig. 2. Traditional agricultural product traceability architecture diagram

Data storage layer: Store all data for the system. The database can be selected from MySQL, Oracle, SQL Server, etc. The table in the database mainly contains user data tables, production entity table, production activity table, traceability information table, etc. User data table stores the account password of the system user. The production entity table stores information on production entities such as greenhouses, fields, crops, etc. The production activity table stores operational information on the production entity, such as fertilization, watering, etc., and the time of operation. The traceability information table stores information such as the number of the product and the source code of the product [10].

Data transmission layer: Information interaction between hardware devices and various software and agricultural product traceability systems, including WLAN, data network, Bluetooth, etc.

Physical layer: Used for environment awareness and system control, including environmental sensors, IoT automatic control terminals, cameras and other hardware. Environmental sensors automatically collect environmental information, the Internet of Things automatic control terminal includes water and fertilizer integrated machine, square fan, roller blind, fill light and other hardware facilities, Camera for real-time image monitoring.

3.2 Disadvantage

The traditional agricultural product traceability system mainly provides services for upper-level applications through the combination of the underlying software and hardware, construct a food quality and safety traceability system covering the entire agricultural product industry chain. In the producer's production process, input data such as planting, processing, transportation and sales into a unified central database, consumers can find out all the production processes that agricultural products have experienced [11].

The traditional agricultural product traceability system focuses on how to improve the coverage of the industrial chain, but ignore a dangerous point: data security. In the traditional agricultural traceability system, Data storage, modification, deletion and query need to operate on the central database, but centralized databases often don't protect data well, database failures and malicious cyber attacks can compromise data security, every piece of production information in the database has been tampered with, This leads to the authenticity of the data, this poses difficulties for consumers to protect their rights and challenges the management of the regulatory authorities; second, because it is a unified database, companies in the agricultural product industry chain cannot store data together, this will expose trade secrets, however, the lack of data will affect the efficiency of traceability of agricultural products, and the government is difficult to supervise and manage it [12].

4 Agricultural Product Traceability System Based on Blockchain Technology

4.1 The Significance of Traceability to Agricultural Products

Blockchain can be seen as a "decentralized" distributed database, traceable data is stored in the block after encryption, every business or organization acts as a node in the blockchain system, have equal status, save and query data in blockchain.

Data Security: In the blockchain system, data is encrypted and saved in the block, each node in the blockchain has its own key, The data saved by this node can only be read by this node, other nodes cannot decipher even if they have acquired data, this mechanism protects the security of data; once the data is uploaded to the blockchain, it will be permanently retained, even if the data is modified, historical archive of data is still retained, this put an end to the tampering of traceability information.

Improve the credibility of traceability information: The data stored in the blockchain is safe and cannot be tampered with, consumers are more convinced of the authenticity of traceability information [13].

Cooperation between enterprises: Blockchain protects data security, this laid a good foundation for cooperation between enterprises. In all aspects of production, companies can store production data in the same blockchain without worrying about data leakage; Companies can collaborate to write smart contracts, determine the agreement between each other in the form of code, the smart contract will automatically execute the relevant instructions when the agreed conditions are met, this improves the efficiency of the company's execution.

Improve the efficiency of traceability of agricultural products: All companies in a production chain store production information in the same blockchain, this will standardize the format of traceability data for each enterprise, forming industry standards, querying traceability data is faster [14].

Facilitate government supervision and management: The government understands the production status of each enterprise and can directly query the blockchain system, and no need to go to each company separately.

4.2   Architecture

The new architecture improves the data storage layer compared to the traditional architecture, adding a smart contract layer (see Fig. 3).

The storage medium in the data storage layer is divided into two parts: database and Hyperledger based blockchain system. The large amount of data stored in the blockchain will burden the system, therefore, data unrelated to the traceability of agricultural products will be stored in each company's own database, key data related to traceability of agricultural products are stored in the blockchain system.

Database stores employee data, environmental data automatically collected by hardware devices, video surveillance data, etc. [15].

Key data related to traceability stored in the blockchain system, Such as processing data, product inspection data, logistics data, etc. these data are generated in the key aspects of production and processing. The query for traceability information is to query these key data from the blockchain and return it to the customer [17].

The intelligent contract layer is written according to the business contract between enterprises. The data operation module performs an increase in data and a query operation.; the fund transaction module is a process of automatically executing the capital transaction process that is negotiated in advance between enterprises, for example, the supplier company delivers raw materials to the receiving company, if the test is correct, the purchaser will automatically pay the payment to the supplier; Security warning module, if the blockchain system detects illegal access or data anomalies, it will be automatically reported to the system administrator [18].

4.3   Agricultural Product Traceability Model

The production of agricultural products is divided into many links, such as planting links, processing links, warehousing links, logistics links, sales links, etc. These links are not monopolized by a single company, they are done by many companies working together (see Fig. 4).

Blockchain: Temporarily in the production process, there are the above five links, every link is chained by itself, save traceability data separately [19].

Enterprise: Each production process is completed by multiple companies, these companies store traceable data into the blockchain of the corresponding link in the production process; products produced by the previous company, will enter the market as a final product, or to the next stage of the business, as a raw material for continued

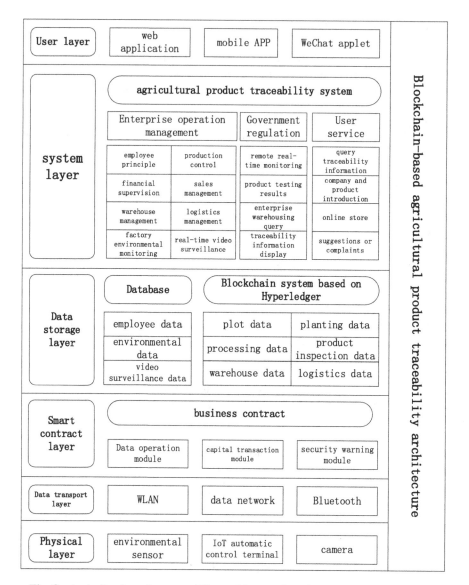

Fig. 3. Agricultural product traceability architecture based on blockchain technology

production; the enterprises in this link get the products of the previous link, the trace source code whose trace source code is used as raw material is stored in the blockchain of this link, after the production of this link, the product will have a new source code, cycle through each link.

Market: All links bring products into the market and consumers buy products.

Consumer: Buy the product and get the source code of the product.

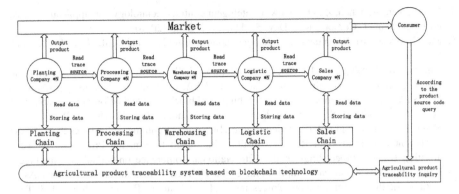

Fig. 4. Agricultural product traceability model

Agricultural product traceability inquiry: Consumers trace the source according to the source code of the product, the system will query the traceability data in the blockchain of each link according to the source code, if the current link is not the first link, it will query the source code of the raw materials in this link, then continue to query in the blockchain of the previous link [20].

Combine the idea of modularity, if the blockchain and the enterprise are combined as a separate module, the input and output of each module are similar, users can make the required modules according to the links they have, then put the selected module into the entire blockchain system, it is equivalent to having its own blockchain system.

5 Summary

Blockchain technology has decentralization and non-tamperable features, blockchain preservation of agricultural traceability data, guaranteed data security. Traditional agricultural product traceability technology has security risks in data storage, combined with blockchain technology, not only solves data security issues, but also provides a new way for cooperation between enterprises. The new agricultural product traceability system is more perfect in terms of system functions, and feedbacks to consumers the true and effective traceability information to ensure people's food safety [21].

References

1. Zhang, Y., Yang, Z., Yang, R., Jin, K., Lin, B., Si, P.: A productivity traceability system based on blockchain. Information Engineering **4**(03), 4–13 (2018)
2. Cheng, Z.: Traceability analysis of cold chain logistics information of fruit and vegetable agricultural products. Mod. Mark. (11), 100 (2018). http://kns.cnki.net/kcms/detail/22.1256.f.20181109.0948.148.html
3. Yang, Y., Xu, Z., Yin, Z.: Design of traceability system for agricultural products. Comput. Knowl. Technol. **14**(04), 235–236 (2018)

4. He, H., Yan, A., Chen, Z.: Overview of intelligent contract technology and application based on blockchain. J. Comput. Res. Dev. **55**(11), 2452–2466 (2018)
5. Ma, C., An, Z., Bi, W., Yuan, Q.: Intelligent contracts in blockchain. Inf. Netw. Secur. (11), 8–17 (2018)
6. Queiroz, M.M., Wamba, S.F.: Blockchain adoption challenges in supply chain: an empirical investigation of the main drivers in India and the USA. Int. J. Inf. Manag. **46**, 70–82 (2019)
7. Wu, S., Yu, C.: Application of internet of things and blockchain technology in traceability of agricultural products. Telecommun. Eng. Technol. Stand. **31**(06), 12–15 (2018)
8. Yang, Z.: Design and implementation of traceable source e-commerce for blockchain. China Intelligent Industrialization Research Institute Intelligent Information Processing Industrialization Branch. Proceedings of the 12th National Conference on Signal and Intelligent Information Processing and Application. China Hi-Tech Industrialization Research Association Intelligent Information Processing Industrialization Branch, China High-Tech Industrialization Research Association, p. 7 (2018)
9. Cheng, X., Xu, J., Zhang, S.: The realization of agricultural food safety to the table by ZHCC's true traceability chain. Food Saf. Guide, (23), 40–45 (2018)
10. Liu, Y., Liu, Y.: The RFID big data security traceability model based on blockchain. Comput. Sci. **45**(S2), 367–368+381 (2018)
11. Yannas, F.: Blockchain promotes a new era of food transparency. Food Saf. Guide, (31), 16–19 (2018)
12. Wang, L.: Discussion on the application of blockchain technology in supply chain tracing. Comput. Fan, (10), 191 (2018)
13. Tao, Q., et al.: Food quality and safety management system based on blockchain technology and its application in rice traceability. China J. Cereals Oils (2019). http://kns.cnki.net/kcms/detail/11.2864.ts.20180817.1024.004.html
14. Mei, L.: Product traceability will be better when it comes to the blockchain. China Qual. Miles, (07), 76–79 (2018)
15. Li, J., Mao, L.: Application research of blockchain technology in traceability system of agricultural products. Mod. Inf. Technol. **2**(06), 192–193+196 (2018)
16. Fu, Y., Liang, Z.: Research on the traceability system of cross-border e-commerce logistics based on blockchain. Chin. Bus. Theory, (14), 7–9 (2018)
17. Chen, W., Feng, G., Zhang, C., et al.: Development and application of big data platform for garlic industry chain. CMC **58**(1), 229–248 (2019)
18. Liu, J., Yang, T., Wang, W.: Anti-counterfeiting traceability system using double blockchain. J. Inf. Secur. **3**(03), 17–29 (2018)
19. Shang, D.: The blockchain in development. Inf. Syst. Eng. (04), 6–9 (2018)
20. Wang, B., Liu, P., Chao, Z., et al.: Research on hybrid model of garlic short-term price forecasting based on big data. CMC **57**(2), 283–296 (2018)
21. Qian, W., Shao, Q., Zhu, Y., Jin, C., Zhou, A.: Blockchain and trusted data management: problems and methods. J. Softw. **29**(01), 150–159 (2018)

Anonymous Authentication Scheme
for Machine-to-machine Communication
Based on Elliptic Curve

Yao Xiong[✉] and Chujun Wu

College of Computer Science and Technology,
Chongqing University of Posts and Telecommunications,
Chongqing 400065, China
807438171@qq.com

Abstract. Recently, the application of the cyber-physical system (CPS) is increasingly widespread. As an important part of CPS, the machine-to-machine communication is also been given a lot of attention. In this paper, we propose a session key agreement scheme bases on elliptic curve for machine-to-machine communication in cyber-physical system. At first, it is easy to calculate, so that it could reduce the occupations of resources; Second, the messages are sent by public channel, which eliminates the cost of encrypted transmission; Third, the using of elliptic curve public key cryptosystem commendably ensures the security of key association. As for feasibility and security, the Burrows–Abadi–Needham (BAN) logic shows the proposed scheme is designed reasonably. The analysis suggest it could resist Replay attack, Man-in-the-middle attack, DoS attack and Impersonation attack.

Keywords: Elliptic curve · Multi-domain · Cyber-physical system · Machine-to-machine · Key agreement

1 Introduction

Nowadays, the area we live is full of interconnection all entities will be able to interconnect and communicate under the CPS environment. The definition of Cyber-physical systems (CPS) is given by papers [1,2], the CPS [2] are integrations of computation and physical processes. The structure of the CPS has three major types of the components [3]. It includes sensing devices, actuators, and controllers. The sensing devices can sense the external environment, the actuator performs the operation, and the controller plays a controlling role. As an important part of CPS, the concept of the machine-to-machine (M2M) was born. The M2M communication [4] causes the emergence of the entire CPS and plays a very important role. The application prospects of M2M are very optimistic, Qi [5] believes.

© Springer Nature Switzerland AG 2019
X. Sun et al. (Eds.): ICAIS 2019, LNCS 11634, pp. 91–103, 2019.
https://doi.org/10.1007/978-3-030-24271-8_9

2   Related Work

In Sect. 2, we are going to discuss related works.

The problem discussed in [6] is more to solve the problem of video transmission networks, While the scheme [7] is also mainly concerning of what conditions are required for the IEEE 802.15.4 standard network to support M2M. Mr. W and his partners [8] proposed a model of M2M certification and corresponding protection, the scheme [9] focuses on the resource-constrained M2M (GLARM) group authentication. As for M2M in multi-domain environment, the paper [10] proposed an anonymous authentication scheme, but there are too many steps. The security and the occupation of resources are also be given conception. The scheme [11] proposes an identity-based security authentication scheme, and could prevent man-in-the-middle attacks and so on. And the scheme [12] uses RSA authentication scheme, the burden on M2M is still heavy. From the perspective of the gateway, the scheme [13] lacks a key escrow mechanism. As for privacy protection, the scheme [14] has done well.

Based on these, there are still several major problems in identity authentication between M2M devices. (1) The authentication steps are complicated, which causes great resource consumption in M2M communication. (2) There is lacking a better privacy protection scheme and measures to prevent message leak from being known by adversary. Therefore, this scheme proposes a session key association basing on the elliptic curve algorithm. In an elliptic curve system, the key is much shorter than RSA to achieve a quite security leave, which is greatly deduce resources.

3   Preliminary

3.1   Discrete Logarithm Problem

Given a prime p and positive integer g, to get the value of $g^x mod\ p$, in order to compute x. For p and g that satisfied certain conditions, in general, if p is carefully chosen, the problem is considered to be difficult to solve, and the algorithm of implementing polynomial to solving discrete logarithm problem has not been found yet.

3.2   Diffie–Hellman Key Exchange

The Diffie–Hellman Key Exchange (DH) is a security protocol for both entities exchange keys in a potentially eavesdropping environment securely. The specific algorithm is as follows:

(1) M and N agree on the values of p and g.
(2) M generates the private key x, and the calculation $g^x mod\ p$ is published as its public key.
(3) N generates the private key y, and the calculation $g^y mod\ p$ is published as the public key.

(4) After M knows $g^y mod\ p$, it calculates $s = (g^y\ mod\ p)^x\ mod\ p = (g^y)^x\ mod\ p = g^{xy}\ mod\ p$

(5) After N knows $g^x mod\ p$, it calculates $s = (g^x\ mod\ p)^y\ mod\ p = (g^x)^y\ mod\ p = g^{xy}\ mod\ p$

(6) Both entities will get the same key s and the key exchange process will be completed.

3.3 M2M System

In real life, the universal M2M system solution means that devices or modules are connected to a centralized management application platform by wireless/wired communication.

4 Proposed Solution

This section will discuss the anonymous authentication scheme for machine-to-machine communication in CPS based on elliptic curve cryptography. We propose five entities in the process: the authentication center MSP, the gateways SG and TG, the sensors SD and TD. The two phases are as follows:

The follow Fig. 1 shows the program framework:

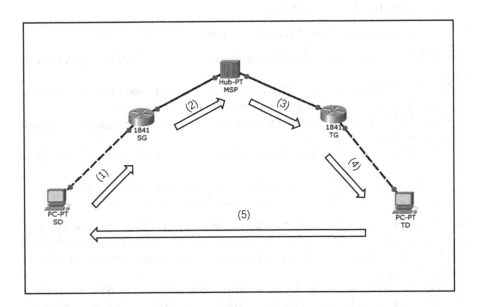

Fig. 1. Program framework

The related notations are briefly defined in Table 1.

Table 1. The notations

Notations	Description
ID_x	Identity of entity x
$E_p(a,b)$	An elliptic curve over a prime finite Z_p defined by the equation $y^2 = x^3 + ax + b \bmod p$
G	An elliptic curve group with the order q, where G is constitutive of all points on E and the point at infinity O
P	A generator of the group G
p, q	Two large prime number
$P = (P^x, P^y)$	An elliptic curve point in a non-singular elliptic curve E_p, $P^{(x)}$ and $P^{(y)}$ are x and y coordinates of P respectively
d_A, Q_A	The private key and the corresponding public key of A respectively
r_x	The random number selected by involved entities x
sk	The secret session key of entities
SK	The secret session key between SD and TD
$\oplus$	The XOR operation
$\parallel$	The message concatenation operation

4.1 System Registration Phase

In this part, the foundation of the scheme will conduct as follows.

MSP. At this stage, the authentication center MSP will conduct performance safely as follows:

(1) The MSP first chooses an elliptic curve E_p over a prime finite Z_p, p should be a large prime. Then, it chooses a generator P of order n over E_p.

(2) The MSP selects d_{MSP} as its private key, then computes $Q_{MSP} = d_{MSP}P$ as the pubic key.

(3) The MSP randomly selects three collision-resistant one-way hash functions $H_1, H_2, h : \{0,1\}^* \rightarrow Z_q$.

(4) After the MSP finishing generating hash functions, it sets public system params $= \{E_p(a,b), p, P, H_1, H_2, Q_{MSP}\}$ and keeps d_{MSP} as a secret.

SD. (1) As for the senior SD, it selects the identity ID_{SD}, private key d_{SD} in order to calculate the public key $Q_{SD} = d_{SD}P$. Then, the SD calculates $MID_{SD} = h(ID_{SD})$ as the registration message and sends it to the MSP over a secret channel.

(2) After the MSP receiving the registration request from the SD, it calculates $M_{SD} = h(MID_{SD}\|d_{MSP})$ and sends it back to the SD via the secret channel.

(3) The SD calculates $M_{SD}^* = M_{SD} \oplus h(MID_{SD}\|d_{MSP})$ to store in its memory and removes M_SD at the same time.

(4) In summary, the information $\{ID_{SD}, d_{SD}, Q_{SD}, M_{SD}^*\}$ is loaded into the memory of the SD and the MSP stores $\{MID_{SD}, M_{SD}\}$ in its database.

TD. (1) The MSP generates ID_{TD}, private key $d_T D$ in order to calculates the public key $Q_{ID} = d_{TD}P$, then it calculates $M_{TD} = h(ID_{TD}||d_{MSP})$ and sends $\{ID_{TD}, d_{TD}, Q_{TD}, M_{TD}\}$ to the TD via a secret channel.
(2) After the TD receiving the information from the MSP, it stores them in memory.
(3) In summary, the information is loaded into the memory of the TD, and the MSP stores $\{ID_{TD}, Q_{TD}\}$ in its database.

SG. (1) The senior SG selects its identity ID_{SD}, private key d_{SG} in order to calculate the public key $Q_{SG} = d_{SG}P$. Then, the SG calculates $MID_{SG} = h(ID_{SG})$ as the registration message and sends it to the MSP over a secret channel.
(2) After the MSP receiving the registration request from the SG, it calculates $M_{SG} = h(MID_{SG}||d_{MSP})$ and sends it back to the SG via the secret channel.
(3) At last, the SG calculates $M_{SG}^* = M_{SG} \oplus (MID_{SG}||d_{MSP})$ to store in its memory and removes M_{SG} at the same time.
(4) In summary, the information $\{ID_{SG}, d_{SG}, Q_{SG}, M_{SG}^*\}$ is loaded into the memory of the SG and MSP stores $\{MID_{SG}, M_{SG}\}$ in its database.

TG. (1) The MSP generates ID_{TG}, private key d_{TG} in order to calculates the public key $Q_{TG} = d_{TG}P$. Then it calculates $M_{TG} = h(ID_{TG}||d_{MSP})$ and sends $\{ID_{TG}, d_{TG}, Q_{TG}, M_{TG}\}$ to the TG via a secret channel.
(2) After TG receiving the information from the MSP, it stores them in its memory.
(3) In summary, The information $ID_{TG}, d_{TG}, Q_{TG}, M_{TG}$ is loaded into the memory of the TG and the MSP stores ID_{TG}, Q_{TG}, M_{TG} in its database.

4.2 Authentication Phase

(1) The SD wants to send a message to the TD, it first calculates:
SD selsct random $r_{SD} \in Z_q^*$
$E_{SD} = r_{SD}P$
$N_{SD} = r_{SD}Q_{MSP} = (N_{SD}^{(x)}, N_{SD}^{(y)})$
$M'_{SD} = M_{SD}^* \oplus h(ID_{SD}||d_{MSP})$
$AID_{TD} = ID_{TD} \oplus N_{SD}^{(y)}$
$AID_{SD} = MID_{TD} \oplus N_{SD}^{(y)}$
$K_{SD} = (r_{TD} + d_{SD})Q_{MSP}$
selects timestamp t_{SD}
$h_{SD} = H_1(K_{SD}||M'_{SD}||t_{SD})$
SD sends to SG:
$h_{SD}, AID_{TD}, AID_{SD}, t_{SD}, E_{SD}$

(2) After the SG receives the message (1), it calculates:
checks $|t_{SD} - t_{SD}| \leq \Delta t$
$Q_{SG} = d_{SG}P$
selects random $r_{SG} \in Z_q^*$

$$E_{SG} = d_{SG}P$$
$$N_{SG} = r_{SG}Q_{MSP} = (N_{SG}^{(x)}, N_{SG}^{(y)})$$
$$M_{SG} = M'_{SG} \oplus h(ID_{SG}\|d_{MSP})$$
$$AID_{SG} = MID_{SG} \oplus N_{SG}^{(y)}$$
selects timestamp t_{SG}
The SG sends to the MSP:
$$E_{SD}, E_{SG}, AID_{SG}, AID_{TD}, t_{SG}, t_{SD}, h_{SD}$$

(3) MSP calculates after receiving message (2):
checks $|t_{SG} - t_{SG}| \le \Delta t$
$$N'_{SG} = d_{MSP}E_{SG} = (N_{SG}^{(x)}, N_{SG}^{(y)})$$
$$M''_{SG} = AID_{SG} \oplus N_{SD}^{(y)}$$
checks $M_{SG} = M''_{SG}$?
$$N'_{SD} = d_{MSP}E_{SD} = (N_{SD}^{(x)}, N_{SD}^{(y)})$$
$$ID'_{TD} = AID_{TD} \oplus N_{SD}^{(y)}$$
checks $ID_{TD} = ID'_{TD}$?
$$MID'_{SD} = AID_{SD} \oplus N_{SD}^{(y)}$$
$$M_{SD} = h(MID'_{SD}\|d_{MSP})$$
$$K'_{SD} = d_{MSP}(E_{SD} + Q_{SD})$$
$$h'_{SD} = H_1(K'_{SD}\|M_{SD}\|t_{SD})$$
checks $h_{SD} = h'_{SD}$?
selects random $r_{MSP} \in Z_q^*$
$$E_{MSP} = r_{MSP}P$$
$$N_{MSP} = r_{MSP}Q_{TG} = (N_{MSP}^{(x)}, N_{MSP}^{(y)})$$
selects timestamp t_{MSP}
$$K_{MSP} = N'_{SD} + r_{MSP}Q_{TD}$$
$$h_{MSP} = H_1(N_{MSP}\|h(ID'_{TD}\|d_{MSP})\|h(ID'_{TG}\|d_{MSP})\|t_{MSP})$$
MSP sends to TG:
$$h_{MSP}, E_{MSP}, E_{SD}, K_{MSP}, t_{MSP}, t_{SD}, N_{SD}$$

(4) After the TG receives the message (3), it calculates:
checks $|t'_{MSP} - t_{MSP}| \le \Delta t$
$$N'_{MSP} = d_{TG}E_{MSP} = (N_{MSP}^{(x')}, N_{MSP}^{(y')})$$
$$h'_{MSP} = H_1(N'_{MSP}\|h(ID'_{TD}\|d_{MSP})\|M_{TG}\|t_{MSP})$$
checks $h_{MSP} = h_{MSP'}$?
selects random $r_{TG} \in Z_q^*$
$$E_{TG} = r_{TG}P$$
$$N_{TG} = r_{TG}Q_{TD} = (N_{TG}^{(x)}, N_{TG}^{(y)})$$
$$AID_{TG} = MID_{TG} \oplus N_{TG}^{(y)}$$
selects timestamp t_{TG}
$$h_{TG} = H_1(N'_{SD}\|h(ID'_{TD}\|d_{MSP})\|M_{TG}\|t_{TG})$$
TG sends to TD:
$$t_{TG}, t_{SD}, E_{SD}, h_{TG}, ID_{TG}, K_{MSP}$$

(5) After the TD receives the message (4), it calculates:

checks $|t'_{TG} - t_{TG}| \leq \Delta t$

$N_{TG}' = d_{TD}E_{TG} = (N_{TG}^{(x)'}, N_{TG}^{(y)'})$

$MID'_{TG} = AID'_{TG} \oplus N_{TG}^{(x)'}$

$M'_{TG} = (MID'_{TG}||d_{MSP})$

$N''_{SD} = K_{MSP} - d_{TD}E_{MSP} = (N_{SD}^{(X)'}, N_{SD}^{(Y)'})$

$h_{TG} = H_1(N''_{SD}||M_{TD}||M_{TG}||t_{TG})$

checks $h_{TG} = h'_{TG}$?

selects random $r_{ID} \in Z_q^*$

$E_{TD} = r_{TD}P$

$sk = (r_{ID} + d_{TD})(E_{SD} + N_{SD})$

selects timestamp t_{TD}

$h_{TD} = H_1(sk||t_{TD})$

$SK = H_2(sk||E_{TD}||E_{SD}||t_{TD}||t_{SD})$

TD sends to SD.

$t_{TG}, t_{SD}, E_{TD}, h_{TD}$

(6) After the SD receives the message (5), it calculates:

checks $|t'_{TD} - t_{TD}| \leq \Delta t$

$sk' = (r_{SD} + N_{SD}^{(x)})(E_{TD} + Q_{TD})$

$h'_{TD} = H_1(sk'||t_{TD})$

checks $h_{TD} = h'_{TD}$?

$SK = H_2(sk'||E_{TD}||E_{SD}||t_{TD}||t_{SD})$

At this point, the authentication phase is completed, the SD and TD can communicate with each other.

5 Belif Derivation

In this part, we give the BAN logic analysis of the protocol. As for BAN logic analysis, the paper [15] shows how to motivate, set out, and exemplify a logic in detail. We elaborate it in four steps: satisfied goals, Idealized form, initiative premises and logical proof.

5.1 Certification Target

$Goal_1.SD \models SD \xleftrightarrow{SK} TD$

$Goal_2.TD \models SD \xleftrightarrow{SK} TD$

$Goal_3.SD \models TD \models SD \xleftrightarrow{SK} TD$

$Goal_4.MSP \models SD \xleftrightarrow{N_{SD}} MSP$

$Goal_5.MSP \models MSP \xleftrightarrow{N_{SD}} TD$

5.2 Idealized Agreement

(1') $SD :< ID_{SD}, ID_{TD} >_{SD \xleftrightarrow{N_{SD}} MSP}, (ID_{SD}, P)_{SD \xleftrightarrow{r_{SD}, h(ID_{SD} \| d_{MSP})} MSP},$
$SD \xleftrightarrow{N_{SD}} MSP$

(2') $SG :< ID_{SG} >_{SG \xleftrightarrow{N_{SG}} MSP}, (ID_{SG}, P)_{SG \xleftrightarrow{r_{SG}, h(ID_{SG} \| d_{MSP})} MSP},$
$SG \xleftrightarrow{N_{SG}} MSP, < ID_{SD}, ID_{TD} >_{SD \xleftrightarrow{N_{SD}} MSP}, (ID_{SD}, P)_{SD \xleftrightarrow{r_{SD}, h(ID_{SD} \| d_{MSP})} MSP},$
$SD \xleftrightarrow{N_{SD}} MSP$

(3') $MSP :< ID_{TG} >_{MSP \xleftrightarrow{r_{MSP}, h(ID_{TD} \| d_{MSP})} TG}, (ID_{TG}, P)_{MSP \xleftrightarrow{r_{MSP}, h(ID_{TG} \| d_{MSP})} TG},$
$MSP \xleftrightarrow{N_{MSP}} TG, < ID_{TD} >_{MSP \xleftrightarrow{r_{MSP}, h(ID_{TD} \| d_{MSP})} TD}, (ID_{TD}, P)_{MSP \xleftrightarrow{N_{SD}, r_{MSP}} TD},$
$MSP \xleftrightarrow{N_{SD}} TD$

(4') $TG :< ID_{TG} >_{TG \xleftrightarrow{N_{TG}} TD}, (ID_{TG}, P)_{TG \xleftrightarrow{N_{TG}} TD}, TG \xleftrightarrow{N_{TG}} TD$

(5') $TD : (SD \xleftrightarrow{SK} TD, P)_{SD \xleftrightarrow{r_{TD}, E_{TD}, N_{SD}} TD},$

5.3 Initialization Hypothesis

(1") $SG \models \sharp \{SD \xleftrightarrow{N_{SD}} MSP\}$

(2") $MSP \models \sharp \{SG \xleftrightarrow{N_{SG}} MSP, SD \xleftrightarrow{N_{SD}} MSP\}$

(3") $TG \models \sharp \{MSP \xleftrightarrow{N_{MSP}} TG, MSP \xleftrightarrow{N_{SD}} TD\}$

(4") $TD \models \sharp \{(MSP \xleftrightarrow{N_{SD}} TD, P)\}$

(5") $SD \models \sharp \{SD \xleftrightarrow{SK} TD\}$

5.4 Logical Reasoning

(1) From (1'), $SG \triangleleft SD \xleftrightarrow{N_{SD}} MSP$ and the message-meaning rule we have, we could get: $SG \models SD \mid \sim SD \xleftrightarrow{N_{SD}} MSP$

(2) Since (1") and (1), according to the freshness rule we have, we could get: $SG \models \{SD \xleftrightarrow{N_{SD}} MSP\}$

(3) Since (2) and the nonce-verification rule we have, we could get: $SG \models SD \models \{SD \xleftrightarrow{N_{SD}} MSP\}$

(4) Since (3) and the belief rule we have, we could get: $SG \models SD \models SD \xleftrightarrow{N_{SD}} MSP$

(5) Since (4) and (7"), as well as the jurisdiction rule we have, we could get: $SG \models SD \xleftrightarrow{N_{SD}} MSP$

(6) From (2'), $MSP \triangleleft MSP \xleftrightarrow{N_{MSP}} TG, SD \xleftrightarrow{N_{SD}} MSP$ and the message-meaning rule, we could get: $MSP \models SG \mid \sim SG \xleftrightarrow{N_{SG}} MSP, SD \xleftrightarrow{N_{SD}} MSP$

(7) Since (2") and (6), according to the freshness rule we have, we could get: $MSP \models \{SG \xleftrightarrow{N_{SG}} MSP, SD \xleftrightarrow{N_{SD}} MSP\}$

(8) Since (7) and the nonce-authentication rule we have, we could get: $MSP \mid\equiv SG \mid\equiv SG \xleftrightarrow{N_{SG}} MSP, SD \xleftrightarrow{N_{SD}} MSP$

(9) Since (8) and the nonce-authentication rule we have, we could get: $MSP \mid\equiv SG \mid\equiv SD \xleftrightarrow{N_{SG}} MSP$

$Goal_4$. According to (9) and (8"), as well as the jurisdiction rule we have, we could get: $MSP \mid\equiv SD \xleftrightarrow{N_{SD}} MSP$

(10) From (3), $TG \lhd MSP \xleftrightarrow{N_{MSP}} TG, MSP \xleftrightarrow{N_{SD}} TD$ and the message-meaning rule we have, we could get: $TG \mid\equiv MSP \mid\sim MSP \xleftrightarrow{N_{MSP}} TG, MSP \xleftrightarrow{N_{SD}} TD$

(11) Since (3") and (7), according to the freshness rule we have, we could get: $TG \mid\equiv \{MSP \xleftrightarrow{N_{MSP}} TG, MSP \xleftrightarrow{N_{SD}} TD\}$

(12) Since (11) and the nonce-authentication rule we have, we could get: $TG \mid\equiv MSP \mid\equiv MSP \xleftrightarrow{N_{MSP}} TG, MSP \xleftrightarrow{N_{SD}} TD$

(13) Since (12) and the belief rule we have, we could get: $TG \mid\equiv MSP \mid\equiv MSP \xleftrightarrow{N_{SD}} TD$

(14) Since (13) and the jurisdiction rule we have, we could get: $TG \mid\equiv MSP \xleftrightarrow{N_{SD}} TD$

(15) From (4), $TD \lhd (MSP \xleftrightarrow{N_{SD}} TD, P)$ and the message-meaning rule we have, we could get: $TD \mid\equiv TG \mid\sim (MSP \xleftrightarrow{N_{SD}} TD, P)$

(16) Since (4") and (16), according to the freshness rule we have, we could get: $TD \mid\equiv \{(MSP \xleftrightarrow{N_{SD}} TD, P)\}$

(17) Since (16) and the nonce-authentication rule we have, we could get: $TD \mid\equiv TG \mid\equiv (MSP \xleftrightarrow{N_{SD}} TD, P)$

(18) Since (17) and the belief rule we have, we could get: $TD \mid\equiv MSP \mid\equiv MSP \xleftrightarrow{N_{SD}} TD$

(19) Since (18) and the jurisdiction rule we have, we could get: $TD \mid\equiv MSP \xleftrightarrow{N_{SD}} TD$

(20) From (5'), $SD \lhd SD \xleftrightarrow{SK} TD$ and the message-meaning rule we have, we could get: $SD \mid\equiv TD \mid\sim SD \xleftrightarrow{SK} TD$

(21) Since (5") and (20), according to the freshness rule we have, we could get: $SD \mid\equiv \{SD \xleftrightarrow{SK} TD\}$

(22) Since (21) and the nonce-verification rule we have, we could get: $SD \mid\equiv TD \mid\equiv SD \xleftrightarrow{SK} TD$

(23) Since (22) and the belief rule we have, we could get: $SD \mid\equiv SD \xleftrightarrow{SK} TD$

6 Safety and Performance Analysis

This part mainly discusses the safety and gives analyses of the scheme. The preliminary knowledge of several common attacks and the security of the scheme under these attacks is separately explained as follows.

6.1 Security Analysis

1. Malicious Attacks

(1) Replay attack

In our scheme, due to the adoption of timestamps, each sent message is time-sensitive. Each entity of this scheme will perform the next calculation only if the verified timestamp is successful, the replay attack cannot succeed.

(2) Man-in-the-middle attack

Since the session key SK is encrypted, due to the difficulty of the elliptic curve discrete logarithm, it will fail. And each device only knows its own private key, so calculating the correct key is almost impossible. Even if the adversary replaces part of the message, the attack will fail because it has no legal identity to entrance authentication. Therefore, the man-in-the-middle attack will not succeed.

(3) DoS attack

Even in the newly appeared big data fields can we find solutions to defend it, like the paper [16], which proposed an abnormal network flow feature sequence prediction approach. And the paper [17] provided a new distributed intrusion detection model for big data. In our scheme, due to the timestamp, the external adversary cannot repeatedly send the intercepted messages to the authentication center MSP for attack. If an external adversary attempts to falsify the authentication message, due to the difficulty of the discrete logarithm of the elliptic curve, it cannot calculate the correct private key d_x. For MSP, only the authentication message can be sent to the gateway, and the communication between the gateway and the sensor device cannot be interfered. DoS Attack could not be successful.

(4) Impersonation attack

If the adversary chooses to fake the senior SD, according to the difficulty of the discrete logarithm of the elliptic curve, the adversary will fail to calculate correct d_{SD}, and N_{SD}. A fake to the gateway SG will also fail because d_{SG} is unknown. If the adversary impersonates the MSP, the authentication message will not be decrypted because the d_{MSP} is not available. For the fake MSP, the final session key is calculated between the two entities. The fake attack is not established.

6.2 Performance Analysis

In this section, the program will do some comparisons with other scenarios to analyze performance (Table 2).

C_{se}: symmetric key encryption's computational cost.
C_{sd}: symmetric key decryption's computational cost.
C_{pe}: public key encryption's computational cost.
C_{pd}: public key decryption's computational cost.
C_s: digital signature generation's computational cost.

Table 2. Comparison of efficiency

	Reference [6]	Reference [12]	Reference [13]	Our scheme
Source device	$6C_{se} + 4C_{sd} + C_{pe} + C_h$	$2C_e + 4C_m + 4C_p + 12C_h$	$2C_{se} + C_{sd} + C_{pe} + 3C_e + 3C_h$	$C_{pe} + C_e + 3C_m + C_h$
Source gateway	$4C_{se} + 3C_{sd} + C_{pe} + 2C_{pd} + 2C_s + C_v$	/	/	$C_{pe} + C_e + 3C_m$
MSP/devices	$3C_{se} + C_{sd} + 2C_{pe} + C_{pd} + 2C_s + C_v + C_h$	$2C_e + 3C_m + 3C_p + 9C_h$	$2C_{se} + 3C_{sd} + C_{pe} + C_{pd} + 5C_e + 4C_h$	$2C_{pd} + C_e + 3C_m + 2C_p + C_h$
Target gateway	$4C_{se} + 5C_{sd} + 2C_{pd} + 2C_v$	/	/	$C_{pd} + 2C_e + 3C_m + C_p + C_h$
Target device	$5C_{se} + 6C_{sd} + C_{pe} + C_h$	$C_e + 3C_m + 3C_p + 9C_h$	$2C_{se} + C_{sd} + C_{pe} + 3Ce + 3C_h$	$C_{pe} + C_{pd} + 2C_e + 3C_m + C_p + 2C_h$

C_v: digital signature authentication's computational cost.
C_e: the modular exponentiation's computational cost.
C_m: the point multiplication's calculation cost.
C_p: the pairing's computational cost.
C_h: the calculation cost of the hash.
/: There is no such party in the scheme.

It can be seen from the above analysis the calculation cost of our scheme is relatively low. As for maximum cost of each calculation, there is no calculation costs of symmetric key encryption and decryption Our scheme greatly reduced the amount of calculation, while the scheme [6] uses almost $6C_{se}$, $5C_{sd}$, the scheme [13] uses almost $2C_{se}$, $3C_{sd}$. About public key encryption and decryption, our scheme just uses nearly c_{pe}, $2C_{pd}$, while the scheme [6] uses $2C_{pe}$, $2C_{pd}$, the scheme [13] uses C_{pe}, C_{pd}, close to the scheme [13] less than the scheme [6]. The computational cost of digital signature generation and authentication shows, without this kind of cost, our scheme could calculate fast and obtain better performance. The max cost of the modular exponentiation in our scheme is $2C_e$, equal to the scheme [12], less than the scheme [13] of $5C_e$. Our scheme's pairing of computational cost is $3C_m$, less than the scheme [12]. The max calculation cost of the hash is $2C_h$, more than the scheme [6] of C_h, less than the scheme [12,13]. Above all, the performance of our scheme relatively works well.

7   Conclusion

This paper proposes an anonymous authentication scheme of M2M session key association based on elliptic curve in CPS. The calculation of elliptic curve encryption consumes small resources, which can greatly alleviate the resource limitation of M2M itself. Based on the discrete logarithm problem, it can defend against man-in-the-middle attack, DoS attack and counterfeit attack. The use of timestamps can resist replay attacks. The BAN logic proves the logical feasibility of the scheme, and the performance analysis also confirms the efficiency of the scheme.

References

1. Yang, L., Yu, P., Bailing, W., Sirui, Y., Zihe, L.: Review on cyber-physical systems. IEEE/CAA J. Automatica Sinica **4**(1), 27–40 (2017)
2. Lee, E.A. Cyber physical systems: Design challenges. In: Proceedings of 11th IEEE International Symposium on Object Oriented Real-Time Distributed Computing (ISORC), May 6, 2008, Orlando, FL, USA, pp. 363–369 (2008)
3. Cardenas, A.A., Amin, S., Sastry, S.: Secure control: towards survivable cyber-physical systems. In: Proceedings of IEEE 28th International Conference on Distributed Computing Systems, pp. 495–500, June 2008
4. Chen, M., Wan, J., Li, F.: Machine-to-machine communications: architectures, standards, and applications. KSII Trans. Internet Inf. Syst. **6**(2), 480–497 (2012)
5. Qi, Q.: Strategic thinking of the internet of Things and M2M Services, ZTE Commun. (01) (2010)
6. Xu, L., Gulliver, T.A.: Performance analysis for M2M video transmission cooperative networks using transmit antenna selection. Multimedia Tools Appl. **76**(22), 23891–23902 (2017)
7. Ma, C., He, J., Chen, H.H., Tang, Z.: Uncoordinated coexisting IEEE 802.15.4 networks for machine to machine communications. Peer-To-Peer Netw. Appl. **7**(3), 274–284 (2014)
8. Ren, W., Yu, L., Ma, L., Ren, Y.: How to authenticate a device? Formal authentication models for M2M communications defending against ghost compromising
9. Lai, C., Lu, R., Zheng, D., Li, H., (Sherman) Shen, X.: GLARM: group-based lightweight authentication scheme for resource-constrained machine to machine communications
10. Qiu, Y., Ma, M., Chen, S.: An anonymous authentication scheme for multi-domain machine-to-machine communication in cyber-physical systems. Comput. Netw. **129**, 306–318 (2017)
11. Chen, S., Ma, M.: An authentication scheme with identity-based cryptography for M2M security in cyber-physical systems. Secur. Commun. Netw. **9**(10), 1146–1157 (2016)
12. Ranjan, A.K., Hussain, M.: Terminal authentication in M2M communications in the context of internet of things. Procedia Comput. Sci. **89**, 34–42 (2016)
13. Chen, H., You, I., Weng, C., Cheng, C., Huang, Y.: A security gateway application for end-to-end M2M communications. Comput. Stand. Interfaces **44**, 85–93 (2016)
14. Kim, J.-M., Jeong, H.-Y., Hong, B.-H.: A study of privacy problem solving using device and user authentication for M2M environments. Secur. Commun. Netw. **7**(10), 1528–1535 (2014)
15. Burrows, M., Abadi, M., Needham, R.M.: A Logic of Authentication, Technical report 39, Digital System Research Center (1989)

16. Cheng, R., Xu, R., Tang, X., Sheng, V.S., Cai, C.: An abnormal network flow feature sequence prediction approach for DDoS attacks detection in big data environment. CMC: Comput. Mater. Continua **55**(1), 095–119 (2018)
17. Xiaonian, W., Chuyun, Z., Runlian, Z., Yujue, W., Jinhua, C.: A distributed intrusion detection model via nondestructive partitioning and balanced allocation for big data. CMC: Comput. Mater. Continua **56**(1), 61–72 (2018)

Linear Complexity of r-ary Sequences Derived from Euler Quotients Modulo $2p$

Rayan Mohammed, Xiaoni Du$^{(\boxtimes)}$, and Li Li

College of Mathematics and Statistics, Northwest Normal University,
Lanzhou 730070, Gansu, People's Republic of China
ymLdxn@126.com

Abstract. Based on the Euler quotient modulo $2p$ (p is an odd prime), we extend the binary sequence with period $2p^2$ to r-ary sequence where r is an odd prime divisor of $(p-1)$. We determine exact values of the linear complexity of the new sequences under the assumption $r^{p-1} \not\equiv 1$ (mod p^2), which are larger than half of the period. For cryptographic purpose, the linear complexities of the sequences in this paper are of desired values.

Keywords: r-ary sequences · Euler quotients · Linear complexity · Finite fields

1 Introduction

With the explosion of multimedia data, more and more data owners would outsource their personal multimedia data on the cloud [17,18]. Secure message transmission plays an main role in the information-based society. Pseudo-random sequences used for stream ciphers are required to have the properties of unpredictability. Linear complexity is one of the main components that indicates this feature. The linear complexity of a sequence is defined as the length of the shortest linear feedback shift register that can generate the sequence [14]. Due to the Berlekamp-Massey algorithm, it is reasonable to suggest that the linear complexity of a good sequence should be at least a half of the period. In the recent years, the sequence derived from the Euler quotients modulo an odd prime power, which is an extension of the Fermat quotients, are a hot spot and much of the sequences possess sound linear complexity, see [1–9,11,12,15,20] and the references therein. While for the study of the sequences derived from the Euler quotients modulo an even number are very rare. For the binary threshold sequence, the linear complexity is derived from Carmichael quotients with even numbers modulus in [16]. In [19], Zhang et al. promoted a class of binary sequences derived from Euler quotients with period $2p^2$ and p is an odd prime and determined the linear complexity and trace function representation of the sequences.

Supported by National Natural Science Foundation of China (61763044).

X. Sun et al. (Eds.): ICAIS 2019, LNCS 11634, pp. 104–112, 2019.
https://doi.org/10.1007/978-3-030-24271-8_10

For an odd prime p and integer $u \geq 0$ with $\gcd(u, 2p) = 1$, the Euler quotient $q_{2p}(u)$ modulo $2p$ can be defined as unique integer with

$$q_{2p}(u) \equiv \frac{u^{p-1} - 1}{2p} \pmod{2p}, \quad 0 \leq q_{2p}(u) \leq 2p - 1,$$

and $q_{2p}(u) = 0$ for $u \in R = \mathbb{Z}_{2p^2} \setminus \mathbb{Z}_{2p^2}^*$, where $\mathbb{Z}_{2p^2}$ denote by the ring of the all the integers modulo $2p^2$ and $\mathbb{Z}_{2p^2}^*$ of the multiplicative group of all the unit in $\mathbb{Z}_{2p^2}$ respectively.

The binary threshold sequence (e_u) defined in [19] as

$$e_u = \begin{cases} 0, & \text{if } 0 \leq \frac{q_{2p}(u)}{2p} < \frac{1}{2}, \\ 1, & \text{if } \frac{1}{2} \leq \frac{q_{2p}(u)}{2p} < 1, \end{cases} \quad u \geq 0. \tag{1}$$

Motivated by the previous work in [15, 19], we extend the binary threshold sequence to r-ary sequence as the following

$$f_u = \begin{cases} 0, & \text{if } 0 \leq \frac{q_{2p}(u)}{2} \leq s, \\ 1, & \text{if } s + 1 \leq \frac{q_{2p}(u)}{2} \leq 2s, \\ \vdots & \quad \vdots \\ r - 1, & \text{if } (r-1)s + 1 \leq \frac{q_{2p}(u)}{2} \leq p - 1, \end{cases} \tag{2}$$

where r is a prime, $r | (p - 1)$ and $s = (p - 1)/r$. In fact, if $r = 2$, then (f_u) is the binary threshold sequence defined in (1). We note that (f_u) is $2p^2$-periodical since $q_{2p}(u)$ is a $2p^2$-periodic sequence modulo $2p$ by the fact

$$q_{2p}(u + 2kp) \equiv q_{2p}(u) + k(p-1)u^{-1} \pmod{2p}, \quad \gcd(u, 2p) = 1.$$

The linear complexity is considered as a primary quality measure for periodic sequences and play an important role in applications of sequences in cryptography. The main aims of this article is to determine the linear complexity of (f_u). We recall that the linear complexity $L((s_u))$ of a T-periodic sequence (s_u) with terms in finite field $\mathbb{F}_q$ with q elements is the least order of L of a linear recurrence relation over $\mathbb{F}_q$

$$s_{u+L} + c_{L-1} s_{u+L-1} + \cdots + c_1 s_{u+1} + c_0 s_u = 0 \quad \text{for } u \geq 0$$

which is satisfied by (s_u) and where $c_0 \neq 0, c_1, \ldots, c_{L-1} \in \mathbb{F}_q$. The polynomial

$$M(x) = x^L + c_{L-1} x^{L-1} + \cdots + c_0 \in \mathbb{F}_q[x]$$

is called the minimal polynomial of (s_u). The generating polynomial of (s_u) is defined by

$$S(x) = s_0 + s_1 x + s_2 x^2 + \cdots + s_{T-1} x^{T-1} \in \mathbb{F}_q[x].$$

It is easy to show that

$$M(x) = (x^T - 1)/\gcd(x^T - 1, S(x)),$$

hence

$$L((s_u)) = T - \deg(\gcd(x^T - 1, S(x))), \tag{3}$$

which is the degree of minimal polynomial, see [13] for more details.

2 Preliminary

The main aims of this article are to determine the linear complexity of (f_u) under the assumption $r^{p-1} \not\equiv 1 \pmod{p^2}$. To achieve our goals we need to describe (f_u) in an equivalent way. For any subset $D \subset \mathbb{Z}_N$, define $aD = \{a \cdot b \pmod{N} : b \in N\}$ for any integer a.

If $\gcd(u, 2p) = 1$, it is easy to verify that

$$q_{2p}(uv) \equiv q_{2p}(u) + q_{2p}(v) \pmod{2p}, \quad \gcd(uv, 2p) = 1. \tag{4}$$

By [19], note that $q_{2p}(u)$ is always even since it can be rewritten as

$$q_{2p}(u) \equiv \frac{(u^{\frac{p-1}{2}} - 1)(u^{\frac{p-1}{2}} + 1)}{2p} \pmod{2p},$$

and two numbers $u^{\frac{p-1}{2}} \pm 1$ are even. Thus we define

$$D_l = \{u : q_{2p}(u) = 2l \pmod{2p} \text{ for } u \in \mathbb{Z}_{2p^2}^*\}$$

for $l = 0, 1, \ldots, p - 1$. We always assume that g be a fixed primitive root modulo $2p^2$ such that $q_{2p}(g) = 2$, we declare such g exists. Otherwise, if $q_{2p}(g) = 2a \neq 2$. It is easy to prove that $\gcd(a, p) = 1$. By (4) we get $q_{2p}(g^{a^{-1}}) = 2$, where a^{-1} is the inverse of a modulo p. Furtherly, we have

$$q_{2p}(g^{a^{-1}+kp}) \equiv 2 \pmod{2p}$$

for all $0 \leq k < p - 1$, then we have

$$D_0 = \{g^{kp} \pmod{2p^2} : 0 \leq k \leq p - 2\}$$

is a subgroup of the multiplicative group $\mathbb{Z}_{2p^2}^*$ and for all $0 \leq l \leq p - 1$, there exists $0 \leq l_0 \leq p - 1$, such that

$$D_l = g^{l_0} D_0 = \{g^{l_0} \cdot a \pmod{2p} : a \in D_0\}$$

and each D_l has the cardinality $\#D_l = p - 1$ and $\mathbb{Z}_{2p^2}^* = \bigcup_{l=0}^{p-1} D_l$.

Now the sequence (f_u) can be written equivalently as

$$f_u = \begin{cases} 0, & \text{if } u \in D_0 \cup D_1 \cup \cdots \cup D_s \cup R, \\ 1, & \text{if } u \in D_{s+1} \cup D_{s+2} \cup \cdots \cup D_{2s}, \\ \vdots & \vdots \\ r - 1, & \text{if } u \in D_{(r-1)s+1} \cup D_{(r-1)s+2} \cup \cdots \cup D_{p-1}. \end{cases} \tag{5}$$

Below, we are devoted to determining the linear complexity of the sequences. The rest of paper is organized as follows. In Sect. 3, we present some Auxiliary lemmas. In Sect. 4, We prove the main results of the paper and give some examples. Finally we conclude the paper.

3   Auxiliary Lemmas

Let $\mathbb{F}_r = \{0, 1, \ldots, r-1\}$ be the finite field of order r and $\overline{\mathbb{F}}_r$ be the algebraic closure of $\mathbb{F}_r$. Below we always let $\beta \in \overline{\mathbb{F}}_r$ be a primitive $2p^2$-th root of unity and the subscripts of D are calculated modulo p.

The following two lemmas are given in [19].

Lemma 1. *For any $0 \le l < p$, if $a \pmod{2p^2} \in D_{l'}$, for some $0 \le l' < p$ we have*

$$D_l \pmod{p} = \{1, 2, \ldots, p-1\} \text{ and } aD_l = D_{l+l'},$$

where $D_l \pmod{p} = \{a \pmod{p} : a \in D_l\}$

Lemma 2. *Let n be a positive integer. Then*

$$\{u \pmod{p^n} : u \in \mathbb{Z}_{2p^n}^*\} = \mathbb{Z}_{p^n}^*.$$

From now we define

$$D_l(x) = \sum_{u \in D_l} x^u \in \mathbb{F}_r[x], \text{ for } 0 \le l \le p-1.$$

From the definition of (f_u) we obtain that the generating polynomial of (f_u) is

$$E(x) = \sum_{u=0}^{2p^2-1} f_u x^u = \sum_{j=1}^{r-1} j \sum_{i=js+1}^{(j+1)s} D_i(x) \in \mathbb{F}_r[x].$$

Lemma 3. *Let $\beta \in \overline{\mathbb{F}}_r$ be a primitive $2p^2$-th root of unity. Then we have*

(1) $D_l(\beta^v) = D_{l+l'}(\beta)$,
(2) $D_l(\beta^u) = D_l(\beta^v)$ and $E(\beta^u) = E(\beta^v)$,

where $u, v \in D_l$ for some $0 \le l \le p-1$.

Proof. From Lemma 1 and the definitions of $D_l(x)$ and $E(x)$, we can obtain the results.

Lemma 4. *Let $\beta \in \overline{\mathbb{F}}_r$ be a primitive $2p^2$-th root of unity.*

(1) For all $v \in \mathbb{Z}_{2p^2}^* \cup 2\mathbb{Z}_{p^2}^*$, we have

$$\sum_{l=0}^{p-1} D_l(\beta^v) = 0.$$

(2) For $0 \le l < p$, we have

$$D_l(\beta^{kp}) = \begin{cases} 0, & \text{if } k \equiv 0 \pmod{p}, \\ -1, & \text{if } k \equiv 0 \pmod{2}, (k, p) = 1. \end{cases}$$

Proof. (1) From the definition of β, we have

$$0 = \beta^{2p^2} - 1 = (\beta - 1) \sum_{j \in \mathbb{Z}_{2p^2}} \beta^j = (\beta^2 - 1) \sum_{j \in 2\mathbb{Z}_{p^2}} \beta^j$$

$$= (\beta^p - 1) \sum_{j \in p\mathbb{Z}_{2p}} \beta^j = (\beta^{2p} - 1) \sum_{j \in 2p\mathbb{Z}_p} \beta^j$$

$$= (\beta^{p^2} - 1)(\beta^{p^2} + 1)$$

(1) of the Lemma is proved by the fact that

$$\mathbb{Z}_{2p^2} = \mathbb{Z}_{2p^2}^* \cup 2\mathbb{Z}_{p^2}^* \cup p\mathbb{Z}_{2p}$$

$$= \mathbb{Z}_{2p^2}^* \cup 2\mathbb{Z}_{p^2}^* \cup 2p\mathbb{Z}_p \cup p\mathbb{Z}_{2p}^* \cup \{p^2\}.$$

(2) If $k \equiv 0 \pmod{p}$, then $k = 0$ or p. It can be easy to see that

$$D_l(\beta^{kp}) = D_l(\beta^{0p}) = D_l(1) = \sum_{u \in D_l} 1^u = p - 1 \equiv 0 \pmod{r}$$

if $k = 0$, and

$$D_l(\beta^{kp}) = D_l(\beta^{p^2}) = D_l(-1) = \sum_{u \in D_l} (-1)^u = 0$$

if $k = p$ from the proof of (1).

If $k \equiv 0 \pmod{2}$ with $(k, p) = 1$, we have β^2 is a primitive p^2-th root of unity, so

$$\{k : k \text{ is an even, with } (k, p) = 1\},$$

then by Lemma 1 and (1) of this lemma, we have

$$D_l(\beta^{kp}) = \beta^{2p} + \beta^{4p} + \ldots + \beta^{2(p-1)}$$

$$= \frac{\beta^{2p} - \beta^{2p^2}}{1 - \beta^{2p}}$$

$$= \frac{\beta^{2p} - 1}{1 - \beta^{2p}}$$

$$= -1 \pmod{r}.$$

$\square$

Lemma 5. *If $r^{p-1} \not\equiv 1 \pmod{p^2}$, then*

$$D_l(\beta^u) \neq 0$$

for all $0 \leq l \leq p - 1$ and all $u \in \mathbb{Z}_{2p^2}^* \cup 2\mathbb{Z}_{p^2}^*$.

Proof. Denote by $d := ord_{2p^2}(r)$ the multiplicative order of r modulo $2p^2$. Thus, $d \mid p(p-1)$ and $d \geq p$ and $r^i \not\equiv r^j \pmod{2p^2}$ for $0 \leq i < j \leq p-1$. Suppose that $r \in D_{l_0 \pmod p}$, using Lemma 1 we have $r^i \pmod{2p^2} \in D_{l_0}$ for all $0 \leq i \leq p-1$ and

$$D_0 \cup rD_0(= D_{l_0}) \cup \cdots \cup r^{p-1}D_0 = D_0 \cup D_1 \cup \cdots \cup D_{p-1} = \mathbb{Z}^*_{2p^2}.$$

Meanwhile the minimal polynomial of β^a over $\mathbb{F}_r$ is given by

$$M(x) = \prod_{k=0}^{d-1} (x - \beta^{ar^k}).$$

Consequently, if there are some $0 \leq l' \leq p-1$ and some $a \in D_k$ such that $D_{l'}(\beta^a) = 0$, then $D_{l'}(\beta^{ar^t}) = 0$ for $0 \leq t \leq d-1$.

Note that

$$D_k \cup rD_k \cup \cdots \cup r^{p-1}D_k = \mathbb{Z}^*_{2p^2}$$

then by Lemma 3(2) we have

$$D_{l'}(\beta^u) = 0 \text{ for all } u \in \mathbb{Z}^*_{2p^2}.$$

Furthermore, Lemma 3(1) leads to that $D_{l'}(\beta^a) = D_{l'+1}(\beta^{a'})$ for some $a' \in D_{k-1}$, we also have $D_{l'+1}(\beta^u) = 0$ for all $u \in \mathbb{Z}^*_{2p^2}$. Seeking this process continually, we will get that

$$D_l(\beta^u) = 0 \text{ for all } 0 \leq l \leq p-1 \text{ and } u \in \mathbb{Z}^*_{2p^2}.$$

By Lemma 2 and notice the fact that $\beta^{p^2} = -1$, we have that for any $l = 0, 1, \ldots, p-1$, the polynomial $D_l(x) \pmod{x^{p^2}+1}$ has at least $p(p-1)$ many roots.

However, in the set $\{u : 0 \leq u \leq p^2 - 1, \gcd(u,p) = 1\}$ there are only $p-1$ many elements, which appear in $D_l(x) \pmod{x^{p^2}+1}$ as exponents for all $0 \leq l \leq p-1$, larger than $p^2 - p$. (Notice that x^{p^2-p} never appears.) So by the pigeonhole principle, there exists at least one $0 \leq l' \leq p-1$, such that $\deg(D_{l'}(x) \pmod{x^{p^2}+1}) < p^2 - p$. This is a contradiction to the fact that the polynomial $D_{l'}(x)$ has at least $p^2 - p$ many different roots. Therefore, for all $u \in \mathbb{Z}^*_{2p^2}$, we always have $D_l(\beta^u) \neq 0$.

For the case of $u \in 2\mathbb{Z}_{p^2}$, by Lemmas 1 and 2, with the fact that $d = ord_{p^2}(r)$ and $(\beta^2)^{p^2} = 1$, following the above approach, we can get desired result. Thus we have finish the proof of the lemma. □

4   Linear Complexity

In this section, we determine the linear complexity of r-ary sequence (f_u) defined in (2) under the assumption $r^{p-1} \not\equiv 1 \pmod{p^2}$.

Theorem 1. *Let* (f_u) *be the* $2p^2$*-periodic* r*-ary sequence defined as in (2). If* $r^{p-1} \not\equiv 1 \pmod{p^2}$, *then the linear complexity* $L((f_u))$ *and the minimal polynomial* $M(x)$ *of* (f_u) *are given by*

$$L((f_u)) = 2p^2 - 2p$$

and

$$M(x) = (x^{2p^2} - 1)/(x^{2p} - 1)$$

respectively.

Proof. We prove this theorem by the following two facts.

(1) $E(\beta^u) \neq 0$ if $u \in \mathbb{Z}_{2p^2}^* \cup 2\mathbb{Z}_{p^2}^*$.

Suppose that there is some $a \in D_k$ for some $0 \leq k \leq p-1$ such that $E(\beta^a) = 0$, similar to the proof of Lemma 5, we have $E(\beta^u) = 0$ holds for all $u \in \mathbb{Z}_{2p^2}^*$. Then we get $E(\beta^{a'}) = E(\beta) = 0$ where $a' \in D_l$. It follows from Lemma 3 and after simple calculation that

$$E(\beta^{a'}) = \sum_{j=0}^{r-1}(j-1) \sum_{i=jl+1}^{(j+1)l} D_i(\beta) - D_0(\beta) + D_l(\beta).$$

Then by Lemma 4, we have

$$0 = -D_l(\beta) = E(\beta) - E(\beta^{a'}) = \sum_{j=0}^{p-1} D_j(\beta) - D_l(\beta).$$

This contradiction with Lemma 5. Then for all $u \in \mathbb{Z}_{2p^2}^*$, we always have $E(\beta^u) \neq 0$.

For all $u \in 2\mathbb{Z}_{p^2}^*$, the results follows directly from Lemma 3.4 in [10].

(2) $E(\beta^u) = 0$ if $u = kp, k \in \mathbb{Z}_{2p}$. Note that each D_l has $p-1$ many elements for $0 \leq l < p$ and $D_l \pmod p = \{1, 2, \ldots, p-1\}$. Then we have two cases. If $k = 0, p$, by Lemma 4 we have

$$E(\beta^{kp}) = E(\pm 1) = \sum_{j=1}^{r-1} j \sum_{i=jl+1}^{(j+1)l} D_i(\pm 1) \equiv 0,$$

and if $u = kp$ for $k \in \mathbb{Z}_{2p}^* \cup 2\mathbb{Z}_p^*$, we have

$$E(\beta^u) = \sum_{j=1}^{r-1} j \sum_{i=jl+1}^{(j+1)l} D_i(\beta^{kp})$$

$$= \sum_{j=1}^{r-1} j \sum_{i=jl+1}^{(j+1)l} (\beta^{pk} + \beta^{2pk} + \cdots + \beta^{(p-1)pk})$$

$$= (\beta^{pk} + \beta^{2pk} + \cdots + \beta^{(p-1)pk}) \sum_{j=1}^{r-1} j \sum_{i=jl+1}^{(j+1)l} 1$$

$$= l(\beta^{pk} + \beta^{2pk} + \cdots + \beta^{(p-1)pk}) \sum_{j=1}^{r-1} j$$

$$\equiv 0 \pmod{r}.$$

Putting every thing together, we have $E(\beta^u) = 0$ if and only if $u \in \{kp : k \in \mathbb{Z}_{2p}\}$, that is, the number of common roots of $E(x)$ and $x^{2p^2} - 1$ is $2p$, so the linear complexity of (f_u) is $2p^2 - 2p$ by (3). Meanwhile, it is easy to see that the minimial polynomial $M(x)$ of (f_u) satisfies $M(x) = (x^{2p^2} - 1)/(x^{2p} - 1)$.   □

Now we provide some examples of $2p^2$-periodic r-ary sequences (f_u) to show the applicability of Theorem 1:

p	r	$L((f_u))$	$L((f_u))$ satisfying
7	3	84	$2p^2 - 2p$
11	5	220	$2p^2 - 2p$
13	3	312	$2p^2 - 2p$
19	3	684	$2p^2 - 2p$
23	11	1012	$2p^2 - 2p$
29	7	1624	$2p^2 - 2p$
31	3 or 5	1860	$2p^2 - 2p$
43	3 or 7	3612	$2p^2 - 2p$

5   Conclusion

For cryptographic purpose, one should construct pseudorandom sequences with high linear complexity according to the Berlekamp-Massey algorithm [14], which tells us that the complete sequences can be deduced from a knowledge of just $2L$ (here L is the linear complexity) consecutive terms from the sequences. So it is desired that the linear complexity should be at least half of the period.

In this article, under the assumption $r^{p-1} \not\equiv 1 \pmod{p^2}$, we give the linear complexity of r-ary sequence derived from Euler quotients modulo $2p$ with p an odd prime. The results show that the linear complexity is equal to $2p^2 - 2p$, which is larger enough to resist the attack from the Berlekamp-Massey algorithm. For the case of $r^{p-1} \equiv 1 \pmod{p^2}$, we leave an open problem since such primes pair are rare.

References

1. Chen, Z.: Linear complexity of some binary sequences derived from Fermat quotients. China Commun. 9(2), 105–110 (2012)
2. Chen, Z.: Trace representation and linear complexity of binary sequences derived from Fermat quotients. Sci. China Inf. Sci. 57(11), 1–10 (2014)

3. Chen, Z., Du, X.: On the linear complexity of binary threshold sequences derived from Fermat quotients. Des. Codes Cryptogr. **67**(3), 317–323 (2013)
4. Chen, Z., Du, X., Marzouk, R.: Trace representation of pseudorandom binary sequences derived from Euler quotients. Appl. Algebr. Eng. Commun. Comput. **26**(6), 555–570 (2015)
5. Dai, Z., Gong, G., Song, H.: A trace representation of binary Jacobi sequences. Discrete Math. **309**(6), 1517–1527 (2009)
6. Dai, Z., Gong, G., Song, H., Ye, D.: Trace representation and linear complexity of binary e-th power residue sequences of period p. IEEE Trans. Inf. Theory **57**(3), 1530–1547 (2011)
7. Dai, Z., Gong, G., Song, H., Ye, D.: Trace representation and linear complexity of binary e-th residue sequences. In: International Workshop on Coding and Cryptography-WCC, pp. 121–133 (2003)
8. Du, X., Klapper, A., Chen, Z.: Linear complexity of pseudorandom sequences generated by Fermat quotients and their generalizations. Inf. Process. Lett. **112**, 233–237 (2012)
9. Du, X., Chen, Z., Hu, L.: Linear complexity of binary sequences derived from Euler quotients with prime-power modulus. Inf. Process. Lett. **112**(14–15), 604–609 (2012)
10. Du, X.: An extension of binary threshold sequences from Fermat quotients. Adv. Math. Commun. **10**(4), 745–754 (2016)
11. Golomb, S., Gong, G.: Signal Design for Good Correlation. Cambridge University Press, Cambridge (2015)
12. Jungnickel, D.: Finite Fields, Structure and Arithmetics. Biblographiches Institute, Mannheim (1993)
13. Lidl, R., Niederreiter, H.: Finite Fields. Cambridge University Press, Cambridge (1997)
14. Massey, J.L.: Shift register synthesis and BCH decoding. IEEE Trans. Inf. Theory **15**(1), 122–127 (1969)
15. Wu, C., Wei, W.: An extension of binary threshold sequences from Fermat quotients. Adv. Math. Commun. **10**(4), 743–752 (2016)
16. Wu, C., Chen, Z., Du, X.: Binary threshold sequences derived from Carmichael quotients with even numbers modulus. IEICE Trans. Fundam. Electron. Commun. Comput. Sci. **E95-A**(7), 1197–1199 (2012)
17. Xiong, L., Shi, Y.: On the privacy-preserving outsourcing scheme of reversible data hiding over encrypted image data in cloud computing. CMC: Comput. Mater. Contin. **55**(3), 523–539 (2018)
18. Xu, W., Xiang, S., Sachnev, V.: A cryptograph domain image retrieval method based on Paillier homomorphic block encryption. CMC: Comput. Mater. Contin. **055**(2), 285–295 (2018)
19. Zhang, J., Zhao, C.: Linear complexity and trace representation of sequences with period $2p^2$. In: IEEE International Symposium on Information Theory, pp. 2206–2210 (2018)
20. Zhao, L., Du, X., Wu, C.: Trace representation of the sequences derived from polynomial quotient. In: Sun, X., Pan, Z., Bertino, E. (eds.) ICCCS 2018. LNCS, vol. 11066, pp. 26–37. Springer, Cham (2018). https://doi.org/10.1007/978-3-030-00015-8_3

Information Hiding

An Improved Steganalysis Method Using Feature Combinations

Zichi Wang, Zhenxing Qian$^{(\boxtimes)}$, Xinpeng Zhang, and Sheng Li

Shanghai Institute for Advanced Communication and Data Science, Key
Laboratory of Specialty Fiber Optics and Optical Access Networks, Joint
International Research Laboratory of Specialty Fiber Optics and Advanced
Communication, Shanghai University, Shanghai, People's Republic of China
zxqian@shu.edu.cn

Abstract. This paper proposes a new feature extraction method for steganalysis. In the improved method, the feature set is equipped with two parts. The first part is obtained by employing an existing feature extraction method on a suspicious image. With a content-correlative operation, differences of the image features are enlarge between the cover and the stego. The second part is obtained by employing the same feature extraction method on the obtained image. The two parts are combined together to form the new feature set. With the new feature set, the modifications made by steganography can be recognized more efficiently. Experimental results show that the detection accuracy of existing feature extraction methods is increased using the proposed method.

Keywords: Information hiding · Steganography · Steganalysis ·
Feature extraction

1 Introduction

Steganography is a technology of hiding secret data into a digital media, aiming at transmitting the secret data through public channels without drawing suspicion [1–3]. On the contrary, steganalysis is a technology of disclosing the secret transmission by analyzing media on public channels [4–6].

The most popular digital image steganography focus on syndrome trellis coding (STC) based embedding [7], which aims to minimize the additive distortion between a cover and a stego using a pre-defined distortion function [8–10]. The distortion function assigns embedding costs for all elements in a cover. These embedding costs are used to quantify the effects when modifying the cover elements. With the development of machine learning, many steganalytic tools were proposed to detect the behaviors of steganography. Modern steganalytic methods use supervised machine learning to investigate the models of the covers and the stegos. As shown in Fig. 1, features are extracted from a set of images to train a common steganalytic classifier, which is then used to distinguish the suspicious image [11]. At present, the ensemble classifier [12] is widely used to measure the feature sets. The feature extraction and machine learning based steganalysis has been proved to be efficient.

© Springer Nature Switzerland AG 2019
X. Sun et al. (Eds.): ICAIS 2019, LNCS 11634, pp. 115–127, 2019.
https://doi.org/10.1007/978-3-030-24271-8_11

Phase of Training

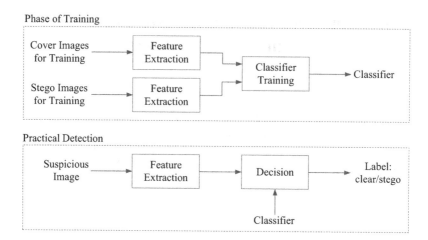

Fig. 1. Sketch of modern steganalysis

Recently, deep learning based steganalysis achieves good performance [13]. But the study of deep-learned features is still in its infancy [14]. Some important operations in the feature extraction process, such as truncation and quantization, cannot be effectively learned by deep networks. Hence, the feature extraction is vital for steganalysis. The most popular feature set is SRM (Spatial Rich Model) [15]. In SRM, the fourth order co-occurrence matrices are calculated to describe the dependencies among different pixels. An image is firstly filtered by many high-pass filters to generate residual images with different shapes and orientations. Then, the fourth order co-occurrence matrices are implemented on the quantized residuals.

After SRM, some improved feature extraction methods are proposed [16, 17]. In PSRM (Projections of Spatial Rich Model) [16], neighboring residual samples are projected onto a set of random vectors and the histograms of the projections are taken as the feature. The feature set maxSRMd2 [17] is a variant of SRM that makes use of the modification probabilities of cover elements during data embedding, which is called probabilistic selection channel. With these feature extraction methods proposed, corresponding optimization methods are needed. A method to improve the detectability of maxSRMd2 is proposed in [18]. However, it is designed to detect CMD (Clustering Modification Directions) steganography [19] directly, not universal for other popular steganographic methods such as HILL [20], SUNIWARD [21], and WOW [22].

This paper proposes a universal feature improving method for steganalysis. The improved feature set is equipped with two parts. An existing feature extraction method is employed on the suspicious image to get the first part, which is as same as the existing feature set. Then an operation correlative to image content is made on this image to enlarge the differences between cover and stego image. After that, the same feature extraction method is employed on the obtained image to get the second part. Finally, the two parts are combined to form the new feature set. Experimental results show that the detection accuracy of existing feature extraction methods is increased using the proposed method.

2 Related Works

Many steganalytic methods have been proposed to defeat steganography. Feature extraction and machine learning based steganalysis has been proved to be efficient. A variety of feature extraction algorithms have been proposed, such as SPAM [23], SRM [15], SRMQ1 [15], and ccJRM [11]. Meanwhile, the ensemble classifier is widely used to measure the feature sets.

In SPAM, the independence of the stego noise is exploited. The differences between adjacent pixels are modeled using first-order and second-order Markov chains. It is postulates that such deviations from this model are due to steganographic embedding. Accordingly, a filter is applied to suppress the image content and exposing the stego noise. Then the dependences between neighboring pixels of the filtered image are modeled as a higher order Markov chain. Finally, the subsets of sample transition probability matrices are used as the feature vector with 686 dimensions.

The dependencies among different pixels can be exploited more exactly. So, the fourth order co-occurrence matrices are employed in SRM. The rich model is consisted of a large number of diverse submodels. These submodels consider various types of relationships among neighboring samples of noise residuals obtained by linear and non-linear filters with compact supports. Many high-pass filters are implemented on an image to generate residual images with different shapes and orientations. Then, the fourth order co-occurrence matrices are implemented on the quantized residuals to form the final feature vector with 34671 dimensions.

The high dimensions of SRM leads to high computational complexity in the process of feature extraction. SRMQ1 is a simplified version of SRM with only 12753 dimensions. In SRMQ1, the quantization factor is not optimized and thus it is not surprising that its performance is generally inferior to the performance of SRM. But the loss is rather small. Comparing with SRM equipped with 106 submodels, the feature extraction time of SRMQ1 is roughly reduced to 1/3 since only 39 submodels need to be calculated.

The rich model feature set for JPEG images has also been studied in [11]. In this steganalyzer, many co-occurrence matrices are calculated to describe the dependencies among different DCT coefficients. The absolute values of DCT coefficients in JPEG are treated as 64 parallel channels with weak dependencies. On the one hand, the 64 channels are modeled using co-occurrence matrices separately and collected together. On the other hand, to find the integral joint statistics among coefficients, co-occurrence matrices constructed from the whole DCT plane with a wider range of values are also collected. Meanwhile, the joint statistics are symmetrized to construct a compact and robust model. The final feature vector is equipped with 22510 dimensions.

Although these feature sets are effective for steganalysis, they still can be improved further. In this paper, we designed a universal method to improve the detection accuracy of the existing feature sets by remaining original feature data and adding some effective information.

3 Proposed Method

3.1 Sketch of Proposed Method

The sketch of the proposed method is shown in Fig. 2. Different from modern steganalysis, in the phase of training, an existing feature extraction method is employed on a cover or stego image firstly. Then an operation correlative to image content is made on this image. After that, the same feature extraction method is employed again on the obtained image. The two feature sets are combined by a combination function to form the new feature set. Finally, the classifier is trained by the combined feature sets. In the phase of practical detection, the same process is repeated to get a combined feature set for decision with the help of trained classifier. The details are as follows.

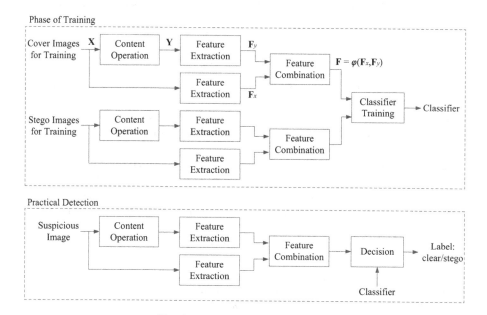

Fig. 2. Sketch of proposed method

For a given image $\mathbf{X}$, denote the feature set extracted from $\mathbf{X}$ using existing feature extraction method as $\mathbf{F}_x$. After a content-correlative operation is made on $\mathbf{X}$, the corresponding image $\mathbf{Y}$ is obtained. Denote the feature set extracted from $\mathbf{Y}$ with the same feature extraction method as $\mathbf{F}_y$. As shown in Eq. (1), $\mathbf{F}_x$ and $\mathbf{F}_y$ are combined together by a combination function $\varphi(\cdot)$ to construct the final feature set $\mathbf{F}$.

$$\mathbf{F} = \varphi(\mathbf{F}_x, \mathbf{F}_y) \tag{1}$$

The details of the content-correlative operation and combination function $\varphi(\cdot)$ would be discussed later. In this way, the differences between cover and stego image are enlarged, and thus more effective information is contained in the combined feature.

Not only the statistical abnormality, but also the variation in feature space caused by steganography are caught. Thus, the detection accuracy of steganography could be increased. Some theoretical proofs are given in next subsection to clarify the feasibility of the proposed method.

3.2   Theoretical Proofs

Theoretically, as shown in Eq. (2), the difference between a cover and stego object can be measured using the KL divergence [24], which is a fundamental concept from information theory measuring the distance of two distributions.

$$D(p_c(x)||p_s(x)) = \sum_x p_c(x) \log \frac{p_c(x)}{p_s(x)} \tag{2}$$

where $p_c(x)$ and $p_s(x)$ are the distributions of cover and stego object respectively. The value of KL divergence is always non-negative [24] and is 0 if and only if the two distributions are equal.

After combination, the distributions of new cover and stego object can be denoted as $p_c(x, y)$ and $p_s(x, y)$. Thus, the KL divergence between the new cover and stego object is,

$$D(p_c(x,y)||p_s(x,y)) = \sum_x \sum_y p_c(x,y) \log \frac{p_c(x,y)}{p_s(x,y)} \tag{3}$$

Then the new KL divergence can be written as,

$$D(p_c(x,y)||p_s(x,y)) = \sum_x p_c(x) \log \frac{p_c(x)}{p_s(x)} + \sum_x \sum_y p_c(x,y) \log \frac{p_c(y|x)}{p_s(y|x)} \tag{4}$$

So,

$$D(p_c(x,y)||p_s(x,y)) = D(p_c(x)||p_s(x)) + D(p_c(y|x)||p_s(y|x)) \tag{5}$$

Due to the non-negativity of KL divergence,

$$D(p_c(y|x)||p_s(y|x)) \geq 0 \tag{6}$$

For the reason that the second part of the combined feature is related to image content instead of produced randomly, the distribution of $p_c(y|x)$ and $p_s(y|x)$ is not equivalent. So, the conditional KL divergence $D(p_c(y|x)||p_s(y|x))$ in formula (6) is not equal to zero. In other words,

$$D(p_c(y|x)||p_s(y|x)) > 0 \tag{7}$$

Therefore,

$$D(p_c(x,y)||p_s(x,y)) > D(p_c(x)||p_s(x)) \tag{8}$$

That means the difference between the new cover and stego object is larger than the original one. That is to say, the new cover and stego object can be distinguished more easily after combination. Therefore, the proposed feature optimization method is effective in theory. Next, the details of the content-correlative operation and combination function of the proposed method will be introduced.

3.3   Content-Correlative Operation

A larger $D(p_c(y|x)||p_s(y|x))$ means larger difference between cover and stego object, and means better performance of the combined feature set. To increase the value of $D(p_c(y|x)||p_s(y|x))$ as possible, as shown in Fig. 2, the content-correlative operation in the proposed method is significant.

A good choice for this operation is Re-Embedding. In other words, $\mathbf{Y}$ is obtained by embedding in $\mathbf{X}$ with the same embedding algorithm and payload of the suspicious image. For modern steganographic schemes which aims to minimize the additive distortion of a cover image, the probability $p(i)$ to modify a cover element $x(i)$ (a pixel for an uncompressed image or a DCT coefficient for a JPEG image) [25] is,

$$p(i) = \frac{e^{-\lambda\rho(i)}}{1 + e^{-\lambda\rho(i)}} \tag{9}$$

where $\rho(i)$ is the embedding cost assigned for $x(i)$, and as shown in Eq. (10), λ is a positive parameter used to make the information entropy of modifying probability equal to the embedding payload m (bits).

$$-\sum_{i=1}^{n} \{p(i)\log_2 p(i) + (1-p(i))\log_2(1-p(i))\} = m \tag{10}$$

Denote the probability to modify a cover or stego element as $p_c(i)$ and $p_s(i)$ respectively. To increase the value of $D(p_c(y|x)||p_s(y|x))$, the difference between $p_c(y|x)$ and $p_s(y|x)$ should be increased. Correspondingly, increasing the difference between $p_c(y|x)$ and $p_s(y|x)$ is equal to increase the difference between $p_c(i)$ and $p_s(i)$.

It can be seen from Eqs. (9) and (10) that the value of modifying probability is determined by embedding cost and payload. After embedding, the cover image is modified with probability $p_c(i)$. According to the proposed method, the obtained image is embedded with the same embedding algorithm and payload. In this way, the value of payload is keep unchanged during the two embedding processes. But the value of embedding cost $\rho(i)$ is changed because that the embedding costs of two different images are calculated by same embedding algorithm. Therefore, the satisfactory difference between $p_c(i)$ and $p_s(i)$ can be guaranteed, and so a large $D(p_c(y|x)||p_s(y|x))$ can be obtained.

To compare Re-Embedding with other content-correlative operation, we conduct a group of experiments over 100 grayscale images arbitrarily selected from BOSSbase ver. 1.01 [26]. We compared Re-Embedding with three content-correlative operations: Wiener Filtering, Sharpening, and Histogram Equalization.

In order to calculate the value of KL divergence, the value of distributions $p_c(x)$, $p_s(y)$, $p_c(x, y)$ and $p_s(x, y)$ should be obtained. Because of the strong pixel correlation in natural images, these values should be calculated using high order statistical properties. Thus, the feature set of modern steganalysis can be used directly since its meaning is equal to distributions and the values of feature set are restricted in (0, 1) after normalization. To save computation complexity, the SPAM feature set [23] with only 686 dimensions is used to get the distribution of image. The comparison of average KL divergence in five cases calculated on the 100 selected grayscale images is shown in Fig. 3. Where "Original" means no operations are employed.

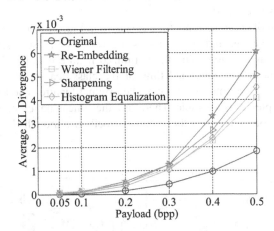

Fig. 3. Comparisons of average KL divergence over 100 images

From Fig. 3 we can see that the Re-Embedding operation achieves the largest increment of KL divergence, which avails steganalysis. Therefore, Re-Embedding is an attractive choice for the content-correlative operation of the proposed method.

3.4 Feature Combination

Another element which determines the performance of the final feature set is the way to combine feature set $\mathbf{F}_x$ and $\mathbf{F}_y$, that is the details of function $\varphi(\cdot)$. We implement $\varphi(\cdot)$ by concatenation, which remains original feature data $\mathbf{F}_x$ and adds some effective information $\mathbf{F}_y$. That is to say,

$$\varphi(\mathbf{F}_x, \mathbf{F}_y) = [\mathbf{F}_x, \mathbf{F}_y] \tag{11}$$

After concatenation, as shown in Eq. (12), the information entropy of the new feature set $\mathbf{F}$ can be calculated as the joint entropy of $\mathbf{F}_x$ and $\mathbf{F}_y$,

$$H(\mathbf{F}_x, \mathbf{F}_y) = H(\mathbf{F}_x) + H(\mathbf{F}_y) - I(\mathbf{F}_x, \mathbf{F}_y) \tag{12}$$

where $H(\cdot)$ is the entropy function, and $I(\cdot)$ represents the mutual information between $\mathbf{F}_x$ and $\mathbf{F}_y$ defined in information theory. So, it is reasonable to combine feature set by concatenation since the maximal amount of information is remained. Other approach cannot obtain higher amount of information than concatenation achieved. The flaw of this operation is that the feature dimensions are increased after concatenation. Fortunately, the computational complexity of feature classification is not increased obviously in spite of the increment of feature dimensions.

The computational time of feature classification using the optimized and original features are respectively tested on a serve with 2.5 GHz CPU, 128 GB memory and windows 7. The type of system is 64 bits and the version of MATLAB is 2013a. We use feature sets SPAM and SRMQ1 to test the computational time of classification with the ensemble classifier [12]. The steganographic algorithm is SUNIWARD, and image dataset is BOSSbase ver. 1.01.

The comparison of computational time is shown in Fig. 4, which is evaluated using the average value over ten independent classification. For most cases, the computational time of the classification using the optimized feature is larger than the original. Numerically, the mean computational time of the classification using the optimized feature is about only 1.16 times as many as the original feature. The tiny increment of computational complexity is tolerable. Therefore, the concatenation operation is a good choice for feature combination in the proposed method although the dimensions are doubled.

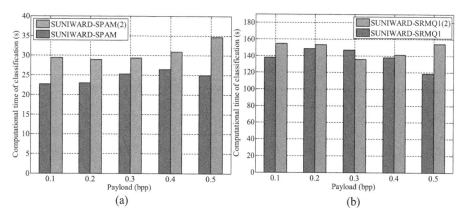

Fig. 4. Comparisons of computational complexity of classification using (a) SPAM, (b) SRMQ1 and their optimized version with SUNIWARD on image dataset BOSSbass ver. 1.01.

Actually, better performance can be achieved by combining more than two feature sets. But feature dimensions and computation complexity would also increased. In addition, the proposed method is universal for both spatial and JPEG steganalysis since the process of feature extraction is unchanged.

4 Experimental Results

4.1 Experiment Setup

The image dataset employed in our experiments is BOSSbass ver. 1.01 [26] which contains 10000 uncompressed grayscale images sized 512×512. All the images are adopted as cover images for experiment comparison.

To get stego images for classifier training and testing, the popular steganographic methods HILL, SUNIWARD and WOW are employed. All embedding tasks are done by the embedding simulator [27] since it is widely used to simulate the optimal embedding. We set the payloads as 0.05, 0.1, 0.2, 0.3, 0.4, and 0.5 bpp, respectively.

Meanwhile, to verify the effectiveness of the proposed method, the popular feature sets SPAM [23], SRMQ1 [15] and SRM [15] are used as benchmark. We employ the ensemble classifier [12] to measure the property of feature sets. One half of the cover and stego feature sets are used for training, while the remaining sets are used for testing. The criterion of evaluating the performance of feature sets is the minimal total error P_E with identical priors achieved on the testing sets [12].

$$P_E = \min_{P_{FA}} \left(\frac{P_{FA} + P_{MD}}{2} \right) \tag{13}$$

where P_{FA} is the false alarm rate and P_{MD} the missed detection rate. The performance is evaluated using the average of P_E over ten random tests. Lower value of P_E means higher detection accuracy.

4.2 Detection Accuracy Against Steganography

For feature sets SPAM, SRMQ1 and SRM, the improved version are denoted as SPAM (2), SRMQ1(2) and SRM(2), respectively. Figure 5 shows the detection accuracy comparisons of these methods. The results indicate that the detection accuracy of all approaches for feature extraction are increased by using the proposed improving method.

Specifically, with the proposed method, the P_E for SPAM is decreased by 2.19% for HILL with 0.5 bpp, 4.47% for WOW with 0.5 bpp, and 4.36% for WOW with 0.4 bpp. For SRMQ1, the P_E is decreased by 1.43% for HILL with 0.3 bpp, 2.12% for WOW with 0.1 bpp, and 1.37% for SUNIWARD with 0.5 bpp. For SRM, the P_E is decreased by 1.36% for HILL with 0.2 bpp, 1.65% for WOW with 0.1 bpp, and 0.79% for SUNIWARD with 0.4 bpp.

In addition, there are some feature selection methods [28, 29] and feature improvement methods, e.g. PSRM [16], maxSRMd2 [17], which also increase the detection accuracy of steganalysis. But these methods and the proposed method are

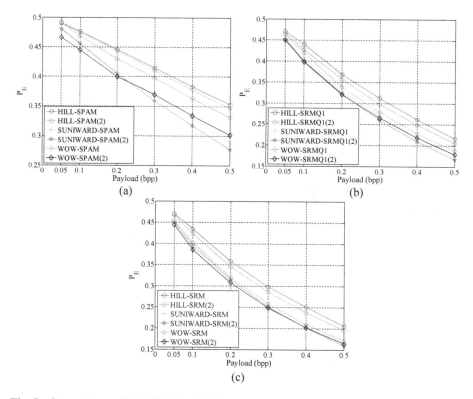

Fig. 5. Comparisons of (a) SPAM, (b) SRMQ1, (c) SRM and its improved version using ensemble classifier with HILL, SUNIWARD, and WOW on image dataset BOSSbass ver. 1.01.

independent and work in different frameworks. These methods aim to improve a feature set itself, while the proposed method combine two feature sets. Where the two feature sets can be improved firstly by these methods. In other words, after these methods are carried out, the obtained feature sets can be improved further using the proposed method.

4.3 Performance on Other Image Dataset

To further verify the effectiveness of the proposed method, we also made comparison on image dataset UCID [30] which contains 1338 uncompressed color images sized 512×384. These images are transformed into grayscale image.

Figure 6 shows the detection accuracy comparisons of SRMQ1, SRM and their improved version using ensemble classifier with HILL on image dataset UCID. It can be seen from Fig. 6 that the detection accuracy of feature sets is also increased after using the proposed method. That means the proposed method is effective in spite of the data source which is significant to the current big data world [31, 32].

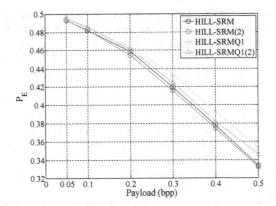

Fig. 6. Comparisons of SRMQ1, SRM and their optimized version using ensemble classifier with HILL on image dataset UCID.

5   Conclusion

This paper proposes a universal feature improving method for steganalysis. The improved feature set is equipped with two parts. The first part is obtained by employing an existing feature extraction method on a suspicious image. Then secret data is embedded in the suspicious image with a certain embedding algorithm and payload. After that, the second part is obtained by employing the same feature extraction method on the embedded image. The two parts are concatenated to form the new feature set. Experimental results show that after the proposed method is employed, the certain steganographic pattern can be recognized more efficient, which results in the increasing of detection accuracy of existing feature extraction methods.

Acknowledgement. This work was supported by the National Natural Science Foundation of China (U1536108, 61572308, U1636206, U1736213, 61525203, and 61602294), the Natural Science Foundation of Shanghai (18ZR1427500), and the Shanghai Excellent Academic Leader Plan (16XD1401200).

References

1. Li, S., Zhang, X.: Towards construction based data hiding: from secrets to fingerprint images. IEEE Trans. Image Process. **28**(3), 1482–1497 (2019)
2. Meng, R., Rice, S., Wang, J., Sun, X.: A fusion steganographic algorithm based on faster R-CNN. CMC: Comput. Mater. Contin. **55**(1), 001–016 (2018)
3. Duan, X., Song, H., Qin, C., Khan, M.: Coverless steganography for digital images based on a generative model. CMC: Comput. Mater. Contin. **55**(3), 483–493 (2018)
4. Li, F., Wu, K., Lei, J., Wen, M., Bi, Z., Gu, C.: Steganalysis over large-scale social networks with high-order joint features and clustering ensembles. IEEE Trans. Inf. Forensics Secur. **11**(2), 344–357 (2016)

5. Wang, Z., Zhang, X., Yin, Z.: Joint cover-selection and payload-allocation by steganographic distortion optimization. IEEE Signal Process. Lett. **25**(10), 1530–1534 (2018)
6. Wang, Z., Lv, J., Wei, Q., Zhang, X.: Distortion function for spatial image steganography based on the polarity of embedding change. In: The 15th International Workshop on Digital-forensics and Watermarking (IWDW 2016), Beijing, China, pp. 487–493, September 2016
7. Filler, T., Judas, J., Fridrich, J.: Minimizing additive distortion in steganography using Syndrome-Trellis codes. IEEE Trans. Inf. Forensics Secur. **6**(3), 920–935 (2011)
8. Wang, Z., Yin, Z., Zhang, X.: Asymmetric distortion function for JPEG steganography using block artifact compensation. Int. J. Digit. Crime Forensics **11**(1), 90–99 (2019)
9. Wang, Z., Yin, Z., Zhang, X.: Distortion function for JPEG steganography based on image-texture and correlation in DCT domain. IETE Tech. Rev. **35**(4), 351–358 (2018)
10. Wang, Z., Zhang, X., Yin, Z.: Hybrid distortion function for JPEG steganography. J. Electron. Imaging **25**(5), 050501 (2016)
11. Kodovsky, J., Fridrich, J.: Steganalysis of JPEG images using rich models. In: Proceedings of the International Society for Optics and Photonics, San Francisco, CA, USA, pp. 83030A–83030A-13, January 2012
12. Kodovsky, J., Fridrich, J., Holub, V.: Ensemble classifiers for steganalysis of digital media. Trans. Inf. Forensics Secur. **7**(2), 432–444 (2012)
13. Ye, J., Ni, J., Yi, Y.: Deep learning hierarchical representations for image steganalysis. IEEE Trans. Inf. Forensics Secur. **12**(11), 2545–2557 (2017)
14. Wang, Z., Qian, Z., Zhang, X., Yang, M., Ye, D.: On improving distortion functions for JPEG steganography. IEEE Access **6**(1), 74917–74930 (2018)
15. Fridrich, J., Kodovsky, J.: Rich models for steganalysis of digital images. IEEE Trans. Inf. Forensics Secur. **7**(3), 868–882 (2012)
16. Holub, V., Fridrich, J.: Random projections of residuals for digital image steganalysis. IEEE Trans. Inf. Forensics Secur. **8**(12), 1996–2006 (2013)
17. Denemark, T., Sedighi, V., Holub, V., Cogranne, R., Fridrich, J.: Selection-channel-aware rich model for steganalysis of digital images. In: Proceedings of the 2014 IEEE International Workshop on Information Forensics and Security, Atlanta, GA, pp. 48–53, December 2014
18. Tan, S., Zhang, H., Li, B., Huang, J.: Pixel-decimation-assisted steganalysis of synchronize-embedding-changes steganography. IEEE Trans. Inf. Forensics Secur. **12**(7), 1658–1670 (2017)
19. Li, B., Wang, M., Li, X., Tan, S., Huang, J.W.: A strategy of clustering modification directions in spatial image steganography. IEEE Trans. Inf. Forensics Secur. **10**(9), 1905–1917 (2015)
20. Li, B., Wang, M., Huang, J., Li, X.: A new cost function for spatial image steganography. In: Proceedings of the IEEE International Conference on Image Processing, Paris, France, pp. 4206–4210, October 2014
21. Holub, V., Fridrich, J.: Digital image steganography using universal distortion. In: Proceedings of the First ACM Workshop on Information Hiding and Multimedia Security, New York, NY, USA, pp. 59–68, June 2013
22. Holub, V., Fridrich, J.: Designing steganographic distortion using directional filters. In: Proceedings of the IEEE International Workshop on Information Forensics and Security, Binghamton, NY, USA, pp. 234–239, December 2012
23. Pevny, T., Bas, P., Fridrich, J.: Steganalysis by subtractive pixel adjacency matrix. IEEE Trans. Inf. Forensics Secur. **5**(2), 215–224 (2010)
24. Cachin, C.: An information-theoretic model for steganography. In: Proceedings of the International Workshop on Information Hiding, Portland, Oregon, USA, pp. 306–318, April 1998

25. Fridrich, J., Filler, T.: Practical methods for minimizing embedding impact in steganography. In: Proceedings of the SPIE, Security, Steganography, and Watermarking of Multimedia Contents IX, San Jose, CA, pp. 2–3, February 2007
26. Bas, P., Filler, T., Pevný, T.: Break our steganographic system: the ins and outs of organizing BOSS. In: Proceedings of the 13th International Conference on Information Hiding, Prague, Czech Republic, pp. 59–70, May 2011
27. Pevný, T., Filler, T., Bas, P.: Using high-dimensional image models to perform highly undetectable steganography. In: Proceedings of the 12th International Conference on Information Hiding, Calgary, AB, Canada, pp. 161–177, June 2010
28. Miche, Y., Roue, B., Lendasse, A., Bas, P.: A feature selection methodology for steganalysis. In: Proceedings of the International Workshop on Multimedia Content Representation, Classification and Security, Istanbul, Turkey, pp. 49–56, September 2006
29. Mohammadi, F.G., Abadeh, M.S.: Image steganalysis using a bee colony based feature selection algorithm. Eng. Appl. Artif. Intell. **31**, 35–43 (2014)
30. Schaefer, G., Stich, M.: UCID - an uncompressed colour image database. In: Proceedings of the Conference on Storage and Retrieval Methods and Applications for Multimedia, San Jose, CA, USA, pp. 472–480, January 2004
31. Guan, Z., Zhang, Y., Wu, L., Wu, J., Ma, Y., Hu, J.: APPA: an anonymous and privacy preserving data aggregation scheme for fog-enhanced IoT. J. Netw. Comput. Appl. **125**, 82–92 (2019)
32. Wu, J., Dong, M., Ota, K., Li, J., Guan, Z.: Big data analysis-based secure cluster management for optimized control plane in software-defined networks. IEEE Trans. Netw. Serv. Manag. **15**(1), 27–38 (2018)

Research on Application of OFD Technology in Secure Electronic Bills

Shaokang Wang, Dan Liu, Jingning Sun, Yinping Bai$^{(\boxtimes)}$, and Zhaofeng Zhou

Beijing Suwell Technology Co., LTD., Beijing 100081, China
{wsk,newdan,sunjn,yinping.bai,zzf}@suwell.cn

Abstract. With the rapid development of e-commerce, electronic bills gradually replace the traditional paper vouchers for electronic information transfer, and the research on the security of electronic bill documents has become more and more important. This paper proposes an electronic document generation method based on OFD (Open Fixed-layout Document) technology, and combines traditional electronic seal, digital signature and multiple digital watermarking techniques to propose a comprehensive security electronic bill solution. The experimental results show that the method of generating electronic document documents proposed in this paper is simple and easy to use with higher security. It can not only realize the integrity, authenticity verification and tampering identification of electronic document content, but also accurately locate the tampering position.

Keywords: OFD · Electronic bill · Digital signature ·
Multiple watermark · Electronic seal

1 Introduction

With the continuous maturity of Internet technology and the increasing popularity of applications, e-commerce activities using the Internet as the main means of information transmission have become more and more active, including advertising, transactions, payments, services and other activities [1]. As the inheritance and development of paper bills, electronic bills gradually replace the traditional paper documents for electronic information transmission by using networks and computers, such as electronic orders, electronic contracts and electronic invoices, etc. [2]. Comparing the electronic bills and the paper bills, the electronic signature replaces the manual signature, the Internet transmission method replaces the manual transmission, and the computer intelligent input replaces the form of the handwriting method. The whole process of bill business, such as the issuance, circulation and payment of bills, can be fully realized electronically with high efficiency, security and convenience. However, the electronic bills are easily falsified, stolen and spread during network transmission, and it brings a great security risk for financial transaction data and personal information leakage [3]. Therefore, how to ensure the integrity and authenticity of the contents of electronic bill

© Springer Nature Switzerland AG 2019
X. Sun et al. (Eds.): ICAIS 2019, LNCS 11634, pp. 128–139, 2019.
https://doi.org/10.1007/978-3-030-24271-8_12

documents has become a key prerequisite for the rapid development of electronic bill business.

The electronic ticket file needs to perform operations such as network transmission, terminal preview and print output. Considering the convenience of file generation and use, and compatibility with application software and operating system, the PDF (Portable Document Format) file becomes the preferred document format for electronic tickets in an e-commerce network environment [4–7]. The electronic ticket generated based on the PDF format has the following advantages [6]: (1) The PDF file is platform-independent and has the perfect system compatibility. (2) The size of PDF file is relatively small for the compact structure and data compression technology, so it is suitable for transmission in a network environment. (3) The PDF file is powerful with beautiful layout effect. In order to ensure the security of electronic bills, the contents of electronic bills are prevented from being illegally falsified by digitally signing PDF files [3]. The digest of the initial digital information is encrypted and then forms a single piece of information. This information is generally different from the initial information. When the initial information is transmitted, the corresponding digest information is attached to verify the authenticity and integrity of initial digital information. However, the digital signature method is prone to the following problems when authenticating digital content: (1) Digital signature technology needs to store the signature information and the information carrier separately, which brings the potential security risks. Once the signature information is lost, it affects the normal use of the information receiver; (2) The digital signature technology can judge whether the digital information content has been intercepted and falsified, but cannot accurately locate the tampering position and restore the falsified content; (3) It can't make any appropriate modification to the digital information content without changing its basic meaning, such as properly lossy compression of JPEG images for transmission efficiency.

In addition, encapsulating electronic tickets and their elements based on XML is also a better choice for electronic ticket generation [7]. This kind of encapsulation helps to protect electronic bills from changes in the technical environment, thus ensuring the authenticity and credibility of electronic invoices, facilitating the retrieval, extraction and utilization of electronic bills and long-term preservation. Fang [8] proposed an electronic invoice in SVG (Scalable Vector Graphic) format, and designed an XML/HTML fragile digital watermarking algorithm for SVG format electronic invoice which has better ability for tamper detection and location. It can apply to the anti-counterfeiting certification of SVG format electronic invoices. The security performance of electronic tickets encapsulated in XML format mainly depends on XML Signature [9,10] or digital watermarking algorithm based on XML/HTML file format [11–14]. At present, considering the degree of content protection, XML/HTML watermarking technology can be roughly divided into the following categories: (1) overall protection of XML/HTML; (2) protection of XML/HTML source files line by line or word by word; (3) protection of XML/ HTML key information. However, since the XML/HTML file only has requirements for the content format, the size and structure of each block is susceptible to a single element. Therefore, there is a common problem of the above algorithms. When the order of the blocks is changed or the XML/HTML file block is additionally added, the result of the watermark extraction and tamper detection by the block order is affected, so that the watermark information cannot be correctly extracted, and it can't locate the tampering position. Some scholars have also converted the electronic bills into digital image files, and used the fragile watermark or semi-fragile digital image authentication algorithms [15–19] to perform electronic bill content integrity authentication and tamper identification. Although the algorithm can accurately detect and locate local malicious tampering of image content without affecting the visual quality of the host image, and it has strong sensitivity and robustness, but the volume of the digital image file is so large. After the image file is compressed lossily, the watermark information in the content of the electronic ticket file may be damaged, thereby affecting the content integrity authentication and tampering identification. Therefore, image file is not well suited as file format carrier for the electronic ticket.

Aiming at the problems of the above methods, this paper proposes an electronic ticket generation method based on OFD file format, and combines XML signature, electronic seal and multiple digital watermarking techniques to realize the content integrity authentication of electronic files. It can not only achieve the purpose of tampering identification of the document content, but also accurately locate the tampering location.

2 Introduction to OFD Technology

2.1 OFD Document Format

OFD Layout technology describes and stores data in a "container + file" manner. A container is a virtual storage system (Virtual Storage System) that aggregates various types of data description files and provides corresponding access interfaces and data compression methods.

To be specific, the basic technical architecture of the OFD document format is divided into four layers:

(a) Virtual storage system: including the package organization structure and the directory organization structure within the package.
(b) File model: including logical organization structure such as documents, pages, outlines and file-level resources, etc.
(c) Page content description: including page level resources, graphics, images and text, etc.
(d) Extended features: including document interactivity and extensibility, etc.

2.2 OFD Technical Characteristics

OFD is an ideal carrier format for serious official documents such as electronic documents, electronic archives, electronic certificates and electronic bills. It is an important guarantee for the standardization and credibility of electronic documents. It has the following characteristics:

(1) The format of the layout document is relatively independent.
    The document format is independent of software, hardware, operating system, rendering and printing devices.
(2) The rendering effect of Layout document is solidified
    In the layout document, the two-dimensional vector image model is adopted, and the coordinates of the objects such as text, graphics, images, and the attributes that affect the rendering effect are accurately described. The layout is solidified according to certain rules with high fidelity to achieve the immediate displaying and printing results. The ability of OFD technology to describe page objects is roughly equivalent to that of PDF technology, which is suitable for most of the business scope of PDF files, but is easier to use.
(3) It supports metadata addition and semantic embedded integration.
    In the OFD layout document, it supports the semantic display and extraction function of electronic bills, realizes semantic retrieval and semantic area positioning through the semantic-navigation-tree, which can greatly improve the efficiency of ticket file exchange and utilization. In order to facilitate electronic ticket exchange sharing and deep utilization, it provides standard interface calls for other applications to write and read ticket metadata and semantic information, such as company name, goods content and ticket validity period, etc.
(4) The design of template file is flexible.
    Due to the wide variety of types of bills, each type of bill has different style and presentation content. For the needs of different types of electronic bills, it is necessary to make corresponding electronic bill template to ensure that each type of bill has a uniform and consistent presentation with the style of paper bills. The OFD technology can be used to provide electronic bill template customization related functions, which can conveniently customize the presentation style of different kinds of bills, set relevant dynamic fill area data items, and generate an electronic template of bills consistent with the paper ticket layout.
(5) It has high security.
    OFD technology does not support the programmability of documents, and improves the security of document content, thus eliminating the security risks caused by programmability. OFD layout documents combined with digital signature technology can realize the non-repudiation, tamper-proof and guarantee the authenticity and reliability of documents. At the same time, it is also possible to process 2D barcode, digital watermark, etc., and further expand the security mechanism of the layout document.

3   Design of Secure Electronic Bills

In this method, an electronic ticket file is generated in an OFD layout file as a carrier format. During the generation process of the OFD file, digital watermarking technology is used to protect the key personalized data loaded into the electronic ticket template file. Finally, the electronic signature is digitally signed by the electronic seal, and the electronic ticket file is obtained by using XML technology to encapsulate the electronic bill file as a whole document.

3.1 Template File Production

For specific types of electronic bills, OFD technology is used to generate a backplane file similar to paper bills, which does not contain specific bills data, but only contains the bills backplane, general text, data domain and other contents of OFD electronic files. The core metadata in each electronic bill is dynamically variable data importing through data domain binding, such as invoicing unit name, cargo name, quantity, amount and the relevant information of the seller, which is the key information of electronic bills and the key object that needs to be protected.

3.2 Authentication Watermark Information Embedding

The watermarking information for content integrity authentication of electronic bills is generated and embedded into variable characters or image data of electronic bills by digital watermarking technology. Once the character data in the electronic bill file is semantically falsified, the bit string of the authentication watermark information will be changed and the tampered position will be located.

Let M be the set of all initial watermarking information m, X be the set of all information carriers x to be protected, W be the set of initial watermarking signal w, K be the set of watermark embedding and extracting key k, and G be the watermark generating algorithm, namely:

$$G : M * X * K \rightarrow W, w = G(m, x, k) \tag{1}$$

The embedding algorithm of embedding watermark information into the information carrier is represented by E_m, that is:

$$E_m = X * W \rightarrow X, x^w = E_m(x, w) \tag{2}$$

Where X represents the original information carrier, x^w represents the carrier with the watermark information embedded, and it can improve the reliability to hide the key in the watermarking scheme.

3.2.1 Authentication Watermarking Information Generation

Read all text information bound to the data domain, and get the text string sequence $T = \{T_1, T_2, ..., T_n\}$, where n is the number of all text characters. The authentication watermark information bit string is generated as follows:

(1) Calculate the sequence of tuple (T_i, i), where $i = 0, 1, \ldots, n-1$ and the first element T_i represents the Unicode encoding value of the character, and the second element i is the index value of T_i to identify the location of T_i in sequence T.

(2) Use the MD5 message digest algorithm to calculate the hash value D of the 128-bit string for the sequence T.

If the electronic bill contains the picture object, a random watermarking information bit sequence is generated based on the Logistic chaotic mapping model [20].

3.2.2 Authentication Watermark Embedding

For the text objects bound in the data domain of electronic bills, the authentication watermark information is embedded by modifying the contents of all text strings using the dual text digital watermarking algorithms. The detailed process is as follows:

(1) By using the text watermarking algorithm of vector font [21], the same character is deformed into different glyphs and saved as different watermark fonts. When imported into the electronic bill page through the data domain, the watermark information is embedded by replacing the corresponding font dynamically according to the 0/1 watermark bit string information of the hash value D of the above string sequence T. Semantically, the characters representing different bit strings of watermark information are the same one, and the corresponding character glyph topology is different. The text watermarking algorithm is robust, the watermark information after printing and scanning still exists, and can be accurately extracted and identified, which is the first-layer robust text watermark.

(2) The corresponding font image data of each character after embedding the watermark is read out from the watermark font library, and the second-layer fragile text watermark is embedded by modifying the edge pixels of the character image.

The image I is the character image block corresponding to T_i read from the watermark font library which is related to the font parameters including font name c, font size γ, font direction θ, font style ρ (deflection, italics and normal) and font thickness σ (bold, fine and normal). For the same character, any different combination of parameters $\{c, \gamma, \theta, \rho, \sigma\}$ will result in different image data. In general, the parameters in electronic bills are set in a fixed format, and any obvious adjustments will attract attention. But with a slight adjustment in font size ($\pm 1\%$) or font angle ($\pm 0.05°$), the human eye is not very sensitive to visual effects. Therefore, a specific parameter combination $\{c, \gamma, \theta, \rho, \sigma\}$ is selected as the key k of watermark embedding and extraction. The watermark information embedded in the character T_i is the i value of the binary sequence (T_i, i). The watermark information is embedded as follows:

Step 1. Perform edge pixel detection of character image I and obtain the set of edge pixel points U.

Step 2. Traverse white pixels or black pixels that collect character image edges.

Suppose in a binary text image, the pixel value of the foreground image (the area occupied by character strokes) is 1, and the pixel value of the background image is 0. The pixel value of the edge pixels locating at (u, v) is $P(u, v)$.

When the edge pixel is black pixel, it satisfies:

$$P(u, v) = 1, |P(u - 1, v) - P(u + 1, v)| = 1, |P(u, v - 1) - P(u, v + 1)| = 1.$$

When the edge pixel is white pixel, it satisfies:

$$P(u, v) = 0, |P(u - 1, v) - P(u + 1, v)| = 1, |P(u, v - 1) - P(u, v + 1)| = 1.$$

As shown in Fig. 1, a black flip-point set U diagram of the character image edge of the Chinese character "一" of FangSong font is shown as pixels marked by gray.

Fig. 1. The black flip-point Set U.

Step 3. According to the watermark information bit string, the white pixels are turned into black pixels or the black pixels are turned into white pixels.

- Flip the black pixels. When the embedded watermark information bit is 0, it keeps the current black pixel unchanged and the pixel value is 1. When the embedded watermark information bit is 1, the current black pixel will be flipped to white pixel, and the pixel value changes from 1 to 0.
- Flip the white pixels. When the embedded watermark information bit is 0, it keeps the current white pixel unchanged, the pixel value is 0. When the embedded watermark information bit is 1, the current white pixel is flipped to black pixel, and the pixel value changes from 0 to 1.

For the capacity of watermark information to be embedded, the pixels to flip can be resampled by adjusting the embedded density parameter t in the set U, where $t \in Z$, $1 \leq t \leq 20$. Not all the edge pixels in the set are used to flip, but only for the pixels with interval $t * s$, $s = 1, 2, 3, \ldots, t * s \leq S$, where S is the number of all pixel points in the set U.

The larger t value is, the smaller the number of pixels used for flipping is, while the distortion of the character image is the smaller, and correspondingly the embedded watermark information capacity is smaller. Conversely, the smaller t value is, the more the number of pixels used for flipping is, while the distortion of the character image is bigger, and the capacity of the embedded watermark information is larger. In this method, the watermark information to be embedded for each character is the index value i, and 16 bits are enough to represent the number of characters in each electronic bill file. Figure 2 is a schematic diagram showing the effect of embedding watermark information in Fig. 1.

Fig. 2. The schematic diagram of effect after embedding watermark information in Fig. 1.

Step 4. It replaces the vector character data of the corresponding position in the electronic bill with the character image I' after embedding the double-layers text watermark information, and finishes the final embedding of the watermark information.

For the bind image object in the data domain of electronic bill, the image block classification model is established by using the image block watermarking technology proposed in reference [21], and the watermark information of multiple image authentication is embedded.

3.3 Digital Signature and Encapsulation

The 2D barcode image is generated to store the necessary information, such as the hash value D of string sequence T, the attribute parameters $\{c, \gamma, \theta, \rho, \sigma\}$ of character typesetting, the combination of watermark key parameters $\{c, \gamma', \theta', \rho, \sigma\}$, the embedded density parameters t and s and other related parameters, and the 2D barcode is inserted into the electronic bill document page.

Using the state-approved electronic signature technology to process and encapsulate the electronic bills in OFD format, a trusted electronic bills is generated to ensure the authenticity, integrity, security and availability.

3.4 Electronic Ticket Verification

Firstly, the electronic seal is used to verify the legitimacy. If the verification is passed, the content of the electronic bill is determined not to have been tampered with. If the check is not passed, the contents of the electronic bill are incomplete, and it continues to locate the tampering position.

Then, all the hidden information in the 2D barcode is extracted, and the key elements of data domain binding in electronic bills are verified:

(1) Extract the first-layer text watermarking information D' from all character image data, and compare the consistency between D and D'. If they are exactly the same, it can be judged that there is no change in the content of the characters, otherwise, it turns to step 2.

(2) The second-layer text watermarking information is extracted according to the attribute parameters $\{c, \gamma, \theta, \rho, \sigma\}$ of text typesetting, the combination of watermark key parameters $\{c, \gamma', \theta', \rho, \sigma\}$, and the embedding density parameters t and s. The specific process is as follows:

According to the combination of parameters $\{c, \gamma', \theta', \rho, \sigma\}$, each character image I is reconstructed and aligned with the character image I', which is extracted from the OFD file, the difference of edge pixels is compared to recover the original watermark information. The edge pixel set U of the collected character image I is traversed in the same way, and the pixel values of the character image I and the character image I' are compared according to the positions of each pixel in the set U. If they are same, the embedded watermark bit string is "0"; otherwise, it will be "1". Whether it is black point flip or white point flip, it is only when the watermark bit string is "1" that the flip operation is carried out. When the watermark bit string is "0", the pixel value remains unchanged, so when the watermark information is extracted, it is only necessary to compare the pixel values at the same position in the character image I and I'.

(3) According to the watermark information extracted in step 2, the position index information of each character is computed to get a new binary sequence (T_j, j), and the sequence $\{1, 2, \ldots, j-1, j, \ldots, n-1\}$ is complete. If it is incomplete, it can determine the location of the tampering by checking the missing location information in the sequence.

Finally, according to the method described in reference [20], the integrity authentication of the image object in OFD electronic bill file is carried out. If the image data is tampered with, the tampered area is located accurately.

4   Experimental Results and Discussion

First of all, We use the OFD-format electronic bill generation platform developed by Beijing Suwell Technology Co.,LTD to carry out the production of electronic invoices, voucher reading and printing, as well as the verification of secure electronic invoices. The Suwell consists of two parts: electronic bill reader and OFD electronic bill service system, which are deployed on the client side and server side respectively. Bill reader includes PC end, mobile end, web plug-in and other product forms; OFD electronic bill service system includes bill template design subsystem, bill production and processing subsystem, paper bill digitization subsystem, bill web page publication subsystem, bill verification subsystem and other five subsystems.

The template file of electronic invoice in OFD format is produced by Suwell platform, as shown in Fig. 3.

The bills data are cleaned and integrated to form the bills data information. The bills data information is combined with the corresponding bills template, and the template-based format conversion technology is used to generate the electronic bills. The generated electronic bills are processed to insert the metadata, two-dimensional barcode, multiple watermark and electronic seal signature, and complete the XML format encapsulation to generate the final electronic bill document containing watermark information as shown in Fig. 4. Figure 5 is an illustration of the effect of the enlarged watermarked character, which contains double watermark information. The way of breaking the stroke is to embed the watermark information by the method shown in [21]. The change of the stroke

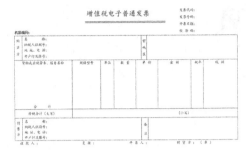

Fig. 3. The electronic invoice template file in OFD format.

Fig. 4. The OFD electronic bill document containing watermark information.

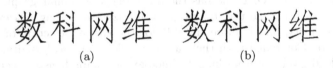
(a)   (b)

Fig. 5. Double watermark embedding effect. (a) Original text image effects. (b) Text image effects embedded with double watermark.

thickness is to embed the second fragile watermark information by the method described in this paper.

After tampering with Fig. 4, electronic seal verification and tamper identification with multiple watermark information are carried out by this method. The identification result is shown in Fig. 6, from which it can be seen that the content tampering operations, such as adding, deleting and modifying on electronic bills can be detected and accurately located.

Fig. 6. The content tampering effect of Fig. 4.

5 Conclusion

This paper presents a method of generating electronic bills based on OFD format files, and discusses the application of OFD format files in secure electronic bills according to the characteristics of OFD technology. The layout of OFD documents is fixed with consistent displaying and printing effects on a variety of platforms. In layout documents, the coordinates of objects such as text, graphics, images, drawing attributes and other parameters that affect the rendering effect are accurately described, so that the layout documents can realize immediate and accurately present the content of the document. Compared with the common PDF file format, OFD file has the advantages of similar graphic element description ability, simple use, template customization, strong retrieval ability and higher security, and is more suitable for the carrier selection of electronic bill documents. Combined with the traditional electronic seal, digital signature and multiple digital watermarking technology, a comprehensive security electronic bill solution is proposed, which can complete the content integrity and authenticity of electronic bill documents, and can accurately locate the tamper location. In short, OFD technology can be used in electronic bills, electronic documents, electronic archives, electronic certificates and other wider areas.

References

1. Yan, Q.: E-Commerce Security Management. China Machine Press, Beijing (2007). (in Chinese)
2. Chen, H.: The impact and influence of electronic bills on China's bill law. J. Guangdong Inst. Social. **41**(4), 101–107 (2010). (in Chinese)
3. Huang, J.: Research on bank electronic document integrity protection based on the watermarking technology. Ph.D. thesis, Guangdong University of Finance and Economics (2016). (in Chinese)
4. Chen, F., Zhang, X., He, H.: Watermarking embedding and authentication method of positioning PDF electronic invoice falsification (2015). China Patent 104,899,822

5. Ding, T.: Design and implementation of electronic bill management system based on list manager. Ph.D. thesis, East China Normal University (2006). (in Chinese)
6. Zhang, G., Peng, X., Sun, Y., Wang, K.: Automatically generating electronic bill technology and application based on PDF. Comput. Eng. Appl. **9**, 23–25 (1999). (in Chinese)
7. Ma, Z.: Construction of the core metadata set of E-invoices. Ph.D. thesis, Zhengzhou University of Aeronautics (2018). (in Chinese)
8. Fang, H.: Electronic invoice trading platform design and implementation based on the digital watermarking technology. Ph.D. thesis, Southwest Jiaotong University (2016). (in Chinese)
9. Chung, Y.D., Kim, J.W., Kim, M.-H.: Efficient preprocessing of XML queries using structured signatures. Inf. Process. Lett. **87**(5), 257–264 (2003)
10. Lu, E.J.-L., Chen, R.-F.: An XML multisignature scheme. Appl. Math. Comput. **149**(1), 1–14 (2004)
11. Li, B., Li, W., Chen, Y.-Y., Jiang, D.-D., Cui, Y.-Z.: HTML integrity authentication based on fragile digital watermarking. In: IEEE International Conference on Granular Computing, Nanchang, pp. 322–325. IEEE Computer Society (2009)
12. Long, X., Peng, H., Zhang, C., Pan, Z., Wu, Y.: A fragile watermarking scheme for tamper-proof of web pages. In: WASE International Conference on Information Engineering, Taiyuan, pp. 155–158. IEEE (2009)
13. Tchokpon, R., Cimato, S., Bennani, N.: Ensuring XML integrity using watermarking techniques. In: Eighth International Conference on Signal Image Technology and Internet Based Systems, Naples, pp. 668–674. IEEE Computer Society (2012)
14. Zhang, Z., Peng, H., Long, X.: A fragile watermarking scheme based on hash function for web pages. In: International Conference on Network Computing and Information Security, Guilin, pp. 417–420. IEEE (2011)
15. Fridrich, J.J.: Security of fragile authentication watermarks with localization. In: Security and Watermarking of Multimedia Contents IV, San Jose. SPIE (2002)
16. Ullah, R., Khan, A., Malik, A.S.: Dual-purpose semi-fragile watermark: authentication and recovery of digital images. Comput. Electr. Eng. **39**(7), 2019–2030 (2013)
17. Wenyin, Z., Shih, F.Y.: Semi-fragile spatial watermarking based on local binary pattern operators. Opt. Commun. **284**(16–17), 3904–3912 (2011)
18. Yang, Z., Huang, Y., Li, X., Wang, W.: Efficient secure data provenance scheme in multimedia outsourcing and sharing. CMC: Comput. Mater. Contin. **56**(1), 1–17 (2018)
19. Xiang, L., Li, Y., Hao, W., Yang, P., Shen, X.: Reversible natural language watermarking using synonym substitution and arithmetic coding. CMC: Comput. Mater. Contin. **55**(3), 541–559 (2018)
20. Li, Z.: Image authentication based on digital watermarking and its key issues. Ph.D. thesis, Beijing Jiaotong University (2008). (in Chinese)
21. Liu, Y., Guo, W., Qi, W.: Researches on text image watermarking scheme based on the structure of character glyph. In: Applied Mechanics and Materials, pp. 163–168. Trans Tech Publications (2015)

Review on Text Watermarking Resistant to Print-Scan, Screen-Shooting

Gaopeng Xie[1], Yuling Liu[1(✉)], Guojiang Xin[2], and Peng Yang[3]

[1] College of Computer Science and Electronic Engineering, Hunan University,
Changsha 410082, China
yuling_liu@126.com
[2] College of Management and Information Engineering,
Hunan University of Chinese Medicine, Changsha 410208, China
[3] Hunan Branch of CNCERT/CC, Changsha 410004, Hunan, China

Abstract. Although the development of the Internet has enabled more and more texts to be transmitted in electronic forms, printed documents are still an irreplaceable form of transmission. Whether it is the copyright protection of book authors or the prevention of the leakage of confidential documents, there is an urgent need for text watermarking resistant to print-scan attacks. Due to the complex influence of print-scan process and the particularity of text carrier, to design a text watermarking method resistant to print-scan is a complex project. The emergence of screen-shooting attacks also brings new challenges and requirements for text watermarking. In this paper, we study the technologies and theories of text watermarking resistant to print-scan in detail and roughly discuss the screen-shooting resilient watermarking, then review the existing research results in text watermarking robust to print-scan operations and digital watermarking robust to screen-shooting. The advantages, disadvantages and contributions of these results are also analyzed.

Keywords: Text watermarking · Printed text · Print-scan attack · Screen-shooting attack

1 Introduction

With the development of the printing industry, the emergence of high-quality input and output devices has brought enormous challenges to digital watermarking technology. High-precision laser scanners and printers make it easier to forge various images, documents and even credentials, etc. Additionally, the print-scan process is a complicated process and hard to be specifically quantified, which may cause large distortions and influences, thus the conventional digital watermarking algorithms do not survive the print-scan process. Besides, text document contains too little redundant information compared to other carriers [1], thus it is difficult to embed print-scan resilient watermarks into text documents. However, the print-scan process is an irreplaceable means of transmission for text

© Springer Nature Switzerland AG 2019
X. Sun et al. (Eds.): ICAIS 2019, LNCS 11634, pp. 140–149, 2019.
https://doi.org/10.1007/978-3-030-24271-8_13

information, therefore, the research on text watermarking technology resistant to print-scan has practical significance.

Moreover, in some sensitive departments, confidential documents can be leaked not only by printing and scanning, but also by means of taking photos. Simply by taking pictures of the screen, perpetrators can easily avoid the monitoring of system logs. Compared to print-scan process, the screen-shooting process is more complicated and introduce more distortions. In order to deal with this new type of attack, related schemes have also been proposed. The complexity of the distortion caused by screen-shooting process make this work extremely difficult and the uncertain content displayed on the screen also adds additional challenges.

This paper focuses on different text watermarking technologies resistant to print-scan and introduces digital watermarking methods resistant to screen-shooting. We provide a review of related research in the field of print-scan resilient watermarking and discuss the latest methods of screen-shooting resilient watermarking. The rest of this paper is structured as follows. Section 2 explains the digital text watermarking in detail. Section 3 summarizes text watermarking technologies resistant to print-scan with their advantages and disadvantages. Section 4 discusses the screen-shooting resilient digital watermarking. Section 5 draws the conclusion.

2   Digital Text Watermarking

The digital text watermarking refers to embedding the related information such as the text creator or the copyright owner into the text. This process will not affect the normal use of the text, and can extract the watermark when a dispute arises to prove the ownership of the copyright or to identify the source of the leakage.

Since Maxemchuk proposed the first text watermarking technology in 1994 [2], there have been many algorithms for text watermarking, and they can be classified into three categories: format-based approach, linguistic-based approach, image-based approach. The specific classification is given in the Fig. 1 below.

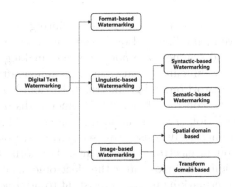

Fig. 1. Digital text watermarking methods

The format-based method embeds watermarks by adjusting some special formats of text, such as the size of characters, the font of text and other physical characteristics. Jalil et al. [3] proposed a word-based text watermarking algorithm using the first letter of all words longer than four characters to embed the watermark. Aman et al. [4] proposed another new text watermarking algorithm based on open space method by using the white spaces in the text to embed the payload. Malik et al. [5] used LZW algorithm to compress the information and then replace the color code to embed the information into email.

The linguistic-based method is based on natural language processing, which embeds watermark by changing the syntactic and semantic properties of text. The meaning of the text remains essentially unchanged during this process. Murphy et al. [6] proposed a sentence structure processing method by shifting noun and verb position to embed the watermark. Chang and Clark [7] proposed two ways to improve the use of synonymous substitution to hide code bits. They use the Google n-gram corpus to check the applicability of synonyms in context and solve problems caused by words with multiple meanings.

The image-based approach is to treat text as a text image. Text content is no longer regarded as an independent text, but as the content of an image. Text images are different from natural images, and the content and background of text images are clearly segmented, thus image watermarking cannot be directly applied to text images. Tirandaz et al. [8] proposed a method which flipped the edge pixels of the connected components. The secret data is embedded in the outer boundary pixels of the connected components so it can preserve minimum visual distortion.

Digital text watermarking can be widely used in many fields. Nowadays, there are huge amounts of user data stored in cloud servers, so relevant security algorithms have been proposed [9], combining with cloud computing is one possible development of text watermarking. However, with the development of steganalysis technology especially binary image steganalysis [10], digital text watermarking also faces more challenges.

3   Text Watermarking Methods Resistant to Print-Scan

The print-scan process is a complicated process. Printing and scanning processes involve multiple uneven sampling and quantization, and the distortions caused by different printers and scanners are not the same, making quantitative analysis of this process very difficult. Usually, the text image after printing will be accompanied by pixel distortion and geometric distortion. Pixel distortions refer to changes in brightness, contrast, tone, etc. Geometric distortions include scaling, rotation and translation. Traditional format-based and linguistic-based text watermarking cannot effectively resist print-scan attacks. Both methods embed watermark information in electronic documents. The format information and the encoded information will be lost after the electronic documents are printed. Therefore, the text watermarking methods resistant to print-scan process usually use text images as the carrier of watermark. Existing image-based text watermarking methods fall into two categories: spatial domain-based and transform domain-based. Figure 2 shows the specific classification.

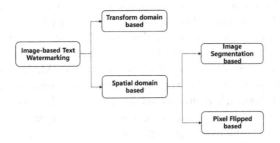

Fig. 2. Image-based text watermarking methods

3.1 Spatial Domain Based Watermark

Spatial domain based watermarking algorithm directly operates on the image in the spatial domain. There are two main classifies: the first one operates directly at the pixel level, embedding the watermark information by flipping the pixel to change the statistical features of the pixel. The other one segments the content in the text image and embeds watermark in the segmented content.

Image Segmentation Based Watermarking Methods. This method usually embeds watermark by adjusting the features of the text image which are difficult to be distinguished by human eyes, such as text strokes, space, etc. It requires precise segmentation of words, characters or strokes and then operates on the segmented object.

The methods of line-shift coding and word-shift coding were proposed by Brassil et al. [11,12]. Line-shift coding uses the line space of the text to embed watermark information. The lines to embed watermark information are slightly adjusted upward or downward according to the bits to be embedded. The previous and the next line of the embedded line remain inactive as references. The method of word-shift coding is basically the same as line-shift coding, but it uses words instead of text lines as the locations of watermark embedding, and the adjacent words also need to keep the position as references. Line-shift coding and word-shift coding can both resist against print-scan attacks. Line-shift coding can achieve blind detection without the need for original text. The word-shift coding method needs the original text as a reference, because the word spacing in the text is not uniform. Although the line-shift coding and the word-shift coding have their own defects at the initial introduction, many scholars have carried out related work on this basis to optimize the algorithms.

Literature [13] made the text line appear sine wave feature by adjusting the word space. The advantage of this method is that the spaces showing sine wave make the invisibility better, and the watermark information to be embedded is encoded as the phase, amplitude and frequency of the sine wave so it is easier to decode by using the periodicity and symmetry of the sine wave. In addition, blind detection can be achieved. However, the drawback is that the capacity is not optimistic. [14] combined line-shift coding and word-shift coding to embed the watermark. The authors also took use of the irregular spacing in the text and introduced spread spectrum technology and BCH coding to combat various noises, so that it can resist a variety of attacks, including print-scan attacks. Zou and Shi [15] proposed an algorithm of Inter-word Space Modulation (ISM). The fundamental concept is to divide the inter-word spaces between adjacent words into two parts. Watermark is embedded by adjusting the spaces. This method is robust to print-scan process but the capacity is only one bit per line. Aiming at the problem of insufficient capacity, [16] improved the method of Zou and Shi [15] by using multi-set modulation technique.

The method of embedding watermark by using the feature of the characters was also proposed. Tan et al. [17] proposed a new method based on stroke direction modulation. By adjusting the angle of rotatable strokes, the watermark is hidden into each character. This method performs well in robustness and watermark capacity, but it only works in Chinese. Varna et al. [18] developed a scheme that adds or removes two groups of pixels from the left edge of a character and the data is encoded by the distance between the two group. This scheme is robust to print-photocopy-scan (PCS) but its invisibility is not satisfying.

The character color can also be used to embed the watermark. Borges et al. [19] proposed a scheme to embed watermark that can resist print-scan process. The payload is embedded by slightly modulating the brightness of characters. The method proposed in [19] is text luminance modulation (TLM), which modifies luminance only in grayscale. [20] hided information in text by quantizing the luminance of each character. The method uses in [20] is text halftone modulation (THM). Compared to TLM, THM has a better performance than TLM. [21] used the text color modulation (TCM) to hide data in documents. TCM is an extension of TLM, the color component of the character is changed according to the data to be embedded. Compared to TLM and THM, TCM needs a color printing device.

Pixel Flipped Based Watermark Methods. The pixel flipped based methods operate directly at the pixel level, which embed the watermark information by flipping the pixel to change the statistical features of the pixels. Wu and Liu [22] developed a high-capacity watermarking method by manipulating flippable pixels based on a particular block-based relationship. At the same time, specific pixel flipping scores and flipping rules were given. This method requires high printing and scanning quality to extract the watermark, so its robustness against print-scan process is not good. Qi et al. [23] found the invariant in the print-scan process. The ratio of the black pixel value contained in each character to the average of the black pixel values of all characters is unchanged before and after the print-scan process. Their pixel flipping strategy used is based on [22], where each character can be embedded with one bit of data. Based on the algorithm of Qi [23], Guo et al. [24] developed a more complex quantization function to flip a single character to embed multi-bit watermark information. Nayak et al. [25] proposed a method to identify the source of leaked confidential documents. This method designs a quick response code for each document and converts it into a one-dimensional matrix containing only 0 and 1. The matrix corresponds to several specific characters in the document, and the number of the matrix represents whether the selected character is replaced by a newly designed character that is difficult to distinguish. When a leak is detected, the quick response code can be extracted to determine which file is leaked. This method is robust and resistant to errors caused by printing, scanning and photocopying. In [26], the authors proposed a feature-based watermarking scheme. Feature extraction is performed in the spatial domain by Fourier descriptors, and the high frequency coefficients of the character boundaries are corrected. The algorithm has achieved a good balance in various aspects. A new special domain-based algorithm was proposed in [27]. The watermark image is first embedded in the blue color component of a white image with the help of a secret key, and then the information to be printed is placed on the image. After printing, the final printed document containing the watermark is produced. This method has a strong robustness against printing, scanning and photocopying, and the watermarks can be extracted even from wrinkled and wet documents. Loc et al. [28] proposed a scheme based on stable regions and object fill. The nonsubsampled contourlet transform (NSCT) is used to detect the stable regions, and the separated objects in stable regions are obtained. The object consists of strokes and fill, but the strokes are easily affected by noises, so only object fill is selected. Then the coordinates of the object fill position are mapped to the gray level value and the watermark information is embedded by adjusting the gray level.

3.2   Transform Domain Based Watermark

Transform domain algorithm inserts the watermark into the spectral coefficients for better invisibility and robustness. Daraee and Mozaffari [29] presented a new watermarking scheme for binary documents based on fractal coding technique. By selecting a specific range segment with predefined conditions, the watermark is added to the fractal code of the selected segment. A double domain watermarking scheme was proposed in [30], the algorithm divides text image characters into embedded part, adjusted part and removed part. In the embedded part, the eigenvalue matrix is constructed by print-scan invariants [23] and the discrete cosine transform is performed. The high frequency coefficients are modified in the transform domain, and then the pixels are flipped in the spatial domain. In the adjusted part, the same pixel amount is flipped to ensure the average black pixel volume unchanged. Double domain watermarking methods implement the use of two domain features in the watermark embedding process to improve the watermark performance. Moreover, it avoids the distortion of text images caused by the transformation in transform domain algorithms.

4   Watermarking Methods Resistant to Screen-Shooting

Obviously, the complex distortions introduced by the photographic process makes the design of screen-shooting resilient watermarking more complicated. The angle, distance, light and so on will affect the results of the shooting. The distortions caused by these factors will make it difficult to extract the watermark.

Two latest methods [31,32] resistant to screen-shooting have been proposed. In literature [31], the authors summarize three important distortions caused by screen-shooting in detail, and design corresponding solutions for each type of distortion. This method is more resistant to screen-shooting than previous methods. However, the algorithm performs the embedding operation in the DCT domain of the image and the text image will produce visible distortion in this process, so it cannot be applied to the text document, which limits the practicability of the algorithm. Literature [32] analyzes the usage scenarios of the watermark and proposes three challenges: the watermark should be presented on any documents at any time; it needs to be robust and invisible; blind detection should be achieved. To solve the three challenges, the authors modify the brightness of the pixels in the spatial domain to ensure that the watermark can be applied to both text and images. They also develop a blind symbol extraction method to achieve blind detection. This method is robust to screen-shooting and basic image manipulation.

The results of screen-shooting resilient methods are far less than the results of print-scan resilient watermarking methods. There are few mature methods that can be really be applied in practice. The information security of confidential institutions cannot be ignored, further related research needs to be carried out.

Finally, we compare the performance of some algorithms discussed in this paper, shown in the following Table 1.

Table 1. Comparisons of different algorithms.

Methods	Robustness	Capacity	Limitations
Inter-word space modulation [15]	Print-photocopy-scan	Low	No
Stroke direction modulation [17]	PCS	High	Stroke-based languages
Shape modification of vertical strokes [18]	PCS	Medium	A requirement of ECC and an additional helper database
Fractal coding [29]	PCS	High	A requirement of the original image
DCT coefficients modification [31]	Screen-shooting	High	Bad performance in simple texture images and binary images
Pixel brightness modification [32]	Screen-shooting	Medium	No

5 Conclusion

This paper studies the work of text watermarking resistant to print-scan and digital watermarking resistant to screen-shooting. It can be found that the research work in both fields are not satisfied, especially digital watermarking resistant to screen-shooting. Many existing watermarking algorithms are still not satisfactory in terms of robustness and generality, and the amount of work done on the two watermarkings is limited. With the development of scanning technology (such as OCR), the text watermarkings will face more serious challenges, thus both two watermarkings need further development to deal with these challenges. Future work needs to focus on robustness, capacity, generality as well as computational complexity.

Acknowledgments. This work was partially supported by National Natural Science Foundation of China (No. 61872134, 61103215), Natural Science Foundation of Hunan Province (No. 2018JJ2062, 2018JJ2301), National Key Research and Development Program (No.2017YFC1703306), and Hunan Key Research and Development Program (2017SK2111).

References

1. Sang, J., Fang, Q., Xu, C.: Exploiting social-mobile information for location visualization. ACM Trans. Intell. Syst. Technol. (TIST) **8**(3), 39 (2017)
2. Maxemchuk, N.F.: Electronic document distribution. AT&T Tech. J. **73**(5), 73–80 (1994)
3. Jalil, Z., Mirza, A.M., Jabeen, H.: Word length based zero-watermarking algorithm for tamper detection in text documents. In: 2010 2nd International Conference, Computer Engineering and Technology (ICCET), vol. 6, pp. 378–382. IEEE, Chengdu (2010)
4. Aman, M., Khan, A., Ahmad, B., Kouser, S.: A hybrid text steganography approach utilizing Unicode space characters and zero-width character. Int. J. Inf. Technol. Secur. **9**(1), 85–100 (2017)
5. Malik, A., Sikka, G., Verma, H.K.: A high capacity text steganography scheme based on LZW compression and color coding. Eng. Sci. Technol. Int. J. **20**(1), 72–79 (2017)
6. Murphy, B., Vogel, C.: The syntax of concealment: reliable methods for plain text information hiding. In: Security, Steganography, and Watermarking of Multimedia Contents IX, p. 65050Y. International Society for Optics and Photonics, San Jose (2007)
7. Chang, C.Y., Clark, S.: Practical linguistic steganography using contextual synonym substitution and a novel vertex coding method. Comput. Linguist. **40**(2), 403–448 (2014)
8. Tirandaz, H., Davarzani, R., Monemizadeh, M., Haddadnia, J.: Invisible and high capacity data hiding in binary text images based on use of edge pixels. In: 2009 International Conference on Signal Processing Systems, pp. 130–134. IEEE, Singapore (2009)
9. Liu, Y., Peng, H., Wang, J.: Verifiable diversity ranking search over encrypted outsourced data. CMC: Comput. Mater. Continua **55**(1), 37–57 (2018)

10. Chen, J., et al.: Binary image steganalysis based on distortion level co-occurrence matrix. CMC: Comput. Mater. Continua **55**(2), 201–211 (2018)
11. Brassil, J.T., Low, S., Maxemchuk, N.F.: Copyright protection for the electronic distribution of text documents. Proc. IEEE **87**(7), 1181–1196 (1999)
12. Brassil, J.T., Low, S., Maxemchuk, N.F., O'Gorman, L.: Electronic marking and identification techniques to discourage document copying. IEEE J. Sel. Areas Commun. **13**(8), 1495–1504 (1995)
13. Huang, D., Yan, H.: Interword distance changes represented by sine waves for watermarking text images. IEEE Trans. Circ. Syst. Video Technol. **11**(12), 1237–1245 (2001)
14. Alattar, A.M., Alattar, O.M.: Watermarking electronic text documents containing justified paragraphs and irregular line spacing. In: Security, Steganography, and Watermarking of Multimedia Contents VI, pp. 685–696. International Society for Optics and Photonics, San Jose (2004)
15. Zou, D., Shi, Y.Q.: Formatted text document data hiding robust to printing, copying and scanning. In: 2005 IEEE International Symposium on Circuits and Systems, pp. 4971–4974. IEEE, Kobe (2005)
16. Culnane, C., Treharne, H., Ho, A.T.S.: A new multi-set modulation technique for increasing hiding capacity of binary watermark for print and scan processes. In: Shi, Y.Q., Jeon, B. (eds.) IWDW 2006. LNCS, vol. 4283, pp. 96–110. Springer, Heidelberg (2006). https://doi.org/10.1007/11922841_9
17. Tan, L., Sun, X., Sun, G.: Print-scan resilient text image watermarking based on stroke direction modulation for Chinese document authentication. Radioengineering **21**(1) (2012)
18. Varna, A.L., Rane, S., Vetro, A.: Data hiding in hard-copy text documents robust to print, scan and photocopy operations. In: 2009 IEEE International Conference on Acoustics, Speech and Signal Processing, pp. 1397–1400. IEEE, Taipei (2009)
19. Borges, P.V.K., Mayer, J.: Text luminance modulation for hardcopy watermarking. Signal Process. **87**(7), 1754–1771 (2007)
20. Villán, R., et al.: Text data-hiding for digital and printed documents: theoretical and practical considerations. In: Security, Steganography, and Watermarking of Multimedia Contents VIII, p. 607212. International Society for Optics and Photonics, San Jose (2006)
21. Borges, P.V.K., Mayer, J., Izquierdo, E.: Robust and transparent color modulation for text data hiding. IEEE Trans. Multimed. **10**(8), 1479–1489 (2008)
22. Wu, M., Liu, B.: Data hiding in binary image for authentication and annotation. IEEE Trans. Multimed. **6**(4), 528–538 (2004)
23. Qi, W., Li, X., Yang, B.: Document watermarking scheme for information tracking. J. Commun. **29**(10), 183–190 (2008)
24. Guo, C., Xu, G., Niu, X., Li, Y.: High-capacity text watermarking resistive to print-scan process. J. Appl. Sci. **29**(2), 140–146 (2011)
25. Nayak, J., Singh, S., Chhabra, S., Gupta, G., Gupta, M., Gupta, G.: Detecting data leakage from hard copy documents. In: Peterson, G., Shenoi, S. (eds.) Advances in Digital Forensics XIV. IAICT, vol. 532, pp. 111–124. Springer, Cham (2018). https://doi.org/10.1007/978-3-319-99277-8_7
26. Tan, L., Hu, K., Zhou, X., Chen, R., Jiang, W.: Print-scan invariant text image watermarking for hardcopy document authentication. Multimed. Tools Appl. 1–23 (2018)

27. Thongkor, K., Amornraksa, T.: Digital image watermarking for printed and scanned documents. In: Ninth International Conference on Digital Image Processing (ICDIP), p. 104203O. International Society for Optics and Photonics, Hong Kong (2017)

28. Loc, C.V., Burie, J.C., Ogier, J.M.: Stable regions and object fill-based approach for document images watermarking. In: 2018 13th IAPR International Workshop on Document Analysis Systems (DAS), pp. 181–186. IEEE, Vienna (2018)

29. Daraee, F., Mozaffari, S.: Watermarking in binary document images using fractal codes. Pattern Recogn. Lett. **35**, 120–129 (2014)

30. Yao, H., Wei, M., Zhou, J., Li, Y.: Document watermarking algorithm combined with print-scan invariants and double domain. J. Huazhong Univ. Sci. Technol. 6 (2018)

31. Fang, H., Zhang, W., Zhou, H., Cui, H., Yu, N.: Screen-shooting resilient watermarking. IEEE Trans. Inf. Forensics Secur. **14**, 1403–1418 (2018)

32. Gugelmann, D., Sommer, D., Lenders, V., Happe, M., Vanbever, L.: Screen watermarking for data theft investigation and attribution. In: 2018 10th International Conference on Cyber Conflict (CyCon), pp. 391–408. IEEE, Tallinn (2018)

A Novel Reversible Data Hiding
Scheme for Encrypted VQ-Compressed Image

Yujie Fu[1], Dongsheng Peng[2], Heng Yao[1], and Chuan Qin[1(✉)]

[1] School of Optical-Electrical and Computer Engineering,
University of Shanghai for Science and Technology, Shanghai 200093, China
tvxq60021995@163.com, {hyao,qin}@usst.edu.cn
[2] Jiangnan Institute of Computing Technology, Wuxi 214083, Jiangsu, China
ds_peng@sohu.com

Abstract. VQ-compressed images have been widely used as an important branch of multimedia, however, there are few reversible data hiding schemes based on VQ-compressed image in encrypted domain. In this paper, a reversible data hiding scheme based on encrypted VQ-compressed image is proposed. On the content owner side, codebook is supposed to be reorganized firstly, and codewords in codebook are then grouped into codeword pair after reorganization. After this process, index table and the new codebook are encrypted separately, using modulo operation to encrypt index table and stream cipher to encrypt codebook. Additional data will be embedded in specific position of index table by modifying their index value. As to the receiver, encrypted index table with addition data and encrypted codebook are decrypted by the encryption key. The additional data can be extracted and image can be recovered effectively according to spatial correlation in natural image.

Keywords: VQ-compressed image · Reversible data hiding · Encrypted image

1 Introduction

Reversible data hiding (RDH) is becoming an emerging technique, attracting researches' interests in recent years. RDH is proposed to reversibly embed pieces of secret data into universal medium, such as images, video, etc. [1, 2]. Reversible data hiding means that the embedded data and cover medium are supposed to be recovered from the marked medium. In the past few years, many classical algorithms [3–7] have been applied in RDH filed, such as Difference expansion (DE) [3], Histogram shifting (HS) [4], Prediction-error expansion (PEE) [5] *et al.* With the development of multimedia technology, RDH is not only applied for gray images, schemes for color images and compressed images are also proposed. Among them, Vector Quantization (VQ) [8] is an especially effective method of data compression and turns out useful for image compression.

In the process of VQ-compression, an image with size of $M \times N$ is divided into multiple non-overlapping blocks with n^2 pixels in each block, where n denotes the size of each block. A VQ-compressed image is consisted of two parts: index table and codebook, in which η codewords are selected in each codebook. (η usually equals to

© Springer Nature Switzerland AG 2019
X. Sun et al. (Eds.): ICAIS 2019, LNCS 11634, pp. 150–160, 2019.
https://doi.org/10.1007/978-3-030-24271-8_14

128, 256, 512, 1024 and the length of each codeword are n^2.) We calculate the Euclidean distance between the image block and codewords and then record the index of the minimum Euclidean distance to the index table. Figure 1 shows the composition of the VQ image, in which a VQ-compressed image has a size of $M \times N$ and index table has a size of $M/n \times N/n$. The values in index table indicate the index of corresponding codeword in codebook.

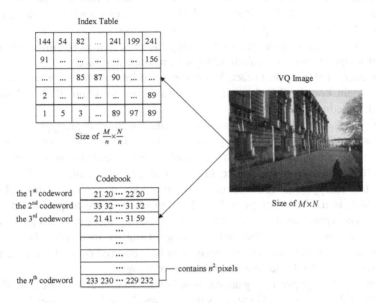

Fig. 1. Construction of VQ image.

A lot of reversible data hiding schemes based on VQ-compressed image were proposed in recent years [9–14]. Chang et al. [9] proposed a data hiding scheme for vector quantization indices based on the search-order coding (SOC) compression method. No extra data distortion existed in this scheme. In work of Lin et al. [10], the similar codewords are grouped together and the additional data with predetermined length is embedded into the group to complete the adaptive embedding. Shie and Jiang [11] proposed a scheme to embed additional data by partially sorting codebook. At the same time, it made good use of SMVQ, guaranteeing the quality of compressed image obtained at the receiver side. In [12], Qin et al. proposed to construct a series of index mappings by using the VQ indexes with 0 occurrence and the largest occurrences in the index table. By analyzing the histogram of the index table, the optimal mapping can be found to achieve the maximum embedding rate. Some schemes based on neighboring were proposed to realize reversible data hiding [13, 14]. In [13], Kieu and Ramroach proposed a scheme based on joint neighboring coding. The difference values between neighboring indexes were utilized for embedding n additional bits. Lee et al. [14] generated specific sub-codebooks by using the nature correlation between neighboring blocks of VQ-compressed image to realize reversible data hiding. The above schemes are based on the plaintext images, in other words, novel schemes were required for an encrypted image.

Different from the conventional approaches utilized for data embedding for plaintext images, RDH in encrypted domain is much more valuable to be followed and researched, which was first proposed by Puech in [15]. Then Zhang proposed a novel scheme in [16] to encrypt image by stream cipher for gray images. Through flipping the 3 least significant bits, the additional bits were embedded into an encrypted image. Based on that, various RDH schemes are designed to resolve such a problem. In [17], Chen et al. proposed a pixel-type-mark generation method based on block-compression, then an iterative recovery strategy is proposed to optimize the marked decrypted image. However, limited RDH schemes are designed for VQ-compressed images in encrypted domain. In fact, VQ-compressed image have been widely utilized as an important branch of multimedia, it is meaningful to design RDH schemes for encrypted VQ-compressed image.

In this paper, we propose a reversible data hiding method in encrypted domain for VQ-compressed image. Before encryption, codewords in VQ codebook are grouping into codeword pair when codebook is reorganized where codewords in each pair are significantly different from each other. In encrypt stage, index table and VQ codebook are separately encrypted. Modulo operation is utilized to encrypt index table and stream cipher, which is used to encrypt codebook. Both of them are helpful to ensure the security of encryption method. A novel data embedding method is designed to hide additional data, which are embedded into index table by modifying their value in selected position. At the receiver side, image can be recovered perfectly and secret data can be extracted through the spatial correlation of image.

The rest of this paper is organized as follows. Section 2 describes the detailed procedures of the proposed scheme. Experimental results and comparisons are given in Sect. 3. Section 4 draws a conclusion of the paper.

2 Proposed Scheme

In this section, the details of the proposed data hiding method based on VQ image are given. In our scheme, image encryption can be divided into two step: codebook encryption and index table encryption, respectively. Then we embed additional data into the encrypted VQ image. On the receiver side, we can extract additional data and restore image.

2.1 Image Encryption

VQ-compressed image consists of index table and codebook, in which index value indicates the position in codebook and codebook contains a series of codewords. We divide encryption into two parts namely, codebook encryption and index table encryption.

For content owner, codebook need to be reorganized first. In general, the codebook in VQ-compressed image is a combination of pixels set in advance. In our scheme, we propose to group the codewords into codeword pair while the codebook is reorganized.

We suppose the number of codewords in codebook is η and the length of codewords is n^2. Euclidean distance between each set of codeword can be written as,

$$d_{u,v} = \sqrt{\left(y_{u,1} - y_{v,1}\right)^2 + \left(y_{u,2} - y_{v,2}\right)^2 + \ldots + \left(y_{u,n^2} - y_{v,n^2}\right)^2}, \tag{1}$$

where y denotes pixel value, u and v represent the uth and the vth index of codewords ($1 \leq u, v \leq \eta$). Euclidean distance $d_{u,v}$ means the difference between the uth codeword and the vth codeword, the arrangement of the new codebook is based on $d_{u,v}$. The construction of the new codebook is described in detail in the following steps.

(1)   Select a codeword from the original codebook randomly, denoting it as C_1.
(2)   Calculate the Euclidean distance between C_1 and the remaining codewords in original codebook using Eq. (1).
(3)   Take out the codeword which has the largest Euclidean distance with C_1, recording it as C_2. C_1 and C_2 constitute a codeword pair and they are the first and second codeword in new codebook. At the same time, C_1 and C_2 are removed from the original codebook.
(4)   Repeat steps (1)–(3) to obtain other $\eta/2$ codeword pairs. These η codewords $\{C_1, C_2, \ldots, C_\eta\}$ construct the new codebook. The new codebook denoted as **C**.

The two adjacent codewords, the lth codeword and the $(l + 1)^{th}$ codeword ($1 \leq l \leq \eta$, mod $(l, 2) = 1$) in the new codebook **C**, are referred to as a codeword pair. The amount of codeword pair in a new codebook **C** is $\eta/2$. According to the construction process of the new codebook **C**, it can be inferred that the codewords in a codeword pair are significantly different from each other. It is worthy to note that not every VQ-compressed image needs to generate a new codebook **C**. In our scheme, **C** is widely applicable and can be applied to all VQ-compressed images. The corresponding index table of VQ-compressed images is generated by **C**, which can be denoted as **T**.

Let $P_{i,j}$ denote the jth pixel in i^{th} codeword and $1 \leq j \leq n^2, 1 \leq i \leq \eta$. Thus, the gray value of the pixel $P_{i,j}$ can be represented as:

$$P_{i,j} = \sum_{k=0}^{7} P_{i,j,k} \times 2^k, \tag{2}$$

where $P_{i,j,k}$ denotes the kth bit of $P_{i,j}$. A sequence of pseudo-random byte $S_{i,j}(1 \leq j \leq n^2, 1 \leq i \leq \eta)$ is generated according to encryption key $K_e^{(1)}$. The operation of bitwise exclusive-or (XOR) is performed on all η codewords for codebook encryption,

$$P_{i,j}^{(e)} = P_{i,j} \oplus S_{i,j}, \tag{3}$$

where $P_{i,j}^{(e)}$ denotes the jth pixel in i^{th} codeword after stream cipher encryption. After all pixels in new codebook encrypted, an encrypted codebook C_e is obtained.

Index table should be encrypted with encryption key $K_e^{(2)}$, which generates a sequence of even numbers, denoting these even numbers as **Z**. There are n^2 even numbers in **Z** and $I_{r,h}$ ($1 \leq r \leq N/n, 1 \leq h \leq M/n$) represents the index of coordinate (r, h) in $\mathbf{T}$. Modulo Operation is used to encrypt index table. Then the index encryption process is described as,

$$I'_{r,h} = \left(I_{r,h} + z\right) \mod \eta, \tag{4}$$

where z is one of even number in $\mathbf{Z}$, $2 \leq z \leq \eta$ and $I'_{r,h}$ is the encrypted index. $I'_{r,h}$ is equal to 0 in the situation of $z = \eta - I_{r,h}$. Since index value should be an integer from 1 to η, a new z is generated to encrypt $I_{r,h}$ in case of $I'_{r,h}$ encrypted as "0". The index table after encryption is denoted as $\mathbf{T}_e$, which is transmitted to data-hider along with $\mathbf{C}_e$.

2.2   Additional-Data Embedding

In this stage, an index value modification scheme is proposed to embed additional data, which can be completed by modifying the value of the indexes in specific position and keeping the value of the rest indexes unchanged.

For index table $\mathbf{T}_e$ with size of $M/n \times N/n$, all the indexes can be divided in to embeddable index and non-embedding index. Then, each non-embeddable index is supposed to be placed between two adjacent embeddable indexes. Therefore, an embeddable index $I'_{r,h}$ should be satisfied:

$$(r + h) \mod 2 = 0. \tag{5}$$

For a vivid description, a simple example can be taken to elaborate the process as follow, Fig. 2 shows the position of embeddable indexes and non-embeddable indexes, in which the gray region denotes $I'_{r,h}$ embeddable while the white region denotes $I'_{r,h}$ non-embeddable. It can be seen that the neighboring indexes of an embeddable index, namely, N(North), W(West), S(South) and E(East), are non-embedding indexes.

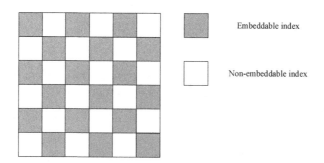

Fig. 2. Distribution of embeddable index and non-embeddable index

In order to obtain a better image quality after decrypting, it is noted that the boundary of index table $\mathbf{T}_e$ cannot be embedded. For the index $I'_{r,h}$ located at gray region, data hider embeds additional data $\mathbf{w}$ into $I'_{r,h}$ through modifying its value. More precisely, 1 bit data will be embedded into $I'_{r,h}$ by modifying its value using

$$\hat{I}_{r,h} = \begin{cases} I'_{r,h}, & w = 0, \\ I'_{r,h} + 1, & w = 1, \ I'_{r,h} \ \text{mod} \ 2 = 1, \\ I'_{r,h} - 1, & w = 1, \ I'_{r,h} \ \text{mod} \ 2 = 0, \end{cases} \tag{6}$$

where $\hat{I}_{r,h}$ is the modified index contains an additional bit, and w is the message to be embedded. Scanning all indexes located at gray region in $\mathbf{T}_e$, if the message embedded is "0", index $I'_{r,h}$ keeps unchanged, if the embedded message is "1", the index $I'_{r,h}$ is modified as the $I'_{r,h} + 1$ or $I'_{r,h} - 1$ to embed additional data "1". In other word, we modify the $I'_{r,h}$ with the index of another codeword of its codeword pair. From above description, we know the codewords in a codeword pair, in which their positions in codebook are adjacent but their codewords are significantly different. According to the value of index, that is to say, the positions in codebook determine $\hat{I}_{r,h} = I'_{r,h} + 1$ or $\hat{I}_{r,h} = I'_{r,h} - 1$. For example, two specific encrypted indexes "21" and "30" will be modified to "22" and "29" when the additional data "1" is embedded. Because the 21th codeword and the 22th codeword constitute a codeword pair and the 29th codeword and the 30th codeword constitute a codeword pair. After all indexes in gray region have been scanned, we obtain a marked, encrypted index table $\mathbf{T}_{ew}$ containing additional data.

In general, if the index table is encrypted with a stream cipher, the decrypted image will be meaningless when an additive operation is performed on an encrypted index. However, because of the special encryption scheme used for the index in our scheme, additional operation will still exist after decryption.

2.3   Data Extraction and Image Recovery

After receiving the marked, encrypted index table $\mathbf{T}_{ew}$ and an encrypted codebook $\mathbf{C}_e$, the receiver first generates a sequence of pseudo-random byte $S_{i,j}$ and a sequence of even numbers $\mathbf{Z}$ according to $K_e^{(1)}$ and $K_e^{(2)}$. Through XOR decryption, a decrypted codebook $\mathbf{C}_d$ is obtained with $K_e^{(1)}$, the decrypted codebook $\mathbf{C}_d$ is exactly the same as $\mathbf{C}$ obviously. $\hat{I}_{r,h}$ in marked, encrypted index table $\mathbf{T}_{ew}$ is decrypted by

$$\tilde{I}_{r,h} = \left(\hat{I}_{r,h} - z \right) \ \text{mod} \ \eta, \tag{7}$$

where $\tilde{I}_{r,h}$ is the directly decrypted index containing additional data. Due to the property of index encryption method, the addition operation is preserved after decryption. When the embedded additional bit is "0", $\tilde{I}_{r,h}$ is the exacted value of decrypted image and when the embedded additional bit is "1", $\tilde{I}_{r,h} + 1$ or $\tilde{I}_{r,h} - 1$ is the correct value for decrypted image. For example, suppose $\eta = 256$ and the original index $I_{r,h}$ is "177", the 177th and 178th codewords constitute a codeword pair. For the encrypted index $I'_{r,h}$ is "21" with $z = 100$, the marked, encrypted index $\hat{I}_{r,h}$ is "22" and the directly decrypted index $\tilde{I}_{r,h}$ becomes "178" after embedding additional data "1". It proves that the additive operation still exists after decryption. Moreover, due to the additive operation, the corresponding codeword has been changed to another codeword in their codeword pair, the corresponding codeword value has changed greatly as well as index value has modified from 177 to 178. Therefore, the receiver can distinguish embedded $\tilde{I}_{r,h}$ from non-embedded indexes by comparing codeword of $\tilde{I}_{r,h}$ index with the predicted $\hat{C}$. The predicted $\hat{C}$ is obtained according to correlation of nature images. For a decrypted embedded index $\tilde{I}_{r,h}$, its neighboring indexes, namely, $\tilde{I}_{r-1,h}$, $\tilde{I}_{r,h-1}$, $\tilde{I}_{r+1,h}$, $\tilde{I}_{r,h+1}$ are non-embedding indexes. As is shown in Fig. 3, C_p is the codeword to be decided by C_{d1}, C_{d2}, C_{d3} and C_{d4}, which are the corresponding codeword of $\tilde{I}_{r-1,h}$, $\tilde{I}_{r,h-1}$, $\tilde{I}_{r+1,h}$ and $\tilde{I}_{r,h+1}$.

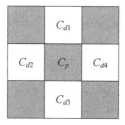

Fig. 3. Distribution of embedded index and non-embedded index after directly decrypted

In our scheme, three different predictors are used for predicting codeword at the position of C_p, denoting the predicted index as $\hat{C}$:

(1) the average of the four neighboring codewords:

$$\hat{C}_1 = \frac{C_{d1} + C_{d2} + C_{d3} + C_{d4}}{4} \tag{8}$$

(2) a weighted average based on local gradients:

$$\hat{C}_2 = \frac{(|C_{d1} - C_{d3}| + 1)\frac{C_{d2} + C_{d4}}{2} + (|C_{d2} - C_{d4}| + 1)\frac{C_{d1} + C_{d3}}{2}}{|C_{d1} - C_{d3}| + |C_{d2} - C_{d4}| + 2} \tag{9}$$

(3) the median

$$\hat{C}_3 = \frac{C(2) + C(3)}{2} \tag{10}$$

where $C(1) \leq C(2) \leq C(3) \leq C(4)$. Noted that, we use the mean value of codewords to calculate instead of all pixels in codeword C_{d1}, C_{d2}, C_{d3} and C_{d4} in (9) and (10).

For an index containing additional bit, the embedded bit may be "0" or "1". During the process of data extraction and image recovery, there are two possible codewords in the position of C_p: C' and C''. Since C' and C'' are in the same codeword pair, the positions of codewords C' and C'' in the codebook are adjacent and their corresponding index value are $\tilde{I}_{r,h}$ and $\tilde{I}_{r,h} + 1$ or $\tilde{I}_{r,h} - 1$, but their codeword values are completely different. According to spatial correlation in natural image, we select the appropriate codeword from C' and C'' based on the predicted $\hat{C}$. In order to obtain more accurate results, we consider the prediction results of three kinds of predictor simultaneously

$$pred(k) = \begin{cases} 1, & if\ D[C', \hat{C}_{(k)}] < D[C'', \hat{C}_{(k)}] \\ 0, & if\ D[C', \hat{C}_{(k)}] = D[C'', \hat{C}_{(k)}], \quad k = 1, 2, 3 \\ -1, & if\ D[C', \hat{C}_{(k)}] > D[C'', \hat{C}_{(k)}] \end{cases} \quad (11)$$

where $D(x, y) = \sqrt{(x_1 - y_1)^2 + (x_2 - y_2)^2 + \ldots + (x_{n^2} - y_{n^2})^2}$, Noted that, it is rare to obtain $pred(k) = 0$, because there are n^2 pixels in a codeword, the recovered index value and extracted data are

$$I_{r,h}^{(r)} = \begin{cases} \tilde{I}_{r,h}, & \sum_{k=1}^{3} pred(k) \geq 0, \\ \tilde{I}_{r,h} - 1, & \sum_{k=1}^{3} pred(k) < 0\ \&\ \tilde{I}_{r,h}\ mod\ 2 = 0, \\ \tilde{I}_{r,h} + 1, & \sum_{k=1}^{3} pred(k) < 0\ \&\ \tilde{I}_{r,h}\ mod\ 2 = 1, \end{cases} \quad (12)$$

$$w_{r,h}^{(r)} = \begin{cases} 0, & \sum_{k=1}^{3} pred(k) \geq 0, \\ 1, & \sum_{k=1}^{3} pred(k) < 0, \end{cases} \quad (13)$$

where $I_{r,h}^{(r)}$ is the recovered index and $w_{r,h}^{(r)}$ is the extracted bit. The additional data w is extracted and then image is recovered at the same time after scanning all index in the gray region.

3 Experimental Results and Comparisons

In this section, a series of experiments were conducted to demonstrate the effectiveness and superiority of our scheme, and the environment of our experiments was based on a personal computer with a 3.20 GHz Intel i5 processor, 4.00 GB memory, Windows 10 operating system, and Matlab R2016a. In order to demonstrate the effectiveness of our scheme, we compared our scheme with Zhang's scheme [16].

3.1 Results of Our Scheme

Figure 4 shows a standard grayscale image *Lena* after VQ-compressing sized 512×512, the length of codebook is 256. Figure 4(b) is the corresponding result of index table and codebook encryption, it can be seen that the content of original VQ-compressed image was effectively masked after encryption. Figure 4(c) shows image after encryption and data embedding, and the embedding rate was 0.4844 bpi (bit per index). Figure 4(d) is the recovered image with PSNR = 32.1 dB (compared with *Lena* after VQ-compression).

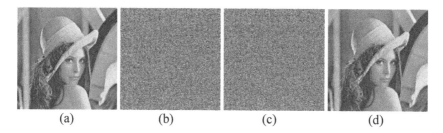

(a)   (b)   (c)   (d)

Fig. 4. Results of the proposed scheme for VQ-compressed image *Lena*. (a) Original VQ compressed image, (b) Encrypted image, (c) Marked, encrypted image ($\tau = 0.4844$ bpi), (d) recovered image (PSNR = 32.10 dB).

Figure 5 shows other 4 different test images sized 512×512, including *Baboon*, *Barbara*, *Peppers* and *Airplane*. Four different size of codebooks ($\eta = 128, 256, 512, 1024$) were used for VQ-compression. Table 1 shows the extracted-bit error rate ζ and embedding rate for the images in Fig. 5 under different codebooks. Extracted-bit error rate ζ is calculated by $\zeta = w_e/w$, where w_e represents the error extracted bits. It can be found from Table 1 that, the proposed scheme achieves a lower extracted-bit error rate. In addition, the maximum embedding rate were kept at 0.4844 bpi under all situation.

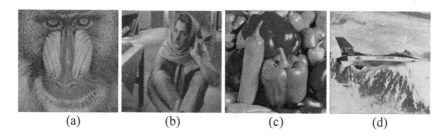

(a)   (b)   (c)   (d)

Fig. 5. Four test images. (a) *Baboon*, (b) *Barbara*, (c) *Peppers*, (d) *Airplane*.

Table 1. Result of extracted-bit error rate and embedding rate for four images under different size of codebook

Size of codebook	Baboon	Barbara	Peppers	Airplane	Embedding rate
	Extracted-bit error rate ζ				τ (bpi)
128	0.0646	0.0262	0.0175	0.0365	0.4844
256	0.0699	0.0336	0.0190	0.0399	
512	0.0700	0.0339	0.0208	0.0418	
1024	0.0805	0.0382	0.0224	0.0451	

3.2   Comparison with State-of-the-Art Scheme

In order to show the superiority of our scheme, we compared our scheme with Zhang's scheme [16] in Table 2. In Zhang's scheme and our scheme, the parameters are selected as $S = 8$ and $\eta = 256$, respectively. It can be found that, the proposed scheme can achieve lower extracted-bit error rate and higher embedding rate compared with [16].

Table 2. Comparisons of Extracted-bit error rate ζ between [16] and proposed scheme

	Baboon	Barbara	Peppers	Airplane	Embedding bits
	Extracted-bit error rate ζ				
Zhang [16]	0.1391	0.0830	0.0231	0.0427	4096 bits
Proposed	0.0697	0.0370	0.0183	0.0403	7938 bits

4   Conclusions

In this paper, we propose a RDH scheme based on encrypted VQ-compressed image. In our scheme, the codebook is divided into a number of codeword pairs and permuted firstly, then index table and new codebook are encrypted separately. Addition data will be embedded into selected indexes by modifying their value. On the receiver side, receiver can extract additional data and recover image perfectly with the aid of spatial correlation in natural image. Experiments result shows our scheme can provide a relative higher embedding rate and a lower extracted-bit error rate.

Acknowledgments. This work was supported by the National Natural Science Foundation of China (61672354, 61702332), the Open Project Program of the National Laboratory of Pattern Recognition (201600003), the Open Project Program of Shenzhen Key Laboratory of Media Security, and Hujiang Foundation of China (C14001, C14002).

The authors would like to thank the anonymous reviewers for their valuable suggestions.

References

1. Vleeschouwer, C.D., Delaigle, J.F., Macq, B.: Invisibility and application functionalities in perceptual watermarking: an overview. Proc. IEEE **90**(1), 64–77 (2002)
2. Duan, X., Song, H., Qin, C., Khan, M.: Coverless steganography for digital images based on a generative model. Comput. Mater. Continua **55**(3), 483–493 (2018)
3. Tian, J.: Reversible data embedding using a difference expansion. IEEE Trans. Circuits Syst. Video Technol. **13**(8), 890–896 (2003)
4. Ni, Z., Shi, Y., Ansari, N., Su, W.: Reversible data hiding. IEEE Trans. Circuits Syst. Video Technol. **16**(3), 354–362 (2006)
5. Thodi, M., Rodriguez, J.: Expansion embedding techniques for reversible watermarking. IEEE Trans. Image Process. **16**(3), 721–730 (2007)
6. Li, X., Zhang, W., Gui, X., Yang, B.: Efficient reversible data hiding based on multiple histograms modification. IEEE Trans. Inf. Forensics Secur. **10**(9), 2016–2027 (2015)
7. Wang, Y., Shen, J., Hwang, M.: A novel dual image-based high payload reversible hiding technique using LSB matching. Int. J. Netw. Secur. **20**(4), 801–804 (2018)
8. Nasrabadi, N., King, R.: Image coding using vector quantization: a review. IEEE Trans. Commun. **36**(8), 957–971 (1988)
9. Chang, C., Chen, G., Lin, M.: Information hiding based on search-order coding for VQ indices. Pattern Recogn. Lett. **25**(11), 1253–1261 (2004)
10. Lin, C., Chen, S., Hsueh, N.: Adaptive embedding techniques for VQ-compressed images. Inf. Sci. **179**(3), 140–149 (2009)
11. Shie, S., Jiang, J.: Reversible and high-payload image steganographic scheme based on side-match vector quantization. Sig. Process. **92**(9), 2332–2338 (2012)
12. Qin, C., Chang, C., Chen, Y.: Efficient reversible data hiding for VQ-compressed images based on index mapping mechanism. Sig. Process. **99**(9), 2687–2695 (2013)
13. Kieu, T., Ramroach, S.: A reversible steganographic scheme for VQ indices based on joint neighboring coding. Expert Syst. Appl. **42**(2), 713–722 (2015)
14. Lee, J., Chiou, Y., Guo, J.: Lossless data hiding for VQ indices based on neighboring correlation. Inf. Sci. **221**(2), 419–438 (2013)
15. Puech, W., Chaumont, M., Strauss, O.: A reversible data hiding method for encrypted images. Proc. SPIE **6819**, 1–9 (2008)
16. Zhang, X.: Reversible data hiding in encrypted image. IEEE Signal Process. Lett. **18**(4), 255–258 (2011)
17. Chen, Y., Yin, B., He, H., Yan, S., Chen, F., Tai, H.: Reversible data hiding in classification-scrambling encrypted-image based on iterative recovery. Comput. Mater. Continua **56**(2), 299–312 (2018)

IoT Security

An Landmark Evaluation Algorithm Based on Router Identification and Delay Measurement

Te Ma$^{(\boxtimes)}$, Fenlin Liu, Fan Zhang, and Xiangyang Luo

State Key Laboratory of Mathematical Engineering and Advanced Computing,
Zhengzhou Science and Technology Institute, Zhengzhou, China
tema_123@163.com

Abstract. City-level landmarks serve as an important foundation for achieving city-level and higher-precision IP geolocation. On the basis of the feature that router host names in network-developed areas often imply geographical location information, this paper proposes a city-level landmark evaluation algorithm based on router identification. Firstly, router host name matching rules are formulated by using plenty of network topology information obtained through probing. Secondly, the matching rules are used to extract router host names; the geographical locations corresponding to routers are queried through the established geographical location dictionary; and the nearest router that can obtain a city-level location in the probing path is reserved. Finally, candidate landmarks are evaluated based on the rule that the physical distance between network entities is less than the delay conversion distance. The experimental results show that the proposed algorithm can effectively evaluate the reliability of landmarks: among the experimental results on 8000 network landmarks in 4 cities in the United States, compared with the typical database query-based landmark obtaining, the city-level accuracy rates of landmarks are increased by 4.4%, 6.85%, 4.35% and 7.05% respectively.

Keywords: IP geolocation · Router identification · City-level landmarks · Candidate landmarks · Landmark evaluation

1 Introduction

The geolocation on the geographical location of a network entity IP refers to determining the geographical location of a network target node at a certain granularity level. Since each host directly connected to the Internet can usually be identified by a unique IP address, the IP address is usually used to find its geographical coordinate mapping. Hence, it is also called IP geolocation [1]. As location-based service (LBS) becomes more widespread, there are increasing applications of IP geolocation technology, such as embedding in web pages the advertisements targeted for visitors' regions (targeted advertisements), adjusting the languages displayed in web pages according to geographical locations, analyzing the access logs of web pages to extract market data, defining the geographical scope of e-tax, formulating the deployment strategies of network infrastructure and finding failed nodes, conducting network forensics on illegal

© Springer Nature Switzerland AG 2019
X. Sun et al. (Eds.): ICAIS 2019, LNCS 11634, pp. 163–177, 2019.
https://doi.org/10.1007/978-3-030-24271-8_15

acts like online fraud and attacks, and providing help for the performance, service continuity and governance of cloud computing [2–4]. The geolocation accuracy and geolocation error of the classical geolocation algorithm often depend on the number and reliability of landmarks, such as city-level geolocation algorithms: the Octant algorithm [5], LBG algorithm [6], geolocation algorithm based on identification router [7]; and street-level geolocation algorithm: the SLG algorithm [8]. As a consequence, the obtaining and evaluation of reliable landmarks have important theoretical and practical significance.

Landmark refers to the network entity with a known geographical location and a stable IP identity. As the important basic data of IP geolocation, landmarks are similar to the reference points in GPS geolocation and Beidou geolocation. Landmarks can be divided into city-level landmarks and street-level landmarks according to geographic granularity. The obtaining of city-level landmarks mainly includes: obtaining landmarks based on IP location database querying [9], which refers to obtaining the geographical location corresponding to an IP by querying the existing database on the network. A large number of landmarks can be obtained in batches through this method, but most IP data in these databases can only guarantee country-level accuracy with demerits in rough and low-precision landmark locations. The network forum-based landmark obtaining algorithm [10] extracts a user's IP address and the geographical area information involved in the forum from the network forum, and uses these IPs as candidate landmarks. When these candidate landmark IPs are gotten to, the geographical locations of the last hop routing IP and its previous hop routing IP in the database are queried. When the query result is in the same city as the candidate landmark IP, the candidate landmark IP is evaluated as a reliable landmark. However, the use of this algorithm is subject to the limitations of network forum privacy protection. Actually, some network topology analysis algorithms can also be used to obtain and evaluate city-level landmarks, The Rocketfuel algorithm [11] uses the geographical location of the router that is closest to the target in the probing path and can estimate location information as the actual area corresponding to the landmark. This algorithm can obtain some reliable landmarks, but it has the following limitations. First, a large number of matching rules provided by the ISP are needed to identify router host names, so the overhead of the algorithm is high. Second, when the number of routing hops between an identifiable router and a candidate landmark is too large, the router and the candidate landmark may be in different cities, which cannot guarantee the reliability of the landmark. In addition, there are some street-level landmark obtaining algorithms, such as Web server-based landmark obtaining algorithm [8] based on data mining, as well as location-based landmark collection algorithm [12] based on the GPS technology.

In network-developed areas (such as the United States), the naming of routers tends to be standardized, and router host names usually contain geographical location identification, namely, the city where the router is located [1, 11]. Obviously, such a router can be used as a benchmark to determine the actual area where a candidate landmark is located. This paper first formulates router host name matching rules by using a large number of probing results, and adopts the matching rules to extract router host names; then obtains the geographical locations corresponding to routers by querying the established geographical location dictionary, and reserves the nearest router that can obtain a city-level location in the probing path, effectively reducing the overhead of router identification; and finally, effectively evaluates candidate landmarks by using delay calculation.

The rest of this paper is organized as follows: Sect. 2 describes the basis for evaluating candidate landmarks by using router identification. Section 3 elaborates on there main parts of matching rule formulation, router identification and candidate landmark evaluation of the proposed algorithm. Section 4 analyzes the feasibility of the key links of the proposed algorithm. Section 5 verifies the effectiveness of the proposed algorithm through experiments, and compares it with existing router identification rules and database query-based city-level landmark obtaining. Finally, the full text is summarized.

2 Problem Formulation

In the network infrastructure construction based on network-developed areas, in order to facilitate the management of the network, the ISP often names the public routers in the network with a router host name that is easy to identify. These host names often imply the types and geographical location information of the routers. As shown in Table 1, a China Telecom probe host located in Beijing (its IP address is 113.59.224.1) is selected to probe the IP address 192.241.254.131 located in New York, USA.

As shown in Table 1, it is known that the IP address 113.59.224.1 of the probe host is located Beijing, and the probing target is located in New York, but the city-level location of the intermediate router in the probing path is unknown. In moderately network-developed areas (China), most routers are not named due to imperfect network construction [11, 13], but after the probing path enters the network-developed areas (USA), the host names of the 10th, 11th and 12th hop routers all include router types and geographical location information. Among them, "core" means the core router; "SanJose" means San Jose, USA; and "NewYork" means New York, USA. It can be determined that the 10th and 11th hop IPs are the core router located in San Jose, USA, and the 12th hop IP is the core router located in New York, USA. ($\varnothing$ Indicates that there is no router hostname).

Table 2 shows the probing results on the 380 PlanetLab nodes in the United States by the probe host in Table 1. The total number of hops before and after the probing path gets to the USA and the number of hops with host names are counted, and the probing target is not included in statistics.

As can be seen from Table 2, after the probing path enters the typical network-developed area USA, a large number of routers have host names, and the ratio increases from 4.4% to 82.1%, that is, a large number of router host names can be extracted through corresponding matching rules. Exactly based on the above features, this paper considers using the router that obtains the city-level geographical location in the probing path as a benchmark, evaluating candidate landmarks by using delay calculation, and finally obtaining reliable city-level landmarks.

Table 1. Probing path information from 113.59.224.1 to 192.241.254.131

Probe host	Router IP	Target	Hop count	Router host names	Location
113.59.224.1	113.59.224.1	192.241.254.131	3	∅	Beijing
	202.80.195.181		4		China
	202.80.192.13		5		China
	42.99.32.9		6		China
	202.97.27.170		7		USA
	202.97.90.250		8		USA
	202.97.50.62		9		USA
	64.86.21.45		10	**ix-xe-8-3-5-0.tcore2.SQN-SanJose.as6453.net**	San Jose
	63.243.205.1		11	**if-ae-1-2.tcore1.SQN-SanJose.as6453.net**	San Jose
	63.243.128.122		12	**if-ae-9-2.tcore1.N75-NewYork.as6453.net**	NY
	66.110.96.26		13	∅	USA
	192.241.254.131		14		NY

Table 2. Counting the number of hops with router host names

The number of target	The number of router hops (before USA)	The number of hops with host names	The number of router hops (enter USA)	The number of hops with host names
380	3943	74	3282	2694

3 Proposed Algorithms

To facilitate the elaboration on subsequent algorithms, this paper defines the following symbols:

Ci is used to represent a certain city, and different subscript i represents different cities;
Ri is used to represent the nearest router that is identifiable in the probing path, and different subscript i represents different routers;
Di is used to represent the city radius of a city, and different subscript i represents different cities.

The proposed algorithm can be divided into three main parts: matching rule formulation, router identification, and candidate landmark evaluation. The framework of the City-Level Landmark Evaluation Algorithm Based on Router Identification is shown in Fig. 1.

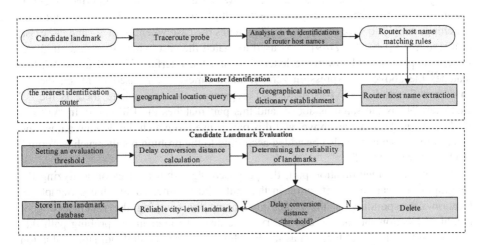

Fig. 1. The basic framework of City-Level Landmark Evaluation Algorithm Based on Router Identification

In the part of matching rule formulation, the proposed algorithm performs plenty of probe on candidate landmarks, analyzes the various types of identifications of the router host names in the probing results, and formulates corresponding router host name matching rules to implement in-batches matching extraction. The steps are specifically as follows:

Step1: Probe host probing. Traceroute probing is performed on candidate landmarks through a plurality of the deployed probe hosts H_1, H_2...H_n in combination with the probing packets under multiple protocols. The probing path information of candidate landmarks is obtained via multi-source probing.

Step2: Analysis on the identifications of router host names. By analyzing the probing results, it can be known that a router host name usually consists of a network interface identification, router type identification, geographical location identification, ISP name and domain name. The locations of the ISP name and domain name are relatively fixed, whereas those of other three identifications are not fixed. The three types of identifications are composed of numbers, English uppercase and lowercase letters, and interface identification "-". Each identification may have multiple segments, and the regular expression is as follows:

$$[a\text{-}zA\text{-}Z0\text{-}9]+(?:[.\text{-}][\text{-}a\text{-}zA\text{-}Z0\text{-}9]+)*(?:\backslash.[\text{-}a\text{-}zA\text{-}Z0\text{-}9]+)+\backslash.(?:net\,|\,NET) \qquad (1)$$

Among them, "$a\text{-}zA\text{-}Z$" matches English uppercase and lowercase letters; "0-9" matches numerical characters; as a result, "$[a\text{-}zA\text{-}Z0\text{-}9]$" matches the case where there are only numbers, English uppercase and lowercase letters but no interface identification "-". "+" matches the above content multiple times; "(?:)" means non-capturing matching, mainly to save memory; "[.-]" matches the case where both "." and "-" exist; as a result, "$(?:[.\text{-}][\text{-}a\text{-}zA\text{-}Z0\text{-}9]+)$" is used to match the case where there are numbers, English uppercase and lowercase letters, "." and the interface identification "-". "$*$" matches the above subexpression zero or more times. "\." is used to match the "." character. Similarly, "$(?:\backslash.[\text{-}a\text{-}zA\text{-}Z0\text{-}9]+)$" represents the case where there is the "." character; "+" is the same as above, and this part matches the ISP name. In "\.(?:net| NET)", "\." is the same as above, and this part is used to match the domain name; and other domain names can also be added according to the probing results, such as "com", "COM", "org", "ORG".

In the router identification part, the proposed algorithm focuses on analyzing the geographical location identification in the router host name, obtains the geographical location corresponding to the router host name by querying the established geographical location dictionary, and reserves the nearest router in the probing path that can obtain the city-level location as the benchmark for candidate landmark evaluation in next step.

Step1: Router host name extraction. Extract all router host names in the probe path through the matching rules formulated in the previous step for the next router identification.

Step2: Geographical location dictionary establishment. The geographical location identification of a router's host name is usually associated with the information of the city where the router is located (city administrative division, an iconic location in the city such as an airport). The proposed algorithm obtains geographical location identifications, including city names, city abbreviations, city airport names and abbreviations of the airport names through existing administrative divisions and public city information, so as to establish a router geographical location dictionary.

Step3: Router host corresponding geographical location query. The geographical location information corresponding to the routers is obtained by querying the dictionary from back to front, and the nearest router that can obtain the city-level location information in the probing path is reserved. For example, the router is Rj, thus completing the router hostname identification.

In the candidate landmark evaluation part, the proposed algorithm calculates the relative time delay between the identified nearest router and the candidate landmark in the same probing path, and compares the delay conversion distance with the set threshold to determine the reliability of landmarks.

Step1: Setting an evaluation threshold. The geographic location of the candidate city-level landmark is the city center, so the nearest identification router should in the geographical location center of the city where it is located. Thus, if $Rj \in Cj$ and $T \in Cj$, and $j = 1, 2 \ldots i$, then the threshold is set to the city radius of the city where is located. Step2: Delay conversion distance calculation. The delay conversion distance between the identified nearest router and the candidate landmark T is calculated, and the relative time delay $RltRTT(Rj, T)$ is as shown in the formula (2), wherein $RTT(P, Rj)$ and $RTT(P, T)$ are the round-trip delays of the probe host P to Rj and T, respectively.

$$RltRTT(Rj, T) = RTT(P, T) - RTT(P, Rj) \tag{2}$$

The empiric value $4/9C$ is used as the conversion coefficient, and the converted delay distance S is(C simples speed of light):

$$S = 1/2(RltRTT(Rj, T) * 4/9C) \tag{3}$$

Step3: Determining the reliability of landmarks. According to the calculation results in the previous step, get the minimum delay of multiple measurements. When the delay conversion distance S is smaller than the city radius Dj, which indicates that the identified nearest router is in the same city as the candidate landmark. The candidate landmark is evaluated as a reliable city-level landmark and stored in the landmark database.

4 Analysis of Proposed Algorithms

The router identification and candidate landmark evaluation parts are the key links of the proposed algorithm. This section elaborates on the feasibility of the two parts in the proposed algorithm.

4.1 Router Identification Feasibility Analysis

The router identification part of the proposed algorithm focuses on the geographical location information implied by the router host names. Consequently, the proposed algorithm uses the matching rules in the formula (1) to extract the router host names, and then further analyzes the geographical location identification part therein, as shown in the following table.

Table 3 shows that the geographical location information of a router is usually composed of four types of identifications: a City Code1 identification, which is relatively simple, namely, the detailed name of a city, such as San Francisco in "corerouter1.SanFrancisco.cw.net"; a City Code2 identification, which is the abbreviation of a city and its state name, such as "Chcil" for Chicago, Illinois; an Airport Code identification, which is the abbreviation of a city airport name, such as "SJC" for San Jose Intl Airport. Besides, there is also a Country Code identification. That is, a router host name only contains a country-level geographical location. For example, "NI" is the abbreviation of Netherlands. The proposed algorithm adds three types of identifications for obtaining city-level geographical locations according to the public administrative

Table 3. Geographical location information implied in router host names

Router host name	Identification	Abbreviation	Corresponding city
corerouter1.SanFrancisco.cw.net	City Code1	SanFrancisco	San Francisco
ccr01.chcil03.atlas.cogentco.com	City Code2	Chcil	Chicago
sjc2-cwoc3.sjc.above.net	Airport Code	SJC	San Jose
asd-nr16.nl.kpnqwest.net	Country Code	Nl	Netherlands

Table 4. Geographical location information implied in router host names

City	City Code1	City Code2	Airport Code
Ashburn, VA	Ashburn	Asbnva	IAD
Atlanta, GA	Atlanta	Atlnga	ATL
Chicago, IL	Chicago	Chcil	ORD, MDW
Dallas, TX	Dallas	Dllstx	DFW
Houston, TX	Houston	Hstntx	IAH
Los Angeles, CA	Los Angeles	Lsanca	LAX
Miami, FL	Miami	Miamfl	MIA
Newark, NJ	Newark	Nwrknj	EWR
New York, NY	New York	Nycmny	JFK, LGA
San Jose, CA	San Jose	Snjsca	SJC

Table 5. Rocketfuel algorithm router host name matching rules

Match status	Regular expression	Router host names
Yes	([a-z]+)[0-9]\.([-a-z]*)([0-9])\.level3\.net	ae-5-5.car1.newyork1.level3.net
No		ae-5-5.car1.newyork.level3.net
		ae-5-5.car1.newyork21.level3.net
Yes	\.([a-z]*\.[a-z]{2})\.(core[0-9]*)\.above\.net	xe-2-2.chicago.il.core1.above.net
No		xe-2.chicago1.il.core1.above.net
		xe2.chicago12.il.core1.above.net

division and city information [14], and creates a geographical location dictionary. Some data are shown in Table 4.

In the existing router identification matching rules, such as the Rocketfuel algorithm [11], a large number of regular expressions are needed to match the router host names. Some matching rules are as shown in the Table 5.

Table 5 shows that the regular expression "([a-z]+)[0-9]\.([-a-z]*)([0-9])\.level3\. net" can only match a relatively simple host name like "ae-5-5.car1.newyork1.level3. net", but it cannot match a more complex host name, such as "ae-5-5.car1.newyork. level3.net" "ae-5-5.car1.newyork21.level3.net". These host names have no digit or one more digit at the geographical location identification. The regular expression "\.([a-z]*\. [a-z]{2})\.(core[0-9]*)\.above\.net" cannot match the router host name with a complex network interface identification or complex number at the geographical location identification, such as "xe-2.chicago1.il.core1.above.net", "xe2.chicago12.il.core1. above.net". Obviously, for the router host name in the foregoing situation, a corresponding regular expression needs to be formulated to match again, resulting in a high algorithm overhead.

4.2   Candidate Landmark Evaluation Feasibility Analysis

In the candidate landmark evaluation part of the proposed algorithm, the candidate landmarks are evaluated by using the rule that the physical distance between network entities is usually smaller than the delay conversion distance, which is specifically shown in the following figure.

As shown in Fig. 2, if the geographical location of a candidate landmark is accurate, its geographical location is the geographical location center of the city where it is located; and if the nearest router is identified to be in the same city as the candidate landmark, the landmark can be evaluated. The proposed algorithm sets the threshold to the corresponding city radius, and identifies the delay conversion distance between the nearest router and the candidate landmark as r. If $r < R$, it indicates that the nearest router is within the radius of the circle centered on the city geographical location, that

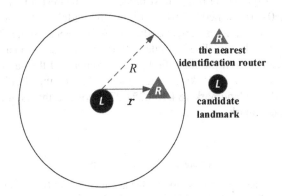

Fig. 2. Setting thresholds to evaluate candidate landmarks

is, the geographical location of the candidate landmark is accurate, and the candidate landmark can be evaluated as a reliable landmark. In actual tests, due to time delay jitter and router swell, the delay conversion distance is not unique. Based on the characteristic that the minimum time delay is corresponding to the minimum distance [15], it is necessary to select the minimum delay measurement result through multiple measurements to convert it to a physical distance, and then compare it with the set threshold (the radius of the city).

Table 6 shows the probing path information of the candidate landmark 184.168.221.27, and the path information of the minimum delay value between the

Table 6. Probing path information from 4.59.233.49 to 184.168.221.27

Probe host	Router IP	Target	Hop count	Router host names	Delay (ms)
4.59.233.49	4.59.233.49	184.168.221.27	3	∅	0.3
	4.69.153.121		4		27.7
	4.53.230.102		5		28.3
	184.168.0.86		6	**ip-184-168-0-86. ip.secureserver. net**	36.7
	184.168.0.85		7	**te0-0-0-7. trmc0215-01.ars. mgmt.phx3.gdg**	37
	184.168.0.81		8	**te0-0-0-7. trmc0215-01.ars. mgmt.phx3.gdg**	**37.1**
	184.168.221.27		9	∅	**37.4**

identified nearest router and the candidate landmark is obtained through multiple measurements.

As can be seen from Table 6, the host name of the nearest router identified in the probing path is "te0-0-0-7.trmc0215-01.ars.mgmt.phx3.gdg". After the matching rules are used for identification, ars is corresponding to Arizona Scottsdale. The threshold is the radius of this city - 40 km. The formulas (2) and (3) are used to calculate the delay conversion distance between the identified nearest router and the candidate landmark, and the calculation result is 15 km, which meets the set threshold. The city-level location of the candidate landmark 184.168.221.27 is correct, that is, it is evaluated as a reliable city-level landmark.

Table 7. Experiment setup

Landmark selection	PlanetLab nodes: 2000 reliable landmarks in New York, Atlanta, Philadelphia, and Orlando respectively
Tool use	IP location database: IP2location, Maxmind, Hostip
	Online map: Google Maps
Probe host deployment	PlanetLab node:2 in Los Angeles and San Francisco respectively, 1 in Seattle
Probe protocol	ICMP, UDP, TCP, ICMP-PARIS, UDP-PARIS

5 Experiments

5.1 Experimental Setup

The experimental setups include four aspects: candidate landmark selection, tool usage (IP location database, online map), probe host deployment and probing policy setting, as specifically shown in Table 7.

Table 7 shows that this paper conducts experiments on New York, Atlanta, Philadelphia and Orlando of USA, a typical network-developed area. In terms of candidate landmark obtaining, 2000 reliable city-level candidate landmarks (detectable) of the above-mentioned each city are selected from the public network platform PlanetLab [16] to verify the effectiveness of landmark evaluation in the proposed algorithm; as regards network probing, one is to adopt multi-source probing to perform Traceroute probing, and the other is to improve the integrity of the obtained path information through multi-protocol probing; in terms of experimental comparison, candidate landmark evaluation results obtained by the proposed algorithm are compared with the respective query results of 3 IP location databases - IP2location [17], Maxmind [18] and Hostip [19]; in addition, Google Map [20] is used to obtain the geographical location radius of each city.

5.2 Router Identification Experiment

In this experiment, through the one-week probing on each city's candidate landmarks in the experimental setups by using the deployed probe hosts, a total of 953,391 pieces of probing path information are collected, which include 87,276 different router host names, and the matching rules of the proposed algorithm are used to extract and query the city corresponding to the geographical location identification. In order to quantify the performance of the proposed algorithm in router identification, according to router type identifications, this paper classifies routers into: core routers (CR, Core, GBR, BB,

Table 8. The experimental results of router identification

Router type	The number of routers	The number of identification routers	Router identification rate
Core routers	48937	40953	83.68%
Border routers	37098	23963	64.61%
Unknown-type routers	1241	945	76.18%

CCR, EBR), border routers (BR, Border, Edge, IR, IGR, Peer, AR, etc.), as well as unknown-type routers, which have no obvious router type identification. Results are shown in the following table.

As can be seen from Table 8, the number of core routers in the probing path is significantly larger than the number of border routers, and only a small number of

Table 9. Candidate landmark evaluation result

City	The number of evaluation landmarks	The number of reliable landmarks	Unable to evaluate/mis-deleted reliable landmarks	Evaluation accuracy
Orlando	2000	1692	308	84.60%
Atlanta	2000	1779	229	88.95%
Philadelphia	2000	1703	297	85.15%
Orlando	2000	1782	218	89.10%

routers do not have a router type identification. From the analysis of the experimental results, it can be known that the number of core routers that the proposed algorithm can identify is larger, and the router identification rate is thus relatively high. Nevertheless, the host names of border routers and unknown routers may not contain geographical location information, and the router identification rate is thus relatively low. In summary, the proposed algorithm can identify the host names of most routers, and then obtain the geographical locations corresponding to the routers.

5.3   Candidate Landmark Evaluation Experiment

In this experiment, the proposed algorithm evaluates the landmarks after the router identification (the minimum delay value is taken after multiple measurements). Results are shown in Table 9.

Table 10. Comparison results on the accuracy rates of the city-level landmarks obtained by two algorithms

City	Proposed algorithm	MaxMind	IP2Location	Hostip
Orlando	**84.60%**	**80.20%**	79.90%	76.60%
Atlanta	**88.95%**	81.70%	**82.10%**	79.30%
Philadelphia	**85.15%**	**80.80%**	79.50%	78.60%
New York	**89.10%**	82.05%	**81.40%**	81.70%

As can be seen from Table 9, among the candidate landmark evaluation results, the evaluation accuracy rates of Atlanta, Philadelphia and New York City are relatively high, all exceeding 88%, but due to delay jitter and the situation that some routers do not contain geographical location information, still a small number of landmarks cannot be evaluated or are mis-deleted. Taken together, the proposed algorithm can effectively evaluate the landmarks.

5.4   Comparison with Database Query-Based Landmark Obtaining

In this experiment, comparison is conducted between the city-level accuracy rate of evaluating landmarks by the proposed algorithm and the city-level accuracy rate of database-based landmark query. The city-level locations of the IPs corresponding to the 2,000 landmarks in experimental setups in the MaxMind, IP2Location and Hostip databases are respectively queried. Results are shown in Table 10.

As can be seen from Table 10, the query results of the three IP location databases are considerably different, but the accuracy rate of evaluating city-level landmarks by the proposed algorithm is significantly higher than that of querying landmarks by the three IP location databases, which further validates the effectiveness of the proposed algorithm.

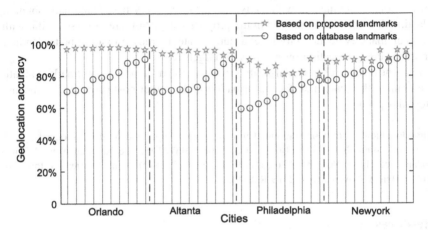

Fig. 3. Comparison on the geolocation results based on two different landmark sets

5.5 Impact on Target IP Geolocation

In order to further verify the influence of the landmarks after the evaluation by the proposed algorithm on target IP geolocation, the 200 reliable landmarks of each city evaluated by the proposed algorithm are randomly selected from the evaluation results. Also, the 200 landmarks belonging to each city are randomly selected from the three IP location database query results. They are respectively used to establish a city delay vector model through a typical city-level LBG geolocation algorithm [6]. The 50 randomly selected reliable landmarks of each city in the experimental setups are geolocated (the landmarks are all detectable and distributed over multiple/24 segments with good representativeness). A total of 10 experiments are performed, and results are shown in Fig. 3. Each line represents the results of one experiment.

As can be seen from Fig. 3, the geolocation accuracy rates of the LBG algorithm change with the selection of different reference landmarks and geolocation targets. However, the geolocation success rate of evaluating reliable landmarks based on the proposed algorithm is always better than that of the geolocation results of querying consistent landmarks based on multiple databases. All this has further verified the high reliability of landmark evaluation by the proposed algorithm.

6 Conclusion and Future Work

On the basis of the feature that router host names in network-developed areas imply geographical location information, this paper proposes a landmark evaluation algorithm based on router identification. The proposed algorithm identifies router host names by formulating matching rules, querying the geographical location dictionary, reserves the nearest router that can speculate a city-level location, and evaluates the reliability of landmarks through delay calculation. Compared with the existing router identification matching rules, the proposed algorithm can effectively reduce the overhead of router identification; and compared with the typical database query-based landmark obtaining, the landmark evaluation strategies in the proposed algorithm are more scientific with a higher landmark evaluation city-level accuracy rate, thereby providing better landmark support for the geolocation on network IP targets.

In the next research, we will further improve the accuracy of landmark evaluation by combining the router interface information in the router host name and by means of router alias parsing.

Acknowledgment. The work presented in this paper is supported by the National Key R&D Program of China (No. 2016YFB0801303, 2016QY01W0105), the National Natural Science Foundation of China (No. U1636219, U1736214 and 61772549), Plan for Scientific Innovation Talent of Henan Province (No. 2018JR0018).

References

1. Padmanabhan, V.N., Subramanian, L.: An investigation of geographic mapping techniques for Internet hosts. ACM SIGCOMM Comput. Commun. Rev. **31**(4), 173–185 (2001)
2. Securing display path for security-sensitive applications on mobile devices. CMC: Comput. Mater. Continua **55**(1), 017–035 (2018)
3. Taylor, J., Devlin, J., Curran, K.: Bringing location to IP addresses with IP geolocation. J. Emerg. Technol. Web Intell. **4**(3), 273–277 (2012)
4. Wang, Z., Chen, Y., Wen, H., et al.: Discovering routers as secondary landmarks for accurate IP geolocation. In: Vehicular Technology Conference on Proceedings, Toronto, pp. 1–5 (2017)
5. Wong, B., Stoyanov, I., Sirer, E.G.: Octant: a comprehensive framework for the geolocation of Internet hosts. In: USENIX NSDI Conference on Proceedings, Cambridge, pp. 23–36 (2007)
6. Eriksson, B., Barford, P., Sommers, J., Nowak, R.: A learning-based approach for IP geolocation. In: Krishnamurthy, A., Plattner, B. (eds.) PAM 2010. LNCS, vol. 6032, pp. 171–180. Springer, Heidelberg (2010). https://doi.org/10.1007/978-3-642-12334-4_18
7. Zhao, F., Song, Y., Liu, F., et al.: City-level geolocation based on routing feature. In: International Conference on Advanced Information Networking and Applications on Proceedings, Gwangju, pp. 414–419 (2015)
8. Wang, Y., Burgener, D., Flores, M., Kuzmanovic, A., Huang, C.: Towards street-level client-independent IP geolocation. In: 8th USENIX Conference on Networked Systems Design and Implementation on Proceedings, Boston, pp. 27–36 (2011)
9. Shavitt, Y., Zilberman, N.: A geolocation databases study. IEEE J. Sel. Areas Commun. **29** (10), 2044–2056 (2011)

10. Zhu, G., Luo, X., Liu, F., et al.: An algorithm of city-level landmark mining based on Internet forum. In: International Conference on Network-Based Information Systems on Proceedings, Taipei, pp. 294–301 (2015)
11. Localization algorithm of indoor Wi-Fi access points based on signal strength relative relationship and region division. CMC: Comput. Mater. Continua **55**(1), 071–093 (2018)
12. Liu, H., Zhang, Y., Zhou, Y., et al.: Mining checkins from location sharing services for client-independent IP geolocation. In: Conference on the Computer Communications on Proceedings, Toronto, pp. 619–627 (2014)
13. Cohen, R., Gonen, M., Wool, A.: Bounding the bias of tree-like sampling in IP topologies. Netw. Heterogen. Med. **3**(2), 323–332 (2017)
14. Political_divisions.https://en.wikipedia.org/wiki/Political_divisions_of_the_United_States
15. Li, D., et al.: IP geolocation mapping for moderately connected internet regions. IEEE Trans. Parallel Distrib. Syst. **24**(2), 381–391 (2013)
16. Planetlab. http://www.planet-lab.org/
17. IP2Location. http://www.ip2location.com/
18. MaxMind. http://www.maxmind.com/
19. Quova. http://www.quova.com/
20. GoogleMaps. https://developers.google.com/maps

Multiplicative Linear Secret Sharing Without Interaction

Bo Mi, Darong Huang$^{(\boxtimes)}$, Jianqiu Cao, Ping Long,
and Hongyang Pan

Institute of Information Science and Engineering,
Chongqing Jiaotong University, Chongqing 400074, China
drhuang@cqjtu.edu.cn

Abstract. As an essential building block in cryptosystem, linear secret sharing is widely used to safeguard the confidentiality and reliability of outsourced data. Though addition and constant multiplication are extremely easy thanks to the linear operation over shared secrets, how to efficiently multiply multiple shares remains an open problem. In this paper, we devised a non-interactive multiplication scheme based on Shamir's secret sharing without parameter constrain. It is proved that our scheme is unconditionally secure if no more than k participants are compromised, meaning that both the security and access structure of Shamir's scheme are immensely retained.

Keywords: Secret sharing · Multiplication · Polynomial convolution · Unconditional security · Q2 access structure

1 Introduction

With the advent of big data era, massive information is collected, accessed and operated all the way. Nevertheless, large amounts of privacies relevant to these data are confronted with the peril of revelation since the communication channels are open and the storages are always consigned [1]. On the other hand, the reliability of stocked data is also prone to damages due to system failure, interference or tampering, which may severely jeopardize the availability of important data [2]. Though functionality and security seem like two contrary goals for information system, lots of cryptographic techs can be used to balance the requirements between them. Oriented to different applications such as secure multi-parity computation) [3], Byzantine agreement [4] and oblivious transfer [5], secret sharing schemes are extensively used as their building block to narrow the gaps of system performance and security [6].

Based on Lagrange polynomial and Chinese remainder theorem, Shamir [7] and Blakley [8] brought about the schemes of secret sharing for the first time. Following their work, a series of secret sharing schemes [9–14] are proposed focusing on specific access structures. Though Ito et al. [15] have devised an universal framework to realize secret sharing on general access structure, it is deemed as impractical since the share size is extraordinary large. However, once the access structure is equivalent to a small monotone span program, efficient secret sharing schemes can easily be achieved [16, 17].

© Springer Nature Switzerland AG 2019
X. Sun et al. (Eds.): ICAIS 2019, LNCS 11634, pp. 178–187, 2019.
https://doi.org/10.1007/978-3-030-24271-8_16

Another research attraction is related to the communication burden and rounds of secret sharing. As proved by Csirmaz [18], to share a ℓ-bits secret within a n-party network, the lower bound of share size is $\Omega(\ell n / log_2 n)$. Though the share sizes of best known schemes [19, 20] are far more larger than such benchmark, the size of shared data can practically approach $n^{\Omega(log_2 n)}$ by linear secret sharing. In order to conserve the confidentiality of shared secrets when compounded with each other, homomorphic computability is also considered as an important requirement for secret sharing [21]. Aiming at minimizing the traffic overhead, linear secret sharing schemes are always exploited in virtue of non-interactive addition and constant multiplication [22, 23]. However, when two shared secrets are multiplied, how to reduce or even eliminate unnecessary communications still remains an open problem [24]. The original homomorphic multiplication for linear secret sharing is presented by Gennaro et al. with $\ell(2k-1)^2$-bits1-round communication [25], which may incur a severe delay when arithmetic circuits are deep. In fact, as proved by Ishai et al. [26, 27], once more that third of the participants are honest, any circuit can be cryptically evaluated via a 2-round secret sharing protocol. That is to say, refraining the communication from homomorphic multiplication is possible. In [28], Barkol et al. presented a multiplication scheme which enables all participants to secretly convert d distinct secrets into an additive sharing of their product. And its verifiable version was then proposed by Yoshida et al. [29]. However, since the circuit depth is strictly limited by the number of participants and security level, their schemes are incapable of fulfilling the property of fully homomorphism. In order to address such defect, Watanabe et al. [30] devised a FHE (Fully Homomorphic Encryption) scheme at the expense of $2n$ extra shares for each secret. Based on the recursive construction, Blackburn et al. [31] presented an efficient multiplicative sharing scheme where the share size will slightly expand along with the increasing of network scales. Thereafter, Wang et al. [32] pointed out that the forementioned scheme is infeasible within MTA (Mutually Trusted Authority)-free environment [33] and disposed the problem of redundantly operating on the same secret. Moreover, numerous secret sharing schemes are successively proposed utilizing different algebraic structures such as discrete logarithm [34], lattice [35] and Abelian codes [36].

Due to the linear nature and Q2 access structure of Shamir's secret sharing, it is widely used as a building block for privacy-preserving implementation. Moreover, since Shamir's scheme is ideal [9], the size of a shared secret is only ℓn-bits uniformly distributed on n participants, which is commendably close to its lower bound. For the sake of homomorphic computation, the trait of its linearity refrained the operations of addition and constant multiplication from interactions. Nevertheless, even if the best multiplicative secret sharing scheme is exploited, non-negligible delay occurs due to a series of communications.

Considering that the multiplicative circuits are inevitable for most practical applications and the characteristics of low communication along with computation overheads must be conserved for real-time implementation, a non-interactive multiplication scheme is proposed for Shamir's secret sharing in this paper. The main idea is, once the identities of all participants are reasonably regulated, polynomial convolution can play a part in reducing the overflowed orders incurred by trivial multiplication. The rest of this paper is organized as below.

In Sect. 2, a formal definition regarding Shamir's secret sharing is given, together with the defect analysis of some previous multiplicative secret sharing scheme. Then, a non-interactive multiplicative method and its correctness proof will be depicted in Sect. 3. Section 4 testified that our method is unconditionally secure and its performance is more preferable compared to related schemes. Finally, the paper will be concluded in Sect. 5.

2 Preliminary of Shamir's Secret Sharing

Based on Q2 access structure, Shamir's secret sharing is always recognized as a (k, n)-threshold scheme, where at least k shares amongst n pieces of a secret s should be gather to for information revealing. Since the essential idea of this threshold scheme is that any polynomial of degree $k - 1$ can be exclusively determined by k points in virtue of Lagrange interpolation [7], a secret s can be divided into a series of shares $(x_i, f(x_i))$, $i = 1, 2, \cdots, n$, according to a stochastic polynomial

$$f_s(x) = s + a_1 x + a_2 x^2 + \cdots a_{k-1} x^{k-1}. \tag{1}$$

Without loss of generality, we assume that the coefficients $a_j, j = 1, 2, \cdots, k - 1$, are independently and uniformly sampled from a finite field $\mathbb{F}_p$, where p is an odd prime. For any secret $s \in \mathbb{F}_p$, the scheme can be formally defined as follows.

Definition 1. The Shamir's secret sharing scheme is a triple function set $\prod = (\text{DIT}, \text{EVL}, \text{REC})$ works on Q2 access structure, where

a. The secret holder computes $\{(x_i, f_s(x_i))\} \xleftarrow{\$} \text{DIT}(s)$ in terms of formula (1) and distributes them to their correspondent receivers via authenticated and private channels. Denoting A as the set of all adversary structures, if $\text{T} \backslash \text{C} \notin \text{A}$ for any $\text{C} \in \text{A}$ where $\text{T} = \{1, 2, \cdots, n\}$, then

$$\Pr\big[\mathcal{A}([s]_\text{C}) = s\big] = 1/p, \tag{2}$$

where $[s]_\text{C}$ represents the set of shares corrupted by adversary $\mathcal{A}$.
b. For any constants c_1, c_2 and a pair of shares $[s_1]_\text{T}, [s_2]_\text{T}$, it is easy to non-interactively compute $[c_1 s_1 + c_2 s_2]_\text{T} \leftarrow \text{EVL}([s_1]_\text{T}, [s_2]_\text{T}, c_1, c_2)$ in terms of trivial addition and multiplication. In order to calculate $[s_1 s_2]_\text{T} \leftarrow \text{EVL}([s_1]_\text{T}, [s_2]_\text{T})$, interactive fully homomorphic schemes do also exist [25]. When executing the function of $\text{EVL}(\cdot)$, it is obvious that the requirements

$$\Pr\big[\mathcal{A}([\cdot]_\text{C}, \text{Com}_\text{T}) = s, s \in \text{S}\big] = 1/p \tag{3}$$

and

$$\Pr\left[\mathcal{A}([\cdot]_C, \mathrm{Com_T}) = \mathrm{REC}(\mathrm{EVL}([S]_T))\right] = 1/p \qquad (4)$$

must hold, where S stands for the set of original secrets and $[\cdot]_C, \mathrm{Com_T}$ are all corrupted shares along with intercepted communications.

c. Within the Q2 structure, the recovery function $\mathrm{REC}(\cdot)$ is capable of revealing the shared secret by

$$\Pr\left[\mathrm{REC}([s]_{\bar{c}}) = s\right] = 1 \qquad (5)$$

where $\bar{C}$ is the complementary set of C.

It is worth noting that the multiplicative secret sharing presented in [25] is feasible only if $n \geq 2k - 1$ with non-negligible communications. Though Barkol et al. [28] achieved a non-interactive scheme which can locally multiply d shared secrets, an auxiliary condition where $n > dk$ should also be satisfied. As for Watanabe's method [30], it is capable of performing multiplication even only k share holders are involved, the share size for each secret are 3 times than that of the primitive scheme and $4\ell k$-bits messages must be collected for each participant to achieve a share of multiplication result. To sum up, no existing multiplicative secret sharing scheme is in a position to avoid both interaction and parameter limitation, and that is why our research cut in.

3   Multiplicative Secret Sharing Without Interaction

The main reason that two shares should not be trivially multiplied can be attributed to the remarkable increment of polynomial order. For instance, when two shares $(x_i, f_a(x_i))$ and $(x_i, f_b(x_i))$ are directly multiplied by participant i, the result is $(x_i, f_a(x_i)f_b(x_i))$, where $f_a(x_i)f_b(x_i)$ can be written as

$$f_a(x_i)f_b(x_i) = ab + r_1 x_i + r_2 x_i^2 + \cdots r_{2k-2} x_i^{2k-2} \qquad (6)$$

which turns the original scheme into a $(2k - 1, n)$-threshold secret sharing. With the help of polynomial convolution, we caught a sight of how to reduce the multiplicative result back to a $k - 1$ order polynomial and maintain its raw threshold without interaction.

Assuming that the polynomials $f_a(x_i)$ and $f_b(x_i)$ is represented as

$$f_a(x_i) = (a, a_1, a_2, \cdots, a_{k-1})(x_i^0, x_i^1, x_i^2, \cdots, x_i^{k-1})^T \qquad (7)$$

and

$$f_b(x_i) = (b, b_1, b_2, \cdots, b_{k-1})(x_i^0, x_i^1, x_i^2, \cdots, x_i^{k-1})^T \qquad (8)$$

respectively. Then $f_a(x_i)f_b(x_i)$ in formula (6) is equivalent to $\alpha + \beta$, where

$$
\alpha = \left(\left(ab, ab_1 + ba_1, \cdots, \sum_{\sigma+\tau=\mu} a_\sigma b_\tau, \cdots, \sum_{\sigma+\tau=k-1} a_\sigma b_\tau \right) \bmod p \right) \cdot \\
\left(x_i^0, x_i^1, \cdots, x_i^\mu, \cdots, x_i^{k-1} \right)^T
$$

(9)

and

$$
\beta = \left(\left(\sum_{\sigma+\tau=k} a_\sigma b_\tau, \cdots, \sum_{\sigma+\tau=\omega} a_\sigma b_\tau, \cdots, a_{k-2}b_{k-1} + a_{k-1}b_{k-2}, a_{k-1}b_{k-1} \right) \bmod p \right) \cdot \\
\left(x_i^{k-1} \left(x_i^1, \cdots, x_i^{\omega=k+1}, \cdots x_i^{k-2}, x_i^{k-1} \right) \right)^T,
$$

(10)

where $a_0 = a$ and $b_0 = b$. Noting that the order of polynomial α is $k - 1$ whose leading coefficient is exactly ab, so if we can figure out β then the share of ab for participant i can be trivially achieved by subtract β from $f_a(x_i)f_b(x_i)$. Based on forementioned observation, we construct a multiplicative secret sharing scheme as below.

Distribution $\{(x_i, f_s(x_i))\} \overset{\$}{\leftarrow} DIT(s)$:

Define $p < x_i < q$ as the identity of participate i, where $q > p + n$ is a positive integer and $\gcd(x_i, p) = \gcd\left(\left(x_i^{-k} - 1 \right)^{-1}, p \right) = 1$. Then calculate $f_s(x_i)$ according to formula (1) modulo $\left(x_i^k - 1 \right)$, which will be distributed to i as her share of secret s.

Multiplication $[ab]_T \leftarrow EVL([a]_T, [b]_T)$:

Participant i locally computes

$$
f_{ab}(x_i) = f_a(x_i)f_b(x_i) - \left(x_i^{-k} - 1 \right)^{-1} \left(\left(f_a(x_i)f_b(x_i) \bmod \left(x_i^k - 1 \right) \right) - f_a(x_i)f_b(x_i) \right) \quad (11)
$$

modulo $\left(x_i^k - 1 \right)$ as her share of ab.

Since participant i is provided with all information about $f_a(x_i), f_b(x_i)$ and x_i, no interaction is necessary for her to calculate formula (11). In order to testify the correctness of our protocol, a Lemma is given in advance.

Lemma 1. For $\forall \theta \in \{0, 1, \cdots, k - 1\}$, if $\left\| \sum_{\sigma+\tau=\theta \bmod k} a_\sigma b_\tau \right\|_\infty < x_i - 1$ then

$$
\alpha + x_i^{-k}\beta < x_i^k - 1. \tag{12}
$$

Proof. Since $\alpha + x_i^{-k}\beta$ is a $k - 1$ order polynomial, which can be written as $\sum_{\theta=0}^{k-1} \left(\sum_{\sigma+\tau=\theta \bmod k} a_\sigma b_\tau \right) x_i^\theta$, we have

$$
0 \le \alpha + x_i^{-k}\beta \le \left\| \sum_{\sigma+\tau=\theta \bmod k} a_\sigma b_\tau \right\|_\infty \left(x_i^0 + x_i^1 + \cdots + x_i^\theta + \cdots + x_i^{k-1} \right). \tag{13}
$$

Once $\left\| \sum_{\sigma+\tau=\theta \bmod k} a_\sigma b_\tau \right\|_\infty < x_i - 1$, then

$$\alpha + x_i^{-k}\beta < (x_i - 1)\left(x_i^0 + x_i^1 + \cdots + x_i^\theta + \cdots + x_i^{k-1}\right) \tag{14}$$

and the formula (12) holds.

Now, we are ready to claim the validity of our multiplicative secret sharing scheme in the following theorem.

Theorem 1. *If $x_i > p$, any participant i is able to non-interactively multiply the shares of two secrets retaining the property of (k, n)-threshold.*

Proof. According to polynomial convolution, the formula $f_a(x_i)f_b(x_i) \bmod \left(x_i^k - 1\right)$ can be represented as $\alpha + x_i^{-k}\beta + t\left(x_i^k - 1\right)$ for some non-positive integer t. Once the condition $\left\| \sum_{\sigma + \tau = 0 \bmod k} a_\sigma b_\tau \right\|_\infty < x_i - 1$ stands, then

$$f_a(x_i)f_b(x_i) \bmod \left(x_i^k - 1\right) = \alpha + x_i^{-k}\beta \tag{15}$$

in terms of Lemma 1. Denoting $\varphi(x_i)$ as

$$\begin{aligned}
\varphi(x_i) &= f_a(x_i)f_b(x_i) \bmod \left(x_i^k - 1\right) - f_a(x_i)f_b(x_i) \\
&= \left(r_0', r_1', \cdots, r_{k-2}', 0, -r_0', -r_1', \cdots, -r_{k-2}'\right) \cdot \\
&\quad \left(x_i^0, x_i^1, \cdots, x_i^{k-2}, x_i^{k-1}, x_i^k, x_i^{k+1}, \cdots, x_i^{2k-2}\right)^T,
\end{aligned} \tag{16}$$

where $r_\delta' = \sum_{\sigma = \delta + 1}^{k-1} a_\sigma b_{\tau = k - \sigma + \delta}$ for $\delta = \{0, 1, \cdots, k - 2\}$, it can be easily seem that

$$\beta = \left(x_i^{-k} - 1\right)^{-1} \varphi(x_i) \tag{17}$$

which is exactly the second term of $\alpha + \beta$. Noting that $\left\| \sum_{\sigma + \tau = 0 \bmod k} a_\sigma b_\tau \right\|_\infty \equiv p - 1 \bmod p$, thus our protocol is correct if $x_i > p$.

4 Security and Performance Analysis

Since the coefficients of polynomial $f_s(x)$ is independently and uniformly sampled from a finite field $\mathbb{F}_p$, the secret s is unconditionally secure if less than k shares are compromised [7]. For clarity, we interpret this property as a formal description.

Lemma 2. *The Shamir's secret sharing scheme is unconditionally secure, where the secret recovery advantage of any adversary $\mathcal{A}$ is*

$$\begin{aligned}
\mathbf{Adv}_{f_s}^{sr}(\mathcal{A}) &= \Pr\left[\mathcal{A}([s]_C) = s, s \in \mathbb{F}_p\right] \\
&= 1/p,
\end{aligned} \tag{18}$$

if $T \backslash C \not\subseteq A$ for any $C \in A$ where $T = \{1, 2, \cdots, n\}$.

It is obvious that because no information is exchanged when multiplying two shares $f_a(x_i)$ and $f_b(x_i)$ in our scheme, the secrets a and b are still unconditionally secure according to Lemma 2.

In order to prove the information-theory security of $[ab]_C$, we consider an experiment where the adversary runs $\mathcal{A}$ as a subroutine to recover ab.

$$\text{Experiment } \mathbf{Exp}^{sr}_{f_{ab}}(\mathcal{B})$$
$$[a]_T \overset{\$}{\leftarrow} \text{DIT}(a), [b]_T \overset{\$}{\leftarrow} \text{DIT}(b)$$
$$[ab]_T \leftarrow \text{EVL}\big([a]_T, [b]_T\big)$$
$$b \leftarrow \text{REC}\big([b]_{\bar{c}}\big)$$
$$a' \leftarrow \mathcal{A}\big([a]_C\big)$$
$$s = a'b$$
$$\text{If } s = ab \text{ return } 1, \text{ else return } 0$$

By contrary, our scheme is also unconditionally secure as below.

Theorem 2. The proposed multiplicative scheme is information-theoretically secure, where the advantage of any adversary $\mathcal{B}$ who expect to reveal ab is

$$\mathbf{Adv}^{sr}_{f_{ab}}(\mathcal{B}) = \Pr\big[\mathcal{B}([ab]_C) = ab, ab \in \mathbb{F}_p\big] \qquad (19)$$
$$= 1/p,$$

if $T\backslash C \not\subseteq A$ for any $C \in A$ where $T = \{1, 2, \cdots, n\}$.

Proof. The proof is straight-forward that if $\mathbf{Adv}^{sr}_{f_{ab}}(\mathcal{B}) > 1/p$, the probability that $\mathcal{B}$ recovers s where $s = ab$ is greater than $1/p$. Since b is plain for him, it implies that $\mathcal{A}$ can reveal a with an advantage $\mathbf{Adv}^{sr}_{f_s}(\mathcal{A}) > 1/p$ as well, which is a contradiction against Lemma 2.

The multiplicative secret sharing scheme in Sect. 3 also suggests that it achieves preferable performance with regard to parameter constrain, share size and communication burden. Three linear secret sharing protocols [25, 28, 30] are investigated for comparison as illustrated in Table 1.

Table 1. Comparison amongst multiplicative secret sharing of [25, 28, 30] and the proposed

Benchmarks	Multiplicative schemes			
	In [25]	In [28]	In [30]	The proposed
Share size (bits)	$n\lceil log_2 p \rceil$	$2n\lceil log_2 p \rceil$	$3n\lceil log_2 p \rceil$	$kn\lceil log_2 q \rceil$
Parameter constrain	$n > 2k - 2$	$n > dk$	\	\
Multiplication traffic load (bits)	$(2k-1)^2\lceil log_2 p \rceil$	0	$4k^2\lceil log_2 p \rceil$	0
Multiplication round	1	0	1	0

As we can see from the above table, each piece of share is $k\lceil log_2 q \rceil$-bits in our scheme to retain all information within α. Fortunately, the threshold parameters k and n are relatively inappreciable compared with p and q is only bounded with $q > p + n$, meaning that the share size of our scheme, which is sub-linearly proportional to that of [25, 28, 30], is reasonable for practical application. Concerning the number of participants who are engaged in secret multiplication, at least $2k - 1$ and dk members are necessary for the schemes of [25] and [28] to multiply d shares correctly. Though the scheme of [30] is capable of multiplying shared secrets only if k participants are involved, massive communications are inevitable since every participant has to collect $4k\lceil log_2 p\rceil$ pieces of information for correct operation. As for our scheme, although the condition of $n \geq k$ must be fulfilled to actualize Q2 access structure, no interaction will be necessary due to the locality of multiplication and the constrain on threshold parameters can be eliminate because each secret is only attached to one piece of shares for each participant.

The computational performance of our scheme is also commendable since the operation of formula (11) is trivial. Noting that, because every participant is provided with her unique identity x_i, she can initially compute $\left(x_i^k - 1\right)$ and $\left(x_i^{-k} - 1\right)^{-1}$ once for all. That is to say, when securely multiplying two pieces of shares, only two integer multiplications and subtractions along with one modular operation need to be executed.

5 Conclusion

In order to privately multiply shared secrets without interaction, a novel multiplicative scheme is presented based on (k, n)-threshold Shamir's secret sharing. The main idea behind the proposed scheme is that we can subtly eliminate the overflowed terms of two plainly multiplied polynomials with the help of convolution. It is proved that our method is capable of correctly retaining the product of secrets as the first coefficient of a $k - 1$ order polynomial with unconditional security. Compared with relevant schemes, our method is preferable since no communication and system parameter constrain are necessary.

Acknowledgments. This work is supported by the National Science Foundation of China P. R. (NSFC) under Grants 61703063, 61573076, 61663008; Chongqing Research Program of Basic Research and Frontier Technology under Grant CSTC2017jcyjAX0411; the Scientific Research Foundation for the Returned Overseas Chinese Scholars under Grant 2015-49; the Program for Excellent Talents of Chongqing Higher School under Grant 2014-18; Science and Technology Research Project of Chongqing Municipal Education Commission of China P. R. under Grants KJ1705139, KJ1600518, KJ1705121 and KJ1605002; Chongqing Municipal Social Livelihood Science and Technology Innovation Project under Grant CSTC2016shmszx30026; Urumqi Science and Technology Plan Project under Grant Y161320008.

References

1. El-Sayed, H., Sankar, S., Prasad, M., et al.: Edge of things: the big picture on the integration of edge, IoT and the cloud in a distributed computing environment. IEEE Access **6**(99), 1706–1717 (2018)
2. SabatÉ, M., Costa, M.A., Kozuma, K., et al.: Survey on various data integrity attacks in cloud environment and the solutions. In: International Conference on Circuits, Power and Computing Technologies, pp. 1076–1081. IEEE (2013)

3. Patel, K: Secure multiparty computation using secret sharing. In: International Conference on Signal Processing, Communication, Power and Embedded System, pp. 863–866. IEEE (2017)

4. Liu, J., Li, W., Karame, G.O., et al.: Scalable byzantine consensus via hardware-assisted secret sharing. IEEE Trans. Comput. 1 (2016)

5. Xie, M.M., Liao, X.F., Zhou, Q.: Generalized oblivious transfer protocol in distributed setting based on secret sharing. Comput. Eng. 40(3), 184–187 (2014)

6. Attasena, V., Darmont, J., Harbi, N.: Secret sharing for cloud data security: a survey. VLDB J. 2017(2), 1–25 (2017)

7. Shamir, A.: How to share a secret. Commun. ACM 22, 612–613 (1979)

8. Blakley, G.R.: Safeguarding cryptographic keys, p. 313. IEEE Computer Society (1979)

9. Brickell, E.F.: Some ideal secret sharing schemes. In: Quisquater, J.-J., Vandewalle, J. (eds.) EUROCRYPT 1989. LNCS, vol. 434, pp. 468–475. Springer, Heidelberg (1990). https://doi.org/10.1007/3-540-46885-4_45

10. Bertilsson, M., Ingemarsson, I.: A construction of practical secret sharing schemes using linear block codes. In: Seberry, J., Zheng, Y. (eds.) AUSCRYPT 1992. LNCS, vol. 718, pp. 67–79. Springer, Heidelberg (1993). https://doi.org/10.1007/3-540-57220-1_53

11. Van Dijk, M., Kevenaar, T., Schrijen, G.J., et al.: Improved constructions of secret sharing schemes by applying (λ, w)-decompositions. In: Proceedings of the IEEE International Symposium on Information Theory, p. 282. IEEE (2003)

12. Beimel, A., Weinreb, E.: Monotone circuits for monotone weighted threshold functions. Elsevier North-Holland, Inc. (2006)

13. Li, H., Liu, H.: Multi-access structure secret sharing schemes without dealer. Nat. Sci. J. Harbin Normal Univ. (2013)

14. Basit, A., Kumar, N.C., Venkaiah, V.C., et al.: Multi-stage multi-secret sharing scheme for hierarchical access structure. In: International Conference on Computing, Communication and Automation. IEEE (2017)

15. Ito, M., Saito, A., Nishizeki, T.: Secret sharing scheme realizing general access structure. Electron. Commun. Jpn. 72(9), 56–64 (2010)

16. Benaloh, J., Leichter, J.: Generalized secret sharing and monotone functions. In: Goldwasser, S. (ed.) CRYPTO 1988. LNCS, vol. 403, pp. 27–35. Springer, New York (1990). https://doi.org/10.1007/0-387-34799-2_3

17. Karchmer, M., Wigderson, A.: On span programs. In: IEEE Conference on Structure in Complexity Theory, pp. 102–111. IEEE Computer Society (1993)

18. Csirmaz, L.: The size of a share must be large. J. Cryptol. 10(4), 223–231 (1997)

19. Jhanwar, M.P., Safavi-Naini, R.: Unconditionally-secure robust secret sharing with minimum share size. In: Sadeghi, A.-R. (ed.) FC 2013. LNCS, vol. 7859, pp. 96–110. Springer, Heidelberg (2013). https://doi.org/10.1007/978-3-642-39884-1_9

20. Tran, T., Rahman, M., Bhuiyan, M.Z.A., et al.: Optimizing share size in efficient and robust secret sharing scheme for big data. IEEE Trans. Big Data PP(99), 1 (2017)

21. Boyle, E., Couteau, G., Gilboa, N., et al.: Homomorphic secret sharing: optimizations and applications. In: ACM SIGSAC Conference on Computer and Communications Security, pp. 2105–2122. ACM (2017)

22. Damgård, I., Fitzi, M., Kiltz, E., Nielsen, J.B., Toft, T.: Unconditionally secure constant-rounds multi-party computation for equality, comparison, bits and exponentiation. In: Halevi, S., Rabin, T. (eds.) TCC 2006. LNCS, vol. 3876, pp. 285–304. Springer, Heidelberg (2006). https://doi.org/10.1007/11681878_15

23. Nishide, T., Ohta, K.: Multiparty computation for interval, equality, and comparison without bit-decomposition protocol. In: Okamoto, T., Wang, X. (eds.) PKC 2007. LNCS, vol. 4450, pp. 343–360. Springer, Heidelberg (2007). https://doi.org/10.1007/978-3-540-71677-8_23

24. Boyle, E., Gilboa, N., Ishai, Y., et al.: Foundations of homomorphic secret sharing. In: 9th Innovations in Theoretical Computer Science Conference, vol. 21, pp. 1–20 (2018)

25. Gennaro, R., Rabin, M.O., Rabin, T.: Simplified VSS and fast-track multiparty computations with applications to threshold cryptography. In: Proceedings of the ACM Symposium on Principles of Distributed Computing, pp. 101–111. ACM Press (1998)

26. Ishai, Y., Kushilevitz, E.: Randomizing polynomials: a new representation with applications to round-efficient secure computation. In: Proceedings of the Symposium on Foundations of Computer Science, pp. 294–304. IEEE (2000)

27. Ishai, Y., Kushilevitz, E., Meldgaard, S., Orlandi, C., Paskin-Cherniavsky, A.: On the power of correlated randomness in secure computation. In: Sahai, A. (ed.) TCC 2013. LNCS, vol. 7785, pp. 600–620. Springer, Heidelberg (2013). https://doi.org/10.1007/978-3-642-36594-2_34

28. Barkol, O., Ishai, Y., Weinreb, E.: On d-multiplicative secret sharing. J. Cryptol. **23**(4), 580–593 (2010)

29. Yoshida, M., Obana, S.: Verifiably multiplicative secret sharing. In: International Conference on Information Theoretic Security, pp. 73–82 (2017)

30. Watanabe, T., Iwamura, K., Kaneda, K.: Secrecy multiplication based on a (k, n)-threshold secret-sharing scheme using only k servers. In: Park, J., Stojmenovic, I., Jeong, H., Yi, G. (eds.) Computer Science and its Applications. LNEE, vol. 330, pp. 107–112. Springer, Heidelberg (2015). https://doi.org/10.1007/978-3-662-45402-2_16

31. Blackburn, S.R., Burmester, M., Desmedt, Y., Wild, P.R.: Efficient multiplicative sharing schemes. In: Maurer, U. (ed.) EUROCRYPT 1996. LNCS, vol. 1070, pp. 107–118. Springer, Heidelberg (1996). https://doi.org/10.1007/3-540-68339-9_10

32. Wang, H., Lam, K.Y., Xiao, G.-Z., Zhao, H.: On multiplicative secret sharing schemes. In: Dawson, E.P., Clark, A., Boyd, C. (eds.) ACISP 2000. LNCS, vol. 1841, pp. 342–351. Springer, Heidelberg (2000). https://doi.org/10.1007/10718964_28

33. Jackson, W.A., Martin, K.M., O'Keefe, C.M.: Mutually trusted authority-free secret sharing schemes. J. Cryptol. **10**(4), 261–289 (1997)

34. Boyle, E., Gilboa, N., Ishai, Y.: Group-based secure computation: optimizing rounds, communication, and computation. In: Coron, J.-S., Nielsen, J.B. (eds.) EUROCRYPT 2017. LNCS, vol. 10211, pp. 163–193. Springer, Cham (2017). https://doi.org/10.1007/978-3-319-56614-6_6

35. Pilaram, H., Eghlidos, T.: An efficient lattice based multi-stage secret sharing scheme. IEEE Trans. Dependable Secure Comput. **14**(1), 2–8 (2017)

36. Shi, M., Guan, Y., Solé, P.: Two new families of two-weight codes. IEEE Trans. Inf. Theory **PP**(99), 1 (2017)

37. Gopinath, V., Bhuvaneswaran, R.S.: Design of ECC based secured cloud storage mechanism for transaction rich applications. CMC: Comput. Mater. Continua **57**(2), 341–352 (2018)

38. Zhong, J., Liu, Z., Xu, J.: Analysis and improvement of an efficient controlled quantum secure direct communication and authentication protocol. CMC: Comput. Mater. Continua **57**(3), 621–633 (2018)

Positioning Improvement Algorithm Based on LoRa Wireless Networks

Longyu Zhou, Ning Yang[✉], and Ke Zhang

University of Electronic Science and Technology of China,
Chengdu, Sichuan, China
ZhoulyFuture@outlook.com, yn@uestc.edu.in

Abstract. Internet of Things (IOT) has been maturing due to multiple applications and high demand, and LoRa technology is hotter and hotter in this area. This paper explains an optimization of positioning accuracy within a certain distance, which is reflected in data processing. This technology is used to update model which is used AHP (The analytic hierarchy process) algorithm, and used data fitting to process received power data, and used GA (Genetic Algorithm) algorithm to iterative. This technology is suitable for long-distance communication positioning. In this paper, it is explained AHP (The analytic hierarchy process) algorithm, data fitting, and GA (Genetic Algorithm) algorithm. The position accuracy can be better by approximately 50% than these algorithms are not used. Finally, the kind of thinking can be used as a reference for the accuracy of long-distance positioning.

Keywords: IOT · LoRa position · The analytic hierarchy process · Genetic algorithm

1 Introduction

Nowadays, due to low-power technology and the advantages of long-distance communication for LoRa [1], the device has been gradually used for outdoor positioning in smart cities and agriculture. The LoRa uses spread spectrum modulation technology and forward correction technology. Compared with traditional OOK (On-Off Keying) modulation techniques, this technology not only expands the transmission range, but also improves the robustness of the communication. The work of data transmission is processed by changing the Spreading Factor (SF) and error correction rate.

The accuracy about positioning is always not ideal, because the accuracy depends on many irresistible elements, such as terrain. Therefore, in the case of encountering obstacles or in a harsh environment, a large amount of power consumption is generated. So the accuracy problem is the focus of attention. There are many positioning algorithms, mainly based on Time Difference of Arrival (TDOA) and Received Strength Signal Indirection (RSSI). TDOA requires strict time synchronization. Nowadays, the positioning technology achieves an accuracy of several hundred meters in the long distance of about 2 km. The TDOA algorithm uses waves of different rates to measure the time difference of arrival, so synchronization is required. For positioning, different values may be received due to interference from obstacles during

© Springer Nature Switzerland AG 2019
X. Sun et al. (Eds.): ICAIS 2019, LNCS 11634, pp. 188–198, 2019.
https://doi.org/10.1007/978-3-030-24271-8_17

transmission, which may cause great interference in receiving correct data. Different paths of data transmission will produce different errors, it is necessary to set a certain transmission interval or a timer to solve [2]. Insufficient power will also cause certain errors, so battery detection devices are needed to detect power.

This paper proposes a scheme that an optimization of precision in data processing. Firstly, according to the RSSI model, gateways receives power values from the unknown node. Obviously, the power values are not all accepted due to the receipt of different values. Secondly, Data Fitting method is used to remove highly deviated power values under the largest residual value. The distance between unknown node and gateway is obtained by Updated Received Signal Strength Indication (RSSI) model in this paper. Finally, in order to improve the positioning accuracy, this paper uses Genetic Algorithm (GA) to get a better coordinate value than before.

2 Overall System Design

LoRa devices are usually used in the outdoor positioning [3], the positioning algorithm is very important. Before explaining the algorithm, we introduce the overall system design. The design consists of end-nodes, gateway and server. And we use the trilateral positioning algorithm to get the distance between unknown node and the gateways (Fig. 1).

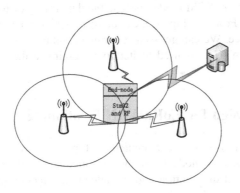

Fig. 1. The overall system consists of one end-node, three gateways and a server. End-node receives the power value from three gateways and sends power values to server.

2.1 End-Node

The end-node consists a STM32L053 microcontroller and a RF. They are connected through the Serial Peripheral Interface (SPI) interface. The end-node is also named unknown node, the STM32L053 microcontroller sends some instructions to RF module, and the RF module send a requested message to gateways so that receive the power value from gateways. The RF module includes the antenna, for the antenna, the antenna gain [4] is proportional to the antenna efficiency, and the antenna gain is proportional to the length of antenna. so negative gain maybe produced after using this logarithm. The antenna gain is as follows:

$$P_{Gain} = 10 * \log \frac{2 * L}{\lambda_0} \tag{1}$$

Where L is the length of the antenna, λ_0 is the central working wavelength.

2.2 Gateway

For gateways, we set the clock reception period and also set the period of receiving power values. The function of gateway is routing and forwarding the power values to the server. Because of the usefulness of the gateways, the distance of communication among the end-nodes can achieve more than about 2–3 km. The gateways play vital roles. The gateway receives requested messages from the end-node and send the information confirmed in return.

The RSSI model is used to calculate the measuring distance between the unknown node and the three gateways. And the RSSI model is used to compute the received power values of unknown node. In current RSSI model, The factor of impacting environment ξ is obeyed Normal distribution. In this paper, the Analytic Hierarchy Process (AHP) is used to improve the RSSI model. This algorithm redefines the factor, the impacting factors are divided into: weather, building, and ground environment. After updating the current RSSI model, we use the data fitting method to remove some terrible power values. From the Fig. 1, it can be seen that we use the trilateral algorithm to compute the distance. We can get some coordinate values through above algorithm. the Genetic Algorithm (GA) is used to iteratively optimize the coordinate values to obtain better values.

3 Algorithm Design for LoRaWAN Positioning

The RSSI model is based on the attenuation of power and distance between the gateways and the unknown node based on the attenuation of power. The standard deviation of the Normal distribution and the attenuation factors in different environment are also different, as shown in Table 1.

Table 1. The attenuation factors and standard deviation values in different environment

Environments	Category	
	Attenuation factors	Standard deviation
Laboratory	1.5–2.2	2.35–3.47
Playground	2.6–3.5	1.65–4.03
Tar road	3.2–3.6	2.95–4.45

The paper explains that the positioning is in a triangle with a side length of 100 m. For example, the gateway nodes are placed at three vertices of the triangle and the unknown node is placed one point of the area. The updated RSSI model and trilateral positioning algorithm are used, the algorithm is simulated with an accuracy of about 10 m.

The algorithm consists of several phases, as shown in Fig. 2.

Fig. 2. Algorithm structure consists above three steps, updated model focus on the impacting factor, and data fitting method focus on power values, and optimization method focus on accuracy.

3.1 Pretreatment

The relationship between the distance and the value of power is expressed through the original RSSI power attenuation model, as shown in Fig. 3.

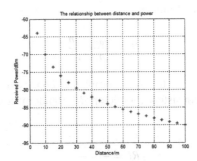

Fig. 3. The relationship between the distance and the power values, we can see that the received power value from gateway decrease as the distance increases.

The paper uses the analytic hierarchy process (AHP) [6] to update the model. The specific process is as follows.

- Problem analysis.
- Constructing judgment matrix.
- Hierarchical single sorting and consistency check.

Firstly, the problem is organized and is clear, and the complex problem is decomposed into the components of the element. The Gaussian distribution variable ξ is redefined, and the proposed problem is divided into three levels.

- The highest layer: the target of the analysis problem, that is the evaluation of signal transmission.
- The middle layer: containing some influence factors. Such as weather, buildings, ground environment.
- The bottom layer: Selecting the corresponding RSSI model.

Secondly, the hierarchy reflects the relationship between the factors. the proportions of the indicators in the target measurement are not the same, and a certain proportion in the minds of policy makers. There are n indicators that needs to be evaluated $A_1, A_2 \cdots A_n$ and their scores are w_i. If they are compared two by two, the ratios will form $n * n$ matrix. The matrix is as follows.

$$A = \begin{bmatrix} w1/w1 & w1/w2 & \cdots & w1/wn \\ w2/w1 & w2/w2 & \cdots & w2/wn \\ \cdots & \cdots & \cdots & \cdots \\ wn/w1 & wn/w2 & \cdots & wn/wn \end{bmatrix}$$

According to the theory of the matrix, A has a unique non-zero maximum eigenvalue $\lambda_{\max} = n$.

Finally, in order to avoid large errors, it is necessary to check the consistency of the matrix. The degree of inconsistency of matrix A measures through the value $\lambda - n$. Consistency indication is as follows.

$$CI = \frac{\lambda_{\max} - n}{n - 1} \tag{2}$$

If the CI equals to zero, so matrix A is completely consistent. To measure the value CI, introduce a random consistency indictor RI. Random consistency indictor is as follows.

$$RI = \frac{\lambda'_m - n}{n - 1} \tag{3}$$

Where λ'_m is the average value of the λ_m. Considering that the deviation of consistency maybe caused by random reasons, it is also necessary to compare CI and RI to obtain the test coefficient CR.

$$CR = \frac{CI}{RI} \tag{4}$$

If $CR < 0.1$, the matrix is considered to pass the consistency test, vice versa.

3.2 Updated Model

According to the interpretation [6] of the analytic hierarchy process (AHP). The impact factor can evaluate, as shown in Fig. 4.

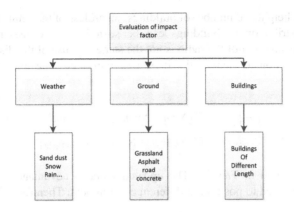

Fig. 4. Chromatographic analysis table displays that the impacting factors are different, including weather, ground and buildings.

According to the requirements of the analytic hierarchy process (AHP), we can get the satisfied feature vector from the 3.1 section. The feature vector is usually set by person, and we can test from formula (2), (3), (4) and matrix A. So we select the feature vector $B = [0.6, 0.3, 0.1]$. This vector satisfies the consistency test.

The next work is to design the three above different algorithms for three influencing factors.

I. Weather Influencing Factors
The densities of the dust, rain, snow, and fog are set to M_i, the impact model for this effect is as follows.

$$P_{weather} = k * M_i * \log(d) \ i = 1, 2, 3, 4 \tag{5}$$

Where k is the density's coefficient, M_i is the density of the weather i, d is the distance. According to Roman Odarchenko [5], k is proportional to the reciprocal of T^4, T is absolute temperature.

II. Ground Influencing Factors
According to Roman Odarchenko [5], for the radio signal transmission, different ground environments have different levels of impact. Therefore, the interference coefficients of grassland, asphalt road and concrete are set to $\gamma = [0.26, 0.3, 0.2]$, the impact model is as follows.

$$P_{ground} = \gamma_i * \log(d) \ i = 1, 2, 3 \tag{6}$$

Where γ_i is the influence factor, from the above formula, it can be concluded that the different ground interference on information transmission is nearly.

III. Building Influencing Factors
The influence of the buildings mainly reflects in height and density. For the consideration of the height and density, we use the Normal distribution to quantify it.

According to the height and number of buildings, regardless of the central cities such as Beijing. The distribution of buildings can be seen it as a Gaussian distribution. However, the transmission of the radio is not the same because of the distance. We use the piecewise function to analyze the impact of buildings. The impact model is as follows.

$$P_{building} = \begin{cases} \frac{1}{\sqrt{2\pi}\delta} * e^{-\frac{x^2}{2\delta^2}} (Num < Num_{max}, \delta = (rand() + 1) * 2) \\ \frac{1}{\sqrt{2\pi}\delta} * e^{-\frac{x^2}{2\delta^2}} (Num >= Num_{max}, \delta = \delta_{min}) \end{cases} \tag{7}$$

Where δ be found in Table 1. The updated model's advantage is that different parameters can be used to position in different environment. Therefore, the model is as follows.

$$P_L(d) = P_L(d_0) + P_{Gain} - 10 * n * \log\frac{d}{d_0} - \chi \tag{8}$$

Where $\chi = \omega_1 * P_{weather} + \omega_2 * P_{floor} + \omega_3 * P_{building}$, ω_1, ω_2, ω_3 consists of vector B, d_0 is reference distance.

3.3 Data Fitting

This section focuses on the content of data fitting. The received power values are divided into several groups. In each process of received data from gateways, because the received data from gateways are statistically independent and each transmission is uncertain. So there will definitely be some terrible power values. We should remove the data that is obviously unsatisfied. There are two methods to solve, one is Data Fitting and other is Confidence level. We firstly find a formula. The formula can make the variance minimum than another formula. We select the logarithmic function as the ideal formula by comparing. Secondly, we use Excel software to fit each set of data and remove the RSSI value with relatively large residuals. This step can increase the credibility of the data. It can also be represented by the Confidence level of the data. Since the level of significant of the confidence level α is specified by human, and it is

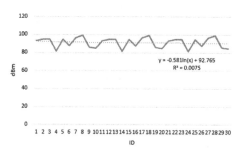

Fig. 5. This figure displays that some power values are farther than another values, these values are not satisfied and they can impact the accuracy of the distance.

not more intuitive than Data Fitting, so Fig. 5 displays that Data Fitting method is adopted.

3.4   Iterative Optimization

This Section [10] introduces the genetic algorithm [7] to iteratively optimize the target coordinates, this algorithm can solve the local optimal problem. This paper sets the result of the last iteration as the target value of the next iteration. Because of complex execution process, the number of external loop must be set. The steps are shown in Fig. 6 as follows.

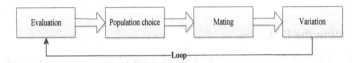

Fig. 6. Algorithm design consists four steps, the evaluation focus on getting better values than before, the population choice focus on getting serval sets of received power values from gateways, the mating focus on mixing power values, the variation focus on removing terrible values.

4   Test and Results

First, the location [11] of the gateway will be analyzed, we can place any position. Secondly, the end-node is placed any area within communication range. Finally, the server will receive the power values from the end-node so that it can process using proposed algorithm. For example, three gateways were placed at three vertices of a triangle, and an unknown node was placed at the hypotenuse. On the day of the test, the temperature is 26° and it is foggy. The software is MATLAB R2015b, the computer's memory is 4G, and the processor is core i5.

4.1   Power Values

Figure 7 displays the RSSI received power values from the gateway. We can also get distance values through the relationship of coordinate among the gateways and end-node. The orange line is the ideal power value. It can be found from the figure that some values are far from the orange line and such values should be kick off. Under normal circumstance, the received power values are near the orange line. However, we cannot get all the satisfied power values due to some other factors, so the values are far from the dotted line.

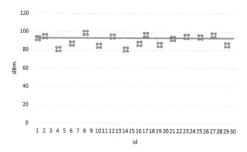

Fig. 7. The power values with blue dots are actual values, we can see that these values are not in the orange line. (Color figure online)

4.2 Computing the Distances

The goal [12, 13] of this step is to detect and remove potential outliers and get the distances among gateways and end-node. First, we should calculate the residual of each value, and we compute the residual of every power value. We set a threshold of the residual. The values what are more than the threshold are named outliers, and vice versa. The outliers are removed through Excel software. In other words, it is not possible directly to use the received power values for the next iterative process. Figure 8 shows the distribution after using the data fitting method. We can use formula (1), (5), (6), (7), (8) to compute the distance among the gateways and end-node. And then we can use the distance to compute the coordinate of unknown node by the trilateral positioning algorithm and centroid algorithm.

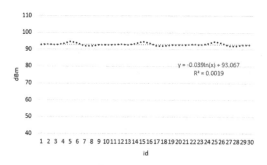

Fig. 8. We test thirty data and the data distribution after data fitting is already displayed, we can see that the power values are near to the blue line, so we can use these values to compute the distances. (Color figure online)

4.3 Iterative Processing

Before describing the iteration [8], we firstly discuss some explanations. Due to the characteristics of the genetic algorithm, we set the value of previous iteration is the target of the next iteration, because the algorithm can only approach the actual coordinate value. It is possible to improve the accuracy of the positioning. We use genetic algorithm to do iterative process, and whether the iterative loop stops or not is determined the frequency of cycle. Due to the complexity of the genetic algorithm [9], the frequency of cycle should not be more than twenty [15, 16]. It does not increase the accuracy because of the high frequency. The comparison of accuracy distribution is shown in the Fig. 9.

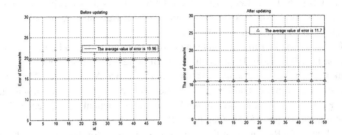

Fig. 9. Abscissa stands for the numbers of iteration (the step size is 5), Vertical coordinate stands for the errors of the distance compared with the actual coordinate. We can see that the accuracy is obvious improved after improving positioning algorithm.

5 Conclusions and Future Work

This paper mainly describes the wireless positioning design to use LoRa module in the IOT system. The main purpose is to provide some ideas about algorithm for long-distance positioning. Of course, this design can also apply to long-distance positioning. The main stress of this design is on the server, which reduces the computational pressure of the LoRa terminal [14, 15]. First, we redefine the original model to improve the model's augmentation, and then define the maximum threshold of the residual to optimize the data, which is easy to implement algorithm. The iterative algorithm is used to approaching the ideal value. In general, the results calculated using the iterative algorithm are better.

There must be new ideas coming up in the future. For future work, it is necessary to apply the current algorithm to the real-time position tracking. Efficiency is a factor that to be considered for real-time tracking. On the one hand, optimizing bases on hardware. For the end-nodes, the spreading spectrum coding can improve the stability of the data, but there may loss packets. The problem should be to avoid for the real-time positioning, because data needs to be token notes and processed in real-time. On the other hand, in terms of communication, it is necessary to improve the accuracy of transmission, especially for long-distance communication. In terms of algorithm, it is necessary to reduce the complexity of the algorithm, which is good for real-time positioning. Another solution is to embed the algorithm into the hardware, which speeds up data processing. It is a good suggestion to implement a real-time tracking scheme for LoRa.

Acknowledgment. This work was supported in part by the National Natural Science Foundation of China under Grant 61731006.

References

1. Fargas, B.C., Petersen, M.N.: GPS-free geolocation using LoRa in low-power WANs. In: Global Internet of Things Summit, pp. 1–6. IEEE (2017)
2. Podevijn, N., Plets, D., Trogh, J., et al.: TDoA-based outdoor positioning with tracking algorithm in a public LoRa network (2018)
3. Lam, K.H., Cheung, C.C., Lee, W.C.: New RSSI-based LoRa localization algorithms for very noisy outdoor environment. In: Computer Software and Applications Conference, pp. 794–799. IEEE Computer Society (2018)
4. Benner, E., Sesay, A.B.: Effects of antenna height, antenna gain, and pattern downtilting for cellular mobile radio. IEEE Trans. Veh. Technol. **45**(2), 217–224 (1996)
5. Odarchenko, R., Dyka, N., Konakhovych, G., Abakumova, A., Vergeles, D.: Estimation and reduction of the climatic conditions influence on the radio signal propagation in the troposphere. In: 2017 4th International Scientific-Practical Conference Problems of Infocommunications, pp. 45–48, October 2017
6. Yang, X., Wang, Y.: Research on the allocation of missile combat missions based on AHP and genetic algorithm. Comput. Digit. Eng. (2018)
7. Maulik, U., Bandyopadhyay, S.: Genetic algorithm-based clustering technique. Pattern Recognit. **33**(9), 1455–1465 (2000)
8. Juang, C.F.: A hybrid of genetic algorithm and particle swarm optimization for recurrent network design. IEEE Trans. Syst. Man Cybern. Part B Cybern. A Publ. IEEE Syst. Man Cybern. Soc. **34**(2), 997–1006 (2004)
9. Su, J., Sheng, Z., Xie, L., Li, G., Liu, A.X.: Fast splitting based tag identification algorithm for anti-collision in UHF RFID system. IEEE Trans. Commun. (2018). https://doi.org/10.1109/tcomm.2018.2884001
10. Su, J., Sheng, Z., Leung, V.C.M., Chen, Y.: Energy efficient tag identification algorithms for RFID: survey, motivation and new design. IEEE Wirel. Commun. (2018)
11. Su, J., Xie, L., Yang, Y., Han, Y., Wen, G.: A collision arbitration protocol based on specific selection function. Chin. J. Electron. **26**(4), 864–870 (2017)
12. Su, J., Hong, D., Tang, J., Chen, H.: An efficient anti-collision algorithm based on improved collision detection scheme. IEICE Trans. Commun. **E99-B**(2), 465–469 (2016)
13. Su, J., Zhao, X., Luo, Z., Chen, H.: Q-value fine-grained adjustment based RFID anti-collision algorithm. IEICE Trans. Commun. **E99-B**(7), 1593–1598 (2016)
14. Jian, S., Wen, G., Hong, D.: A new RFID anti-collision algorithm based on the Q-ary search scheme. Chin. J. Electron. **24**(4), 679–683 (2015)
15. Meng, R., Rice, S.G., Wang, J., Sun, X.: A fusion steganographic algorithm based on faster R-CNN. CMC: Comput. Mater. Continua **55**(1), 001–016 (2018)
16. Cui, J., Zhang, Y., Cai, Z., Liu, A., Li, Y.: Securing display path for security-sensitive applications on mobile devices. CMC: Comput. Mater. Continua **55**(1), 017–035 (2018)

Time-Aware and Energy Efficient Data Collection Mechanism for Duty-Cycled Wireless Sensor Networks

Zhiqiang Ruan[1,2(✉)], Haibo Luo[1,2], and Ge Xu[1]

[1] Minjiang University, Fuzhou 350108, China
rzq_911@163.com, robhappy@qq.com, xuge@pku.edu.cn
[2] Digital Fujian IoT Laboratory of Intelligent Production, Fuzhou 350108, China

Abstract. Wireless sensor networks (WSNs) are composed of huge amount of battery powered sensor nodes, which usually adopt sleep strategy to save energy and prolong network lifetime. Although appealing, such network faces the problem of data availability when nodes switch to the sleep mode. One alternative is to replicate data from the sleep sensor to other active nodes before hibernation. We explore reliable data replication over Named Data Networking (NDN) architecture and propose DSGC, an efficient Data Synchronization protocol for duty-cycled WSNs by integrating node Grouping knowledge and in-network Caching capabilities. In particular, sensors are organized into different groups according to their respective regions, through name-based data synchronization mechanism, we ensure that the newly updated shared data are always accessible within each group and can be retrieved through the active nodes. We also consider packet loss and node failures that happen frequently in WSNs. Simulation results verify that DSGC can guarantee data availability nearly 100% under different network conditions with negligible overhead.

Keywords: Wireless sensor network · Sleeping mechanism · Data collection · Energy efficiency

1 Introduction

Wireless sensor networks (WSNs) often include a lot of battery-supplied sensor nodes to be continuous monitor the environment over several months or years. Nodes can apply sleep scheduling strategy periodically, by shutting down the radio and switching to an ultra-low power state, to conserve energy and prolong network lifetime. The network vision in this mode is referred to as duty-cycled WSNs (DC-WSNs hereafter) [1, 2].

In DC-WSNs, if a node in the delivery path is dormant, the packet has to be buffered on the current node until the next hop resumes, which inevitably increase the time delay. In addition, the duration of active/sleep nodes have different effects on the network, e.g., increasing the sleep time of a sensor will save more energy for that node while incur a larger time delay for the data receiver and vice versa. Although the researchers have devoted to dynamically adjusting the duty cycle to make a better

© Springer Nature Switzerland AG 2019
X. Sun et al. (Eds.): ICAIS 2019, LNCS 11634, pp. 199–210, 2019.
https://doi.org/10.1007/978-3-030-24271-8_18

tradeoff between energy consumption and time delay [3–5], they cannot guarantee 100% of data availability over the long run of the system.

We investigate the resilient data availability problem in DC-WSNs over Named Data Networking (NDN) paradigm [6]. Inherited by increasing mentioned Information Centric Networking (ICN) or Content-centric Networks (CCN), NDN addresses scalable data distribution, security, and mobility problems exist in current Internet. It shifts the network communication model from host-centric to data-centric, and makes immutable data with hierarchical names.

CoCa [7] is the first distributed cooperative data caching scheme in the context of NDN to handle data availability in DC-WSN. Unfortunately, this work emphasizes best-effort caching but not reliable data replication, thus it provides data availability only for some specific applications. VectorSync [8] classified each data with a unique prefix and a growing digital number, which facilitates the use of a state vector to express reachable path on the shared dataset in an innovative way. However, it enforces all group members to always keep online to agree with dataset synchronization, and thus introduces extra energy and communication time. Instead of associating a unique identifier to each packet in [9], DSGC represents each data object by a two-dimensional array consists of sensor name and data serial number. DSGC also utilizes NDN's in-network caching and Interest aggregation to lower data transmission. Moreover, multipath forwarding protocol is used to avoid node failures, and collision avoidance mechanism is employed to reduce energy consumption.

2 Models and Design Goals

To illustrate the applications of WSN and benefits of NDN, we consider the representative use cases in the buildings such as hotel room safety detection, smart homes and/or personal health and wellness. In these applications, there are a number of battery-powered wireless sensors/devices operate on monitoring the temperature, humidity, solar, health level conditions in a room. For energy-saving purposes, sensors switch to sleep mode periodically. We assume that sensors in the same room and adjacent rooms can directly communicate with each other via WiFi channel, and sensor nodes may fail due to various reasons. To handle these cases, we apply multipath forwarding to avoid single point of failure and maintain seamless connection for the network, as shown in Fig. 1, where the solid arrow is the best path or shortest path, and the dotted arrow is an alternative path or semi-best path enroute to the sink.

In DSGC, sensors are divided into various groups according to their room numbers, for simplicity, we use term room and group interchangeably in the following. Figure 1 shows n groups of sensors and each group has 6 sensors. The sensors in group 1 can directly communicate to all sensors in group 1, 2 and m ($m < n$). Sensors generate sensed data every 5 s. There is a sink node located in the n-th group and it is responsible for gathering sensed data from all groups in the building every 10 min. Data are transmitted hop by hop from sensors to the sink node [10–13].

Data synchronization (DS) is a basic requirement for a large number of distributed applications, including IP networks, WSN, and NDN. DSGC performs DS within each

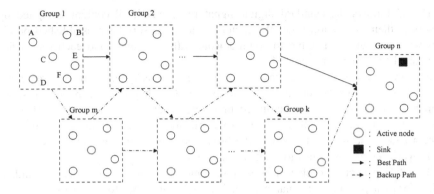

Fig. 1. Network model.

group rather than the entire WSN, because it can greatly reduce the involved replicated data and thus save a lot of energy. There are three design goals for DSGC:

(1) Shared namespace description: Group communication requires a shared namespace for members to information interaction for DS. A namespace for data should be received and identified by all other members in a group.

(2) Dataset representation: Each sensor in the DS group holds a local set of shared dataset with others, it also maintain a state list of the local dataset, which maps to the corresponding dataset namespace. A node can compare its dataset status with others to determine which part of data that needs to be updated.

(3) Synchronous mechanism: at a given time, each sensor may produce new data and add to its shared dataset, leading to dataset and/or status difference with others. The DS mechanism has to announce other sensors about dataset and/or state update and trigger a certain module to synchronize dataset status, so that the group has an overall agreed dataset state.

3 DSGC Design

NDN employs the hierarchical structure for naming convention with semantically meaning, for instance, "Apollo Hotel" is named "/hotel/fuzhou/apollo", associating the affiliation similar to DNS. Thus, each group in WSN can be uniquely identified by naming with "building name + room number", e.g., room/group 8821 is named "/hotel/fuzhou/apollo/8821". Similar to [8], each node names the generated data by a unique name and an increasing integer, namely, "sensor name + data serial number". Each sensor is distributed with a unique identifier (e.g. $A \sim F$) to indicate its group affiliation and endued a unique name, represented by "group name + sensor ID". e.g., sensor B is named "/hotel/fuzhou/apollo/8821/B", and the latest data is "/hotel/fuzhou/apollo/8821/B/500". One salient feature of such naming convention is that NDN considers all objects as name prefixes regardless of node heterogeneity, enables the application of DSGC to the Internet of Things (IoT).

DSGC follows the standard digital signature of NDN, all content is signed by sensors at their generation time. We assume that all sensors have established public keys with each group member to communicate with each other and each sensor has established trust relationships with the sink.

To facilitate group communication, each group is assigned with a name prefix "/hotel/fuzhou/apollo/<group ID>", if no packet loss happens, each sensor sends Interests or Data via one-hop multicast under its group namespace, and it also can receive the content from all the other group members. The content is sent through multicast face, the second layer uses the broadcast address to send frames, while the third layer uses group names to multicast and filter packets.

The data packet of each sensor is monotonically increased by a serial number, which forms a part of entire namespace. We use a State Vector (SV) to record the dataset status of its group members. The SV is a pair of [sensor ID: serial number], where the serial number represents the latest data the owner sensor generated until the last synchronization. The SV allows group members to explicitly list data producer and serial number, so that a sensor can distinguish each item in the list, which avoids the need of group membership management. Take an example of the SV owned by sensor B in room 8821, as shown in Fig. 2, where sensor B has the dataset of itself and A, C, D, E, suppose sensor F is in the sleep mode. The least data sensor B knows about itself and, A, C, D, E is 502, 500, 503, 504, and 503, respectively. It must be noted that a node has a SV of the dataset does not mean that it has captured all the packets in the dataset, it is a separate problem to discuss whether fetch a packet or not and when to fetch it.

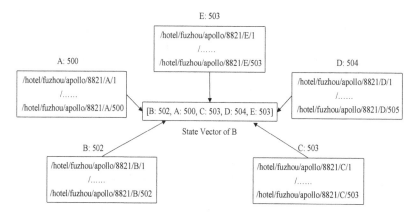

Fig. 2. State vector of sensor B.

The initiator of the synchronization starts the DS process, while other active group members act as responders. Different sensors could have different SV when knowing that the group's dataset have not been synchronized yet. In view of this, the DS includes two steps. First, the initiator sends a sync packet, namely, "/[group-name]/sync/[initiator-id]/[initiator-SV]". After receiving the initiator's latest SV in the sync packet, other active sensors compare its own SV with the initiator's, if there are new components in the initiator's SV, it merges two SVs into a new one and update its own SV with it. Second, each responder adds all new items into PIT and later sends them to get these new data.

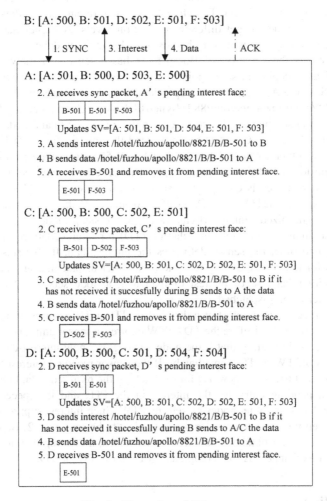

Fig. 3. Illustration of DS process.

In fact, there is another problem needs to be serious considered. That is, how does the initiator know that all its data has been successfully replicated before switching to the sleep mode? To address this problem, at least one responder needs to inform the initiator that it has fetched all the missing data by constructing an ACK packet, which consists of "/[group name]/ACK/[initiator-id]/[initiator-SV]/[responder-id]", and send to the initiator. The initiator can go to sleep when the first ACK received, or it can wait a little longer until receives acknowledgment messages from more responders.

Note that, each active node does not possess all data declared by the group, and after how many ACK packets are received before the initiator goes to sleep has no impact on data availability. The sink can successfully fetch all data, as long as the union of each active sensor's local dataset has complete data of the group, incorporating the sleeping sensor's data. Therefore, DSGC can dynamically adjust the selection of replicating nodes to get different replication levels. A higher data reliability requires more data migrations, but at the cost of a longer time delay.

Figure 3 shows the DS process. Room 8821 has 6 sensors, namely A ~ F. Suppose E and F are sleeping at some point, A, B, C and D are active. Sensor B is the initiator of DS, while A, C and D are responders. B first multicasts sync packet in the group, named "/hotel/fuzhou/apollo/8821/sync/B/[B-SV]". Upon receiving B's Interest packet, A, C and D add pending interest faces on the missing data and update their SVs correspondingly. Later, A, C and D begin to send the Interest for 'B-501'. Sensor B sends back data to them, whom delete Interest for 'B-501' from their pending Interest faces and begin to fetch the next missing data. This process is repeated until A, C, or D's pending Interest face is empty, at least one of them sends an ACK packet: i.e., "/hotel/fuzhou/apollo/8821/ACK/A/[A-SV]/B", to inform B that their data have been successfully synchronized. Finally, B can switch to the sleep mode.

Each sensor maintains a timer of delaying (TD) for interest/data pairs, if TD ran over the specified time, the sensor deliveries the interest/data. It also sets a timer of waiting (TW) for the corresponding reception data after dispatching an interest; if the TW expires either because of interest or data lost, a node sets a TD for the new generated packet to be dispatched.

If a sensor receives an interest or a data before TD or TW expires, it needs to take corresponding actions. (1) Before the TD or TW expires, a sensor announces an interest from other sensors, indicating that some node has begun a new interest-data exchange process, it calls off TW or TD immediately. If the sensor received interest for the data from other nodes, it triggers a new TD for dispatching the required data. Otherwise, the node creates a pending entry for the interest in the PIT, and it expects to receive corresponding data from other nodes by setting a TW. Such interest suppression avoids sensors interested the same interest for the same data to be sent out. (2) Before the TD or TW expires, a sensor obtains a data from other nodes, indicating that another round of request-data exchange has just completed, it calls off TW or TD.

4   Evaluation

We choose a single group of sensors with sizes ranges from 6 to 22, sensors adopt IEEE 802.15.4 2.4 GHz to communication with each other. The packet sizes of Interest and Data are 640 bytes and 216 bytes, respectively. The active sensors periodically publish data per 5 s. Each simulation lasts 15 min for sensors to generate enough DS rounds and data packets. Packet loss is simulated by a predefined error rate on the received packets. Every 10 s, 30% ~ 50% of sensors in the group take turns to sleep based on predefined patterns. The initiator enters the sleeping mode after receiving the first ACK packets. When a sensor wakes up, it works for 20 s and then returns to sleep again (15 s for regular operating, the remaining time for synchronizing data).

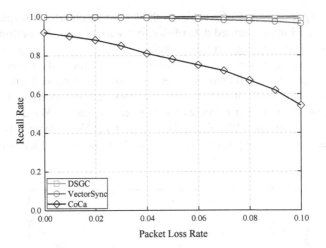

Fig. 4. Recall rate.

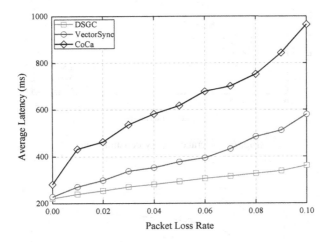

Fig. 5. Average response time

We examine DSGC under different TD threshold, group size, and packet loss rate, and compare DSGC with CoCa [7] and VectorSync [8]. We define recall rate (RR) as the number of Data available in all active sensors divides all generated Data in the group; we also define synchronization time (ST) as the time a sensor spends on migrating data before switching to sleep mode, and the corresponding synchronization time overhead (STO) which represents the ratio of ST account for a sensor's whole working time. For default, we set TW = 50 ms, group size = 10, and TD = 45 ms.

Figure 4 investigates the recall rate under different packet loss rate of all three schemes. We can see that DSGC achieves the highest recall rate, even with a larger packet loss rate of 10%, it still has nearly 100% of RR, indicating that our mechanism can immune to packet loss. CoCa achieves the lowest recall rate as it selects cooperating nodes for caching the sensed data of sleeping sensors at the best-effort, regardless of the sensors' residual energy and duty cycle.

Figure 5 shows that the average latency of three methods increase with the increases of packet loss rate, if there is no sensor failure in the network and the collision probability is negligible, greater value of packet loss rate will increase the number of packet retransmissions, which increases the average time delay. We also observe that DSGC can further improve retrieval speed than CoCa and VectorSync, this is attributed to the DS mechanism we applied to improve the data exchange efficiency.

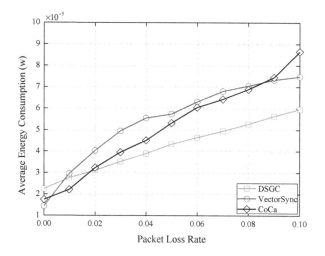

Fig. 6. Average energy consumption

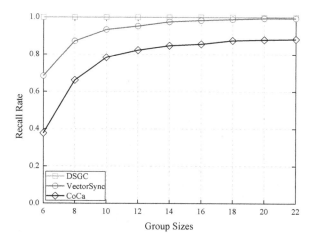

Fig. 7. Recall rate vs. group sizes

Figure 6 shows that the average energy consumption of all three mechanisms increases as packet loss rate increases, and energy consumption of our proposed mechanism increase slower than that of CoCa and VectorSync when packet loss rate larger than 1%. This is because, DSGC take advantage of NDN's Interest aggregation and content caching to lower packet transmissions, and adopts techniques for collision prevention, thus reduce energy consumption in a wireless environment.

Figure 7 shows RR for different group sizes, where TW = 50 ms, TD = 60 ms, and packet loss = 0%. RR in DSGC maintains relatively stable within the range between 99.91% and 100% under different group sizes, this is because, DSGC perform DS in the group, data transmission is restricted within the group, thus, it incurs a much higher RR than CoCa. For VectorSync, it has to keep a certain number of sensors online to synchronize data, a larger group sizes, a better RR achieves.

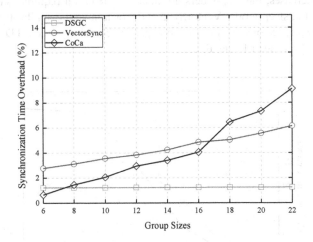

Fig. 8. Synchronization time overhead vs. group sizes

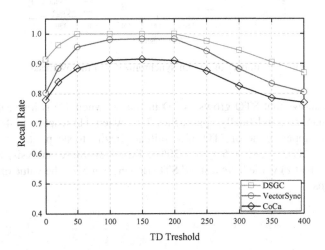

Fig. 9. Impact of TD on recall rate

Figure 8 shows that STO in DSGC basically keeps constant at 1.25%, the reason is, in the DC-WSN, if a responder is not the newly wake-up sensor, the size of its pending Interest face is small and not affected by group size, thus it can fetch all missing data within a short time, resulting in a small and stable STO. Furthermore, the number of sensors and data packets in VectorSync is greater than DSGC, thus the STO of data packets increases significantly given the same packet loss rate.

Figure 9 investigates RR under different TD values, as we can see that when TD is less than 20 ms, RR is unable to achieve 100%, this is due to the fact that a lot of packets collision occurs in the group, and the time of replicating a packet exceeds its maximum limitation; when TD is larger than 20 ms but less than 200 ms, RR is almost reaches 100% because the larger the TD, the lower the collision possibility; however, when TD keeps growing, RR begins to drop again, as the exchange periodicity of Interest/Data increases, the responders are unable to fetch all required data before the initiator enters the sleep mode. VectorSync and CoCa have the similar trend as that of DSGC. However, VectorSync incurs more packet collisions when TD smaller than 20 ms, leading to a much lower RR.

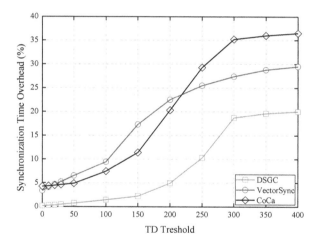

Fig. 10. Impact of TD on synchronization time overhead

Figure 10 shows that STO grows as TD increases, when TD is lower than 50 ms, STO is less than 1%, and finally approaches 20% when TD reaches to 400 ms (note that 20% is the upper bound of STO; if an initiator begins to sleep when a new sensor wakes up, then STO = 5/(5 + 5 * 4) = 20%). Based on those analysis, to ensure a better RR (i.e., 100%) while have a small STO (lower than 5%), the value of TD should be 20 ~ 200 ms.

5 Conclusion

This work proposes DSGC, a data synchronization mechanism for duty cycled WSNs based on NDN architecture. DSGC adopts group knowledge for sensors and explicitly named each sensor's data by a growing serial number, and builds a vector for representing the dataset' state, which records the data's current state and facilitate to synchronize the dataset of a sensor group. DSGC exploits efficient dataset state synchronization in the context of inconsistent status between sensors or packet losses caused by collision. Evaluation results verify that DSGC can guarantee data availability nearly 100% with negligible energy consumption and traffic. In the future, we plan to consider communication collision between groups and different sleeping strategies in DSGC design to make it more promising to be applied in the real environment.

Acknowledgements. This work is supported by the National Nature Science Foundation of China (61871204); the Natural Science Foundation of Fujian Province (2018J01544); the Key Project of Natural Foundation for Young in Colleges of Fujian Province (JZ160466); Fujian College of Outstanding Young Talent Support Program; Fujian College of New Century Excellent Talent Support Program; Fujian Provincial Leading Project (2017H0029); and the Science and Technology Project of Fuzhou City (2017-G-106).

References

1. Park, P., Ergen, S.C., Fischione, C., Sangiovanni-Vincentelli, A.: Duty-cycle optimization for IEEE 802.15.4 wireless sensor networks. ACM Trans. Sens. Netw. **10**(1), 1–12 (2013)
2. Carrano, R.C., Passos, D., Magalhaes, L.C.S., Albuquerque, C.V.N.: Survey and taxonomy of duty cycling mechanisms in wireless sensor networks. IEEE Commun. Surv. Tutor. **16**(1), 181–194 (2014)
3. Xie, R., Liu, A., Gao, J.: A residual energy aware schedule scheme for WSNs employing adjustable awake/sleep duty cycle. Wirel. Pers. Commun. **90**(4), 1859–1887 (2016)
4. Luo, H., He, M., Ruan, Z., Zeng, X.: Optimal sleep time controller based on traffic prediction and residual energy in duty-cycled wireless sensor networks. Int. J. Distrib. Sens. Netw. **13**(12), 1–14 (2017)
5. Ayele, E.D., Wen, J., Ansar, Z., Dargie, W.: An adaptive sleep-time management model for wireless sensor networks. In: 24th International Conference on Computer Communications and Networks, Las Vegas, NV, USA, pp. 1–7 (2015)
6. Zhang, L., et al.: Named data networking. ACM SIGCOMM Comput. Commun. Rev. **44**(3), 66–73 (2014)
7. Hahm, O., Baccelli, E., Schmidt, T., Wahlisch, M., Adjih, C., Massoulie, L.: Low-power internet of things with NDN & cooperative caching. In: 4th ACM Conference on Information-Centric Networking, Berlin, Germany, pp. 1–10 (2017)
8. Shang, W., Afanasyev, A., Zhang, L.: VectorSync: distributed dataset synchronization over Named Data Networking, NDN, Technical Report NDN-00 (2018)
9. Dubey, B.B., Chauhan, N., Chand, N., Awasthi, L.K.: Incentive based scheme for improving data availability in vehicular ad-hoc networks. Wirel. Netw. **23**(6), 1669–1687 (2017)
10. Ruan, Z., Liang, W., Sun, D., Luo, H., Cheng, F.: An efficient and lightweight source privacy protecting scheme for sensor networks using group knowledge. Int. J. Distrib. Sens. Netw. **14**(5), 1–14 (2013)

11. Wang, B., Gu, X., Yan, S.: STCS: a practical solar radiation based temperature correction scheme in meteorological WSN. Int. J. Sens. Netw. **28**(1), 22–33 (2018)
12. Liu, Y., Yang, Z., Yan, X., Liu, G., Hu, B.: A novel multi-hop algorithm for wireless network with unevenly distributed nodes. Comput. Mater. Continua **58**(1), 79–100 (2019)
13. Liu, X., Liu, Q.: A dual-spline approach to load error repair in a HEMS sensor network. Comput. Mater. Continua **57**(2), 179–194 (2018)

An Implementation of CoAP-Based Semantic Resource Directory in Californium

Yao Wang$^{(\boxtimes)}$ and Gengyu Wei

Beijing University of Posts and Telecommunications, Beijing 100876, China
samuelyo12@163.com, weigengyu@bupt.edu.cn

Abstract. Although Resource Directory (RD) is proposed and still under standardization by IETF CoRE WG for resource discovery in constrained networks, Californium as an open-source platform of CoAP is short of the RD functions and could not well support CoAP-based semantic applications to do data analysis and security related to discoveries and allocations. This paper demonstrates an implementation of RD entity with basic mechanisms including URI discovery, resource registration and resource lookup in Californium, and improves the semantic-based resource discovery through adding several sematic attributes such as reference ontology (ro), semantic description (sd) and annotation type (at). The experimental results show that the implementation works are feasible and consistent with CoRE WG's RD specification. Also its performance is given and achieves satisfactory results in semantic application. By realizing the semantic RD functions in Californium, this paper could promote CoAP based on IoT semantic researches on the Californium framework in the future.

Keywords: Semantic Sensor Network · Resource Directory · CoAP · Californium · IoT

1 Introduction

There are resource-constrained nodes and restricted networks in The Internet of Things (IoT), such as 8-bit microprocessors and limited nodes with small ROM and RAM [1]. Constrained Application Protocol (CoAP) is a generic protocol for the special requirements of this constrained environment which realizes a subset of Representational State Transfer (REST) that is common with HTTP but optimized for M2M applications. In many M2M scenarios, direct discovery of resources is not practical because a resource-constrained IoT has the characteristics of sleepy nodes, wide range of networks, low-performance multicast. The entity of Resource Directory (RD) based on CoAP has been proposed by IETF CoRE working group to achieve the purpose of resource discovery in the resource-constrained IoT. The Semantic Sensor Network (SSN) semantically annotates the information of endpoints and builds an ontology that supports semantic annotation enabling the endpoint to perform semantic reasoning based on the relationship between the semantic markup of the information indicated by this ontology and other information.

© Springer Nature Switzerland AG 2019
X. Sun et al. (Eds.): ICAIS 2019, LNCS 11634, pp. 211–222, 2019.
https://doi.org/10.1007/978-3-030-24271-8_19

The IETF CoRE working group published the first version draft of Resource Directory in 2011 and has been keeping updating its definition and function and making changes in a new version draft since then. Californium, an open source CoAP framework, is now available on the Eclipse platform widely used in CoAP research and has implemented most capabilities of RFC 7252 [2]. However functions of Resource Directory defined in draft-ietf-core-resource-directory-12 have not been fully realized in Californium which causes some limitations on future work. The diversity of ontology information representation and the limited nature of the subject become the inherent contradiction that restricts the further intelligent development of semantic IoT. This paper describes the basic mechanisms for Resource Directory to discover resources which includes discovery of Resource Directory addresses, registration of resources, operation of registered resources and the resource discovery with the Resource Directory and adds several sematic attributes such as ro, sd and at to enhance the sematic resource discovery. Also an implementation of semantic Resource Directory entity is proposed in Californium and experiments are executed in order to clarify and validate this implementation of the Resource Directory with the Copper CoAP user-agent which is an add-on for the Firefox Web browser. The performance of the proposed implementation is given and it proves that Resource Directory with this implementation can achieve satisfactory performance.

The rest of the paper is as follows. Related work is discussed in Sect. 2, while Sect. 3 describes the basic mechanism and sematic attributes of Resource Directory based on CoAP in detail. Section 4 presents the implementation of semantic Resource Directory in Californium and relevant numerical experimental results which show the feasibility of the Resource Directory and the performance of the proposed implementation. The paper is concluded by Sect. 5.

2 Related Work

The use of Web Linking for the description and discovery of resources hosted by constrained web servers is specified by the CoRE Link Format [RFC 6690]. It defines that resource discovery in CoRE is accomplished through the use of a well-known resource URI that returns a list of links about resources hosted by that server and other link relations [3]. CoRE Link Format [RFC 6690] also points out that it makes sense to deploy resource directory entities that store links to resources stored on other servers thinking of this as a limited search engine for constrained M2M resources.

Michele Ruta, Floriano Scioscia et al. proposed a SWoT framework based on Wireless Sensor Networks (WSNs) to enable cooperative resource discovery between sensors that enables CoAP resource discovery to be more personalized through semantic matching through semantic reasoning. Richard Mietz, Philipp Abraham et al. introduced a new option in the CoAP protocol, High-level States (HLS), which enables the generation of high-level state resources based on raw sensor readings with bandwidth-saving resources and enhancements [4]. Cai and Zhang et al. presented a prototype intelligent system SWMRD (Semantic Web-based manufacturing resource discovery) for distributed manufacturing collaboration across ubiquitous virtual enterprises via a new, multidisciplinary manufacturing ontology is proposed on the semantic web to convert resources into machine understandable knowledge.

There are several kinds of open-source implementations of Resource Directory by different languages. Jelmer Tiete has implemented the Resource Directory using JavaScript which is compatible with [draft-ietf-core-resource-directory-10] and this implementation uses node-coap and levelDB as key value storage for the different resources [5]. Henning Mueller introduce a CoAP RD node that can be used to implement a local CoAP Resource Directory supporting to Node-RED with Ruby [6]. Californium, an open-source CoAP framework developed by the Federal Institute of Technology in Zurich, Switzerland, is now available on the Eclipse platform and follows a well-structured, modular design with well-written comments and documentation. However semantic-based Resource Directory functions have not been achieved in Californium which causes resource registration or discovery are not supported semantically by Californium. So it is important to implement Resource Directory in Californium in order to make full use of it in the further semantic CoAP research and applications.

3 Semantic Resource Discovery Mechanism for Resource Directory

Resource Directory hosts descriptions of resources held on other servers, allowing lookups to be performed for those resources [7]. Following part demonstrates the resource discovery mechanism for Resource Directory (Fig. 1).

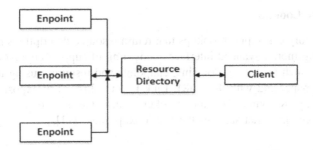

Fig. 1. The architecture of Resource Directory

3.1 Finding a Resource Directory

Resource Directory is configured with a specific IP address for the simplicity of usage. That IP address may also be an any-cast address which can allow the network to forward Resource Directory requests to the Resource Directory that is topologically close [8].

3.2 URI Discovery

An endpoint uses the well-known interface of the CORE Link Format [RFC 6690] for the discovery of the Resource Directory and its URIs. Discovery of the Resource Directory registration URI path is accomplished by sending either a multicast or unicast GET request to "/.well-known/core" and including a Resource Type (rt) parameter [RFC 6690] with the value "core.rd" in the querying string. [9].

3.3 Registration

After finding the location of the Resource Directory, the other resource server endpoint can use the registration interface to register its resources. This registration interface accepts a POST from endpoints that contain a list of resources to add to the directory which has a message payload in the CoRE Link Format [RFC 6690], as well as query parameters that indicate endpoint names or optionally their domain and the lifetime of the registration.

3.4 Operations on the Registration Resource

Endpoint should keep the returned location of the registration resource for further operations. Resource Directory should continue to provide access to the registration resources so that the registration endpoint can eventually refresh the registration source. Registration resources can also be used to check the registration resources using GET, update the contents of the registration link using POST or remove the registration using DELETE [10].

3.5 Resource Lookup

Resource Directory can support lookups that return resource descriptions in alternative formats or using more advanced interfaces consisting of support context or semantic-based lookups, such as finding domains, endpoints and resources using the attributes defined in this paper and with the CoRE Link Format. Instead of exposing registered resources directly, Resource Directory Lookup returns the link content from the registration resource entry that satisfies the RD lookup query [11].

3.6 Semantic Attributions

The reference ontology (ro) is a new type of attribute that contains the URI of the ontology pointed to by the resource description. This attribute is mandatory in resource registration (POST) and query (GET) requests. Its presence allows the CoAP server to distinguish between standard requests and semantic-enhanced requests. The semantic description (sd) is an annotated description of the resource. It is a compressed concept expression Web Ontology Language(WOL) that performs RDF/XML syntax. The annotation type (at) is a new property that implies coding conventions for ontology language, grammar, and semantic annotations. It is defined in the same way as the standard type (media type) attribute. For each language, grammar and encoding, the associated MIME category should be added to the CoAP Media Class Registration, which can match the MIME category string to the 16-bit encoding. For example, the unregistered code "30004" corresponds to the category of application/rdf (Table 1).

Table 1. The function of Resource Directory

Function	Interaction	Method	URI template
URI discovery	EP -> RD	GET	/.well-known/core?{?rt}
Registration	EP -> RD	POST	{+rd}{?ep,d,lt,con,extra-attrs}
Registration update	EP -> RD	POST	{+location}{?lt,con,extra-attrs*}
Registration removal	EP -> RD	DELETE	{+location}
Read Endpoint links	EP -> RD	GET	{+location}{?href,rel,rt,if,ct}
Lookup	EP -> RD	GET	{+type-lookup-location}{search*}

4 Implementation and Experiments

Californium is a Java based framework which adopts a completely object-oriented programming idea and implements a detailed and layered implementation of the CoAP protocol. It divides the whole structure into Resource, Endpoint and Connector according to the workflow in the communication process, follows a well-structured, modular design with well-written comments and documentation which is useful for Resource Directory implementations [12]. For example, CoapEndpoint implements the Endpoint interface, implements message reception through the RawDataChannel interface which belongs to elements-connector, and implements message sending through the Outbox interface. A CoapEndpoint is usually associated with a Connector to implement the sending and receiving of the transport layer (Fig. 2).

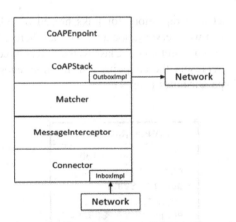

Fig. 2. The implementation of CoAP Endpoint in Californium

4.1 Implementation

Based on Californium, there are serval problems we need to focus on when we design and implement Resource Directory. For example, registration interface must be idempotent, so registering serval times with the same endpoint parameters, endpoint name and domain will not create multiple registration resources. Lookup filtering can include multiple search criteria in one request lookup. The search criteria is matched allowing trailing "*" wildcard operators. To solve these problems, we designed following key Class such as KeyValuePair, RDNodeResource, RDResource and LookUpResource.

KeyValuePair

To avoid create multiple registration resource with the same endpoint parameters and make sure the high accuracy of matchup for resource discovery, we design Class KeyValuePair which consists of name and value attributes (Fig. 3).

```
┌─────────────────────────────────────────────────┐
│                  KeyValuePair                    │
├─────────────────────────────────────────────────┤
│ - name : String                                 │
│ - value : String                                │
├─────────────────────────────────────────────────┤
│ + KeyValuePair()                                │
│ + KeyValuePair(name : String, value : String)   │
│ + KeyValuePair(name : String, value : int)      │
│ + KeyValuePair(name : String)                   │
│ + parse(str : String) : KeyValuePair            │
│ + isFlag() : boolean                            │
│ + getName() : String                            │
│ + getValue() : String                           │
│ + getIntValue() : int                           │
└─────────────────────────────────────────────────┘
```

Fig. 3. The implementation of Class KeyValuePair

RDNodeResource

Resource Directory is set as a repository for links hosted on other resource servers called endpoints which is a web server associated with a scheme, IP address and port, and can be identified by its endpoint name. Class RDNodeResource extends from basic Class CoapResource to represent the endpoint with lifetime, endpointName, domain, context and endpointType attributes (Fig. 4).

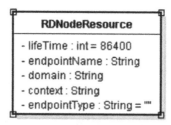

Fig. 4. The implementation of Class RDNodeResource

RDResource

Resource Directory implements a set of REST interfaces for endpoints to register and maintain sets of Web Links called Resource Directory registration resource and for other web clients to lookup resources from the Resource Directory. Class RDResource represents the registration resource which can handle POST and GET two kinds of request (Fig. 5).

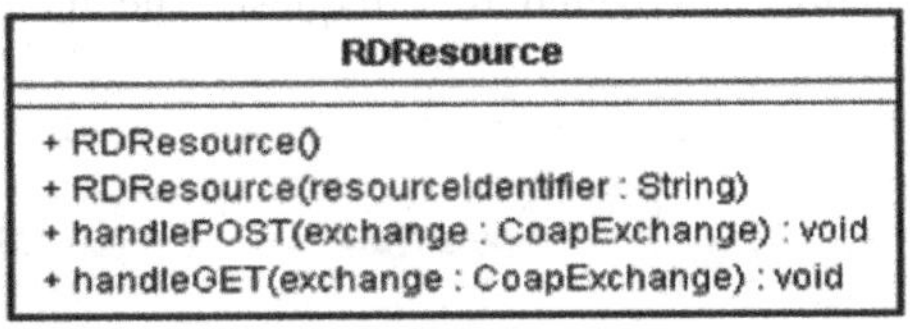

RDResource
+ RDResource()
+ RDResource(resourceIdentifier : String)
+ handlePOST(exchange : CoapExchange) : void
+ handleGET(exchange : CoapExchange) : void

Fig. 5. The implementation of Class RDResource

LookUpResource

For the resource lookup function, we design three different kinds of discovery results resource Class such as RDLookUpDomainResource, RDLookUpEPResource and RDLookUpResResource all of which is extended from basic Class CoapResource.

Semantic Attributions

Reference ontology (ro) is a new type of attribute that contains the ontology URI pointed to by the resource description, and its presence allows the CoAP server to distinguish between standard requests and semantic-enhanced requests. For example, "ro=http://somewhere/LM70TemperatureSensor".

Annotation type (at) is a new attribute that implies coding specifications for ontology language, syntax, and semantic annotations. For each language, syntax and encoding, the associated MIME category should be added to the CoAP Media Category registration. For example, "at=30004".

Semantic description (sd) attribute is set by applying Semantic Sensor Network Ontology (SSN) to RDF namespace and using the GZIP compression algorithm to compress the RDF/XML expression. SSNO follows a horizontal and vertical modular architecture, including a lightweight but self-contained core ontology called SOSA (Sensor, Observation, Sample, and Actuator) for its base class and attributes designed to extend the target audience and application areas that can leverage the semantic Web ontology.

4.2 Experiments

The Copper (Cu) CoAP user-agent for Firefox installs a handler for the CoAP URI scheme and allows users to browse and interact with Internet of Things devices. We use the Copper as a client to validate the Resource Directory basic discovery mechanism with a visible interface [13]. We run the Californium framework in a laptop which has an Intel(R) Core(TM) i5-3210M CPU @2.50 GHz and a 4.00 GB RAM. The experimental network is IPv6 local area network and we configured a specific IPv6 address

"2001:da8:215:3f0:99b1:e5ca:b253:bc5e" for the Resource Directory which allows the network to forward RD requests to the Resource Directory that is topologically close.

Figure 6 shows we register a resource whose endpoint name is "node1". This mechanism is from endpoint to the Resource Directory with the POST method. This URI template can have serval variables such as "ep", "d", "lt" and so on. This example shows an endpoint with the name "node1" registering a resource to an Resource Directory using Registration interface and the location "/rd" is an example Resource Directory location discovered in a request. The returned location path is "/rd/node1".

Fig. 6. Registration

Figure 7 shows we use the Resource Directory with a lookup request from the client to the Resource Directory. We use the Copper as a client to send a lookup interface URI with the GET method which consists of several template variables and lookup filters. Results shows we discover the registration resource with "temperature-c" value through the Resource Directory lookup filtering whose search criterion value is "rt=temperatue*".

Figure 8 shows we use the Copper as a client to send a lookup interface URI with the GET method which consists of several semantic template variables and lookup filters. Results shows we discover the registration resource with specific semantic description value compressed by GZIP through the Resource Directory lookup filtering whose search criterion semantic SPARQL value is also compressed.

In conclusion, the proposed semantic Resource Directory implementation has followed the specified web interfaces in the draft of Resource Directory and fulfilled following basic functions in CoAP such as finding a Resource Directory, Resource Registration, Resource Lookup and so on. Also it can meet the basic semantic requirements of resource discovery through adding several semantic attributes. This provides basements and more probabilities for more future CoAP semantic research in Californium.

Fig. 7. Lookup filtering

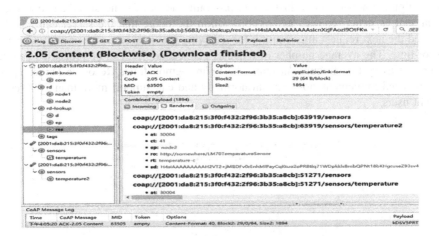

Fig. 8. Semantic lookup filtering

4.3   Performance Testing

To test the performance of the proposed implementation of Resource Directory, we can simplify the operations process of the CoAP client and execute a large number of repetitive requests. We defined a CoAP client's Resource Discovery request operation as a Callable or Runnable task, and then initialized a properly sized thread pool in Java so that each thread repeatedly repeats the above Callable or Runnable tasks. We simulated different numbers of concurrent requests by setting different thread numbers to test the Resource Directory server capabilities in a laptop which has an Intel(R) Core (TM) i5-3210M CPU @2.50 GHz and a 4.00 GB RAM. The experimental network is IPv6 Wi-Fi network simulated as a constrained network environment and we configured a specific IPv6 address "2001:da8:215:3f0:99b1:e5ca:b253:bc5e" for the Resource Directory, the URI of request of Resource Discovery is "coap://[2001:-da8:215:fa33:edc6:10e:495f:5905]:5683/rd-lookup/res?rt=temperature-c".

Table 2 shows we tested average response time under two different methods of resource discovery, use of a well-known resource URI and Resouce Directory of the proposed implementation. The test program begins with the client making a request and ends with receiving the response. We repeated 10 times and took the average of response time. The figure demonstrates that the response time is significantly shorter using the Resource Directory compared to the use of a well-known resource URI.

Table 2. Resource discovery response times under different methods

Discovery resource methods	Response time (ms)
use of a well-known resource URI	10.020
Resource directory of the proposed implementation	8.062

Figure 9 shows we created a specified number of virtual client concurrently based on configuration parameters in the test program and within the specified time each client sent as many requests as possible within the range that the server can handle, initiated the next request after waiting for receiving previous response or not waiting if out-of-time. The average number of requests per second that can be processed can be computed as system throughput rate. The figure demonstrates Resource Directory of the proposed implementation can run normally and can support more than 1000 concurrent users.

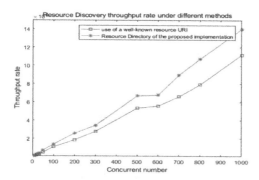

Fig. 9. Resource Discovery throughput rate under different methods

5   Conclusion and Future Works

The paper demonstrates and implements a novel semantic Resource Directory which can be used to discovery constrained resource in the resource-constrained IoT. It is based on CoAP and includes backward-compatible CoAP extension. The basic mechanism of the proposed Resource Directory is discussed such as finding a Resource Directory, URI discovery, registration and operations on the registration resource including registration update, registration removal and read endpoint links and resource lookup using the Resource Directory. Also several semantic attributes are added to improve the semantic-based Resource Directory such as ro, sd, at. The implementation of Resource Directory is accomplished on the Californium, a framework which is now available on the Eclipse platform and widely used among the CoAP research. The basic mechanism and function is validated with the Copper Firefox plus. The experimental results demonstrate that the proposed implementation of semantic Resource Directory can meet the basic requirements and has some feasibility according to the draft of IETF CoRE working group which can promote CoAP research based on the Californium framework in the future.

Future work includes more semantic applications due to the more attention paid to Semantic Sensor Network. For the elderly nursing home application scenario, based on the relevant sensor data, the semantic enhanced resource directory is used to discover the sensor resources that satisfy the preset query semantic conditions [14]. Design experiments to validate and compare resource discovery performance before and after the introduction of semantic attributes, such as accuracy, throughput, and real-time [15].

References

1. Xia, F., et al.: Internet of things. Int. J. Commun. Syst. **25**(9), 1101 (2012)
2. Yang, S.-H.: Internet of things. In: Yang, S.H. (ed.) Wireless Sensor Networks. SCT, pp. 247–261. Springer, London (2014). https://doi.org/10.1007/978-1-4471-5505-8_12
3. Shelby, Z., Hartke, K., Bormann, C: The constrained application protocol (CoAP) (2014)
4. Shelby, Z., Krco, S., Bormann, C.: CoRE Resource Directory, draft-shelby-core-resource-directory-02, vol. 13 (2013). http://toolsietf.org/html/draft-shelby-core-resource-directory-04 . Accessed 3 June 2014
5. Bull, J.W., et al.: Strengths, weaknesses, opportunities and threats: a SWOT analysis of the ecosystem services framework. Ecosyst. Serv. **17**, 99–111 (2016)
6. Shelby, Z., van der Stok, P.: CoRE Resource Directory draft-ietf-core-resource-directory-13. Consultant (2018)
7. Kovatsch, M., Lanter, M., Shelby, Z.: Californium: scalable cloud services for the internet of things with coap. In: 2014 International Conference on the Internet of Things (IOT). IEEE (2014)
8. Mietz, R., Abraham, P., Romer, K.: High-level states with CoAP: giving meaning to raw sensor values to support IoT applications. In: 2014 IEEE Ninth International Conference on Intelligent Sensors, Sensor Networks and Information Processing (ISSNIP). IEEE (2014)
9. Ruta, M., et al.: Cooperative semantic sensor networks for pervasive computing contexts
10. Ruta, M., et al.: Resource annotation, dissemination and discovery in the Semantic Web of Things: a CoAP-based framework. In: 2013 IEEE and Internet of Things (iThings/CPSCom), IEEE International Conference on and IEEE Cyber, Physical and Social Computing, Green Computing and Communications (GreenCom). IEEE (2013)
11. Shelby, Z.: Constrained RESTful environments (CoRE) link format (2012)
12. Kovatsch, M., Mayer, S., Ostermaier, B.: Moving application logic from the firmware to the cloud: towards the thin server architecture for the internet of things. In: 2012 Sixth International Conference on Innovative Mobile and Internet Services in Ubiquitous Computing (IMIS). IEEE (2012)

13. Liu, M., et al.: Distributed resource directory architecture in Machine-to-Machine communications. In: 2013 IEEE 9th International Conference on Wireless and Mobile Computing, Networking and Communications (WiMob). IEEE (2013)
14. Rahman, A., Dijk, E.: Group communication for the constrained application protocol (CoAP). Group (2014)
15. Villaverde, B.C., et al.: Service discovery protocols for constrained machine-to-machine communications. IEEE Commun. Surv. Tutor. 16(1), 41–60 (2014)
16. Liu, J., Sun, N., Li, X., Han, G., Yang, H., Sun, Q.: Rare bird sparse recognition via part-based gist feature fusion and regularized intraclass dictionary learning. CMC: Comput. Mater. Continua 55(3), 435–446 (2018)
17. Shi, C.: A novel ensemble learning algorithm based on D-S evidence theory for IoT security. CMC: Comput. Mater. Continua 57(3), 635–652 (2018)

A Survey of Simulators for Home Energy Management: System Architecture, Intelligence, UI and Efficiency

Mingxu Sun[1], Williams Dannah[2(✉)], Qi Liu[3], and Xiaodong Liu[3]

[1] School of Electrical Engineering, University of Jinan, Jinan, China
[2] Jiangsu Collaborative Innovation Center of Atmospheric Environment and Equipment Technology (CICAEET), Nanjing University of Information Science and Technology, Nanjing 210044, China
20185132003@nuist.edu.cn
[3] School of Computing, Edinburgh Napier University, Edinburgh, UK

Abstract. The ever-increasing demand for comfort in the home has continually given rise to the level of electricity consumption thereby opening up more opportunities for home energy management systems (HEMS). HEMS play vital roles both on the demand side and the supplier side of the electricity supply chain as well as in the environmental protection arena. The major focus of HEMS has been to improve energy efficiency in the home without negatively impacting the comfort levels. To prove the feasibility of HEMS implementation in real homes, demonstration in a simulation environment using virtual appliances and devices are used to emulate the real smart home situation. Various simulation tools have been used to emulate electrical home appliances with the aim of demonstrating how HEMS can be beneficial when utilized in homes. This paper presents a review of home energy simulation tools considering system architecture, intelligence, user interface (UI) as well as efficiency.

Keywords: Home energy management · Appliance simulation · Artificial intelligence

1 Introduction

Home energy management simulation tools have proved their importance in diverse ways including the emulation of real household electricity usage to provide a basis for decision making by players in the energy market [1], aiding people who conduct various research works in that regard to corroborate their models for electricity consumption control and optimization as well as their ability to help establish ways by which consumers can save energy and money through the use of HEMS in their households [2, 3]. The power consumption pattern as modeled in these simulators gives users a fair idea of how their appliances consume energy, thereby helping them understand concepts such as peak demand and their effect on energy consumption and cost. On the demand side management, the monitoring and management of power consumption has become one of the most concerned setups [4]. To this effect, some of the simulators visualize household electricity consumption with the use of their

X. Sun et al. (Eds.): ICAIS 2019, LNCS 11634, pp. 223–231, 2019.
https://doi.org/10.1007/978-3-030-24271-8_20

visualization engines and based the consumption pattern detected, provide energy-saving recommendations to end-users [5].

While smart residential load simulators help customers to understand the dynamics involved in residential energy demand and supply, they also prove useful to educators in their quest to better explain the concepts involved in energy management. Smart algorithms such as the HEC algorithm when integrated into Demand response (DR) operations put more control in the hands of users, enabling them to better manage the most common electrical appliances in the home by ensuring a minimum rate of energy consumption especially during peak hours of the day [6]. This is achieved by switching the appliances in the home based on their level of priority without compromising the comfort of the user. It is clear in [7] that besides the concerns related to consumer savings, energy shortage especially during peak periods, and the importance of home energy management systems also extend to issues of global warming which has been one of the major long-standing hot topics of the twenty-first century. Although conducting experiments in a simulator is easier than working in the real environment especially when dealing with electrical energy, simulator experiments still help to foresee the challenges ahead [8, 9].

2   Overview on Home Energy Management Simulation Tools

This chapter discusses works conducted by various researchers with respect to the design and development of intelligent home energy management simulators and their impact on the identification of good practices towards energy efficiency [1] (Fig. 1).

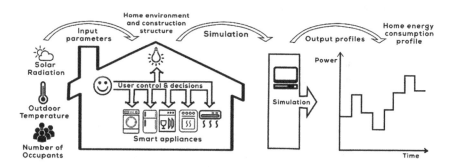

Fig. 1. General simulation setup overview of HEMS [10]

Various research works hinging on the demand side management of electrical energy have been conducted since the 1970s [10] and still continues to attract attention especially due in recent times due to high rising demand and cost of electricity as well as the increase in CO_2 emissions. Simulators have certain properties that contribute to the achievement of their intended objectives, thus in this paper, we focus on a few pivotal ones including the systems architecture, intelligent mechanisms, UI and general performance.

3 Simulator Properties

This chapter discusses some vital features of various home energy management simulators under consideration with regards to their architecture, intelligent algorithms, affordance, and general performance.

3.1 Architecture of Simulators

The various architectural components and development environments employed in the various simulation tools under discussion are outlined in Table 1.

Table 1. System architecture and components of home energy simulators.

Reference	Architecture/components	Development environment
[1]	SaaS paradigm with multiple modules (i.e. agent, CSN, aggregation, web service and end-user modules)	
[2]	Neural network, DOPF, appliances and energy source models	Simulink toolbox
[3]	Individual appliance models	MATLAB
[8]	Virtual sensors, context retriever, reasoning, appliances, home server, home environment, weather, and people	.NET and Sharp Develop
[11]	HAN, WAN, communication backbone, real-time database	Java and SQL
[12]	4 layered architecture (individual simulator, adapter, communication, and simulation manager layers)	MATLAB/Simulink, Python
[13]	4 layered architecture (producer, distributor, substation and end-user layers)	Java
[14]	HAN, WAN, communication backbone, real-time database	Java and SQL
[15]	Bottom-up approach	JAVA/JADE
[16]	Distributed deployment	Java RMI, CoObRA

The design of the CASSANDRA platform [1] follows the Software-as-a-Service (SaaS) paradigm and consists of five modules including the Agent module, CSN module, aggregation module, web service modules and the end-user module. The SRLS [2] which was developed using the MATLAB-Simulink toolbox models residential load dataset through an aggregation of the load and the results then used in creating a Neural Network Model. This is further integrated into a DOPF model to obtain ideal Demand Response (DR). The simulator proposed in [3] integrates the individual appliance models and RTP. In [11], a simulation tool which encompasses a Household Area Network (HAN) [8] is linked to a Wide Area Network (WAN) which is further connected to the internet serving as the communication backbone. Each HAN contains some appliances which are either specified by the user or the system, linked to the measuring device and then to a larger network. The simulation tool presented in [12] has a layered architecture of five interoperable sub-simulators with an individual simulation layer being a core component of each simulator. Besides the sub-simulator which models the physical environment, the rest of the four sub-simulators namely the house simulator, human simulator, home appliance simulator, and electric power simulator are all developed under Python environment.

The architecture of the smart grid household's profile simulator as proposed in [13] has four layers namely; the producer layer, distributor layer, substation layer and the consumer layer. The system architecture presented in [14] has similar features as that presented in [11] considering the relationship, and interconnectivity among the various components of the simulation platform. Figure 2 shows the architecture of the bottom-up method which enables the end-user to ascertain each device energy profile's effect [15].

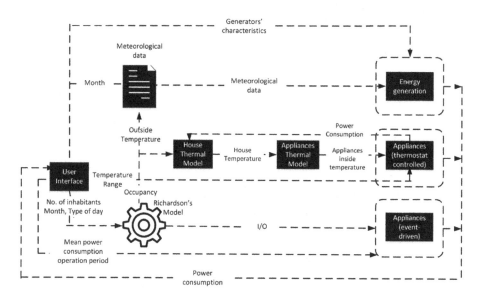

Fig. 2. The architecture of agent-based simulator based on Richardson's model [15]

The eHomeSimulator presented in [16] allows deployment in multiple environments. To this effect each deployment site represents a gateway that executes its services in relation to the various devices present in the corresponding environment.

3.2 Intelligence Mechanisms in Simulators

The HEMS simulation platforms considered in this paper have certain intelligence mechanisms that play pivotal roles in the optimization of energy consumption. Table 2 outlines the algorithms and models that compose the intelligence mechanisms of the tools under discussion.

Table 2. Intelligence mechanisms of home energy management simulators

Reference	Intelligence mechanism
[1]	K-means, hierarchical clustering
[2]	NN Model, DOPF model
[3]	Genetic algorithm (GA)
[5]	Control engine, recommendation engine, visualization engine
[8]	Context register
[11]	PSO algorithm
[12]	Trust region reflective algorithm
[13]	SDO toolbox
[14]	BPSO algorithm
[15]	Richardson's model
[16]	Detector sensors

In the CASSANDRA platform as presented in [1] the CSN module is able to model and group consumers based on mutually exploitable loading ranks and their interaction with other consumers using clustering methods such as the k-means and hierarchical clustering. The consumer networks in the CSN module are symbolized as an undirected graph: $G = (V; E)$ wherein each of the nodes is represented by a vertex $v \in V$. The SRLS [2] serves as a tool to help consumers comprehend and experts give details on the dynamics of household power request and resource, as well as help to help researchers test and validate their energy management and optimization models. A study [3] developed an interactive simulation tool for demonstrating ways by which home energy users can save energy by employing it in their household. The simulation tool uses an intelligent algorithm known as Genetic Algorithm (GA) for the purpose of power optimization by searching for the best possible results. The GA algorithm models the organic theory of natural selection through population and growth [5]. As indicated in Eq. 1 the GA algorithm which is executed to find the topmost possible outcomes in the optimization problem takes into consideration battery lifetime, cost of battery-life.

$$f(x) = P_{RTP,total}(t) + a_f.f + a_e.|A_{vol} - B_{vol}| \tag{1}$$

The Interactive Smart Home Simulator as proposed by [8] has an intelligent feature of reasoning which helps the simulator to query and conclude the appropriate actions to take in a given context using roles and case-based reasoning. To achieve this, a web server helps to integrate context-aware into the ISS using the Context Server Discovery Protocol (CSDP). This approach facilitates the change of ways to reason.

The PSO algorithm presented in [11], functions as a heuristic method to optimize energy management. The home simulator presented in [12] combines situation-specific information which are obtained using the numerous intelligent sensor networks installed on both the internal and external parts of the home environment.

Electricity consumption levels differ among various households, hence the study in [13] proposed a prototype to forecast the behaviour of a household as well as find out sudden power usage. The demand response simulation tool as presented in [14] makes use of Demand-Side Management and BPSO for device choice in order to attain optimized consumption. In the agent-based simulator presented in [15], the simulation is able to do a real-time adaptation of its behavior to any changes made. The simulator uses Richardson's model which is a stochastic model that allows the system to deduce at a 1-min resolution. The eHomeSimulator presented in [16] uses an intelligence some intelligence features to detect the presence of a person and activate the services needed to make the person comfortable and then off when the person is out. These features include the person-detector service, the light-follow-person service, heating service, and the music-follows-person service.

3.3   Affordances and Interactivity of GUI

A user-friendly interface which provides a good level of affordance and usability is a required feature especially for non-technical users. In Table 3, the GUI affordance and user interactivity features of the simulators are briefly outlined.

Table 3. User interactivity of various HEMS GUI

Reference	Affordance/interactivity
[1]	Allows user control in project and scenario creation, the definition of number of appliances and consumption models
[2]	User defines states of already defined appliances, peak level, temperature, and family characteristics
[8]	Prompt messages on user's screen to keep the user updated on the states of various appliances. Less technical and highly intuitive interface with good design aesthetics
[11]	Allows user to easily navigate appliances and displays info on energy consumption and costs
[12]	Real smart home scenario with user control. Prompt messages displayed in real time to the user
[14]	Gives user options to select appliances and their properties. Continuous automatic update of information at a 10 s interval
[15]	Good level of abstraction. Easier interaction even without deep knowledge on devices
[16]	2D graphical simulation of the home environment. 3 graphical layers (i.e. persons, devices and background)

The CASSANDRA platform's GUI [1] comes with great aesthetics and intuitive features, allowing the user to create projects and scenarios with ease. In their quest to promote awareness of SHEMS and also to demonstrate how residential users can enhance their savings by reducing their power consumption to the barest minimum, researchers in [2] proposed a graphical user interface with easy-to-use features that allow users to input the preliminary data and parameters needed. The graph component presents real-time pricing information that give the user an insight into how they could manage their rate of consumption to improve their savings. The interactive Smart Home Simulator [8] provides quite an intuitive and less technical GUI with modernized aesthetics. The interface presented clearly shows the pictorial view of a smart home. Prompt messages relating to various occurrences in the home are also displayed in real-time on the user interface in order to keep the user constantly updated. The user interface presented in [11] looks quite simple and intuitive enough for all users regardless of their technical background. This feature enhances the user-friendliness of the simulator and its ability to attract all the intended target users. The GUI introduced by [15] has a good level of affordance, making easier for a user to set up a new simulation without a deep knowledge on the devices involved. The eHomeSimulator presented in [16] uses a 2D graphical design to model the home environment with three layers which include persons, devices and background (floor and walls) which does not change throughout the whole simulation process, the devices which are static but can change color, and the persons who are allowed to freely move in all accessible areas of the simulation environment.

3.4   Efficiency

Table 4 briefly outlines the efficiency level of the various tools simulated based on their energy optimization and cost saving results during simulation.

Table 4. Performance of home energy management simulators

Reference	Performance
[1]	6% reduction in peak load (from 2824 MWs to 2652 MWs)
[2]	Takes 20 s to solve model equations
[11]	16.4% cost saving
[12]	Approximates thermal energy and temperature with a 1.2 °C margin of error
[14]	33% cost saving
[15]	31% saving on electricity bill

Energy management programs when implemented on a larger scale have the potential to shift the demand of electricity from on-peak periods to off-peak [17] thereby reducing the pressure on the power grid as well as saving consumers some cost. This necessitates the use of proficient algorithms that support this objective. Based on the demand-side experiment conducted in [1] using the CSN module, a 6% decrease in peak consumption (from 2824 MW to 2652 MW) was realized in addition to a decrease in the standard deviation related to the amount of energy consumed within 96 quarters of the day (from 573 MW to 549 MW). It could be a basis for enhanced poor demand forecasting as a result of the minimal difference in the resultant curve. Averagely, the Smart Residential Load Simulator as proposed by [2] takes about 20 s to resolve the model equations, with 24 s of time recesses, producing data to enable the consumer analyze the behavior of the appliances under simulation. The use of the PSO algorithm in the DSM simulator [11] leads to an improvement in the efficiency level of power consumption by a factor of 16.4%, bringing about a substantial yearly savings for the residential user. In [12], the proposed home simulation platform was validated using an experiment conducted in a real experimental house. Results of the experiment proved the capability of the simulator to emulate and approximate the temperature of different rooms with a 1.2 °C margin of error. It was also able to simulate electrical energy usage established on the schedule of the activities of residents and usage of appliances in the home. The use of DSM and BPSO in [14] leads to a 33% cost saving for the consumer and a further 19–21% cost savings through enhanced choice of appliance and improved resource control, depicting quite a substantial savings in annual electricity expenditure. According to the simulation conducted in [15] it is shown that by automatically rescheduling the working period of some appliances to a time period when more renewable energy was available, the household was able to save 31% of the electricity bill.

4 Discussion

Although the various simulation tools as discussed are capable of imitating the household consumption environment and aiding researchers to validate optimization models as well as demonstrating ways of controlling appliances to minimize energy consumption, most of these simulators lack the feature of extensibility. These tools are therefore limited to the features, appliances, energy sources and scenarios specified by the developers, hence may not have the capacity to allow users specify new scenarios, appliances and environmental conditions. Software portability also needs to be considered since most of these simulators discussed are restricted to specific execution environments, thus not allowing for cross-platform execution.

5 Conclusion

This paper discussed various simulation tools for modeling home energy management. The underlying architectures and user interface designs of the various simulation platforms were discussed. Various intelligence mechanisms integrated into the simulators to ensure efficiency as well as the overall performance of these simulation tools were discussed. From the analysis future simulation tools to be developed need to be based on more personalized data. Future developments should also incorporate compatibility and portability onto Android and IOS platforms to allow easy accessibility by a cross-section of users especially those who may lack access or the required skills to run simulations in MATLAB or other technically inclined environments.

Acknowledgements. This work is funded by the European Union's Horizon 2020 research and innovation programme under the Marie Sklodowska-Curie grant agreement No 701697.

References

1. Vavliakis, K.N., Chrysopoulos, A.C.: CASSANDRA - a simulation-based, decision-support tool for energy market stakeholders (2015)
2. Gonzalez, J.M., Pouresmaeil, E., Canizares, C.A., Bhattacharya, K., Mosaddegh, A., Solanki, B.: Smart residential load simulator for energy management in smart grids (2018)
3. Hu, Q., Chan, J., Li, F., Chen, D.: A comprehensive user interactive simulation tool for smart home application. In: Proceedings of the 2014 Australasian Universities Power Engineering Conference, AUPEC 2014, pp. 1–6 (2014)
4. Liu, X., Liu, Q.: A dual-spline approach to load error repair in a HEMS sensor network. Comput. Mater. Contin. **57**, 179–194 (2018)
5. Murugesan, L.K., Hoda, R., Salcic, Z.: Toward visualising and controlling household electrical appliances. In: Proceedings of the 2015 6th International Conference on Automation, Robotics and Applications, ICARA 2015, pp. 591–596 (2015)
6. Abdelwahed, A.S., Zekry, A.H., Zayed, H.L., Sayed, A.M.: Controlling electricity consumption at home smart home. In: Proceedings of the 2015 10th International Conference on Computer Engineering and Systems, ICCES 2015, pp. 49–54 (2016)
7. Shareef, H., Ahmed, M.S., Mohamed, A., Al Hassan, E.: Review on home energy management system considering demand responses, smart technologies, and intelligent controllers. IEEE Access **6**, 24498–24509 (2018)
8. Van Nguyen, T., Kim, J.G., Choi, D.: ISS: the interactive smart home simulator. In: 2009 11th International Conference on Advanced Communication Technology, ICACT 2009, vol. 3, pp. 1828–1833 (2009)
9. Tang, X., Xu, J., Duan, B.: A memory- efficient simulation method of Grover's search algorithm. Comput. Mater. Contin. **57**, 307–319 (2018)
10. Et-Tolba, E.H., Ouassaid, M., Maaroufi, M.: Smart home appliances modeling and simulation for energy consumption profile development: application to Moroccan real environment case study. In: Proceedings of 2016 International Renewable and Sustainable Energy Conference, IRSEC 2016, pp. 1050–1055 (2017)
11. Gudi, N., Wang, L., Devabhaktuni, V., Shekara, S., Reddy, S.: A demand-side management simulation platform incorporating optimal management of distributed renewable resources, pp. 1–7 (2011)
12. Makino, Y., Lim, Y., Tan, Y.: Development of home simulation with thermal environment and electricity consumption (2016)
13. Bouderraoui, H.: Smart grid household's profiles simulator
14. Gudi, N., Wang, L., Devabhaktuni, V., Depuru, S.S.S.R.: Demand response simulation implementing heuristic optimization for home energy management. In: North American Power Symposium, NAPS (2010)
15. Sa, A., Lopes, R.A., Martins, J.F.: Design of an agent-based simulator for real-time estimation of power consumption/generation in residential buildings, pp. 3832–3838 (2015)
16. Armac, I., Retkowitz, D.: Simulation of smart environments. In: 2007 IEEE International Conference on Pervasive Services, ICPS, vol. 3, pp. 322–331 (2007)
17. Peruzzini, M., Capitanelli, A., Papetti, A., Germani, M.: Designing and simulating smart home environments and related services, pp. 1145–1156 (2014)

Relay Location Optimization and Relay Coordination in Multi-hop Cognitive Radio Networks

Yinghua Zhang[1,3]([✉]) [iD], Yanfang Dong[2] [iD], Lei Wang[1] [iD], Jian Liu[1],
and Yunfeng Peng[1]

[1] School of Computer and Communication Engineering,
University of Science and Technology Beijing,
Beijing 100083, People's Republic of China
82774807@qq.com, zhangyh@sugon.com, ustb_wl16@163.com,
{liujian,pengyf}@ustb.edu.cn
[2] School of Opto-Electronic Information Science and Technology,
Yantai University, Yantai 264005, People's Republic of China
dyfytu12@163.com, ytwzx3@126.com
[3] Dawning Information Industry Co., Ltd., Beijing 100193,
People's Republic of China

Abstract. Relay cooperative transmission can increase the transmission distance and reduce the transmit power. In this paper, three transmission modes are discussed: direct mode, single relay mode and dual relay mode. Each of the transmission schemes is optimized to obtain the maximum channel capacity. The theoretical formula of the channel capacity is derived and the effectiveness is verified through simulation. The paper also discusses a tradeoff between transmission delay and transmission distance. When the balance between transmission delay, distance and power is established, maximum channel capacity is achieved.

Keywords: Cognitive Radio · Multi-hop · Optimal relay selection · Outage probability

1 Introduction

Cooperative communication is one of the fastest developing research fields in recent years [1,2]. Its main idea is to share resources among multiple nodes in the network so as to achieve the overall resources efficiency [3].

Multi-hop relay technology and optimal relay location will provide an ideal solution to achieve high-speed and long distance transmission for the wireless systems. Its main feature of the multi-hop relay technology is to divide the

This work is supported by National Major Project (No. 2017ZX03001021-005) and 2018 Sugon Program of Intelligent-Factory on Advanced Computing Devices initiated by MIIT.

direct transmission path into several short paths by relays along the end to end path from source node to its destination [4–8]. Compared with the direct end to end transmission, the multi-hop transmission technology can reduce the transmit power, extend coverage and improve the channel capacity of the system. To choose the appropriate criteria is important for relay selection [9–11]. The different scheme will obtain different results. Toward this end, a model for the outage probability of the secondary user [12] has been proposed to find the optimal relay position by minimizing the outage probability. In [13,14], the authors have considered the outage performance and optimal relay location in bidirectional relay networks. However, most of these works have focused on the performance evaluation of the quality of transmitted data. The most classic criteria are the highest channel capacity criterion, and it is also the goal of most selection schemes. The number of relay nodes as well as the location has a great influence on the channel capacity [15–17]. This paper concentrates on the relay node location and multi-hop relay cooperative.

In this paper, the channel capacity formula of the system is provided for three transmission modes: direct mode, single relay mode and dual relay mode. A specific non-linear function is constructed. From the characteristics of this function, the expression of the optimal relay location is derived. Through analysis and simulation, it can be seen that the relay node location has the only optimal value that maximizes the channel capacity. Then the appropriate transmission mode is selected according to the transmission distance and the transmit power. Thus the data is transmitted through an optimal path and the performance of the secondary transmission is improved.

The paper is organized as follows. Section 2 gives a brief introduction of a system model. Section 3 gives a description of the relay cooperative transmission optimization model with maximum channel capacity. Section 4 depicts the optimal relay selection in the transmission mode. Section 5 provides simulation results and validates the theoretical analysis in this paper. This part also evaluates the optimal algorithm of relaying selection transmission systems. Section 6 concludes the present paper with a summary and some final remarks.

2   System Model

We consider a system mode as shown in Fig. 1, where S can transmit data to S_0 either by direct mode or relay mode. As for relay mode, there is Dual-hop with single best relay mode, Three-hop with dual best relay mode, etc. Suppose that there are m relays in the system, and the DF protocol is used in wireless communication.

As shown in Fig. 1, the impact of the Primary User (PU) on the Secondary User (SU) is considered in this scenario. The Cognitive Radio Network (CRN) consists of a primary transmitter receiver pair P-P_0, a secondary transmitter receiver pair S-S_0 and secondary relays $r_i \in \{r_1, \ldots, r_m\}$. S transmits data x_s to S_0 through the candidate relays r_{1i} and r_{2i}. To ensure the quality of service (QoS) of PU, the power E_S should be constrained. Besides, E_S cannot exceed

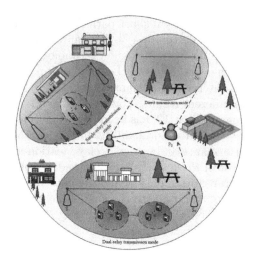

Fig. 1. The system model of relay selection mechanism

the maximum power allowed by the secondary system. Similarly, the relay power is defined as E_R, the power of the main user defined as E_P, channel attenuation coefficient defined as α and Gaussian noise (AWGN) defined as $\sigma_0{}^2$. Then the SNR of the threshold value is respectively given as $\gamma_c = \frac{E h_0{}^2}{\sigma_n^2}$. Hence, the SNR of these transmissions is:

$$\gamma_{LN} = \frac{E h_{LN}{}^2}{\sigma_n^2} \tag{1}$$

Where $L \in \{P, S, r_{1i}, r_{2j} | i, j = 1, \ldots, m\}, N \in \{P_0, S_0, r_{1i}, r_{2j} | i, j = 1, \ldots, m\}$, h_{LN} denote fading coefficient of the channel from L to N with the fading variance , and σ_{LN}^2 represent the additive white Gaussian noise (AWGN) at N with zero mean and variance σ_0^2. Relays $r_i (i = 1, \ldots, m)$ transmit data from source S to destination S_0. As shown in Fig. 1, in the process of dual relay selection which allows the measurements fading coefficient of the channel between S and r_{1i}, i.e. $h_{\mathrm{sr}_{1i}}$, between r_{1i} and r_{2j}, i.e. $h_{r_{1i}r_{2j}}$, as well as between r_{2j} and S_0, i.e. $h_{r_{2j}s_0}$.

Similar to (1), we denote the distance transmitted from L to N as d_{LN}. The distance transmitted can be expressed as

$$d_{LN}(L \in \{P, S, r_{1i}, r_{2j} | i, j = 1, \ldots, m\}, N \in \{P_0, S_0, r_{1i}, r_{2j} | i, j = 1, \ldots, m\}) \tag{2}$$

Thus, $r_{1i}(x_{1i}, y_{1i})$, $r_{2j}(x_{2j}, y_{2j})$ denote the position of the relay when assuming the positions of the source and the destination are $S(x_S, y_S)$ and $S_0(x_{S0}, y_{S0})$. Unless specified, the relay area is assumed to be a specific area with geographic characteristics between the source and the destination. While these assumptions based on the ideal state, they do enable us to gain insight into the design of cooperative relaying systems. The formula of distance between two points can be written as

$$d_{LN} = \sqrt{((x_L - x_N)^2 + (y_L + y_N)^2)} \tag{3}$$

Among them $L \in \{P, S, r_{1i}, r_{2j} | i, j = 1, \ldots, m\}$, $N \in \{P_0, S_0, r_{1i}, r_{2j} | i, j = 1, \ldots, m\}$.

3 Optimal Model with Maximum Channel Capacity

In this chapter, the following three transmission modes are discussed: direct mode, single relay mode and dual relay mode.

3.1 Direct Mode

S transmits data to S_0 by direct transmission, which is called direct mode. In this mode, the distance is within proper scope and the transmission power is strong enough. So the best transmission path is also the shortest path. This greatly reduces the delay and improves the efficiency of data transmission. The channel capacity, in this case, is represented as

$$C_1 = \log_2(1 + SNR_{SS_0}) \tag{4}$$

where $SNR_{SS_0} = \gamma_{SS_0} d_{SS_0}{}^{-\alpha}$ denotes the signal to noise ratio of the channel.

3.2 Single Relay Mode

S transmits data to S_0 through relay r_i $(i = 1, \ldots, m)$, which is called single relay mode. Relay cooperative transmission can effectively reduce transmission power, which not only ensures the reliability of transmission, but also extends the distance. The channel capacity can be written as

$$C_2 = \frac{1}{2}\log_2(1 + t) \tag{5}$$

where $1/2$ indicates that only half of the channels are used for each transmission by the source or relays, $t = \min(SNR_{sr_i}, SNR_{r_is_0})$, and t represents the smaller SNR in the two hops of the transmission link.

3.3 Dual Relay Mode

Similar to single relay mode, S transmits data to S0 through relay r_{1i} (x_1, y_1) and $r_{2j}(x_2, y_2)$, called dual relay mode. When the transmission distance is far away, the path loss of the wireless channel is very large. If transmitting power of the user is increased without any restraint, the energy loss will increase respectively. In order to further expand the coverage of the communication, the dual relay mode is needed. The channel capacity can be formulated as

$$C_3 = \frac{1}{3}\log_2(1 + t) \tag{6}$$

where $1/3$ indicates that only one third of the channels are used for each transmission by the source or relays, C_3 is the optimal relay channel capacity, t represents the smaller SNR in the three hop of the transmission link, i.e., $t = \min(SNR_{sr_{1i}}, SNR_{r_{1i}r_{2j}}, SNR_{r_{2j}s_0})$.

4 Analysis of Optimal Relay Selection

In this section, we will study the formulas of channel capacity given in three different cases when S to S_0 distance has been determined. In direct mode, S can access to S_0 either by direct transmission, i.e. $C_1 = \log_2(1 + \gamma_{SS_0} d_{SS_0}^{-\alpha})$ .Under the known parameters; C_1 is a known value at this time. And 2D coordinate of the optimal relay location is shown by numerical calculation.

4.1 Problem for Single Relay Mode

We assume that the coordinates of S, S_0 and optimal relay r_i are $S(0,0), S_0(d,0)$, and $r_i(x,y)$, respectively. The 2D coordinate of optimal relay location can be expressed as follows:

$$[x, y, t] = \underset{x,y,t}{\operatorname{argmax}}(\frac{1}{2}\log_2(1 + t)) \tag{7}$$

When the transmission distance d is bigger enough, the effect of P on S can be ignored. Channel attenuation coefficient is set as $\alpha = 4$. From formula (5), we assume that the SNR of these links can be obtained by the following formula:

$$SNR_{sr_i} = \gamma_{sr_i} d_{sr_i}^{-4} \tag{8}$$

$$SNR_{r_i s_0} = \gamma_{r_i s_0} d_{r_i s_0}^{-4} \tag{9}$$

Therefore, the optimal relay with maximum channel capacity can be described as following equations.

$$\max_{x,y,t} f = t \tag{10}$$

$$s.t. \ \frac{\gamma_{sr_i}}{(x^2 + y^2)^2} \geq t \tag{11}$$

$$\frac{\gamma_{r_i s_0}}{((d - x)^2 + y^2)^2} \geq t \tag{12}$$

4.2 Analysis of Optimal Relay Selection for Single Relay Mode

First, the optimization model with maximum channel capacity is transmitted into a variational inequality. Then we transmit the variational inequality into Karush Kuhn Tucker (KKT) condition, and describe the optimal relay selection under KKT condition.

For simplicity, we assume that the transmit power between the source and the relays is the same, i.e., $2E_S = E_R$. In the single relay mode, the Lagrangian function for the optimal relay of the secondary user can be obtained

$$L(x, y, t) = -t + \mu_1(t - \frac{\gamma_c}{(x^2 + y^2)^2}) + \mu_2(t - \frac{2\gamma_c}{((d - x)^2 + y^2)^2}) \quad (13)$$

$\mu_1 \geq 0, \mu_2 \geq 0$ is Lagrange factor, respectively.

The KKT condition can be further decomposed as

$$
\begin{aligned}
\frac{\partial L}{\partial x} &= \frac{\mu_1 x}{(x^2+y^2)^3} - \frac{2\mu_2(d-x)}{((d-x)^2+y^2)^3} = 0 \\
\frac{\partial L}{\partial y} &= \frac{\mu_1 y}{(x^2+y^2)^3} - \frac{2\mu_2 y}{((d-x)^2+y^2)^3} = 0 \\
\frac{\partial L}{\partial t} &= -1 + \mu_1 + \mu_2 = 0 \\
\mu_i &\geq 0 (i = 1, 2) \\
\mu_1(t &- \frac{\gamma_c}{(x^2+y^2)^2}) = 0 \\
\mu_2(t &- \frac{2\gamma_c}{((d-x)^2+y^2)^2}) = 0
\end{aligned}
\quad (14)
$$

The relationship between μ_1 and μ_2 can be expressed as

$$\mu_1 = \frac{2(d - x)(x^2 + y^2)^3}{x((d - x)^2 + y^2)^3} \cdot \mu_2 \quad (15)$$

Function $\frac{2(d-x)(x^2+y^2)^3}{x((d-x)^2+y^2)^3} \neq 0$, where if $\mu_1 = 0, \mu_2 = 0$, and $\mu_1 \neq 0, \mu_2 \neq 0$. Hence, in order to transmit data to destination, the SNR of each hop must satisfies

$$t - \frac{\sqrt[4]{2}+1}{(x^2 + y^2)^2} = 0 \quad (16)$$

$$t - \frac{2\gamma_c}{((d - x)^2 + y^2)^2} = 0 \quad (17)$$

Therefore, relay is the best choice when the noise ratio of two relays signal is equal. By conditioning on the inter relay link, the Lagrange multiplier can be calculated as:

$$\mu_1 = \frac{1}{\sqrt[4]{2}+1} \quad (18)$$

$$\mu_2 = 1 - \frac{1}{\sqrt[4]{2}+1} \quad (19)$$

It can be seen that 2D coordinate of the relay location $r_i(u_{1d}, 0)$ of optimal relay can be determined.

4.3   Problem for Dual Relay Mode

In the dual relay mode, we assume that the coordinates of S, S_0, r_{1i} and r_{2j} are $S(0,0)$, $S_0(d,0)$, optimal relay $r_{1i}(x_1, y_1)$ and optimal relay $r_{1i}(x_2, y_2)$, respectively. The relay location 2D coordinate of the optimal relay can be expressed as follows:

$$[x_1, y_1, x_2, y_2, t] = \underset{x_1, y_1, x_2, y_2, t}{\mathrm{argmax}} \; (\frac{1}{3}\log_2(1+t)) \tag{20}$$

The SNR in case of DF relaying is determined by the SNR of the bottleneck link. Hence, the optimal relay with maximum channel capacity can be described as

$$\underset{x_1, y_1, x_2, y_2, t}{\max} f = t \tag{21}$$

$$s.t. \; \frac{\gamma_{sr_{1i}}}{(x_1^2 + y_1^2)^2} \geq t \tag{22}$$

$$\frac{\gamma_{r_{1i}r_{2j}}}{((x_2 - x_1)^2 + (y_2 - y_1)^2)^2} \geq t \tag{23}$$

$$\frac{\gamma_{r_{2j}s_0}}{((d - x_2)^2 + y_2^2)^2} \geq t \tag{24}$$

4.4   Analysis of Optimal Relay Selection for Dual Relay Mode

For simplicity, we assume that the transmit power of the source and the relays is the same, i.e., $E_S = E_{R1} = E_{R2}$. In the dual relay mode, the Lagrangian function for optimal relay of the secondary user can be obtained.

$$L(x_1, y_1, x_2, y_2, t) = -t + \lambda_1(t - \frac{\gamma_c}{(x_1^2 + y_1^2)^2}) + \lambda_2(t - \frac{\gamma_c}{((x_2 - x_1)^2 + (y_2 - y_1)^2)^2}) \\ + \lambda_3(t - \frac{\gamma_c}{((d - x_2)^2 + y_2^2)^2}) \tag{25}$$

Where $\lambda_1 \geq 0$, $\lambda_2 \geq 0$ and $\lambda_3 \geq 0$ are Lagrange factors corresponding to formula (22), (23), and (24) respectively.

Similar to the case of two hops, relay solution is the best choice when SNRs between three hops are equal to each other. By conditioning on the inter relay link, the Lagrange factor can be calculated as:

$$\lambda_1 = \lambda_2 = \lambda_3 = \frac{1}{3} \tag{26}$$

It can be seen that 2D coordinates of the relay location are $r_{1i}(\frac{1}{3}d, 0)$ and $r_{2j}(\frac{2}{3}d, 0)$.

4.5   Analysis of Three Models

In this section we discuss the channel capacity of three transmission modes. The channel capacity of these modes are compared with each other using Matlab. For simplicity, we assume that the transmission power of the source is equal to the relays, $E_S = E_{R1} = E_{R2}$.

In case of the direct mode and single relay mode, the relay with maximum channel capacity is selected as the best relay to receive a message from S and transmit it to S_0. With the change of transmission distance d, the channel capacities of the two transmission modes are equal, i.e., $C_1 = C_2$. Based on this description, we can obtain

$$\log_2(1 + \frac{\gamma_C}{d_1{}^4}) = \frac{1}{2}\log_2(1 + \frac{\gamma_C}{\mu_1^4 d_1{}^4}) \tag{27}$$

After calculation, the transmission distance d1 can be expressed as:

$$d_1 = \sqrt[4]{\frac{\gamma_C \mu_1^4}{1 - \mu_1^4}} \tag{28}$$

Similarly, if $d = d_2$, the channel capacities of the direct mode were exactly the same as the dual relay mode.

$$\log_2(1 + \frac{\gamma_C}{(\mu_1 d_2)^4}) = \frac{1}{3}\log_2(1 + \frac{\gamma_C}{(1/3 d_2)^4}) \tag{29}$$

Thus, the transmission distance d_2 is given by:

$$d_2 = \sqrt[4]{\frac{4\gamma_C}{\sqrt{321} - 3}} \tag{30}$$

In case of dual relay mode and single relay mode, if $d = d_3$, the channel capacities of the two transmission modes are equal, i.e., $C_2 = C_3$. Based on this description,

$$\frac{1}{3}\log_2(1 + \frac{\gamma_C}{(1/3 d_2)^4}) = \frac{1}{2}\log_2(1 + \frac{\gamma_C}{(\mu_1 d_2)^4}) \tag{31}$$

where, $w = \frac{\gamma_C}{d_2^4}$. After some simplifications, we obtain a quadratic equation that can be simplified as:

$$\frac{w^2}{\mu_1^{12}} + (\frac{3}{\mu_1^8} - 3^8)w + \frac{3}{\mu_1^4} - 162 = 0 \tag{32}$$

Find the solutions of the quadratic equation, and give up the solution of the equation that is always negative. Thus, the solution of the quadratic equation is calculated as:

$$w = \frac{\mu_1^{12}(-(\frac{3}{\mu_1^8} - 3^8) + \sqrt{(\frac{3}{\mu_1^8} - 3^8)^2 - 4\frac{1}{\mu_1^{12}}\frac{3}{\mu_1^4} - 162})}{4} \tag{33}$$

And the transmission distance d_1 can be written as:

$$d_3 = \sqrt[4]{\frac{4\gamma_C}{\mu_1^{12}(-(\frac{3}{\mu_1^8} - 3^8) + \sqrt{(\frac{3}{\mu_1^8} - 3^8)^2 - 4\frac{1}{\mu_1^{12}}\frac{3}{\mu_1^4} - 162})}} \tag{34}$$

In order to simplify the analysis of transmission mode, conditioning on the transmission links, will be carried out first. Thus, according to the channel capacity of the transmission links we will obtain the optimal path. In fact, the path transmits data from S to S_0 through optimal relay will serve as optimal path. Given some parameters, according to formula (4) (5) and (6), we can get the channel capacity C_1, C_2, C_3 of three transmission mode. If $d < d_1$, the relationship among the channel capacity of three transmission modes is $C_1 > C_2 > C_3$. When $d_1 < d < d_2$, likewise, we get $C_2 > C_1 > C_3$. When $d_2 < d < d_3$, we get $C_2 > C_3 > C_1$. If $d > d_3$, we get $C_3 > C_2 > C_1$.

5   Simulation Results and Discussion

In the simulation, we propose a DF protocol for a multiple-node (source, relay, and destination) wireless cooperative communication system. We assume that the source node S is at the origin, i.e., $S(0,0)$, and the destination node is located at d in the positive direction of the x-axis, i.e. $S_0(d,0)$. According to theoretical analysis, the optimal locations of relays are located on the x-axis towards the destination node. In single relay mode, the optimal relay coordinates $r_i(x,0)$. In dual relay mode, the optimal relay coordinates $r_{1i}(x_1,0)$, $r_{2j}(x_2,0)$. Other simulation parameters are given as $E_S = 10$, $N_0 = 10^{-13.4}$, $\alpha = 4$.

Figure 2 illustrates the secondary channel capacity versus d under different settings for three transmission mode. d denotes the distance between S and S_0, and the distance d varies from 1000 to 6000. As can be seen from the graph, with gradual increase of the distance d, the channel capacity of the system under the three modes is reduced. It is obvious that the distance d is the dominant factor that affects the secondary channel capacity. When $d < d_1$, the direct mode has the highest channel capacity. While $d_1 < d < d_3$, the channel capacity of the single relay mode is superior to other transmission modes. When $d > d_3$, the channel capacity of the dual relay mode is greater than all other transmission modes. Under the condition of different distance d, the maximum effective system capacity is obtained by selecting the transmission mode with the highest channel capacity.

In single relay mode, the data is transmitted from S to S_0 through the optimal relay $r_i(x,0)$. Similarly, in dual relay mode, data is transmitted to S_0 through the relay $r_{1i}(x_1,0)$ and $_{2j}(x_2,0)$. Formula (23) shows that $x = \mu_1 d$, $x_1 = \frac{1}{3}d$, $x_3 = \frac{2}{3}d$, $y_1 = y_2 = y = 0$, where $\mu_1 = \frac{1}{\sqrt[4]{2}+1}$. As shown in the Fig. 3, The distance

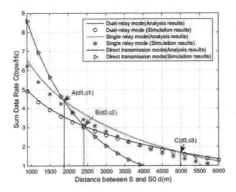

Fig. 2. The secondary channel capacity C as a function of the distance between S and S_0.

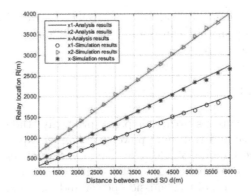

Fig. 3. The relay location as a function of distance between S and S_0

between the optimal relay and S node increases linearly with distance d. The simulation results are in good agreement with the numerical analysis.

Figure 4 depicts the secondary channel capacity versus E_S (i.e., the transmit power of Source node S) under different settings for three transmission mode. The transmit power ES varies from 0 to 10^E. The transmit power E_S of S is the dominant factor to affect the secondary channel capacity.

According to formula (28) (30) and (34), three intersection points of D, F, G can be calculated for three transmission modes. In the simulation results of Fig. 4, the transmit power is smaller when $E_S < E_{S1}$ and the dual relay mode obtains the maximum channel capacity at this time. In regions that meet $E_{S1} < E_S < E_{S3}$, the maximum channel capacity can be obtained by selecting single relay mode. In regions that meet $E_S > E_{S3}$, The direct mode should be selected. Simulations show that the data can be transmitted reliably by corresponding multi hop relay cooperation transmission in low transmission power situation. According to the relationship between the transmit power and the transmission

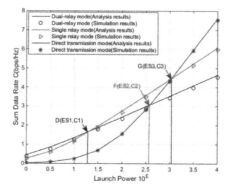

Fig. 4. The secondary channel capacity C as a function of the transmit power E_S

distance d in the wireless network, we can select the corresponding cooperative transmission mechanism that can obtain the maximum channel capacity, and achieve reliable data transmission.

6   Conclusions

On the basis of previous research, this paper primarily studies the influence of transmission distance and transmits power on channel capacity of three transmission modes, direct mode, single relay mode and dual relay mode. We can obtain the maximum channel capacity of the three transmission modes respectively through the control of transmission power and distance. Theoretical analysis and simulation shows that we can choose different cooperative transmission mechanisms to obtain maximum channel capacity and improve the performance of the system according to actual situation in the wireless network.

References

1. Abualhaol, Y., Matalgah, M.: End-to-end performance analysis of cooperative relay-based wireless system over generalized Gaussian-Finite-Mixture fading channels. In: 2007 Global Telecommunications Conference, GLOBECOM 2007, pp. 3942–3947. IEEE (2007)
2. Lu, X., Cheng, W.: Cooperative communication based regular topology to achieve coverage and K-connectivity for WSNs. In: IEEE Conference on Industrial Electronics and Applications (ICIEA) (2018)
3. Duangsri, W., Somrobru, M.: Performance enhancement for co-channel interference cancellation with smart antenna and power adaptive in cooperative communication. In: 2018 International Conference on Advanced Communication Technology, p. 1 (2018)
4. Li, Y., Vucetic, B.: Distributed turbo coding with soft information relaying in multihop relay networks. IEEE J. Sel. Areas Commun. **24**(11), 2040–2050 (2006)

5. Chang, B., Liang, Y.: Dynamic connection admission control in 4G LTE-advanced multihop relaying networks. In: IEEE International Conference on Consumer Electronics-Taiwan (ICCE-TW) (2016)
6. Hong, N., Maric, I.: Short message noisy network coding with sliding-window decoding for half-duplex multihop relay networks. IEEE Trans. Wirel. Commun. 15(10), 6676–6689 (2016)
7. Kim, T., An, K.: Performance analysis of centralised and distributed scheduling schemes for mobile multihop relay systems. IET Commun. 11(1), 69–75 (2017)
8. Gui, J., Deng, J.: Multi-hop relay-aided underlay D2D communications for improving cellular coverage quality. IEEE Access 2018, 99 (2018)
9. Li, S., Yang, K.: Joint power allocation and location optimization for full-duplex amplify-and-forward relay networks. In: International Symposium on Wireless Personal Multimedia Communications. IEEE (2017)
10. Kamouch, A., Chaoub, A.: Optimum relay location and power allocation of cooperative decode-and-forward dual-hop ARQ networks. In: International Conference on Multimedia Computing and Systems, pp. 344–348. IEEE (2017)
11. Kim, S., Chae, S.: Relay location considering in-band emission for OFDMA-based D2D overlay systems. In: 2017 International Conference on Ubiquitous Future Networks, pp. 528–530 (2017)
12. Thampy, H., Babu, V.: Relay location optimization in cognitive full-duplex relay networks. In: 2007 IEEE Region 10 Symposium, pp. 1–5. IEEE (2017)
13. Khalil, I., Berber, M.: Energy efficiency and spectrum efficiency trade-off over optimal relay location in bidirectional relay networks. In: Antennas and Propagation in Wireless Communications, pp. 298–302. IEEE (2016)
14. Yadav, S., Chawla, R.: Outage performance and location optimization for traffic-aware two-way relaying with direct link. In: International Conference on Signal Processing and Communications. IEEE (2016)
15. Wang, B., Gu, X.: A code dissenmination approach to energy efficiency and status surveillance for wireless sensor networks. J. Internet Technol. 8(4), 877–885 (2017)
16. Jiang, Y., Zhong, X.: Communication mechanism and algorithm of composite location analysis of emergency communication based on rail. CMC: Comput. Mater. Contin. 57(2), 321–340 (2018)
17. Liu, W., Luo, X.: Localization algorithm of indoor Wi-Fi access points based on signal strength relative relationship and region division. CMC: Comput. Mater. Contin. 55(1), 071–093 (2018)

Subspace Extension Algorithm for Joint DOA and DOD Estimation in Bistatic MIMO Radar

Sheng Liu$^{(\boxtimes)}$, Jing Zhao, and Wei Li

Tongren University, Tongren 554300, China
liushengtrxy@126.com

Abstract. A subspace extension algorithm for joint direction of departure (DOD) and direction of arrival (DOA) estimation in bistatic multiple-input multiple-output (MIMO) radar is proposed. A two-level nested array is employed as receive array. The signal subspace can be got by eigenvalue decomposition (EVD) of covariance matrix. Then the signal subspace can be extended without additional EVD, and the DOD and DOA can be estimated by ESPRIT algorithm. Because of subspace extension, the proposed algorithm has higher precision than the traditional ESPRIT algorithm. Numerical simulations demonstrate the performance of the proposed design technology.

Keywords: Subspace extension · DOA estimation · DOD estimation · MIMO radar

1 Introduction

One of the main functions of radar is to locate the position of target [1, 2]. As a new radar system, multiple-input multiple-output (MIMO) radar has attracted lots of attention. It employs multiple antennas to simultaneously transmit orthogonal wave-forms and multiple antennas to receive the reflected signals. Compared with the traditional phased-array radars, MIMO radars have many obvious advantages [3, 4] such as enhanced spatial resolution, improved target detection performance, and more degrees of freedom. In recent years, many direction of arrival (DOA) estimation algorithms [5–8] for monostatic MIMO radar have be proposed by scholars. For the monostatic MIMO radar, the transmit array and receive array are closely located, so only the DOA of targets should be considered. Unlike the monostatic MIMO radar, the transmit array and receive array of bistatic MIMO radar are far apart. Hence, both the DOA and DOD need to be estimated. Numerous joint DOA and DOD estimation algorithms [9–18] in bistatic MIMO radar have be presented. In [9], Capon method is applied for the estimation of DOD and DOA, but two-dimensional (2D) spectrum peak searching increases the computation cost. In order to reduce the computational burden caused by 2D spectrum peak searching, the reduced-dimensional Capon (RD-Capon) [10] and reduced-dimensional MUSIC (RD- MUSIC) [11] were proposed, where the DOD and DOA can be estimated by one-dimensional (1D) spectrum peak searching. In [12], the cost function in traditional MUSIC was transformed into a constrained quadratic form. Then, the DOA and DOD can be estimated by minimizing this

© Springer Nature Switzerland AG 2019
X. Sun et al. (Eds.): ICAIS 2019, LNCS 11634, pp. 244–252, 2019.
https://doi.org/10.1007/978-3-030-24271-8_22

quadratic form. In [13, 14], ESPRIT method was presented to accomplish the estimation of DOD and DOA which does not need spectrum peak searching. In [15], the polynomial root finding technique was used for joint DOD and DOA estimation, and this technique is combined with ESPRIT in [16]. In [17], an ESPRIT-based algorithm was proposed, where the DOA and DOD can be estimated and paired automatically by singular value decomposition (SVD) of cross-correlation matrix of the received data from two transmit subarrays. For avoiding eigenvalue decomposition (EVD) or SVD, propagator method (PM) is used to estimate the DOA and DOD in [18]. But for these algorithms, the covariance matrix of receive signals is directly used to estimate the DOA or DOD. In fact, in this way, the receive data has not been fully utilized. If the receive data can be used more sufficiently, we can obtain more accurate DOA and DOD estimation.

In order to make good use of the received data, we propose a subspace extension algorithm for joint DOD and DOA estimation. For this algorithm, a two-level nested array [19, 20] is employed as receive array. To facilitate express, we call it as subspace extension ESPRIT (SE-ESPRIT) algorithm.

Notation: The operators $[\bullet]^{+}$, $[\bullet]^{T}$, $[\bullet]^{H}$ and $\otimes$ stand for the Moore-Penrose generalized inverse, the transpose, the conjugate transpose, and the Kronecker product respectively. The operator $E[\bullet]$ is the statistical expectation. The superscript $\mathbf{A}_{i:j,:}$ denotes a matrix consisting of the ith column to the jth column of matrix $\mathbf{A}$.

2   Subspace Extension Algorithm

See Fig. 1.

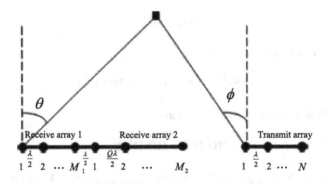

Fig. 1. The second bistatic MIMO radar structure

2.1   Data Model

Consider a bistatic MIMO radar consisting of N-element transmit array and M-element receive array as shown in Fig. 2, where $M_1 + M_2 = M$. The transmit array is a ULA with half-wavelength ($\lambda/2$) spacing between adjacent sensors. The receive array is comprised by two ULAs with half-wavelength ($\lambda/2$) spacing between the two subarray. The element interval of the first sub array is $\lambda/2$, and the element interval of the second sub array is $Q\lambda/2$, where Q is a positive integer. Assume that there are $K(K \leq \min\{(N-1)M, M_1 N\})$ uncorrelated targets, and $\phi_k, \theta_k, k = 1, 2, \cdots, K$, are the DOD and DOA of the kth target. Let $\mathbf{y}(t) = [y_1(t), y_2(t), \cdots, y_{MN}(t)]^T \in C^{MN \times 1}$ be the output of the matched filters from the receive array, and it can be expressed as [13]

$$\mathbf{y}(t) = \mathbf{B}(\boldsymbol{\theta}, \boldsymbol{\phi})\mathbf{s}(t) + \mathbf{e}(t), \ t = 1, 2 \cdots T \tag{1}$$

where $\mathbf{B}(\boldsymbol{\theta}, \boldsymbol{\phi}) = [\mathbf{b}_r(\theta_1) \otimes \mathbf{b}_t(\phi_1), \mathbf{b}_r(\theta_2) \otimes \mathbf{b}_t(\phi_2), \cdots, \mathbf{b}_r(\theta_K) \otimes \mathbf{b}_t(\phi_K)] \in C^{MN \times K}$ is the array manifold matrix, $\mathbf{b}_t(\phi_k) = [1, e^{-j\pi \sin \phi_k}, \cdots, e^{-j\pi(N-1)\sin \phi_k}]^T \in C^{N \times 1}$ and $\mathbf{b}_r(\theta_k) = [1, e^{-j\pi \sin \theta_k}, \cdots, e^{-j\pi(M_1-1)\sin \theta_k}, \cdots, e^{-j\pi(M_1 + M_2 Q - Q)\sin \theta_k}]^T \in C^{M \times 1}$ are the transmit and receive steering vectors of the kth target; $\mathbf{s}(t) = [s_1(t), s_2(t), \cdots, s_K(t)]^T$, $\mathbf{e}(t) = [e_1(t), e_2(t), \cdots, e_{MN}(t)]^T \in C^{MN \times 1}$ is Gaussian white noise vector with zeros mean and covariance matrix $\delta^2 \mathbf{I}_{MN}$.

2.2   Algorithm Description

Denoting $\mathbf{R}_y = E[\mathbf{y}(t)\mathbf{y}^H(t)]$, implementing EVD on $\mathbf{R}_y$ yields

$$\mathbf{R}_y = \mathbf{W}_s \mathbf{D}_s \mathbf{W}_s^H + \mathbf{W}_n \mathbf{D}_n \mathbf{W}_n^H \tag{2}$$

where $\mathbf{D}_s = diag\{\lambda_1, \lambda_2, \cdots, \lambda_K\}$, $\lambda_1, \lambda_2, \cdots, \lambda_K$ denote the K biggest eigenvalues of matrix $\mathbf{R}_y$ and the columns of $\mathbf{W}_s$ are the corresponding eigenvectors.

Since span$\{\mathbf{W}_s\}$ = span$\{\mathbf{B}\}$, there must be a reversible matrix $\mathbf{H} \in C^{MN \times MN}$ meeting

$$\mathbf{W}_s = \mathbf{B}\mathbf{H} \tag{3}$$

According to (3), we can know

$$\mathbf{W}_s \mathbf{D}_s \mathbf{W}_s^H = \mathbf{B}\mathbf{H}\mathbf{D}_s \mathbf{W}_s^H = \mathbf{B}\mathbf{H}\mathbf{D}_s \mathbf{H}^H \mathbf{B}^H \tag{4}$$

Because $\mathbf{B}$ is a full rank matrix, we have

$$\mathbf{H}\mathbf{D}_s \mathbf{W}_s^H = \mathbf{H}\mathbf{D}_s \mathbf{H}^H \mathbf{B}^H \tag{5}$$

Let $\mathbf{W}_1 = [\mathbf{W}_s]_{1:M_1 N,:}$, $\mathbf{W}_2 = [\mathbf{W}_s]_{N+1:M_1 N+N,:}$, $\mathbf{W}_3 = [\mathbf{W}_s]_{M_1 N+1:MN,:}$, $\mathbf{B}_1 = [\mathbf{B}]_{1:M_1 N,:}$, $\mathbf{B}_2 = [\mathbf{B}]_{N+1:M_1 N+N,:}$, $\mathbf{B}_3 = [\mathbf{B}]_{M_1 N+1:MN,:}$, then we can obtain

$$\mathbf{B}_2 = \mathbf{B}_1 \boldsymbol{\Phi} \tag{6}$$

From (3), we have

$$\begin{cases} \mathbf{W}_1 = \mathbf{B}_1 \mathbf{H} \\ \mathbf{W}_2 = \mathbf{B}_2 \mathbf{H} \end{cases} \tag{7}$$

Combining (6), (7), we can get

$$(\mathbf{W}_1)^+ \mathbf{W}_2 = \mathbf{H}^{-1} \mathbf{\Phi} \mathbf{H} \tag{8}$$

From (8), we have

$$\mathbf{W}_3[(\mathbf{W}_1)^+ \mathbf{W}_2]^{Nq} = \mathbf{B}_3 \mathbf{H}(\mathbf{H}^{-1}\mathbf{\Phi}\mathbf{H})^{Nq} = \mathbf{B}_3 \mathbf{\Phi}^{Nq}\mathbf{H} = \mathbf{B}_{3q}\mathbf{H}, q = 0, 1, \cdots, Q-1 \tag{9}$$

where $\mathbf{B}_{3q} = \mathbf{B}_3 \mathbf{\Phi}^{Nq}$.

Denote matrix $\mathbf{F}_{ij} \in C^{Q \times M_2}$, $i = 1, 2, \cdots, Q$, $j = 1, 2, \cdots, M_2$ with only nonzero element 1 on the cross position of the ith row and the jth column.

Denote matrix $\mathbf{E}_q$ as

$$\mathbf{E}_q = \begin{bmatrix} \mathbf{F}^T_{q+1,1} & \mathbf{F}^T_{q+1,2} & \cdots & \mathbf{F}^T_{q+1,M_2} \end{bmatrix}^T \otimes \mathbf{I}_N, q = 0, 1, \cdots, Q-1 \tag{10}$$

where $\mathbf{I}_N$ is an $N \times N$ identity matrix.

We construct a new matrix $\mathbf{R}_{ynew} \in C^{(M_1 N + Q M_2 N) \times (M_1 N + M_2 N)}$ as

$$\mathbf{W}_{new} = \begin{bmatrix} \mathbf{W}_s \\ \displaystyle\sum_{q=0}^{Q-1} \mathbf{E}_q \mathbf{W}_3[(\mathbf{W}_1)^+ \mathbf{W}_2]^{Nq} \end{bmatrix} \tag{11}$$

Substituting (3) and (9) into (11), $\mathbf{W}_{new}$ can be rewritten as

$$\mathbf{W}_{new} = \mathbf{J}\mathbf{H} \tag{12}$$

According to (5), $\mathbf{B}_3$ can be rewritten as

$$\mathbf{B}_3 = \begin{bmatrix} e^{-j\pi M \sin\theta_1}\mathbf{b}_t(\phi_1) & e^{-j\pi M \sin\theta_2}\mathbf{b}_t(\phi_2) & \cdots & e^{-j\pi M \sin\theta_k}\mathbf{b}_t(\phi_k) \\ e^{-j\pi(M+Q)\sin\theta_1}\mathbf{b}_t(\phi_1) & e^{-j\pi(M+Q)\sin\theta_2}\mathbf{b}_t(\phi_2) & \cdots & e^{-j\pi(M+Q)\sin\theta_k}\mathbf{b}_t(\phi_k) \\ \vdots & \vdots & \ddots & \vdots \\ e^{-j\pi(M+(N-1)Q)\sin\theta_1}\mathbf{b}_t(\phi_1) & e^{-j\pi(M+(N-1)Q)\sin\theta_2}\mathbf{b}_t(\phi_2) & \cdots & e^{-j\pi(M+(N-1)Q)\sin\theta_k}\mathbf{b}_t(\phi_k) \end{bmatrix} \tag{13}$$

According to (9), $\mathbf{B}_{3q}$ can be rewritten as

$$\mathbf{B}_{3q} = \begin{bmatrix} e^{-j\pi(M+q)\sin\theta_1}\mathbf{b}_t(\phi_1) & e^{-j\pi(M+q)\sin\theta_2}\mathbf{b}_t(\phi_2) & \cdots & e^{-j\pi(M+q)\sin\theta_k}\mathbf{b}_t(\phi_k) \\ e^{-j\pi(M+Q+q)\sin\theta_1}\mathbf{b}_t(\phi_1) & e^{-j\pi(M+Q+q)\sin\theta_2}\mathbf{b}_t(\phi_2) & \cdots & e^{-j\pi(M+Q+q)\sin\theta_k}\mathbf{b}_t(\phi_k) \\ \vdots & \vdots & \ddots & \vdots \\ e^{-j\pi(M+(N-1)Q+q)\sin\theta_1}\mathbf{b}_t(\phi_1) & e^{-j\pi(M+(N-1)Q+q)\sin\theta_2}\mathbf{b}_t(\phi_2) & \cdots & e^{-j\pi(M+(N-1)Q+q)\sin\theta_k}\mathbf{b}_t(\phi_k) \end{bmatrix} \tag{14}$$

Combining (10) and (14), we can get

$$
\mathbf{E}_q\mathbf{B}_{3q}\mathbf{H} = \mathbf{E}_q \begin{bmatrix} e^{-j\pi(M+q)\sin\theta_1}\mathbf{b}_t(\phi_1) & e^{-j\pi(M+q)\sin\theta_2}\mathbf{b}_t(\phi_2) & \cdots & e^{-j\pi(M+q)\sin\theta_k}\mathbf{b}_t(\phi_k) \\ e^{-j\pi(M+Q+q)\sin\theta_1}\mathbf{b}_t(\phi_1) & e^{-j\pi(M+Q+q)\sin\theta_2}\mathbf{b}_t(\phi_2) & \cdots & e^{-j\pi(M+Q+q)\sin\theta_k}\mathbf{b}_t(\phi_k) \\ \vdots & \vdots & \ddots & \vdots \\ e^{-j\pi(M+(N-1)Q+q)\sin\theta_1}\mathbf{b}_t(\phi_1) & e^{-j\pi(M+(N-1)Q+q)\sin\theta_2}\mathbf{b}_t(\phi_2) & \cdots & e^{-j\pi(M+(N-1)Q+q)\sin\theta_k}\mathbf{b}_t(\phi_k) \end{bmatrix}\mathbf{H}
$$

$$
= \begin{bmatrix} 0 & 0 & 0 & 0 \\ \vdots & \vdots & \vdots & \vdots \\ e^{-j\pi(M+q)\sin\theta_1}\mathbf{b}_t(\phi_1) & e^{-j\pi(M+q)\sin\theta_2}\mathbf{b}_t(\phi_2) & \cdots & e^{-j\pi(M+q)\sin\theta_K}\mathbf{b}_t(\phi_K) \\ 0 & 0 & 0 & 0 \\ \vdots & \vdots & \vdots & \vdots \\ e^{-j\pi(M+Q+q)\sin\theta_1}\mathbf{b}_t(\phi_1) & e^{-j\pi(M+Q+q)\sin\theta_2}\mathbf{b}_t(\phi_2) & \cdots & e^{-j\pi(M+Q+q)\sin\theta_K}\mathbf{b}_t(\phi_K) \\ 0 & 0 & 0 & 0 \\ \vdots & \vdots & \vdots & \vdots \\ e^{-j\pi(M+(N-1)Q+q)\sin\theta_1}\mathbf{b}_t(\phi_1) & e^{-j\pi(M+(N-1)Q+q)\sin\theta_2}\mathbf{b}_t(\phi_2) & \cdots & e^{-j\pi(M+(N-1)Q+q)\sin\theta_K}\mathbf{b}_t(\phi_K) \\ \vdots & \vdots & \vdots & \vdots \end{bmatrix}\mathbf{H}
$$

$$(15)$$

From (9), we have

$$
\mathbf{E}_q\mathbf{W}_3\left[(\mathbf{W}_1)^+\mathbf{W}_2\right]^{Nq} = \mathbf{E}_q\mathbf{B}_{3q}\mathbf{H} \tag{16}
$$

Then, we can obtain

$$
\sum_{q=0}^{Q-1}\mathbf{E}_q\mathbf{W}_3\left[(\mathbf{W}_1)^+\mathbf{W}_2\right]^{Nq} = \begin{bmatrix} e^{-j\pi M\sin\theta_1}\mathbf{b}_t(\phi_1) & e^{-j\pi M\sin\theta_2}\mathbf{b}_t(\phi_2) & \cdots & e^{-j\pi M\sin\theta_k}\mathbf{b}_t(\phi_k) \\ e^{-j\pi(M+1)\sin\theta_1}\mathbf{b}_t(\phi_1) & e^{-j\pi(M+1)\sin\theta_2}\mathbf{b}_t(\phi_2) & \cdots & e^{-j\pi(M+1)\sin\theta_k}\mathbf{b}_t(\phi_k) \\ \vdots & \vdots & \ddots & \vdots \\ e^{-j\pi(M+NQ-1)\sin\theta_1}\mathbf{b}_t(\phi_1) & e^{-j\pi(M+NQ-1)\sin\theta_2}\mathbf{b}_t(\phi_2) & \cdots & e^{-j\pi(M+NQ-1)\sin\theta_k}\mathbf{b}_t(\phi_k) \end{bmatrix}
$$

$$(17)$$

Then, it's easy to get

$$
\mathbf{W}_{new} = \begin{bmatrix} \mathbf{W}_s \\ \sum_{q=0}^{Q-1}\mathbf{E}_q\mathbf{W}_3\left[(\mathbf{W}_1)^+\mathbf{W}_2\right]^{Nq} \end{bmatrix} = \mathbf{JH} \tag{18}
$$

where
$\mathbf{J}(\boldsymbol{\theta},\boldsymbol{\phi}) = [\bar{\mathbf{b}}_r(\theta_1)\otimes\mathbf{b}_t(\phi_1), \bar{\mathbf{b}}_r(\theta_2)\otimes\mathbf{b}_t(\phi_2), \cdots, \bar{\mathbf{b}}_r(\theta_K)\otimes\mathbf{b}_t(\phi_K)] \in C^{(M_1+QM_1)\times K}$,
$\bar{\mathbf{b}}_r(\theta_k) = [1, e^{-j\pi\sin\theta_k}, \cdots, e^{-j\pi(M_1+QM_1-1)\sin\theta_k}] \in C^{(M_1+QM_1)\times K}$.

Obviously, compared with $\mathbf{W}_s$, $\mathbf{W}_{new}$ can be seen as an extended signal subspace. This process is inspired by the subspace extension algorithm [19]. Dealing with the $\mathbf{W}_{new}$ with the ESPRIT algorithm [13], we can get the estimation of DOD and DOA.

3   Simulation Results

In this subsection, several simulations are carried out to prove the effectiveness of proposed algorithm. Since this algorithm can be considered as the improved algorithm of ESPRIT. So, we only compare it with ESPRIT [13]. In these simulation experiments, we suppose $N = 5$, $M = 5$. For the SE-ESPRIT, we let $M_1 = 3$, $M_2 = 2$. The root-mean-square error (RMSE) of joint DOD and DOA estimation is defined as

$$\text{RMSE} = \sqrt{\frac{1}{JK} \sum_{k=1}^{K} \sum_{j=1}^{J} (\hat{\theta}_{jk} - \theta_k)^2 + (\hat{\phi}_{jk} - \phi_k)^2} \qquad (19)$$

where $J = 500$, and $\hat{\theta}_{jk}$, $\hat{\phi}_{jk}$ are the DOA and DOD estimations of the kth target in the jth Monte Carlo trial.

Experiment 1. In this experiment, we compare the performance of ESPRIT [13] and proposed ESPRIT algorithm for three targets. Consider three target signals with $[\theta_1, \theta_2, \theta_3] = [10°, 20°, 30°]$ and $[\phi_1, \phi_2, \phi_3] = [15°, 25°, 35°]$. Figure 2 shows the RMSE comparison versus SNR for ESPRIT algorithm and proposed ESPRIT algorithm with T = 200. Figure 3 shows the RMSE comparison versus snapshots for ESPRIT algorithm and proposed ESPRIT algorithm with SNR = 5 dB.

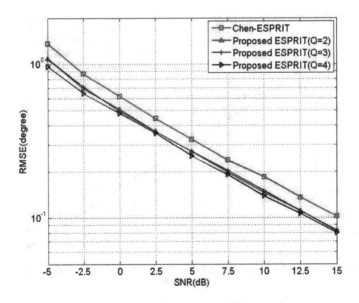

Fig. 2. RMSE versus SNR for three targets.

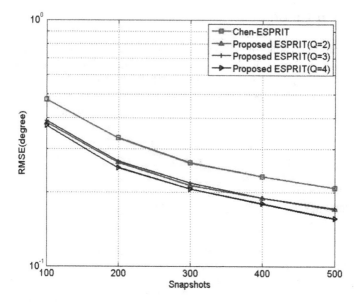

Fig. 3. RMSE versus snapshots for three targets.

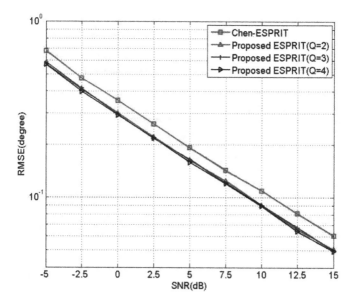

Fig. 4. RMSE versus SNR for four targets.

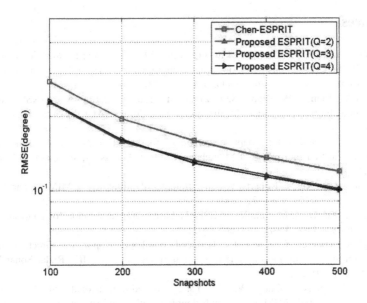

Fig. 5. RMSE versus snapshots for four targets.

Experiment 2. In this experiment, we compare the performance of SE-ESPRIT and ESPRIT for four targets. The DOA and DOD of four targets are $[\theta_1, \theta_2, \theta_3, \theta_4] = [-10°, 10°, 20°, 35°]$ and $[\phi_1, \phi_2, \phi_3, \phi_4] = [-20°, 0°, 10°, 25°]$. Figure 4 presents the RMSE of three method versus SNR with T = 200. Figure 5 presents the RMSE of three method versus snapshots with SNR = 5 dB. It is indicated in Figs. 4 and 5 that SE-ESPRIT has better estimation performance than ESPRIT.

4 Conclusions

In this paper, the SE-ESPRIT algorithms are proposed for joint DOA and DOD estimation. A two-level nested array is employed as receive array. According to the special array construction, an extended signal subspace can be got without additional calculated amount. Simulation results show the proposed algorithm has higher accurate than the traditional ESPRIT algorithm because of the extended signal subspace.

Acknowledgments. This work was supported by the Cooperation Agreement Project by the Department of Science and Technology of Guizhou Province of China (LH [2017]7320, LH [2017]7321), the Foundation of Top-notch Talents by Education Department of Guizhou Province of China (KY [2018]075), the Innovation Group Major Research Program Funded by Guizhou Provincial Education Department (KY [2016]051) and PhD Research Startup Foundation of Tongren University (trxyDH1710).

References

1. Liu, W.Y., Luo, X.Y., Liu, Y.M., Liu, J.Q., Liu, M.B., Shi, Y.Q.: Localization algorithm of indoor Wi-Fi access points based on signal strength relative relationship and region division. CMC: Comput. Mater. Contin. **55**(1), 071–093 (2018)
2. Zhou, T.Y., Lian, B.W., Yang, S.Q., Zhang, Y., Liu, Y.Y.: Improved GNSS cooperation positioning algorithm for indoor localization. CMC: Comput. Mater. Contin. **56**(2), 225–245 (2018)
3. Xu, L., Li, J., Stoica, P.: Adaptive techniques for MIMO radar. In: 4th Proceedings of Workshop on Sensor Array and Multichannel Signal Processing, Waltham, MA, pp. 258–263 (2006)
4. Li, J., Stoica, P., Xu, L., Roberts, W.: On parameter identifiability of MIMO radar. IEEE Sig. Process. Lett. **14**(12), 968–972 (2007)
5. Zhang, X., Xu, D.: Low-complexity ESPRIT-based DOA estimation for collocated MIMO radar. Electron. Lett. **47**(4), 283–285 (2011)
6. Zhang, X., Huang, Y., Chen, C.: Reduced-complexity Capon for direction of arrival estimation in a monostatic multiple-input multiple-output radar. IET Radar Sonar Navig. **6**(8), 796–801 (2012)
7. Li, J.F., Zhang, X.F., Chen, W., Hu, Y.T.: Reduced-dimensional ESPRIT for direction finding in monostatic MIMO radar with double parallel uniform linear arrays. Wirel. Pers. Commun. **77**(1), 1–19 (2014)
8. Wang, W., Wang, X.P., Song, H.G., Ma, Y.H.: Conjugate ESPRIT for DOA estimation in monostatic MIMO radar. Sig. Process. **93**(7), 2070–2076 (2013)
9. Yan, H., Li, J., Liao, G.: Multitarget identification and localization using bistatic MIMO radar systems. EURASIP J. Adv. Sig. Process. **2008**(8), 1–8 (2013)
10. Zhang, X., Xu, D.: Angle estimation in MIMO radar using reduced-dimension Capon. Electron. Lett. **46**(12), 860–862 (2010)
11. Zhang, X.F., Xu, L.Y., Xu, D.Z.: Direction of departure (DOD) and direction of arrival (DOA) estimation in MIMO radar with reduced-dimension MUSIC. IEEE Commun. Lett. **14**(12), 1161–1164 (2010)
12. Xie, R., Liu, Z., Wu, J.X.: Direction finding with automatic pairing for bistatic MIMO radar. Sig. Process. **92**(1), 198–204 (2012)
13. Chen, D.F., Chen, B.X., Qin, G.D.: Angle estimation using ESPRIT in MIMO. Electron. Lett. **44**(12), 770–772 (2008)
14. Chen, J.L., Guo, H., Su, W.M.: Angle estimation using ESPRIT without pairing in MIMO radar. Electron. Lett. **44**(24), 1422–1423 (2008)
15. Bencheikh, M.L., Wang, Y.D., He, H.Y.: Polynomial root finding technique for joint DOA and DOD estimation in bistatic MIMO radar. Sig. Process. **90**(9), 2723–2731 (2010)
16. Bencheikh, M.L., Wang, Y.D.: Joint DOD-DOA estimation using combined ESPRIT-MUSIC approach in MIMO radar. Electron. Lett. **46**(15), 1081–1082 (2010)
17. Chen, J.L., Hong, G., Su, W.M.: A new method for joint DOD and DOA estimation in bistatic MIMO radar. Sig. Process. **90**(2), 714–718 (2010)
18. Zhang, X.F., Wu, H.L., Li, J.F., Xu, D.Z.: Computationally efficient DOD and DOA estimation for bistatic MIMO radar with propagator method. Int. J. Electron. **99**(9), 1207–1362 (2012)
19. Liu, S., Yang, L.S., Li, D., Cao, H.L.: Subspace extension algorithm for 2D DOA estimation with L-shaped sparse array. Multidimension. Syst. Sig. Process. **28**, 315–327 (2017)
20. Liu, S., Zhao, J., Xiao, Z.G.: DOA estimation with sparse array under unknown mutual coupling. Prog. Electromagnet. Res. Lett. **70**, 147–153 (2017)

Under-Determined Blind Source Separation Anti-collision Algorithm for RFID Based on Adaptive Tree Grouping

Xiaohong Zhang[1(✉)], Qiuli Wang[2], and Yungang Jin[1]

[1] School of Information Engineering, Jiangxi University of Science and Technology, Ganzhou 341000, People's Republic of China
xiaohongzh@263.net
[2] Shanghai Technical Institute of Electronics Information, Shanghai 201411, People's Republic of China

Abstract. Under-determined blind separation becomes poorer with increasing number of tags, to the point where it cannot separate source tag signals, reducing overall system performance. This paper proposes a parallelizable identification anti-collision algorithm based on non-negative matrix factorization and adaptive ID sequence grouping of binary tree slots. The number of tags in each group can be controlled within the optimum range by selecting a reasonable number to retained source signal separation in the RFID system, which will greatly improve system performance. With the Matlab software numerical calculation and simulation, the results show that tag identification rate improves from 152.8% to 359.2% compared with the blind separation and dynamic bit-slot group algorithm using the same multi-antenna technology for 4–16 antennas, while increasing tag identification speed from 60% to 78.4%. Thus, the proposed algorithm provides high efficiency and low cost and will have very good application for fast identification of large numbers of tags.

Keywords: RFID technology · Under-determined blind separation · Non-negative matrix factorization · Anti-collision algorithm · Identification efficiency

1 Introduction

Radio frequency identification (RFID) is an automatic recognition technology by way using non-contact induction of electromagnetic waves [1, 2]. With the rapid development of networking technologies and applications as the core technology for the internet of things, RFID technology has become an important research area, widely used in many fields, including military, industrial automation, public management, logistics management, etc. [3–5].

In practical applications, readers need to identify a large number of tags in a short time, but these tags and the readers share the radio communication channel when they communicate with each other. If multiple tags simultaneously receive query signals sent by the reader, tag collision problems can seriously affect tags identification speed

© Springer Nature Switzerland AG 2019
X. Sun et al. (Eds.): ICAIS 2019, LNCS 11634, pp. 253–265, 2019.
https://doi.org/10.1007/978-3-030-24271-8_23

and correctness. Therefore, effective anti-collision algorithms are essential to ensure fast and efficient communication between readers and multiple tags [6, 7].

Tag anti-collision algorithms for RFID system can be divided into code division multiple access, time division multiple access (TDMA), frequency division multiple access and space division multiple access, etc. systems [8, 9]. Two TDMA anti-collision algorithms are commonly used due to cost and resource constraints: the ALOHA algorithm, based on uncertainty, and the deterministic algorithm, based on trees [10, 11]. The ALOHA anti-collision algorithm uses EPC Gen2 dynamic frame slotted random algorithm based on the Q algorithm [12]. Although this provides some adaptability, the Q algorithm maximum tag identification rate is only ∼50%. On the other hand, the enhanced binary search tree anti-collision (EBS) algorithm is based on the binary numbers deterministic anti-collision algorithm [13]. However, although tag identification rate can approach 100%, the algorithm is bit-by-bit identification, hence search depth is related to tag ID-digit length, and recognition rate declines sharply with increasing tag bits. Therefore, it is crucial to find a new multi-tags anti-collision algorithm.

Blind source separation (BSS) [14, 15] is an emerging method that can separate source signal from observed signals without knowing the source signal or transmission parameters. BSS can be divided into under-determined BSS [16] and non-under-determined BSS [17]. Non-under-determined BSS usually adopts independent component analysis (ICA) [18], such as the blind separation and dynamic bit-slot grouping (BSDBG) algorithm [19]. However, the BSDBG algorithm requires that the number of antennas is greater than the number of tags, but the cost is too high and the restriction is obvious. On the other hand, although under-determined BSS has achieved BSS when the tag number was greater than the number of antennas conditions. Based on multi-standard anti-collision [20], separation and tag identification rates are greatly reduced with increasing number of tags. To solve this problem, this paper proposes an under-determined BSS adaptive packet anti-collision algorithm tree, combining under-determined BSS with tag ID number sequence binary grouping. Simulation results show that tag recognition rate and performance are greatly improved in shorter time with increasing number of tags.

2 Algorithm System Description

2.1 Multi-antenna Blind Source Separation System Model

The proposed multi-antenna under-determined BSS anti-collision system consists of three parts: tag, reader, and computer system (Fig. 1). Multiple reader antennas simultaneously transmit query information to tags, then the tags modulate the carrier signals to provide reverse transfer signals. When the reader receives a response signal, it uses restraint non-negative matrix factorization (NMF) [21] BSS to process the responsive tags and simultaneously stores the appropriate information, then sends the stored information to the information processing system.

Supposing there are N tags in the scope of the reader, source signal of the tags can be expressed as $S = [s_1(t), s_2(t), \cdots, s_N(t)]^T$, where: $s_i(t)$ $(1 \leq i \leq N)$ is the i th tag

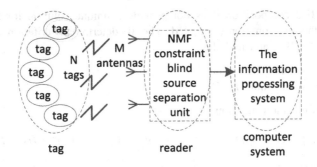

Fig. 1. Antenna system model of under-determined blind source separation.

signal sample value. Similarly, M mixed signal received by the reader, that is to say observed signal can be represented as $X = [x_1(t), x_2(t), \cdots, x_M(t)]^T$, and $x_j(t)$ $(1 \leq j \leq M)$ is the received signals of j th reader antenna.

The mathematical model of blind source separation can be expressed as:

$$X = AS + R \tag{1}$$

Among them, A is mixing coefficient matrix, matrix R stands for interfering noise. Ignoring the noise Eq. (1) can be expressed as:

$$X = AS \tag{2}$$

In the case of multi-tag anti-collision, classical ICA approach is often used to tags blind source separation, namely to separate out the source tag signal S by obtaining an inverse matrix A^{-1}.

However, this method is only applicable to the case that the number of tags is less than or equal to the number of antenna. When the number of tags is more than the number of receiving antennas of reader, namely $N > M$, even if it can estimate the mixing matrix A, but it cannot separate the source signals due to the A^{-1} matrix does not exist. In practical applications often encounter that tags number N is greater than the number of antenna M, in order to reduce the costs and improve efficiency in the multi-antenna RFID systems, the use of under-determined blind separation algorithm is more realistic.

2.2 Constraint Under-Determined Blind Source Separation Algorithm

Non-negative matrix factorization can be described as follows. A non-negative limiting matrix $V = [v_1, v_2, \ldots, v_N] \in R^{m \times N}$ decomposes into the non-negative matrix product of $W = [w_1, w_2, \ldots, w_n] \in R^{m \times n}$ and $H = [h_1, h_2, \cdots, h_N] \in R^{n \times N}$, i.e.,

$$V = W \times H, \tag{3}$$

where the matrix dimensions satisfy $(m + N)n < mN$.

Since NMF decomposition does not provide a unique solution for $\mathbf{S}$, the triple constraint method is commonly adopted. The W determinant criterion constraint is denoted as $vol(\varphi(W))$ and includes

1. $\mathbf{H}$ sparse constraint, $J(H)$; and
2. $\mathbf{H}$ correlation constraint, $R(H)$.

Hence, the optimization function is

$$F(V\|WH) = \partial_D D(V\|WH) + \partial_\varphi vol(\varphi(W)) + \partial_J J(H) + \partial_R R(H) \tag{4}$$

where $D(V\|WH)$ is the objective function, $\partial_D, \partial_\varphi, \partial_J, \partial_R$ are constraint parameters, and the optimization is to minimise the $D(V\|WH)$ reconstruction error. To ensure algorithm convergence, we set

$$D(V\|WH) = \frac{1}{2}\|V - WH\|^2 = \frac{1}{2}\sum_{i,j}(V_{i,j} - [WH]_{i,j})^2 \tag{5}$$

where $1 \leq i \leq m, 1 \leq j \leq N$.

Using the gradient descent method [22] to update $\mathbf{W}$ and $\mathbf{H}$, updated rules can be expressed as

$$W_{ik} = W_{ik}\left(\frac{[VH^T]_{ik}}{[WHH^T]_{ik} + \xi} - \partial_\varphi \det(WW^T)\frac{[(WW^T)^{-1}W]_{ik}}{[H^THW]_{ik} + \xi}\right) \tag{6}$$

$$H_{kj} = H_{kj}\frac{[W^TV]_{kj} - \partial_J - \partial_R(\frac{h_{kj}}{h_k h_k^T} - [(HH^T)^{-1}H]_{kj})}{[W^TWH]_{kj} + \xi} \tag{7}$$

where $W_{ik}, H_{kj} > 0$, $\sum_i W_{ik} = 1, 1 \leq k \leq n$, and ξ is a sufficiently small positive constant to prevent the denominator becoming zero.

Negative $\mathbf{W}$ and $\mathbf{H}$ elements are set to zero after every iteration, and W is normalized

$$W_{ik} = \frac{W_{ik}}{\sum_k W_{ik}}$$

Equations (6) and (7) are iterated until $F(V\|WH)$ is less than a given (small) threshold, and the correct $\mathbf{W}$ and $\mathbf{H}$ obtained.

Under non-negative conditions, $\mathbf{X}$ (see (2)) is decomposed following (3), i.e., $X = WH$, hence $\mathbf{W}$ is the estimate for $\mathbf{A}$ and $\mathbf{H}$ is the estimate for $\mathbf{S}$.

2.3   Adaptive Grouping Decomposition Based on Binary Tree

Under normal circumstances, set the number of tags $= N$, number of reader antennas $= M$, optimal number of tags $= L$, and tag ID number sequence length $= J$, then j is the number of tags associated with the optimal parameter,

$$j = ceil(\log_2 L), \tag{8}$$

where ceil() is the rounding up function. Table 1 shows the relationship between j and L.

Table 1. Relationship between the optimal number of tags (L) and number of tags (j)

L	j
4	2
$5 \leq L \leq 8$	3
$9 \leq L \leq 16$	4
$17 \leq L \leq 32$	5
$32 \leq L \leq 64$	6

Access code length sent by the reader $= (J - j)$, and the number of slots assigned $=$, as shown in Fig. 2. Larger $(J - j)$ implies more detailed distributed labels and less tag numbers in each slot.

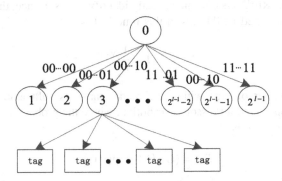

Fig. 2. Initial slot allocation for adaptive grouping

Suppose $J = 8$, i.e., the ID number sequence for each tag is 00000000–11111111. For this particular under-determined BSS RFID systems, each tag's ID number is uniquely determined. Figure 3 shows that the reader sends 0000 to 1111, a total of 16 4 bit query codes, to the initial allocation slots. Since the first 4 bits of the ID sequence are the same as the query code, this tag is assigned to the corresponding time slot and transmits a response signal to reader. Depending on the number of time slots in response to tag, time slots can be divided into read and idle slots. When tag

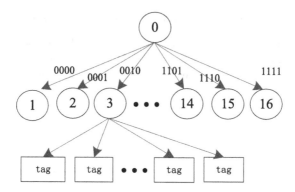

Fig. 3. Adaptive grouping when the optimal number of tags is $L = 16$

number ≥ 1, the time slot is deemed as read, other cases as idle slots. Since the slot-readable tag ID sequence only differs in the last 4 bits in each slot, the number of tags in each slot ≤ 16, hence can be used to enhance RFID system performance requirements when $L = 16$.

2.4 Selection of the Optimal Number of Tags

The conventional anti-collision under-determined BSS assumes the reader has M antennas, the number of recognizable tags within one time slot within the reader range = N, and the RFID system can correctly identify n tags. Hence, the mean number of successfully identified RFID tags in this time slot is

$$N_s = N(1 - \frac{1}{n})^{N-1}. \tag{9}$$

When the number of tags within the reader range is sufficient, the tag arrival process can be considered a Poisson distribution, where the probability distribution tag arrive within a time slot is

$$P_N = (G^N/N!) \exp(-G), \tag{10}$$

where G is the load. Therefore, the throughput of a time slot can be expressed as

$$S_N = \sum_{N=0}^{\infty} N_s P_N \tag{11}$$

and substituting (9) and (10) into (11),

$$S_N = \sum_{N=0}^{\infty} N(1 - \frac{1}{n})^{N-1} * (G^N/N!)\exp(-G)$$

$$= G\exp(-G) * \exp((1 - \frac{1}{n})G) = G\exp(-\frac{G}{n}).$$

(12)

If we set the derivative of (12) equal to zero, then maximum throughput is $S_{N\max} = n/e$ when $G = n$.

Figure 4(a) shows that when $M = 3$ throughput increases with increasing number of tags, and maximum throughput (2.208 from [12]) occurs when $N = 6$. If N continues to increase, system throughput decreases, and hence performance deteriorates rapidly. Similarly, maximum throughput for $M = 4$ and 5 are 2.944 and 3.678, respectively, which correspond to $L = 8$ and 10, respectively (see Fig. 4(a)). Figure 4(b) shows that the optimal number of tags reaches approximately twice the number of antennas, i.e.

$$L = 2M.$$

(13)

Thus, combining (8) and (13),

$$j = ceil(\log_2 L) = ceil(\log_2(2M))$$

(14)

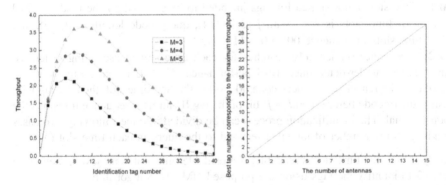

(a) The throughput comparison(the number of antenna is $M = 3, 4, 5$)

(b) Relationship between the number of antenna and the best tag number L

Fig. 4. Throughput and optimal tag number (L) for different (a) number of antennas (M), and (b) M and L

3 Adaptive Tree Grouping

Although under-determined BSS can solve the problem where $N > M$, RFID system performance declines rapidly when $N > L$, to the point where it cannot separate **S**. Therefore, we propose an algorithm that combines under-determined BSS with binary tree grouping based on the tag ID number sequences, to ensure that $N \leq L$ in any time slot, hence ensuring near optimal system performance can be maintained.

3.1 Tag Identification Description of NMF Ddaptive Tree Grouping Algorithm

The proposed NMF BSS algorithm is based on NMF and adaptive tree grouping, where number of queries is related to the J and M, but is independent of N, such that the number of collision does not increase when N increases. Suppose $S(N)$ is the number of queries,

$$S(N) = 2^{J-j} \tag{15}$$

Then the tag identification rate is

$$E(N) = N/S(N) = N/2^{J-j}. \tag{16}$$

3.2 Proposed Algorithm Implementation

Figure 5 shows the proposed algorithm flow chart, and details are as follows.

Step 1: Time slots are assigned for tags intended to be grouped by the reader. Initial allocation of time slots is 2^{J-j}, with j as in (14), query code length = $(J - j)$, and $1- 2^{J-j}$ time slots in sequence $00...00 - 11...11$.

Step 2: The reader sequentially searches for each time slot in ascending order. To ensure optimal under-determined BSS performance, $N \leq L$ in each time slot. To achieve this, the reader sends query code $00...00$ in the first time slot, then the tag with the same query code before the $(J - j)$ bit of the tag ID number sequence transmits the response signal. The identification process can be divided into the following two cases depending on the number of tags that respond to the query in each time slot (N).

1. $N \geq 1$, i.e., the time slot is readable. If a readable time slot is retrieved, then go to step 3 to identify the tags using the proposed NMF BSS algorithm.
2. $N = 0$, i.e., the time slot is idle. Go immediately to the next time slot retrieval.

Step 3: The algorithm determines the number of responding tags from the rank of **X**, or the number of eigenvalues. If $N > M$, initialize **W** and **H** as non-negative matrices, and employ the NMF algorithm to separate the blind source, and obtain the final **W** and **H**. Then **H** is the isolated source signal, **S**, and the source tags can be successfully identified. The reader then reads the tag data in the time slot, records them, and returns to step 2 to retrieve the next time slot.

Step 4: After retrieving all time slots, the algorithm ends.

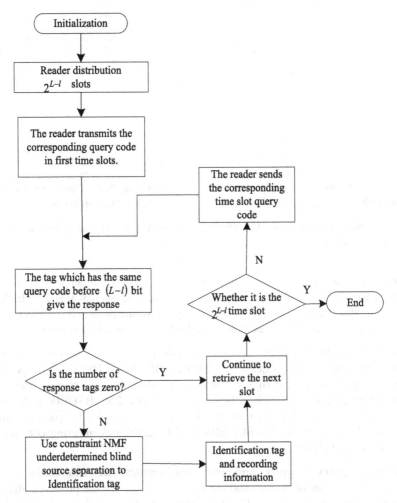

Fig. 5. Proposed under-determined blind source separation anti-collision algorithm based on adaptive tree grouping

4 The New Algorithms Performance

Experiments were performed for $N = 32$–256 with $N > M$. NMF algorithm constraints were is set following [15]: minimum correlation constraint parameter $\partial_R = 0.01$, determinant constraint parameter $\partial_\varphi = 1$, sparseness constraint parameter $\partial_J = \frac{1}{4 \times 1000}$, iterative error $\sigma = 10^{-6}$. If the difference between simulation successive iterations $\leq \sigma$ then the result is considered as correct and unique solution for **W** and **H**, otherwise, continue iterating. We found the following general outcomes.

(1) Tag Identification Rate. Figure 6(a) compares the proposed and BSDBG, EBS, and Q algorithm tag identification rates. The proposed NMF BSS algorithm identification rate

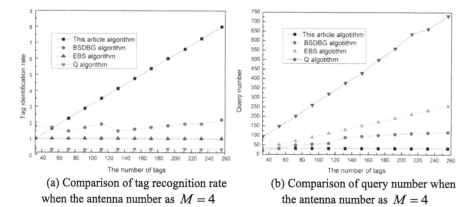

(a) Comparison of tag recognition rate
when the antenna number as $M = 4$

(b) Comparison of query number when
the antenna number as $M = 4$

Fig. 6. Algorithm performances when number of antenna $M = 4$ (a) tag recognition rate and (b) number of queries

continues to increase with increasing number of tags, whereas the other algorithms. When $N = 256$, the proposed algorithm tag identification rate ≈ 8, whereas BSDBG, EBS, and Q algorithm rates ≈ 2.17, 1, and 0.3, respectively. Thus, the proposed algorithm performance is more ideal, and provides a more stable and efficient RFID system.

(2) Query Number. Figure 6(b) shows that when $M = 4$, the proposed algorithm maintains the number of queries = 32, whereas BSDBG, EBS, and Q algorithm's queries rise rapidly with increasing N. The proposed algorithm advantage is particularly evident for large N. For example, when $M = 4$ and $N = 256$, BSDBG, EBS, and Q queries = 117.7, 256, and 731.4 respectively. Thus, the proposed algorithm requires significantly less time than BSDBG, EBS, and Q algorithms, meeting core requirements for practical RFID systems.

(3) Antenna, Query Number, and Tag Identification Rate Correlations. Fig. 7 shows that the number of queries and tag recognition rate for the proposed algorithm are significantly superior to the BSDBG, EBS, and Q algorithms, particularly for increasing number of antennas. For example, when $M = 16$, average tag recognition rate for the proposed algorithm ≈ 18, whereas BSDBG, EBS, and Q algorithms ≈ 5.16, 1, and 0.33, respectively (see Fig. 7(a)). For $M = 4–16$, tag identification rate for the proposed algorithm improves from 152.8% to 359.2% compared with the BSDBG algorithm, with even larger increases for EBS and Q algorithms.

Figure 7(b) shows that when $M = 16$, the number of queries for the proposed algorithm = 8, whereas BSDBG, EBS, and Q 28.23, 256, and 731.4, respectively. For $M = 4–16$, the proposed algorithm tag identification rate increased from 60% to 78% compared with the BSDBG algorithm. Thus, the proposed algorithm has good practical value and high efficiency to support fast and stable RFID systems.

When N is too large, e.g. $N = 1000$, adjusting the tag sequence ID number (J) can solve tag recognition problems. For example, if $J = 10$, i.e., the ID sequence for each tag is 0000000000–1111111111, the system can simultaneously identify 1024 tags. Figure 8 shows that when $N = 1000$, and $M = 4–16$, the proposed algorithm has significant query

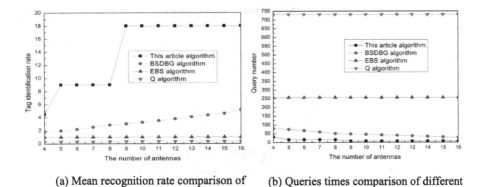

(a) Mean recognition rate comparison of
different antenna number

(b) Queries times comparison of different
antenna number

Fig. 7. Antenna number effects on (a) mean recognition rate and (b) query number

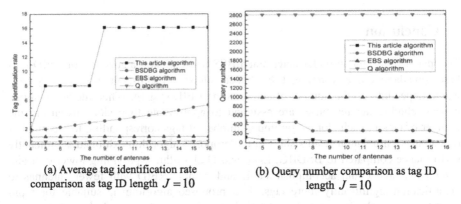

(a) Average tag identification rate
comparison as tag ID length $J = 10$

(b) Query number comparison as tag ID
length $J = 10$

Fig. 8. Effect of increasing tag number sequence length J = 10 for (a) tag recognition rate and
(b) query number

number and tag recognition rate advantages compared with BSDBG, EBS, and Q algorithms. For example when $M = 16$, Fig. 8(a) shows that tag recognition rate for the proposed algorithm ≈ 16.1, whereas BSDBG, EBS, and Q algorithms $\approx 5.39, 1$, and 0.33, respectively. Similarly, Fig. 8(b) shows that when $M = 16$, the proposed algorithm query number = 32, whereas BSDBG, EBS, and Q algorithms = 134.9 1000, and 2816.8, respectively (and the Q algorithm does not change with increasing M).

(4) Proposed Algorithm Query Map. Figure 9 shows the query number for the proposed algorithm for different M and J. with the change of the number of antennas and the length of the tag ID, when the number of antenna and tag ID sequence is shorter, the number of query of the proposed algorithm is less, it can quickly identify the tags and improve the system efficiently.

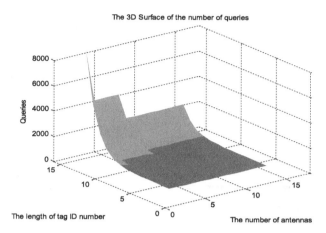

Fig. 9. Antenna number (M) and tag sequence length (J) effects on query number for the proposed algorithm

5 Conclusion

This paper proposed an under-determined BSS anti-collision algorithm for RFID tags based on adaptive tree grouping. The proposed algorithm adjusts the reader query code length depending on the number of antennas the RFID system. When the query signal is sent, eligible tag responses are assigned to appropriate time slots, to ensure the number of tags in each slot $\leq$ optimum number of tags corresponding to the number of antennas. Simulation results showed the proposed algorithm exhibited significantly performance compared to BSDBG, EBS, and Q algorithms, providing lower cost and complexity, and could accomplish stable and reliable RFID with fewer antennas to identification significantly more tags. This proposed algorithm is suitable for rapid identification of the large number of tags in medium and large scale enterprise warehouses and logistics.

Acknowledgments. This work is jointly supported by the National Natural Science Foundation of China (Nos. 61763017, 51665019), Natural Science Foundation of Jiangxi Province (Nos. 20161BAB202053, 20161BAB206145).

References

1. Guo, Z.X., Ngai, E.W.T., Yang, C., Liang, X.D.: An RFID-based intelligent decision support system architecture for production monitoring and scheduling in a distributed manufacturing environment. Int. J. Prod. Econ. **159**(1), 16–28 (2015)
2. Zhang, X.H., Zhang, L.Y.: Research on RFID anti-collision algorithm of a lot responding in real-time and co-processing. Acta Electronica Sinica **42**(6), 1139–1146 (2014)
3. Qu, Z.G., Zhu, T.C., Wang, J.W., Wang, X.J.: A novel quantum stegnagraphy based on brown states. Comput. Mater. Continua **56**(1), 47–59 (2018)

4. Wang, L., Xu, L.D., Bi, Z.M., Xu, Y.C.: Data cleaning for RFID and WSN integration. IEEE Trans. Ind. Inf. **10**(1), 408–418 (2014)
5. Zhang, D., Wang, X., Song, X., Zhao, D.: A novel approach to mapped correlation of ID for RFID anti-collision. IEEE Trans. Serv. Comput. **7**(4), 741–748 (2014)
6. Pang, Y., Peng, Q., Lin, J.Z., Zhou, Q.N., Li, G.Q., et al.: Reducing tag collision in radio frequency identification systems by using a grouped dynamic frame slotted ALOHA algorithm. Acta Physica Sinica **62**(7), 496–503 (2013)
7. Li, Z., Li, J., He, C.: Artificial immune network-based anti-collision algorithm for dense RFID readers. Expert Syst. Appl. **41**(10), 4798–4810 (2014)
8. Wu, H., Zeng, Y., Feng, J., Gu, Y.: Binary tree slotted ALOHA for passive RFID tag anticollision. IEEE Trans. Parallel Distrib. Syst. **24**(1), 19–31 (2013)
9. Zhang, X.H., Xiao, J.F.: Passive RFID system tag anti-collision optimization algorithms. J. Syst. Simul. **26**(6), 1320–1326 (2014)
10. Zhang, D.G., Li, W.B.: Novel ID-based anti-collision approach for RFID. Enterp. Inf. Syst. **10**(7), 771–789 (2016)
11. Zhao, J.M., Li, N., Li, D.A., et al.: Collision alignment: an RFID anti-collision algorithm assisted by orthogonal signal detection and analogy principle. Telecommun. Syst. **66**(1), 131–144 (2017)
12. Chuang, P.J., Tsai, W.T.: Switch table: an efficient anti-collision algorithm for RFID networks. IET Commun. **11**(14), 2221–2227 (2017)
13. Zheng, F., Kaiser, T.: Adaptive aloha anti-collision algorithms for RFID systems. EURASIP J. Embed. Syst. **1**, 7–20 (2016)
14. Wang, C.H., Liu, C.S., Xu, H., Tu, Y.X.: An enhanced tree-based anti-collision algorithm. J. Hunan Univ. (Nat. Sci.) **40**(8), 97–101 (2013)
15. Liu, W.J., Chen, Z.Y., Liu, J.S., Su, Z.F., Chi, L.H.: Full-blind delegating private quantum computation. Comput. Mater. Contin. **56**(2), 211–223 (2018)
16. Djeddou, M., Khelladi, R., Benssalah, M.: Improved RFID anti-collision algorithm. AEU-Int. J. Electron. Commun. **67**(3), 256–262 (2013)
17. Fu, W.H., Wang, L., Ma, L.F.: Improved laplace mixed model potential function algorithm for UBSS. J. Xidian Univ. **41**(12), 1–5 (2014)
18. Arjona, L., Landaluce, H., Perallos, A., Onieva, E.: Fast fuzzy anti-collision protocol for the RFID standard EPC Gen-2. Electron. Lett. **52**(8), 663–665 (2016)
19. Gao, B., Bai, L., Woo, W.L., Tian, G.Y., Chen, Y.H.: Automatic defect identification of eddy current pulsed thermography using single channel blind source separation. IEEE Trans. Instrum. Meas. **63**(4), 913–922 (2014)
20. Bagheri, N., Alenaby, P., Safkhani, M.: A new anti-collision protocol based on information of collided tags in RFID systems. Int. J. Commun Syst **30**(3), 231–240 (2017)
21. Yue, K.Q., Sun, L.L., You, B., Lou, L.H.: Parallelizable identification anti-collision algorithm based on under-determined blind separation. J. Zhejiang Univ. (Eng. Sci.) **48**(5), 865–870 (2014)
22. Gillis, N., Luce, R.: Robust near-separable nonnegative matrix factorization using linear optimization. J. Mach. Learn. Res. **15**(1), 1249–1280 (2014)

Design of a Peristaltic Pump Driven by Pneumatic Artificial Muscles

Hua Yan[1(✉)], Zhengyu Yang[1], Fei Ding[2], Shijie Xu[1],
and Dengyin Zhang[2]

[1] Nanjing Institute of Technology, Nanjing 211167, China
yanhua@njit.edu.cn
[2] Jiangsu Key Laboratory of Broadband Wireless Communication and
Internet of Things, Nanjing University of Posts and Telecommunications,
Nanjing 210003, China

Abstract. This paper designs an air-type peristaltic pump driven by pneumatic artificial muscles. It consists of a pump head assembly, an artificial muscle unit, a flange and an air duct. The outer wall is a plexiglass tube, one end of which is sealed with a pump cover and the other end is open. The artificial muscle unit is built into the plexiglass tube, and there are gaps in the perimeter. One end of each of the six air ducts leads to each artificial muscle unit, and the other end is connected to each of the reversing valves. Design the lower computer control system through PLC to control proportional pressure valve and reversing valve; using the configuration software to write the upper computer control interface, the interface is designed with buttons, switches and text boxes. We can monitor the operation of the peristaltic pump in real time by the communication of configuration software and PLC.

Keywords: Artificial muscle · Peristaltic pump · Configuration software · PLC · Proportional pressure valve · Reversing valve

1 Introduction

Peristaltic pump is a new kind of fluid transport pump after rotor pump, centrifugal pump and diaphragm pump, which has been widely popularized and applied in various industries such as medical treatment, medicine, food, beverage, chemical industry and metallurgy. Peristaltic pumps delivering a fluid at present are required for multiple industries, such as plant transportation systems, fields and emergencies. These fluids are usually transmitted by positive displacement pumps and vane pumps. However, the fluid is easy to collide with the impeller of the vane pump to damage the pump, while the positive displacement pump must be large to adapt to the high pressure of the transferred fluid, which leads to its inconvenient outdoor application and excessive space. Therefore, the existing peristaltic pump needs to be improved in terms of working principle, space occupation and so on. In addition, more and more research began to add data processing or big data technologies, in order to further optimize the existing information system [1–3].

© Springer Nature Switzerland AG 2019
X. Sun et al. (Eds.): ICAIS 2019, LNCS 11634, pp. 266–275, 2019.
https://doi.org/10.1007/978-3-030-24271-8_24

According to the above mentioned shortcomings of the peristaltic pump, we introduce the concept of earthworm peristalsis to solve these problems and apply it as a model to the new peristaltic pump. Through data review, we learned that an earthworm consists of 110–200 body segments with independent tissues and two layers of muscles: ring muscle distributed under the skin and longitudinal muscles distributed along the length of the ankle under the ring muscle. When the anterior body segment elongates, the posterior body segment contracts in the opposite direction [4–7]. Firstly, the longitudinal muscle contraction is used to contract the anterior body segment. The contraction is then transmitted to the posterior portion, while the anterior segment is then stretched by the ring muscle. The movement is transmitted through the segments of earthworms. In this way, the earthworm can be moved forward by repeated expansion and contraction, while the body segments on the outer wall can remain fixed. It has been explored that, as a new material, pneumatic artificial muscles with simple structure and large power-to-weight ratio can be directly driven without decelerator and transmission mechanism, so we decided to use the pneumatic artificial muscle to build the model of earthworm peristalsis. The principle of transporting fluids using pneumatic artificial muscle volume changes can prevent damage to the pump blades caused by fluids and transporting fluids with a small pump body can save plant space and make outdoor applications possible. At the same time, such a new peristaltic pump is not only easy to carry, but also highly adaptable.

2 Peristaltic Pump Design

Since the 1960s, American doctor McKibben has invented a pneumatic actuator that drives prosthetic movement. After several decades, pneumatic artificial muscles has made considerable progress, but because of the particularity of this design which is applied to peristaltic pumps (higher requirements to the radial and axial volume change), the prevailing pneumatic artificial muscles on the market do not meet the requirements. In view of this, we can try to make pneumatic artificial muscles according to the following solutions.

The pneumatic artificial muscle is mainly composed of an inner tube, a shell and a joint at both ends. The simplest material is available with two lengths of hard plastic hose of appropriate length, slightly larger than the inner diameter of the inner tube, or other materials, such as a metal cylindrical plug at one end and a metal or plastic fitting at the other end. Insert two pieces of hard plastic hose into the ends of the rubber inner tube. Since the outer diameter of the plastic hose is slightly larger than the inner diameter of the inner tube, a good seal can be ensured after assembly. Then, the plastic hose at one end is heated and softened with a soldering iron to form a plug, and one end of the inner tube is sealed. Then, the wire and the end of the jacket are tightly wound together, and a wire of appropriate length is left as a connecting line to facilitate connection with the driven component. The plastic hose of the other end serving as a pneumatic artificial muscle supply port is suitably long to connect with the quick pipe joint. The shell and the end portion are also tightly wound with a wire, and a wire of a proper length is left to be fixed on the base.

As shown in Fig. 1, a peristaltic pump consists of a pump head assembly, six artificial muscle units, a flange and an air duct. The outer wall is a glass pipe, one end of which is sealed by a pump cover and the other end is open. The artificial muscle unit is built into the glass tube with a gap around it. One end of the six air ducts leads to each of the artificial muscle units, and the other end is connected to each of the reversing valves.

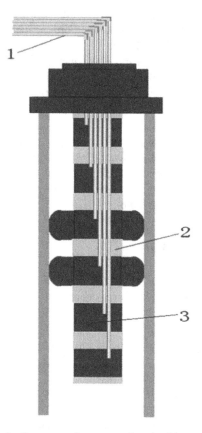

Fig. 1. Structure of a proposed peristaltic pump.

Pneumatic artificial muscle units are used to simulate the body segments of the earthworm, and the flanges connect the pneumatic artificial muscle units. The working principle of the peristaltic pump is shown in Fig. 2. Firstly, the last part of the pneumatic artificial muscle unit is inflated to seal the pipe to prevent backflow. Then, the liquid is discharged due to expansion of the other section in the discharge direction. Since at least one expansion joint prevents backflow, the liquid is forced back out in the direction of discharge. In addition, the draining action causes the reverse expansion joint to contract. The liquid is drawn into the same volume of vacuum as the expansion joint. Finally, the next expansion joint expands to expel the liquid. By repeating such an action, the pump can transport fluids.

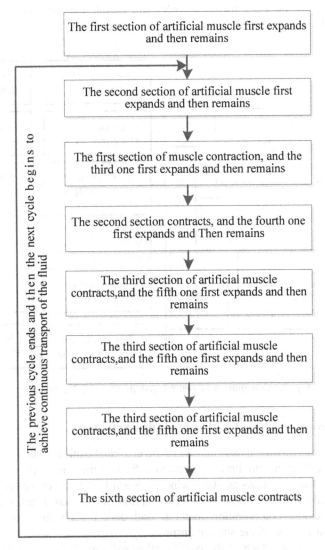

Fig. 2. Peristaltic pump working principle.

3 Peristaltic Pump Control System Implementation

The peristaltic pump is internally composed of six artificial muscle parts. Each artificial muscle part is pneumatically expanded and contracted. Six artificial muscle parts are respectively connected to six three-position and five-way reversing valves, and the reversing valve controls the expansion sequence of different muscles. The three states of each reversing valve are intake, hold, and exhaust. The proportional pressure valve is connected to the reversing valve to control the expansion speed of the artificial muscle part. This reaches the adjustments of order and speed. The constitution of control system on peristaltic pump is shown in Fig. 3.

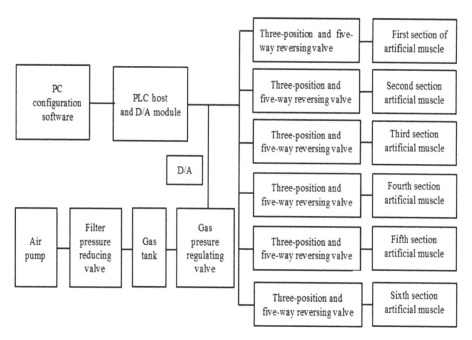

Fig. 3. Constitution of control system on peristaltic pump.

3.1   Interface Design Based on Configuration Software

The configuration software makes full use of the graphical editing function of Windows to conveniently form the monitoring screen, and displays the state of the control device in an animated manner. It has an alarm window, a real-time trend curve and so on, and can conveniently generate different types of reports. It also has a rich set of device drivers and flexible configuration methods and data linking functions. Real-time monitoring and control of the site are ensured.

First, in the left interface of the configuration software engineering browser, left-click the device, then create a new device on the right screen, the device using Mitsubishi's FX3U to be communicated by the configuration software; then, left-click the data dictionary in the left of the project browser, create the required variables in the right interface, and associate the variables with the relevant parameters in the PLC, including the auxiliary relay M, data register D, the configuration software can write the values of each variable to parameters of the PLC. The tool then create a screen, using the configuration software related to the drawing screen, and specify the width and height of the screen. After the picture shown in the figure is drawn; finally, the buttons, switches, and parts of the picture to be animated are associated with the variables. Control interface based on configuration software is shown in Fig. 4.

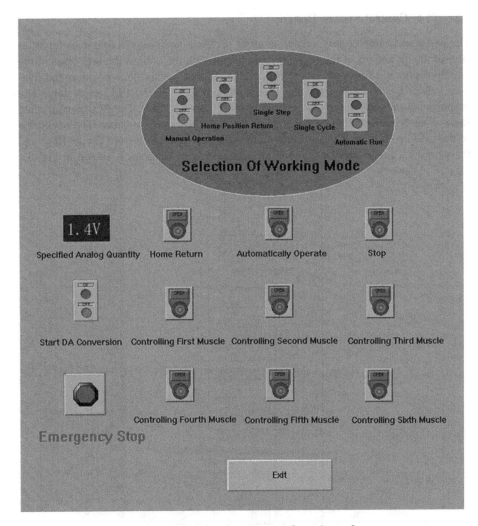

Fig. 4. Control interface based on configuration software.

Above the control panel is the choice of working mode, which is manual, homing, single step, single cycle, automatic operation; analog quantity is specified below; auxiliary relay M0-M4 is the working mode selection, it should be noted that M0-M4 cannot be turned on at the same time; under normal circumstances, the selection of working mode should be connected to the selection switch. Due to the limitation of the configuration software, we use the button switch instead of the selection switch, so we should pay attention to the five button switches, which should only be connected to one button switch at the same time. Before controlling the muscle action sequence, you must first enter the corresponding analog quantity (for example, 1.4 V), and then Press the "Start DA Conversion" switch.

3.2   PLC Control System Design

The peristaltic pump control system requires six three-position and five-way valves to control the on and off of the two gas passages through the coils at the both ends of the three-position and five-way valve. The twelve coils of the six three-position and five-way valves are controlled by the 12 output terminals of the PLC separately. The proportional pressure valve requires one analog output control. The PLC is connected to the FX2 N-2DA analog output module through the extension cable. The resolution of the module is 2.5 mv, the output voltage adjustment range is from 0 v to 10 v, and the working voltage is 24DC. The PLC terminal wiring diagram is shown in Fig. 5.

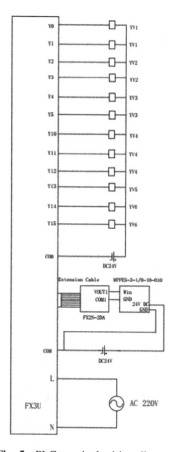

Fig. 5. PLC terminal wiring diagram.

In the PLC programming, the initialization instruction in the convenient instruction is used. The program has four parts: the initialization program, the manual operation program, the homing program, and the automatic operation program. In addition to the most basic parts, the initialization program also includes analog output, muscle expansion time, PLC emergency stop, etc. The digital-anlog conversion is to convert the value of data register D100 into analog output. The value of D100 is not given in the PLC program, but specified by the user in the control interface of configuration software.

In Fig. 4, the function and operation of each button are as follows:

(1) Press the "manual operation" switch in the control interface, the working mode is switched to the manual mode, and the PLC performs the manual operation procedure. The inflating and deflation of each muscle can be separately controlled by 6 buttons.

(2) Press the "Return to origin" switch in the control interface, and the working mode is switched to the homing mode. At this time, press the "home return start button" and the PLC executes the homing program. The origin of our setting is that all 6 muscles are in contraction. In order to achieve this state, first disconnect all 6 coils responsible for inflating the muscles, then energize the 6 muscles responsible for muscle deflation, then add a 1.5 s delay to fully deflate the muscles. The muscles return to the initial state, and the coils are all powered off.

(3) Press the "single step" switch in the control interface to switch to the single step mode. At this point, press "Automatically start" button, the program will follow the automatic running program to go to a state, and then click the "automatically operate the start button". The program continues to the next state.

(4) Press the "single cycle" switch in the control interface to switch to the single cycle mode. At this point, press "Automatically start" button, the program will complete a cycle according to the automatic running program (do not cycle).

(5) Press the "Auto Run" switch in the control interface to switch to the automatic operation mode. At this point, press "Automatically Run Start" button, the PLC executes the automatic running program, the program will run according to the automatic running program, and continue to cycle; if you do not want the program to continue running, press the "Stop" button, the program will finish the last step of the automatic running program and then stop.

3.3 Debugging and Actual Control

Under the condition of completing PLC control program and monitoring interface, actual debugging and control are required to be done. Before the actual control, simulation debugging has been completed and the program can run as required. First of all, the hardware wiring is completed. Refer to Fig. 5 for specific wiring details. Pay attention not to short circuits in the course of actual wiring. When connecting the 4 wires of proportional pressure valve to PLC, attention should be paid to the color correspondence. Then, use the software GXWorks-2 to write the correct debugged PLC program into PLC. Since there is no communication interface with PLC on the computer, an additional RS232 adapter is needed to write the program. When the computer communicates with PLC, firstly open the device manager in the computer to see which port is connected to PLC. The port here is COM1. Then open the connection target option in GXworks, select the connection on the computer side, select "Serial USB", the port number is COM1, and the transfer rate is 115.2kbs. Click OK.

Open the correct debugged PLC program and select online PLC in the menu bar to write the program into PLC. After the program is written into PLC, GXWorks-2 needs to be closed and the connection with PLC is stopped to prepare for the following monitoring interface and PLC communication. Finally, open the Kingview, it is necessary to notice that the port number should be the same as the port number of USB adapter, otherwise the communication will fail.

Open the configured monitoring interface and switch to the running system. At this time, we can see from the system log that Kingview communicates with PLC successfully. According to the actual requirements, we can control the solenoid valve and proportional pressure valve, indirectly control the artificial muscle, and achieve the purpose of conveying fluid. After the communication is successful, you will see the value in the analog input box is 0, indicating that no value has been specified at this time. Firstly, we designate a suitable analog value of 1.4 V to the proportional pressure valve. Then press the button to start DA and measure the voltage of the analog output module of 1.4 V with an ammeter. Switch the work pattern to the manual mode, press the button manually to test whether the expansion of each muscle is running according to the preset conditions. After the test in the manual mode has no problem, switch the selection switch to the automatic mode to check whether the artificial muscle is working normally. After the normal operation of the artificial muscle is confirmed, fluid is introduced into the pipeline to realize the function of conveying fluid.

4   Conclusion

This paper proposes a new type of peristaltic pump that can transmit high-viscosity and solid-liquid mixed fluids, which can effectively avoid the problems of equipment damage and inconvenient installation caused by the current peristaltic pump in the process of transporting high-density fluids. The peristaltic pump can be used in a variety of transportation systems, such as pipeline transportation in the factory. This new type of pneumatic artificial muscle-driven peristaltic pump not only occupies less space in the transportation system, but also is expected to play a greater role in pipeline transportation, under the hypothesis of ensuring that its transportation efficiency can be controlled.

Acknowledgements. This work is partially supported by the Ministry of Education-China Mobile Research Foundation, China (No. MCM20170205), the Scientific Research Foundation of the Higher Education Institutions of Jiangsu Province, China (Nos. 15KJA510002 and 17KJB510043), Six Talent Peaks Project in Jiangsu Province (No. DZXX-008), the Research Foundation for Advanced Talents of Nanjing University of Posts and Telecommunications (No. NY217146), and the Practice Innovation Training Project for the Jiangsu College Students, China (No. 201711276031Y).

References

1. Ding, F., Song, A., Li, J., Song, G.: An adaptive localisation algorithm of mobile node in wireless sensor network. Int. J. Sens. Netw. **14**(1) (2013). https://doi.org/10.1504/ijsnet.2013. 056342
2. Li, D.H., Zhang, G.Z., Xu, Z.: Modelling the roles of cewebrity trust and platform trust in consumers' propensity of live-streaming: an extended TAM method. CMC-Comput. Mater. Continua **55**(1), 137–150 (2018)
3. Jayaprakash, G., Muthuraj, M.P.: Prediction of compressive strength of various SCC mixes using relevance vector machine. CMC-Comput. Mater. Continua **54**(1), 83–102 (2018)
4. Antoine, N., Raphael, G., Ricardo, A., et al.: Non-muscular structures can limit the maximal joint range of motion during stretching. Sports Med. **47**(10), 1925–1929 (2017)
5. Liu, W., Liu, X., Tan, R.: Design of peristaltic pump based on patent analysis. J. Eng. Des. **20**(5), 361–382 (2013)
6. Chen, A., Wang, M., Zou, Y.: Design and application of peristaltic pump control software. Exp. Sci. Technol. (2010)
7. Wei, L., Duan, J., Wang, C., Lu, L.: Peristaltic pump flow precise control system based on host link protocol. Institute of Energy and Power Engineering, Lanzhou University of Technology (2017)

An Approach to Deep Learning Service Provision with Elastic Remote Interfaces

Mingxu Sun[1], Zhiyun Yang[2], Hao Wu[3], Qi Liu[4(✉)], and Xiaodong Liu[4]

[1] School of Electrical Engineering, University of Jinan, Jinan, China
[2] Jiangsu Collaborative Innovation Center of Atmospheric Environment and Equipment Technology (CICAEET), Nanjing University of Information Science and Technology, Nanjing 210044, China
[3] School of Computer and Software, Nanjing University of Information Science and Technology, Nanjing 210044, China
[4] School of Computing, Edinburgh Napier University, 10 Colinton Road, Edinburgh EH10 5DT, UK
q.liu@napier.ac.uk

Abstract. Deep learning has been widely applied for computer vision, natural language processing, and information retrieval etc. Using a deep learning framework can reduce learning curve of beginners facilitating them to get involved with deep learning algorithms. Current deep learning frameworks can mainly be divided into traditional local deployment and cloud-based platforms. However, the two forms cannot be considered at the same time in terms of debugging and remote access. This paper focuses on the logical isolation between deep learning algorithm design and actual business execution, and it proposes an elastic framework that can resolve the contradiction between internal improvement and external access, which can improve the efficiency of both algorithm design researchers and business requirements department engineers.

Keywords: Deep learning · Cloud platform · Logical isolation · Remote access · Elastic framework

1 Introduction

Deep learning is one of the most important methods in the field of machine learning. It is a kind of multi-layer neural network learning algorithm, which alleviates the local minimum of traditional training algorithm. The main applications of in-depth learning in computer vision are image recognition [21], character recognition [22], sentiment analysis [1] and so on. The success of deep learning in this area has also attracted the attention of researchers in other fields, such as the application of deep learning to identify cancer cells in the medical field [2], financial sector using it to predict the stock market [3], the commercial use of recommending products to users and analysis of user evaluation [4]. It can be seen that deep learning has great application and demand for more and more fields.

© Springer Nature Switzerland AG 2019
X. Sun et al. (Eds.): ICAIS 2019, LNCS 11634, pp. 276–286, 2019.
https://doi.org/10.1007/978-3-030-24271-8_25

It is precisely because deep learning has a wide range of applications in various fields that more and more people are exposed to the field of deep learning. Using a deep learning framework reduces the barrier to entry into deep learning area. The current major deep learning frameworks include TensorFlow [5], MXNet [6], Caffe [7], etc. For debugging convenience, these frameworks are generally deployed locally, selecting algorithms to extract features, classify and train operations locally. For algorithm designers this method can improve the algorithm at any time, but there is great inconvenience when it is necessary to remotely access the data results of training and testing in the future. In addition to local deployment, there is public cloud solution now. The three world-famous public cloud providers are Amazon, Microsoft Azure and Google [8, 18]. These public cloud providers offer users a wide range of deep learning product services, such as Amazon Polly [9] for text-to-speech, Microsoft Azure's Emotion API can be used to analyze human emotions, and the Recognition API verifies speaker recognition [10], Google's Dialogflow chat bot can be used for teaching [11]. The deep learning modules of these public cloud providers are almost all provided to users in the form of encapsulation into API. Users use the provider's services by calling API. This method emphasizes remote debugging and flexible scheduling of resources. For some design researchers of deep learning algorithms, it is difficult to directly access the source code, and the algorithm cannot be improved at any time during the research and debugging process, and the data is stored on the server of the public cloud provider, privacy of the data cannot be guaranteed. The problems caused by these two methods decrease the implementation efficiency of deep learning and business and limit the improvement of algorithms to a certain extent.

Focusing on the contradiction between internal improvement and external access, this paper proposes an elastic framework that can resolve this contradiction. This framework uses web services and RPC middleware technology to isolate the algorithm design from the actual business. With this method, the deep learning algorithm design researchers deploy, debug, improve, and propose new deep learning algorithms locally. Based on the deep learning algorithm online, business requirements department engineers, select appropriate algorithms to train and test actual business data to meet actual business requirements.

The remainder of this paper is organized as follows, and Sect. 2 describes the related work. Section 3 describes the design of this system. Section 4 describes system usage, user interface design, and the benefits of this system.

2   Related Work

There are many deep learning frameworks currently. In order to facilitate debugging, local deployment and local access are widely used. Here are a few simple introductions and comparisons of several common deep learning frameworks.

2.1 Deep Learning Framework

TensorFlow

TensorFlow is an open source framework developed by the Google brain team for numerical computing. It uses a data flow graph, the nodes represent mathematical operations in the graph, and the lines in the graph represent multidimensional data arrays that are interconnected between nodes [12]. TensorFlow is highly flexible, and it can be used as long as it can represent the calculation as a data flow graph. The underlying core engine of TensorFlow is implemented in C++ and provides Python, C++, Java, and Go API.

Caffe

Caffe was developed by the Berkeley Center for Visual and Learning and community contributors. Caffe is an open source framework written in C++, Python, with CUDA for GPU computing that deploys deep learning architecture [13]. Caffe seamlessly switches between GPU and CPU. The Caffe model and corresponding optimizations are given in text form rather than code.

MXNet

MXNet is a deep learning framework chosen by Amazon. The author is Li Mu. MXNet is a portable, scalable deep learning framework with data flow diagrams similar to Theano and TensorFlow. MXNet supports Python, R, Julia, C++, Scala APIs. MXNet combines the advantages of imperative and declarative programming for easy debugging. MXNet compute optimization and memory configuration resource management is good, can run on a variety of heterogeneous systems [6].

Pytorch

PyTorch [14] is an open source Python machine learning framework developed by Facebook's AI team. It uses Python API to implement programming. Unlike TensorFlow's static computational graph, PyTorch's computational graph is dynamic and can be changed at any time according to computational needs. PyTorch provides CUDA API for tensors and Autograd libraries.

2.2 Public Cloud Provider

There are also many deep learning services based on cloud platforms, but these cloud platforms emphasize remote access debugging and resource elastic scheduling. The world's most famous public cloud providers are Amazon, Microsoft, and Google. AWS [15] is a cloud computing provider operated by Amazon that has great flexibility in the amount of resources customers need, and users can expand or reduce the resources they need at any time. Azure is a public cloud service platform developed by Microsoft that allows applications to run from a remote connection system. The host is located in the Microsoft data center and the data is stored on the cloud platform. With Azure, you can debug your application locally and deploy it on the cloud [16]. In addition to different virtual machines, the Azure environment provides a distributed, massive storage environment for applications. Google developed the Google Cloud Platform [17]. Using this platform, developers can build and test deployments with using Google's highly reliable architecture, while hardware assembly and maintenance is handed over to Google's experts [14]. The services provided by the three public cloud providers in the field of deep learning are shown in the Table 1.

Table 1. Deep learning services provided by three public cloud providers

	Amazon AWS	Microsoft Azure	Google Cloud
Image recognition	Rekognition Image	Computer Vision API Custom Vision Service Face API Emotion API Content Moderator	Vision API AutoML Vision
Video analysis	Rekognition Video	Computer Vision API Video Indexer Content Moderator	Video Intelligence API
Speech to text	Transcribe	Bing Speech API Custom Speech Service Speaker Recognition API	Speech API
Text to speech	Polly	Bing Speech API	Text-to-Speech API
Translation	Translate	Translator Text API	Translation API
Language analysis	Comprehend	Text Analytics API Content Moderator Language Understanding Web Language Model API Linguistic Analysis API	Natural Language API
Chatbot	Lex	Azure Bot Service	Dialogflow

2.3 Comparison and Analysis

We compare the local deployment and cloud-based deep learning services of the deep learning framework. The former is convenient for researchers of deep learning algorithms to improve and propose new deep learning algorithms based on research, debugging, but for engineers of practical business departments, they do not need to have a deep understanding of deep learning algorithms, only need packaged deep learning algorithms to achieve remote access by calling API. Using the deep learning service based on cloud platform, engineers can reduce the difficulty, but for researchers of deep learning algorithm, they can no longer access the source code of deep learning algorithm. It brings inconvenience to the improvement of the original algorithm and the proposal of the new algorithm. At the same time, using these cloud platforms cannot guarantee the security of data.

This paper focuses on the contradiction between in-depth deployment framework local deployment, local debugging and cloud-based deep learning services, internal improvement and external access, and proposes an elastic framework that isolates algorithm design from actual business. This framework solves this contradiction by using web services and RPC middleware technology, enabling deep learning algorithm design researchers to deploy, debug, improve, and propose new deep learning algorithms. Based on the deep learning algorithm online, business requirements department engineers, selecting appropriate algorithms to train and test actual business data. This solution improves the efficiency of both aspects.

3   System Design

This part introduces the system built by this elastic framework proposed in this paper, and uses RESTful API and ICE API as examples to realize remote access to deep learning resources.

3.1   System Introduction

The core design idea of the system is the logical isolation between the deep learning algorithm design and the actual business execution. The structure of the whole system is shown in Fig. 1.

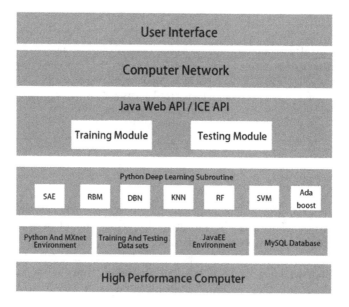

Fig. 1. System structure

The system is divided into two parts: the service provider side and the third-party user side. The host is a high-performance computer, and we need to deploy the software and deep learning framework environment we need on this computer. In addition, there are several deep learning algorithm Python files that have been written on this computer. The extension of future algorithms is also extremely simple. If algorithm researchers improve and propose new algorithms int the future, they only need to modify and add algorithm code files on the host. The system consists of two modules for training and testing. We provide RESTful style Java Web and ICE APIs for remote access and invocation. A third-party user is generally an engineer in the actual business requirements department. They use deep learning algorithm by calling specified API without understanding the specific principles of the algorithm. This system uses the computer network, and its execution efficiency mainly depends on the network response speed, so the code running time is not much different from that deployed locally.

The system operation is shown in Fig. 2. When the system service is opened, the third-party user calls API to transfer the parameters of the deep learning subroutine to the host, ¡and the deep learning subroutine reads these parameters and runs the code. After the code runs, the run result file is saved on the host or cloud, and the data is returned to the user. The relevant operational history are recorded in specialized databases.

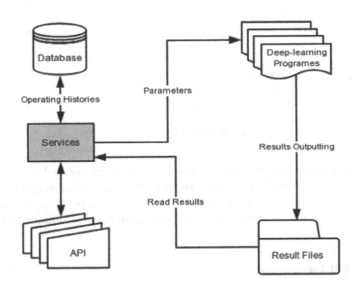

Fig. 2. System server-side operation

3.2 RESTful API Introduction

REST means Resource Representational State Transfer, it does not create new technologies, components, or services by itself, but rather an architectural style or specification of web services that better utilizes some of the guidelines and constraints of existing web technologies. Resources in the RESTful [19] architecture can be identified and adhere to the Uniform Resource interface principle. The system uses JavaEE technology to implement a web-based interface, and the interface style is RESTful. A separate API for deep learning subroutines written in Python is called directly by a Java program. The RESTful architecture of this system is shown in Fig. 3.

There are many advantages to using the RESTful API in this system. It follows the semantics of the HTTP protocol itself, and the client operates on server resources by using four HTTP verbs. It is suitable for a wide-open API and is suitable for a wide range of front-end devices. RESTful API users' behavior is separate from resources. When users call an API and get access to operational resources, the current state is not need to be considered. In addition to the advantages of RESTful itself, each operation

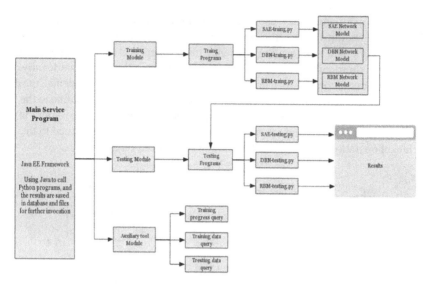

Fig. 3. RESTful architecture

of the deep learning resources in the system is asynchronous, non-online, and the user does not have to wait for a long deep learning training time when using the user, and can perform other operations during training. By using Java programs to call Python deep learning subroutines, algorithm researchers can improve algorithms and propose new algorithms.

3.3   ICE API Introduction

ICE [20] (Internet Communications Engine) is a middleware platform for object-oriented distributed systems. It describes the interface of the service through a neutral language slice that is independent of the specific programming language. Therefore, the language used by the client can be different from the language written by Server. Compared with other object-oriented middleware technologies, ICE has many advantages such as high performance, lightweight, multi-programming language and cross-platform. The way the ICE framework Server communicates with the Client is shown in Fig. 4.

The system uses the API provided by ICE to implement the client's access to deep learning resources on server, but this access method is not a direct solution. This method essentially uses the ICE API to access the RESTful API. Using the ICE API, parameters related to deep learning training can be input on the client side. These parameters are transmitted to the server according to the ICE framework communication, and then transmitted to the web API, and the relevant deep learning subroutine is called. Similarly, the system can acquire deep learning training records and results through such methods.

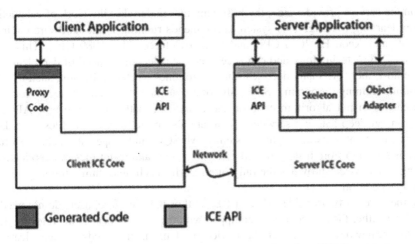

Fig. 4. Communication between client and server based on ICE framework

4 System Implementation

The system is designed to logically isolate the algorithm design researchers from the actual business department engineers. The system uses Java to program, and uses the JFinal framework, provides a RESTful-style API based on the HTTP protocol, and an ICE API that provides services indirectly by calling the RESTful API. The system realizes the call of various deep learning modules, and it has the function of remote access to deep learning resources. The whole system framework is shown in Fig. 5.

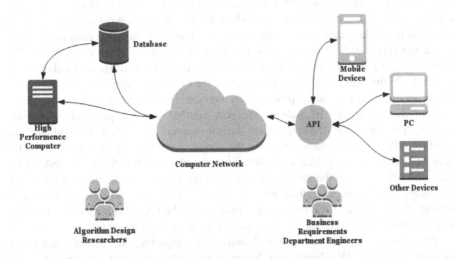

Fig. 5. System implementation framework

On the service provider side, the host computer undertakes the work of calculation of deep learning training. This system recommends running in the hardware environment of Intel Xeon E5-2620 CPU and Nvidia Geforce GTX 1080 GPU. This GPU supports CUDA technology and can accelerate the calculation speed of deep learning. On the host, there are many deep learning subroutines written in Python, such as SAE algorithm training program, SAE algorithm testing program, etc. Algorithms researchers can put algorithm code on the designated path, and write new APIs, so users can get deep learning services. There are also multiple test data files. The database management software of this system is MySQL, and a special database storage device is set up to store history record files, status files and result files of deep learning training. This system provides the only interface for each algorithm's training, testing or query operation.

In the third-party user side, whether RESTful or ICE interface, users do not need to consider whether the device used is equipped with the environment of the relevant deep learning framework, or whether the device used meets the needs of deep learning computing. All they need is a computer network to access deep learning resources. And the factor that determines the time of deep learning training is only the network response speed, so the operation execution time of these trainings is almost the same as that of local deployment.

Using the RESTful API, and computer network, the user can input the parameters of the corresponding module of deep learning. The parameters are transmitted to the specific deep learning program of the corresponding module, and the corresponding result data is returned to the user.

Using the ICE API, access to deep learning resources can be achieved more efficiently. The ICE API also requires a computer network, and the programming languages used by the Server and Client can be different. But first you need to place a same file written in Slice on the Server and Client side, which contains the module name, interface name, and abstract methods in the interface. Then compile the Slice file according to the language used by the server and client. In the same path as the Slice file on the server side, you can write the server-side service resource program. We define the class method for accessing the RESTful API in the corresponding class in the server file. In the same path as the Slice file on the client side, you can write the client-side program access resource provided by service. In the program, there are proxy name of the server, the IP address, the port number, and the protocol of the port number, you can call the parameter in the server. The class method for the RESTful API gets the data returned by the server. As shown in Fig. 6, we write the class method for training SAE algorithm in the interface of the relevant module of the Slice file. After starting the server, we can input the relevant parameters on the client-side program to start SAE training. The train's information will be returned after training. Then we start SAE test, the test process can be long, but we can get train log during testing. The figure shows the asynchrony of our system.

The system only realizes the isolation of the algorithm design and the actual business execution. Developers can design framework codes that directly calls deep learning subroutines by using the ICE API based on actual conditions. Apart from it, UI is not specially designed for the user in this system, and the developers can design the UI according to the actual business needs.

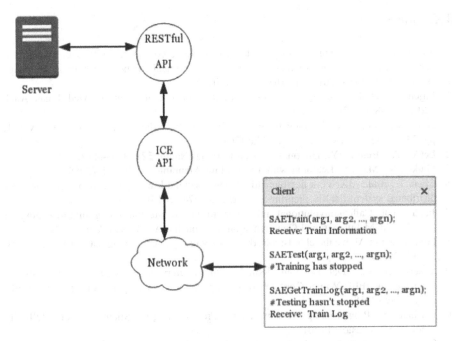

Fig. 6. Get deep learning resources by using ICE API

5   Conclusion

Deep learning has a wide range of applications in many fields today and it is one of the important methods in the field of machine learning. This paper compares the two common methods of deep learning resource deployment. Local deep learning environment deployment or use of public cloud platforms have advantages and disadvantages for both algorithm design researchers and actual business department engineers.

This paper combines the advantages and disadvantages of two kinds of deep learning resources on different roles, focusing on the logical isolation of algorithm improvement, design and actual business execution, and proposes an elastic framework that can meet the contradiction between internal improvement and external access, and designs a system is implemented. The system is divided into two parts, service provider side and the third-party user side. The service provider side provides related deep learning resource services and external access APIs. The third-party user side uses the API provided by service provider to get access to deep learning service. With this method, this paper realizes the logical isolation between the improved design of the algorithm and the actual business execution.

Acknowledgement. This work has received funding from the European Union Horizon 2020 research and innovation programme under the Marie Sklodowska-Curie grant agreement no. 701697, Major Program of the National Social Science Fund of China (Grant No. 17ZDA092), Basic Research Programs (Natural Science Foundation) of Jiangsu Province (BK20180794), 333 High-Level Talent Cultivation Project of Jiangsu Province (BRA2018332) and the PAPD fund.

References

1. Socher, R., et al.: Recursive deep models for semantic compositionality over a sentiment treebank. In: Proceedings of the Conference on Empirical Methods in Natural Language Processing, EMNLP 2013, pp. 1631–1642 (2013)
2. Litjens, G., et al.: A survey on deep learning in medical image analysis. Med. Image Anal. 42(9), 60–88 (2017)
3. Ding, X., et al.: Deep learning for event-driven stock prediction. In: IJCAI 2015, vol. 1, pp. 2327–2333. AAAI Press, Palo Alto (2015)
4. LeCun, Y., Bengio, Y., Hinton, G.: Deep learning. Nature 521, 436–444 (2015)
5. Shukla, N.: Machine Learning with TensorFlow. Manning, Greenwich (2018)
6. Chen, T., et al.: MXNet: a flexible and efficient machine learning library for heterogeneous distributed systems. arXiv preprint arXiv:1512.01274 (2015)
7. Jia, Y., et al.: Caffe: convolutional architecture for fast feature embedding. In: Proceedings of the 22nd ACM International Conference on Multimedia. ACM, New York (2014)
8. Fox, A., et al.: Above the clouds: a Berkeley view of cloud computing. UCB/EECS, vol. 28, no. 13 (2009)
9. Vasudevan, A.B., Dai, D., Van Gool, L.: Object referring in visual scene with spoken language. In: IEEE Winter Conference on Applications of Computer Vision 2018. IEEE, Piscataway (2018)
10. Krishnan, S.: Programming Windows Azure: Programming the Microsoft Cloud. O'Reilly Media Inc., Sebastopol (2010)
11. Sato-Shimokawara, E., et al.: A cloud based chat robot using dialogue histories for elderly people. In: 24th IEEE International Symposium on Robot and Human Interactive Communication (RO-MAN), pp. 206–210. IEEE, Piscataway (2015)
12. Abadi, M., et al.: TensorFlow: a system for large-scale machine learning. In: OSDI, vol. 16, pp. 265–283. USENIX, Berkeley (2016)
13. Sherkhane, P., Vora, D.: Survey of deep learning software tools. In: International Conference on Data Management, pp. 236–238. IEEE, NJ (2017)
14. Ketkar, N.: Deep Learning with Python. Apress, Berkeley (2017)
15. Tajadod, G., Batten, L., Govinda, K.: Microsoft and Amazon: a comparison of approaches to cloud security. In: 4th IEEE International Conference on Cloud Computing Technology & Science, pp. 539–544. IEEE, Piscataway (2012)
16. Microsoft Azure Homepage. https://azure.microsoft.com/. Accessed 08 Oct 2018
17. Google Cloud Homepage. https://cloud.google.com/. Accessed 01 Oct 2018
18. Peng, J., et al.: Comparison of several cloud computing platforms. In: Second International Symposium on Information Science and Engineering, vol. 1, pp. 1631–1644 (2009)
19. Richardson, L., Ruby, S.: RESTful Web Services. O'Reilly Media Inc., Sebastopol (2008)
20. Henning, M.: A new approach to object-oriented middleware. IEEE Internet Comput. 8(1), 66–75 (2004)
21. Zhou, S., Liang, W., Li, J., Kim, J.-U.: Improved VGG model for road traffic sign recognition. CMC: Comput. Mater. Continua 57(1), 11–24 (2018)
22. Tu, Y., Lin, Y., Wang, J., Kim, J.-U.: Semi-supervised learning with generative adversarial networks on digital signal modulation classification. CMC: Comput. Mater. Continua 55(2), 243–254 (2018)

Design of an IoT-Based Efficient Security Scheme in Home Wireless System

Fei Ding[1,2], Zhiliang Li[1], Chengwan Ai[1], Ruoyu Su[1],
Dengyin Zhang[1,2(✉)], and Hongbo Zhu[2]

[1] Jiangsu Key Laboratory of Wireless Communications, Nanjing University
of Posts and TeleCommunications, Nanjing 210003, China
zhangdy@njupt.edu.cn
[2] Engineering Research Center of Health Service System Based on Ubiquitous
Wireless Networks, Ministry of Education, Nanjing University of Posts
and Telecommunications, Nanjing 210003, China

Abstract. Home security is a typical Internet of Things application with a broad market prospect. This paper proposes a framework for building a home security system based on the IoT three-tier architecture. Under the architecture of this system, the home sensor node communicates with the home gateway through wireless communication, and the platform-level business cloudization solution can facilitate the expansion of home security services. A testbed of a simple home network application system that includes a gateway and multiple sensors is created to test its user interaction capabilities. Experimental results show that the proposed test system can run stably; it can be applied to other monitoring areas and simultaneously supports a multi-ubiquitous sensor network.

Keywords: Home security · IoT · Home gateway · SMS

1 Introduction

In the future construction and decoration industry, smart home projects will show the biggest growth. Hardcover housing is an inevitable trend in the future development of real estate. The rise in housing prices also provides market space for smart homes to enter hardcover homes, and second-time buyers have a more realistic need for hard-wearing homes in terms of both safety and comfort. As an important application area of the Internet of Things (IoT), the smart home brings new services, redefines the customer experience, and stimulates the expansion of market demand. Its broad market value will enable it to be widely applied to hotels, villas, residential communities, factories, office buildings, commercial centers, large venues, and other areas, greatly changing our existing lifestyle. In addition, the state's requirements for energy conservation and emission reduction, as well as the society's advocacy for low-carbon life, also provide potential requirements for policy background and social background for the popularization of smart homes. The development of smart homes will undoubtedly lead to the upgrading of traditional home appliances, furniture, security, and other industrial structures, resulting in a broader market.

© Springer Nature Switzerland AG 2019
X. Sun et al. (Eds.): ICAIS 2019, LNCS 11634, pp. 287–296, 2019.
https://doi.org/10.1007/978-3-030-24271-8_26

Nowadays, there are an increasing number of research achievements in the field of home security architecture and service systems [1, 2], such as a PZT based home safety monitoring system [3], and a GSM (Global System for Mobile Communication) based home security scheme [4], respectively. A home security system for the elderly is proposed in [5]. A DIY security protection against invasion was proposed in [6]. There are also some studies on the optimization for home security systems, such as increasing the methods and steps of face recognition in the home security system [7]; security mechanism of family security system with multi-level authentication [8]; strengthening the home management efficiency based on the method of logic sensing [9]; and optimizing the efficiency and robustness of the home security system [10]. More and more research began to add data processing or big data technologies, in order to further optimize the existing information system [11, 12].

This paper fully considers the application requirements of the home security system. Based on the three-layer architecture of the IoT, a design framework of the home security system is proposed. The third part analyzes and sorts out the business function classification of the home security system, including wireless landline security, gateway security, wireless camera security, security alarm, and home environmental quality monitoring. On this basis, the fourth part builds a home security test system and verifies the home security related business functions. Finally, the conclusions are given.

2 Design Methods

2.1 System Overview

The system architecture is shown in Fig. 1. Home security service is an intelligent information product combining traditional communication technology and Internet of Things technology. Through a mobile phone client and portal website, it mainly provides Wi-Fi routing, security alarm, video surveillance, home appliance control, and other functions to optimize lifestyle. The living environment of the smart home must meet the needs of users for the modern life.

The door, smoke detector, gas detector, air detection, camera, and other equipment through wired/wireless access security controller, security controller to LAN/USB/Wi-Fi connected to the home gateway, and the home gateway communicates with the service platform. When the security external plug-in is connected to the home gateway with the USB method, the external plug-in is only responsible for the communication function, and the home gateway will undertake a part of the security service function.

Users can arm/disarm operation via the PC/mobile phone client login platform, view real-time video footage, and simultaneously when the alarm condition is triggered, the business platform can be set by mobile phone short/MMS to send alarm information to user.

The home security platform does not realize the functions of video storage, transcoding, distribution, and so on. These functions are undertaken by the video surveillance capability platform (such as Ali video cloud platform), and the security business platform is only the related functions provided by the call capability platform.

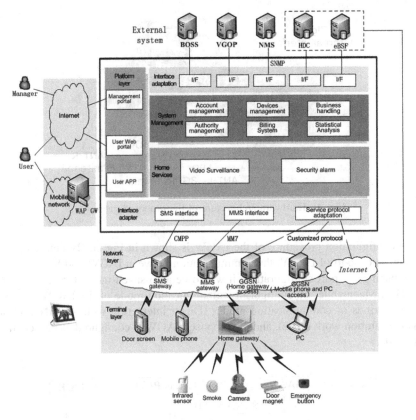

Fig. 1. Home security system structure

2.2 IAGW Design

The IAGW prototype is designed to provide easy access to the CNs deployed in the HNA system. Figure 2 shows the stack structure hardware architecture of the proposed IAGW gateway [13].

The mainboard is the core unit of the gateway which designed with an ARM11 processor, 512 Mbytes SDRAM, 2 GByte NAND flash, and runs Linux 2.6 or later operating system. The USB interface is used to connect a memory card for local data storage, especially for video monitoring data. The 4 LED indicators of the IAGW represents different working states, corresponding with gateway power on, network connect/disconnect, data transmission and alarm on/off, respectively. The IAGW proposes an onboard 22 pin internal interface and a RS232/485 external interface connected to the mainboard, which are convenient for ZigBee SN development and integration. If users need to connect and control other wireless standard home devices, it can develop the corresponding SN node and also integrated through the two interfaces. If users use this interface to integrate SN node, then, must comply with the dimensions.

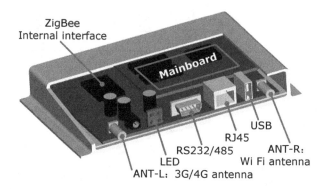

Fig. 2. Hardware architecture of the proposed gateway.

The configuration procedure of the IAGW is shown in Fig. 3. By configuring the communication port of IAGW, the communication between IAGW and SN is secured. After finishing the port configuration, it would be auto-saved into internal memory of the IAGW. Meanwhile, by configuring communication mode of the IAGW, it mainly includes 2 kinds of communication modes (Direct interaction with the HNASC platform or separation work mode), and the proposed IAGW is configured as the separation work mode.

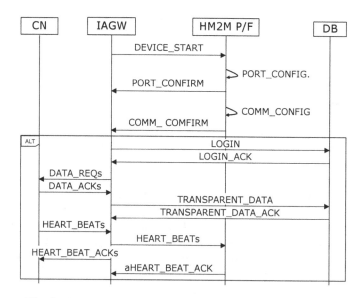

Fig. 3. Control flow of the HM2 M platform to IAGW gateway.

If the HMMP-S communication configuration is finished, then, we can configure the communication parameters of the HMMP-A. The main parameters include IP address, port, and secret keys of HNASC platform should be configured. The IAGW also can be configured encrypt mode. When the COMM_CONFIG data is executed, IAGW is send communication key request to HM2M P/F, and automatically assigned by the latter. Between CNs and IAGW, IAGW and M2M P/F, monitoring and maintaining of communication is implemented by HEART_BEAT and HEART_BEAT_ACK packet. Hence, data transmission link of the HNA system has been established, HM2M P/F can implement the remote management for IAGW and CNs, and HNASC can support the business service for users.

2.3   Home Security Service Classification

Under the support of home security business system, we integrate the Internet of things and communication technology, as well as implement various kinds of sensor terminals, to monitor and protect houses and vehicles, providing users with comprehensive information services for security.

Target users mainly include family users – families and small shops, street shops, and other families with family attributes.

On this basis, a series of home oriented security business is launched, which includes five kinds of businesses: security alarm, video surveillance, air detection, tracking and anti-theft, and third party applications (Table 1).

Table 1. Service classification of home security system.

Typical service	Service content
Security alarm	Information is obtained through the sensing equipment, such as the magnetic and smoke sense of doors and windows, and provides a stable and reliable security alarm function
Video surveillance	Service can be provided based on video cloud platform and intelligent video analysis platform, video monitoring, and intelligent alarm
Indoor environmental quality monitoring	The indoor CO_2 and VOC (Volatile Organic Compounds) concentration are detected. The sensor data is transmitted to the platform through the security controller and the home gateway, and actively synchronized to the user service terminal
Positioning and tracking	GPS (Global Position System) and other positioning technology are combined with short distance communication technology to realize the tracking and anti-theft of cars and assets
Third party business	Based on the home security open platform, the third party security category applications that meet the requirements can be quickly introduced

3 Home Security Scheme and Its Services

The home security services mainly provides Wi-Fi routing, security alarm, video surveillance, home appliance control, and other functions, including various terminal forms, such as home gateway, smart set-top box, Wi-Fi camera (or wired camera), and magnetic door and window magnetism. Security sensors/controllers are available to meet the needs of different users. The business functions of each form of product have different emphases, resulting in a more comprehensive series of products.

3.1 Wireless Landline Security

The product uses a traditional wireless landline as a carrier to increase security functions.

(1) Voice communication: realizes voice call and short message of traditional wireless landline based on the telecom operators network.
(2) Security alarm: Detects environmental changes through sensors, such as door magnets, and sends alarm information to specified security numbers.
(3) Appliance control: realizes the function of controlling air conditioner activation and temperature setting through mobile phone.

3.2 Gateway Based Home Security

Based on the traditional home router, the product incorporates security features and expands Wi-Fi video surveillance.

(1) Wi-Fi routing: Forwards broadband signals to nearby wireless network devices in the form of Wi-Fi.
(2) Security alarm: Detects environmental changes through sensors, such as door magnets, and sends alarm information to specified security numbers.
(3) Appliance control: realizes the function of controlling air conditioner activation and temperature setting through mobile phone.
(4) Wi-Fi video surveillance: Video surveillance is achieved by connecting to a Wi-Fi camera.

3.3 Wireless Camera Based Home Security

The product is based on the 3G/4G network of the telecom operator and provides remote wireless video images for viewing the video and controlling the camera on the security client or portal.

(1) Video surveillance: View camera monitoring screens, monitor sounds, video screenshots, or videos through the mobile client or portal.
(2) Camera control: Control the camera head position through the mobile client or portal.

(3) Security alarm: Detects environmental changes through sensors, such as door magnets, and sends alarm information to specified security numbers.
(4) Appliance control: realizes the function of controlling air conditioner opening and temperature setting through mobile phone.

3.4   Security Alarm

Through the door magnet, window magnet, smoke and other equipment to arm the designated area, when an alarm occurs, the platform will notify the user by voice, SMS, mobile client, or another specified method. According to the mode set by the user, the home host will also prompt corresponding to the alarm status.

3.5   Terminal Management

Through this function module, we manage the security host (home gateway) and peripheral sensors, and combine all kinds of devices freely into business sales suite, so as to facilitate the salesmen entering the room. The administrator can log onto the business platform, and then add, delete, or modify the information of security host and sensor, including device name, device type, device manufacturer, equipment quantity, equipment price, and relative remarks information.

Then business and management platform saves the host security serial number, manufacturer number, host types, parts information, sensor serial number, sensor type, host security switch state, disarm state, sensor state, home gateway information, network information, Family Customs set USB (Universal Serial Bus) security information platform, and other external plug-ins required for the physical information terminal.

3.6   Business Logic Control

It provides alarm logic, terminal configuration logic, data synchronization logic, and other main business logic, and the corresponding alarm module, terminal configuration module interface, to achieve alarm, terminal configuration, and other functions. The home security service platform must have the function of checking the alarm white list.

3.7   Interface Adaptation

The platform needs to provide interface modules with BOSS system, family business center, network management system, VGOP (Value-added Service General Operation Platform) system, and video monitoring system, so as to realize all kinds of functions of billing, network management, monitoring, and so on.

The video surveillance capabilities provided by the home security service platform are provided by the third party video cloud platform (such as the Ali video cloud).

3.8 System Self-management

It mainly includes the functions of user management, equipment management, alarm setting, and alarm processing.

4 System Implementation

Based on the above architecture, a home security test system was built (as shown in Fig. 4), which mainly consisted of a home gateway, a camera, a door/window contact sensor, an alarm, and two indoor air quality (IAQ) nodes. All security sensors communicate wirelessly with the gateway (GW) node through radio frequency technology. The camera communicates with the GW node through Wi-Fi, and other nodes communicate with the GW node through the 433 MHz radio frequency.

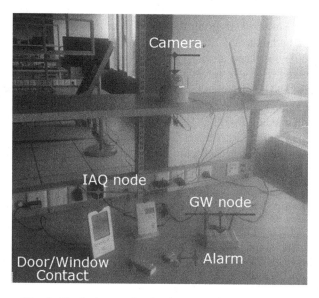

Fig. 4. Testbed setup for the demonstration experiments.

Figures 5 and 6 show the results of continuous sampling of temperature and VOC parameters over 24 h, with a sampling period of 9 s and a total of 407 packets. According to the extra 7 data packets, it is caused by the retransmission of the wireless communication packet loss established by the system.

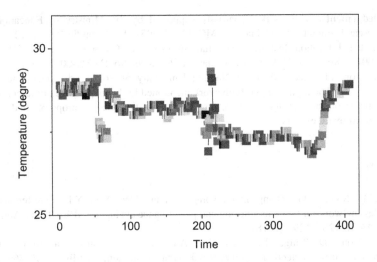

Fig. 5. Continuous temperature sampling results in 24 h (Starting at 12 noon).

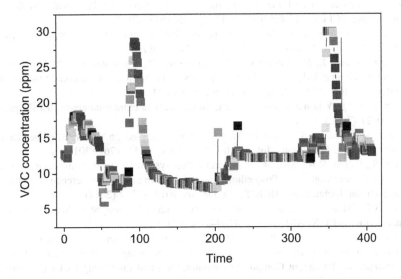

Fig. 6. Continuous VOC sampling results in 24 h (Starting at 12 noon).

5   Conclusion

This paper proposes a framework for building a home security system based on the IoT three-tier architecture. Under this system architecture, the home sensor nodes communicate with the home gateway through wireless communication. The business cloudization solution through the platform layer can simplify the function expansion of the future home security system, as well as verify the stability of the test system through continuous environmental parameter sampling. The system architecture proposed in this paper can be replicated and promoted in many IoT systems in the future.

Acknowledgements. This work is partially supported by the Ministry of Education-China Mobile Research Foundation, China (No. MCM20170205), the Scientific Research Foundation of the Higher Education Institutions of Jiangsu Province, China (nos. 15KJA510002 and 17KJB510043), Six talent peaks project in Jiangsu Province (No. DZXX-008), and the Research Foundation for Advanced Talents of Nanjing University of Posts and Telecommunications (No. NY217146). The home service framework mentioned in this paper partially refers to China Mobile's home business system, and we are grateful for the relevant proposals and technical guidance from many experts.

References

1. Ding, F., Song, A.G., Zhang, D.Y., Tong, E., Pan, Z.W., You, Y.H.: Interference-aware wireless network for home monitoring and performance evaluation. IEEE Trans. Autom. Sci. Eng. **15**(3), 1286–1297 (2018)
2. Su, J., Hong, D., Tang, J.L., Chen, H.P.: An efficient anti-collision algorithm based on improved collision detection scheme. IEICE Trans. Commun. **E99-B**(2), 465–469 (2016)
3. Sultana, S., Akand, T., Dey, M.: Design and implementation of home security system using PZT. In: Proceedings of the 9th International Conference on Electrical and Computer Engineering (ICECE), 13 February 2017, pp. 554–557 (2017)
4. Isa, E., Sklavos, N.: Smart home automation: GSM security system design & implementation. J. Eng. Sci. Technol. Rev. **10**(3), 170–174 (2017)
5. Kulsiriruangyos, J., Rattanawutikul, V., Sangsartra, P., Wongsawang, D.: Home security system for alone elderly people. In: Proceedings of the 5th ICT International Student Project Conference (ICT-ISPC), 22 July 2016, pp. 65–68 (2016)
6. Wayt, G.W.: DIY home security: deter intruders with an extra loud alarm. IEEE Spectr. **53**(1), 20–21 (2016)
7. Sahani, M., Subudhi, S., Mohanty, M.N.: Design of face recognition based embedded home security system. KSII Trans. Internet Inf. Syst. **10**(4), 1751–1767 (2016)
8. Peter, S., Gopal, R.K.: Multi-level authentication system for smart home-security analysis and implementation. In: Proceedings of the International Conference on Inventive Computation Technologies (ICICT), 18 January 2017, vol. 2 (2017)
9. Jose, A.C., Malekian, R.: Improving smart home security: integrating logical sensing into smart home. IEEE Sens. J. **17**(13), 4269–4286 (2017)
10. Chilipirea, C., Ursache, A., Popa, D.O., Pop, F.: Energy efficiency and robustness for IoT: Building a smart home security system. In: Proceedings - IEEE 12th International Conference on Intelligent Computer Communication and Processing (ICCP), 7 November 2016, pp. 43–48 (2016)
11. Li, D.H., Zhang, G.Z., Xu, Z.: Modelling the roles of cewebrity trust and platform trust in consumers' propensity of live-streaming: an extended TAM method. CMC Comput. Mater. Continua **55**(1), 137–150 (2018)
12. Jayaprakash, G., Muthuraj, M.P.: Prediction of compressive strength of various SCC mixes using relevance vector machine. CMC Comput. Mater. Continua **54**(1), 83–102 (2018)
13. Ding, F., Song, A.G., Tong, E., Li, J.Q.: A smart gateway architecture for improving efficiency of home network applications. J. Sens. **2016**, 10 (2016). Article ID 2197237

Discussion on the Application
of Industrial Internet

Yanruixuan Ma[1($\boxtimes$)], Zhendan Li[3], Yanglijuan Liu[4], Huijie Liu[2],
and Shengqian Ma[2($\boxtimes$)]

[1] University of Electronic Science and Technology of China,
Chengdu 611731, Sichuan, China
2055653378@qq.com
[2] School of Physics and Electronic Engineering, Taishan University,
Taian 271000, Shandong, People's Republic of China
shqma@126.com
[3] Shandong Taikai High Voltage Switch Co., Ltd.,
Taian 271000, Shandong, China
[4] NanJing Institute of Industry Technology, Nanjing 210000, Jiangsu, China

Abstract. This article introduces the origin, development, main technologies platform and bottlenecks encountered in the application of industrial Internet. It reveals the inevitability and strong development momentum of industrial internet, makes a comparative study on the application and promotion of the current platform at home and abroad, and looks forward to the future of industrial internet.

Keywords: Industrial Internet platform · IaaS · PaaS · APP

1 Introduction

In the digital economy environment, with the extensive use of advanced technologies such as cloud computing, big data, mobile social networking, the Internet of Things, and artificial intelligence, the manufacturing resources of individuals, enterprises, and even the entire production system have been widely and real-time connected. Not only has it changed the way people live, but it is changing the nature of business. Digital transformation is an inevitable choice for all enterprises. The purpose of digital transformation is to better create value for users and achieve the best customer experience, and to disrupt the production process of enterprise product realization and delivery. Through the user data insight in product-related activities, systematically carry out knowledge precipitation and inheritance, improve the digital design capability and service level of products, and optimize the product delivery mechanism to meet the customer's personalized experience. In all these business activities, the complete commercial realization process that produces the demand of the product until the product is delivered, the data is effectively, continuously, and closed-loop, and the resources of the product design, manufacturing, and even the entire supply chain are closely coordinated. The industrial Internet platform is an open platform that faces the demands of digital and networked intelligence in manufacturing industries, and builds a

X. Sun et al. (Eds.): ICAIS 2019, LNCS 11634, pp. 297–308, 2019.
https://doi.org/10.1007/978-3-030-24271-8_27

collection, convergence analysis, and service system based on massive data to support manufacturing resources in connection, elastic supply, and efficient allocation. Industrial Internet is the strategic direction of the digital transformation and development of the industrial economy and the commanding height of competition. It is speeding up the development of industrial Internet innovation. Industrial Internet is in a crucial period of industrialization and is implementing the strategy of industrial Internet innovation and development. It is of great significance to break through the bottleneck of key core technologies, accelerate the application and popularization of technological achievements, and build an advanced and complete industrial Internet technology industry system for promoting the high-quality development of industrial economy, promoting the transformation of China from a big manufacturing country to a strong manufacturing country, and realizing the transition from a big network country to a strong network country. The Industrial Revolution has driven the rapid development and replacement of machines and equipment. The increasingly perfect new Internet technologies such as cloud computing, big data, and artificial intelligence have triggered an upsurge in the Internet revolution. Intelligent machines and people are connected through the Internet and combined with big data analysis to create more efficient, safer and cleaner. It is the general trend to build more efficient, safer and cleaner advanced productive forces and an industrial Internet platform.

2   The Origin of Industrial Internet

Industrial Internet is a key infrastructure linking the whole industrial system, the whole industrial chain and the whole value chain, and supporting the development of industrial intelligence. It is a new form of business and application model formed by the deep integration of the new generation of information technology and manufacturing industries. It is the core carrier of the Internet from the consumption field to the production field and from the virtual economy to the real economy. A new round of scientific and technological revolutions and industrial changes are booming around the world. In 1998, the Massachusetts Institute of Technology first proposed the concept of the Internet of Things (this is the starting point of today's industrial Internet). Initially, the Internet of Things almost exclusively included radio frequency identification technology - also known as "electronic tags." After more than a decade, the Internet of Things is still largely like a computer in the 1960s and 1970s – it has excellent applications in many fields, but it is an "application island". The Industrial Internet was proposed by GE in 2012. As the third wave of great change after the Industrial Revolution and the Internet Revolution, it is the integration of advanced computing power, data analysis, low-cost sensing technology, wide-ranging connections and global industrial systems promoted by the Internet. It is the depth of the digital world and the machine world. Degree intertwined will bring far-reaching changes to the global industrial system. GE is not the only player in the game of using cloud computing technology to develop industrial Internet to help itself grow rapidly in energy, manufacturing, health care, aircraft manufacturing and other industries. IBM, Amazon and other cloud service companies are also describing their Internet of Things strategy and other cloud-based industrial data processing solutions to developers, while startups like SAP, Siemens and Machineshop are trying to apply their business analysis capabilities to large data generated by machines and sensors. The fuel for the next industrial revolution will consist of data: manufacturing will not only be automated, but will be driven by data to permanently change factory production methods. As a product of the deep integration of the new generation of information technology and manufacturing, the industrial Internet has increasingly become the key support for the new industrial revolution and an important cornerstone for deepening the "Internet + advanced manufacturing industry", which has had an all-round, profound and revolutionary impact on the development of industrial manufacturing. It is an important basis for promoting the construction of a powerful manufacturing country and a powerful network country. In November 2017, the State Council issued the Guiding Opinions on Deepening the "Internet + Advanced Manufacturing Industry" to Develop Industrial Internet, which clearly set out the goal of fostering 300,000 industrial APPs for specific industries and scenes by 2020. The industrial Internet platform is an important foundation for promoting the development of industrial APP and building an industrial APP ecosystem. It plays an important supporting role in the process of industrial APP cultivation. Lenovo data has been deeply implementing the national policy. Since 2011, it has established a large platform for industrial data and industrial Internet. In the rapidly advancing industry 4.0 era, Lenovo data expects to unite production, research and research forces with an open, collaborative and win-win attitude. Comprehensive support for the development of industrial APP, through the activation of industrial data and knowledge resources, enabling the industry to improve quality, efficiency and transformation and upgrade.

3 Main Technologies Platform

The Industrial Internet builds a service system based on massive data collection, aggregation, and analysis, supporting the ubiquitous link, flexible supply, and efficient configuration of manufacturing resources. The industrial Internet platform can be divided into four parts: (1) Edge layer: Forming an effective data collection system through protocol transformation and edge calculation, thereby making the invisible data of the physical space explicit in the network space. (2) IaaS layer: virtualize basic computing network storage resources to realize infrastructure resource pooling; (3) industrial PaaS layer: industrial operating system, downward docking of massive industrial equipment, instruments, products, supporting industrial intelligent applications Rapid development and deployment; (4) Industrial APP: mainly for industry users and third-party developers, industry users such as Foxconn, Zoomlion and other industrial verticals, third-party developers mainly based on PaaS layer to do industrial APP. The development work creates applications for industries and scenarios by calling and packaging open tools on the industrial PaaS platform.

(1) Asset optimization platform – the commanding heights of platform competition.

Asset optimization platform is mainly used in the management and operation of equipment assets. It connects intelligent terminals through modern sensing and mobile communication technologies, collects data and information about equipment and environment from terminals, and then uses large data, artificial intelligence and other technology and industry experience knowledge in the cloud based on these data. Real-time intelligent analysis of equipment operation status and performance status, and then in the form of industrial App program to provide corresponding intelligent services for production and decision-making. The main participants in the asset optimization platform are often industrial control companies and large equipment manufacturers. Asset optimization platform is the commanding height of future manufacturing dominance competition. It can not only fully integrate advanced technologies such as big data and artificial intelligence, but also provide a development environment for third parties. For example, Siemens's MindSphere and GE's Predix platform provide software development environments and tools. It aims to form a third-party development application ecology similar to the Apple Store through the access of third-party developers and applications. At present, the industrial giant is the main impetus for such platforms, such as GE, Siemens, ABB, etc. China's Sanyiyun and Xugong Industrial Cloud also belong to such platforms, but the degree of development is relatively lagging behind. In the case of Siemens's MindSphere, MindSphere is an open ecosystem. It can make full use of Siemens equipment installed around the world (30 million automated systems, 70 million smart instruments, 800,000 associated products) and rich applications (APIs) to obtain massive data. And based on its deep industry knowledge and experience to provide digital services, the MindSphere platform includes three levels of edge connection layer, development and operation layer, and application service layer, corresponding to three core elements of MindConnect, MindClub, and MindApps, respectively. MindConnect is responsible for data transmission to the cloud platform. The MindCourt provides users with data analysis, application development environment and application development tools. MindApps provides users with industrial intelligent applications that integrate industry experience and data analysis results, such as combining equipment historical data with real-time running data, building data twins, and timely monitoring of equipment performance. We will ensure the preventive maintenance of equipment, make rational plans for the use of energy efficiency such as equipment production lines based on the collection and analysis of on-site energy consumption data, optimize energy data management and improve energy efficiency.

(2) Resource allocation platform – the important starting point of supply side reform.

The resource allocation platform is mainly embodied in the organization and scheduling of resources. It gathers a large amount of industrial data, model algorithm, R&D and design resources and capabilities in the application process. It disperses these accumulated resources through cloud access and cloud processing technology, optimizes the resource management, business process, production process, supply chain management and other links of manufacturing enterprises, and realizes manufacturing enterprises and supply chain management. The docking of external user needs, innovation resources and production capacity. Such platforms can effectively promote capacity optimization and regional synergy, and also support new business such as C2M customization to meet the diversified market demand and provide support for supply-side reform. China has a number of such platforms at the leading level, such as INDICS platform of Aerospace Science and engineering, COSMO Plat of Haier, etc.

Take the INDICS platform of the aerospace industry as an example: The INDICS platform builds its own data center on the IaaS layer, provides rich data storage, product analysis and services on the DaaS layer, and provides various industrial service engines on the PaaS layer. For example, the process engine for software definition and manufacturing, the data analysis engine, the simulation engine and the artificial intelligence engine, as well as the public service component library for developers and more than 200 API interfaces, its open to the public self-research software and public research application APP A total of more than 500 species, It covers the industrial application capabilities of smart R&D, lean manufacturing, smart services, smart enterprises, ecological applications, and other industrial chains and products throughout their life cycle. More than 600 INDICS platform access groups share design models, professional software, and more than 13,000 equipment facilities, which can effectively solve the problem of idle production capacity and overloaded operation of production units. For example, Henan Aerospace Hydraulic Pneumatic Technology Co., Ltd. implements collaborative R&D and process design based on the INDICS platform with the General Design Department and the assembly plant, shortening the R&D cycle by 35%, increasing the utilization rate of resources by 30%, and improving production efficiency by 40%. In addition, industrial enterprises can also open up their spare manufacturing capabilities through the platform to realize online leasing of manufacturing capabilities, further releasing production capacity.

(3) General enabling platform - Asset Optimization and resource allocation platform support.

Universal Enabling Platform mainly provides basic and universal services for cloud computing, Internet of Things and big data, mainly provided by ICT enterprises. Some of the platforms focus on data computing and storage of cloud services, such as Azure of Microsoft, HANA of SAP, AWS of Amazon, Aliyun and Tencent Cloud of China, and others focus on device connection management of Internet of Things, such as Jasper of Cisco, Ocean Connect of Huawei, etc. Such platforms provide technical support for asset optimization and resource allocation-based industrial Internet. For example, GE's Redix is deployed on Microsoft's Azure platform. In addition, Universal Enabling Platform is also widely used in finance, entertainment, life services and other industries. Taking HUAWEI's OceanConnect platform as an example, its technical architecture is divided into two directions: vertical and horizontal. Vertical direction can be divided into three layers: connection management layer, mainly providing SIM card life cycle management, billing, statistics and enterprise portal functions; equipment management layer, to provide equipment connection, equipment data acquisition and storage, equipment maintenance and other functions; application enabler layer, mainly providing open API capabilities, while having data. Analysis, rule engine, business layout and other capabilities. Horizontally, the distributed IoT agent connected to the platform docks with the industry intelligent device gateway and provides edge computing capability to achieve collaboration with cloud computing. The OceanConnect platform provides cloud gateways, supporting all kinds of codec plug-ins, enabling devices to plug and play. FAW has realized effective connection and management of tens of millions of vehicles after using Ocean Connect platform, and can process millions of vehicles' information concurrently. At the same time, the platform also supports the development of FAW's new business and the rapid integration of new equipment, providing large data capability for real-time analysis.

(4) Comparative analysis and future development trend of three kinds of platforms.

All three types of industrial Internet platforms connect physical carriers directly or indirectly through the industrial Internet to provide differentiated services. Among them, the asset optimization platform takes the terminal equipment and production process as the direct optimization object. It interacts most deeply and frequently with the underlying physical equipment. The data types and volumes it obtains are also very large. For example, when GE's Prex platform is used in steam turbines, thousands of types of data such as pressure, temperature and speed should be collected in real time. The volume of data collected by each machine can reach TB level. At the same time, the processing and analysis of these data need to integrate large data, artificial intelligence and other innovative technologies, so the construction of such platforms is difficult, not only need to master the new generation of information technology, but also need to have full coverage of intelligent products, high-end equipment and integrated solutions.

Resource allocation platforms are often based on mature network information technology. They pay more attention to the cross-regional and cross-link reorganization and integration of resources, focusing on network collaboration and front-end docking of personalized customization to provide precise services. This kind of platform has strong vertical industry attributes, and has high requirements for information integration application and supply chain management level. Universal Enabling Platform mainly provides low-level technical support for industrial Internet, such as connection, computing, storage, and so on. It basically involves the edge layer and IaaS layer of industrial Internet industrial system. Generally, ICT giants provide more clear division of labor for future platforms. Asset optimization platform provides optimization services for high-end products, promotes high-end manufacturing from high-value products to "high-value products + high-value services". Resource allocation platform promotes capacity optimization, drives consumption balance, and drives the transformation of enterprise development mode. Universal enabling platform provides technical support for the upper platform, thus enabling it to provide technical support for the upper platform. The upper platform can focus on services directly related to production, and achieve specialization of all platforms. In the future, the cooperation between various platforms will be closer and the purpose is to provide complete solutions for customers. Through cooperation, it can not only realize the flexible deployment of the platform, such as the cooperation between GE, Siemens, Microsoft, and Amazon, it can effectively optimize the deployment of basic resources, but also strengthen the ability to collect data on the spot, such as the cooperation between the aerospace department and SAP and Siemens. Through Siemens huge stock base, reduce the difficulty of equipment access, achieve a wider range of data acquisition. In addition, the cooperation can also improve its own data analysis capabilities. For example, ABB, Siemens and IBM's cooperation are all aimed at improving the computing and analysis capabilities of their own platforms. Relying on the cooperation of various platforms, provide complete solutions for customer applications.

4 Bottlenecks to Be Addressed

The Industrial Internet Platform leverages data-based capabilities as a link to create an open, shared value network. The industrial Internet platform is a professional service platform with data as the driving force and manufacturing capability as the core. Firstly, data is the core element of the platform, and cooperation based on data capabilities is the driving force for platform business development and mode innovation. Major industrial Internet platforms around the world are actively competing for data resources and data capabilities, such as GE's acquisition of Bit Stew Systems and Wise.io, PTC's acquisition of Coldlight and so on. Secondly, building an open and shared value network is the basis for the development of industrial Internet platform. At present, no company can provide end-to-end solutions such as "cloud infrastructure + terminal connection + data analysis + application services" for industrial Internet platform independently. Building partnership and ecosystem is the main development of the platform. Companies such as GE, Siemens, Schneider, and Aerospace Cloud Network work together with platform vendors, component vendors, and integrators to bridge the gap and provide customers with more powerful services. Thirdly, from the platform function and product as the center, the Industrial Internet Platform is gradually changed to create value as the center. As the platform gradually has the ability to automatically quantify service value, it will revolve around the market demand, realize the transformation from selling products or services to selling quantifiable value results, drive the change of service pricing, financial instruments, risk prevention and control mechanism, and redefine the competition pattern and industrial structure.

PaaS, known as the operating system of industrial Internet platform, is gradually becoming the focus and key breakthrough of platform development, and its commercial value is still in the exploratory stage. On the one hand, the industrial Internet platform architecture IaaS and PaaS are gradually loosely coupled, and the mutual influence is weakening. On the other hand, PaaS is the enabling platform for SaaS. Only when the maturity and capabilities of PaaS are greatly improved, SaaS has the potential to prosper. At present, industrial PaaS construction is in its infancy, requiring deep integration of manufacturing, ICT industry in technology, management, and business models. First, the PaaS platform requires a deep accumulation of manufacturing technologies in specific fields, and it also needs to transform industry knowledge and experience into digital general manufacturing technology rules through ICT technology. The two thresholds of technology and cost of the GE Predix platform limit the number of platform users and developers. Availability and ease of use are common problems that the platform needs to solve. Second, the PaaS market system has not yet been established. The platform mainly completes cloud migration of traditional services and processes. The main business is still an offline solution, and more than 90% of the users transferred from traditional channels. Third, the business model is not clear, most of the platforms are in the input period, transaction costs are high, and the exploration of transaction standardization, security, and user credit systems has not yet begun or just started. For example, the cost of Predix applications is too high, GE is adjusting its business architecture, and the business prospects of the platform are unknown. MindSphere mainly provides services for Siemens customers, and the problem of openness has not yet been resolved. Roots interconnection mainly depends on the profit of the post-service market, and the platform's core services are relatively slow to advance.

China's industrial data collection and analysis capabilities are insufficient. First, China has a large gap between digitalization and networking in terms of equipment. In 2017, the digitalization rate of equipment in China was 44.8%, and the networking rate of digital equipment was 39.0%. Especially the foundation of small and medium-sized enterprises was weak, and equipment transformation and data collection were difficult. Second, the industrial equipment products of developed countries occupy a dominant position in the global market. Leading enterprises such as GE and Siemens can collect huge amounts of data across regions, industries and fields based on their own products. Third, the United States and Germany have a large number of senior and start-up data analysis companies, which can help the platform to rapidly improve its capabilities through cooperation. However, the Chinese market is huge. Once the basic links such as data collection are solved, the network effect will inevitably bring a late-comer advantage. China, the United States and Germany have their own advantages and characteristics in the development of industrial Internet platform. China and the United States have strong IaaS infrastructure capabilities, and are expanding from the Internet industry to other industries. The know-how and equipment digital base in the United States and German industry are superior to China. China has the best Internet ecological base, and SaaS has the greatest application potential. The gap between China and the United States in terms of industrial base and industrial know-how is significant. The German industry has a deep accumulation of industrial products, equipment and automation systems, industrial control and process processes in the world's well-known old industrial companies and invisible championship SMEs. The United States is a global leader in software and platform technology for industrial knowledge experience. It has global software service oligarchs such as IBM, Microsoft, and Oracle. China's industrialization has a short history, insufficient experience in manufacturing technology and management knowledge, and the level of integration and development of industrial enterprises is uneven. However, the complete industrial system has brought huge application needs and development potential, providing the soil for platform cultivation and growth. China, the United States and Germany have their own strengths in information infrastructure and ICT technology capabilities. China and the United States are relatively strong in terms of information infrastructure. In the area of NB-IoT, China will build the world's largest NB-IoT network this year, which can effectively support the construction of industrial Internet platforms, promote massive terminal access, and expand application scenarios. In the IaaS field, Amazon, Microsoft, IBM, and others are far ahead in technology, products, and market size. China's Ali and Tencent's combined strength is in the top 10 in the world. In the PaaS field, the underlying technology of the PaaS platform in the United States has absolute advantages. Almost all of the world's industrial Internet platforms PaaS core architecture uses open source technologies such as Cloud Foundry and Docker in the United States. The United States has the ability to solidify core experience knowledge into modular microservice components and tools development, but China's industrial PaaS is just beginning and is in the exploration stage.

The industrial Internet strategy of various enterprises has many problems at the implementation level. This has led to the very difficult landing of industrial Internet, poor practicality, and a large number of "air clouds". The difficulty of landing on the industrial Internet has three main problems:

Firstly, data security. Unlike individual customers, corporate customers have very high data security requirements. This is mainly due to corporate data, especially production data, which contains a large number of corporate processes and business secrets. Industrial Internet mostly uses the centralized industrial cloud platform, and the data is concentrated in the cloud service provider's storage and management. This has huge security risks for user companies. Industrial enterprises are generally risk-averse rather than innovation-oriented. Any single-point safety problem may lead to major safety accidents. Therefore, the safety and reliability of data is an indicator that can not be compromised by industrial enterprises.

Secondly, there is the problem of excessive costs. The so-called industrial Internet is actually an upgraded version of enterprise informatization. About 300,000 Chinese manufacturing companies, of which 97.4% are small and medium-sized manufacturing companies, have the same problem – the lack of information technology and the lack of Internet of Things technology. For SMEs, they do not have too much capital, technology, talent and other resources to complete the upgrade, and there is no sense of urgency to complete the upgrade. Survival is the first priority for them. Most of the industrial Internet adopts the centralized industrial cloud scheme, and the operating and maintenance costs are too high and can not be borne by the general manufacturing companies.

Thirdly, there is the question of flexibility. Industrial Internet is usually accompanied by large-scale automation and information upgrading, and the higher the level of automation and informatization of a production system, the worse the flexibility of manufacturing. At present, the common problem facing manufacturing enterprises is the rapid change of the external market at all times. Traditional industrial Internet solutions cost tens of millions of dollars, the system functions are complex, and they can not respond quickly. Small and medium-sized enterprises can not choose flexibly according to the changes in the current situation.

China's industrial Internet platform has the world's most robust market demand and the most complete Internet ecology. On the one hand, virtue regards large enterprises as the main user group of the platform, and China regards the industrial Internet platform as a new carrier for the integrated development of large and medium-sized enterprises, through the modularization of platform technology and the softwareization of knowledge experience. Large enterprises will mature effective technology, management, application and other knowledge and experience, quickly replicate and promote to small and medium-sized enterprises, reduce technology barriers and application costs, and promote their transformation and upgrading. On the other hand, the United States is weaker than China in the fields of Internet application innovation and market size, and there is no Internet ecosystem that covers the entire society. German practices and capabilities on Internet platforms are still in a period of adaptation. China's Internet development concept, business model, and application practice are relatively mature. It basically forms an Internet ecology that covers all members and the whole society. It has unique advantages in promoting industrial Internet platforms and seizing opportunities for industrial development to "change roads". To meet the needs of enterprises in the government sector, we will build a digital map of the industrial Internet operation on the industrial Internet platform. At the same time, we will focus on the improvement of industrial APP innovation and supply capabilities such as dedicated enterprises. At the same time, we will also build and improve the smart manufacturing evaluation service platform for enterprises. We will provide manufacturing transformation to a large number of manufacturing enterprises and help them to plan and implement appropriate industrial Internet applications.

5 Development Prospects

The Internet access project will be implemented for manufacturing equipment and facilities, and laid a solid foundation for terminal data connectivity for industrial Internet platforms. Through special funds such as technology renovation, smart manufacturing, and industrial Internet, the requirements of central enterprises and leading enterprises for the entry of suppliers, as well as the formulation of standards and norms, we will fully guide and help enterprises to accelerate the upgrading of automation, digitization and networking of equipment and facilities. Eliminate the bottleneck of inadequate terminal connection in our country. For the existing equipment and facilities of the enterprise, data connection is achieved by installing sensors. At the same time, accelerate the development and application of intelligent domestic equipment and facilities.

The inclusive development of "manufacturing + Internet + finance" will be promoted and a favorable environment for SaaS be created to flourish independently. We will carry out pilot projects for the development of the "manufacturing industry, the Internet and finance", and explore key elements and basic rules for the development of industrial Internet platforms. "Manufacturing + Internet" can better solve the problem of information asymmetry, but the credit system is not perfect, and online transactions of resources and capabilities are still difficult to reach. Financial innovation provides credit guarantees for the conclusion of online, convenient and efficient service transactions, establishes a reliable new mechanism for credit sharing among participating parties, and realizes the dynamic allocation of resources according to needs, laying a solid foundation for SaaS prosperity.

We should comprehensively and thoroughly promote "mass entrepreneurship and multitude innovation", break the constraints of traditional industrial system and mechanism, and stimulate the innovative vitality, motivation and potential of talents. Through the two-mode integrated management system, the participating enterprises are guided to take the new type of capacity-building as the main line, data as the driving force, and service as the direction, breaking the shackles of traditional industrial institutions and mechanisms, and forming a new value network that conforms to the laws of the information age. Through the interactive innovation of management systems and technologies, it will fully stimulate and unleash the vitality, motivation and potential of talents, and provide a huge amount of talent resources for the open source community construction of industrial Internet platforms and SaaS services.

Pay attention to the information security of the industrial Internet platform and ensure the healthy development of the industrial Internet platform. First, we will improve relevant policies, regulations and industry regulatory systems, study and formulate an overall information security plan for industrial Internet platforms, establish working mechanisms for platform risk notification, inspection and evaluation, and security review, and establish a national emergency command system for security incidents on major industrial Internet platforms. We will formulate plans for the emergency handling of security on classified platforms. Second, focusing on key areas such as equipment, networks, platforms, and data, we will build situational awareness, simulation tests, and offensive and defensive training platforms. We will conduct testing, risk assessment, verification and verification of technology products and solutions, and improve the technical support capabilities of industrial Internet platforms. Avoid embarrassing situations of "connecting without connecting", "connecting without connecting with each other" and "connecting without the Internet".

The Information Research and Promotion Center of the National Industrial Information Security Development Research Center investigated more than 20 domestic and foreign mainstream industrial Internet platforms such as GE, Siemens, Aerospace Cloud Network, Haier, Huawei, Ali, and Tencent. Industrial PaaS (platform is a service) is gradually becoming the focus and key breakthrough for the development of the platform. In this field, the leading manufacturing enterprises with a high level of informatization are the main forces, and ICT enterprises are the pioneers of key enabling technologies. The Internet leader with ecological advantages is likely to emerge. Industrial Internet refers to the result of the integration of global industrial systems with advanced computing, analysis, induction technology, and Internet connectivity. Industrialization has created numerous networks of machines, equipment groups, facilities and systems, the Internet revolution has brought about advances in computing, information and communication systems, and the industrial Internet has brought together the results of two major revolutions, bringing together various machines, equipment groups, facilities and systems in the world. network, connecting to advanced sensor, control and software applications offers new growth opportunities for a variety of enterprises, industries and macroeconomics. By connecting intelligent machines to each other and eventually connecting human and human machines, and combining software and large data analysis, China will make further use of its advantages, base itself on cutting-edge research in policy, industry, standards and other aspects, build high-end think tanks for industrial Internet, and deepen and expand its application. Integrate multiple resources, create a new ecology of industrial Internet, restructure global industry, and stimulate productivity to make the world a better, faster, safer, cleaner and more economical place.

References

1. Zheng, X.: Industrial Internet: Industrial Transformation in the Internet + Times. Machinery Industry Press, Beijing (2015)
2. Yanna, X., Sheng, Z.: Industry 4.0: The Present Future. Machinery Industry Press, Beijing (2015)

3. Schwab, K.: The Fourth Industrial Revolution. China CITIC Press, Beijing (2016)
4. Ma, S., Meng, F., Ma, Y., Su, J.: Automatic integrated exhaust fan based on AT89S51 single chip microcomputer. In: Sun, X., Pan, Z., Bertino, E. (eds.) ICCCS 2018. LNCS, vol. 11067, pp. 118–127. Springer, Cham (2018). https://doi.org/10.1007/978-3-030-00018-9_11
5. Meng, R., Rice, S.G., Wang, J., Sun, X.: A fusion steganographic algorithm based on faster R-CNN. CMC Comput. Mater. Continua **55**(1), 001–016 (2018)
6. Cui, J., Zhang, Y., Cai, Z., Liu, A., Li, Y.: Securing display path for security-sensitive applications on mobile devices. CMC Comput. Mater. Continua **55**(1), 017–035 (2018)

Performance Analysis of a NB-IoT Based Smart Lamp Solution with Application Enabled Platform

Sijia Lou[1,2], En Tong[2], and Fei Ding[1(✉)]

[1] School of Internet of Things, Nanjing University of Posts
and Telecommunications, Nanjing, China
dingfei@njupt.edu.cn
[2] China Mobile Group Jiangsu Co., Ltd., Nanjing, China

Abstract. The NB-IoT (Narrow Band Internet of Things) network is proved be suitable for connecting everything with low energy consumption, high concurrency at a low cost. In this paper, we proposed a NB-IoT based smart lamp scheme to solve the problems of traditional street lamps, such as large electricity consumption, difficult maintenance and inconvenient management. Random access, staggered peak communication and reasonable heartbeat mechanism are proposed to improve the soft capacity of the system. The commercial project shows solution we proposed can effectively manage every single lamp. The online rate and the communication success rate are all up to expectations.

Keywords: Internet of Things · NB-IoT ·
Application Enabled Platform (AEP) · Smart lamp

1 Introduction

Massive connectivity is one of the major goals of 5G mobile communications. NB-IoT systems are emerging as a way to achieve this goal [1]. The NB-IoT (Narrow Band Internet of Things) network is proved more suitable than RFID for connecting everything with low energy consumption, while also being robust and having high concurrency [2–4].

Embedded sensors and automatic control devices are becoming widespread, being used in a number of applications such as consumer devices [5], farming [6], environment [7], utilities [8] and industrial internet [9, 10]. In order to decrease the number of road accident rate and increase flow of the vehicles and the safety, the street lamps are lighted for more than 13 h, which requires a plenty of electric power [11]. Nearly

This work is partially supported by the Ministry of Education - China Mobile Research Foundation, China (No. MCM20170205), the Communication Soft Science Research Project of Ministry of Industry and Information Technology, China (No. 2017-R-34), "333 High Level Talent Training Project" of Jiangsu Province, China (BRA2016341), the Scientific Research Foundation of the Higher Education Institutions of Jiangsu Province, China (No. 17KJB510043), the Research Foundation for Advanced Talents, Nanjing University of Posts and Telecommunications (No. NY217146).

© Springer Nature Switzerland AG 2019
X. Sun et al. (Eds.): ICAIS 2019, LNCS 11634, pp. 309–318, 2019.
https://doi.org/10.1007/978-3-030-24271-8_28

30% electrical power of a medium-sized city is utilized lightning the streets. This results in a waste of electricity. Studies show that using LED can reduce 50% of power consumption, and single lamp controller can provide extra 10% energy saving [12]. In [13], authors provide a better solution for streetlight control and automation through WIFI, which is difficult to implement because of need for relay equipment. Scheme proposed in [14] reduced 100% of manual work using an automatic switch. Single lamp control can detect lamp malfunction in time, prevent street lamp from being damaged or stolen, and realize effective asset management [15].

Researchers in [16] pointed out that under the condition of limited NB-IoT network, additional technology was needed to ensure the performance of the system. In this paper, we proposed a NB-IoT based smart lamp scheme with OneNET, which is AEP developed by China Mobile, to solve the problems of traditional street lamps.

In Sect. 2, we describe NB-IoT infrastructure of Chine Mobile, including network and AEP called OneNET. In Sect. 3, we propose a smart lamp solution. We also describe parameters and key technologies we used in a commercial project. Then we analyses performance of the proposed scheme in Sect. 4. Finally, we conclude this paper in Sect 5.

2   The NB-IoT Infrastructure of Chine Mobile

2.1   NB-IoT Network

The NB core network includes mobility management device (MME), service gateway (S-GW), PDN gateway (P-GW), HSS/HLR used to store user signing information, mobile switching center server (MSC sever), and short message service center (SMS-SC) Fig. 1. In the NB-IoT network system of China Mobile, HSS/HLR, SMS-SC, and P-GW are the centralized, and the MME, S-GW, and MSC severs are deployed locally by different provinces.

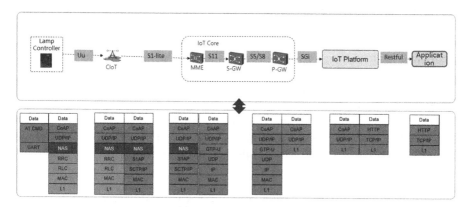

Fig. 1. The NB-IoT infrastructure of China mobile.

2.2 IoT Application Enabled Platform

The Application Enabled Platform (AEP), which helps users build hardware and maintain equipment at low cost, is necessary in NB-IoT network architecture. The application can communicate with AEP through APIs by https protocol, realize real-time communication and ensure the security of communication. Meanwhile, AEP aggregates cloud computing, big data and other cutting-edge technologies to provide value-added services to customers. Additionally, the platform uses cloud technology, such as virtual technology and distributed storage, provide program independence and secure access [17].

As shown in Fig. 2, OneNET is a PaaS layer IoT open platform developed by China Mobile, which can help developers easily access device and realize device connections, it can quickly complete product development and deployment. Main advantages of OneNET are as following.

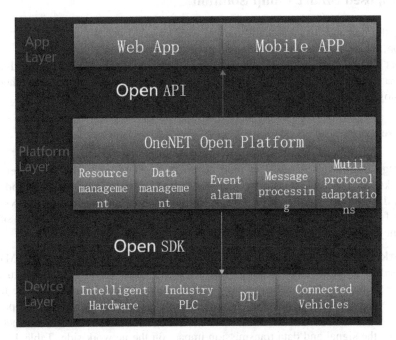

Fig. 2. Three layers of OneNET.

Seamless Access. Compatible with a variety of mainstream protocols and network channels, realize quick deployment.

Stable Connection. To ensure stable connection, carrier-class equipment cluster to provide you with high-performance, high concurrent cloud connectivity services.

Data Security. Passed the "trusted cloud" security certification, based on a variety of international standard encryption algorithms, provided carrier-class security services for corporate data.

Rule Engine. Realized various rules setting up, more convenient and efficient.

Application Development. More than 300 APIs and application incubator enable the developers complete developing lamp APP within 10 min.

Device Management. Provide device inspection, online debugging, group management, firmware upgrades and other visual operations.

IoT system have high concurrency and real-time data transmission, and each server has a fixed amount of device access, in order to meet business needs, applications have to expand capacity and increase operation costs, meanwhile inevitably reduce the stability of platform. OneNET provides multi-protocol adaptation SDK, a wide range of APIs and light application incubator to achieve stable and reliable terminal connection service, supports millions of massively concurrent connections.

3 Proposed Smart Lamp Solution

Facing the demand of smart lamp market, we proposed a NB-IoT based end-to-end solution, which is suitable for national application promotion.

This scheme clarifies the system parameters and functional requirements of the NB-IoT smart lamp of China Mobile from the network, platform, terminal and other key technologies.

3.1 Network

Coverage Planning. Standard of road coverage is set to −85 dBm for current NB Networks, then we made capacity planning based on street lamp spacing and base station distribution in urban area. Due to current equipment constraints, the NB network of China Mobile adopts hetero-frequency network, each cell uses a single-frequency, which is different with neighbors.

Network Configuration. Smart lamp should close Power Saving Mode (PSM) and Extended Discontinuous Reception (eDRX) figure. It is recommended to turn on accurate paging, to meet high real-time performance request. In addition, due to the existence of large-scale concurrent services, signaling and data transmission impact on the network, so different access and downlink transmission controls should be adopted to reduce the signal and data transmission impact on the network side. Table 1 shows the key parameters we used (Table 2).

Table 1. Network parameter.

Index	Parameters
MCL	147 dB
SNR	>−3 dB
Uplink RSSI	<−124 dB

Table 2. Network configuration.

Parameters	Name	Description
APNNI	Appointed APN	According the HSS, usually different business will adopt different APN
RAUTAUTMRSRC	Long period RAU/TAU timer source	When the terminal carries a long period timer, the MME can be configured to use the terminal timer or specify by network Recommends: specify by network
LONGRAUTAUTMR	Long period RAU/TAU timer (hours)	Recommends: 60 min
PSMSW	PSM Switch	Recommends: off
ACTIVETIMER	Active Timer	Recommends: none
CPOPSW	CP optimization	Recommends: support

3.2 Traffic Model

Terminal Message Reporting (Periodic/Aperiodic). An uplink message initiated by the terminal, which is used to collect data, for example on/off time, voltage, current, active power, power factor and fault information. It is also used to monitor the usability of the network. The ACK, which is waiting for the response of the IOT platform after sending the message, is considered to be successful, without the need for the application platform to reply the platform confirmation message.

Downlink Control Strategy. The system realizes lamping management (control and dimming), system query and parameter command, which includes two types: real-time control instruction and parameter configuration offline.

Software Upgrade. Remote download and upgrade software, including MCU upgrade and firmware upgrade over the air. Full and differential upgrades are need to support, and the process will roll back once upgrade fails.

3.3 Key Technologies

The capacity and concurrency of the cell are limited due to the use of a single frequency point network. In this paper, the soft capacity of the system is improved effectively by random access, staggered peak communication and reasonable heartbeat mechanism.

If all controllers attempt to register when the street lamps are turned on, it causes network congestion and lead to difficulties of access. In this scheme, lamp controllers are proposed to turn off automatic access and to register in the network after a random delay t. After a few months of testing, we believe that t = 100 s can meet customer requirements and effectively improve the success rate at the same time.

After the terminal enters the network, it needs to send the status update information to the platform periodically. In order to avoid network congestion caused by all terminals heartbeat at the same time, we set the access time as base line, and update periodically. In this scheme, we choose 300 s as heartbeat period after balancing cell capacity with customer needs of renewal frequency.

Every download message would cause paging in NB-IoT core network. The OneNET carries on the batch flow control to the data transmission, avoids simultaneously paging massive terminals cause network congestion. The terminals are grouped according to the cell identification reported when accessing the network, then OneNET selects the group discretely to send data.

4 Performance Analysis

In this section, we analyze the performance of end-to-end NB-IoT system in practical application through a commercial smart street lamp case. We have installed 4000 street lamps in this case, most of them in urban areas. The street lamps are about 30 m apart, served by more than 40 cells. So each cell has an average of 80–100 terminals.

Terminal heartbeat interval is set to 5 min, Application inquiry terminal status every 20 min, simulating heavy stress test for the whole NB-IoT system. And the uplink/downlink timeout time is set to 20 s, and OneNET attempt to retransmit twice before the link close.

Figures 3 and 4 shows the Transaction Per Second (TPS) curve, which reflects the concurrent pressure of the AEP platform, which is OneNET in this case. Obviously, the peak of tps value of the whole system decreases after using the random access and

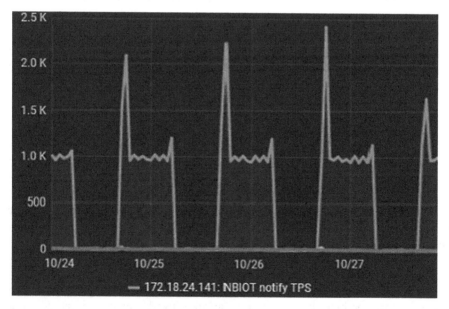

Fig. 3. The Transaction Per Second (TPS) curve before accessing without random delay.

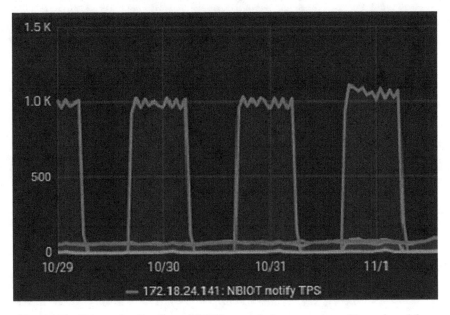

Fig. 4. The Transaction Per Second (TPS) curve before accessing with random delay.

staggered peak communications. Under the current traffic model, tps is only 1000, far from the design capacity of OneNET.

Table 3 shows the downlink message success rate of the platform for extracting time at any time. The downlink success rate keeps above 99.5%.

Table 3. The downlink message success rate.

	Trial 1	Trial 2	Trial 3	Trial 4
Communications attempted	25991	27960	27407	28972
Paging failed	47	37	34	79
Heartbeat failed	80	93	75	63
Success rate	99.51%	99.54%	99.6%	99.51%

Figure 5 shows online rate of street lamp through GSM, CDMA and NB-IoT networks. After 6 months of commercial project, the online rate of NB street lamp is same as that of traditional GSM and CDMA network, using only one 200 kHz frequency. In the long run, with the performance improvements brought by the R14 new features and the use of more frequency resource, the capability of NB-IoT networks is certainly much stronger than that of GSM networks.

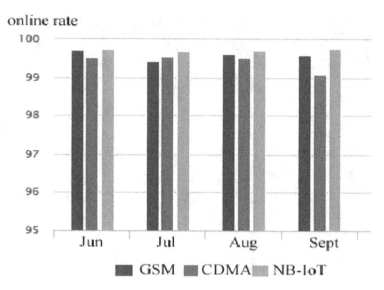

Fig. 5. Online rate of street lamp through GSM, CDMA and NB-IoT networks.

We selected a period of time of NB downlink delay data for statistical analysis. As shown in Fig. 6, 77.8% of downlink communication can be completed in 2 s, in which the range between 500 ms and 1000 ms takes the greatest probability, about 44.9%.

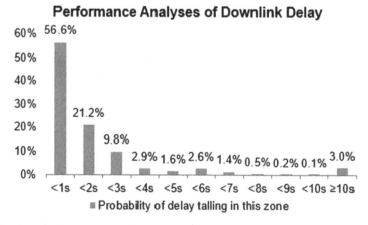

Fig. 6. Online rate of street lamp through GSM, CDMA and NB-IoT networks.

5   Conclusion

This paper proposed a NB-IoT based smart lamp solution enabled by OneNET. This scheme is applied to Nanjing smart lamp commercial project. It can verify and guide the NB-IoT network optimization and IoT platform function iteration, and lay a practical foundation for the commercialization of NB-IoT such as water and gas metering, parking, agriculture and so on.

References

1. Overall Description: Stage 2, document 3GPP TS 36.300 v13.4.0 Release 13, 3GPP, June 2016
2. Cellular System Support for Ultra Low Complexity and low Throughput Internet of Things, document 3GPP TR 4S.820 v1.3.1 Release 13, 3GPP, June 2015
3. Oh, S.-M., Jung, K.-R., Bae, M., Shin, J.: Performance analysis for the battery consumption of the 3GPP NB-IoT device. In: Information and Communications Technology Council (ICTC), pp. 981–983 (2017)
4. Chen, H., Liu, K., Ma, C., Han, Y., Su, J.: A novel time-aware frame adjustment strategy for RFID anti-collision. CMC: Comput. Mater. Continua 57(2), 195–204 (2018)
5. Opperman, C.A., Hancke, G.P.: Using NFC-enabled phones for remote data acquisition and digital control. In: IEEE Africon 2011 (2011)
6. Kumar, C.A., Hancke, G.P.: A zigbee-based animal health monitoring system. IEEE Sens. J. 15(1), 610–617 (2015)
7. Phala, S.E., Kumar, A., Hancke, G.P.: Air quality monitoring system based on ISO/IEC/IEEE 21451 standards. IEEE Sens. J. 16(12), 5037–5045 (2016)
8. Mudumbe, M.M., Abu-Mahfouz, A.M.: Smart water meter system for user-centric consumption measurement. In: IEEE International Conference on Industrial Informatics (2015)
9. de Silva, D.B., Fisher, R., Kumar, A., Hancke, G.P.: Experimental link quality characterization of wireless sensor networks for underground monitoring. IEEE Trans. Ind. Inform. 11(5), 1099–1110 (2015)
10. Chiwewe, G.T., Mbuya, C., Hancke, G.P.: Using cognitive radio for interference-resistant industrial wireless networks: an overview. IEEE Trans. Ind. Inform. 11(6), 1466–1471 (2015)
11. du Toit, P., Kruger, C., Hancke, G.P., Ramotsoela, T.D.: Smart street lights using power line communication. In: IEEE Africon 2017 Proceedings, pp. 1581–1586 (2017)
12. Badgelwar, S.S., Pande, H.M.: Survey on energy efficient smart street light system. In: International Conference on IoT in Social, Mobile, Analytics and Cloud (I-SMAC), pp. 866–869 (2017)
13. Dheena, F., Raj, G.S., Dutt, G., Jinny, S.V.: IOT based smart street light management system. In: Proceedings of 2017 IEEE International Conference on Circuits and Systems (ICCS), pp. 368–371 (2017)
14. Monika, H.R., et al.: Internet of things based intelligent street lighting system for smart city. Int. J. Eng. Basic Sci. Manag. Soc. Stud. 1(1) (2017)
15. Deo, S., Prakash, S., Patil, A.: Zigbee-based intelligent street lighting system. In: 2014 2nd International Conference on Devices, Circuits and Systems (ICDCS), pp. 1–4 (2014)

16. Kim, H., Cho, S., Oh, J., Jo, G.: Uplink scheduling technique for the LTE system to improve the performance of the NB-IoT system. In: The 10th International Conference on Ubiquitous and Future Networks (ICUFN), pp. 613–615(2018)
17. Xie, X., Yuan, T., Zhou, X., Cheng, X.: Research on trust model in container-based cloud service. CMC: Comput. Mater. Continua **56**(2), 273–283 (2018)

Mining Hypernym-Hyponym Relations from Social Tags via Tag Embedding

Mengyi Zhang[1,2], Tianxing Wu[3], Qiu Ji[4,5(✉)], Guilin Qi[1,2], and Zhixin Sun[4,5]

[1] School of Computer Science and Engineering, Southeast University, Nanjing, China
[2] Key Laboratory of Computer Network and Information Integration,
Southeast University, Ministry of Education, Nanjing, China
`zhangmengyi_0429@163.com, gqi@seu.edu.cn`
[3] School of Computer Science and Engineering, Nanyang Technological University,
Singapore, Singapore
`wutianxing@ntu.edu.sg`
[4] School of Modern Posts and Institute of Modern Posts,
Nanjing University of Posts and Telecommunications, Nanjing, China
[5] YuanTong Express Co., LTD., Shanghai, China
`{qiuji,sunzx}@njupt.edu.cn`

Abstract. With the rapid development of Internet of Thing, mobile Internet, cloud computing and other technologies, network data increases dramatically and Folksonomy plays an important role in web systems. How to obtain valuable knowledge, especially hypernym-hyponym relations, becomes a popular research topic in the field of artificial intelligence. For Folksonomy, hypernym-hyponym relation identification aims to recognize the "is-a" relation between two social tags. Most existing works about identifying hypernym-hyponym relations are based on statistical and heuristic approaches, but their performance still needs to be improved. In this paper, we propose a novel supervised learning approach to identify hypernym-hyponym relations from social tags using tag embeddings. First, we use a neural network model to learn tag embeddings. This model relies on not only the hypernym and hyponym tags, but also the contextual information between them. We then apply such embeddings as features to identify hypernym-hyponym relations using a supervised learning method. Our experimental results demonstrate that the proposed approach significantly outperforms other state-of-the-art approaches over a labeled dataset. The accuracy and F1-score of our approach achieve 0.91 and 0.86 respectively.

Keywords: Social tags · Hypernym-hyponym relation ·
Word embedding · Folksonomy

1 Introduction

With the rapid development of Internet of Thing, mobile Internet, cloud computing and other technologies [6,29,32], network data (e.g., the data in social

© Springer Nature Switzerland AG 2019
X. Sun et al. (Eds.): ICAIS 2019, LNCS 11634, pp. 319–328, 2019.
https://doi.org/10.1007/978-3-030-24271-8_29

networks) increases dramatically and Folksonomy[1] plays an important role in web systems [30]. Folksonomy is a shared and evolving classification structure, where a folk taxonomy is a lightweight conceptual structure created by the users. Folksonomy has been applied to a growing number of web systems (e.g., Flickr[2] for photo-sharing and del.icio.us[3] for social bookmarking) and allows users to apply a set of words (also called tags) to label online resources (e.g., web pages, images and videos) without relying on a controlled vocabulary or a previously defined structure. However, it does not provide explicit hierarchical structures to describe the relationship among social tags. Thus, the accuracy of many tag-based tasks like resource navigation and information retrieval may be largely influenced [19,23,33].

To deal with the above mentioned problem and obtain valuable knowledge from the tags used in Folksonomies, various approaches (surveys can be found in [11,13]) have been proposed to generate hypernym-hyponym relations. They generally can be divided into two categories: statistical approaches and heuristic ones. The statistical approaches mainly include clustering [17], co-occurrence analysis [14,25] and distribution inclusion hypothesis [22] based approaches. Although such approaches are efficient, the accuracies are still low [3]. The heuristic approaches [2,15,16] usually identify hierarchical structures by means of predefined similarity measures.

Recently, a few works make use of word embeddings [4] to find hierarchical structures between two terms or words [3,31]. They have been proved to be effective in exploring both linguistic and semantic relations. However, these approaches either do not consider the cases of tags, or ignore the contextual information which is an important factor for extracting hierarchical structure [3]. In the case of finding hierarchical structures between tags, how to define the contextual information and reflect the characteristics of tags is challenging.

In this paper, we use a neural network model to learn tag embeddings. This model encodes not only the information of hypernym and hyponym tags, but also the contextual information between them. We then apply the identified embeddings as features to find the positive hypernym-hyponym relations using the supervised method Support Vector Machine (SVM) [7]. To see the performance of our approach, we compare it with the state-of-the-art approaches over a real-life dataset by exploiting various measures.

The rest of the paper is organized as follows. In Sect. 2, we apply a neural network to learn tag embeddings based on hypernym, hyponym and their contextual information. We then provide a supervised method to identify hypernym-hyponym relations in Sect. 3 by using the learned embeddings as features. Section 4 presents the details of our experiments and Sect. 6 finally concludes this paper.

---

[1] https://en.wikipedia.org/wiki/Folksonomy.

[2] http://www.flickr.com/.

[3] http://del.icio.us/.

2   Tag Embedding Learning

Inspired by the work given in [3], our approach to learn tag embeddings consists of two steps: extracting training data and training a neural network.

2.1   Training Data Extraction

Our training data is in the form of triples $(hype, hypo, cont)$, where $hype$ is a hypernym tag, $hypo$ is a hyponym tag and $cont$ indicates a set of tags representing contextual information. Before extracting the contexts, the tag pairs, in the form of $(hype, hypo)$, with hypernym-hyponym relations, need to be obtained from a given dataset.

First, a set of tag pairs representing hypernym-hyponym relations need to be constructed. This can be done manually by domain experts or automatically with the help of external resources. For example, the hierarchical structure given in WordNet [21] between noun words and the concept taxonomies given in some top ontologies could be used.

According to the characteristics of Folksonomy data, the contextual information can be extracted from the resources with tags. Usually, a resource can have more than one tag and we call its tags as a tag group. For a given tag pair $(hype, hypo)$, its contextual information includes all tags in the tag groups containing both $hype$ and $hypo$, except the two tags themselves in the pair. Figure 1 gives an example on generating the contextual information (i.e., $(zoom, northeast\_tiger, forest, carnivore)$) of the given tag pair $(tiger, animal)$.

The given tag pair: (tiger, animal)   ⟹   Tag groups:
#1: (tiger, animal, zoom)
#2: (tiger, animal, northeast_tiger, forest)
#3: (tiger, animal, carnivore)

⟱

Contextual information:
(zoom, northeast_tiger, forest, carnivore)

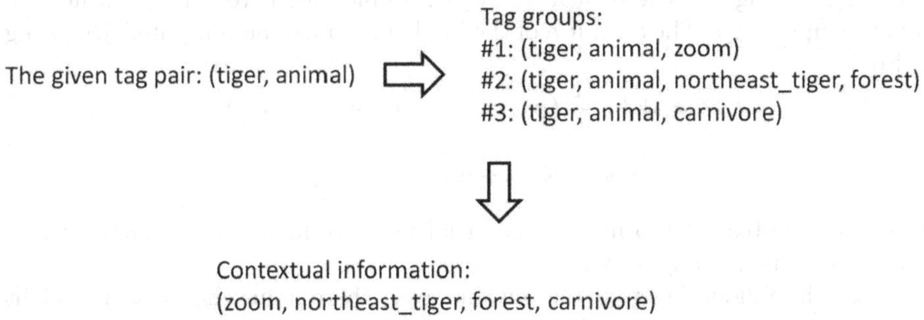

Fig. 1. An example on generating the contextual information of the given tag pair.

2.2   Neural Network Training

Based on the extracted training data, we utilize a neural network model which is similar to the one proposed in [3] to predict the hypernym tag from the given hyponym tag and contextual information. The model takes training triples as inputs and output tag embeddings. Its architecture is presented in Fig. 2. This model consists of an input layer, a hidden layer and an output layer, whose sizes are $(k+1) \cdot V$, N, and V respectively. Here, k is the number of contextual tags, V is the vocabulary size, and N is the size of tag embeddings to be learned.

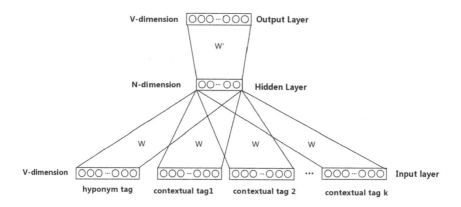

Fig. 2. The architecture of tag embedding model.

In the input layer, the hyponym tag *hypo* and k contextual tags $c_1, c_2, \ldots, c_k$ in a training triple are taken as inputs, where each tag t is represented by a one-hot V-dimensional vector x_t.

From the input layer to the hidden layer, a $V \times N$ matrix W is used to indicate the weights, where each row is a N-dimensional vector representation v_t of the input tag t. The output h of the hidden layer can be computed according to Eq. 1:

$$\begin{aligned} h &= W^T \cdot \frac{1}{2k}(k \times x_{hypo} + x_{c_1} + \ldots + x_{c_k}) \\ &= \frac{1}{2k}(k \times v_{hypo} + v_{c_1} + \ldots + v_{c_k}) \end{aligned} \tag{1}$$

To reduce the bias of too many contextual tags, we multiply the vector representation of the hyponym by k.

From the hidden layer to the output layer, there is another $N \times V$ weight matrix W'. We use this matrix to compute an output score u_t for each tag in the vocabulary:

$$u_t = v_t'^T \cdot h \tag{2}$$

Here, $v_t'^T$ is the output vector of tag t in a training triple. Next, a log-linear classification model soft-max is applied to obtain the posterior distribution of hypernym tags:

$$p(hype|hypo, c_1, c_2, \ldots, c_k) = \frac{e^{u_{hype}}}{\Sigma_{i=1}^V e^{u_i}}$$

$$= \frac{e^{v'^T_{hype} \cdot \frac{1}{2k}(k \times v_{hypo} + \Sigma_{j=1}^k v_{c_j})}}{\Sigma_{i=1}^V e^{v'^T_i \cdot \frac{1}{2k}(k \times v_{hypo} + \Sigma_{j=1}^k v_{c_j})}} \quad (3)$$

Through maximizing the log-likelihood objective function below over the entire training data, we obtain the tag embeddings.

$$O = \frac{1}{T} \Sigma_{t=1}^T log(p(hype_t|hypo_t, c_{1t}, \ldots, c_{kt})) \quad (4)$$

Here, T indicates the number of training triples.

3   Hypernym-Hyponym Relation Identification

Based on the learned tag embeddings, a classifier with such embeddings as features is built to determine if two tags have the hypernym-hyponym relation. In this paper, the commonly used and one of the best classifier [9], i.e., SVM, is applied.

Specifically, for a given tag pair $(hype, hypo)$, the input features include not only the concatenated embedding vectors (v_{hype}, v_{hypo}), but also the offset vector $(v_{hype} - v_{hypo})$ which contains the information of all contextual tags between $hype$ and $hypo$. In addition, two similarity metrics to measure (v_{hype}, v_{hypo}) are also added as the input features of SVM, since we believe that two tags should be similar if they have the hypernym-hyponym relation. The similarity metrics are cosine and Euclidean Distance. Therefore, the feature vector is a $3d + 2$ dimensional vector consisting of $v_{hype}, v_{hypo}, v_{hype} - v_{hypo}, sim_{cos}(v_{hype}, v_{hypo}), sim_{euc}(v_{hype}, v_{hypo})$, where d is the dimension of tag embeddings.

4   Experiments

In this section, we compare our approach with the state-of-the-art approaches over a real-life dataset. All experiments have been performed on a computer with 2.7 GHz Intel(R) Core(TM) i7-6820HQ CPU and 16 GB RAM using Windows 10.

4.1   Experimental Setup

In our experiments, we use the well-known Folksonomy dataset BIBSONOMY [5]. It is crawled from the website of bibsonomy.org[4] which is a system to share the tags and literatures with regards to the users' publications and bookmarks. This dataset contains $7,234$ users, $216,094$ tags and $852,292$ relations. To remove

---

[4] https://www.bibsonomy.org/.

the noisy data, we use some heuristic strategies like removing those tags that are too long or non-English. After filtering, we have more than 450 distinct tags and about 240, 000 resource-tag pairs.

To see the performance of our approach **SVM+Our**, namely the approach with our model to learn tag embeddings and SVM for classification, we compare it with the two representative baselines **SVM+Feature** and **SVM+Word2vec**. **SVM+Feature** [8] first extracts features and then uses the training data to train a SVM model. **SVM+Word2vec** [10] uses the tag embeddings obtained by applying the Skip-gram model [20] and then applies SVM. Its input is also a $3d + 2$ dimensional vector as our approach.

To evaluate these approaches, we use the following measures: accuracy, precision, recall and F1-score. Here, accuracy is the probability of a correct prediction in all samples; Precision is the probability of a correct prediction in all predicted positive samples; Recall is the probability of correct prediction of the true positive samples in the test set; F1-score is the weighted harmonic mean of the precision and recall.

4.2   Experimental Results

In the experiments, for **SVM+Our** and **SVM+Word2vec**, the vector dimension is set to be 100, and the learned embedding vector is used as the input of SVM for training the classifier. As for **SVM+Feature**, we first extract the features of the training data from the given dataset and then use the training data to train SVM.

Table 1. Comparison of our approach with existing ones.

Model	Accuracy	Precision	Recall	F1-score
SVM+Feature	0.39	0.37	0.30	0.33
SVM+Word2vec	0.58	0.60	0.49	0.53
SVM+Our	0.91	0.88	0.84	0.86

Table 1 presents the experimental results of the comparison. From the table, we first observe that **SVM+Word2vec** outperforms **SVM+Feature**. It is mainly because the latter just uses 7 features which are not enough to produce good results. The best result of **SVM+Feature** is no more than 0.4. Second, comparing with **SVM+Word2vec**, our approach achieves much better performance. Each value of the measures is at least 0.84, especially the accuracy (i.e., 0.91). This should owe to the usage of contextual information and the highlight of hyponym to reduce the bias of too many contextual tags.

5   Related Work

To generate hypernym-hyponym relations or taxonomies, various approaches have been proposed. We describe the relevant approaches with respect to the statistical approaches, ontology based approaches and heuristic ones for deriving hierarchical structures for tags. We also present the work about applying word embeddings for finding such structures for any pair of terms.

The statistical approaches make use of the technologies like clustering, co-occurrence analysis and distribution inclusion hypothesis. In [27], a topic model based learning approach is proposed to capture the hierarchical semantic structure of Folksonomies which are collections of user-defined tags. In [18], an integrated method is given to extract ontological structures from Folksonomies by using the power of low support association rule mining, where an ontology could provide both shared vocabularies and semantic relations that facilitate the translation and integration of different sources [26]. In [28], a semi-supervised method incorporating rules is presented to capture subsumption relations among the categories from taxonomies and tags from Folksonomies. The work in [23] proposed methods by using the co-occurred tags and the content of annotated document. Besides, an algorithm to construct a layered Directed Acyclic Graph of tags is given for eliminating the redundant relations. Among these approaches, the most relevant work given in [8] proposed a supervised method with tag-tag similarity measures as the learning features. It regards the problem of determining the hypernym-hyponym relation of two tags as a classification problem.

The heuristic approaches often make use of predefined similarity measures. The work in [2] proposes an automatic approach based on a similarity measure to enrich folksonomy tags with the help of online ontologies, where subsumption relationships are included. The approach given in [15,16] derives the subsumption relations between tags with the help of Wikipedia[5]. In this approach, each tag is first mapped to a relevant Wikipedia text and then uses a defined metric to decide the relationship between two tags. The method proposed in [1] employs measures of similarity and generality. In [12], the proposed approach relies on non-descending order of closeness centrality in a similarity graph of tags, where tags are represented by vectors and the similarity between two tags is calculated by the cosine similarity measure.

The word embedding-based approaches make use of linguistic and semantic relations between words. The work in [10] uses Mikolov's word embedding model [20] to obtain vector representations of words. Then, it learns the hypernym-hyponym relations by estimating projection matrices which map words to their hypernyms. The work in [3] uses dynamic weighting neural network to learn term embeddings for identifying taxonomic relations from sentences. This work leverages contextual information of words from text. The authors in [31] proposed a dynamic distance-margin model to learn embeddings, and applied such embeddings as term features. Our work also uses a word embedding model and considers not only the contextual information. The main difference between the existing word embedding-based approaches and ours is that we deal with the social tags provided in Folksonomies. This task is important since finding the appropriate contextual information between a hypernym tag and a hyponym one is non-trivial.

---

[5] https://en.wikipedia.org/wiki/Main_Page.

6   Conclusions

In this paper, we utilize a neural network model to learn tag embeddings. Its prominent feature is to encode not only the hypernym tags and hyponym tags, but also the contextual information between the tags. Based on this prominent feature, the learned tags have great generalization capability. The experimental results show that our approach significantly outperforms other state-of-the-art approaches in terms of accuracy, F1-score, recall and precision, where the accuracy and F1-score achieve 0.91 and 0.86 respectively.

As for the future work, we first consider to assign the weight of each tag in contextual information to better model the hypernym-hyponym relations among tags, and plan to apply our proposed approach to mine large-scale hypernym-hyponym relations from different social Web sites to contribute and publish a knowledge base. We will also integrate such built knowledge base with existing datasets in linked open data, such as DBpedia[6], Yago[7], Linked Open Schema[8], etc., to facilitate the development of semantic Web and artificial intelligence. Furthermore, in order to improve the quality of derived hierarchical structures and find the problem at an early stage, we could borrow the idea from [24] to filter the candidate subsumption relationships.

Acknowledgements. This work is supported by National Science Foundation of China (61602259 and 61672299), National Natural Science Foundation of China Key Project (U1736204), National Key R&D Program of China (2018YFC0830200, 2017YFB1002801), and National Engineering Laboratory for Logistics Information Technology, YuanTong Express co. LTD.

References

1. Almoqhim, F., Millard, D.E., Shadbolt, N.: An approach to building high-quality tag hierarchies from crowdsourced taxonomic tag Pairs. In: Jatowt, A., et al. (eds.) SocInfo 2013. LNCS, vol. 8238, pp. 129–138. Springer, Cham (2013). https://doi.org/10.1007/978-3-319-03260-3_12
2. Angeletou, S., Sabou, M., Motta, E.: Semantically enriching folksonomies with FLOR. In: Proceedings of the 1st International Workshop on Collective Semantics: Collective Intelligence & the Semantic Web (CISWeb 2008) at the 5th European Semantic Web Conference (2008)
3. Anh, T.L., Tay, Y., Hui, S.C., Ng, S.K.: Learning term embeddings for taxonomic relation identification using dynamic weighting neural network. In: Proceedings of the Conference on Empirical Methods in Natural Language Processing, pp. 403–413 (2016)
4. Bengio, Y., Ducharme, R., Vincent, P.: A neural probabilistic language model. In: Proceedings of Annual Conference on Neural Information Processing Systems, pp. 932–938 (2000)

---

[6] https://wiki.dbpedia.org/.

[7] https://www.mpi-inf.mpg.de/departments/databases-and-information-systems/research/yago-naga/yago/.

[8] http://los.linkingopenschema.info/.

5. Benz, D., et al.: The social bookmark and publication management system bibsonomy. Int. J. Very Large Data Bases (VLDB) **19**(6), 849–875 (2010)
6. Chen, H., Liu, K., Ma, C., Han, Y., Su, J.: A novel time-aware frame adjustment strategy for RFID anti-collision. CMC: Comput. Mater. Contin. **57**(2), 195–204 (2018)
7. Cortes, C., Vapnik, V.: Support-vector networks. Mach. Learn. **20**(3), 273–297 (1995)
8. da Cunha Rego, A.S., Marinho, L.B., Pires, C.E.S.: A supervised learning approach to detect subsumption relations between tags in folksonomies. In: Proceedings of Annual ACM Symposium on Applied Computing, pp. 409–415 (2015)
9. Fernández-Delgado, M., Cernadas, E., Barro, S., Amorim, D.: Do we need hundreds of classifiers to solve real world classification problems? J. Mach. Learn. Res. **15**(1), 3133–3181 (2014)
10. Fu, R., Guo, J., Qin, B., Che, W., Wang, H., Liu, T.: Learning semantic hierarchies via word embeddings. In: Proceedings of Annual Meeting of the Association for Computational Linguistics, pp. 1199–1209 (2014)
11. Garcia-Silva, A., Corcho, O., Alani, H., Gomez-Perez, A.: Review of the state of the art: discovering and associating semantics to tags in folksonomies. Knowl. Eng. Rev. **27**(1), 57–85 (2012)
12. Heymann, P., Garcia-Molina, H.: Collaborative creation of communal hierarchical taxonomies in social tagging systems, Stanford (2006)
13. Jabeen, F., Khusro, S., Majid, A., Rauf, A.: Semantics discovery in social tagging systems: a review. Multimed. Tools Appl. **75**(1), 1–33 (2016)
14. Lawrie, D.J., Croft, W.B.: Generating hierarchical summaries for web searches. In: Proceedings of International ACM SIGIR Conference on Research and Development in Information Retrieval, pp. 457–458 (2003)
15. Lee, K., Kim, H., Jang, C., Kim, H.J.: Folksoviz: a subsumption-based folksonomy visualization using Wikipedia texts. In: International Conference on World Wide Web, pp. 1093–1094 (2008)
16. Lee, K., Kim, H., Shin, H., Kim, H.J.: Folksoviz: a semantic relation-based folksonomy visualization using the Wikipedia corpus. In: ACIS International Conference on Software Engineering, Artificial Intelligences, Networking and Parallel/Distributed Computing, pp. 24–29 (2009)
17. Li, B., Liu, J., Lin, C.Y., King, I., Lyu, M.R.: A hierarchical entity-based approach to structuralize user generated content in social media: a case of Yahoo! Answers. In: Proceedings of the Conference on Empirical Methods in Natural Language Processing, pp. 1521–1532 (2013)
18. Lin, H., Davis, J., Zhou, Y.: An integrated approach to extracting ontological structures from folksonomies. In: Aroyo, L., et al. (eds.) ESWC 2009. LNCS, vol. 5554, pp. 654–668. Springer, Heidelberg (2009). https://doi.org/10.1007/978-3-642-02121-3_48
19. Marinho, L.B., Pires, C.E.S.: A supervised learning approach to detect subsumption relations between tags in folksonomies. In: Proceedings of Annual ACM Symposium on Applied Computing, pp. 409–415 (2015)
20. Mikolov, T., Sutskever, I., Chen, K., Corrado, G., Dean, J.: Distributed representations of words and phrases and their compositionality. In: Proceedings of Annual Conference on Neural Information Processing Systems, pp. 3111–3119 (2013)
21. Miller, G.A., Hristea, F.: WordNet nouns: classes and instances. Comput. Linguist. **32**(1), 1–3 (2006)

22. Roller, S., Erk, K., Boleda, G.: Inclusive yet selective: supervised distributional hypernymy detection. In: Proceedings of International Conference on Computational Linguistics (2014)

23. Si, X., Liu, Z., Sun, M.: Explore the structure of social tags by subsumption relations. In: Proceedings of International Conference on Computational Linguistics, pp. 1011–1019 (2010)

24. Solskinnsbakk, G., Gulla, J.A., Haderlein, V., Myrseth, P., Cerrato, O.: Quality of hierarchies in ontologies and folksonomies. Data Knowl. Eng. **74**(6), 13–25 (2012)

25. Specia, L., Motta, E.: Integrating folksonomies with the semantic web. In: Franconi, E., Kifer, M., May, W. (eds.) ESWC 2007. LNCS, vol. 4519, pp. 624–639. Springer, Heidelberg (2007). https://doi.org/10.1007/978-3-540-72667-8_44

26. Staab, S., Studer, R.: Handbook on Ontologies. International Handbooks on Information Systems, vol. 2, pp. 227–255. Springer, Berlin (2004). https://doi.org/10.1007/978-3-540-24750-0

27. Tang, J., Leung, H., Luo, Q., Chen, D., Gong, J.: Towards ontology learning from folksonomies. In: Proceedings of International Joint Conference on Artificial Intelligence, vol. 9, pp. 2089–2094 (2009)

28. Tianxing, W., Wang, H., Qi, G., Zhu, J., Ruan, T.: On building and publishing linked open schema from social web sites. J. Web Semant. **51**, 39–50 (2018)

29. Xiao, B., Wang, Z., Liu, Q., Liu, X.: SMK-means: an improved mini batch K-means algorithm based on mapreduce with big data. CMC: Comput. Mater. Contin. **56**(3), 365–379 (2018)

30. Xu, S., Bao, S., Fei, B., Su, Z., Yu, Y.: Exploring folksonomy for personalized search. In: Proceedings of the 31st Annual International ACM SIGIR Conference on Research and Development in Information Retrieval, pp. 155–162 (2008)

31. Yu, Z., Wang, H., Lin, X., Wang, M.: Learning term embeddings for hypernymy identification. In: Proceedings of International Joint Conference on Artificial Intelligence, pp. 1390–1397 (2015)

32. Zhang, J., Xie, N., Zhang, X., Yue, K., Li, W., Kumar, D.: Machine learning based resource allocation of cloud computing in auction. CMC: Comput. Mater. Contin. **56**(1), 123–135 (2018)

33. Zhou, M., Bao, S., Wu, X., Yu, Y.: An unsupervised model for exploring hierarchical semantics from social annotations. In: Aberer, K., et al. (eds.) ASWC/ISWC -2007. LNCS, vol. 4825, pp. 680–693. Springer, Heidelberg (2007). https://doi.org/10.1007/978-3-540-76298-0_49

Accurate and Fast DV-Hop Localization Algorithm in Irregular Networks

Xiaoyong Yan[1,2(✉)], Xiang Feng[2], and Zhixin Sun[1,2]

[1] Broadband Wireless Communication and Sensor Network Technology
Key Lab of Ministry of Education,
Nanjing University of Posts and Telecommunications,
Nanjing 210003, China
{xiaoyong_yan,sunzx}@njupt.edu.cn
[2] YuanTong Express Co. LTD., Shanghai 201705, China

Abstract. The DV-hop localization algorithm does not depend on any measurement hardware, which only uses hop-counts to describe the Euclidean distance between nodes, it will not generate any additional burden, and thus this lightweight localization algorithm is economical and effective. Unfortunately, nodes generally have irregular distribution in reality, which tends to make deviations during the conversion between hop-counts and Euclidean distance, and as a result, the final estimated locations of nodes tend to deviate from the right location. Therefore, we analyzed the error during the hop-counts and Euclidean distance conversion, derived that the variance of error is related to hop-counts, and used the weighted least square method to correct the deviation. On this basis, we also limit the estimation location range of normal nodes according to the distances relationship between the estimated distances of normal nodes to anchor nodes and the distances of normal nodes estimated location to anchor nodes. Both the theoretical analysis and experimental results show that the proposed algorithm has not only maintained the economic characteristics of DV-hop localization, but also has the high localization accuracy and it can be adapted to various networks with different deployment of nodes.

Keywords: DV-hop localization algorithm ·
Optimal weighting function · Geometric constraint

1 Introduction

The position data is critical natural characteristics of people or objects in the physical world, which is also the information that people are really care about in real life. With the fast development of wireless technology, the technology that determines the location information of wireless network nodes becomes great important [1]. The GPS is the earliest widely used outdoor wireless positioning technology. However, when the receiving equipment is moved to the enclosed environment such as indoors and forest, the GPS signal will be constrained

© Springer Nature Switzerland AG 2019
X. Sun et al. (Eds.): ICAIS 2019, LNCS 11634, pp. 329–340, 2019.
https://doi.org/10.1007/978-3-030-24271-8_30

by various factors such as penetration loss and multipath interference, and the intensity of GPS signal received by the receiver is significantly lower than the minimum intensity of $-160\,\mathrm{dBw}$ required by the Interface Control Document (ICD) [2]. Therefore, it is difficult to carry out GPS localization in enclosed environment. With the emergence of multi-hop wireless network technology, the localization technology has also upgraded from one-hop localization to multi-hop localization correspondingly. The emergence of multi-hop localization can extend outdoor localization to the indoors environment [3].

We assume that in a network, among where nodes are evenly distributed. The minimum hop-counts from the node i to the node j is h_{ij}, and d_{ij} is defined as corresponding physical distance between two nodes. We easily find that d_{ij} is proportional to h_{ij}, i.e. $d_{ij} \propto h_{ij}$. Inspired by this feature, Niculescu et al. [4] proposed the well-known multi-hop distributive localization algorithm, namely DV-hop localization algorithm.

The DV-hop consists of the following three steps. I: In the network, each anchor nodes has broadcasted its location information within the network using flood routing protocol (Distance Vector Protocol); after receiving the information of anchor nodes, the node maintains an information table, and records anchor nodes' location information and corresponding least hop-counts form itself to anchor nodes. II: According to the calculated distance to another anchor node j in the network and corresponding hop value h_{ij} , anchor node i estimates its average per-hop distance $HopDist_i$ (also called hop-distance transformation model) in accordance with Eq. 1. III: According to the average per-hop distance to the nearest anchor node and the hop-count h_{ki} to this anchor node, the normal node k calculates the estimated distance $\hat{d}_{ki} = HopDist_i \times h_{ki}$ between the normal node and anchor node. Then, the multilateration method is employed to estimate the location of normal node.

$$HopDist_i = \frac{\sum_{i \neq j} d_{ij}}{\sum_{i \neq j} h_{ij}} \tag{1}$$

However, the neighborhood relationship of nodes in the real network is usually limited by the surrounding objects. For example, due to the topographic factors and existence of barrier, the path which could previously be achieved in one-hop has to be achieved in multiple hops, and the shortest path of approximate straight line became polygonal line, which results in irregular distribution of nodes. If a network presents irregular distribution of nodes, the hop-counts between nodes may not be able to well match the Euclidean distance, and in other words, the Euclidean distance between nodes cannot be directly estimated according to the hop-counts between them. Therefore, in the network with nodes irregular distribution, it will generate high localization error by directly using the traditional hop-based localization algorithm. In this paper, we analyzed the error generated during the hops-distance conversion process, obtained the error correction function (weighted function), and estimated the error generated by error correction during the estimation process based on that. Without increasing the computational complexity, the algorithm adopts the weighted method to effectively correct the error of estimated distance from the normal node to the anchor node, which can increase the algorithm's adaptability to different environment and improve the localization precision.

2   The Problem Analysis of DV-Hop Localization Algorithm

A total of $m+n$ nodes are randomly deployed and constituted a network in the 2D space. n nodes are normal nodes, which do not have their location information, and m nodes are anchors that their locations are known exactly.

In III of DV-hop algorithm, the multilateration method is generally employed to compute the coordinate of non-anchor nodes. Suppose that a node normal N_u coordinates (x, y) is localizing itself. Let $\hat{d}_i$ represents the estimated distance between N_u and anchor i whose locations are $(x_i, y_i), i = 1, \cdots, m \text{ and } m > 3$, we can construct the relationship equation between non-anchor and anchors, $i.e.$,

$$\begin{cases} (x_1 - x)^2 + (y_1 - y)^2 = \hat{d}_1^2 \\ \quad\vdots \\ (x_m - x)^2 + (y_m - y)^2 = \hat{d}_m^2 \end{cases} \tag{2}$$

In Eq. 2, the new equations can be obtained by subtracting one equation from various equations (here, we choose the m-th equation as the base equation) and becomes

$$\begin{cases} 2(x_m - x_1)x + (y_m - y_1)y = \hat{d}_1^2 - \hat{d}_m^2 + y_m^2 + x_m^2 - y_1^2 - x_1^2 \\ \quad\vdots \\ 2(x_m - x_{m-1})x + (y_m - y_{m-1})y = \hat{d}_{m-1}^2 - \hat{d}_m^2 + y_m^2 + x_m^2 - y_{m-1}^2 - x_{m-1}^2 \end{cases} \tag{3}$$

Then Eq. 3 can be rewritten in the Matrix-Vector form as

$$Ax = b \tag{4}$$

where

$$A = 2 \times ((x_1 - x_m)(y_1 - y_m)); \cdots ; ((x_{m-1} - x_m)(y_{m-1} - y_m))]^T$$

$$x = [x, y]^T, \quad b = \begin{bmatrix} \hat{d}_1^2 - \hat{d}_m^2 + y_m^2 + x_m^2 - y_1^2 - x_1^2 \\ \vdots \\ \hat{d}_{m-1}^2 - \hat{d}_m^2 + y_m^2 + x_m^2 - y_{m-1}^2 - x_{m-1}^2 \end{bmatrix}$$

Therefore, we can see that the final localization precision of normal nodes depends on the precision of the estimated distance in vector b. If the error contained in vector b satisfies the following conditions: the mean value is 0, the error variance is a constant, the error terms are independent from each other, and the error terms present normal distribution, then, the location of normal node can be obtained through Eq. 5:

$$\hat{x} = [\hat{x}, \hat{y}]^{\mathrm{T}} = \left(A^{\mathrm{T}}A\right)^{-1} A^{\mathrm{T}}b \tag{5}$$

In practical application, the average per-hop distance is directly related to other factors such as the node connectivity and node distribution. According to literatures [5], it has been proven that when the nodes are randomly distributed in the monitored area, the nodes present Poisson distribution. Therefore, the error variance of average hop-counts can be regarded as a constant, which can be denoted as σ^2. At the same time, we can find that for any two nodes within the network, with the change of hop-counts, the error variance between them will also change accordingly. The estimated distance error between different nodes can be expressed as:

$$\delta = \epsilon \times h \tag{6}$$

where ϵ is the error of average per-hop distance; h denotes the shortest hop-counts between nodes. Therefore, it is easy to know $var\left(\delta\right) = var\left(\epsilon \times h\right) = h^2\sigma^2$. In the meantime, we can also find that the error variance of estimated distance between nodes with different hop-counts is also different. This phenomenon of variance instability is called "heteroscedasticity" in theory.

According to the statistics Theorem, due to heteroscedasticity, the estimation results no longer have the minimum variance characteristic anymore. Therefore, in the position estimation process, we must correct the heteroscedasticity of the position estimate to make the estimated value closer to the optimal linear unbiased estimate, thus improving the positioning accuracy.

3   Related Study

The hop-based localization algorithm generally uses information exchange between nodes to collect information required by the algorithm. According to the source of localization information, the hop-based localization algorithm can be divided into the local-based information and global-based information algorithm. Considering that the further the anchor node is from the normal node, the higher accumulative error will be generated, and the heteroscedasticity problem will be severer, some localization algorithms which only collect the neighborhood information for localization have been proposed (*i.e.*, the local-based information localization algorithm). Classic algorithms include Reliable Anchor-based Localization (RAL) [6], Anchor Supervised (AnSuper) [7], and DV-maxHop [8] *etc.* The RAL algorithm would filter out the anchor nodes with improper location estimation through the pre-established lookup table first. Due to irregular distribution, these anchor nodes would cause the estimated distance to deviate from the actual length of distance. By using the lookup table, it requires to know related information of the network first, such as the node distribution, node density and node communication range, and this requires pre-computation, which will result in high computational complexity. In the AnSuper algorithm, every anchor selects a set of friendly anchors which are consisting of multiple anchor node according to the residuals of the estimated distance between itself and other anchors. And then the normal nodes conduct location estimation based on the near friendly anchor set. However, the friend set selected in the AnSuper method depends on the artificial setting, which results in poor adaptability to different scenarios. The latest DV-maxHop method adopts the adaptive multi-objective particle swarm optimization method [9] to find the maximum hop-count range for even distribution of nodes. Through experiments, the DV-maxHop is used to find that nodes have relatively even distribution within the hop-count range of 5–15. However, according to the evolution state of Pareto entropy monitoring population, the adaptive multi-objective particle swarm optimization method adaptively adjusts the inertia weight and learning factors. Based on the characteristics of Pareto solution set, direct detection of population convergence state is more complicated than the single-target problem, and this method tends to cause the algorithm to be trapped in local problem which the algorithm cannot be jumped out from, so the DV-maxHop problem also has the stability problem. In addition, the localization algorithms based on local information all fail to fundamentally solve the heteroscedasticity problem of distance estimation among nodes with different hop-counts, and they have high requirement for the number of neighbor anchor nodes. When there are a small number of anchor nodes in the network, the algorithm has very poor localization precision, and it also tends to have the coverage loss problem.

The global-based localization method collects the hop-counts information of entire network for localization, and the classic algorithms include DV-hop, MDS-MAP [10], *etc.* Because the hop-counts information of each normal node came from the entire network, this kind of algorithm requires smaller proportion of anchor nodes. However, during random deployment of nodes, especially under irregular distribution of nodes, the existence of heteroscedasticity would result in significant deviation of the distance information collected by the normal node from the actual distance. According to the heteroscedasticity problem generated under irregular distribution of nodes, the original model should be corrected, so that after correction, the error term of hops-distance conversion model has a constant variance. The correction of hops-distance conversion model depends on the relation between error variance and hop-counts. Assume the variance of error vector ϵ is generally proportional to the function $W(h)$ of hop-counts vector h, *i.e.*,

$$\delta_\epsilon^2 = W(h) \times \sigma^2 \tag{7}$$

Here, σ^2 is a finite constant. Therefore, $\sqrt{W(h)}$ is used to eliminate the original model, so that the error vector of new mode has a constant variance, and this kind of method is also called the weighted least square method. Song *et al.* [12] designed an improved weighted centroid DV-Hop (IWC-DV-hop) that employs global hop-counts information for location estimation. IWC-DV-hop uses Eq. 8 weaken the influence of heteroscedasticity on distance estimation *i.e.*,

$$w(h_i) = \frac{\sum_{i=1}^{m} h_i}{m \times h_i} \tag{8}$$

where $W(h) = diag(w(h_i))$.

Recently, Kaur et $al.$ [13] designed another weighted hop-based localization method (enhanced weighted centroid DV-Hop, EWC DV-hop) which is based on Song's method, and this method has considered various factors, including the number of anchor nodes, communication range and the distance between the normal node and the nearest anchor node. The weighted function of EWC DV-hop is:

$$w(h_i) = \left(\frac{\sum_{i=1}^{m} h_i}{m \times h_i} \right)^{\frac{r}{HopDist_i}} \tag{9}$$

where $HopDist_i$ refers to the average per-hop distance between the normal node N_u and the nearest anchor node j; r is the communication range of nodes.

4   Localization Algorithm with Weighted Least Square

According to the description of Sect. 2, we can clearly find out that among the DV-hop and its improved localization algorithms, they are all interfered by the heteroscedasticity problem during the hops-distance conversion process. The existence of heteroscedasticity will result in unstable results of the final estimation location. In order to solve this problem, we employ the weighted least square method in which the weight function is optimal. Under the optimal weight function help, the estimated distance with bigger variance of error term is assigned to smaller weight value, while the estimated distance with smaller variance of error term is assigned with bigger weight value, which makes it a stable model without heteroscedasticity.

How to select weight function in the weighted least square method is crucial to the whole algorithm. The literature [11] have proven that the reciprocal of error vector variance is the optimal weight function. For this reason, we need to obtain the variance of error vector which can help obtain the optimal location estimation. Let Δ is an error vector of Eq. 4 and it can be expressed as:

$$\Delta = Ax - b$$

$$= 2 \times \begin{bmatrix} (x_1 - x_m) & (y_1 - y_m) \\ \vdots & \vdots \\ (x_{m-1} - x_m)(y_{m-1} - y_m) \end{bmatrix} - \begin{bmatrix} x_1^2 - x_m^2 + y_1^2 - y_m^2 + \hat{d}_m^2 - \hat{d}_1^2 \\ \vdots \\ x_{m-1}^2 - x_m^2 + y_{m-1}^2 - y_m^2 + \hat{d}_m^2 - \hat{d}_{m-1}^2 \end{bmatrix}$$

$$= \begin{bmatrix} (x - x_1)^2 + (y - y_1)^2 - \hat{d}_1^2 \\ \vdots \\ (x - x_{m-1})^2 + (y - y_{m-1})^2 - \hat{d}_{m-1}^2 \end{bmatrix} - \begin{bmatrix} (x - x_m)^2 + (y - y_m)^2 - \hat{d}_m^2 \\ \vdots \\ (x - x_m)^2 + (y - y_m)^2 - \hat{d}_m^2 \end{bmatrix} \tag{10}$$

where $\hat{d}_i$ represents the estimated distance from the normal node N_u to the anchor node i, and $\sqrt[.]{(x - x_i)^2 + (y - y_i)^2} = d_i$ denotes the exact distance. Therefore, the error variance of the distance between the ith anchor node and the unknown node N_u can be described as:

$$var\left(((x - x_i)^2 + (y - y_i)^2 - \hat{d}_i^2) - ((x - x_m)^2 + (y - y_m)^2 - \hat{d}_m^2)\right)$$

$$= var\left((x - x_i)^2 + (y - y_i)^2 - \hat{d}_i^2\right) + var\left((x - x_m)^2 + (y - y_m)^2 - \hat{d}_m^2\right)$$

$$= var\left(d_i^2 - \hat{d}_i^2\right) + var\left(d_m^2 - \hat{d}_m^2\right) \tag{11}$$

Since d_i^2 is unique, its variance is zero. And the reference node m is specified in advance, so its variance is zero. Then, the error variance between the d_i and $\hat{d}_i$ is:

$$var\left(\delta_i\right) = var\left(\hat{d}_i^2\right) = var\left((HopDist_i \times h_i)^2\right)$$

$$= h_i^4 var\left(HopDist_i\right) \tag{12}$$

Because $var(HopDist_i) = \sigma^2$, and σ^2 can be cancelled-out during the operation. Thus, the weight function $\boldsymbol{W}(h)$ can be formulated simply as

$$\boldsymbol{W}(h_i) = diag\left(\frac{1}{h_i^4}\right) \qquad where \; i = 1, \cdots, m - 1 \tag{13}$$

Then, the estimated location of normal node can be re-expressed as

$$\hat{\boldsymbol{x}} = [\hat{x}, \hat{y}]^{\mathrm{T}} = \left(\boldsymbol{A}^{\mathrm{T}} \boldsymbol{W} \boldsymbol{A}\right)^{-1} \boldsymbol{A}^{\mathrm{T}} \boldsymbol{W} \boldsymbol{b} \tag{14}$$

In addition, we also consider the scene as showed in the Fig. 1. It is assumed that the estimated location of normal node U is determined by the three anchor nodes A, B, C, wherein the estimated distances (per-hop distance $\times$ hop-counts) from the anchor nodes A, B, C to the normal nodes U are $\hat{d}_{AU}$, $\hat{d}_{BU}$, and $\hat{d}_{CU}$, respectively. Considering that the distances $\tilde{d}$ from the estimated location of normal nodes U to any anchor nodes should be less than or equal to the corresponding estimated distances $\hat{d}$. So, we choose the shortest estimation distance $\hat{d}_{CU}$ as the constraint, that is, $\tilde{d}_{CU} \leq \hat{d}_{CU}$. If the relational $\tilde{d}_{CU} \leq \hat{d}_{CU}$ does not hold, the location of the normal node U is estimated to be the location of anchor C.

5   Performance Evaluation

In this section, the performance of the proposed algorithm is compared with the same type of localization algorithms. Assume the nodes are randomly deployed

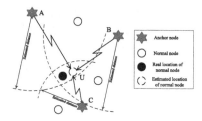

Fig. 1. The relationship between the estimated location of a normal node and the neighboring anchor nodes

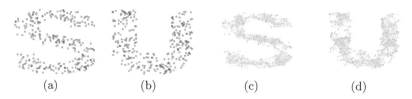

| (a) | (b) | (c) | (d) |

Fig. 2. Node distribution. (a) S-shaped network; (b) U-shaped network; (c) The neighbor relationship between nodes in S-shaped network; (d) The neighbor relationship between nodes in U-shaped network

in two irregular networks, as illustrated by the U-shaped and S-shape [15] networks in Fig. 2a and b, and the neighbourhood relationship between nodes is as illustrated in Fig. 2c and d.

We consider the Root Mean Square (RMS) as the criterion for localization precision, and RMS can be expressed as:

$$RMS = \sqrt{\frac{1}{n}\sum_{i=1}^{n}\left((\hat{x}_i - x_i)^2 + (\hat{y}_i - y_i)^2\right)} \tag{15}$$

where n means the total number of localized nodes, (x, y) means the true location of the normal node, $(\hat{x}, \hat{y})$ means the estimated location of the normal node.

In addition, the localization performance was mainly analyzed in the experiments based on indices such as the proportion of anchor nodes and node density in the network. In the meantime, considering the algorithm proposed in this paper is an improved algorithm based on DV-hop, in addition to comparing it with the classic DV-hop algorithm [4], we also compared its performance with that of DV-maxHop [8] based on local information and the latest EWC DV-hop [13] based on global information on multiple aspects.

5.1 Irregular Distribution of Nodes Impact

In this group of experiments, 300 nodes are uniformly deployed in S-shaped and U-shaped networks of 300-by-300, 20 of them are anchor nodes (as illustrated in

Fig. 3, circles represent normal nodes, and hexagons represent anchor nodes.).
Let the communication range R [14] of nodes stay constant, which is $R = 40$.
Figure 4 describes the localization results of the proposed method and similar
algorithms under the node distribution as shown in Fig. 3. The results of location estimation are described with 3-D stem plot, the stem height represents the
absolute error of estimation, and the higher the height is, the bigger the localization error. According to the results in Fig. 4, we can see that in an irregular
network, due to use of fixed hops-distance conversion model in DV-hop, deviation
is generated during the hops-distance conversion, which will result in extremely
high localization error. DV-maxHop is a multi-hop localization method based on
local information, which only depends local anchor node information for localization, and it will have poor localization precision when only a small number
of local anchor nodes with poor distribution quality can be obtained. For example, there are very few anchor nodes on the upper left part of S-shaped and
U-shaped networks in Fig. 3; in the corresponding area in Fig. 4, the localization
precision of DV-maxHop has been significantly improved. Both EWC DV-hop
and DV-hop are global-based information localization methods, and this kind of
algorithm only requires a small proportion of anchor nodes to realize node local-
ization(In theory, only 3 anchor nodes are needed). However, the method based
on global information has a strict requirement for the node distribution area.
The EWC DV-hop method weakens the error generated during hops-distance
conversion through the weighted method, but the weight function in the EWC
DV-hop method fails to find the error relationship between hop-counts and distance, so it has a low localization precision. The proposed method in this paper
explores the error relationship between hop-counts and distance through theoretical derivation, so it can obtain higher localization precision than previous
methods.

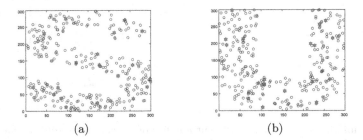

(a)   (b)

Fig. 3. The distribution of normal nodes and anchor nodes. (a) S-shaped network; (b)
U-shaped network

5.2 Anchor Number Impact

In this group of experiments, the communication range R of nodes remains
unchanged, still 40. We set the number of anchor nodes in the range from 15

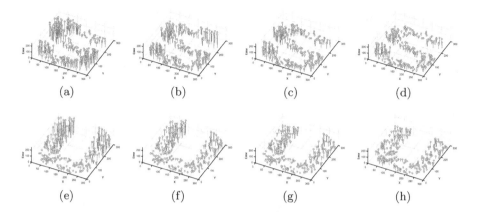

(a)   (b)   (c)   (d)

(e)   (f)   (g)   (h)

Fig. 4. Location results. (a) DV-hop, RMS=119.89; (b) DV-maxHop, RMS=89.42; (c) EWC DV-hop, RMS=70.64; (d) Proposed method, RMS=51.37; (e) DV-hop, RMS=95.0106; (f) DV-maxHop, RMS=67.1546; (g) EWC DV-hop, RMS=49.13; (h) Proposed method, RMS=39.57

to 30 (each experiment increases by 5) and observe its impact on the proposed algorithm in this paper, as well as the DV-hop, DV-maxHop and EWC DV-hop methods. In order to reduce the inconsistency of performance evaluation caused by random deployment of nodes in the experiment, for a constant number of anchor nodes, the experiment was repeated for 150 times, and the box-plot was used to describe the distribution of each location estimation result.

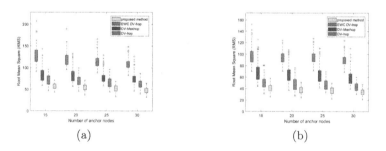

(a)   (b)

Fig. 5. Simulation results under different number of anchors for the (a) S-shaped and (b) U-shaped networks

As can be seen in Fig. 5, DV-hop, DV-maxHop, EWC DV-hop and the proposed method display their different performance in localization accuracy based on various numbers of anchor nodes. The experimental results show that the error medians of DV-hop are higher than 100 in S-shaped networks and close to 100 in U-shaped networks. Since the DV-Maxhop, EWC DV-hop, and proposed method all suppress errors during converting hop-counts into distances, thus their error distribution is appreciably lower than those of DV-hop. Moreover, the error medians of them are relatively lower than the DV-hop method. Since the proposed method correctly calculates the errors during converting hopcounts into distances, it has the highest localization accuracy among them. In the S-shaped network, compared to the DV-hop, DV-Maxhop and EWC DV-hop methods, the mean localization precision of proposed method has increased by 120.56%, 49.55%and 25.77% respectively. In the U-shaped network, compared to the DV-hop, DV-Maxhop and EWC DV-hop methods, the mean localization precision of proposed method has increased by 151.97%, 71.81% and 25.89%, respectively.

6 Conclusions

In this paper, we have proposed a novel weighted DV-hop localization algorithm suppress the heteroscedasticity problem in the hops-distance conversion process. Based on the error during the localization process, we find that the optimal weight function only related to hop-counts between nodes. In addition, we ensure the stability of localization performance based on the relationship between the estimated location of normal nodes and the estimated distances. It has been demonstrated though computer simulations that in the network with irregular distribution of nodes, the proposed method in this paper has higher localization precision than the DV-Hop algorithm and its improved method proposed recently, and it is also the least affected by the number of anchor nodes.

Acknowledgments. Xiaoyong Yan is indebted to the overseas training program for outstanding young teachers in Jiangsu for its financial support as a visiting scholar at The Hong Kong Polytechnic University, Hong Kong. National Engineering Laboratory for Logistics Information Technology, YuanTong Express co. LTD. This work was partially supported by the NSFC (61672299), the China and Jiangsu Postdoctoral Science Foundation (2016M601861 and 1701049A), the Natural Science Foundation of Jiangsu Higher Education Institutions (16KJB520033) and the NUPTSF (NY218144).

References

1. Zhou, T., Lian, B., Yang, S., Zhang, Y., Liu, Y.: Improved GNSS cooperation positioning algorithm for indoor localization. CMC: Comput. Mater. Continua 5(2), 225–245 (2018)
2. Dedes, G., Dempste, A.G.: Indoor GPS positioning: challenges and opportunities. In: Proceedings of IEEE Conference on Vehicular Technology, pp. 412–415. IEEE, Dallas (2005)
3. Wang, Z., Zhang, B., Wang, X., Jin, X., Bai, Y.: Improvements of multihop localization algorithm for wireless sensor networks. IEEE Syst. J. (Early Access) 13, 1–12 (2018)
4. Niculescu, D., Nath, B.: DV based positioning in Ad Hoc networks. Telecommun. Syst. 22, 267–280 (2003)
5. Takagi, H., Kleinrock, L.L.: Optimal transmission ranges for randomly distributed packet radio terminals. IEEE Trans. Commun. 32, 246–257 (1984)

6. Xiao, B., Lin, C., Xiao, Q.J., Li, M.L.: Reliable anchor-based sensor localization in irregular areas. IEEE Trans. Mobile Comput. **9**, 60–72 (2009)
7. Liu, X., Zhang, S.G., Bu, K.: A locality-based range-free localization algorithm for anisotropic wireless sensor networks. Telecommun. Syst. **62**, 3–13 (2016)
8. Shahzad, F., Sheltami, T.R., Shakshuki, E.M.: DV-maxHop: a fast and ac-curate range-free localization algorithm for anisotropic wireless networks. IEEE Trans. Mobile Comput. **16**, 2494–2505 (2017)
9. Hu, W., Yen, G.G.: Adaptive multiobjective particle swarm optimization based on parallel cell coordinate system. IEEE Trans. Evol. **19**, 1–18 (2015)
10. Shang, Y., Rumi, W., Zhang, Y.: Localization from connectivity in sensor networks. IEEE Trans. Parallel Distrib. Syst. **15**, 961–974 (2004)
11. Strutz, T.: Data Fitting and Uncertainty: A Practical Introduction to Weighted Least Squares and Beyond. Vieweg+Teubner, Germany (2010)
12. Song, G., Tam, D.: Two novel DV-Hop localization algorithms for randomly deployed wireless sensor networks. Int. J. Distrib. Sens. Netw. **2015**, 1–9 (2015)
13. Kaur, A., Kumar, P., Gupta, G.P.: A weighted centroid localization algorithm for randomly deployed wireless sensor networks. J. King Saud Univ.-Comput. Inf. Sci. (2017, in press)
14. Lee, S., Kim, K.: Determination of communication range for range-free multi-hop localization in wireless sensor networks. In: Proceedings of 20th International Conference on Computer Communications and Networks (ICCCN), pp. 1–4. IEEE Maui (2011)
15. Liu, W., Luo, X., Liu, Y., Liu, J., Liu, M., Shi, Y.Q.: Localization algorithm of indoor Wi-Fi access points based on signal strength relative relationship and region division. CMC: Comput. Mater. Continua **55**(1), 071–093 (2018)

Shape Recognition with Recurrent Neural Network

Songle Chen[1], Xuejian Zhao[1], Zhe Sun[1], Feng Xiang[2],
and Zhixin Sun[1(✉)]

[1] Nanjing University of Posts and Telecommunications, Nanjing 210003, China
{chensongle,zhaoxj,zhesunny,sunzx}@njupt.edu.cn
[2] YuanTong Express Co. LTD., Shanghai 201705, China

Abstract. Shape recognition is a fundamental problem in the field of computer vision and is important to various applications. A number of methods based on deep CNN has acquired state-of-the-art performance in shape recognition. Among them, model-based methods perform convolutions with 3D filters on the voxels or point cloud in continuous 3D space, and the volumetric representation makes them exploit complete structure information. Unfortunately, in order to train the deep network with available samples in a reasonable amount of time, these methods have to use a coarse representation, typically $30 \times 30 \times 30$ grid, which will inevitably sacrifice much discriminate detail information. This paper presents a novel approached based on recurrent neural network to solve this problem. In each step, the model selects the location of the subvolume from where the local 3D CNN feature is extracted, and the hypothesis is formulated by merging the features of subvolumes of each step. In this way, the proposed approach can explore the shape with high resolutions and exploit the fine-grained 3D structure information. Primary experimental results on the public dataset verify the effectiveness of the proposed method.

Keywords: Shape · Recognition · Recurrent neural network

1 Introduction

Shape recognition is a fundamental problem in the field of computer vision and is important to various applications. The challenges of shape recognition lay in wide variety of transformations, meaningful data only spreading on surface, containing deformable parts, existing holes, etc. Recently, instead of using conventional hand-craft features, deep convolution neural networks incorporate the feature representation learning into an end-to-end learning framework and have had great success in significantly advancing the state-of-the-art on shape recognition.

Depending on how the addition of the third spatial dimension is treated, these methods can be coarsely categorized into view-based and model-based. View-based methods render shapes from multiple different viewpoints and utilize the 2D CNN network to extract feature representation for single view, then employ max pooling or other strategies to form the final decision across multiple views [1]. The main advantage of view-based methods lies in the available 2D CNN pre-trained on huge

X. Sun et al. (Eds.): ICAIS 2019, LNCS 11634, pp. 341–350, 2019.
https://doi.org/10.1007/978-3-030-24271-8_31

image dataset such as ImageNet [2], and lots of methods based on which have achieved state of art performance in many tasks of computer graphics and computer vision [3, 4]. Model-based methods usually represent shapes as a binary occupancy grid or 3D point cloud, and then apply 3D CNN to train a classification model [5–8]. The key advantage of model-based methods is that the volumetric representation in continuous 3D space makes them can exploit complete structure information.

However, convolving 3D voxels or point cloud of model-based CNN methods has cubical complexity with respect to the spatial resolution. In order to train the deep network with available samples in a reasonable amount of time, these methods have to use a coarse representation, typically $30 \times 30 \times 30$ grid. Moreover, to get high performance, model-based methods usually average predictions across from 10 to 24 multiple rotated copies of each input shape for data augmentation. As the result, it often takes several days to train the network on GPU server. For instance, although single VRN [7] model has achieved comparable performance to view-based methods, as the author reported, a single training epoch takes around 6 h on a single Titan X, and it requires around 6 days of training to converge. The testing computational cost of VRN model is also high because it averages predictions across 24 rotated copies of each input shape.

Our key observation is that coarse resolution usually neglects too much fine-grained discriminative information which may help enhance the performance of shape recognition. Figure 1 shows a concrete example. It can be seen that the right rear wheel of car can hardly be recognized under the coarse resolution of $30 \times 30 \times 30$ grid while it remains rich information for discrimination under high resolution of $128 \times 128 \times 128$. However, tremendous computation cost prevent us from performing full 3D CNN on such high voxel resolution.

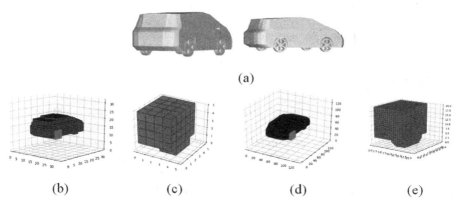

Fig. 1. An example of car with different resolution representation. (a) Gray Image rendered from two different viewpoints. (b) Voxels of car with resolution of $30 \times 30 \times 30$ grid, the right rear wheel is in the subvolume of $5 \times 5 \times 5$ grid highlighted with red color. (c) Amplified right rear wheel shown in (b). (d) Voxels of car with resolution of $128 \times 128 \times 128$ grid, the right rear wheel is in the subvolume of $20 \times 20 \times 20$ grid highlighted with red color. (e) Amplified right rear wheel shown in (d). (Color figure online)

Inspired by recent attention model, this paper presents a novel approached based on recurrent neural network to solve this problem. In each recurrent step, the model selects the location of the subvolume from which the local CNN feature is extracted, and the hypothesis is formulated by merging the features of subvolumes of each steps. In this way, the proposed approach can explore the shapes with high resolutions and exploit the fine-grained 3D structure information for discrimination.

2 Method

2.1 Subvolume Encoding with 3D CNN

We first need to encode the subvolume extracted from shape and there are various deep neural network available for selection, such as 3D ShapeNets [5], VoxNet [6] and so on. For effectiveness of adjusting the layers of the network according to the over-fitting or under-fitting, we adopt 3D ResNet [9] as the 3D CNN network. ResNet [10] is one of the most successful architectures in image classification, provides shortcut connections that allow a signal to bypass one layer and move to the next layer in the sequence. Since these connections pass through the networks' gradient flows from the later layers to the early layers, they can facilitate the training of very deep networks.

In theory, we can embed 3D ResNet network into recurrent neural network and learn the parameters of 3D ResNet with the recurrent neural network simultaneously. However, it is time-consuming process because there is no pre-trained network can be used for initializing the network. For efficiency, we train 3D ResNet separately.

Figure 2 presents the workflow of subvolume 3D CNN feature extraction. Shapes in the training set are with the high resolution of $128 \times 128 \times 128$. The resolution of subvolume is $32 \times 32 \times 32$. For each shape, we sample the subvolume with stride 16. As a result, there are total 7^3 subvolumes extracted from each shape. We exclude the empty subvolumes for they have no contribution for shape recognition. All other

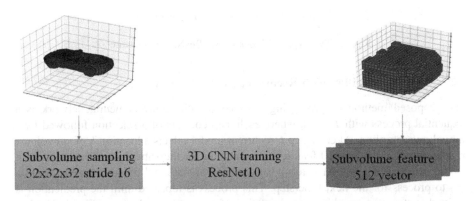

Fig. 2. Workflow of subvolume 3D CNN feature extraction.

subvolumes with their shape category compose the training set for 3D ResNet network learning.

The depth of layers of 3D ResNet can be from 10 to 152, and from experiment, we found 10 layers is enough for encoding the subvolume. Two types of block of 3D ResNet architecture are shown in Fig. 3. In this work the first type is adopted. The training process is converge at accuracy of about 82%. This indicates that most of the subvolumes have the ability to discern the category of the shape. So combining several subvolumes and merging them by recurrent neural network has the potency to achieve high performance for shape recognition. We extract the feature of each subvolume with the trained 3D ResNet10, and the final representation of each subvolume is 512 dimension of vector. Notice that we don't use any data in the validation set and the training is in end-to-end framework.

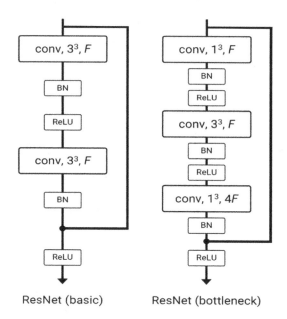

Fig. 3. Two types of block of 3D ResNet architecture

2.2 Shape Recognition with Recurrent Neural Network

The proposed method of processing a shape x with recurrent neural network is a sequential process with T steps, where each step consists of a selection followed by a subvolume sampling. At each step t, recurrent model selects a location l_t of subvolume x_t and extract 3D ResNet10 feature representation for the subvolume. Then, recurrent model uses the observation x_t to update its internal state and output the new location l_{t+1} to process for the next time step. This process is repeated until the predication is emitted at step T. A graphical representation of our model is shown in Fig. 4. The key components of the model are described below.

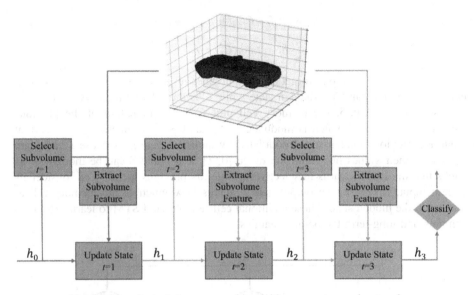

Fig. 4. Flowchart of shape recognition with recurrent neural network.

Recurrent Neural Network: The proposed approach is based on recurrent neural network (RNN). The model maintains an internal state which summarizes information extracted from the history of past observations. This internal state is formed by the hidden units h_t of the recurrent neural network and updated over each time step with the subvolume feature vector x_t. Though RNNs have proven successful on tasks such as speech recognition [11], text generation [12] and action recognition from video [13] or 3D data, it can be difficult to train them to learn long-term dynamics, likely due in part to the vanishing and exploding gradients problem that can result from propagating the gradients down through the many layers of the recurrent network, each corresponding to a particular time step. Long-Short-Term Memory units (LSTMs) provide a solution by incorporating memory units that allow the network to learn when to forget previous hidden states and when to update hidden states given new information. We adopt Long-Short-Term Memory units [14] for the non-linearity Recurrent because of their ability to learn long-range dependencies and stable learning dynamics. LSTM calculates a hidden state h_t as follows.

$$i_t = \sigma(x_t U_i + h_{t-1} W_i) \tag{1}$$

$$f_t = \sigma\left(x_t U_f + h_{t-1} W_f\right) \tag{2}$$

$$o_t = \sigma(x_t U_o + h_{t-1} W_o) \tag{3}$$

$$\sim C_t = tanh\left(x_t U_g + h_{t-1} W_g\right) \tag{4}$$

$$C_t = \sigma(f_t * C_{t-1} + i_t * \sim C_t) \tag{5}$$

$$h_t = tanh(C_t) * o_t \tag{6}$$

Here, i, o, f are the input, forget and output gates respectively. U and W are weight matrix. $\sim C$ is the candidate hidden state while C is the internal memory of the unit.

As shown in Fig. 5, the memory cell unit C_t is a summation of the previous memory cell unit C_{t-1} which is modulated by f_t, and $\sim C_t$, a function of the current input and previous hidden state, modulated by the input gate i_t. Because i_t and f_t are sigmoidal, their values lie within the range $[0, 1]$, and i_t and f_t can be thought of as knobs that the LSTM learns to selectively forget its previous memory or consider its current input. Likewise, the output gate o_t learns how much of the memory cell to transfer to the hidden state. These additional cells enable the LSTM to learn extremely complex and long-term temporal dynamics.

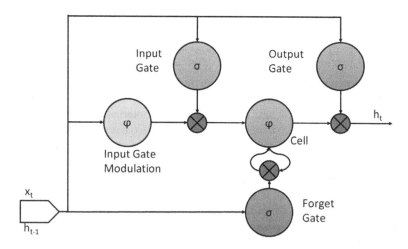

Fig. 5. A diagram of LSTM memory cell.

Next Subvolume Selection: The model takes the current state h_t of recurrent network as input and makes a prediction on where to extract the subvolume to observe. It consists of a fully connected hidden layer that maps the feature vector h_t from the recurrent network to a coordinate triple $l_{t+1} = (p_x, p_y, p_z)$. The location network can be denoted as

$$l_{t+1} = ReLU(FC(h_t)) \tag{7}$$

where FC is the linear full connect layer and $ReLU$ is the activation function. In the training phase, l_{t+1} is resampled stochastically from a Gaussian distribution with a mean of l_{t+1}, and a fixed variance for reinforce learning.

Classification Network: The classification network outputs a prediction for the class label y based on the final internal state h_T which summarizes information extracted from the history of past observations. The classification network has one fully connected hidden layer and a *softmax* output layer for the class y, namely

$$P(y|X) = softmax(FC(h_T)) \tag{8}$$

Learning: Although we can design a function mapping the location l_t to the subvolume directly and obtain a continuous function for standard back propagation training. However, the function is too complicated and the gradient vanishing problem is very easy to happen which prevents training convergence. To solve this problem, we combine the back propagation and REINFORCE [15] to train the model in end-to-end fashion. REINFORCE is a powerful approach that enables learning in non-differentiable settings. Given a space of action sequences A and $p(a)$, a distribution over a $\in A$ and parameterized by θ, we wish to learn network parameters that maximize the expected reward of a sequence of actions. The gradient of the objective is

$$\nabla J(\theta) = \sum_{a \in A} p_\theta(a) \nabla \log p_\theta(a) r(a) \tag{9}$$

Here $r(a)$ is a reward assigned to each possible action sequence. However, this is a non-trivial optimization problem due to the high-dimensional space of possible action sequences. REINFORCE addresses this by learning network parameters using Monte Carlo sampling. After running an agent's current policy π_θ in its environment and obtaining K interaction sequences of length T, the approximation to the gradient equation is

$$\nabla J(\theta) \approx \frac{1}{K} \sum_{i=1}^{K} \sum_{t=1}^{T} \nabla \log \pi_\theta(a_t^i | s_{1:t}; \theta)(R_t^i - b_t) \tag{10}$$

Here, policy π_θ maps the history of past interactions with the environment $s_{1:t}$ to a distribution over actions for the current time step t. R_t is the cumulative future reward from the current time step to time step T, b_t is a baseline reward to reduce the variance of the gradient estimation, and it is natural to select b_t as the mathematics expectation of R_t of K samples. We refer to [15] and [16] for a detail RNN based REINFORCE.

3 Experiments and Results

Our network is implemented using Torch [17, 18] on the platform with NVIDIA GeForce TITAN X GPU. It needs about 1000 epochs for training, as shown in Fig. 6. The learning rate is set to 0.0001 in the first 300 epochs, then decreases linearly to minimum 0.00001 at epoch 600. Momentum is set to 0.9, batch size is set to 20, and optimization is done through stochastic gradient descent. Based on grid search, the fixed variance of Gaussian distribution for reinforce learning is set to 0.10, the reward scale is set to 1. Time steps T is fixed for each shape.

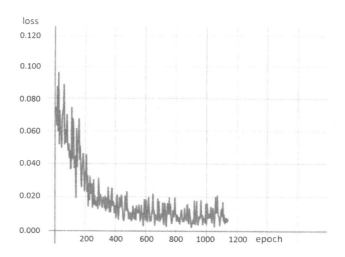

Fig. 6. Training loss of the proposed method.

At present, we made the first attempt on ModelNet10 [5], shapes of which are well annotated and can be downloaded from the web. ModelNet10 contains 10 shape categories with 4,899 unique shapes. The authors provide a training and testing split on the website. Meanwhile, all shapes have been aligned in their canonical orientation. We assume every shape keeping this orientation for fair comparison.

We report the performance of our method on all shapes in the test set with instance-level accuracy, which is the ratio of the number of shapes that are classified correctly to the number of the total shapes in the test set. Figure 7 shows the comparison of the performance of the state-of-the-art model-based methods for shape recognition. It can be seen that So-Net [8] with the accuracy 95.7% achieves the best performance. Our method outperforms 3D ShapeNets [5] and VoxNet [6] and gets the comparable performance to VRN [7], 93.5% vs. 93.6 instance-level accuracy. However, VRN averages predictions across 24 rotated copies of each input shape, while our method achieves such high performance without any strategy of data augmentation.

Time steps T in the proposed method is a super parameter and it determines how many subvolumes need to be processed before emit the classification predication. Recurrent neural network uses the same parameters and network for different time steps, so that the total number of parameters will not expand with the increase of T. Figure 8 shows the best accuracy our method obtained on ModelNet10 with different time steps T from 1 to 10. It can be seen that the performance can quickly converge within few time steps. In our experiments, the model achieves the best accuracy 93.5% on ModelNet10 with $T = 8$.

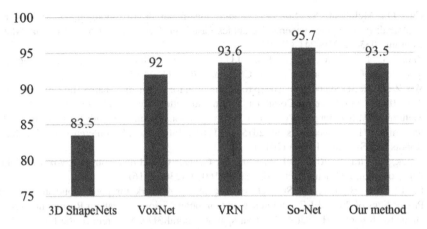

Fig. 7. Comparison of the performance of model-based methods.

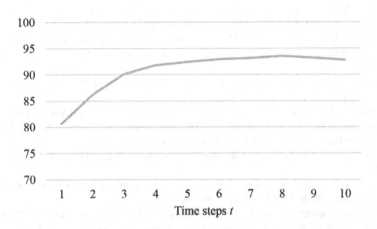

Fig. 8. Accuracy on ModelNet10 with different time steps T from 1 to 10

Acknowledgment. This work was partially supported by the National Natural Science Foundation of China (No. 61373135, No. 61672299), Natural Science Foundation of Jiangsu Province of China (No. BK20160913) and National Engineering Laboratory for Logistics Information Technology, YuanTong Express co. LTD.

References

1. Su, H., Maji, S., Kalogerakis, E., Learned-Miller, E.: Multiview convolutional neural networks for 3D shape recognition. In: Proceedings of International Conference on Computer Vision (2015)
2. Deng, J., Dong, W., Socher, R., Li, L.J., Li, K., Fei-Fei, L.: ImageNet: a large-scale hierarchical image database. In: Proceedings of IEEE Conference on Computer Vision and Pattern Recognition (2009)

3. Cui, Q., McIntosh, S., Sun, H.: Identifying materials of photographic images and photorealistic computer generated graphics based on deep CNNs. CMC: Comput. Mater. Continua **055**(2), 229–241 (2018)
4. Zhou, S., Liang, W., Li, J., Kim, J.U.: Improved VGG model for road traffic sign recognition. CMC: Comput. Mater. Continua **57**(1), 11–24 (2018)
5. Wu, Z., et al.: 3D ShapeNets: a deep representation for volumetric shapes. In: Proceedings of 2015 IEEE Conference on Computer Vision and Pattern Recognition (2015)
6. Maturana, D., Scherer, S.: VoxNet: a 3D convolutional neural network for real-time object recognition. In: Proceedings of 2015 IEEE/RSJ International Conference on Intelligent Robots and Systems (IROS) (2015)
7. Brock, A., Lim, T., Ritchie, J., Weston, N.: Generative and discriminative voxel modeling with convolutional neural networks. arXiv:1608.04236 (2016)
8. Li, J., Chen, B., Lee, G.: SO-Net: self-organizing network for point cloud analysis. In: Proceedings of 2018 IEEE Conference on Computer Vision and Pattern Recognition (2018)
9. Hara, K., Kataoka, H., Satoh, Y.: Can spatiotemporal 3D CNNs retrace the history of 2D CNNs and ImageNet. In: Proceedings of 2018 IEEE Conference on Computer Vision and Pattern Recognition (2018)
10. He, K., Zhang, X., Ren, S., Sun, J.: Deep residual learning for image recognition. In: Proceedings of 2016 IEEE Conference on Computer Vision and Pattern Recognition (2016)
11. Vinyals, O., Ravuri, S.V., Povey, D.: Revisiting recurrent neural networks for robust ASR. In: 2012 IEEE International Conference on Acoustics, Speech and Signal Processing (ICASSP) (2012)
12. Soomro, K., Zamir, A.R., Shah, M.: UCF101: a dataset of 101 human actions classes from videos in the wild. arXiv:1212.0402 (2012)
13. Donahue, J., Hendricks, A., Guadarrama, S., Rohrbach, M.: Long-term recurrent convolutional networks for visual recognition and description. In: Proceedings of 2015 IEEE Conference on Computer Vision and Pattern Recognition (2015)
14. Hochreiter, S., Schmidhuber, J.: Long short-term memory. Neural Comput. **9**(8), 1735–1780 (1997)
15. Williams, R.J.: Simple statistical gradient-following algorithms for connectionist reinforcement learning. Mach. Learn. **8**(3–4), 229–256 (1992)
16. Wierstra, D., Foerster, A., Peters, J., Schmidhuber, J.: Solving deep memory POMDPs with recurrent policy gradients. In: Proceedings of International Conference on Artificial Neural Networks (2007)
17. Collobert, R., Kavukcuoglu, K., Farabet, C.: Torch7: a Matlab-like environment for machine learning. In: BigLearn, NIPS Workshop (2011)
18. Léonard, N., Waghmare, S., Wang, Y., Kim, J.-H.: RNN: recurrent library for torch. arXiv preprint arXiv:1511.07889 (2015)

WSN Multi-hop Routing Algorithm Based on Path Quality Comparison in New Energy Consumption Distance Node Relation Model

Huizong Li[1], Xiagnqian Wang[2(✉)], Bin Ge[2], Jie Wang[2], Yujie Ma[2], Chaoyu Yang[2], and Haixia Gui[2]

[1] Nanyang Normal University, Nanyang 473061, China
[2] Anhui University of Science and Technology, Huainan 232001, China
xqwaust@163.com

Abstract. The wireless sensor network is an important technology of the Internet of things. In the sensor network, the limited energy and uneven distribution of nodes lead to unbalanced load of nodes, and reduce the quality of network and the survival time. In order to eliminate the lack of space distance relationships between two nodes, this paper makes an improvement to the node relation model and proposes the concept of Energy Consumption Distance (ECD). According to the relation model, a multi-hop routing algorithm based on path goodness degree (MRPGD) is proposed. The core idea of the algorithm is that the path lifetime combines with the data redundancy to form the link quality index after the path failure, and the link quality index is the path goodness degree (PGD). The source node uses the higher PGD path to return data, and accurately calculates the transmission paths of all nodes in the network, which can completely draw the network topology. This method can effectively suppress the hot spots in the network and effectively prolong the lifetime. The results show that the proposed algorithm has a 36% increase in the network lifetime compared with the related algorithms.

Keywords: WSN · Routing · Energy Consumption Distance · Link lifetime

1 Introduction

WSN is an important technology of the Internet of things, which is composed by many sensors. WSN plays a vital role in the fields of object tracking, military reconnoitering, biological conservation, etc. Limited by the volume of senor nodes, the energy carried by a single senor node is very little, and the node's energy cannot get a timely supplement because the senor nodes are usually deployed in complex environments. Many scholars propose different solutions from different research perspectives. For example, in data aggregation field, Mohanty et al. propose an energy efficient and unstructured data aggregation and delivery protocol, named ESDAD [1]. ESDAD is utilized to determine the costly functional calculations of an unstructured next hop node. ESDAD can accurately calculate the waiting time of packets on every intermediate node, which makes the data aggregating has efficiently on routing paths. For another example, in sleeping algorithm field, Mostafaei et al. propose a sleep scheduling algorithm, named

© Springer Nature Switzerland AG 2019
X. Sun et al. (Eds.): ICAIS 2019, LNCS 11634, pp. 351–361, 2019.
https://doi.org/10.1007/978-3-030-24271-8_32

PCLA, which relies on learning automata to realize [2]. The main idea of PCLA is that the quantity of activated sensors is minimized to cover the interesting sections, and the connectivity of sensors is preserved perfectly. In addition, there are many other technologies are utilized to solve this question, such as secondary node [3], multi-sink coordination [4], and mobile agent [5].

Such solutions have great limitations for improving network lifetime and balancing nodes load. For example, PCLA algorithm still reduces the perception range of the network when it reduces the network traffic to improve the network lifetime. Recent years, to improving network lifetime and balancing nodes load, many researchers make great efforts in improving the network protocol, in which clustering algorithm is the research focus. Early, Heinzelman et al. propose a clustering routing algorithm, LEACH [6]. LEACH algorithm optimizes the network communication architecture in some ways, and eliminates hot pints in the network by introducing the mechanism of Rotary. However, this routing algorithm utilizes probability and threshold to judgment the cluster head, which leads that the cluster head far away from sink nodes in the network will consume more power, and leads that the node load is not balance. There are also many improved protocols based on LEACH, such as energy efficient routing protocol TEEN [7], self-adaptive periodic energy efficient routing protocol APTEEN, energy efficient data protocol PEGASIS, and so on. Besides these clustering algorithms, there are many other algorithms are proposed to solve the application problems [8, 9].

The classical and newer algorithms by improving the network protocol to promote the network lifetime are briefly introduced on the above. The existing routing algorithms mainly utilize the space distance [10–12] to describe the relationship between two nodes. This relation model depends on GPS position. Therefore, the production costs of nodes will be increased. Beyond that, because electromagnetic waves have different reflection and attenuation in different transmission mediums, the space distance applied in practical scenarios is very limited. In order to eliminate the communication's adverse effects caused by network deployment environment, and save the complex distance measurement soft hardware, the Energy Consumption Distance (*ECD*), namely the communication energy consumption of each unit data, is utilized for replacing the space distance to describe the relationships of nodes.

2 Model Construction

2.1 Network Model Hypothesis

H1: In target area, N wireless sensors distribute randomly in the range of a circle, where the center of this circle is the Sink node and the radius of this circle is R.

H2: Each node including Sink node has a unique identifier, namely *ID*.

H3: All source nodes (ordinary nodes) have the same data processing ability and communication ability, and have the same sensing data in unit time.

H4: Data transmission power $(0 - p_{max})$ can be adjusted.

H5: Sink node has infinite energy and strong data processing ability. Source nodes have limited energy and the initial energy of them is same.

2.2   Node Relation Model

In this paper, an energy consumption distance (*ECD*) node relation model is proposed. The core idea of this model is that the data transmission power of nodes in the system is equally divided into n segments, which are sorted from small to large in sequence, and the sequence is $M_1, M_2, \ldots, M_n$. If the data transmission power of which a_i sends to a_j is within M_k, the *ECD* from a_i to a_j can be represented as $ECD(i,j)$, and its calculation formula is shown in formula (1).

$$ECD(a_i, a_j) = P(M_k) = \frac{p_{max}}{n} k \tag{1}$$

According to the symmetry of radio transmission, if node a_j is in the M_k field of node a_i, node a_i must also be in the M_k field of node a_j. We can draw the conclusion as shown in formula (2).

$$ECD(a_i, a_j) = ECD(a_j, a_i) \tag{2}$$

ECD list is the basis of the link selection. Formula (1) and formula (2) give the expression of *ECD* and its property, and provide parameters to sink node for building the *ECD* list. The element structure of the *ECD* list is shown in Fig. 1, and the *ECD* list can reflect the connection relationships of any nodes that can be connected. The elements of the *ECD* list include the *ID*, the Energy (*E*), and the Energy Consumption Distance (*ECD*) of the two connected nodes, and the information is necessary and complete to the link selection.

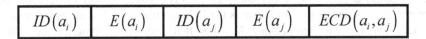

$ID(a_i)$	$E(a_i)$	$ID(a_j)$	$E(a_j)$	$ECD(a_i,a_j)$

Fig. 1. The structure of *ECD* list

According to the symmetry of *ECD* (formula 2), if a network has N source nodes, we can find that the final constructed *ECD* list has $C_N^2 + N$ element items, including N relationships for each source node to Sink node. When the senor nodes are arranged and do not move, which means that *ECD* list only need to update the residual energy of nodes each time, and do not need to update the *ECD* information of nodes at every moment. The structure of *ECD* list effectively saves the nodes energy and improves the response speed of the network.

2.3   Energy Consumption Model

The related energy consumption algorithms mainly adopt the wireless communication energy model proposed by Heinzelman et al. On the basis of Heinzelman's model, an improved model combined the formula (1) is proposed in this paper. The improved energy consumption model expressions are shown as follow.

(i) Energy consumption of sending node a_i is shown in formula (3).

$$E_T\left(l, ECD\left(a_i, a_j\right)\right) = l \cdot ETX + l\frac{ECD\left(a_i, a_j\right)}{L} \tag{3}$$

(ii) Energy consumption of receiving node is shown in formula (4).

$$E_R(l) = l \cdot ERX \tag{4}$$

Where L represents the amount of data transferred in unit time, l represents the amount of data in which a_i sends to a_j, ETX represents the energy consumption in unit data circuit of the data sending node, and ERX represents the energy consumption in unit data circuit of the data receiving node.

3   The Multi-hop Routing Algorithm Based on the Path Goodness Degree

The multiple hop routing sensor network is composed by links, and two links will be interacted mutually by common nodes. During network operation, for any source node in the network, there is one link to overload this node's perceived data and sent data to Sink node. A routing algorithm (MRPGD) is proposed in this paper, and the core idea of the MRPGD is that all source nodes in the network utilize the path contrast strategy to select the best quality link. To eliminate hot spots caused by paths crossing, the process of link selecting is executed continually. The implementation of the path contrast strategy is quantifying paths and contrasting them. Here, we define Q as the path goodness degree to quantify the path quality. Now, we will analyze the two important parameters of Q, which one is the link survival time T, and the other one is the node average data redundancy R. After that, we will summarize the routing implement algorithm based on Q.

3.1   The Analysis of Link Model

The link model constructed by ECD relations among nodes is shown in Fig. 2. Where the longitudinal direction represents the residual energy of nodes, and the transverse direction represents the ECD relations in nodes. It should be pointed out that the ECD in nodes of this model does not apply to the arithmetic addition operations. For example, assuming there are three nodes a_i, a_j, and a_k, according to the formula (1), we can draw the conclusion that $ECD\left(a_i, a_j\right) \neq ECD\left(a_i, a_j\right) + ECD\left(a_j, a_k\right)$. This model provides an intuitive analysis for the link survival time T and the node average data redundancy R.

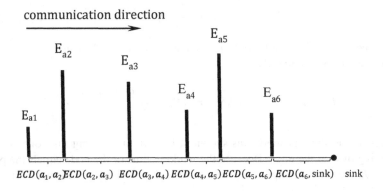

Fig. 2. The link model without data fusion

3.2 The Link Survival Time

The quality of a link is decided by the nodes life in this link. If the survival time of each node is relatively longer in this link, it shows that this link can undertake much more data relay transmission service. Assuming that there are m source nodes in the link, the link survival time can be acquired by analyzing the energy consumption model and the link model (as shown in Fig. 2) in the network.

Definition 1: The link survival time T represents the running time when the link does not have any dead node, l_R represents the receiving data of node a_n when the link runs stably in t time, and l_n represents the sensing data of node a_n in t time.

According to energy consumption model, the energy consumption E_n of the node a_n equals the sum of the data receiving energy consumption E_R and the data sending energy consumption E_T. Leaded l_R and l_n into E_n, we can acquire the expression of E_n as shown in formula (5).

$$E_n = E_R(l_R) + E_T[(l_R + l_n), ECD(a_n, a_{n+1})] \tag{5}$$

Introduced formulas (3) and (4) into formula (5), the energy consumption E_n of the node a_n in the link can be further inferred, and its expression is shown in formula (6).

$$E_n = l_R \cdot ERX + (l_R + l_n) \cdot ETX + (l_R + l_n)\frac{ECD(a_n, a_{n+1})}{L} \tag{6}$$

According to the hypothesis of the network model, the sensing information of all nodes in the network is same. Also considering the state without data fusion in information retransmission process, the conclusion can be inferred that l_R should be represented as the sum of the information sensing amount of the former $n - 1$ nodes except the node a_n in the link. And l_n represents the self-information sensing amount of the node a_n in the link. Therefore, the relation expression between l_R and l_n can be shown in formula (7).

$$l_R = (n-1)l_n \tag{7}$$

Introduced formula (7) into formula (6), the expression of E_n can be further inferred again as shown in formula (8).

$$E_n = l_n\left[(n-1)\cdot ERX + n\cdot(ETX) + \frac{ECD(a_n, a_{n+1})}{L}\right] \tag{8}$$

According to the link model (as shown in Fig. 2), the running time of the link t is the working time of the node. Because the working time of the node equals the product of l_n and L, the relation expression between t and l_n is shown in formula (9).

$$l_n = t\cdot L \tag{9}$$

Introduced formula (9) into formula (8), the relation expression between E_n and t can be inferred as shown in formula (10).

$$E_n = t[(n-1)ERX\cdot L + ETX\cdot L + ECD(a_n, a_{n+1})] \tag{10}$$

Based on the above, the relationship between the link lifetime and the node energy consumption can be obtained under the link stable running condition (definition 1). When the network run t_n time ago, and the energy $E(n)$ of the node a_n is exhausted, we call t_n is the max survival time of the node a_n in the link. Therefore, t_n and $E(n)$ are suitable for formula (10). Introduced t_n and $E(n)$ into formula (10), the expression can be acquired as shown in formula (11).

$$t_n = \frac{E(n)}{(n-1)ERX\cdot L + n\cdot[ETX\cdot L + ECD(a_n, a_{n+1})]} \tag{11}$$

By analyzing the Fig. 2, we know that the link is composed of limited nodes. From source node to sink node, if an arbitrary node failed, we can judge that the link is dead. Therefore, the link's survival time T should be the minimum of all nodes max survival time. The expression of T is shown in formula (12).

$$T = \min\{t_1, t_2, \cdots, t_n\} \tag{12}$$

3.3   The Link Average Data Redundancy

The link average data redundancy means the average value of the non-failed node's remaining communication data when the link loses its effectiveness. The expression of the average data redundancy R is shown in formula (13).

$$R = \frac{1}{n}\sum_{i=0}^{n} L(t_i - t_k) \tag{13}$$

Suppose a_k is the least longevity node in the link, therefore, $L(t_i - t_k)$ represents the data amount of which the node a_i sends to the next node when the node a_k loses its effectiveness.

The path goodness degree (PGD) is represented as $Q(T, R)$. For the two paths of the same source node, the PGD are as $Q_1(T_1, R_1)$ and $Q_2(T_2, R_2)$ respectively, and the expression of the comparison algorithm is shown in formula (14).

$$
\left.\begin{array}{l} T_1 < T_2 \\ T_1 = T_2 \&\& R_1 < R_2 \end{array}\right\} Q_1 < Q_2 \\
\left.\begin{array}{l} T_1 > T_2 \\ T_1 = T_2 \&\& R_1 > R_2 \end{array}\right\} Q_1 > Q_2
\tag{14}
$$

If the survival time and the average data redundancy of two links or more links are equal, namely $T_1 = T_2 \&\& R_1 = R_2$. Which means the link quality is same. To protected the Uniqueness of the link selection and the rigorism of the algorithm, and to reduce the complexity of the algorithm, the link of which firstly acquires the Q value is utilized as the data transmission path of this sources node.

4 Simulation Experiment

In order to evaluate the performance of the algorithm, this paper uses MATLAB R2016a as the experimental platform to evaluate the proposed MRPGD algorithm, and simulates the three algorithms LEACH, DEEC, UCDP [13] under the same experimental conditions. For a better discussion, we control the maximum path length of the MRPGD algorithm as 2 and 5 to form the MRPGD-2 and MRPGD-5 algorithms.

The experiment is divided into two groups. The first group of experiments is used to test the survival of the nodes of the four algorithms in the effective time of the network (this article assumes that 50% of the nodes are dead network failure). The second group of experiment compares the standard deviation of the node's transmission data.

4.1   Unified Energy Consumption Model and Parameter Settings

Since the routing algorithm proposed in this paper is based on the node ECD relationship model, any two nodes in the implementation only need to obtain the energy consumption distance value through the tentative connection. The implementation of LEACH, DEEC, and UCDP algorithms relies on node coordinates. Free space and multipath attenuation energy consumption models are used by this algorithm. The relationship expression of two modes is shown in formula (15).

$$
E_T(l, d) = \begin{cases} l \cdot ETX + l \cdot Efs \cdot d^2, d < d_0 \\ l \cdot ETX + l \cdot Emp \cdot d^4, d \geq d_0 \end{cases}
\tag{15}
$$

$$
E_R(l) = l \cdot ERX
$$

In order to ensure the consistency of the environment of the two algorithms, a unified spatial distance relationship model is used in the experiment. Therefore, the reference relationship between the ECD and the spatial distance d needs to be established, which is shown in formula (16).

$$ECD = \begin{cases} L \cdot Efs \cdot d^2, d < d_0 \\ L \cdot Emp \cdot d^4, d \geq d_0 \end{cases} \tag{16}$$

The simulation parameters of reference [1], the experimental parameters are defined as shown in the following Table 1.

Table 1. WSN simulation parameter

Parameter name	Value	Unit
Network_area	$R = 200$ m $O = (200, 200)$ m	Node distribution area
N	1. 100	2. Number of nodes
E	3. 1 J	4. Initial energy of the node
Sink_xy	5. (200, 200) m	6. Sink node coordinates
ETX	7. 50 Nj/bite	8. RF energy consumption coefficient
ERX	9. 50 Nj/bite	10. Receive data energy dissipation factor
Efs	11. 10 Pj/(bite * m^4)	12. Power amplifier circuit energy factor
Emp	13. 0.0013 Pj/(bite * m^4)	14. Power amplifier circuit energy factor
d_0	15. 87.7 m	16. Threshold
pack	17. 6400 bite	18. Datagram size

Before the experiment, firstly, N nodes are generated in Network area (Table 1) and randomly deployed, so that a unified node distribution parameter can be generated. Then, under the same simulation parameters and the distribution parameters of the node, the LEACH algorithm, DEEC algorithm, UCDP algorithm and the proposed algorithm are simulated respectively. The unified node distribution parameters can ensure the fairness of the experimental results analysis.

4.2 Node Lifetime Within the Network Validity

Figure 3 reflects the relationship between the failed nodes and the network running time in the effective time of the network. The figure shows that the first dead node of the LEACH and DEEC algorithms appears in 100 rounds. Compared with the UCDP algorithm and the MRPGD algorithm proposed in this paper, the first node death time is significantly earlier. Analysis of LEACH algorithm shows that although the algorithm adopts a certain energy equalization strategy (network clustering and cluster head rotation), it is limited by the random selection of cluster heads, which is easy to generate hotspots. Although the DEEC algorithm optimizes the election of cluster heads based on the LEACH algorithm, the probability of occurrence of hotspots is reduced. It can be seen from the figure that the first dead node in the algorithm appears 41 times later than LEACH, and the network survival time is extended by 68 rounds. The UCDP algorithm has a greater improvement in LEACH and DEEC than the LEACH and DEEC in the first node, mainly due to its distributed clustering strategy using dynamic partition load balancing. In the process of clustering, the residual energy and the "integrated distance factor" are fully considered, and the nodes in the network are divided into common nodes, routing nodes and head nodes; effectively taking advantage of multi-hop routing.

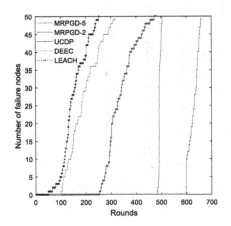

Fig. 3. The relationship between the failed nodes and the network running time in the effective time of the network

The first node dead time of the proposed algorithm is significantly longer than the other three algorithms, and the network lifetime is longer than other algorithms. The result is that the algorithm accurately calculates the link quality. The precise link selection makes the nodes with lower energy not forward data for other nodes, and the node will get the services of other nodes in the network to the maximum extent.

4.3   Energy Balance

The second set of experiments is a comparative discussion of the standard deviation of node data transmission in the network effective time by various algorithms. The definition of standard deviation is shown in formula (17).

$$a = \sqrt{\frac{\sum_{i=1}^{n}(K_i - u)}{n}} \tag{17}$$

Here, the n represents the number of data-aware nodes in the network's effective time, and K_i represents the data-aware amount of node a_i. The average data perception of nodes within the network is $u = \left(\sum_{i=1}^{n} K_i\right)/n$. It can be seen from the above definition that the standard deviation can directly reflect the difference in the perceived amount of node data in each network effective time, and can be used as an important evaluation basis for node load balancing in the network. It can be seen from Fig. 4 that the MRPGD-5 algorithm proposed in this paper is one order of magnitude lower than the other three algorithms, and the MRPGD-2 is even lower. This shows that the MRPGD algorithm performs better in controlling load balancing.

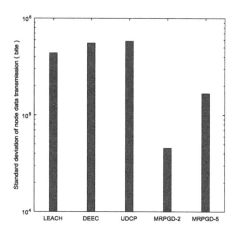

Fig. 4. Standard deviation of node data transmission in different algorithms

5 Conclusion

This paper proposes a novel *ECD* relationship model, which effectively solves the problem of the spatial distance relationship of nodes–non-standard attenuation of signals and node inability to locate under complex conditions. Discussed the classic algorithms for solving load imbalance problems in the field of WSN, as well as the latest research results. And proposed a multi-hop routing algorithm based on path superiority. The core idea of the algorithm is to use path lifetime and path data redundancy as the optimal number to select the best data transmission path for the source node. Although the algorithm proposed in this paper shows better performance advantages in simulation experiments, but with the wider application of network, the diversity and complexity of network structure increase. In order to better adapt to the new form of sensor network, such as heterogeneous network, multi-Sink node, event-driven, etc. The next step is to make improvements to the needs of the algorithm in different network environments, making it more suitable for practical situations.

Acknowledgments. This work is supported by the National Natural Science Foundation of China (No. 51474007, 51874003, 61703005), the MOE Humanities and Social Science Research on Youth Foundation of China (No. 13YJCZH077), and the Natural Science Foundation of Anhui Province of China (NO. 1808085MG221). The authors are grateful to the anonymous referee for a careful checking of the details and for helpful comments that improved this paper.

References

1. Mohanty, P., Kabat, M.R.: Energy efficient structure-free data aggregation and delivery in WSN. Egypt. Inform. J. **17**(3), 273–284 (2016)
2. Mostafaei, H., Montieri, A., Persico, V.: A sleep scheduling approach based on learning automata for WSN partialcoverage. J. Netw. Comput. Appl. **80**(C), 67–78 (2017)
3. Bakr, B.A., Lilien, L.T.: Extending lifetime of wireless sensor networks by management of spare nodes. Proc. Comput. Sci. **34**, 493–498 (2014)
4. Shi, X.-B., Zhang, Y., Zhao, B.: Discrete multi-objective optimization of particle swarm optimizer algorithm for multi-agents collaborative planning. J. Commun. **37**(6), 29–37 (2016)
5. Zhang, X.-W., Shen, L., Jiang, Y.-F.: Optimizing path selection of mobile Sink nodes in mobility-assistant WSN. J. Commun. **34**(2), 85–93 (2013)
6. Heinzelman, W.R., Chandrakasan, A.: Energy-efficient communication protocol for wireless microsensor networks. Adhoc Sens. Wirel. Netw. **2**(10), 10–18 (2000)
7. Manjeshwar, A., Agrawal, D.P.: TEEN: a routing protocol for enhanced efficiency in wireless sensor networks. In: International Parallel & Distributed Processing Symposium, pp. 189–194. IEEE Computer Society (2001)
8. Wang, J., Ju, C., Gao, Y., Sangaiah, A.K., Kim, G.J.: A PSO based energy efficient coverage control algorithm for wireless sensor networks. CMC Comput. Mater. Continua **56**(3), 433–446 (2018)
9. Jaideep, K., Kamaljit, K.: A fuzzy approach for an IoT-based automated employee performance appraisal. CMC: Comput. Mater. Continua **53**(1), 23–36 (2017)
10. Zhang, D., Zhao, C., Li, G.: A kind of routing protocol based on forward-aware factor for energy balance. Acta Electronica Sinica **42**(1), 113–118 (2014)
11. Weng, C.E., Lai, T.W.: An energy-efficient routing algorithm based on relative identification and direction for wireless sensor networks. Wireless Pers. Commun. **69**(1), 253–268 (2013)
12. Du, H., Li, Q., Ding, G.: The research of AODV routing protocol based on link quality and node energy in WSN. Chin. J. Sens. Actuators **29**(7), 1042–1048 (2016)
13. Sun, Y., Peng, J., Liu, T.: Uneven clustering routing protocol based on dynamic partition for wireless sensor network. J. Commun. **1**, 198–206 (2014)

Tobacco Intelligent Management System Based on Internet of Things

Lining Liu, Pingzeng Liu$^{(\boxtimes)}$, Chao Zhang, Xueru Yu,
Jianyong Zhang, Yang Li, and Jainghang Fu

Shandong Agricultural University, Tai'an 271018, China
lpz8565@126.com

Abstract. In the context of the information age, Internet of Things technology has become the best way to change traditional farming methods. A tobacco intelligent management system suitable for various working environments such as tobacco cultivation and processing is developed based on the analysis of the actual tobacco planting process of the current tobacco company and combined with the current Internet of Things technology. The purpose of the system is to improve the current tobacco planting management level, improve the scientific tobacco leaf quality analysis standards, and further strengthen the effective supervision of tobacco leaf processing. The system realizes real-time monitoring and visual display of each link information through a unified network platform, and provides scientific guidance analysis for users. The system operation results show that the system has good environmental adaptability and stability.

Keywords: Internet of Things (IOT) · Tobacco ·
Flue-cured tobacco · Intelligent management

1 Introduction

In recent years, with the transformation of science and technology and people's consumption consciousness, high-quality products have become the new demand of consumers. With the rapid development of the tobacco industry and the widespread application of the current Internet of Things technology, people began to consciously apply the Internet of Things technology to different aspects of the tobacco industry to improve the production efficiency and quality of tobacco leaves, thereby improving economic efficiency. In this process, people have encountered various problems, such as low information perception accuracy and insecure information transmission. In response to the above problems, scholars from various countries have proposed different solutions and developed a variety of practical systems for different needs. The research results are mainly based on the information perception of logistics industry and warehousing environment, and have achieved relatively gratifying results under the efforts of scholars from various countries [1–3].

Liu et al. [4] systematically analyzed the importance and necessity of the Internet of Things information perception and transmission technology represented by RFID technology in realizing the comprehensive perception, comprehensive coverage and comprehensive control of tobacco intelligent management, by analyzing the future

© Springer Nature Switzerland AG 2019
X. Sun et al. (Eds.): ICAIS 2019, LNCS 11634, pp. 362–372, 2019.
https://doi.org/10.1007/978-3-030-24271-8_33

RFID technology. The application of the Internet of Things to build a beautiful blueprint for the intelligent management of the tobacco industry; Ling et al. [5] proposed to use the Internet of Things to develop a tobacco anti-counterfeiting and quality traceability system to improve the level of tobacco anti-counterfeiting and achieve accurate traceability of tobacco quality. Through the development of chaotic encryption algorithm for RFID, the data model of tobacco anti-counterfeiting and quality traceability system is established to realize the monitoring and tracking of the production, circulation and sales of tobacco products, improve the level of tobacco anti-counterfeiting and achieve accurate traceability of tobacco quality; Based on the actual needs of Chongqing Tobacco Company, Wu et al. [6] explored and established a set of Lean Logistics Management System for Tobacco Lean from three aspects: optimizing business process, enriching quality data collection means and improving logistics tracking. It has achieved remarkable results in standardizing tobacco purchase order, improving operation efficiency, reducing labor and cost. The establishment of the system laid the foundation for the realization of comprehensive lean tobacco production.

Based on the above research, it is not difficult to find that people have achieved more achievements in the automation and intelligence of tobacco production process [7–13]. In particular, it has made outstanding achievements in logistics management, tobacco storage, and traceability of finished products. The production and processing of tobacco leaves is a very complicated process. It also involves a large number of complex production and processing processes, especially in the intelligentization and automation of high-quality tobacco cultivation and selection, processing, etc., which still needs improvement. The cultivation of high-quality tobacco leaves determines the quality of tobacco leaves and the yield and quality of high-end products. Its selection determines the proportion of products in the final tobacco products. The tobacco processing process determines the number of high quality tobacco leaves in the final product. Digital, intelligent production, classification and processing methods help tobacco companies optimize product mix, increase economic income, and build high-end brands.

2 The Demand

Tobacco companies began to focus on the automation and intelligence of tobacco planting management. They hope to achieve efficient and precise management of tobacco leaf cultivation, processing and warehousing through scientific means. At present, the research on tobacco intelligent management system mainly focuses on some aspects of tobacco production and processing. It lacks comprehensive and in-depth research on the entire production system of tobacco leaves, and lacks information communication between different systems, which cannot achieve information sharing. In addition, the existing system does not comprehensively acquire information on the basic links, and lacks the collection of key factors. This brings great inconvenience to the later data mining analysis and correlation analysis. The main process of tobacco leaf production is shown in Fig. 1 in combination with the actual needs of enterprises and the scientific needs of later data analysis.

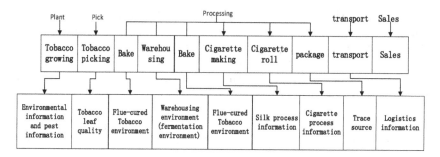

Fig. 1. The process of tobacco production

The system needs to have the following features:

(1) Environmental information perception
Tobacco production, processing, warehousing, transportation and other processes require a certain environmental foundation. The accurate perception of environmental information in different links is the basic guarantee for the healthy growth of tobacco, efficient processing, reliable storage and safe transportation. Because there is a big gap in the basic information that needs to be obtained in different links, and the adaptation environment has great differences, there is a high demand for the adaptability and scalability of the basic system. It is necessary to analyze the actual needs of each link of the enterprise, analyze its specific needs, and develop an information collection system that adapts to different environmental conditions to achieve accurate perception of information in different situations.

(2) Tobacco leaf component perception
The quality of tobacco leaves affects the economic income of tobacco farmers intuitively. The traditional way of judging is based on the experience of tobacco farmers. By observing the size and color of tobacco leaves, the quality of the tobacco leaves is judged. High, difficult to start, easy to make mistakes. Combining the correlation between tobacco leaf components and tobacco leaf quality, combined with the current information acquisition methods of Internet of Things, the paper analyzes the main components of tobacco leaves, digitizes the quality of tobacco leaves, and intuitively tells farmers the results.

(3) Data sharing
Realizing data sharing is the basis for information analysis of the whole process of tobacco production. For example, if the tobacco leaf processing link obtains the main component information of the tobacco leaf, the information such as the baking time and temperature of the tobacco leaf can be adjusted according to the difference of the main components of the tobacco leaf, thereby greatly ensuring the quality of the tobacco leaf and avoiding the quality loss of the artificial processing process. At the same time, the storage environment of the storage and transportation links can be further adjusted according to the basic information after processing the tobacco leaves to provide suitable temperature, humidity and carbon dioxide content for its storage.

(4) Data analysis

The deep mining and correlation analysis of tobacco leaf production data is the fundamental guarantee for the intelligent management of tobacco leaves. The production management of tobacco leaves involves multiple links. Each link has its own needs and characteristics. Combining the actual needs and data foundations of each link manager, it provides scientific environmental guidance and personnel distribution opinions through the use of algorithm models. Early warning and other services.

3 The Design of System

3.1 The Design of Architecture

With the development of science and technology, in order to adapt to the different needs of people, the Internet of Things architecture has been continuously updated with the changes of people's needs [14]. It has passed through the three-layer architecture of the Internet of Things, four-tier architecture, five-tier architecture, and eight layers. Structure and domain structure.

At present, combined with the actual needs of the tobacco industry, according to the results of demand analysis, the tobacco intelligent management system based on the Internet of Things is designed. The system needs to have good characteristics of data perception, expansion, sharing and analysis. According to the above requirements, the existing characteristics of the Internet of Things architecture are analyzed. Finally, the domain structure is selected as the basic framework. According to the specific needs of users, the system architecture is partially adjusted as follows. The specific structure is shown in Fig. 2.

As can be seen from Fig. 2, the system mainly consists of a user domain, a service domain, a resource switching domain, an information processing domain, a sensing control domain, and an object domain. The user domain is the window for the system to display data to the user; the service domain is the key to realize data analysis; the resource exchange domain is the key to realize data sharing; the information processing domain is the key to realize the basic information preprocessing; the sensing control domain is to realize each The core of class traceability information acquisition; the target object domain contains the source object of the information that the system wants to perceive.

3.2 The Design of System Module

The system adopts the current Internet of Things technology, and realizes the scientific guidance of tobacco planting and processing through data analysis and mining technology, thereby realizing the management mode of changing traditional tobacco planting and processing, realizing the scientific, digital planting and management of high-quality tobacco leaves machining. On the basis of efficient collection of data information, the system realizes reliable transmission and sharing of data through resource sharing domains, which facilitates the understanding of each other's basic

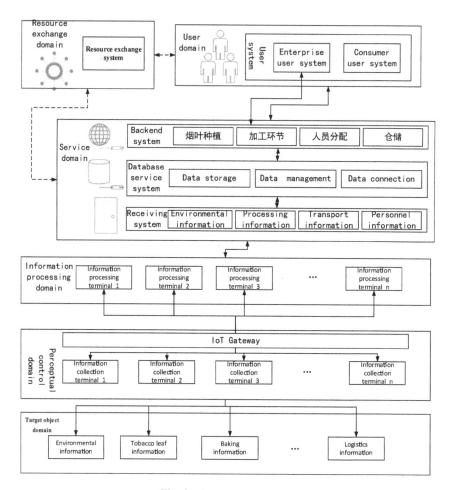

Fig. 2. System architecture

information. The system can be divided into six parts according to the function. The structure framework mainly consists of six parts: user domain, service domain, resource switching domain, information processing domain, sensing control domain and target object domain. The basic sensing object and the control object are allocated in the object domain; the developed system-aware control terminal is allocated in the sensing control domain; the terminal device that performs preliminary classification and summary of the original information is allocated in the information processing domain; The analyzed server and database, and the data pool are allocated in the service domain; the resource exchange domain is the key to realize the server data exchange within each enterprise. It is mainly composed of the Internet; the platform, system, and APP for displaying system analysis results and data information. The program is assigned to the user domain. Its specific composition is shown in Fig. 3.

In order to achieve intelligent management of tobacco planting management, accurate access to basic information is a top priority. The system mainly realizes

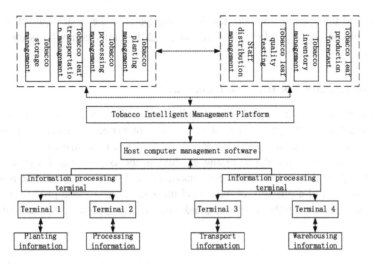

Fig. 3. The design of system function module

accurate acquisition of various information such as environmental information, processing information and warehousing information through research and development of information-aware terminals installed in different links, and provides a comprehensive and stable data source for later data analysis. There are great differences in the types of information and access methods obtained in each link. For example, the information acquisition methods and types of tobacco growing process and tobacco leaf baking process are quite different. In the tobacco growing process, the environment for tobacco growth is mainly obtained through environmental sensors. Information, which is mainly based on illumination, wind speed, air temperature and humidity, combined with pest detection equipment to achieve precise control of the tobacco planting environment; the baking process is to obtain the drying of the tobacco leaves inside the tobacco baking equipment through the weight sensing equipment and the temperature equipment. Roasting state, so that the temperature and time of baking are accurately controlled. In order to realize the real-time transmission and sharing of basic data, the system combines the distance and environment characteristics of data information transmission between various links, and finally selects the combination of wired and wireless to realize the reliable transmission of local area and global data information. On the basis of obtaining basic data, the service domain realizes the scientific analysis of the basic data through data pool and data analysis model, and uses the visualization method to display the analysis result to the user through the user domain, providing scientific analysis guidance for the user.

4 System Implementation

Based on the rational IoT architecture system and the actual Internet of Things technology and big data analysis technology, the system finally designed and completed the tobacco intelligent management system. The system is mainly composed of the upper computer and the upper computer. The lower computer is the basic equipment for the system to obtain the original data information; and the upper computer is the core for data sharing, data analysis and visual display.

4.1   Implementation of the Lower Computer

The lower computer is a general term for all terminal devices that sense information, control, and basic data processing. It is mainly composed of a central processing module, an information sensing module, an information transmission module and a control module. The central processing module is the core of the lower computer, which determines the function and performance of the lower computer. The module is mainly composed of a plurality of functional units such as a central processing unit, a timer, an information number converter, and a trigger. Its specific structure is shown in Fig. 4.

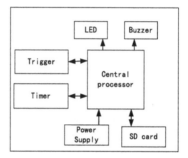

Fig. 4. The structure of lower computer terminal

In addition, the function of the system's information-aware module is determined by the central processing module. According to the difference in information acquired in different links, the central processing module will choose to obtain different types of information, combined with the data types required by the central processor and the field installation environment. Characteristics, the information-aware module will use different sensing devices. For example, the outdoor environmental information acquisition equipment needs to have good waterproof performance and corrosion resistance, while the equipment applied in the warehouse does not need the above performance; Hyperspectral equipment for accurate analysis of blade components, while other components do not require hyperspectral equipment.

The lower position machine for obtaining the tobacco planting environment information, the lower position machine obtains the living environment of the tobacco by intermittently supplying power to ensure the stable operation of the equipment outdoors. In addition, the information obtained by the system mainly includes digital information such as wind speed, air temperature and humidity, soil moisture and other environmental information, and image information mainly based on pest and disease images.

The detection of tobacco leaf components is mainly based on hyperspectral detection equipment. The device uses eight different bands of light to achieve accurate detection of different components of the tobacco leaf. The system adopts a trigger mode. Once a page enters the detection range, the system automatically detects the component content of the blade and provides the user with the level of the leaf based on the analysis result.

The first step in the processing of tobacco leaves when baking leaves is also a very important part. In this link, the lower computer system mainly obtains the temperature of the baking box and the weight change of the internal tobacco leaves, and provides scientific temperature and time for the flue-cured tobacco personnel by analyzing the relationship between the weight change trend of the tobacco leaves and the quality of the tobacco leaves guide.

In addition to the above systems, the lower computer terminal also contains many different types, such as warehousing, transportation, etc. In each link, the system will adjust the specific structure and function of the lower computer according to specific needs to meet the needs of users.

4.2 Implementation of the Host Computer

The host computer is the key and core of the system to achieve data analysis and sharing. The upper computer system is mainly divided into three parts, one is the system platform that presents the data analysis result to the user; the second is the background system that realizes the data analysis, processing and storage; the third is the basic layer service system that realizes the basic data receiving and sharing. Its structure is shown in Fig. 5.

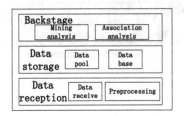

Fig. 5. The structure of upper computer

As can be seen from Fig. 5, the base layer service system is the basis of the host computer system. It acquires the raw data of the lower computer through the data receiving channel, performs basic permissions on it, and stores it as a data pool.

The back-end system is the core of the entire host computer system. Through the pre-recorded algorithm, it analyzes whether the current environmental state is suitable for the growth of tobacco in this period, or whether the current oven temperature is suitable, how long it needs to be baked at this temperature, or the storage environment. Whether it is suitable for long-term storage of tobacco leaves, how long the current stock of tobacco leaves is stored, whether it is suitable for continued storage, and so on.

The system platform will report the environmental information, blade information and production information of each link in the form of graphic and text to the user according to the needs of the user. The user can view the data information according to their own authority, or according to the graphic prompts, the site The device makes adjustments.

5 System Application

At present, the system has passed the laboratory simulation test for half a year and the field test for five months. The experiment shows that the system has good stability and reliability, the experimental data obtained is accurate and reliable, and the automated

(a) The lower computer

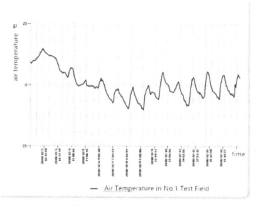

(b) The host computer

Fig. 6. The diagram of system operation

operation process is greatly reduced. The flat rate of human operation is suitable for on-site use. The system adopts a unified information management platform and integrates multiple subsystems including data analysis, monitoring and early warning, personnel management, etc., to facilitate management personnel to fully understand the entire process of tobacco production. The system operation interface is as shown (Fig. 6).

6 Conclusion

(1) The IoT information collection terminal suitable for each link was developed. We fully consider the specific needs of the actual production and processing of tobacco, and combine the traditional farming methods and work habits of tobacco farmers. Finally, the information acquisition system for the lower machine suitable for different tobacco processing links was developed, which realized the accurate perception of different links of tobacco planting, processing, warehousing and transportation. It greatly improves the accuracy and reliability of data information.

(2) The host computer system covering the entire production line was developed. Through the construction of a data sharing and analysis platform covering the whole tobacco production and processing process, the system analysis and deep mining of tobacco pre-production, post-production and post-production information are realized. And the system realizes the scientific sharing of information in all aspects of production. This facilitates the breadth and breadth of data analysis, and further enhances the scientific and comprehensive nature of data analysis.

(3) A component detecting device for the information of the tobacco leaf itself has been developed. The system can obtain the specific composition information of tobacco leaves, and achieve accurate acquisition of tobacco leaf quality information. This makes up for the gap in the current crop information of the tobacco itself. While avoiding human judgment errors, it improves the scientific nature of system analysis and provides valuable data support for the analysis and guidance of later data.

Acknowledgements. This work was financially supported by the following project:

(1) Shandong independent innovation and achievements transformation project (2014ZZCX07106).

References

1. Wang, J., Jiang, M., Dai, S.: Design of outbound and logistics process for tobacco business enterprises based on RFID technology. J. Logist. Sci. **31**(5), 97–100 (2008)
2. He, M.: Development direction of tobacco logistics in China. Co-Op. Econ. Technol. **2011** (9), 67–68 (2011)
3. Zhu, F., Wu, L., Chen, F., et al.: Application and development of intelligent video surveillance terminal in Internet of Things. J. Chin. Acad. Electron. **06**(6), 561–566 (2011)

4. Liu, J., Chen, L.: Application of RFID technology in tobacco Internet of Things. Mod. Bus. Ind. **24**(04), 242–243 (2012)

5. Ling, J., Liu, D., Zhu, Y.: Tobacco anti-counterfeiting and quality traceability system based on Internet of Things. FOOD Ind. **2014**(12), 247–250 (2014)

6. Wu, B., Ma, G., Ai, J.: Exploration and practice of lean logistics management based on Internet of Things Technology——taking Chongqing as an Example. J. Chin. Tob. **23**(5), 114–120 (2017)

7. Xu, Z., Wu, Z., Cai, C., et al.: Application of Internet of Things in modern tobacco agriculture. Anhui Agric. Sci. **40**(1), 603–605 (2012)

8. Sun, W., Zheng, A., Jiao, Y.: Analysis and design of tobacco leaf logistics management system under Internet of Things. Logist. Technol. Appl. **19**(3), 114–116 (2014)

9. Wang, B., Liu, P., Chao, Z., et al.: Research on hybrid model of garlic short-term price forecasting based on big data. CMC **57**(2), 283–296 (2018)

10. Huo, B., He, M.: On the construction of tobacco supply chain logistics. J. Chin. Tob. **20**(2), 1–8 (2014)

11. Yan, M., Cai, W., Wen, Y.: Exploration and practice of deep integration of Hunan tobacco business informationization and industrialization. Chin. Tob. Sinica **21**(2), 90–93 (2015)

12. Shi, C.: A novel ensemble learning algorithm based on D-S evidence theory for IoT security. CMC **57**(3), 635–652 (2018)

13. Ji, X., Jiang, M., Wu, X.: Research on tobacco leaf life cycle management system based on Internet of Things. Logist. Technol. **32**(11), 399–401 (2013)

14. Sun, Q.B., Jie, L., Shan, L.I., et al.: Internet of Things: summarize on concepts, architecture and key technology problem. J. Beijing Univ. Posts Telecommun. **33**(3), 1–9 (2010)

Research on Fault Self Diagnosis Technology of Agricultural Internet of Things Information Collection System

Jianyong Zhang, Pingzeng Liu$^{(\boxtimes)}$, Xueru Yu, and Jianhang Fu

Shandong Agricultural University, Tai'an 271018, China
lpz8565@126.com

Abstract. In order to realize the accurate and effective collection and acquisition of agricultural production environment information by the information acquisition system of the agricultural Internet of Things, the information acquisition system of the agricultural Internet of Things was developed and designed, and the fault self-diagnosis of the whole information acquisition system of the Internet of Things was studied and processed. This paper mainly considers the soft and hard faults of the acquisition system, analyses the causes and classifications of the hard and soft faults, and detects and treats the faults according to their respective problems. The whole set of fault self-diagnosis system of agricultural Internet of Things has been realized in practical application, and the system is stable and reliable. The system can monitor all kinds of faults in the collection system of the Internet of Things in real time, and send short messages to professional technicians for timely maintenance and repair of the faults.

Keywords: The Internet of Things · Information collection ·
Soft fault and hard fault · Fault self diagnosis

1 Introduction

With the rapid development of Internet of Things technology and its popularization and application in agriculture, a large number of information collection systems of Internet of Things in farmland and greenhouse are all over the country. However, due to the harsh agricultural production environment and the complex and changeable climate, the stability and working life of the collection system of the Internet of Things will be affected to a large extent, resulting in the collection of information deviation and lack of problems. In order to solve the problems, on-site fault detection and repair are needed, which costs a lot of time and manpower. Therefore, it is particularly important to study the self-diagnosis technology of system fault.

There are many research on Fault Diagnosis Technology of wireless sensor nodes in the world, but there are few research on Fault Diagnosis Technology of agricultural Internet of Things. Venkataraman [1] proposes a clustering-based fault management mechanism for wireless sensor networks (WSNs) in view of the energy loss type faults of infinite sensor network nodes. When the node faults occur in WSNs, the algorithm

© Springer Nature Switzerland AG 2019
X. Sun et al. (Eds.): ICAIS 2019, LNCS 11634, pp. 373–383, 2019.
https://doi.org/10.1007/978-3-030-24271-8_34

has fast responsiveness and ensures network connectivity, and can prolong the lifetime of the whole WSNs. Naidu et al. [2] established a three-layer feedforward neural network model based on back propagation algorithm, which is suitable for sensor fault diagnosis in first-order linear systems and second-order nonlinear systems. Menke et al. [3] used the method of multi-model adaptive estimation to diagnose sensor faults, and achieved good results. Scholkopf et al. [4] proposed a fault identification method based on Kernel Principal Component Analysis (KPCA). This method maps input variables into high-dimensional space and carries out linear principal component analysis (PCA) in high-dimensional space, which provides a great reference for the research of fault diagnosis methods. Lei et al. [5] proposed a node fault diagnosis algorithm based on rough theory for wireless sensor networks. Rough set theory was applied to simplify the fault attributes, reduce the network overhead in the process of system diagnosis, and detect the hard faults of infinite sensor network nodes by message inquiry. Zhang et al. [6] used Greenhouse Wireless Sensor Network (WSN) as algorithm test system, studied the fault diagnosis and detection methods of WSN nodes by signal principal component analysis method, established the wavelet analysis method to explore the fault location and identification method of WSN nodes, and calculated various factors affecting the operation status of indoor WSN by fuzzy analytic hierarchy process. Determine the weight and establish the WSN health evaluation system, and evaluate the operation state of the system.

At present, there are relatively many research on fault diagnosis of wireless sensor networks, and there are many research on software fault diagnosis technology of information acquisition system of agricultural Internet of Things. There is a lack of research on fault self-diagnosis of the whole set of information acquisition system of agricultural Internet of Things. Combined with the completion of the project, this paper comprehensively summarizes, studies and treats the fault types in the process of collecting information of the agricultural Internet of Things, and realizes the remote monitoring and fault diagnosis of each node equipment of the lower computer by using the management platform of the upper computer of the agricultural Internet of Things [7]. On this basis, the equipment of the agricultural Internet of Things is classified, and judgment methods are found and processed according to different fault types of different equipment. Different methods are used to realize the diagnosis of hard and soft faults, and the application of fault diagnosis technology in the agricultural Internet of Things is realized.

2 System Principle and Problem Analysis

2.1 Work Principle of Information Collection System of Internet of Things

The information collection system based on the Internet of things consists of two parts: the lower computer acquisition terminal and the host computer software. The lower computer acquisition terminal is generally composed of core processor, power supply module, acquisition module, communication module and so on. In this paper, the acquisition terminal uses MSP430F5438 low-power MCU as the core processor, solar panel and battery power supply as the power supply module, various sensors and multi-channel data acquisition card as the acquisition module, GPRS DTU as the communication module, acquisition module and communication module through RS485 and processor string. The information acquisition process of the lower computer acquisition system is shown in Fig. 1.

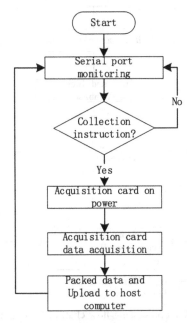

Fig. 1. Flow chart of information acquisition for lower computer

The upper computer software is installed on the target server. After receiving the data uploaded by the lower computer acquisition terminal, the upper computer software is normalized and stored in the corresponding tables in the database. The workflow is shown in Fig. 2.

2.2 Fault Classification and Cause Analysis

The faults of the collection node of the Internet of Things can be divided into two kinds: hard fault and soft fault. Hard fault refers to the situation that the communication can not be achieved due to insufficient power supply and hardware damage. Soft fault refers to the situation that the communication function of the collection system is normal, but the data uploaded appears abnormal in value, format or instantaneous communication fault [8].

Node failure: It is caused by various sensors, hardware design of acquisition card, production defects, external environment and other factors. As far as the hardware structure of sensor and acquisition module is concerned, as long as one component of a sensor node fails, such as the sensor is disturbed by noise, aging itself, the power

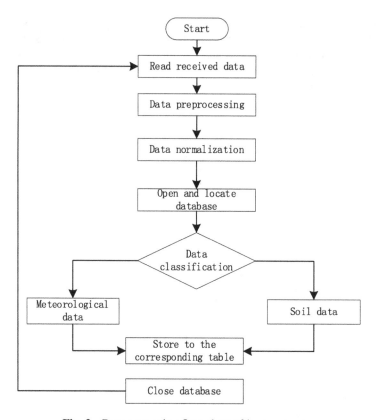

Fig. 2. Data processing flow chart of host computer

supply voltage is insufficient or exhausted, it will lead to the failure or failure of the sensor network acquisition node. If we consider the software design of the acquisition system, it is usually the operating system, programming code, its own defects or errors, which will also cause the failure of wireless sensor nodes.

Network failure: including communication link failure and routing path failure. Communication link failure refers to the fact that the channel between sending node and receiving node can not be established normally under the condition of good communication signal in wireless network, which results in the network communication link being blocked or channel attenuation being too large. Its inducement is closely related to bad environment, interference wave and node movement. Routing path failure is due to the movement or failure of the node, which causes the information of the source node not to be transmitted to the expected node correctly, thus causing data delay, data packet destruction or loss and other phenomena.

Summarize the possible faults. According to the structure, the faults of power supply module mainly include battery damage or loss, solar controller damage. This kind of fault will cause the whole system without power supply or the supply voltage is lower than the rated voltage, so that the whole or part of the system can not work properly. Faults of acquisition module mainly include power failure of acquisition card, faults of acquisition card, faults of sensor, faults of serial communication between acquisition card and processor, etc. The results of such faults include that all or part of the data collected are obviously abnormal. Communication module failures mainly include communication serial port problems, GPRS module failures, weak signals and other issues, which will result in the failure to upload data or scrambling of uploaded data. Processor faults include failure of crystal oscillator, which can lead to failure to process received instructions, failure to send acquisition instructions to acquisition card, and failure to upload data.

According to the classification of soft faults and hard faults, the above faults can be classified and processed, as shown in Table 1.

Table 1. Common faults and attribute definition of WSN nodes

Attribute	Fault performance	Attribute value
P1	Whether the measured nodes are continuous or N cycle without information return	Hard fault
P2	Does the measured node regularly return information?	Hard fault, Soft fault
P3	Can the measured nodes respond to the query order of the sink node?	Soft fault
P4	Change the sending frequency of the collection command and issue whether the query command has response	Soft fault
P5	Are the instructions issued by the sink node correctly executed by the tested nodes?	Soft fault
P6	Collecting data is always zero	Hard fault
P7	Data collection is always full value	Hard fault
P8	...	...
P9	...	...

From the above table, it can be seen that the terminal with hard fault can not send data, while the terminal with soft fault can upload some or all of the information to the server. Therefore, when diagnosing these faults, data can be received from the host computer for fault diagnosis.

3 Improved Design

Through the analysis of the previous part, it can be found that the results of soft fault are all data upload errors, but the failure modes are different, and the manifestations of data errors are also different. When diagnosing, we can judge the fault according to the erroneous form of data received by the host computer, and determine the type and cause of the fault. But the result of hard fault is no data upload, and there are many possible reasons, so it is difficult to determine the specific cause of the fault. To solve this problem, we add a variety of key nodes and key links detection functions from the perspective of system design.

Aiming at the expansibility, reusability, security and reliability of the construction principles of the agricultural Internet of Things architecture, combined with the latest conceptual model of the Internet of Things proposed by the National Standardization Management Committee of China in 2016, it consists of the target object domain, the perceptual control domain, the service delivery domain, the resource exchange domain, the operation and maintenance control domain and the user domain. In the design of fault self-diagnosis for the information acquisition system of the agricultural Internet of Things, the functional domains and corresponding entities of the reference architecture of the Internet of Things are selected, and different functional domains are combined, split and optimized concretely. A functional diagnosis domain is added between the perceptual control domain and the service delivery domain to realize the research and design of fault self-diagnosis for the information acquisition system of the agricultural Internet of Things. The corresponding functions are realized by designing the upper computer and the lower computer respectively. The latest concept model of the Internet of things is shown in Fig. 3.

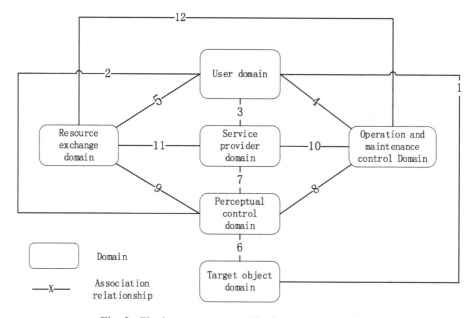

Fig. 3. The latest concept model of the Internet of things

3.1   Processor State Detection

The possible faults of the processor include chip damage, crystal vibration damage and watchdog timer overflow caused by program loopholes. If the chip is damaged, the processor does not run any programs and the system is in a standstill state. If the crystal oscillator is damaged and the system clock will be disordered, the serial program of the timer will be affected, which will cause the system to stop at a certain step and start executing from the main function repeatedly. If a program bug causes the watchdog timer to overflow, the program will start running from the main function again and again. Therefore, the boot instruction is set in the main function. After the system is powered on, the main function first sends a boot instruction to the host computer, indicating that the system has just started.

If the system repeats the main function program due to the above reasons, it will continuously send boot instructions to the host computer. The host computer can judge that this situation belongs to processor failure according to the received instructions. When the fault occurs, its state flow is shown in Fig. 4.

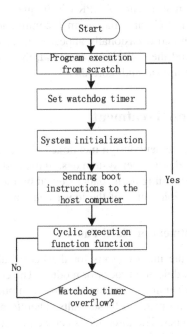

Fig. 4. State flow chart for collecting terminal failure

3.2 System Voltage Detection

The power supply voltage of the IOT information acquisition system is 12 V DC power supply. The solar panels collect electricity and store it in the storage battery. The solar controller is needed to control the output voltage. The 12 V voltage is responsible for supplying power to the main circuit board, acquisition card, sensors and GPRS communication module where the processor is located. In order to keep abreast of the real-time state of the system supply voltage, the system supply voltage is connected to the AD conversion pin of the core processor, so that the system power supply is also regarded as a variable to be collected and uploaded to the host computer with other data to provide data support for detailed fault diagnosis.

3.3 Communication Module Detection

The remote communication module uses H7210 GPRS DTU, which communicates with the central controller through UART serial port. Its Tx pin is connected to P5.5 of the central controller, and its RX pin is connected to P5.4 of the central controller. The DTU uses 12 V power supply, VCC pin is connected to VCC of the central controller, and GND pin is connected to GND of the central controller. Communication module (GPRS DTU) embedded PPP, TCP/IP protocol stack, supports transparent data transmission between RTU and DSC, TCP/UDP link supports heartbeat function, and communicates with PC program through wireless signal. The upper computer can monitor the online status of GPRS DTU in real time. If GPRS is not online, the power supply problem of GPRS may occur. If GPRS is frequently online or dropped, the stability of communication link and the normal communication signal should be detected. If the data transmitted occasionally appears packet loss, the upper computer should resend the data. Send the collection command, the lower machine terminal re acquisition and get data to upload and store data.

4 Fault Diagnosis and Treatment

Through the pertinent improvement design mentioned above, the collection terminal of the Internet of Things provides a better system design method and key data support for accurate fault diagnosis. According to the data received by the upper computer, we can preliminarily judge the possible faults of the lower computer system.

4.1 Diagnosis and Treatment of Hard Faults

From the above analysis, the main reasons for the hard fault include power supply module, communication module and processor module. The common feature is that the acquisition terminal can not transmit data to the host computer. In the last part, corresponding improvements are made to these faults. Therefore, we receive the voltage data through the host computer. The three faults can be judged. The flow chart of hard fault diagnosis is shown in Fig. 5.

4.2 Diagnosis and Treatment of Soft Faults

The cause of soft fault is usually due to the damage of acquisition module, i.e. acquisition card or sensor. The common cause of soft fault is that data is uploaded to the host computer. On the one hand, there will be some obvious fluctuations in some data or data. On the other hand, when the data range exceeds the set threshold, the host computer automatically determines that soft faults occur, including constant deviation faults, fixed faults, jump faults, drift faults and precision decline faults.

According to the various fault types, corresponding fault diagnosis is carried out. Constant deviation fault: refers to a constant deviation between the output value of the sensor and the measured true value. In this case, after a long period of operation of the

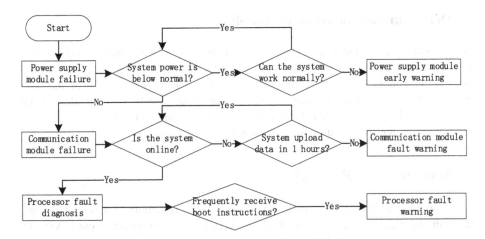

Fig. 5. The flow chart of hard fault diagnosis

system, the specific standards of all kinds of sensors are found, and the calibration and calibration of sensors are carried out.

Fixed fault: the sensor output signal has always been a fixed value. It may be caused by blockage, fouling or internal failure. When the system detects the fault of some kind of sensor or some kind of sensor, the host computer sends short messages to professional technicians in time to maintain or replace the sensor, and retest, calibrate and install the corresponding sensor.

Jump fault: refers to the fault that the output value of the sensor runs randomly at a certain range on the basis of the measured true value. This is usually due to external electromagnetic interference, vibration or poor contact of sensor interfaces. When the system detects a large jump in data, it is necessary to send a short message to the user in time to clean up the electromagnetic interference source near the acquisition system, and to re-contact the interface of the corresponding sensors with faults in the acquisition system.

Drift fault: refers to a fault in which the deviation between the output of the sensor and the real value of the measured variable varies with temperature or time because of temperature change and aging. Due to the complexity and harshness of the agricultural production environment, sensors and other electronic components will have such failures when they work for a long time or are operated artificially improperly. When the system detects such faults in data, it can send short messages to professional technicians to replace the faulty sensors.

4.3   The Initiation Strategy of Diagnostic Mechanism

Because this strategy will increase the workload of the host computer, if it is kept open, it will cause unnecessary redundant workload. Therefore, periodic self-diagnosis can be selected, and the diagnosis cycle can be determined according to the installation time of IOT acquisition equipment, such as opening at a fixed time every day to detect whether there is a fault.

5 Determination of Data Threshold

Since the data are collected every other short period of time, the meteorological data will not change dramatically in a short period of time, but should be a relatively stable process. Therefore, we can use time series model to predict the range of the next acquisition data based on the data collected in previous rounds. If the quality of the model is good, we can predict the range of the next acquisition data more accurately and determine the threshold of the detection data.

6 Summary and Prospect

Based on the field information acquisition system of the agricultural Internet of Things, the fault self-diagnosis of the whole Internet of Things system is carried out in view of the abnormal environmental parameters detected by the host computer. Aiming at the abnormal situation of data asynchronism, time asynchronism and data loss in the data transmission process between wireless communication module and server and data acquisition unit, network fault diagnosis is carried out. On the basis of the information acquisition system of the agricultural Internet of Things, the fault diagnosis function module and the short message reminder function are added to realize the fault self-diagnosis of the power supply module, the acquisition module, the communication module and the processor module of the whole collection system of the Internet of Things. When problems or faults occur in the corresponding modules are detected, the system can send short messages in time to inform professional and technical personnel for the maintenance and repair of the whole system. The results of the normal operation of the system preliminarily verify the practicability and timeliness of the fault self-diagnosis of the information acquisition system of the Agricultural Internet of Things.

I plan to conduct in-depth research in the following aspects:

(1) Study on Spatial-temporal correlation of environmental parameters of Agricultural Internet of things. Spatial-temporal correlation research is carried out. Spatial similarity analysis is based on temporal correlation and spatial similarity analysis. Spatial similarity includes spatial similarity analysis based on homogeneous sensors and spatial similarity analysis based on heterogeneous sensors. The time series prediction algorithm is used to predict the temporal correlation of environmental data, and the spatial similarity of environmental parameters is predicted by using the characteristics of homogeneous and heterogeneous sensors.

(2) Research on sensor fault recognition method based on Spatial-temporal information comparison. correlation research is carried out. Research and design a sensor fault identification method to judge the accuracy of environmental information collected by sensors in the information acquisition system of the Agricultural Internet of Things.

(3) The integrated application and system test for the fault diagnosis function of the information collection system of the Agricultural Internet of things are carried out. For sensor faults, fault detection, fault identification, fault diagnosis and recovery of anomalous data based on temporal and spatial information will be carried out.

Aiming at the network faults and data packet loss in the data transmission process of the agricultural Internet of Things (IOT) information acquisition system, the remote data asynchronous and time asynchronous fault identification and repair will be carried out.

Acknowledgements. The project is funded by Elion Resources Group.

References

1. Venkataraman, G., Emmanuel, S., Thambipillai, S.: A cluster-based approach to fault detection and recovery in wireless sensor networks. In: International Symposium on Wireless Communication Systems (2007)
2. Naidu, S.R., Zafiriou, E., Mcavoy, T.J.: Use of neural networks for sensor failure detection in a control system. IEEE Control Syst. Mag. **10**(3), 49–55 (2002)
3. Menke, T.E., Maybeck, P.S.: Sensor/actuator failure detection in the Vista F-16 by multiple model adaptive estimation. In: American Control Conference, pp. 3135–3141. IEEE Xplore (1993)
4. Scholkopf, B., Smola, A., Muller, K.R.: Kernel principal component analysis. In: Advances in Kernel Methods: Support Vector Learning, pp. 327–352. MIT Press, Cambridge (1999)
5. Lei, L., Dai, C., Wang, H.: Rough set theory based fault diagnosis of node in wireless sensor network. J. Beijing Univ. Ports Telecommun. **4**, 69–73 (2007)
6. Zhang, F.: Indoor wireless sensor network node failure and health diagnosis. University of Jiangsu (2007)
7. Shi, C.: Novel ensemble learning algorithm based on D-S evidence theory for IoT security. Comput. Mater. Continua **57**(3), 635–652 (2018)
8. Wang, J., Ju, C., Gao, Y., Sangaiah, A.K., Kim, G.: A PSO based energy efficient coverage control algorithm for wireless sensor networks. Comput. Mater. Continua **56**(3), 433–446 (2018)

Analysis of Antenna Array Parameter Effect for Massive MIMO Transmission

Lin Guo[1($\boxtimes$)] and Lijun Yang[2]

[1] Key Laboratory of Broadband Wireless Communication
and Sensor Network Technology, Ministry of Education,
School of Modern Posts, National Laboratory of Solid State Microstructures,
Nanjing University of Posts and Telecommunications, Nanjing University,
Nanjing 210003, People's Republic of China
guolin@njupt.edu.cn
[2] College of Internet of Things, School of Computer Science,
Nanjing University of Posts and Telecommunications, Nanjing 210003
People's Republic of China

Abstract. This paper presents a study on beam division multiple access (BDMA) with performance parameters of the antenna array. For this work, firstly we introduce BDMA for massive multiple-input multiple-output (MIMO) transmission. Then the actual antenna model is proposed, and a simple application scenario is established. In the case that antenna parameters are changed, this work shows that the sum-rate simulation results are different. We combine the performance parameters of the antenna with the BDMA channel model of free space, and then we can build the actual network layout. The channel simulations based of the sum-rate will be performed in this paper respectively. The simulation results show that the parameters such as the coupling effect between elements in the antenna array will affect the BDMA channel model of large-scale MIMO systems for typical mobile scenarios, which should be considered in the subsequent channel model analysis.

Keywords: Massive MIMO system · Beam division multiple access (BDMA) · Element coupling · Sum-rate

1 Introduction

In recent years, with the rapid development of wireless communication, it has brought a lot of impact on our lives. But the demand for high speed data communication services is growing at a high speed [1, 2]. For the single input single output system, the channel capacity formula proposed by Shannon C.E. in 1948. It determines the upper limit rate of reliable transmission in noisy channels, which has become a bottleneck of the development of wireless communication system. So MIMO communication system has gained more and more attention and a lot of research in academia. Massive MIMO transmission scheme deploys a large number of antenna elements at the base stations

© Springer Nature Switzerland AG 2019
X. Sun et al. (Eds.): ICAIS 2019, LNCS 11634, pp. 384–393, 2019.
https://doi.org/10.1007/978-3-030-24271-8_35

(BSs) to simultaneously serve multiple user terminals (UTs) and can significantly improve the system spectrum efficiency [4, 5]. The massive MIMO transmission scheme is one of the key technologies to realize high speed broadband wireless communication.

The topic of massive MIMO communication systems was initiated by the prospective research work in [4] which elaborated a multi-cell multi-user time-division duplex (TDD) communication model. The analysis shows that, under the influence of the law of large numbers, the adverse effects of uncorrelated receiver noise and fast fading on communication systems will decrease with the increase of the number of transmitting antennas. In this way, only the pilot contamination effect remains in the communication system, that is, the interference caused by the reuse of the same pilot sequence in adjacent units. The most advanced survey on SM–MIMO research was showed in [2]. The novel beam division multiple access (BDMA) transmission decomposes complex massive MU-MIMO channels into low dimensional SU-MIMO interference channels via user scheduling [6]. Based on the large-scale antenna arrays deployed by base stations, a transmission scheme suitable for different users is designed by utilizing the unique characteristics of large-scale MIMO channels [7].

So far, based on the assumption that the number of antennas increases unrestrictedly, the academia pays more attention to the scale growth of antenna arrays, and has realized some asymptotic capacity scaling laws under the ideal conditions. However, the number of antennas in the actual system should be limited owing to physical constraints. If the number of transmitting antennas and receiving antennas tends to be infinite, the ideal mathematical model we have built will collapse [8]. With the continuous miniaturization of the antenna unit, the increasing number of antenna elements and the decrease of the antenna unit spacing, the mutual coupling effect between the antenna elements will become an important factor for the MIMO transmission performance. Therefore, the performance parameters of the antenna array should be considered to build the wireless communication systems channel model, which makes our channel model more accurate and more practical. In this paper, based on the BDMA, the coupling parameters of the antenna array element will be studied in depth.

The rest of this paper is organized as follows. In Sect. 2, we will introduce the BDMA. In Sect. 3, we will introduce channel model. In Sect. 4, we will present simulation results for three different cases and the paper is concluded in Sect. 5.

2 Introduction of BDMA

In this section, we will introduce the novel BDMA transmission. The key point of BDMA is that after appropriate user scheduling such that users are separated in the beam domain, the BS communicates with users through non-overlapping beams. The communication scheme includes the following phases:

(1) The BS acquires all user statistical channel state information (CSI) in the cell. Statistical CSI acquisition contains two steps: the first is in the uplink, Multiusers

transmit their voice signals on independent subcarriers for the base station to estimate the instantaneous CSI and calculate the statistical CSI. The statistics is the Eigen mode channel coupling matrices in the beam domain. Separate sub-carriers lead to no interference among users.

(2) BS enables users to be sufficiently separated in the beam domain by user scheduling scheme. Based on statistical CSI, the approximate sum-rate can be calculated. User scheduling maximizing the sum-rate by selects users with the constraints that different user beams are non-overlapping and the maximum number of beams is not exceeded.

(3) The complex MU-MIMO link is decomposed into low dimensional SU-MIMO links. Beams at the BS are also divided into different groups by user scheduling. In the uplink and downlink transmissions, the BS uses one beam set to receive from and transmit to one user, in a SU-MIMO interference channel.

(4) Uplink and downlink sequences include pilot training and data. In the training step, for the training procedure, users are divided into different beam groups at the BS, pilot sequence can be shared among the selected users. The overhead of uplink and downlink training is proportional to the amount of antenna elements at each user or the amount of beams in each beam set. The receivers estimate the reduced low dimensional channel matrices and the instantaneous correlation of interference for data detection.

Because of the reduced-dimensional of MIMO links, BDMA significantly reduces the channel estimation overhead and the computational complexity of transceiver.

3   Channel Model

In this section, the wideband channel model of massive MIMO is firstly introduced. For this channel, we present the wideband channel model with antenna array performance parameters. And then we apply the channel model with antenna array performance parameters to BDMA.

3.1   System Configuration

Consider a single-cellular system which consists of one BS equipped with M antennas. K users, each with N antenna elements, are randomly and uniformly distributed throughout the cell. Figure 1 shows the schematic diagram of MIMO channel. In this paper, we focus on the one-dimensional uniform linear array (ULA) with a half wavelength antenna spaced at BS, and multiple uncorrelated antennas at each user [9]. Throughout the paper, we allow receivers to have instantaneous CSI, whilst the transmitter only has access to statistical CSI.

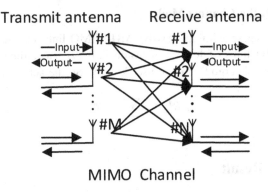

Fig. 1. Schematic diagram of MIMO channel.

3.2 MIMO Channel Mode

Here we consider jointly correlated MIMO channel model [10–12]. We analyze the downlink channel, while the uplink channel analysis is similar. For a physical channel model, it is assumed that P physical paths exist between BS and users, and the p_{th} path of the k_{th} user has an attenuation of $a_{p,k}$, an angle of $\varphi_{p,k}$ with the transmit antenna array and an angle of $\theta_{p,k}$ with the receive antenna array. Then the physical MIMO channel matrix associated with the p_{th} of the k_{th} user can be described as [13]

$$\mathbf{H}_{p,k} = a_{p,k}e^{-j2\pi d_{p,k}/\lambda_c}e_r\left(\theta_{p,k}\right)e_t^H\left(\varphi_{p,k}\right) \tag{1}$$

$d_{p,k}$ is the distance between transmit antenna element and receive antenna element along the path p, and λ_c is the signal carrier wavelength. In addition, $e_r(\theta)$ is the user antenna array response vector corresponding to the angle of arrival $(AoA)\theta$ satisfying $||e_r(\theta)||_2 = 1$, and $e_t(\varphi)$ is the BS antenna array response vector corresponding to the angle of departure $(AoD)\varphi$ satisfying $||e_t(\varphi)||_2 = 1$.

3.3 Channel Model with Antenna Array Performance Parameters

When we consider the performance parameters of the antenna array elements, the physical MIMO channel matrix associated with the p_{th} path of the k_{th} user can be modeled as

$$\mathbf{H}_{a,p,k} = \mathbf{T}_r\mathbf{H}_{p,k}\mathbf{T}_e \tag{2}$$

Here $\mathbf{T}_r$ is the matrix between the input and output vectors of the receive antenna. And $\mathbf{T}_e$ is the matrix between the input and output vectors of the transmit antenna.

3.4   BDMA with the Channel Model

After appropriate user scheduling, massive MU-MIMO links can be decomposed into multiple SU-MIMO links of lower dimension [14–19]. According to BDMA transmission, the achievable ergodic rate at user k is R_k^d. So the achievable sum-rate is

$$R_{sum}^d = \sum_{k=1}^{K_s} R_k^d \qquad (3)$$

4   Simulation Result

In this section, we build the actual network layout and we add different antenna performance parameters to the MIMO model. Then channel simulations based on the sum-rate will be performed. Finally we will get the simulation results.

4.1   Network Layout

This paper considers a single-cellular system, including a base station (BS) with 12 antennas. Figure 2 shows the antenna physical model, Fig. 3 shows the coupling relations between the. A user with 4 antennas is randomly distributed in the cell. For simplicity, we choose three adjacent cells, each cell has 10 randomly distributed users. Figure 3 shows the network layout.

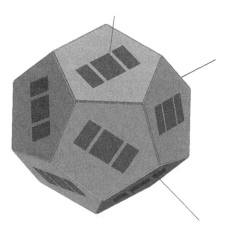

Fig. 2. Antenna physical model.

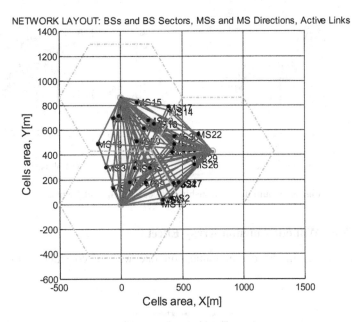

Fig. 3. Network layout.

4.2 Coupling Relationship Simulation

Figure 4 shows the coupling relationship between antenna elements, and Fig. 5 shows the amplitude and phase of coupling parameters between the antenna elements.

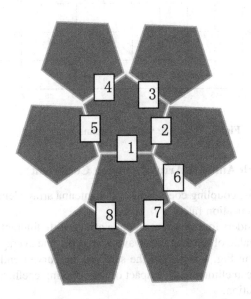

Fig. 4. Coupling relationship between antenna elements.

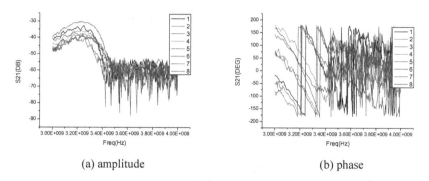

(a) amplitude   (b) phase

Fig. 5. Coupling relationship between antenna elements.

4.3   Sum Rate Without Antenna Array Effect

Figure 6 shows the simulated communication rate without considering the antenna array effect.

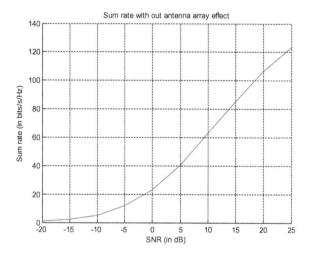

Fig. 6. Sum rate without antenna array effect.

4.4   Sum Rate with Antenna Array Coupling Coefficient

In consideration of the coupling coefficient of the antenna array elements, Fig. 7 shows the resulting communication rate.

This section considers four different antenna arrays with different port S parameters. And the maximum value of the standing wave is −20 dB, the average value is −25 dB.

The curve trend in Fig. 4 is clearly the same as the curve trend in Fig. 5. So, our new channel model can eliminate the impact of the coupling coefficient on the sum rate performance degradation.

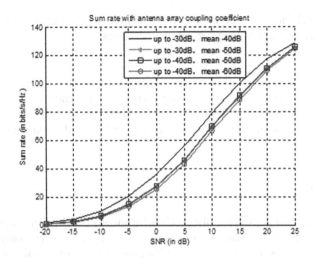

Fig. 7. Sum rate with antenna array coupling coefficient.

4.5 Sum Rate with Antenna Array Coupling Coefficient

In consideration of the coupling coefficient of the antenna array element and the reflection attenuation of the port, Fig. 8 shows the resulting communication rate. This section also considers four different antenna arrays with different port S parameters. And the maximum value of the standing wave is −20 dB, the average value is −25 dB.

From Fig. 8, we can know our new channel model can greatly reduce the impact on the sum rate performance degradation when we consider the all effect of the antenna array. And Through the comparison of Figs. 6, 7, and 8, the curve trend in Fig. 5 is more consistent with the curve trend in Fig. 5 than the curve trend in Fig. 8. So, We

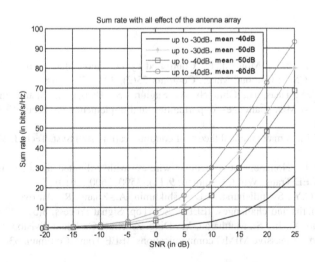

Fig. 8. Sum rate with all effect of the antenna array.

can get the conclusion that the reflection attenuation is more critical to the sum rate performance degradation than the coupling coefficient.

4.6 Simulation Results

From the simulation results can be seen, our channel model with performance parameters of the antenna array has excellent performance when we consider the coupling coefficient of the antenna array element and the reflection attenuation of the port.

5 Conclusion

In this paper, we have introduced the BDMA for massive MIMO transmission system with implant performance parameters of the antenna array, where only CSI at the transmitter is available. Firstly, the physically motivated beam domain channel model is investigated. And shown that antennas have coupling and reflection attenuation properties. Therefore, we propose the channel model with antenna array performance parameters. We have further applied the channel model to BDMA. Channel simulations based for the sum-rate has been performed. The effect of antenna array physical structure for the channel model based on BDMA has been verified by the simulation result, which will be conducive to the actual massive MIMO systems in typical mobility scenarios.

Acknowledgment. This work is supported by The National Natural Science Foundation of China for Youth (Grant No. 61602263), The Natural Science Foundation of Jiangsu Province, China (Grant No. BK20160916), The National post-doctoral fund (Grant No. 2017M621798), The Jiangsu Planned Projects for Postdoctoral Research Funds (Grant No. 1701132B), and NUPTSF (No. NY214189, NY215146 and NY216020).

References

1. Wang, M., Yang, C., Mousoli, R.: Controlled cyclic remote state preparation of arbitrary qubit states. CMC: Comput. Mater. Continua **55**(2), 321–329 (2018)
2. Di Renzo, M., Haas, H., Ghrayeb, A., Sugiura, S., Hanzo, L.: Spatial modulation for generalized MIMO: challenges, opportunities, and implementation. Proc. IEEE **102**(1), 56–103 (2014)
3. Shannon, C.E.: A mathematical theory of communication. Bell Syst. Tech. J. **27**(3), 379–423 (1948)
4. Marzetta, T.L.: Noncooperative cellular wireless with unlimited numbers of base station antennas. IEEE Trans. Wirel. Commun. **9**(11), 3590–3600 (2010)
5. Lu, L., Li, G.Y., Swindlehurst, A.L., Ashikhmin, A., Zhang, R.: An overview of massive MIMO: benefits and challenges. IEEE J. Sel. Top. Signal Process. **8**(5), 742–758 (2014)
6. Sun, C., Gao, X., Jin, S., Matthaiou, M., Ding, Z., Xiao, C.: Beam division multiple access transmission for massive MIMO communications. IEEE Trans. Commun. **63**(6), 2170–2184 (2015)

7. Jiang, Y., Zhong, X., Guo, Y., Duan, M.: Communication mechanism and algorithm of composite location analysis of emergency communication based on rail. CMC: Comput. Mater. Continua 57(2), 321–340 (2018)
8. Rusek, F., et al.: Scaling up MIMO: opportunities and challenges with very large arrays. IEEE Signal Process. Mag. 30(1), 40–60 (2013)
9. Akyildiz, I.F., Wang, X., Wang, W.: Wireless mesh networks: a survey. Comput. Netw. 47(4), 445–487 (2005)
10. Gao, X., Jiang, B., Li, X., Gershman, A.B., McKay, M.R.: Statistical eigenmode transmission over jointly-correlated MIMO channels. arXiv preprint arXiv:0903.1952 (2009)
11. Weichselberger, W., Herdin, M., Ozcelik, H., Bonek, E.: A stochastic MIMO channel model with joint correlation of both link ends. IEEE Trans. Wirel. Commun. 5(1), 90–100 (2006)
12. Tulino, A.M., Lozano, A., Verdú, S.: Impact of antenna correlation on the capacity of multiantenna channels. IEEE Trans. Inf. Theory 51(7), 2491–2509
13. Tse, D., Viswanath, P.: Fundamentals of Wireless Communication. Cambridge University Press, New York (2005)
14. Veeravalli, V.V., Liang, Y., Sayeed, A.: Correlated MIMO rayleigh fading channels: capacity, optimal signaling, and asymptotics (2005)
15. Christensen, S.S., Agarwal, R., De Carvalho, E., Cioffi, J.M.: Weighted sum-rate maximization using weighted MMSE for MIMO-BC beamforming design. IEEE Trans. Wirel. Commun. 7(12), 4792–4799 (2008)
16. Negro, F., Shenoy, S.P., Ghauri, I., Slock, D.T.: On the MIMO interference channel. In: Information Theory and Applications Workshop (ITA), pp. 1–9. IEEE (2010)
17. Shin, J., Moon, J.: Weighted sum rate maximizing transceiver design in MIMO interference channel. In: 2011 IEEE Global Telecommunications Conference (GLOBECOM 2011), pp. 1–5. IEEE (2011)
18. Evolved Universal Terrestrial Radio Access: Physical channels and modulation. 3GPP TS, 36, V8 (2009)
19. Li, X., Jin, S., Gao, X.: Multi-user MIMO downlink eigen-mode transmission over jointly correlated MIMO channels. Sci. China Inf. Sci. 54(10), 2124 (2011)

Intelligent Irrigation System of Balcony Flowers Based on Internet of Things

Jianhang Fu, Pingzeng Liu[✉], Chao Zhang, Xueru Yu,
Jianyong Zhang, and Yang Li

Shandong Agricultural University, Tai'an 271018, China
lpz8565@126.com

Abstract. With the gradual maturity of the Internet of Things technology, production intelligence and information has become more common. The level of automation in irrigation systems represents a major factor in the efficiency of agricultural development. This article has studied the intelligent automatic irrigation system of balcony flowers based on Internet of Things. MSP430F5438A single-chip microcomputer is used as the core microcontroller to collect soil moisture information through soil moisture sensors. The humidity information is uploaded to the server by the wireless communication module. The server responds to the client's instructions and the real-time soil temperature and humidity to water the balcony flowers. The GPRS module sends the control command to the lower position machine, and the microcontroller transfers the instructions through the wireless transmission module. And to control the operation of the switch of solenoid valve. The entire irrigation system is based on the MSP430 single-chip microcomputer and has good features such as low power consumption and high stability.

Keywords: Internet of things · MSP430 microcontroller · Intelligent irrigation system · GPRS

1 Introduction

In China, at present, irrigation is carried out in many areas in the agricultural production process, and irrigation method is still dominated by diffusion irrigation, so the water resource consumption is very huge and the overall utilization rate is not high. Agriculture occupies a large proportion of water in China's industrial and agricultural production. The total amount of water used for agriculture accounts for 70% of the country's total water consumption. Therefore, it has become a long-term and arduous task to increase the effective utilization rate of irrigation water, improve soil environment and crop yield, and become the key to the development of agriculture in China at the present stage. With strong support from the government, some areas have begun to implement automatic irrigation systems, which play an important role in saving time, manpower and cost in agricultural production. At the same time automatic irrigation system also has the same outstanding contribution to the flower planting industry, the future application prospect is very broad.

© Springer Nature Switzerland AG 2019
X. Sun et al. (Eds.): ICAIS 2019, LNCS 11634, pp. 394–402, 2019.
https://doi.org/10.1007/978-3-030-24271-8_36

At present, people hope to have a green living environment, many people will plant a variety of flowers in the home, to achieve the goal of improving indoor air quality. At present, plant vegetable on the balcony also very welcome, such people can afforest the environment in the home again can eat the green healthy vegetable that oneself grows in the home. Yet the hectic pace of life often makes office workers miss out. Especially when we meet the holidays or visit the elderly relatives, flowers and vegetables are not watered in time, people often see a withered after returning from a long holiday. Therefore, people urgently need a self-made intelligent irrigation device to timely solve the irrigation problem of crops such as flowers and vegetables [1]. At present, the automatic control of irrigation system in China is still immature. In addition, the connection accessories and water valve required by the intelligent irrigation system are all substitute products, and the compatibility of the whole irrigation system is poor.

In this design, the single-chip computer control system is added to the traditional irrigation system. Through accurate measurement to conduct watering, real-time soil moisture detection can be achieved perfectly, and the system can determine whether watering is needed according to the measured humidity. If the test results show that the soil is about to run out of water, the system will automatically start watering, ensuring soil moisture and keeping the plants growing normally.

MCU is small in size, but powerful in function and very low in power consumption. It can expand various sensors for different control. MCU can carry out the development of various types.

2 Design Background

2.1 Development of IoT Technology

The Internet of Things [2] literally means the Internet is connected to things. The Internet of things was proposed in this century, and the main principle is to connect other sensors via radio frequency identification (RFID) [3] to form a distributed network. With the Internet as the core, the world Internet of things is an extended application of the Internet, realizing multi-network communication and achieving the connection between things and things, people and things.

With the constant development and maturity of IoT technology, IoT technology is called the third wave of the information industry, and is one of the greatest technologies in this century. At present, the development of IoT has been involved in all aspects of our life, including agriculture, education, medical care, transportation and so on.

2.2 Agricultural Internet of Things and Intelligent Irrigation

Agricultural Internet of things (IoT) is a technology that brings convenience to agricultural production on the basis of the Internet of things, which is also a technology that technology changes the world. Agriculture is the foundation of human survival, and how to expand agricultural production is a research topic of tireless efforts of all countries. The growth of crops needs to be taken care of carefully, but the large area of farmland is difficult to be managed manually. At this time, the introduction of IoT technology can greatly improve the efficiency, reduce human cost and finally improve the production of crops. The development and use of the Internet of things has brought great changes to agricultural development, especially intelligent irrigation systems for farmland.

The concept of intelligent irrigation have been proposed for many years, the main is a micro controller, sensor, automatic watering and other parts, is the collection many kinds of technology management system, at present our country's intelligent irrigation system is still in the preliminary stage of development, a lot of technology is not mature enough, in recent years, some developed countries have been introduced into China the advanced irrigation control devices, but due to various factors such as high price, the maintenance difficulties, it is mainly used in institutions of higher learning, scientific research units and agricultural demonstration zone, and is not in conformity with the Chinese characteristics of the application of soil [4]. Therefore, it is very important for China to perfect the control of plant planting environment through scientific and technological means. It is inevitable for future development to replace manpower with low-cost and powerful control system.

2.3 Intelligent Irrigation System of Balcony Flowers Based on Internet of Things

In the development of the Internet of things technology [5] and intelligent greenhouse irrigation systems, inspired by the ideas of the Internet of things and abstracted model of intelligent greenhouse irrigation system, the study design a set of balcony flowers intelligent irrigation system, using the sensor measurement of soil moisture and temperature, the proper irrigation by microcontroller control irrigation system, to ensure that the plant enough moisture is appropriate, the system can not only guarantee the optimal growth of plants, also can maximum level of saving water [6].

3 System Design

3.1 Overall System Planning

The intelligent balcony flower irrigation system based on the Internet of things takes MSP430F5438A single chip computer [7] as the core micro controller, including the lower machine part and the upper machine part. The lower part mainly includes information acquisition system and irrigation control system. As shown in Fig. 1, the information collection system mainly consists of soil temperature and humidity sensor and collection card, which is responsible for the collection of various data to prepare for the later control. Irrigation control is mainly composed of LED display module, electromagnetic valve, pump, MSP430 MCU module and GPRS module. The upper computer is mainly composed of server and client.

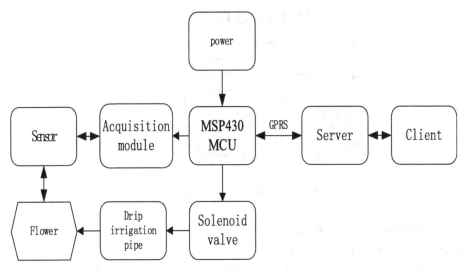

Fig. 1. Overall system structure diagram

3.2 Main Controller

Microcontroller, namely microcontroller, is the most core part of the system design. Therefore, choosing appropriate microcontroller is the primary task of the design. At present, the most common microcontroller is the 51 series. Although the functions of the 51-series MCU have been very perfect at present, there are still some deficiencies. The internal hardware resources of the 51-series MCU are relatively few and the power consumption is relatively large. Therefore, it is necessary to expand the peripheral circuits to achieve the purpose of users. Based on the design for real-time acquisition of flower soil data, considering the actual power consumption and specific functions, a relatively low power microcontroller was selected for design. The manufacturer of MSP430 series MCU is Texas instruments (TI), a famous microprocessor company. MSP430 has the characteristics of ultra-low power consumption, and the power supply voltage is 1.8–3.6 v [8].

By compared with other microcontroller, MSP430 MCU integrates a variety of functional modules, including 3 16-bit timers, analog comparator, 12 DAC, a 12 bit ADC, analog comparator, DMA controller and so on, also including, asynchronous I/O ports, I2C bus to accept/send device (UART), serial peripheral interface (SPI) three multi-function serial interface, the watchdog timer use watchdog (WDT) & constant ramp/LCD drive, USB hardware multiplier, 2 KB–10 KB of RAM, and a variety of the interrupt function.

The single chip microcomputer can be programmed in time online. Only when the single chip microcomputer is connected with the JTAG simulator, the program can be simulated and debugged in time. This technology can save a lot of development time and improve efficiency for development. The program after debugging through JTAG can be directly downloaded to the FLASH memory of the single chip. The four wire system is adopted, and the specific pin interface is shown in Fig. 2.

MSP430-JTAG

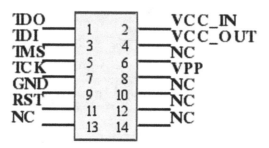

Fig. 2. The interface way of JTAG

3.3 Information Acquisition System

3.3.1 Acquisition Card DAM-3000

DAM-3000 supports the EIA-485 communication protocol, which USES the bidirectional balanced circuit standard to achieve true multi-point two-way communication. The DAM-3000 can connect 8 different signal sources, support 8 different signals, read the voltage or current signal generated by the sensor, and convert the data that the user wants to measure through the 16 bit ADC on the DAM-3000, which satisfies the diversity of the sensor. The eight channels of DAM-3000 can be respectively set as different data acquisition modules, while one module can be achieved through DAM-3000, saving hardware costs. DAM-3000 is applicable to various working environments, and the working temperature of the product module is $-10 \sim +70°$. DAM-3000 series of modules are all made of industrial-grade components, and the products can work at the limit temperature of $-40 \sim +85°$. At the same time, 10–30 VDC power input range is provided, which has very high reliability and security, meeting the field needs of various applications.

In addition, excellent control software is built into the modules, and users can easily use the software to control the system I/O modules.

3.3.2 The Sensor

In normal growth of crops, air temperature and humidity, as an important environmental factor, play a very important role. Plants cannot grow without water, sunlight and inorganic salts, and the proper temperature is an important factor, but the growth of plant temperature and humidity are not fixed in a value, but there is one of the most suitable growth temperature, minimum and maximum temperature between a best temperature, in the best temperature range is most suitable for plant growth and reproduction of [9].

At the same time, soil moisture and crop can grow normally important environment factor, the soil humidity is small, if enough abundance of soil water content, then plants will have enough water to participate in all metabolism, especially the transpiration of water is plentiful, can moments for plants absorb nutrients from the soil, the growth of plants can be better. However, if the humidity in the air is too high in the environment where the plant grows, the biological activities inside the plant will be restricted, resulting in the growth limitation. If the relative humidity is too low, the soil will become dry and even the atmosphere will become dry. When the temperature is higher and the water is less, the plant will start its own protection system to protect the water in the body from evaporation and thus stop growing. In conclusion, we can understand how important temperature and humidity are to the growth of plants.

Air temperature and humidity and soil moisture (also known as soil moisture content) are two important preconditions for automatic irrigation system. Therefore, a sensor for measuring air temperature and humidity and two soil moisture sensors for measuring humidity are designed in this design.

The measurement sensor selected in this system design is a sensor based on FDR frequency domain reflection technology. High-frequency electronic technology is widely used in soil moisture measurement [10], and has become one of the most popular humidity measurement methods in the world at present due to its high-precision and high-sensitivity characteristics [11]. Its measurement distance is that electromagnetic pulse will have different frequency in soil with different water content, and the proportion of water in the total volume can be obtained by measuring the frequency, so as to reflect the soil moisture and measure the volume percentage of soil moisture, so as to obtain the soil temperature and humidity status through the inversion of a certain corresponding relation.

3.4   GPRS Signal Transmission Module

GPRS communication technology relative to its bricks and networking communication technologies such as Bluetooth, ZigBee, radio frequency communication technology such as RF and WIFI, GPRS communication technology the most suitable for use in a sudden, intermittent or frequent small amounts of data transmission, and the communication technology to support the data transfer rate will be higher, in the practical application of limit peak of 115 kbps, can also be applied to the occasional big data transmission.

GPRS communication technology is a wireless communication transmission technology based on TCP/IP protocol [12]. GPRS system is mainly composed of the main entity, logical structure, protocol structure and channel of GPRS network. In practical operation, the data transmitted by GPRS module has two parts, one is the measured data, which belongs to user data, and the other is the control signaling to control and provide transmission support for user data.

The main function of the GPRS communication module is to set up the data transmission channel between the upper computer and the lower computer to complete information processing communication [13]. Core chip adopts H7210 DTU. The modules of H7200 series have high reliability and wide range of use, and are the best choice for wireless communication of many systems [14].

As the most commonly used wireless communication module, its internal built-in PPP and TCP/IP protocol stack, to meet most of the wireless communication protocol requirements; Can support fixed IP address and domain name; There are three different communication modes: TCP, UDP and SMS. Able to support private networks using mobile operator APN; In order to ensure the network patency and reduce power consumption, it also has idle offline and timed offline functions; SMS number support international area code and local number two modes; Debugging information can be set via a serial port.

3.5 Irrigation System Design

Irrigation systems are divided into manual and automatic systems. The control circuit mainly controls the opening and closing of the pump by relay. When the system works, the soil moisture sensor begins to detect the current soil moisture [15]. The data measured by the soil moisture sensor is converted into digital signals and transmitted to the microcomputer through AD conversion. MCU compares the acquisition value with the set value. When the collected value is less than the humidity lower limit set, the control relay is connected to the pump to water the flowers and plants. When the pump is turned on, if the measured value is greater than the set humidity upper limit or reaches the maximum watering time, the pump is closed [16, 17]. In the watering

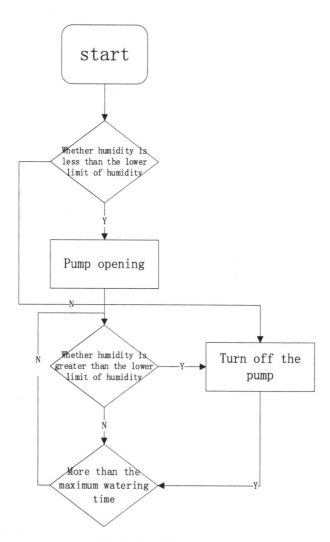

Fig. 3. Workflow diagrams

process, if the measured value of soil temperature and humidity is greater than the set value of humidity upper limit, the control relay closes the water pump. Its workflow is shown in Fig. 3. When switched to manual, the relay is automatically closed and the pump is closed for manual watering.

4 The System Test

Due to the limitations of time and conditions in the system design, field testing and debugging were not carried out. All tests and debugging were carried out in the laboratory. Experiments were conducted through the established simulation model:

(1) In the display module of the system, the upper and lower limits of humidity, watering duration and other relevant parameters are set manually, which gives the water demand of flowers and plants. Then, the command is transmitted to the downward machine to test whether the water pump can be opened normally for irrigation and shut down automatically after irrigation is completed.
(2) The soil moisture sensor is inserted into the dry soil to test whether the water pump can be automatically opened for irrigation, and then inserted into the wet soil to test whether the water pump can automatically shut off irrigation.
(3) After power on, the system can automatically detect the soil temperature and humidity, and timely control the water pump for irrigation according to the collected data.

After the design is completed, the system is tested and debugged through the actual test. The actual test results show that the system designed in this design can work normally and independently, and the effect is good. It achieves the expected design effect and can effectively conduct intelligent irrigation.

5 Conclusion

In the system design, based on consulting a large number of relevant data and documents, and combining the actual requirement of the design to carry on the design, encountered many problems during, but have been conducted to solve the guidance of the teacher carefully, after two months of efforts finally according to the design requirements expected only irrigation system are designed. The whole system can be divided into two main parts, one is the measurement and control of the machine, the other is for display and artificial control of PC, to achieve the intelligent control of the system, MSP430F5438A microcontroller as the microcontroller in the system, solved the normal most of the crops can't timely watering flowers of life's problems, and can according to different soil moisture data were collected during different water irrigation, let flower growing in a proper soil temperature and humidity environment.

References

1. Sun, Q., Ma X.: A simple economical and practical scheme which according to the soil resistance for automatic watering. Dev. Innov. Mech. Electr. Products **24**(5) (2011)
2. ITU Internet Reports 2005: The Internet of Things, ITU (2005)
3. Chen, H., Liu, K., Ma, C., Han, Y., Su, J.: A novel time-aware frame adjustment strategy for RFID anti-collision. CMC: Comput. Mater. Continua. **57**(2), 195–204 (2018)
4. Zhan, J., Song, Z., Li, F., et al.: Japan, Netherlands and Israel's development of facility agriculture to China's inspiration. Tianjin Agricultural Science (2011)
5. Shi, C.: A novel ensemble learning algorithm based on D-S evidence theory for IoT security. CMC: Comput. Mater. Continua. **57**(3), 635–652 (2018)
6. Yan, S., Shen, Y., Zhou, M., et al.: Home automatic watering device based on soil timing test. The North Garden (2011)
7. Hong, L., Zhang, Y., Shibao, L.: MSP430 MCU principle and application examples detailed. Beijing university of Aeronautics and Astronautics Press (2010)
8. Ming, T., Deng, P., Ma, X.: Design of temperature acquisition system based on MSP430 MCU. Instrum. User **25**(03), 5–7 +76 (2018)
9. Qian, L.: Research on soil moisture detection device based on FDR technology. Heilongjiang University (2016)
10. Skierucha, W., Wilczek, A.: A FDR sensor for measuring complex soil dielectric permittivity in the 10–500 MHz frequency range. Sensors **10**(4), 3314–3329 (2010)
11. Jie, C., Chen, H.: Design and implementation of temperature and humidity detection system based on single chip microcomputer. Electronic test (2011)
12. Pescapè, A., Ventre, G.: A simulation environment for GPRS traffic in an advanced travellers information system (ATIS). In: Simulation Modelling Practice and Theory (2004)
13. Shangming, C., Yue, S., Xiaofeng, H., Xiaoyuan, H.: Hardware design of automatic irrigation system based on GPRS. Lab. Res. Explor. **31**(06), 10–13 (2012)
14. Ma, Y.: Research on optimization of GPRS wireless network. Beijing University of Posts and Telecommunications (2009)
15. Jing, D.: Research design and application of automatic irrigation control system with single chip microcomputer. Beijing Agricultural Engineering University (1994)
16. Rui, L., Yuan Jun, G., Haiying, T.H., Zhengzhi, H.: Automatic irrigation and fertilization system can be realized by single chip microcomputer. Comput. Appl. **S1**, 219–221 (2001)
17. Peng, X.: Design of automatic control system for water-saving irrigation in farmland. Hebei Agricultural University (2014)

Multimedia Forensics

The Impact of Using Facebook on the Academic Performance of University Students

Sajida Karim[1], Hui He[1(✉)], Ghulam Ali Mallah[2], Asif Ali Laghari[1],
Hina Madiha[3], and Raja Sohail Ahmed Larik[2]

[1] School of Computer Science and Technology, Harbin Institute of Technology,
Harbin, China
{sajidakarim,hehui,asiflaghari}@hit.edu.cn
[2] Shah Abdul Latif University of Khairpur, Sindh, Pakistan
{gulam.ali,raja.mscs2011}@salu.edu.pk
[3] Shaanxi Normal University, Xian, China
madiha41@live.com

Abstract. The Advancement of technology has changed the social and academic lives. It provides a facility for people to communicate anywhere at any time diversely such as electronic mail, instant messages and social networks. A use of social network is common among the students' and also builds a distraction for students. It is crucial for researchers to get an attention to investigate the role of social network (Facebook) in academic areas where its influences on students' live with various activities and involves them in a different process of channels. To determine the multitasking inversely affect health and academic performance while using Facebook with different activities i.e. sharing, posting, chatting and playing games with access of internet and use of different devices during class time and study time. This study investigates the impact of using Facebook on the academic performance of university students. We conducted Correlation analysis, and Regression analysis extracted using Statistical Package for the Social Sciences (SPSS) to examine the correlation between students using Facebook in the higher academic career. The results show Facebook with academic performance has a negative relationship and medium correlation with Multitasking has positive that Facebook is not the only factor to enhance multitasking but also enhance other activities of Facebook that can effect on students which mean there is relationship between multitasking and using Facebook where Health factor has low correlation and negative relationship might get the cause to indirectly affect the students' academic performance.

Keywords: Social network · Students · Academic performance

1 Introduction

Education has adopted electronic technologies with different aspects of usage to refurnish with innovative environments and integrate with effective learning processes such in library, faculty, and administration where students have been socializing and

© Springer Nature Switzerland AG 2019
X. Sun et al. (Eds.): ICAIS 2019, LNCS 11634, pp. 405–418, 2019.
https://doi.org/10.1007/978-3-030-24271-8_37

interacting with each other especially in the field of education where people of all ages and genders are available to communicate and create relationships with others. Academic performance is one of the essential functions of student that widely researched over the years where passive students indicates the lack of understanding in their learning, writing and lack of gain in other activity; it will deficit the adult's academic performance [1–3].

Nowadays, the use of social network site makes robust connectivity of the internet to transform learning processes where Technology is an essential need of students where student immersed in technology day by day with different flavors of activities. Social media is not only used for entertainment purposes but it is also used for educational and documentation purposes [4]. As Facebook is one of the latest current tools of social networks all over the world and a great source to learn new information and share among the students. Social networks are a recognizable source of channels to inform and educate the learners as well as teachers where each and every time the unlimited number of students takes a part on social networks [3, 5]. The logical hierarchy of social network with users' activities is well defined with interaction between students' and academic performances are showed in Fig. 1.

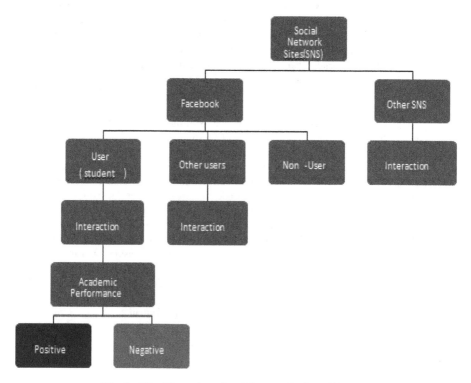

Fig. 1. The Hierarchy of social network site with users

No doubt, the current use of the social network has been influenced in the academic areas with the advancement of technology to facilitate the users. The use of Facebook in today's world vision is positive because it has made gaining of knowledge much easier with the access of internet over the worldwide area. It seems to have good results on educationalist especially students' academic performance. Many Researchers indicate Facebook as a cause of bad results in academic performance. Is it myth or not? Still, it's invisible fact and remains largely unanswered [6].

To the research of fact in reality, nowadays academic performance is more important in education but students show great interest in using Facebook because it is easy to use, very popular social network site and it can be logged into through different devices like mobiles, tablets, laptops and desktops for performing of independent activities of students. We conduct the research based on unanswered facts that technology as social media may cause of students' failure in academic field as a part of our community.

The contribution of this paper is presented into three folds.

- This study investigates the impact of using Facebook on the academic performance of university students.
- Statistically, Hypothesis Analysis a significant point from the present research is acquired by comprehensive analysis results extracted using SPSS.
- This study examines the correlation between students using Facebook performed different activities and higher health risks.

This paper is organized into V sections. In the next Sect. 2, we will describe the literature review. Section 3 based on the Survey methodology and In Sect. 4 provides to results and discussion. Finally, the paper is concluded in Sect. 5.

2 Literature Review

This section presents the literature review and furthermore is divided into two sections. Background of social network (Facebook) and existing Facebook relationship with students.

2.1 Background of Social Network (Facebook)

Social networks began to grow popularity as more users become connected to cellular networks and the internet and were widespread as well as ever modified dynamically [7, 8]. The number of social networks had perceptibly enlarged over the last fifteen years. Social network sites like Friendster, Myspace and Facebook were ultimately the most social network sites to grow the analysis background to rise perceive backgrounds [9]. In the year of 2004 and month of February, Mark Zuckerberg created Facebook in a dorm at Harvard University. Facebook allowed users from the college. Facebook found in manners to allowed work and anyone to join Facebook in the year of 2006. People joined SNS to share info concerning them and learn additional information regarding those they think about "friends". Facebook as a social network permits the users to determine new connections, maintain relationships and present information regarding them. Facebook users use the positioning to contact with their current friends, explore for old friends and meet new individuals. Facebook users produce a web profile to share information: post comments regarding themselves, post comments on alternative friends, pages, share photos and videos, play games, and update others on their life occurrences [10].

Facebook friends are able to confine bit and share what they're presently doing in their lives? In the year of 2005, Facebook expanded outside of the U.S to include high schools and schools. In the year of 2006, Facebook found its manner into the work and allowed anyone to join Facebook and users share intimate, mundane and interesting moments with their online friends. Facebook users actively stay online for a long time, therefore, disbursement to time with friends in a virtual community sense [9, 11]. Facebook was attained status as the world's largest and most profitable social network till up to now. It encourages people to begin communication and eventually form relationships with people of similar backgrounds and interests. However, the visibility of users' profiles can be set at their own discretion. Profiles display user's information to connect with other friends using messages or instant chatting features, share photographs and videos, and interest groups within the social network site to connect with those of similar goals and opinions [12].

Once users engaged in Facebook and became an active member, they have the ability to receive information that may not be available to them in any other form. Facebook features also give the chance to participate and perform multitasking into other activities and come across the opportunities either they may not have the advantage of gaining access [13].

2.2 Existing Facebook Relationship with Students

Students grew up in a world of technology that makes the Internet as "a central key element" in their daily lives. Recent research has focused on the relationship between Facebook and Academic performance. The findings identified the effect of internet on the academic performance of the students under the age of teen group more addicted and getting wrong use of it. Considered 47% of Facebook addicted users reflected the academic performance. It is very essential part of an individual's life for every level of students [13].

Tariq et al. and A'lamElhuda et al. [14, 15] investigated the Facebook usage among undergraduate students performance that examined the different style of Facebook usage research was aimed to identify a style of Facebook usage. The Find out effects of gender on Facebook that how a Facebook affected by students. Many online tools are available on the Internet for communication channels where Facebook is one of them. It can be dangerous to increase the students' addiction and its effects on their academic performance as well as student future.

Ahn et al. and Singh et al. [16, 17] determined technology and health unexpected truth that a decade of research showed media as a tool that had not any effects on students' learning's and very difficult and complex to analyze the statement that Media effects on health. Findings identified the effect of internet addiction on mental health (stress) of the students that are more addict and getting wrong use of it.

Krin et al. [18] explored the fact on Rehearsals of task accumulate the recall the data as human consciously engaged in a repetitive task to do multitasking the effectiveness of worth become slows and tiredness made to lose the control of rehearsal and forget easily. However, a cause of stress associated with tiredness came through multitasking activities. Different Researchers found that Facebook affects the human factors.

Bijari et al. [19] investigate on the effects of social networking site impact on the academic achievements of those students who used social network site at night time rather than on a day-time. Larik et al. [20] research on effects on human body, those used excess use of technology they cannot fully concentrate on their tasks that point immediately negative impact on their academic performance due to sleepless cause disturbance and impacts on mental health of the user.

Junco et al. [21] whenever user engaged to complete more than one task at the same time. Those amount of multi-tasked decrease their cognitive abilities and decreased their potential of productive work. The fact of studies covered the coat of arrangement and to make multitasking besides hiding the impact of self-features that many researchers demonstrate the impact of multitasking on human information.

Bieler et al. [22] and Ellison et al. [9] found complex survey data on negative connection between multitasking under the study of different activities like Facebook usage and text messaging, chit chat on a mobile phone, Emailing & internet surfing, while the focus on their academic performance, Using of Facebook was the least content informing. surveyed that 34.54% of male spent three to four hours daily on using Facebook and 27.27% of female spent one to two hours daily, pointed that Features of Facebook involve through the multitasking and direct the effect on students' outcomes due to impairment of cognitive learning becomes overloaded and energy waste in different activities of task and not focus on one-task of academic performance.

According to [23] found the students, almost have a Facebook account and more used to do varieties of activities on Facebook. Thus, the impact of Facebook decreases the level of focus and timeframe by multitasking. Rehearsals of task accumulate the recall the data as human consciously engaged in a repetitive task and do multitasking the effectiveness of worth become slower and tiredness made to lose the control of rehearsal and forget easily, however, cause of stress associated with tiredness came through multitasking.

The literature review discovered the necessary knowledge concerning social networks such as Facebook, academic performance, and still not work done on Facebook connection with human factors on students. Facebook is also one of the tools of media that most adults attract to use in their daily life routine. It provides a platform for adults to develop personal and social identities. This feature and adoption of cultural norms and social capital of social network communities may cause an effect on human behaviors. However, the literature with reference to show social networks and Facebook continues to be raised the students' lives as a result of it should be a relatively new theme in studious research.

3 Methodology and Design

The sample is represented by a convenient random sample technique. The sample consists of 375 participants of students enrolled in an undergraduate program at Shah Abdul Latif University (SALU). The research questionnaire is primarily developed on the basis of literature, existing survey and previous studies. A pilot study was conducted before distribution of instrument. Pearson Correlation method is used to test the reliability of the question items. This Study examines (Cronbach's alpha = 0.860) reliable. Self-administrated structure method is used to collect the data from participants. SPSS tool is used to perform data analysis of the survey. All the data are keyed in an Excel spreadsheet before using the Statistical Package for the Social Sciences (SPSS) software. This Study employed the Pearson Moment Correlation test and Regression to examine the relationships between dependent and independent variables presentation model given below in Fig. 2.

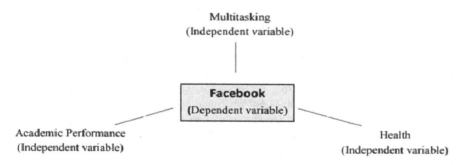

Fig. 2. Variables presentation model.

4 Results and Discussions

This section describes the results in two parts (a) Descriptive statistics and (b) inferential statistics and furthermore is discussion related to study.

4.1 Descriptive Statistics

A total of 375 respondents are surveyed about the impact of using Facebook on the academic performance of students. The result shows (69.6%) of the respondents were Male and (30.4%) Female, with different age group (42.4%) of the respondents are 17–18 years, (47.2%) are 19–21 years, and (9.6%) are 22–24 years and (.8%) are 25 years or above and their undergraduate level with previous CGPA information details are given in Table 1.

The main development of Facebook was to use for academic purposes, It was important to collect data about Facebook is a dependent variable and it is used for academic as well or not where (92%) of respondents have a Facebook account and (8%) were against Whenever, Facebook is measured in an hour per day. students

Table 1. The demographic characteristics of Facebook users.

Demographic characteristics	Sample size N = 375	%
Gender		
• Male	261	69.6
• Female	114	30.4
Age group		
• Less or equal to 18 years old	159	42.4
• 19–21 years	177	47.2
• 22–24 years	36	9.6
•25 years or above	3	0.8
Undergraduate level		
• First year	64	17.1
• Second year	93	28.8
• Third year	122	32.5
• Fourth year	96	25.6
CGPA		
• 1.5–2.0 CGPA	25	6.7
• 2.1–2.5 CGPA	78	20.8
• 2.6–3.0 CGPA	163	43.5
• 3.1–3.5 CGPA	85	22.7
• 3.6–4.0 CGPA	28	6.4

responses that (35%) of respondents use Facebook less than one hour per day, (16%) of respondents are using Facebook 1–5 h per day, (10%) of respondents are using Facebook 6–10 h per day, (7%) are using Facebook 11–16 h per day, (69%) of respondents are using Facebook 16–18 h per day.

Academic performance is an independent variable of this study. To measure the study timings as the use of Facebook is being affected by study timings resultant (68%) of the respondents indicates the positive response that Facebook affects their study timings and (32%) of respondents represents negative response that has no any impact of using Facebook on study timings. When the compare the Facebook activity on during class times the respondents the majority (71%) of the respondents indicated that they use Facebook during class time of study and (29%) of the respondents were against of statements. Many students are like to do work with multiple activities, (57%) of the respondents' activity performed use of Facebook on multitasking, it decrease their focus level and concentration in Demographic characteristics Sample. Define the purpose and different activities of Facebook: (66%) prefer Chat with Friends/family, (15%) of Discussion on Group board, (50%) of Group chatting, (9%) of Play games, (11%) of Share personal views, (87%) of shared photos, (53%) of share post on Groups, (27%) of use Facebook apps and (70%) of Watch friends status/news.

Multitasking is one of the variable of that support their lives students like to do task many tasks at same time, when measuring the item, strongly Disagree (3%), Disagree

(20%), Uncertain (8%), Agree (43%) and Strongly agree (26%). Health is independent variable of Facebook that 71% of respondents' response that Facebook can effects on health, 29% were against that were not affected on health. Hence,

Health has been effecting by Facebook, students faced some of health issues while using of Facebook, respondents response that (47%) were Eyesight issue, (13%) were Headache issue, (10%) of Stress, (2%) of Depression and (28%) of response Sleeping disorderly.

4.2   Inferential Statistics

This section presents the inferential statistics and further is divided into two parts, (a) correlation Analysis and (b) Regression Analysis.

Correlation Analysis

Correlation analysis is a part of testing the linear relationship between dependent variable to independent variables. This study used method of Bivariate Pearson correlation and technique was used to test the hypothesis between the relationships. Furthermore, it was used to test hypothesis. The correlation shows Pearson correlation (p) value level 0.01 and correlation Pearson two tailed test method used by using SPSS to find out the relationships between two variables and r values are the coefficients of Pearson [24].

This research shows the relationships between variables of value (r, p) and r values identifies the sign of positive or negative range from (+1 to −1) and even if r value 0.5 to 0.1 or −0.5 to −0.1 that examined the strong relationship between two variables exits, if r value is 0.3 to 0.5 or −0.3 to −0.5 that shows the medium relationship even if the r value 0.1 to 0.3 or −0.1 to −0.3 that to considered low and weak relationship [25].

However main function is to provide and decide the case of positive or negative correlation coefficient relationship (if significant level less than 0.05 is rejected and equal to Null hypothesis).

Facebook correlations with Academic performance Hypothesis

H_0 - *There is no relationship between students using Facebook and Academic performance*
H_1 - *There is a relationship between students using Facebook and Academic performance*

When we compute the relationship between Facebook and Academic performance variables examined the result (−0.417**) of negative relationships are indirectly proportional exists when the independent variable increase indirectly another side dependent variable should be decreased. Increase and decrease of variables should be based on the nature of students'. Computing the relationship between Facebook and academic performance variables examined the result r = (−0.417**) of negative relationship.

Significant level is (p = 0.000 < 0.05) that means there is a relationship between students' academic performance and using Facebook that rejects the null hypothesis (H_0). The results showed in Table 2 to defined the Correlation is medium that also showed that Facebook is one of the factor that impact on academic performance of the university students (H_1).

Table 2. Correlation between Facebook and Academic performance.

Correlations		Facebook	Academic performance
Facebook	Pearson correlation	1	$-.417^{**}$
	Sig. (2-tailed)		.000
	N	375	375
Academic performance	Pearson correlation	$-.417^{**}$	1
	Sig. (2-tailed)	.000	
	N	375	375

**. Correlation is significant at the 0.01 level (2-tailed).

Facebook correlation with Multitasking

H_0 - There is no relationship between students using Facebook and Multitasking.
H_1 - There is a relationship between students using Facebook and Multitasking.

Second computation of result is to measure the relationship between Facebook and multitasking see that research to measure the activities of users on Facebook. It shows the (0.393**) positive correlation between Facebook and Multitasking, independent variable increase also dependent variable increase, it is directly correlation of variables. The results showed in Table 3, medium correlation signifies that Facebook is not only factor to enhance multitasking but also enhance other activities of Facebook that can effect on students. In this correlation, when university of students increase the using of Facebook that also increase user activities as multitasking on Facebook however relationship is moderate to reject the (H0) null hypothesis and accept the H1 hypothesis because of the significance level is p = 0.000 < 0.05 which means there is relationship between multitasking and using Facebook.

Table 3. Correlations between Facebook and multitasking.

Correlations		Facebook	Multitasking
Facebook	Pearson correlation	1	$.393^{**}$
	Sig. (2-tailed)		.000
	N	375	375
Multitasking	Pearson correlation	$.393^{**}$	1
	Sig. (2-tailed)	.000	
	N	375	375

**. Correlation is significant at the 0.01 level (2-tailed).

Facebook correlation with Health

H_0 - *There is no relationship between students using Facebook and health*
H_1 - *There is a relationship between students using Facebook and health*

Health factor might get the cause of indirectly affect the students' academic performance measuring the Health factor in relationship between Facebook results are working out on the relationship between dependent variable, and independent variable outcomes (r = −0.200**) that signifies negative correlation between these two variables results and it shows there is low correlation that pointed out the dependent variable increase, and independent variable decrease, which means the usage of Facebook may effect on health and may cause to bad health, students may addict to use Facebook. However, the Facebook is not the only factor that has negative impact on the health. In addition, the final results of correlation shows (r = 0.200, p = 0.000 < 0.05) that signifies there is negative correlation exist and reject Null hypothesis therefore accept alternative H1. The results are shown in Table 4.

Table 4. Correlations between Facebook and Health.

Correlations

		Facebook	Health
Facebook	Pearson correlation	1	−.200**
	Sig. (2-tailed)		.000
	N	375	375
Health	Pearson correlation	−.200**	1
	Sig. (2-tailed)	.000	
	N	375	375

**. Correlation is significant at the 0.01 level (2-tailed).

Measuring the Health factor in relationship between Facebook results are working out on the relationship between dependent variable and independent variable outcomes (r = −0.200**) and signifies negative correlation between these two variables results shows there is low correlation that pointed out the dependent variable increase the independent variable decrease which means the using of Facebook may effect on health and may cause to bad health, students may addict to use Facebook however the Facebook is not only factor that has negative impact on the health. In addition, the final results of correlation shows (r = −0.200, p = 0.000 < 0.05) that signifies there is negative correlation exist and reject H_0 hypothesis therefore accept alternative H_1.

Regression Analysis
Regression analysis is a method to use for many independents variables that are correlated with dependent variables and linear regression technique [26, 27]. It is used to interpret the regression coefficients as the above correlation analysis outcomes in this research showed all the null hypothesis rejected but not make sure the accepted hypothesis support and not on concerned research. Furthermore, in this study simple

and Linear regression model created in SPSS which Standard multiple linear regression and the enter method are used to analyze the all independent variables at the same time into the model. Related to this survey, Regression analysis is interpreted the standardized coefficient beta (β) and R Square (R2) to provide the vivid transparency of independent variable and dependent variable are correlated in a relationship or not in relationships. Regression coefficients determined the analysis of variables in relation. The finding results and analysis showed the all of variables rejected the null hypothesis which is 0.000 significant level is less than 0.05. Furthermore, this study conducted Linear multiple regression analysis to predict the variables of values of the dependent variable (Facebook) known through independent variables (Academic performance, Multitasking, and Health issues).

Table 5. Model summary of study.

Model summary				
Model	R	R Square	Adjusted R Square	Std. error of the estimate
1	.417[a]	.174	.172	.247
2	.430[b]	.185	.180	.246
3	.608[c]	.369	.364	.217

a. Predictors: (Constant), Academic performance
b. Predictors: (Constant), Academic performance, Health
c. Predictors: (Constant), Academic performance, Health, Multitasking

In Table 5, presented the Model summary Results which extract from SPSS software, Model summary represent the Predicator in columns defined the relationship of R-Pearson correlation, RSquare coefficient determinations value, Adjusted R Square and Std. the error of the Estimate values.

Table 6. ANOVA results take out from SPSS.

ANOVA[b]					
Model	Sum of squares	df	Mean square	F	Sig.
1 Regression	10.191	3	3.397	72.398	.000[a]
Residual	17.409	371	.047		
Total	27.600	374			

a. Predictors: (Constant), Multitasking, Academic performance, Health
b. Dependent Variable: Facebook

The result of Anova-F-test showed in Table 6 is (72.398) positive and significant showed the all of variables rejected the null hypothesis which is 0.000 significant level is less than 0.05 which also support of model fitness.

In each table of results extracted form SPSS that indicates the Coefficients of determination explains the power of formulas that determine the strength of values changes in the dependent variable with the relation of independent variables. Table 5 Results of Model summary presented the linear regression analysis and Model testing exposes the value of R-Square so Model is 0.369 and the correlation of Coefficient 0.369. It indicates a low and weak positive linear correlation that means the R-Square explains 36.9% of the variance in the dependent variables which is Facebook while the remaining 63.1% did not clarify the variance in the dependent variable and might be other factors used to determine the negative impact of using Facebook on university students.

In Table 7 Regression coefficients determined the analysis of variables in relation however, the finding results and analysis showed the all of variables rejected the null hypothesis which is 0.000 significant level is less than 0.05. All independent variables has a relationship with using dependent variable (Facebook) form table of Model summary $R2 = 0.369$ or 36.9% results shown by the contribution of regression coefficients values the academic performance ($\beta = -0.352$), Multitasking ($\beta = 0.447$), health ($\beta = -0.235$).

Table 7. Regression coefficients results take out from SPSS.

Variables	Beta	Std. error	t-stat	Sig.
Constant	1.185	0.058	20.431	0.000
Academic performance	−0.352	0.025	−8.251	0.000
Health	−0.235	0.026	−5.321	0.000
Multitasking	0.447	0.035	10.415	0.000

After the interpretation of results, the highest contribution of results saying multitasking is a significant positive relationship that means the usage of Facebook increases, the amount of multitasking also increases. The academic performance and health have a negative significant relationship this means the usage of Facebook increase, Health and academic performance of the students will be decreased. In this study when Facebook is frequently used by students that may cause to decrease in academic performance and academic performance depends on students' usage that how much Facebook is being used by students in a day.

5 Conclusion and Future Work

This research has examined and evaluated the underlying impact of using Facebook on student's academic performance. Facebook has been increased day by day like a mushroom growth i.e. Facebook is becoming a need of social culture to stay live in the society. This study investigates the impact of using Facebook on the academic performance of University students. Facebook provides a significant role in academic areas and constructs a distraction for students at many universities but many of students don't know about the adverse impact on academic performance as these type of social networks badly damaged the system of education as well as the career of students.

The main idea of the current study was to create the awareness and make suggestions that what will be a better way to manage use of Facebook at university or during study times. It was focused on the dependent variable (Facebook) showed the results with independent variables (academic performance and multitasking). Directly or indirectly, Communication tools such as Facebook plays an important role in developing relationships either it impacts positive or negative on student's lives.

This study examines the relationship between Facebook and academic performance although it investigates that Facebook would impact on academic performance of the university students'. Findings of Result that indicates (69%) of students are engaged to use Facebook more than 16–18 h in a day when the students will divert to use Facebook on different activities obviously it will be affected on academic performance negatively. This research shows that Facebook has a positive relationship with multitasking (44.7%). However, when the multitasking is increased other side academic performance (35.2%) and health (−23.5%) will be decreased vice versa although the disadvantages are outweighed of advantages especially when it is done by without management and control. Finally, Misuse of Facebook damages the structure of education that directly effects on the students' academic performance with heavily used by students. Limitations of the present study are designed to examine the correlations between students and using Facebook. Statistically, Findings of the present study presents with ($p < 0.5$) significant level.

Future research will be added with a qualitative element to present study of mixed methods. This study was conducted an Undergraduate level of students that would be expanded for a higher level of students and other stakeholders. Future research will be a comparison between students GPA/percentage of before and after of using Facebook. This study was limited in selected areas of the institute, therefore, Future research and similar study should be conducted at schools, colleges, other universities of Sindh and the entire country.

Acknowledgment. The work is supported by the National Key Research & Development Plan under grant No. 2017YFB0801801, the National Science Foundation of China (NSFC) under grant No. 61472108 and 61672186.

References

1. Roblyer, M.D., McDaniel, M., Webb, M., Herman, J., Witty, J.V.: Findings on Facebook in higher education: a comparison of college faculty and student uses and perceptions of social networking sites. Internet Higher Educ. **13**(3), 134–140 (2010)
2. Al-Rahmi, W., Othman, M.: The impact of social media use on academic performance among university students: a pilot study. J. Inf. Syst. Res. Innovation **4**(12), 1–10 (2013)
3. Ainin, S., Naqshbandi, M.M., Moghavvemi, S., Jaafar, N.I.: Facebook usage, socialization and academic performance. Comput. Educ. **83**, 64–73 (2015)
4. Mehmood, S., Taswir, T.: The effects of social networking sites on the academic performance of students in college of applied sciences, Nizwa, Oman. Int. J. Arts Commer. **2**(1), 111–125 (2013)

5. Seely Brown, J., Adler, R.P.: Open education, the long tail, and learning 2.0. Educause Rev. **43**(1), 16–20 (2008)
6. Ogedebe, P.M., Emmanuel, J.A., Musa, Y.: A survey on Facebook and academic performance in Nigeria Universities. Int. J. Eng. Res. Appl. **2**(4), 788–797 (2012)
7. Laghari, A.A., He, H., Shafiq, M., Khan, A.: Assessment of quality of experience (QoE) of image compression in social cloud computing. Multiagent Grid Syst. **14**(2), 125–143 (2018)
8. Li, Y., Li, J., Chen, J., Minchao, L., Li, C.: Seed selection for data offloading based on social and interest graphs, CMC: computers. Mater. Continua **57**(3), 571–587 (2018)
9. Boyd, D.M., Ellison, N.B.: Social network sites: definition, history, and scholarship. J. Comput.-Mediated Commun. **13**(1), 210–230 (2007)
10. Laghari, A.A., He, H., Karim, S., Shah, H.A., Karn, N.K.: Quality of experience assessment of video quality in social clouds. Wirel. Commun. Mobile Comput. **2017**, 10 (2017)
11. Ziedonis, D., et al.: Tobacco use and cessation in psychiatric disorders: National Institute of Mental Health report, pp. 1691–1715 (2008)
12. Junco, R., Cotten, S.R.: No A 4 U: the relationship between multitasking and academic performance. Comput. Educ. **59**(2), 505–514 (2012)
13. Jafarkarimi, H., Sim, A.T.H., Saadatdoost, R., Hee, J.M.: Facebook addiction among Malaysian students. Int. J. Inf. Educ. Technol. **6**(6), 465 (2016)
14. Tariq, W., Mehboob, M., Khan, A., Ullah, F.: The impact of social media and social networks on education and students of Pakistan. Int. J. Comput. Sci. Issues (IJCSI) **9**(4), 407 (2012)
15. A'lamElhuda, D., Dimetry, D.A.: The impact of Facebook and others social networks usage on academic performance and social life among medical students at Khartoum University. Int. J. Sci. Technol. Res. **3**(5), 41–46 (2014)
16. Ahn, J.: The effect of social network sites on adolescents' social and academic development: current theories and controversies. J. Am. Soc. Inf. Sci. Technol. **62**(8), 1435–1445 (2011)
17. Singh, N., Barmola, K.C.: Internet addiction, mental health and academic performance of school students/adolescent. Int. J. Indian Psychol. **2**, 98–108 (2015)
18. Kirn, W.: The autumn of the multitaskers. Atlantic, 66–80 (2007)
19. Bijari, B., Javadinia, S.A., Erfanian, M., Abedini, M., Abassi, A.: The impact of virtual social networks on students' academic achievement in Birjand University of Medical Sciences in East Iran. Procedia-Soc. Behav. Sci. **83**, 103–106 (2013)
20. Larik, R.S.A., Mallah, G.A., Talpur, M.M.A., Suhag, A.K., Larik, F.A.: Effects of wireless devices on human body. J. Comput. Sci. Syst. Biol. **9**, 119–124 (2016)
21. Junco, R., Cotten, S.R.: Perceived academic effects of instant messaging use. Comput. Educ. **56**(2), 370–378 (2011)
22. Bieler, G.S., Brown, G.G., Williams, R.L., Brogan, D.J.: Estimating model-adjusted risks, risk differences, and risk ratios from complex survey data. Am. J. Epidemiol. **171**(5), 618–623 (2010)
23. Karim, S., Madiha, H., Mallah, G.A., Abbasi, S.K., Larik, R.S.A.: Utilization of Facebook website in avoiding academic performance and health hazards: a study of Khairpur Medical College Students. Int. J. Sci. Eng. Res. **7**(11), 2229–5518 (2016)
24. Sekaran, U., Bougie, R.: Business research methods: a skill-building approach (2011)
25. http://www.statisticssolutions.com/directory-of-statistical-analyses-correlationanalysis/correlation/. Accessed 5 Nov 2017
26. Xi, X., Sheng, V.S., Sun, B., Wang, L., Fuyuan, H.: An empirical comparison on multi-target regression learning, CMC: computers. Mater. Continua **56**(2), 185–198 (2018)
27. http://www.statisticssolutions.com/directory-of-statistical-analysesregressionanalsis/regression/. Accessed 5 Nov 2017

Robust Audio Watermarking Algorithm Based on Moving Average and DCT

Jinquan Zhang[✉], Xizi Peng, and Shibin Zhang

School of Cybersecurity, Chengdu University of Information Technology,
Chengdu, China
zhjqcom@163.com

Abstract. Noise is often brought to host audio by common signal processing operation, and it usually changes the high-frequency component of an audio signal. So embedding watermark by adjusting low-frequency coefficient can improve the robustness of a watermark scheme. Moving Average sequence is a low-frequency feature of an audio signal. This work proposed a method which embedding watermark into the maximal coefficient in discrete cosine transform domain of a moving average sequence. Subjective and objective tests reveal that the proposed watermarking scheme maintains highly audio quality, and simultaneously, the algorithm is highly robust to common digital signal processing operations, including additive noise, sampling rate change, bit resolution transformation, MP3 compression, and random cropping, especially low-pass filtering.

Keywords: Audio watermarking · Robust watermarking ·
Moving average sequence · Discrete cosine transform

1 Introduction

With the development of Internet network, more and more resources are fully shared on Internet. But some copyrighted digital products are also spread in unauthorized circumstances, which seriously harmed the creators' interests, and hurt the author's creative passion. An important method to track piracy is to embed robust digital watermark in the works.

Audio watermarking has been attracting the researchers' attention [1]. Some audio watermarking algorithms embedded information in a single domain. For examples, literature [2–4] embedded information in time domain, and literature [5–7] embedded watermark in frequency domain. Usually, algorithm which embeds information in time domain has high efficiency, and algorithm which embeds information in the frequency domain has good robustness to a variety of signal processing operations.

For signal processing transformations have respective advantages, some researchers combined good properties of two or three kinds of transformations and embedded watermark into hybrid domain. Making use of the multi-resolution of discrete wavelet transform (DWT) and the energy compression of discrete cosine transform domain (DCT), Wang and Zhao [8] argued embedding the watermark into the hybrid domain. Literature [9] proposed an improved algorithm based on literature [3], which combined

X. Sun et al. (Eds.): ICAIS 2019, LNCS 11634, pp. 419–429, 2019.
https://doi.org/10.1007/978-3-030-24271-8_38

characteristics of DWT and histogram. The robustness to MP3 compression and low-pass filter was increased. Literature [10] performed DWT on a frame audio, then, singular value decomposition (SVD) was done on the approximation coefficients, and embedded watermark into the SVD coefficients. Literature [11] segmented audio signal and SVD was performed on each segment, then first SVD coefficient in every block were grouped together and DCT was done, and the watermark was embedded into DCT coefficients. These algorithms all had good robustness.

To a robust audio watermarking algorithm, the watermark information is required to survive common signal processing operations, such as MP3 compression, low-pass filter and so on. As we known, the time delay will take place when low-pass filtering is done on a watermarked audio, and about 1000 zero samples will be added at the front of the audio signal when MP3 compression is performed on. At the same time, the random-clipping may be happen to a watermarked audio. It is necessary to embed synchronization code into a watermarked audio [2, 10–12].

For common signal operations mainly change the high frequency component of a signal, embedding message in low frequency component of an audio signal is important to improve the robustness of an algorithm. In literature [13–17], DWT was performed on audio signal segment, then, the message was embedded in approximate coefficient. In literature [8, 10, 18], DWT was performed the audio signal frame first, and other transformation are carried out on the approximate coefficient, then, the message was embedded in the coefficient of hybrid domain.

Decreasing the embedding capacity is also a way to improve the robustness, for decreasing the capacity means that embedding a bit message involves more samples, the characteristic of the signal segment is more stable. In literature [2], embedding one bit message needs 1020 samples. If the sampling frequency of an audio signal is 44.1 kHz, the embedding capacity of the algorithm is about 43 bps. In literature [3], the value is 2 bps. In literature [19], it is 80 bps and in literature [11], it is 43 bps.

In our scheme, a moving average sequence (MAS) of audio signal is obtained first. It is the low-frequency feature of an audio signal. Then, DCT is performed on a long sequence segment to get a stable feature. The maximal coefficient of DCT is chosen to embed message by quantization index modulation (QIM). At the same time, synchronization code is used to locate the watermark and improve the accuracy of the detecting algorithm.

The rest of this paper is organized as follows: In Sect. 2, we defines the moving average sequence, describes its properties, and presents a rapid calculation of MAS. Section 3 separately describes the watermark embedding and watermark extraction of the proposed watermarking method. In Sect. 4, the experimental results are presented to show the performance of the proposed watermark. The conclusion of this paper is drawn out in Sect. 5.

2 Definition of MAS and Its Property

2.1 Definition of MAS and Its Properties

Assume the sample number of an audio clip is R, and the value of them are denoted as $x_1, x_2, \ldots, x_R$. Choose an integer b, and the MAS M_B is defined as Eq. (1).

$$M_{B_i} = \frac{1}{b}(x_i + x_{i+1} + \cdots + x_{i+b-1}) = \frac{1}{b}\sum_{k=i}^{i+b-1} x_k, \ i \in (1, R - b + 1) \qquad (1)$$

It is easy to know from the Eq. (1) that the sequence has good low-pass characteristic. As we all know, common signal processing, such as additive noise, sampling rate change, bit resolution transformation and so on, usually mainly changes high-frequency component of an audio signal, and the low-frequency component is slightly distorted.

Our experimental results shows that, for an audio clip, the MAS is nearly unchanged after it undergo common signal processing operations, such as additive noise, sampling rate change, bit resolution transformation, and so on, even the audio waveform has obviously different. That is, their MASs are nearly overlapping, which means their low-frequency components are almost the same.

In the following experiment, the low-pass filter operation is done to a certain audio clip. In the experiment, the integer b = 30, the cutoff frequency of low-pass filter is 8 kHz. The waveform of the original audio clip and its MAS, the waveform of audio clip after low-pass filtering and its MAS are all shown in Fig. 1. As we all know, the time delay will take place when low-pass filter is done to a time signal. In order to compare the shapes of these waveforms, the waveform after low-pass filter processing and its MAS are both shift to left 3 sampling periods. As can be seen from Fig. 1, the waveform of the audio clip changed obviously after low-pass filtering, but their MASs are almost overlapping.

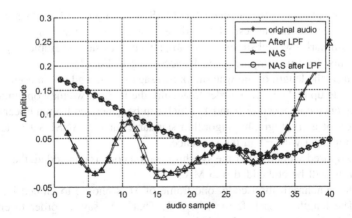

Fig. 1. audio waveform and its MAS before and after low-pass filtering

2.2 Rapid Calculation of MAS

The following method is used to obtain the MAS of an audio segment quickly. Assume an audio signal $X = (x_1, x_2, \ldots, x_R)$. For a given integer $b > 0$,
Let

$$M_{B_i} = (x_i + x_{i+1} + \ldots + x_{i+b-1})/b \tag{2}$$

Now, we will compute $M_{B_{i+1}}$. In fact, compare with M_{B_i}, when the $M_{B_{i+1}}$ is computed, the ith sample is excluded, and the $(i + b)$th sample is included.
Then

$$M_{B_{i+1}} = M_{B_i} + x_{i+b}/b - x_i/b \tag{3}$$

From Eq. (3), we can obtain Eq. (4) as follows.

$$M_{B_{i+1}} = M_{B_i} + (x_{i+b} - x_i)/b \tag{4}$$

The method will reduce the computation load dramatically.

3 Embedding and Extracting Watermark

Because the shape of MAS of an audio clip is almost the same before and after signal processing operations, our scheme embeds message in DCT domain of MAS. The rule of the synchronization code described in literature [20] is adopted to locate the watermark information. If the audio clip is very long, the synchronization code and watermark are embedded repeatedly.

3.1 Embedding Watermark

We choose an integer b to calculate the MAS M_B following Eq. (1) according to definition in Sect. 2. In the rest of this paper, for convenient writing, we substitute M for M_B. Similarly, we substitute M_i for M_{B_i}. That is to say, b samples, $x_i, x_{i+1}, \ldots, x_{i+b-1}$, are involved in computing the M_i according to Eq. (1).

We assume the length of the watermark message w is L, and w is a pseudo-random sequence made up of $\{-1, 1\}$. In order to acquire the w, first, we may obtain a pseudo-random sequence composed of 0 and 1, which can be generated from a linear feedback shift register, or a cryptographic algorithm standard, such as ANSI X9.32 and so on. Then, 0 is replaced with -1 in the sequence.

In the proposed scheme, after the synchronization code is embedded, the watermark information w will be embedded into MAS.

After the synchronization code, one frame of M is chosen to embed into one bit message. The length of each frame is $n \times b$. That is to say, in order to embed the message w, the length $n \times b \times L$ of M is needed. How to choose the parameters n and b is presented in Sect. 4.1.

For the 1-th frame of M after the synchronization code, we denoted it as $(M_1, M_2, \ldots, M_{n \times b})$ which involves $n \times b + b - 1$ samples, denoted as $(x_1, x_2, \ldots, x_{n \times b + b - 1})$. Then, For a certain frame of M, such as i-th frame, it is denoted as $(M_{n \times b \times i + 1}, M_{n \times b \times i + 2}, \ldots, M_{n \times b \times (i+1)})$, which involves $n \times b + b - 1$ samples, denoted as $(x_{n \times b \times i + 1}, x_{n \times b \times i + 2}, \ldots, x_{n \times b \times (i+1) + b - 1})$.

These expressions in the previous paragraph weren't simplified because it is helpful to understand our scheme, such as $n \times b \times i + b + 1$, $n \times b \times i + n \times b$ and so on.

In our scheme, for avoiding the interference which is brought by the previous bit message embedding, the sequence $(M_{n \times b \times i + 1}, M_{n \times b \times i + 2}, \ldots, M_{n \times b \times i + b})$ keeps unchanged, and DCT is performed on $(M_{n \times b \times i + b + 1}, M_{n \times b \times i + b + 2}, \ldots, M_{n \times b \times i + n \times b})$. Then, the QIM is adopted to embed watermark message by modifying the maximal coefficient of DCT. That is to say, the length of DCT is $(n-1) \times b$.

For the i-th frame of M_B, the detailed procedure of embedding one bit message into it is described as follows.

(1) Set the embedding strength $S > 0$. Let $d[-1] = 3S/4$, $d[1] = S/4$.

(2) If the number of the remaining audio samples may embed the whole watermark message w one time, go to step (3), if not, the embedding procedure is over.

(3) DCT is performed on $(M_{n \times b \times i + b + 1}, M_{n \times b \times i + b + 2}, \ldots, M_{n \times b \times i + n \times b})$. Assume the coefficient with the largest absolute value is t in DCT coefficients. So, t is a signed number. According to the properties of DCT, it must be a low frequency coefficient and relatively stable to common signal processing operation. Then, the i-th bit watermark information $w(k)$ will be embedded. The embedding rule is shown in Eq. (5).

$$t' = \begin{cases} round((t + d[1])/S) \times S - d[1], & if \ w(i) = 1 \\ round((t + d[-1])/S) \times S - d[-1], & if \ w(i) = -1 \end{cases} \tag{5}$$

Where round $(\cdot)$ means rounding to nearest integer.

(4) The t' may not be the maximal one now, so we must adjust coefficients whose absolute value is larger than $|t'|$. To improve the robustness of the scheme, coefficients whose absolute value is close to $|t'|$ are also slightly reduced. An optional approach is that, if the $|t'| > S$, these coefficients are changed to $|t'|-S/8$, if not, changed to $0.8S$. The sign of these coefficients is unchanged, and $|\cdot|$ means the absolute value function. Other adjustment ways may be also acceptable.

(5) IDCT is performed and $(M'_{n \times b \times i + b + 1}, M'_{n \times b \times i + b + 2}, \ldots, M'_{n \times b \times i + n*b})$ is obtained. Then, subtract $(M_{n \times b \times i + b + 1}, M_{n \times b \times i + b + 2}, \ldots, M_{n \times b \times i + n \times b})$ from $(M'_{n \times b \times i + b + 1}, M'_{n \times b \times i + b + 2}, \ldots, M'_{n \times b \times i + n*b})$ correspondingly. Set the variation of sequence $(M_{n \times b \times i + 1}, M_{n \times b \times i + 2}, \ldots, M_{n \times b \times i + n \times b})$ is v, then

$$\begin{aligned} v &= (M_{n \times b \times i + 1} - M_{n \times b \times i + 1}, M_{n \times b \times i + 2} - M_{n \times b \times i + 2}, \ldots, M_{n \times b \times i + b} - M_{n \times b \times i + b}, \\ & \quad M'_{n \times b \times i + b + 1} - M_{n \times b \times i + b + 1}, M'_{n \times b \times i + b + 2} - M_{n \times b \times i + b + 2}, \ldots, M'_{n \times b \times i + n*b} - M_{n \times b \times i + n \times b}) \\ &= (v_1, \ldots, v_b, v_{b+1}, \ldots, v_{n \times b}) \\ &= (0, \ldots, 0, v_{b+1}, \ldots, v_{n \times b}). \end{aligned}$$

There are b zeros in the front of the sequence because $(M_{n \times b \times i+1}, \ldots, M_{n \times b \times i+b})$ isn't involved into DCT.

The variation of corresponding audio samples should satisfy Eq. (6):

$$\sum_{j=k}^{k+b-1} z_j = b \times v_k, k = 1, \ldots n \times b \tag{6}$$

z_j denotes variation of the $(n \times b \times i + j)$-th audio sample.

Now, we solve the equation set made up of the last b equations. That is, the equation set is made up of equations from $((n-1) \times b+1)$-th to $(n \times b)$-th.

From the last equation, that is,

$$\sum_{j=n \times b}^{n \times b+b-1} z_j = bv_{n \times b} \tag{7}$$

We let $z_{n \times b+j} = v_{n \times b}, j = 0, 1, 2, \ldots, b - 1$.

Then, the other $b-1$ equations is solved,

$$z_{(n-1) \times b+j} = b(v_{(n-1) \times b+j} - v_{(n-1) \times b+j+1}) + z_{n \times b+j}, j = 1, 2, \ldots, b - 1 \tag{8}$$

Then, the equation set, which is made up of equations from $(n-2) \times b+1$ to $(n-1) \times b$, is solved,

$$z_{(n-2) \times b+j} = b(v_{(n-2) \times b+j} - v_{(n-2) \times b+j+1}) + z_{(n-1) \times b+j}, j = 1, 2, \ldots, b \tag{9}$$

The rest equations can be solved in the same manner.

Assume the solution of Eq. (6) is z_j, $j \in [1, n \times b + b - 1]$. Then, z_j, $j \in [1, n \times b + b - 1]$ plus x_r, $r \in [n \times b \times i + 1, n \times b \times i + n \times b + b-1]$ correspondingly, for example, $x'_{n \times b \times i+1} = x_{n \times b \times i+1+z_1}$. Then the watermarked audio is obtained.

3.2   Watermark Extraction Algorithm

Parameters which are used in embedding watermark phase are obtained first, including parameters used in the embed phase of synchronization code, the integer b, the length of frame $n \times b$, the embedding strength S, the length of the watermark L, and so on. The extraction scheme is described as follows.

The synchronization code is searched first. Then, the position where message is embedded into is located.

Similar to the embedding phase, After the synchronization code, the MAS M'' (In fact, it is M''_B) is gotten by the watermarked audio according to Eq. (1) in Sect. 2. Then, the MAS is chosen to detect message. The length of frame is also $n \times b$, and DCT is performed on each frame.

For a certain frame M_B'', set the maximal data of DCT coefficient is t^*, one bit message may be detected as follows,

$$w_i = \begin{cases} 1, & t^* - \lfloor t^*/S \rfloor \times S \geq S/2 \\ -1, & t^* - \lfloor t^*/S \rfloor \times S < S/2 \end{cases} \tag{10}$$

The similar procedure is performed until all data are extracted.

Assume the number of watermark extraction is n, and the i-th message which is extracted from the watermarked audio is denoted as $(w_1^i, w_2^i, \ldots, w_L^i)$. L is the length of the watermark. Then, according to majority principle, the k-th bit watermark is obtained by the following equation.

$$w_k = \begin{cases} 1, & if \left(\sum_{j=1}^n w_k^j \right) \geq 0 \\ -1, & otherwise \end{cases} \tag{11}$$

So the watermark information is obtained.

4 Experimental Results and Discussions

In our experiments, a random sequence with 128 bits is adopted as watermark message, which is generated by the pseudo-random number generator in ANSI X9.32. The number of 1 and -1 are both 64 bits in the watermark. Various styles of audio clips are chosen to accomplish the experiments. Each audio clip is a 16-bit mono audio clip in the WAVE format sampled at 44 100 Hz.

4.1 Choice of B and N

Assume the number of zero-crossing of M_{10} is $z_{M_{10}}$, M_{10} is obtained according to Eq. (1) in Sect. 2. L is the sample number of the original audio clip. Let $num = L/z_{M_{10}}$. The integer b in embedding phase in Sect. 3 is less than num a little.

The parameter n is an experimental value. We choose many various styles of audio clips to accomplish the experiments. According to our experimental results, the algorithm have good compromise between robustness and audibility when $n \in [8, 10]$.

4.2 Imperceptibility Test

In order to evaluate the quality of the watermarked audio, signal-to-noise ratio (SNR) and perceptual evaluation of audio quality (PEAQ), an assessment tool recommended by ITU BS1387, are both used in objective evaluation tests, and Mean Opinion Score (MOS), suggested by ITU-T P.800, is used in the subjective listening test. Here, we only report the results with three audio clips which are pop music, country music and blues music.

The parameters of the three chosen audio clips are as follows. For pop music clip, the length is 15 s, $b = 60$, $n = 10$, $S = 0.18$. For country music clip, 15 s, $b = 60$,

$n = 10$, $S = 0.18$. For blues music clip, 16 s, $b = 50$, $n = 9$, $S = 0.2$. For each clip, use PEAQ to measure the watermarked audio quality to adjust embedding parameters, especially the embedding strength S. In our experiments, the ODG (Objective Difference Grades) is less than -1, and the SNR is more than 30 dB.

For those coefficients whose absolute value are larger than or close to $|t'|$, the way which is used to adjust these coefficients is as described in Sect. 3.1. In our experiments, the largest coefficient is often the 3–12-th alternating current (AC) coefficient of the DCT domain.

In order to assess the algorithm, a comparative experiment which embed message in DCT is carried out. In the contrastive experiment, the parameters and location of synchronization code are unchanging. The same message is embedded at the same location, and the embedding capacity is identical. The message is embedded into the maximal DCT coefficients by QIM. The embedding strength was adjusted according to the similar SNR.

The SNR and ODG of the watermarked audio are obtained in test. The subjective test is done by a team composed of 10 audiences. As shown in Table 1, in the case of nearly SNR, our scheme have greater ODG than the contrastive scheme which message is embedded in the DCT domain directly, especially for smooth music. For example, pop music.

Table 1. Imperceptibility test.

	SNR (dB)	ODG	MOS
Pop music (Proposed scheme)	31.7	−0.75	4.85
Pop music (DCT)	31.5	−1.41	4.15
Country music (Proposed scheme)	30.6	−0.08	4.95
Country music (DCT)	30.6	−0.12	4.90
Blues music (Proposed scheme)	30.5	−0.42	4.91
Blues music (DCT)	30.7	−0.53	4.89

4.3 Embedding Capacity

Assume the sampling frequency of the audio clip is fs, the embedding capacity is about fs/nb bits, b is the integer which is used to compute the MAS, and n is as described in Sect. 4.1.

As mentioned above, the synchronization code is embedded before the message, as described in literature [20]. In proposed scheme, embedding one bit synchronization code involves about $2b$ samples. For one bit message, it is about $10b$ samples. At the same time, the length of the synchronization code is much less than the length of the watermark information. So the embedding capacity is mainly determined by the watermark embedding algorithm.

4.4 Robustness Tests

In experiments, the processing operations shown in Table 2 are performed on the watermarked audio signals which are mentioned in Sect. 3.1. These operations include:

(1) Additive white Gaussian noise (AWGN): white Gaussian noise is added to the watermarked signal until the resulting signal has an SNR of 55 dB/45 dB/35 dB.

(2) Re-quantization: the 16-bit watermarked audio signals are re-quantized down to 8 bits/sample and then back to 16 bits/sample.

(3) Resampling: The watermarked signal, originally sampled at 44.1 kHz, is re-sampled at 22.05 kHz/11.025 kHz, and then restored back by sampling again at 44.1 kHz.

(4) Low-pass filtering: A six order Butterworth filter with cut-off frequency 10 kHz/8 kHz/4 kHz/2 kHz is used.

(5) Cropping: Segments of one second are removed from the watermarked audio signal randomly.

(6) MP3 Compression 128 kbps/96 kbps/80 kbps/64 kbps: The MPEG-1 layer-3 compression is applied. The watermarked audio signal is compressed at the bit rate of 128 kbps/96 kbps and then decompressed back to the WAVE format.

The experimental results for above three audio clips are shown in Table 2. As can be seen in the table, the number of embedding message in the watermarked audio is 8, even the number of detecting watermark message is only 2–4, such as Additive noise

Table 2. Imperceptibility test.

	SNR (dB)		ODG		MOS	
	DT	BER	DT	BER	DT	BER
No attack	8	0	8	0	10	0
Additive noise (55 dB)	7	0	8	0	10	0
Additive noise (45 dB)	8	0	8	0	8	0
Additive noise (35 dB)	3	0	4	0.0078	5	0.0078
Re-quantization	8	0	8	0	10	0
Resampling (22050 Hz)	8	0	8	0	10	0
Resampling (11025 Hz)	8	0	8	0	8	0
Low-pass filtering (10 kHz)	7	0	6	0	10	0
Low-pass filtering (8 kHz)	7	0	7	0	9	0
Low-pass filtering (6 kHz)	7	0	6	0	10	0
Low-pass filtering (4 kHz)	6	0	5	0	7	0
Low-pass filtering (2 kHz)	5	0	3	0	7	0
Random cutting	7	0	6	0	9	0
MP3 (128 kbps)	7	0	5	0	8	0
MP3 (96 kbps)	7	0	5	0	7	0
MP3 (80 kbps)	5	0	2	0.0156	5	0
MP3 (64 kbps)	4	0	2	0.0156	6	0.0156

(35 dB), or MP3(64 kbps), the bit error rate (BER) of the proposed algorithm is close to zero, or equal to zero, which means the algorithm has strong robustness.

In Table 2, DT means the detected times of the information in watermarked audio.

To evaluate the performance of our scheme, we compare with literature [10–12, 19] against low-pass filter processing. Our scheme and comparative schemes give results for lots of audio clips in experiments. Here, we adopt the average value as the way in literature [11], and indicate different cutoff frequencies, as Table 3 shows. As we can see, our algorithm have better performance against low-pass filter processing in the case of close embedding capacity.

Table 3. Performance comparison against low-pass filter.

	Scheme [10]	Scheme [11]	Scheme [12]	Scheme [19]	Our scheme
Capacity (bps)	45.9	43	30.7	80	76
SNR (dB)	24.4	32.5	25.7	37.4	30.9
ODG	-	−0.57	−0.63	−0.75	−0.42
Synchronization code	Yes	Yes	Yes	No	Yes
Low-pass BER (%) (cutoff frequency, kHz)	0(11.025)	0(44.1)	11.0(10)	2.7(6)	0(2)

-: the literature didn't give the experimental data.

5   Conclusion

A robust audio watermark algorithm is proposed in the paper. The algorithm combines the low-pass characteristics of moving average and energy concentration characteristics of DCT, embeds watermark by adjusting the largest coefficient of DCT domain. Experimental results show that the watermarked audio have high SNR and good audibility. The algorithm is strongly robust against common signal processing operations such as additive noise, re-quantization, resampling, low pass filtering, random cutting, and MP3 compression. Next, we will try our scheme in image watermarking [21, 22].

Acknowledgments. This work is supported by the National Key Research and Development Project of China (No. 2017YFB0802302), the National Natural Science Foundation of China (No.61572086, No.61402058), the Scientific Research Foundation of CUIT (No. KYTZ 201420), and the Scientific Research Project of Department of Education in Sichuan Province (No. 16ZA0221).

References

1. Hua, G., Huang, J., Shi, Y.Q., et al.: Twenty years of digital audio watermarking – a comprehensive review. Signal Process. **128**, 222–242 (2016)
2. Lie, W.N., Chang, L.: Robust and high-quality time-domain audio watermarking based on low-frequency amplitude modification. IEEE Trans. Multimedia **8**(1), 46–59 (2006)

3. Xiang, S.J., Huang, J.: Histogram-based audio watermarking against time-scale modification and cropping attacks. IEEE Trans. Multimedia 9(7), 1357–1372 (2007)
4. Erçelebi, E., Subaşı, A.: Robust multi-bit and high quality audio watermarking using pseudo-random sequences. Comput. Electr. Eng. 31(8), 525–536 (2005)
5. Al-Nuaimy, W., El-Bendary, M., Shafik, A., et al.: An SVD audio watermarking approach using chaotic encrypted images. Digit. Signal Process. 21(6), 764–779 (2011)
6. Wang, J., Healy, R., Timoney, J.: A robust audio watermarking scheme based on reduced singular value decomposition and distortion removal. Signal Process. 91(8), 1693–1708 (2011)
7. Fallahpour, M., Megías, D.: High capacity audio watermarking using the high frequency band of the wavelet domain. Multimedia Tools Appl. 52(2), 485–498 (2011)
8. Wang, X., Zhao, H.: A novel synchronization invariant audio watermarking scheme based on DWT and DCT. IEEE Trans. Signal Process. 54(12), 4835–4840 (2006)
9. Xiang, S., Kim, H., Huang, J.: Audio watermarking robust against time-scale modification and MP3 compression. Signal Process. 88(10), 2372–2387 (2008)
10. Bhat, K.V., Sengupta, I., Das, A.: An adaptive audio watermarking based on the singular value decomposition in the wavelet domain. Digit. Signal Process. 20(6), 1547–1558 (2010)
11. Lei, B.Y., Soon, I.Y., Li, Z.: Blind and robust audio watermarking scheme based on SVD-DCT. Signal Process. 91(8), 1973–1984 (2011)
12. Megías, D., Serra-Ruiz, J., Fallahpour, M.: Efficient self-synchronised blind audio watermarking system based on time domain and FFT amplitude modification. Signal Process. 90(12), 3078–3092 (2010)
13. Shaoquan, W., Huang, J., Huang, D.: Efficiently self-synchronized audio watermarking for assured audio data transmission. IEEE Trans. Broadcast. 51(1), 69–76 (2005)
14. Wang, X., Niu, P., Yang, H.: A robust digital audio watermarking based on statistics characteristics. Pattern Recognit. 42(11), 3057–3064 (2009)
15. Lei, M., Yang, Y., Luo, S.: Semi-fragile audio watermarking algorithm in DWT domain. China Commun. 7(4), 71–75 (2010)
16. Chen, S.-T., Hsu, C.-Y., Huang, H.-N.: Wavelet-domain audio watermarking using optimal modification on low-frequency amplitude. IET Signal Process. 9(2), 166–176 (2015)
17. H-T, H., Hsu, L.: A DWT-based rational dither modulation scheme for effective blind audio watermarking. Circuits Syst. Signal Process. 35(2), 553–572 (2016)
18. Lei, B., Soon, I.Y., Zhou, F., et al.: A robust audio watermarking scheme based on lifting wavelet transform and singular value decomposition. Signal Process. 92(9), 1985–2001 (2012)
19. Kang, X., Yang, R., Huang, J.: Geometric invariant audio watermarking based on an LCM feature. IEEE Trans. Multimedia 13(2), 181–190 (2011)
20. Zhang, J., Wang, H., Li, X.: Robust audio watermarking algorithm based on neighborhood averaging method. J. China Railw. Soc. 34(7), 43–48 (2012)
21. Gong, D., Chen, Y., Haoyu, L., Li, Z., Han, Y.: Self-embedding image watermarking based on combined decision using pre-offset and post-offset blocks. Comput. Mater. Continua 57(2), 243–260 (2018)
22. Jayashree, N., Bhuvaneswaran, R.S.: A robust image watermarking scheme using z-transform, discrete wavelet transform and bidiagonal singular value decomposition. Comput. Mater. Continua 58(1), 263–285 (2019)

Computer Evidence Analysis Technology Based on Weighted Frequent Pattern Growth Algorithm

Tianxiao Xue, Qingbao Li, Ping Zhang, Zhifeng Chen[✉],
Peijun Feng, and Nan Luo

State Key Laboratory of Mathematical Engineering and Advanced Computing,
Zhengzhou, China
736274187@qq.com, xiaohouzi06@163.com

Abstract. The current analysis of computer forensics is still dependent on the investigation personnel, leading to the problem of heavy workload and low efficiency. At the same time, computer evidences have the characteristics of complex structure and large amount of data, which is prone to the problem of association rules redundancy. In order to improve the efficiency of computer evidence analysis, this paper uses association analysis technology to analyze the user's behavior habits from the obtained computer system log, browser records, file operation traces and other information; combined with the idea of weighted features, the weight set was generated according to the difference of attribute importance, and the Frequent Pattern Growth (FP-Growth) algorithm is improved. The experimental results show that the improved FP-Growth algorithm can effectively remove the redundant rules in evidence analysis, and is more practical for user behavior analysis.

Keywords: Computer forensics · Association analysis ·
FP-Growth algorithm · User behavior

1 Introduction

On January 31, 2018, China Internet Network Information Center (CNNIC) released *the 41st Statistical Report on Internet Development in China* in Beijing [1]. As of December 2017, the number of Internet users in China reached 772 million, with a penetration rate of 55.8%, exceeding the global average (51.7%) by 4.1% points, exceeding the Asian average (46.7%) by 9.1% points.

With the continuous development of computer network technology, various types of new criminal activities with network information systems are increasing, and the harm caused by them is increasing. How to obtain evidence related to computer crime and bring criminals to justice has become a new topic in the field of computer science and justice. As an interdisciplinary subject in the field of computer science and law, computer forensics has become a hot spot in the field of computer security.

Data mining algorithms are an important technology for data analysis, including classification, association, cluster, and anomaly analysis. The development of data

Project 61802432 supported by National Natural Science Foundation of China.

X. Sun et al. (Eds.): ICAIS 2019, LNCS 11634, pp. 430–441, 2019.
https://doi.org/10.1007/978-3-030-24271-8_39

mining technology makes the analysis of forensic data no longer limited to the processing of structured data and character information, but can be extended to the visualization of audiovisual materials, video information [2, 3], etc. From single structured processing to heterogeneous, semi-structured, even unstructured text information [4]. The characteristic of data mining is to extract the pattern law from its own data, give its own data connotation value, and refine the data into knowledge [5].

In the field of digital evidence analysis, the use of correlation analysis to find potential association rules from a large number of behavioral information, such as the literature [6] applies correlation rules to evidence analysis to analyze the similarities of computer anomalies. Literature [7] proposes a log association model to track network attacks. The experimental results show that the method can accurately locate the attacker in the controllable network. Literature [8] uses a network sniffer to monitor the data in the network, and uses the Apriori algorithm to mine the association rules to find some keywords. However, its algorithm has limited application and does not have good universality. Literature [9] analyzes user behavior rules by studying business flow time series relationship. A user behavior analysis method is proposed and divided into three parts: based on fractal model, improved Apriori algorithm and maximum distance clustering method. Segmentation clustering and time series analysis, and finally obtain user behavior rules from user data exchange. However, the time complexity of this method is high, and the memory overhead required for the experiment is large. Literature [10] combines traditional statistical analysis technology and data mining technology, the search log is analyzed and researched in detail makes a detailed analysis and study of the search logs by combining traditional statistical analysis and data mining. A search log analysis system based on data mining is designed. A user-click-based query term proximity algorithm is used to input the user. The query word is used to refer to the word recommendation to improve the user experience. Literature [11] proposes an internal access method based on association rules and clustering algorithm. Through the analysis of the opening and running time of different processes in memory, the improved Apriori association algorithm is used to correlate the user's behavior habits and obtain the behavior of the user in a certain period of time or one hour. Using the improved K-means clustering algorithm, clusters different users according to intimacy. Literature [12] applies the association algorithm to the Named Entity Recognition (NER) technology, through the association analysis of the entity recognition results in the communication text, mining the hidden relationship between the entities, but not optimizing and improving the Apriori algorithm, and only generating binary frequent patterns, the correlation strength is not obvious.

To solve the problem that the computer electronic evidence structure is complex, the data volume is large and the analysis efficiency is low, this paper uses the appropriate association mining algorithm to mine the association relationship among the attribute data in the data set, generate the association rules, and analyze the user behavior habits. Aiming at the problem that the traditional FP-Growth algorithm is not sensitive to the key anomaly behavior, the algorithm is optimized and improved. According to the characteristics of electronic evidence, an analysis technique based on Weighted FP-Growth algorithm is proposed, which greatly improves the timeliness of electronic evidence analysis. Through the analysis of evidence, the investigators are helped to portray the suspect's behavior and habits, and explore the correlation between them to provide technical support for the next step of the public security department.

2 Problem Description

2.1 Traditional FP-Growth Algorithm

The FP-Growth algorithm is an association analysis algorithm proposed by Jiawei Han et al. It adopts the following divide and conquer strategy: compressing the database of frequent itemsets into a Frequent Pattern Tree, but retaining the item set association information. FP-tree is a special prefix tree consisting of a frequent item header table and an item prefix tree. The FP-Growth algorithm speeds up the entire mining process based on the tree structure.

The FP-Growth algorithm is based on Apriori, but uses an advanced data structure to reduce the number of scans, greatly speeding up the algorithm. The algorithm only needs to scan the database twice, and the Apriori algorithm scans the database for each potential frequent item set to determine whether the given mode is frequent, so the FP-Growth is faster than the Apriori.

2.2 Limitations of Traditional Algorithms Applied to Evidence Analysis

According to the previous section, the FP-Growth algorithm has two major advantages: (1) Only two database scans are performed. (2) No overly large candidate sets are generated. However, due to the particularity of computer forensics, the application of the algorithm to evidence analysis still has the following three problems:

First, Time and Space Overhead Is Large. When using the FP-Growth algorithm for electronic evidence mining, the FP-Tree generated by the algorithm will still be very large due to the massive data of the computer. In the mining process of frequent patterns, it is necessary to read and traverse the entire FP-Tree from the memory, and the time and space overhead required is still large.

Second, the Data Structure Types Are Numerous. Computer evidence is complex, and there are many attribute values. Only the system log has more than a dozen attributes. The attribute value is also very complicated, only one attribute of the *operation time* is accurate to the second, and there are 86,400 value possibilities every day. If the memory space cannot meet the requirements of constructing FP-Tree, subsequent frequent pattern mining will become very difficult.

Third, It Is Easy to Generate Redundant Association Rules. As mentioned above, there are multiple attribute values in computer data, and a large number of association rules are generated between attributes. However, there are usually many distracting items in these rules, such as "administrator $\Rightarrow$ N/A", "log $\Rightarrow$ "owner" and similar useless rules in system log mining. Not only increase the space-time overhead, but also overwhelm those important association rules.

For the mining of computer crime information, the investigators are mainly interested in the crime characteristics related to the crime data. Some unrelated frequently appearing attributes will have a huge adverse effect on the results of the mining. Therefore, it is necessary to select the attributes of interest before excavation so that the mining has certain goals.

Aiming at the problems encountered in applying the traditional FP-Growth algorithm to forensic analysis, this paper removes redundance, discretizes the collected data, and generates weighted attribute items to be mined according to the attention of the investigators. WFP-Growth, a weighted association algorithm for computer forensics analysis, explores the behavioral habits of criminals and speculates on suspicious activities in the future.

3   Improved FP-Growth Algorithm (WFP-Growth)

The implementation of the WFP-Growth algorithm is similar to that of the traditional FP-Growth algorithm. The normalization process is performed before the WFP-Tree is established, and the weight of the terminal node is used to constrain the corresponding path. The implementation of the algorithm mainly includes two steps: (1) Normalize the original transaction database and construct a WFP-Tree. (2) Perform frequent pattern mining on the WFP-Tree. The specific algorithm steps are as shown in Algorithm 1, Algorithm 2.

Algorithm 1. WFP-Tree Construction Algorithm

Algorithm: WFP-Tree Construction Algorithm
Input: transaction dataset D, minimum support threshold *min_sup*, weight set $W(A)$; **Output:** WFP-Tree 1   Scan dataset D ,obtain a set F of weighted frequent items, calculate the weighted support degree of each frequent item, the result is a weighted frequent item list L; 2   Create a root node T of the *FP-Tree* => "*null*"; 3   **for** each transaction in the transaction data set D *Trans* **do** 4   items in *Trans* are sorted in descending order of L; 5   *[p|P]* format express the sorted weighted frequent items table, where p is the first element, and P is the item list of the remaining elements in the table after removing p; 6   call function *insert_tree([p|P], T)*; 7   **end for** **insert_tree([p|P], root)** 1   **if** root has children node N and N.*item-name*=p.*item-name* **then** 2   N.count++; 3   **else** 4   Create a new node N; 5   N.item-name=p.item-name; 6   N.count++; 7   p.parent=root; 8   Point N.*node-link* to the node in the tree with the same project name; 9   **end if** 10 **if** $P \neq \Phi$ **then** 11   the first item of $P = p$ and remove it from P; 12   recursive call *insert_tree([p|P], N)*; 13 **end if**

Algorithm 2. WFP-Tree Mining Algorithm

Algorithm: Weighted frequent tree mining algorithm *WFP-Growth(WFP-Tree, α)*;
Input: *WFP-Tree*, item set *α=Φ, min_sup*;
Output: frequent item set *L* in transaction dataset *D*;
1   initial value L=*Φ*;
2   **if** *Tree* only contains a single path *P* **then**
3   **for** each combination of nodes in path *P* (denoted as *β*) **do**
4   generate a project set *α ∪β* ,*support* is equal to *min_sup* of the node in *β*;
5   **return** *L = L ∪* (items greater than *min_sup β ∪α*)
6   **else** // contains multiple paths
7   **for** each frequent item *α_f* in *Tree* **do**
8   produces a set of items *β = α_f ∪ α*, the support of *β* = the support of *α_f*;
9   constructing a conditional pattern base *B* of *β*,and WFP tree *Treeβ* of *β*;
10   **if** Tree*β≠Φ* **then**
11   recursive call *WFP-Growth (Treeβ, β)*;
12   **end if**
13   **end for**
14 **end if**

4   Correlation Mining in Computer Forensics

The goal of association rule mining is to find potential rules for data sources that are shaped like "The probability that something will happen, when something happens." Association mining finds connections between different attributes in a data set and finds dependencies between trusted and valuable multiple attribute domains. By applying association rules to forensic analysis, it is possible to effectively analyze the connections between events in massive data and to discover hidden relationships that cannot be detected by manual analysis. As shown in Fig. 1, it is the implementation framework of the weighted association algorithm in user behavior analysis.

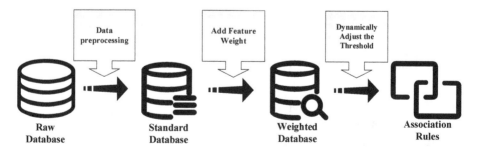

Fig. 1. User behavior association mining implementation framework

4.1   Data Preprocessing Steps

Data preprocessing is the induction and merging of raw data of different types and structures to better utilize the association mining method. For the forensic data to be analyzed, the attributes that reflect the user's behavior should be extracted as much as possible, so as to improve the efficiency of mining.

(1) Remove useless attributes, select feature attributes
The association rule analysis algorithm is used to mine frequent itemsets and strong association rules for data. In the analysis, you need to determine which attributes must be analyzed and which are useless. Computer evidence contains many attributes, but not all attributes are suitable for association analysis. At the same time, some unrelated attributes appear frequently, which not only reduces the efficiency of the algorithm, but also affects the results of data mining. Therefore, before data mining, we must clearly define the target, select reasonable and effective data items for mining.

(2) Transform unstructured data into a unified transaction database
Association rule mining can be applied in many aspects of forensic analysis, and the data formats obtained by computer forensics are also different. It is not practical to repeatedly write modules for all formats, so the data to be mined needs to be converted. So that, the association mining algorithm can analyze data items in different formats. In order to facilitate mining, in the data preprocessing process, this paper converts the basic properties of data records into a transaction database.

(3) Continuous data discretization
Some of the data obtained from the computer forensics process is relatively accurate, such as the time attribute, which can be accurate to the second. But these precise attributes have no meaning in the correlation analysis, so continuous data needs to be discretized. The purpose of discretization is to replace the low-level concept with a higher-level concept. Discretization is to divide the data of the data attribute range into several intervals.

4.2   User Behavior Analysis Module Implementation

Currently, computer forensics mainly includes the following steps: data collection, data analysis, evidence identification, preservation of evidence and evidence submission. For these massive and diverse data, computer forensics systems must be able to correctly analyze normal and abnormal data, and extract evidence related to computer crime quickly and efficiently.

In this paper, the association mining technology is applied to computer forensics analysis. The four main steps are as follows: Firstly, the original evidence information of the suspect is obtained from the target computer. Secondly, the original database is preprocessed to form a standard database that is easy to mine. Thirdly, according to the historical electronic crime record, select the characteristic attributes that need to be analyzed and set the attribute weight values respectively. Finally, use the association mining technology to mine the weighted feature database, and generate association rules to analyze the behavior habits of the criminal suspects. As shown in Fig. 2, the process of applying association mining to user behavior analysis is as follows:

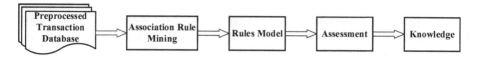

Fig. 2. The process of association mining applied to user behavior analysis

In this paper, the windows user operation trace information of the previous forensics, such as system log, browser record, modified file trace, program access record, etc., the data is unified and unified, and the transaction database {*transaction ID, user name, operation time, activity, Activity path*}, and then dig out the association between user activities.

5 Experiment and Result Analysis

5.1 Data Collection

This paper tests the computer forensics system developed by the research group. Due to the confidentiality of computer crime information, this test only simulates the analysis of ordinary computer systems. Based on the Windows operating system, the evidence is extracted from the three hosts in the research group, and log information, file information, webpage information, process information, deleted file information, etc. are obtained, and these records are organized into a transaction database. The database records the evidence of three computers for nearly two months, sorted according to the access time, a total of 25030 records. As shown in Fig. 3, part of the data information is structured as follows, and the file type is the extension of the operation file. To protect privacy of users, the Windows account name is replaced by User1, User2, and User3, and the sensitive words in the path are blurred.

ID	User	Activity name	Type	Creation time	Operation time	Modify time	Path
1	user1	Application of data m	DOC	2018/9/10 8:35	2018/9/14 9:22	2018/9/14 9:22	C:\Users\zhyt\Desktop\papers\Application of data mining in computer forensics.doc
2	user2	CRIS.exe	EXE		2018/9/14 9:16		E:\CRIS\bin\Release\CRIS.exe
3	user3	Weka.exe	EXE	2018/9/13 21:46	2018/9/13 21:47	2018/9/13 21:47	D:\Program Files (x86)\Weka
4	user3	WekaManual.pdf	PDF	2018/9/13 21:46	2018/9/13 21:46	2018/9/13 21:46	D:\Program Files (x86)\Weka\WekaManual.pdf
5	user3	weka.exe	EXE	2018/9/13 21:46	2018/9/13 21:46	2018/9/13 21:46	D:\Program Files (x86)\Weka\weka.ico
6	user1	Forensic information		2018/9/13 20:18	2018/9/13 21:01	2018/9/13 21:01	C:\Users\zhyt\Desktop\Forensic information
7	user1	System services.xls	XLS	2018/9/13 20:20	2018/9/13 20:20	2018/9/13 20:20	C:\Users\zhyt\Desktop\Forensic information\System services.xls
8	user1	Program loaded.xls	XLS	2018/9/13 20:20	2018/9/13 20:20	2018/9/13 20:20	C:\Users\zhyt\Desktop\Forensic information\Program loaded.xls
9	user1	Document access.xls	XLS	2018/9/13 20:19	2018/9/13 20:19	2018/9/13 20:19	C:\Users\zhyt\Desktop\Forensic information\Document access.xls
10	user1	Switching time.xls	XLS	2018/9/13 20:19	2018/9/13 20:19	2018/9/13 20:19	C:\Users\zhyt\Desktop\Forensic information\Switching time.xls
11	user1	System search.xls	XLS	2018/9/13 20:19	2018/9/13 20:19	2018/9/13 20:19	C:\Users\zhyt\Desktop\Forensic information\System search.xls
12	user1	Running record.xls	XLS	2018/9/13 20:19	2018/9/13 20:19	2018/9/13 20:19	C:\Users\zhyt\Desktop\Forensic information\Running record.xls
13	user1	Recycle bin history.x	XLS	2018/9/13 20:19	2018/9/13 20:19	2018/9/13 20:19	C:\Users\zhyt\Desktop\Forensic information\Recycle bin history.xls
14	user1	Program access.xls	XLS	2018/9/13 20:19	2018/9/13 20:19	2018/9/13 20:19	C:\Users\zhyt\Desktop\Forensic information\Program access.xls
15	user1	Hardware configuratic	XLS	2018/9/13 20:18	2018/9/13 20:18	2018/9/13 20:19	C:\Users\zhyt\Desktop\Forensic information\Hardware configuration.xls
16	user1	Internet information.	XLS	2018/9/13 20:18	2018/9/13 20:18	2018/9/13 20:18	C:\Users\zhyt\Desktop\Forensic information\Internet information.xls
17	user1	Application of data m	DOC	2018/9/12 9:02	2018/9/13 19:03	2018/9/13 19:03	C:\Users\zhyt\Desktop\papers\Application of data mining in computer forensics.doc
18	user1	papers		2018/6/28 10:14	2018/9/13 19:02	2018/9/13 19:02	C:\Users\zhyt\Desktop\papers
19	user1	1.jpg	JPG	2018/7/27 21:53	2018/9/13 16:37	2018/9/13 16:37	C:\Users\zhyt\Desktop\papers\ReliefF algorithm based on crime characteristics analys
20	user2	CRIS.vshost.exe	EXE		2018/9/13 15:47		E:\CRIS\bin\Release\CRIS.vshost.exe
21	user1	Opening report (final	DOC	2018/6/15 10:00	2018/9/13 15:35	2018/9/13 15:35	C:\Users\zhyt\Desktop\Opening report (final version)
22	user2	360Restore.exe	EXE		2018/9/13 14:47		F:\Program Files (x86)\360\360Safe\360Restore.exe
23	user3	The application of de	CAJ		2018/9/13 14:31		I:\XTX\The application of deep learning in text categorization - CSDN blog. HTML
24	user2	WeChat.exe	EXE		2018/9/13 10:47		F:\WeChat\WeChat.exe
25	user3	Romantic maple leaf	PPT		2018/9/13 10:40		I:\Item S3- pevan e-business - romantic maple leaf \ romantic maple leaf X6 template
26	user3	Login QQ mailbox	HTML		2018/9/13 9:32		https://accounts.google.com/Login?hl=zh-CN&continue=https://scholar.google.com/schol
27	user3	Qq mailbox _baidu se	HTML		2018/9/13 9:32		https://scholar.google.com/scholar?hl=zh-CN&as_sdt=0%2C5&q=Document+analysis+with+te
28	user1	1035985847_7753304891	EXE		2018/9/13 9:17		F:\1035985847_7753304891522668?2cf754318db43d86.exe
29	user1	Baidu map.sln	SLN		2018/9/13 8:59		C:\Users\zhyt\Desktop\Baidu map\Baidu map.sln
30	user1	Design and implement	CAJ		2018/9/13 8:55		C:\Users\zhyt\Desktop\New folder (3)\ pattern matching forensics\Design and implemen

Fig. 3. Integrated transaction database

5.2 Data Preprocessing

User behavior is mined based on the information of the transaction database. Through the analysis of Fig. 5, it is found that the aggregated database data is still very messy, the information is incomplete, and there is more redundancy. Therefore, the transaction database data is preprocessed according to the data preprocessing method in Sect. 3.1.

The First Step Is to Fill or Delete the Missing Attributes. Through the analysis of the transaction database, it can be found that the file creation time and modification time are missing more, because some modules cannot obtain these two times. At the same time, creation, modification and access are file operations, so this paper uniformly integrates them into operational time. So that the time information for each module can be unified into a single time attribute item. The user's active content is generated according to the file type. For example, the HTML type indicates that the user browses the webpage; the DOC type indicates that the user is editing the Word document; the XLS type indicates that the user is processing the Excel table; the JPG, PNG type indicates that the user is opening the image; the CPP and SLN types indicates that the user is programming.

The Second Step Is to Select the Feature Attributes. To ensure that the access time, activity type and other data generate association rules around specific users, "*user*" is the most important, followed by "*activity type*" and "*operation time*". The "*path*" attribute is complex and meaningless, does not participate in the association analysis experiment. In order to facilitate the investigator to quickly find suspicious files, the "*path*" is used as the remark information as the last column in the database.

The Third Step Is to Discretize the Data. Since the purpose of this experiment is to analyze user behavior habits, the date in the time attribute can be omitted and divided only for time. For example, the access time of the first record is 09:22:34.

After the above preprocessing steps, the generated transaction database is as shown in Fig. 4.

ID	User	Activity name	Type	Activity	Operation time	Path
1	user1	Application of data	DOC	Word	9	C:\Users\zhyt\Desktop\papers\Application of data mining in computer forensics.d
2	user2	CRIS.exe	EXE	Program	9	E:\CRIS\bin\Release\CRIS.exe
3	user3	Weka.exe	EXE	Program	21	D:\Program Files (x86)\Weka
4	user3	WekaManual.pdf	PDF	PDF	21	D:\Program Files (x86)\Weka\WekaManual.pdf
5	user3	weka.exe	EXE	Program	21	D:\Program Files (x86)\Weka\weka.ico
6	user1	System services.xls	XLS	XLS	20	C:\Users\zhyt\Desktop\Forensic information\System services.xls
7	user1	Program loaded.xls	XLS	XLS	20	C:\Users\zhyt\Desktop\Forensic information\Program loaded.xls
8	user1	Document access.xls	XLS	XLS	20	C:\Users\zhyt\Desktop\Forensic information\Document access.xls
9	user1	Switching time.xls	XLS	XLS	20	C:\Users\zhyt\Desktop\Forensic information\Switching time.xls
10	user1	System search.xls	XLS	XLS	20	C:\Users\zhyt\Desktop\Forensic information\System search.xls
11	user1	Running record.xls	XLS	XLS	20	C:\Users\zhyt\Desktop\Forensic information\Running record.xls
12	user1	Recycle bin history.xls	XLS	XLS	20	C:\Users\zhyt\Desktop\Forensic information\Recycle bin history.xls
13	user1	Program access.xls	XLS	XLS	20	C:\Users\zhyt\Desktop\Forensic information\Program access.xls
14	user1	Hardware configurati	XLS	XLS	20	C:\Users\zhyt\Desktop\Forensic information\Hardware configuration.xls
15	user1	Internet information	XLS	XLS	20	C:\Users\zhyt\Desktop\Forensic information\Internet information.xls
16	user1	Application of data	CAJ	CAJ	19	C:\Users\zhyt\Desktop\papers\Application of data mining in computer forensics.d
17	user1	1.jpg	JPG	Picture	16	C:\Users\zhyt\Desktop\papers\ReliefF algorithm based on crime characteristics s
18	user2	CRIS.vshost.exe	EXE	Program	15	E:\CRIS\bin\Release\CRIS.vshost.exe
19	user1	Opening report (fina	DOC	Word	15	C:\Users\zhyt\Desktop\Opening report (final version)
20	user2	360Restore.exe	EXE	Program	14	F:\Program Files (x86)\360\360Safe\360Restore.exe
21	user3	The application of d	CAJ	CAJ	14	I:\XTX\The application of deep learning in text categorization - CSDN blog. HTM
22	user2	WeChat.exe	EXE	Program	10	F:\WeChat\WeChat.exe
23	user3	Romantic maple leaf	PPT	PPT	10	I:\Item 83- pevan e-business - romantic maple leaf \ romantic maple leaf X6 tem
24	user3	Login QQ mailbox	HTML	Webpage	9	https://accounts.google.com/Login?hl=zh-CN&continue=https://scholar.google.com/
25	user3	Qq mailbox _ baidu s	HTML	Webpage	9	https://scholar.google.com/scholar?hl=zh-CN&as_sdt=0%2C5&q=Document+analysis+wi
26	user1	103595847_7753304891	EXE	Program	9	F:\103595847_7753304891S226872cf754318db43d86.exe
27	user1	Baidu map.sln	SLN	Program	8	C:\Users\zhyt\Desktop\Baidu map\Baidu map.sln
28	user1	Design and implement	CAJ	CAJ	8	C:\Users\zhyt\Desktop\New folder (3)\ pattern matching forensics\Design and imp
29	user3	Deep search prototyp	CAJ	CAJ	8	E:\papers\FGX\research related\injection module\deep search prototype code
30	user2	SectorEdit2000.sln	SLN	Program	8	E:\papers\FGX\research related\injection module\deep search prototype code\Sect

Fig. 4. Preprocessed transaction database

5.3   Data Association Rules Mining

After the data is ready, through the association mining process, a strong association rule is generated, from which the user's behavior habits are analyzed, and the relationship between different behaviors of the user is found.

First, use the traditional FP-Growth algorithm for mining

In data mining, set the minimum support degree *min_sup* to 0.1 and the minimum confidence *min_conf* to 0.5. Through experiment mining, the generated strong association rules are as follows:

No.	Association rules	Support	Confidence
1	User = User1 $\Rightarrow$ Activity = Word	0.17	0.53
2	Activity = Word $\Rightarrow$ Time = 10	0.15	0.68
3	Activity = Program $\Rightarrow$ User = User2	0.12	0.65
4	Time = 10 $\Rightarrow$ User = User1	0.11	0.51
5	Activity = Webpage $\Rightarrow$ Time = 21	0.10	0.52
6	Time = 15 $\Rightarrow$ Activity = CAJ	0.10	0.51
7	Time = 15 $\Rightarrow$ User = User3	0.10	0.56

After analysis, it is found that in the generated 7 association rules. "Word $\Rightarrow$ 10", "Webpage $\Rightarrow$ 21" and "15 $\Rightarrow$ CAJ", the three rules are not related to the user and have little meaning for behavior analysis; "10 $\Rightarrow$ User1", "15 $\Rightarrow$ User3", two rules indicates the time period during which the user frequently operates, but does not involve specific activity content.

Second, use the improved WFP-Growth algorithm for mining

According to the analysis in the previous section, this paper analyzes the user behavior and assigns a greater weight to the "*user*" attribute. According to past analysis experience, the investigators are more concerned about the type of activity than the access time. Therefore, the "*user*" attribute is weighted $W_1 = 5.0$, the "*activity type*" attribute is weighted $W_2 = 3.0$, the "*operation time*" attribute is weighted $W_3 = 1.5$, and normalized in the algorithm. Set the minimum support *min_sup* to 0.1 and the minimum confidence *min_conf* to 0.5. Through experiment mining, the strong association rules generated under weighted conditions are as follows:

No.	Association rules	Support	Confidence
1	User = User1 $\Rightarrow$ Activity = Word	0.17	0.53
2	Activity = Program $\Rightarrow$ User = User2	0.12	0.65
3	Activity = CAJ $\Rightarrow$ User = User3	0.11	0.62
4	Activity = Webpage $\Rightarrow$ User = User3	0.10	0.52

In order to further more association rules, the threshold of support is lowered, the minimum support degree *min_sup* is set to 0.03, the minimum confidence *min_conf* is 0.5, and 46 strong association rules are generated through experiment mining. This article only lists the more typical 3-frequent item association rules, as shown below:

No.	Association rules	Support	Confidence
5	User = User1 ∧ Time = 10 ⇒ Activity = Word	0.06	0.51
6	Time = 20 ∧ Activity = Program ⇒ User = User2	0.05	0.62
7	User = User3 ∧ Activity=CAJ ⇒ Time = 15	0.03	0.52
8	User = User1 ∧ Activity=Webpage ⇒ Time = 21	0.03	0.50

5.4 Analysis of Results

Analysis of the excavated rules can give the following results:

- Rule1 indicates that 17% of all transactions are User1 editing Word documents, and 53% of User1's activities are editing Word documents.
- Rule2 indicates that 12% of all transactions are User2 programming, and 65% of all programming records are from User2.
- Rule3 indicates that 11% of all transactions are User3 reading CAJ documents, and 62% of all CAJ open records are from User3.
- Rule4 indicates that 10% of all transactions are User3 browsing the webpages, and 52% of all online records are from User3.
- Rule5 indicates that 6% of all transactions are User1's Word document editing from 10:00 to 11:00, and User1 has a 51% probability of editing Word documents between 10:00 and 11:00.
- Rule6 indicates that 5% of all transactions are User2 written at 20:00 to 21:00, of which 62% of all records programmed from 20:00 to 21:00 are from User3.
- Rule7 indicates that 3% of all transactions are User3 reading CAJ documents from 15 to 16 h, and User3 reading CAJ documents has a 52% probability of being between 15:00 and 16:00.
- Rule8 indicates that 3% of all transactions are User1 browsing the webpage between 21:00 and 22:00, and the User1 online behavior has a 50% probability of occurring between 21:00 and 22:00.

After analyzing the results of two mining results with different thresholds, we can find that:

Username	Behavioral habits	Speculation
User1	Frequently edits Word documents, occasionally opens CAJ documents, usually online at night	Writing a thesis recently
User2	Often writes programs, most in the evening, occasionally online in the morning	Participating in the project recently
User3	Often opens the CAJ file, most in the afternoon, and the online behavior is more than the other two users, but the time is random	Reading the literatures currently

Comparing with the experimental results, it can be found that the data preprocessing and the improved FP-Growth algorithm can effectively improve the redundancy of evidence association rules. Due to the large weight assigned to the *"user"* attribute, most of the rules excavated by the experiment are generated around the user. For the attributes such as "*user*" and "*activity*" that are more concerned by forensic investigators, the weighted and improved FP-Growth algorithm shows greater practicability. At the same time, by dynamically adjusting the threshold, some association rules of small probability events can be found, which helps to analyze the multi-transaction relevance. Investigators can also adjust the feature attribute weights according to the changes in the points of interest to achieve different forensic analysis purposes.

In summary, the association analysis method is applied to the field of computer forensics analysis, and it has powerful advantages compared with manual analysis. The improved FP-Growth algorithm is more purposeful and practical, and can better dig out the information that investigators need.

6 Conclusion

This paper analyzes the two association mining algorithms of Apriori and FP-Growth, and compares the running time and memory overhead of the latter. In order to solve the limitation problem of traditional algorithm applied to evidence analysis, the FP-Growth algorithm is weighted and optimized, and the data such as system log, browser record and file operation trace are analyzed. The experimental results show that the results obtained by weighted optimization are more accurate and effective, and can be used in the forensic analysis of investigators to realize the portrayal of user behavior habits and speculate on the identity and activity trends of suspects.

References

1. Statistical Report on the Development of China's Internet Network. China Sci. Technol. Inf. **41**(5), 6–7 (2018)
2. Cui, Q., McIntosh, S., Sun, H.: Identifying materials of photographic images and photorealistic computer generated graphics based on deep CNNs. CMC: Comput. Mater. Continua **55**(2), 229–241 (2018)
3. Tang, Z., et al.: Robust image hashing via random gabor filtering and DWT. CMC: Comput. Mater. Continua **55**(2), 331–344 (2018)
4. Su, H.: Research on electronic forensics system based on user behavior correlation analysis. Telecommun. Sci. **8**(12), 7–78 (2012)
5. Wang, X., Zhao, C., Heng, X., Wang, Y., Zhang, Q.: Application of time series based association analysis in technology monitoring. J. Intell. **32**(4), 10–15 (2013)
6. Jiwen, Z., Shijing, W.: Application of association rules technology in computer crime forensics. Microcomput. Appl. **12**(7), 776–779 (2012)
7. Liu, B., Wei, L.: A model of network attack tracking system based on log association. J. Chongqing Univ. Sci. Technol. **9**(4), 81–84 (2017)
8. Zadgaonkar, A., Balpande, M.: Optimizing live digital evidence mining using structural subroutines of apriori algorithm. Int. J. **18**(3), 88–96 (2016)
9. Chang, H., Shan, H., Man, Y.: User behavior analysis based on segmentation clustering and time series correlation analysis. Appl. Res. Comput. **5**(2), 526–531 (2014)

10. Chen, P.: Research on data analysis and processing of mobile terminal service data based on data mining. Beijing University of Posts and Telecommunications (2015)
11. Ping, D., Yongping, G.: A new improvement of Apriori algorithm for mining association rules. In: 2010 International Conference on Computer Application and System Modeling (ICCASM), pp. 529–532. IEEE (2010)
12. Yang, M.: Document analysis with text mining approaches in digital forensics. HKU Theses Online (HKUTO) (2017)

Reversible Data Hiding in JPEG Images Based on Multiple Histograms Modification

Xing Lu[1], Fangjun Huang[1($\boxtimes$)], and Hyoung Joong Kim[2]

[1] Guangdong Provincial Key Laboratory of Information Security Technology,
School of Data and Computer Science, Sun Yat-sen University,
Guangzhou 510006, Guangdong, China
huangfj@mail.sysu.edu.cn
[2] Graduate School of Information Security, Korea University,
Seoul 136-701, South Korea

Abstract. The joint photographic experts group (JPEG) is the most popular image on the internet nowadays. Therefore, reversible data hiding (RDH), which can be used to ensure the widely used JPEG images' originality and integrity, has attracted more and more attention. However, when performing RDH in JPEG images, besides the embedding capacity and visual quality, which have to be considered for uncompressed images, the storage size of the marked JPEG file should also be considered. In this paper, a new JPEG RDH scheme based on multiple histograms modification is proposed. Firstly, according to zero run length (ZRL) of the discrete cosine transform (DCT) coefficients, multiple DCT coefficient histograms are generated. Then, the message bits are embedded via the histogram shifting algorithm. In order to improve the efficiency of the proposed method, a new adaptive embedding strategy based on the ZRL and the number of zero coefficients in each 8×8 block is also proposed. Experimental results show that our method can effectively reduce the increase of image storage size caused by information embedding.

Keywords: JPEG · Reversible data hiding (RDH) · Multiple histograms · Image storage size

1 Introduction

RDH is an important branch of data hiding, by which the original image as well as the embedded message can be completely restored from the marked image without any loss. The reversibility in RDH is quite desirable and helpful in some practical applications such as medical imagery, military imagery, and law forensics, where the original signal is so precious that it cannot be damaged.

RDH for uncompressed images can be roughly classified into three fundamental strategies: lossless compression [1], difference expansion [2] and histogram shifting (HS) [3, 10–14]. Compared with uncompressed images, the compressed images have less redundancy, thus are considerably more difficult for RDH. Among all the formats of compressed images, JPEG is the most popular one, thus JPEG RDH has received more and more attention in recent years.

© Springer Nature Switzerland AG 2019
X. Sun et al. (Eds.): ICAIS 2019, LNCS 11634, pp. 442–454, 2019.
https://doi.org/10.1007/978-3-030-24271-8_40

There are mainly three approaches having been proposed in JPEG RDH. The first approach is based on the modification of the JPEG quantization tables [1, 4], via dividing some elements of the quantization table by an integer k and multiplying the corresponding quantized DCT coefficient with the same integer k, the space for embedding information can be obtained. However, the original quantization table of a JPEG file provides a considerable tradeoff between the file size and the perceptual quality of the encoded image. Once a non-standard quantization table is utilized as that in [1, 4], the size of the marked image may increase significantly. The second approach is based on modifying the Huffman table [5]. Through mapping a used variable length-code (VLC) to an unused VLC to embed information, the storage size of the JPEG file can be well preserved. However, the embedding capacity is rather limited and only can be applied to JPEG images encoded with non-optimized Huffman tables. The third approach is based on modifying the quantized DCT coefficients [6–9]. In 2016, Huang *et al.* [8] proposed a new HS-based RDH scheme for JPEG images. In this method, the 0 coefficients remain unchanged and only the ± 1 alternating current (AC) coefficients are selected to carry messages. With a new block selection strategy, high performance in image visual quality and file storage size can be obtained. In [9], via estimating unit distortion for each frequency of AC coefficients and then utilizing block selection strategy, Hou *et al.* [9] improved Huang *et al.*'s [8] scheme with better visual quality and less file size increase. Generally speaking, modifying the quantized DCT coefficients is the most popular approach among the above three approaches because of its higher embedding capacity, better image visual quality and less file size increase.

In this paper, a new JPEG RDH scheme is proposed. Our new method is based on the modification of multiple histograms, which are generated according to zero run length (ZRL) of the discrete cosine transform (DCT) coefficients. Further more, a new adaptive embedding strategy with considering the ZRL and the number of zero coefficients in each 8×8 block is also provided to improve the efficiency of the proposed method. The experimental results demonstrate that compared with the existing algorithms, such as Huang *et al.* [8] and Hou *et al.* [9], our algorithm can greatly reduce the storage size of the marked images.

The rest of this paper is organized as follows. We briefly introduce the related work in Sect. 2. In Sect. 3, the proposed RDH scheme is presented in details. Experimental results are given in Sect. 4. Finally, we conclude in Sect. 5.

2 Related Work

2.1 Overview of JPEG Compression

The JPEG compression codec flow is shown in Fig. 1. The JPEG encoder mainly includes three parts, namely, forward discrete cosine transform (FDCT), quantization and entropy encoder. And the JPEG decoding is the reverse process of encoding and also includes three components, that is, entropy decoding, de-quantization, and inverse discrete cosine transform (IDCT).

Since in our method, only the AC coefficients are utilized for RDH, the run length encoding (RLE) for AC coefficients will be described first in brief. In JPEG

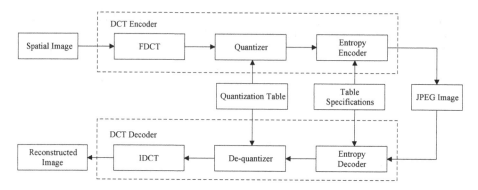

Fig. 1. Block diagram of JPEG compression process.

compression process, the AC coefficients are encoded in a specific intermediate format as (R/C, V). Here, R denotes the zero run length (i.e., the number of consecutive zero coefficients between two non-zero coefficients) and C denotes the category of the non-zero AC coefficients (i.e., the number of bits needed to represent the amplitude of the non-zero AC coefficient) and V denotes the value of the non-zero AC coefficient. For more detailed information, please refer to the JPEG guidelines published by the International Telecommunication Union [15].

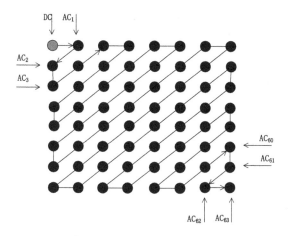

Fig. 2. Zig-zag scanning order.

In Table 1, the code lengths and code words corresponding to some R/C combinations are illustrated. It is observed from Table 1 that in general for the R/C combinations with the same zero run length value R, the corresponding code lengths will increase with the magnitudes of the coefficients (i.e., the value of C). It can also be observed from Table 1 that for the R/C combinations with the same category value C, the corresponding code lengths will increase with the value of R.

Table 1. Luminance AC coefficients

R/C	Code length	Code word
0/0(EOB)	4	1010
0/1	2	00
0/2	2	01
0/3	3	100
...	...	...
1/1	4	1100
1/2	5	11011
1/3	7	1111001
...	...	...
2/1	5	11100
2/2	8	11111001
2/3	10	1111110111
...	...	...

2.2 Overview of HS-Based RDH Scheme

The HS-based RDH algorithm usually consists of three steps. The first step is to generate a histogram from the host signal. It can be the original histogram, the difference histogram, or the prediction error histogram. The second step is to divide the histogram into the inner region and the outer region. The inner region consists of pixels associated with the peak values, while the outer region consists of the rest. The last step is to embed the message by modifying the inner bins. What's more, the outer bins will be shifted to make room for information embedding.

Suppose in the given JPEG image, the quantized non-zero AC coefficients sequence is $(c_1, \ldots, c_M)$, and the corresponding histogram H can be established as:

$$H(k) = \sum_{i=1}^{M} f(c_i, k), k \in [C_{min}, C_{max}] \tag{1}$$

where C_{min} is the minimum value of quantized non-zero AC coefficient and C_{max} is the maximum value of quantized non-zero AC coefficient and

$$f(x, y) = \begin{cases} 1, & x = y \\ 0, & otherwise \end{cases} \tag{2}$$

In [8] the 0 coefficients remain unchanged and only coefficients with values "1" and "−1" are selected to carry messages via using the histogram shifting strategy. Note that in the embedding process, the AC coefficients with magnitudes greater than 1 are shifted by 1 unit to make room for information embedding. Suppose that the quantized AC coefficients are scanned in a *zig-zag* order, as shown in Fig. 2. Figure 3 exemplified the embedding process based on the HS scheme. Figure 3(a) illustrates the original JPEG quantized coefficients and Fig. 3(b) is the corresponding coefficients after data hiding, where the binary stream $(101010101)_2$ is embedded.

28	1	-6	2	2	-1	0	0
0	-1	0	1	1	3	0	0
-3	2	5	-1	0	0	0	0
4	1	0	0	0	0	0	0
1	-1	0	0	0	0	0	0
0	2	0	0	0	0	0	0
0	0	0	0	0	0	0	0
0	0	0	0	0	0	0	0

(a)

28	2	-7	3	3	-1	0	0
0	-1	0	2	2	4	0	0
-4	3	6	-1	0	0	0	0
5	1	0	0	0	0	0	0
2	-2	0	0	0	0	0	0
0	3	0	0	0	0	0	0
0	0	0	0	0	0	0	0
0	0	0	0	0	0	0	0

(b)

Fig. 3. An example of HS-based scheme. (a) Original quantized coefficients. (b) Coefficients after data embedding.

3   Proposed Scheme

This section mainly considers how to reduce the increase in image size caused by information embedding, and then proposes a JPEG image RDH scheme based on multiple histograms modification.

3.1   Multiple Histograms

As can be seen from Table 1, the smaller the ZRL, the shorter the corresponding code length. Therefore, we will divide the original non-zero AC coefficients into multiple histograms according to ZRL.

Definition. (1) For quantized DCT coefficients, each non-zero AC coefficient is associated with a ZRL value. The ZRL value is determined as the number of consecutive zero coefficients between the current non-zero AC coefficient and its previous non-zero coefficient according to the *zig-zag* scanning order; (2) Since the DC coefficient and the zero AC coefficient are kept unchanged in the embedding process, no ZRL value is associated with the DC and zero AC coefficients in our scheme.

According to the above definition, the ZRL values corresponding to those *zig-zag* scanned non-zero AC coefficients $(1,-3,-1,-6,2,2,4,1,1,5,1,2,-1,1,-1,-1,2,3)$ in Fig. 3(a) are $(0,1,0,0,0,1,0,0,0,0,0,0,0,0,0,1,2,3)$. In the light of the ZRL values, four sub-histograms can be obtained, which are corresponding to the ZRL values of 0, 1, 2, and 3, respectively. Since the DC coefficients and the 0 AC coefficients remain unchanged during the embedding process, the ZRL values associated with the non-zero AC coefficients remain unchanged after embedding.

Suppose in the given JPEG image, the quantized non-zero AC coefficients sequence is $(c_1, \ldots, c_M)$, and the associated ZRL sequence is $(z_1, \ldots, z_M)$. According to the ZRL values, the sequence $(c_1, \ldots, c_M)$ can be divided into N sub-groups, and the coefficients associated with the same ZRL value will be divided into the same sub-group. Suppose there are N sub-groups, and thus N sub-histograms $H_0(k), H_1(k), \ldots, H_{N-1}(k)$ can be generated according to Eq. (1)–(2). For ease of explanation, some sub-histograms resulted from the standard 512×512 Lena image with quality factors (QF) 100 is illustrated, which are shown in Fig. 4. Figure 4(a) illustrates the global histogram of all non-zero AC coefficients, and Fig. 4(b)–(g) illustrate the sub-histograms associated with different ZRL values, i.e., from 0 to 5. In our algorithm, the information is embedded via modifying those sub-histograms $H_n(k)(0 \leq n \leq N-1)$.

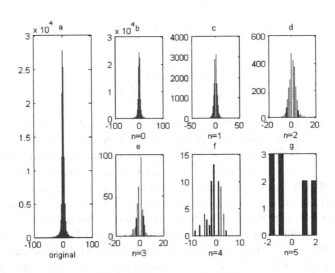

Fig. 4. Original histogram and sub-histograms.

3.2   The Proposed Algorithm

This paper proposes a JPEG image RDH scheme based on multiple histograms modification. The main idea is described as follows.

Scanning the quantized DCT coefficients by *zig-zag* order to obtain the histogram of non-zero AC coefficients and computing the corresponding ZRL for each coefficient. Then dividing the original histogram into multiple sub-histograms according to ZRL. In the embedding process, coefficients belonging to the sub-histograms with smaller ZRL will take precedence (i.e., in the sequence of $H_0(k), H_1(k), \ldots, H_{N-1}(k)$) for data hiding. Moreover, for those coefficients associated with the same sub-histogram, the coefficients belonging to those 8×8 blocks with more zero coefficients will take precedence for data hiding.

The information is embedded according to (3) and (4). Here, C and C' are the AC coefficients before and after the information embedded, respectively. And $b \in \{0, 1\}$ is the information to be embedded.

$$C' = \begin{cases} C + sign(C) * b & if \ |C| = 1 \\ C + sign(C) & if \ |C| > 1 \end{cases} \tag{3}$$

$$sign(x) = \begin{cases} 1 & if \ x \geq 0 \\ 0 & if \ x = 0 \\ -1 & if \ x < 0 \end{cases} \tag{4}$$

The message extraction and image restoration can be described as:

$$b^* = \begin{cases} 0 & if \ C' = \pm 1 \\ 1 & if \ C' = \pm 2 \end{cases} \tag{5}$$

$$C^* = \begin{cases} sign(C') \ if \ 1 \leq |C'| \leq 2 \\ C' - sign(C') \ if \ |C'| \geq 3 \end{cases} \tag{6}$$

where b^* and C^* are extracted bit and restored AC coefficients, respectively.

An example of the embedding process of our proposed scheme is illustrated in Fig. 5. To better distinguish the difference between our method and the HS-based method [8], the same coefficient block is utilized, which is shown in Fig. 3(a). There are 9 AC coefficients with a magnitude of 1, and we embed the same binary stream $(101010101)_2$ as in Sect. 2.2. From our above discussion in Sect. 3.1, we know that the coefficient block in Fig. 3(a) can be divided into four sub-histograms. And the coefficients with a magnitude of 1 are only distributed in the sub-histograms with ZRL of 0 and 1. Therefore, only this two sub-histograms need to be modified, while the sub-histograms with ZRL of 2 and 3 remain unchanged. In the embedding process, we first embed the sub-histogram with ZRL of 0 and then embed the sub-histogram with ZRL of 1. It can be found that while embedding the same binary stream, the HS-based method [8] needs 9 invalid moves, and our method only needs 7 invalid moves.

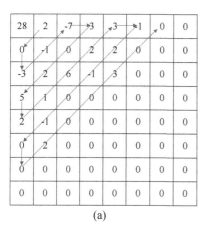

(a)

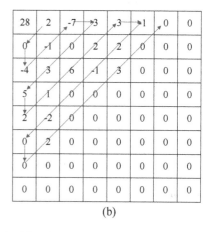

(b)

Fig. 5. An example of the proposed scheme. (a) Embedding in sub-histogram with ZRL of 0. (b) Embedding in sub-histogram with ZRL of 1.

3.3   Embedding, Extraction, and Restoration Steps

(1) Embedding Steps

Step (1) Entropy-decode the original JPEG file to get the quantized DCT coefficients, and then compute the number of zero AC coefficients for each 8×8 block.

Step (2) According to Sect. 3.2, for each 8×8 block, the DCT coefficients are scanned in a *zig-zag* sequence, and the ZRL of each non-zero AC coefficient is calculated. Then divide the original histogram into multiple sub-histograms according to the coefficients' ZRL values.

Step (3) The secret information (including the length of the secret information L, which can be represented by a 24-bit binary sequence), is embedded into the DCT coefficients sequentially. Note that in the embedding process, coefficients belonging to the sub-histogram with smaller ZRL will take precedence (i.e., embedding the messages in the sequence of $H_0(k), H_1(k), \ldots, H_{N-1}(k)$). Furthermore, for those coefficients associated with the same sub-histogram, the coefficients belonging to those 8×8 blocks with more zero coefficients will take precedence for data hiding.

Step (4) After the information is embedded, all the modified coefficients are entropy-encoded to get the marked JPEG file.

(2) Extraction and Restoration Steps

Step (1) Entropy-decode the marked JPEG file to get the quantized DCT coefficients, and then compute the number of zero AC coefficients for each 8×8 block.

Step (2) For each 8×8 block, the DCT coefficients are scanned in a *zig-zag* sequence, and the ZRL of each non-zero AC coefficient is calculated. Then divide the original histogram into multiple sub-histograms according to the coefficients' ZRL values.

Step (3) Extract the secret information and restore the original DCT coefficients according to Eqs. (5) and (6) with the same order as that described in the embedding process.

Step (4) After all the secret message bits are extracted and all the marked coefficients are restored, entropy-encode the restored coefficients again to get the original JPEG file.

4   Experimental Results

In our experiments, the original images are downloaded from USC-SIPI database[1]. And we use the IJG toolbox[2] to get the JPEG images with QF = 70, 80, 90,100. The secret message bits are randomly generated and the JPEG images are compressed with the optimized Huffman table. The experiments are conducted on six grayscale images as shown in Fig. 6.

To evaluate the performance of the proposed new scheme, two current state-of-the-art RDH methods [8, 9] designed for JPEG images are selected for comparison. The peak signal-to-noise ratio (PSNR) is utilized to measure the perceivable difference

---

[1] http://sipi.usc.edu/database/database.php?volume=misc.

[2] http://www.ijg.org/.

(a) Lena   (b) Baboon   (c) Boat

(d) Lake   (e) Splash   (f) Tank

Fig. 6. Test images.

between the original and the marked JPEG image. Generally, a high PSNR means better visual quality. Moreover, the increased file size is also calculated. In Fig. 7, the horizontal axes represent the effective embedding capacity, and the vertical axes represent the PSNR value or increased file size value.

Visual Quality. From Fig. 7, we can see that the PSNR values obtained by the proposed method are lower than those obtained by Huang *et al.* [8] and Hou *et al.* [9]. The reason is that the modified coefficients may belong to higher frequencies. Since the coefficients belonging to high frequencies are associated with relatively large quantization steps, which may introduce more distortion.

File Size Preservation. It is observed from Fig. 7 that the proposed method can preserve the file size better than Huang *et al.* [8] and Hou *et al.* [9], which implies that the proposed algorithm can achieve better file size preservation in general. Although the visual quality of the secret image is insufficient, while there is a clear advantage in the preservation of the image storage size, especially when the QF is 70, 80, 90.

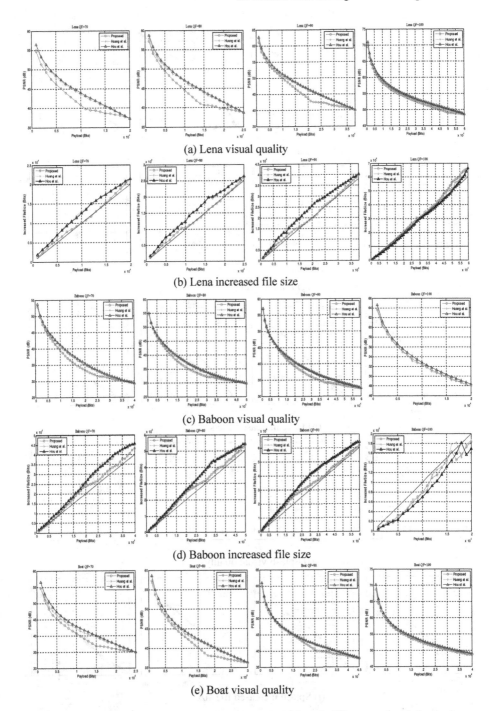

(a) Lena visual quality

(b) Lena increased file size

(c) Baboon visual quality

(d) Baboon increased file size

(e) Boat visual quality

Fig. 7. Visual quality and storage size of dense images with different embedded capacity.

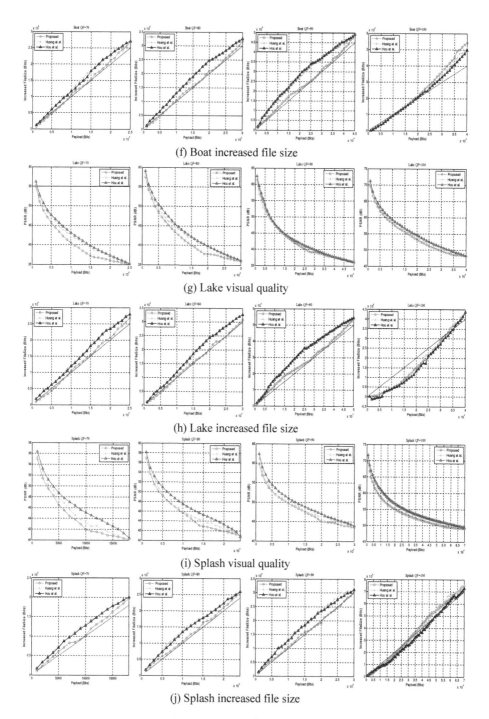

(f) Boat increased file size

(g) Lake visual quality

(h) Lake increased file size

(i) Splash visual quality

(j) Splash increased file size

Fig. 7. (*continued*)

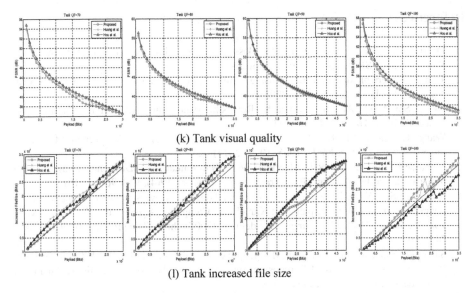

(k) Tank visual quality

(l) Tank increased file size

Fig. 7. (*continued*)

5 Conclusion

As one of the most popular image formats how to ensure the originality and integrity of JPEG image has received more and more attention in recent years. However, any modification in JPEG images may introduce considerably more distortion than that in an uncompressed image and invalid modification may lead to the serious problem of bit stream expansion.

In this paper, a new JPEG image RDH algorithm based on the multiple histograms modification is proposed. For each non-zero AC coefficient, its ZRL value is first computed according to the number of consecutive zero coefficients between the current non-zero AC coefficient and its previous non-zero coefficient, then multiple histograms are generated according to the ZRL value. Finally, data embedding is implemented according to the proposed embedding strategy based on multiple histograms modification. A large number of experimental results show that, compared with the current mainstream HS-based JPEG image RDH algorithm, our algorithm can effectively reduce the file size increase caused by information embedding.

Acknowledgments. This work is partially supported by the National Natural Science Foundation of China (61772572), the NSFC-NRF Scientific Cooperation Program (61811540409), the Natural Science Foundation of Guangdong Province of China (2017A030313366), and the Fundamental Research Funds for Central Universities (17lgjc45).

References

1. Fridrich, J., Goljan, M., Du, R.: Lossless data embedding for all image formats. In: Proceedings of SPIE, pp. 572–583, April 2002
2. Tian, J.: Reversible data embedding using a difference expansion. IEEE Trans. Circuits Syst. Video Technol. **13**(8), 890–896 (2003)
3. Ni, Z., Shi, Y.-Q., Ansari, N., Wei, S.: Reversible data hiding. IEEE Trans. Circuits Syst. Video Technol. **16**(3), 354–362 (2006)
4. Wang, K., Lu, Z.-M., Hu, Y.-J.: A high capacity lossless data hiding scheme for JPEG images. J. Syst. Softw. **86**(7), 1965–1975 (2013)
5. Mobasseri, B.G., Berger, R.J., Marcinak, M.P., NaikRaikar, Y.J.: Data embedding in JPEG bitstream by code mapping. IEEE Trans. Image Process. **19**(4), 958–966 (2010)
6. Xuan, G., Shi, Y.Q., Ni, Z., Chai, P., Cui, X., Tong, X.: Reversible data hiding for JPEG images based on histogram pairs. In: Kamel, M., Campilho, A. (eds.) ICIAR 2007. LNCS, vol. 4633, pp. 715–727. Springer, Heidelberg (2007). https://doi.org/10.1007/978-3-540-74260-9_64
7. Sakai, H., Kuribayashi, M., Morii, M.: Adaptive reversible data hiding for JPEG images. In: Proceedings of International Symposium on Information Theory Applications, Auckland, New Zealand, pp. 1–6, December 2008
8. Huang, F., Qu, X., Kim, H.J., Huang, J.: Reversible data hiding in JPEG images. IEEE Trans. Circuits Syst. Video Technol. **26**(9), 1610–1621 (2016)
9. Hou, D.D., Wang, H.Q., Zhang, W.M., Yu, N.H.: Reversible data hiding in JPEG image based on DCT frequency and block selection. Sig. Process. **148**, 41–47 (2018)
10. Ou, B., Li, X., Zhao, Y., Ni, R., Shi, Y.-Q.: Pairwise prediction-error expansion for efficient reversible data hiding. IEEE Trans. Image Process. **22**(12), 5010–5021 (2013)
11. Sachnev, V., Kim, H.J., Nam, J., Suresh, S., Shi, Y.Q.: Reversible watermarking algorithm using sorting and prediction. IEEE Trans. Circuits Syst. Video Technol. **19**(7), 989–999 (2009)
12. Li, X., Zhang, W., Gui, X., Yang, B.: A novel reversible data hiding scheme based on two-dimensional difference-histogram modification. IEEE Trans. Inf. Forensics Secur. **8**(7), 1091–1100 (2013)
13. Li, X., Zhang, W., Gui, X., Yang, B.: Efficient reversible data hiding based on multiple histograms modification. IEEE Trans. Inf. Forensics Secur. **10**(9), 2016–2027 (2015)
14. Ma, B., Shi, Y.Q.: A reversible data hiding scheme based on code division multiplexing. IEEE Trans. Inf. Forensics Secur. **11**(9), 1914–1927 (2016)
15. Information Technology—Digital Compression and Coding of Continuous–Tone Still Images: Requirements and Guidelines, document T.81 (1992)

Image Hashing Based on CS-LBP and DCT for Copy Detection

Qi Shen and Yan Zhao[✉]

Department of Electronics and Information Engineering,
Shanghai University of Electric Power, 2588 Changyang Road,
Shanghai 200090, People's Republic of China
yanzhao79@hotmail.com

Abstract. In order to improve the accuracy and speed of copy detection, we propose an image hashing algorithm based on local feature and global feature in this paper. Firstly, input image is converted to a normalized image. Then, wavelet decomposition is applied to the preprocessed image to produce approximate image and high-frequency information. Center symmetric local binary pattern (CS-LBP) is applied to approximate image to produce a CS-LBP texture image. The local feature is extracted by dividing blocks and selecting mean, variance, third moment, fourth moment statistics feature in CS-LBP texture image. The global feature is extracted by selecting the discrete cosine transform (DCT) coefficients of high frequency-information. Finally, local features and global features are combined to generate image hashing. Experiment with open images are carried out and the results show that the proposed algorithm is robust and discriminative. The precision rate and the recall rate (P-R) curve comparisons show that our hashing algorithm outperforms some existing hashing algorithms in copy detection.

Keywords: CS-LBP · Statistics · DCT coefficient · Copy detection

1 Introduction

Digital images are easily edited and copied by image processing software, leading to many copied images appearing in the web. However, digital watermarking technique can only detect images containing the watermark. Thus copyright protection of images becomes an important issue.

As far, many hash algorithms have been reported. These hashing algorithms can be roughly classified into the following categories: discrete cosine transform (DCT) [1–3], discrete wavelet transform (DWT) [4, 5], Radon transform [6, 7], Gabor transform [8, 9], dimensionality reduction [10, 11], feature point [12, 13], and other methods [14–16]. Literature [1] proposed an image hashing based on image blocks and DCT. But its recognition performance in copy detection is not good enough. Literature [4] exploited the statistics of DWT coefficients to construct image hash. The algorithm has poor performance on gamma correction and contrast adjustment. Literature [7] proposed to extract the statistical feature after Radon transform to generate a robust hash. The algorithm is robust to rotation. But its efficiency needs to be improved. Literature [11]

© Springer Nature Switzerland AG 2019
X. Sun et al. (Eds.): ICAIS 2019, LNCS 11634, pp. 455–466, 2019.
https://doi.org/10.1007/978-3-030-24271-8_41

proposed to construct the hash by principal component analysis (PCA) dimension reduction after image reconstruction. The algorithm is robustness to the conventional operation such as JPEG compression and contrast adjustment, but its efficiency needs to be improved. Literature [12] proposed Multi-scale SIFT feature points, which improve the discrimination of the local feature. Literature [17] proposed to construct a hash by combining multiple features to achieve better recognition performance. Literature [18, 19] proposed to combine the local features and global features to achieve better copy detection performance. The proposed algorithm is different with literature [18, 19]. Global feature is context information around local features in literature [18]. Thus, local and global features are extracted from space feature. Our global feature is extracted from frequency feature. Local and global features are extracted from frequency feature in literature [19]. Our local feature is extracted from space feature.

In this paper, we propose a hashing algorithm based on local and global features. To improve the efficiency of the detection, we obtain the approximate image and high-frequency information by wavelet decomposition. Then the CS-LBP texture image is obtained by using CS-LBP. The local feature is the statistics feature extracted from each texture image block. The global feature is the DCT coefficients extracted from high-frequency information after wavelet decomposition. Finally the obtained local and global features are concatenated to form an intermediate hash. The intermediate hash is rearranged by a secret key to produce the final hash. Several experiments show that proposed algorithm has good robustness and discrimination. The accuracy and efficiency of image copy detection are better than some algorithms. The rest of this paper is organized as follows. Section 2 introduces proposed image hashing algorithm and Sect. 3 discusses experimental results. Conclusions are given in the Sect. 4.

2 Proposed Algorithm

The proposed algorithm includes preprocessing, wavelet decomposition, local feature extraction, global feature extraction and generate hash, as shown in Fig. 1. The detailed steps will be explained in the following section.

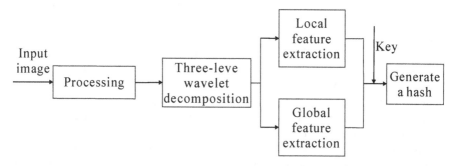

Fig. 1. Diagram of our hash

2.1 Preprocessing

The input image is firstly converted to a normalized size $N \times N$ by bilinear interpolation. Then, Gaussian low-pass filter is applied to the normalized image for reducing the influence of minor image processing operation. If the input image is an RGB color image, we convert the normalized image to gray image.

2.2 Wavelet Decomposition

The three-level wavelet decomposition is applied to the preprocessed image to produce approximate image and high-frequency information.

2.3 Local Texture Feature

The CS-LBP [20] is applied to the three-level approximate image to produce the CS-LBP texture image. We divide the CS-LBP texture image into $M \times M$ non-overlapping blocks. To obtain the robust feature matrix V, four statistics are extracted from each block as features, i.e., mean, variance, third moment, fourth moment [21], which are defined as follows:

$$m_k = \frac{1}{N_k} \sum_{i=1}^{N_k} B_k(i) \tag{1}$$

$$v_k = \frac{1}{N_k - 1} \sum_{i=1}^{N_k} (B_k(i) - m_k)^2 \tag{2}$$

$$t_k = \frac{1}{N_k} \sum_{i=1}^{N_k} (B_k(i) - m_k)^3 \tag{3}$$

$$f_k = \frac{1}{N_k} \sum_{i=1}^{N_k} (B_k(i) - m_k)^4 \tag{4}$$

Where B_k is the set of pixels of the k-th image block, N_k is the number of pixels in B_k, and $B_k(i)$ is the i-th pixels of B_k.

Data normalization is applied to V to obtain V'. The reference matrix C is the mean of each row of the matrix V'. The feature matrix Q is calculated by the Eq. (5). Then, matrix Q is expanded by column. It is quantized to binary sequences according to Eq. (6). Thus, local feature sequence H_T is obtained.

$$Q_{i,j} = \sqrt{(V'_{i,j} - C_i)^2} \tag{5}$$

In Eq. (5), $V'_{i,j}$ is the i-th row and the j-th column of V', C_i is the i-th row of C.

$$H(i) = \begin{cases} 0, & H(i) < H_{mean} \\ 1, & otherwise \end{cases} \tag{6}$$

In Eq. (6), $H(i)$ is the i-th element of feature sequence H and H_{mean} is the mean of feature sequence H.

2.4   Global DCT Coefficients Feature

The three-level high-frequency information after wavelet decomposition is transformed by 2D-DCT. The first K DCT coefficients of each direction are selected with zigzag scanning as features matrix $G = [g_1, g_2, g_3]$. And, g_1, g_2, g_3 are horizontal direction, vertical direction and diagonal direction respectively. The mean of the matrix G is named by GM. Thus, we obtain a feature matrix H_G by the Eq. (7). It is quantized to binary sequences according to Eq. (6). The global feature sequence H_D is obtained.

$$H_G(i) = \sqrt{(G(i) - GM)^2} \tag{7}$$

In Eq. (7), $G(i)$ is the i-th element of the feature matrix G.

2.5   Hash Generation

Local and global features are united as hash sequence according to the Eq. (8). Then the columns of H are rearranged to produce a secure hash sequence by using a pseudo-random generator under the control of a key. According to the above, e can know that hash sequence length is $4 \times M^2 + 3K$ bits.

$$H = [H_T, H_D] \tag{8}$$

In Eq. (8), H_T, H_D are the local feature sequence and global feature sequence respectively.

2.6   Image Copy Detection

The flow chart of image copy detection is shown in Fig. 2. The image is mapped into hash sequence through the hash function. Hamming distance is used to evaluate similarity between two images. If the distance between the two hash sequences is less than the threshold, the image is considered as copied image.

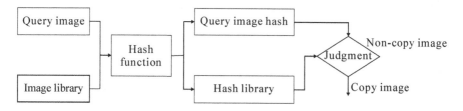

Fig. 2. The flow chart of image copy detection

3 Experiments and Results Analysis

In the experiment, $N = 256$, $M = 8$ and $K = 64$. Thus, The hash length is $4 \times 8^2 + 3 \times 64 = 448$ bits.

3.1 Robustness Test

Five standard color images sized 512×512 were used in robustness test: Airplane, House, Peppers, and Baboon. NeoImaging, Matlab and Photoshop were applied to attack five images. The types of attacks and the parameters are listed in Table 1.

Table 1. Attack setting

Attack	Parameter	Parameter values	Number
Brightness adjustment	Level	−20 −10 10 20	4
Contrast adjustment	Level	−20 −10 10 20	4
Gamma correction	Gamma	0.75 0.9 1.1 1.25	4
JPEG compression	Quality	30 40 50 60 70 80 90 100	8
Rescaling	Ratio	0.5 0.75 1.1 1.5	4
Salt & Pepper	Noise density	0.002 0.004 0.006 0.008	4
Speckle	Variance	0.002 0.004 0.006 0.008	4
Gaussian Noise	Variance	0.002 0.004 0.006 0.008	4
Gaussian filtering	Variance	0.2 0.4 0.6 0.8	4
Mean Filter	Neighborhood	3×3 5×5	2
Median Filter	Neighborhood	3×3 5×5	2
Watermark	Transparency	0.3 0.4 0.5 0.6 0.7 0.8	6
Mosaic	Square size	4 6 8 10	4
Plus subtitles	Font size	10 12 14 16 18 20	6
Total	\	\	60

Hamming distances between the original images and their attacked versions are calculated. The results are presented in Fig. 3. The abscissa is various attacks on the original image. The ordinate is the Hamming distance between the original and attacked image. From the Fig. 3, the maximum distance is no more than 100. Thus, the proposed algorithm is robust against to convention digital processing.

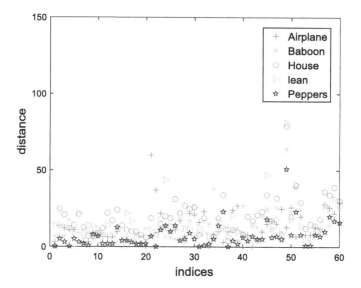

Fig. 3. Robustness test result

3.2 Discrimination Test

Discrimination means that two hash sequences from two different images should be low collision probability (*CP*) [22], The CP is calculated by Eq. (9). To analyze the discrimination, hashes of 1000 different images are obtained. The 499500 results are obtained by calculating Hamming distance among hashes. Collision probabilities with different thresholds are listed in Table 2. As can be seen from Table 2, the collision probability of proposed algorithm is very small. Thus, the different images can be accuracy recognized by proposed algorithm.

Table 2. Collision probabilities with different thresholds

Threshold	97	100	105	110	115
CP	0	2.00×10^{-6}	6.00×10^{-6}	1.00×10^{-5}	1.80×10^{-5}

$$CP = \frac{N_{ds}}{N_T} \tag{9}$$

In Eq. (9), N_{ds} is the number of different images judged as similar images and N_T is the total number of different images.

3.3 Image Copy Detection

The proposed algorithm can be used in image copy detection. 1000 images are downloaded from the website [23]. In database, 100 images are selected as the query images randomly. We exploited NeoImaging, Matlab and Photoshop to produce copied versions of query images. The parameters are shown in Table 3. We obtained 2800 copied images and then added them into the database. Thus, there are 3800 images in image databases.

Table 3. Attack setting

Attack	Parameter	Parameter values
Brightness adjustment	Level	−20 20
Contrast adjustment	Level	−20 20
Gamma correction	Gamma	0.75 1.25
JPEG compression	Quality	40 80
Rescaling	Ration	0.5 1.5
Salt & Pepper	Noise density	0.002 0.006
Speckle	Variance	0.002 0.006
Gaussian Noise	Variance	0.002 0.006
3 × 3 Gaussian low-pass filtering	Variance	0.2 0.6
Mean Filter	Neighborhood	3 × 3 5 × 5
Median Filter	Neighborhood	3 × 3 5 × 5
Watermark	Transparency	0.3 0.8
Mosaic	Square size	6 10
Plus subtitles	Font size	10 20
Total	\	28

The recall rate (R) and the precision rate (P) [24] are used to evaluate the performance of the proposed algorithm. the formulas are shown in (10) and (11). The recall rate and the precision rate with different thresholds are listed in Table 4. With the increase of the recall rate, the precision rate is reduced. When the threshold is 113, the algorithm has a good recall rate and a precision rate.

$$R = \frac{N_1}{N_2} \tag{10}$$

$$P = \frac{N_1}{N_3} \tag{11}$$

Table 4. The recall rate and precision rate with different thresholds

Threshold	Recall	Precision
103	0.9961	1
105	0.9971	0.9997
107	0.9975	0.9997
113	0.9996	0.9997
122	0.9996	0.9986
124	1	0.9980

In Eqs. (10) and (11), N_1 is the number of the correctly copies that are considered as the copies of the corresponding query images, and N_2 is the number of all copies in the image databases. N_3 is the number that are considered as the copies of the corresponding query images.

3.4   Effect of Parameters on Image Copy Detection

The effect of parameters M and K on image copy detection is discussed. The query images and image databases are same with Sect. 3.2. During experiments, only one parameter (M or K) is changed and other parameter are unchanged. The P-R graph is exploited to evaluate the accuracy of copy detection. In the P-R graph, the x-axis is R, the y-axis is P. And, a P-R curve is plotted by coordinates (R, P) with different thresholds. Among all P-R curves, the curve which are closest to the top-right corner has best accuracy.

In the experiment, the value of M are 4, 8 and 16 respectively, when the K value is 64. Figure 4 is the P-R graph with different M values. It can be seen from the graph that the curve is more closer to top-right than other curves, when the M value is 8. And the hash length is calculated and listed in Table 5. From the Table 5, Although the hash length of $M = 4$ is small, its performance of copy detection is not enough. And, hash length of $M = 16$ is too long. Thus. the hash length and performance are suitable when the M value is 8.

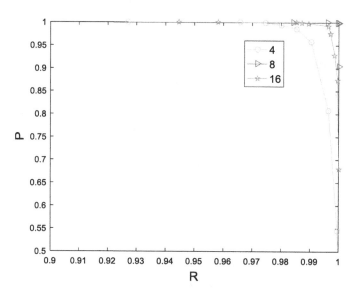

Fig. 4. P-R curve with different M values

Table 5. The hash length with different M values

M value	4	8	16
Hash length (bits)	256	448	1216

The value of K are 32, 64 and 512 respectively, when the M value is 8. The P-R graph with different K values is shown in Fig. 5. It can be seen that the curve is more closer to top-right than other curves when the K is 64. And, the hash length is calculated. Table 6 is the hash length with different K values. From the Table 6, the hash length is too long when the K values is 512. Although the hash length of $K = 32$ is small, its curve is below the curve of $K = 64$. Thus the algorithm has good performance when the $M = 8$ and $K = 64$.

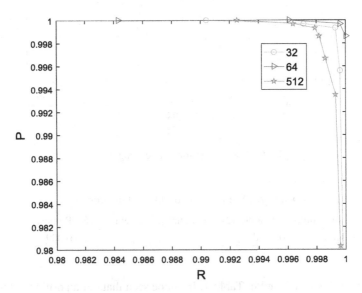

Fig. 5. P-R curve with different K values

Table 6. The hash length with different K values

K value	32	64	512
Hash length (bits)	352	448	1792

3.5   Performance Comparisons

We compared our algorithm with the literature [2, 3, 6]. In the experiment, query images and image databases are the same with proposed algorithm. And the parameters of the compared algorithms are the same with their reported settings. All algorithms are implemented in the same computer. P-R curves with different algorithms are shown in Fig. 6. It is obvious that the proposed algorithm is better than the compared algorithm in recognition performance.

Moreover, the efficiency of algorithm is evaluated. The total time of extracting hashes of image databases in image copy detection test is recorded. Thus, the average time of different algorithms for generating a hash is calculated. The average time of

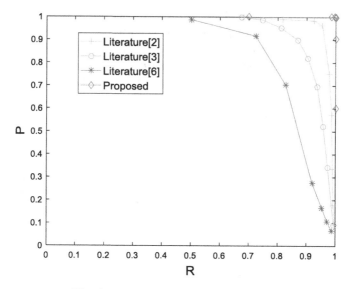

Fig. 6. P-R curves for different algorithms

Table 7. Average time of different algorithms

Algorithms	Literature [2]	Literature [3]	Literature [6]	Proposed
Time (s)	0.1238	0.03	0.72	0.009

different algorithms are listed in Table 7. It can be seen that our algorithm is faster than all other compared algorithms.

4   Conclusions

In this paper, we propose an image hashing algorithm based on local and global features for image copy detection. The experimental results demonstrate that the proposed algorithm is robust against most conventional digital operations. Moreover, the algorithm has a low collision probability. The performance in image copy detection is better than the compared algorithms both in accuracy and efficiency. However, the proposed algorithm has its limitation. Proposed algorithm is not robust to crop and rotation. The reason is that local feature is based on image blocks. Further study is how to enhance the robustness when dealing with these drawbacks.

Acknowledgements. This work was supported by National Natural Science Foundations of China under Grant (61802250).

References

1. Kim, C.: Content-based image copy detection. Sig. Process. Image Commun. **18**(3), 169–184 (2003)
2. Tang, Z., Yang, F., Huang, L., Wei, M.: DCT and DWT based image hashing for copy detection. ICIC Express Lett. **7**(11), 2961–2967 (2013)
3. Tang, Z., Yang, F., Huang, L., Zhang, X.: Robust image hashing with dominant DCT coefficients. Optik-Int. J. Light. Electron Opt. **125**(18), 5102–5107 (2014)
4. Venkatesan, R., Koon, S.M., Jakubowski, M.H., Moulin P.: Robust image hashing. In: International Conference on Image Processing, vol. 663, pp. 664–666 (2000)
5. Hsieh, S.L., Chen, C.C., Chen, C.R.: A Novel Approach to Detecting Duplicate Images using Multiple Hash Tables. Kluwer Academic Publishers, Hingham (2015)
6. Ou, Y.: Rhee, K.H.: A key-dependent secure image hashing scheme by using Radon transform. In: International Symposium on Intelligent Signal Processing and Communication Systems, pp. 595–598 (2009)
7. Srivastava, M., Siddiqui, J., Ali, M.A.: Robust image hashing based on statistical features for copy detection. In: IEEE Uttar Pradesh Section International Conference on Electrical, Computer and Electronics Engineering, pp. 490–495 (2017)
8. Li, X.-W., Xia, X.Z.: Robust image hashing based on content structure diagram. J. Appl. Sci. **34**(6), 691–701 (2016)
9. Tang, Z., et al.: Robust image hashing via random Gabor filtering and DWT. CMC: Comput. Mater. Contin. **55**(2), 331–344 (2018)
10. Monga, V., Mihcak, M.K.V.: Robust and secure image hashing via non-negative matrix factorizations. IEEE Trans. Inf. Forensics Secur. **2**(3), 376–390 (2007)
11. Tang, Z., Yang, F., Huang, Z., Lao, H.: Image hashing algorithm based on PCA feature distance. J. Guangxi Norm. Univ. (Nat. Sci. Ed.) **34**(4), 9–18 (2016)
12. Ling, H., Cheng, H., Ma, Q., Zou, F., Yan, W.Q.: Efficient image copy detection using multiscale fingerprints. IEEE Multimed. **19**(1), 60–69 (2012)
13. Baber, J., Satoh, S.I., Keatmanee, C., Afzulpurkar, N.: Improving the performance of SIFT and CSLBP for image copy detection. In: International Conference on Telecommunications and Signal Processing (2013)
14. Zhou, Z., Wang, Y., Wu, Q.M.J., Yang, C.N., Sun, X.: Effective and efficient global context verification for image copy detection. IEEE Trans. Inf. Forensics Secur. **12**(1), 48–63 (2016)
15. Wu, Q., Li, Y., Lin, Y., Zhou, R.: Weighted sparse image classification based on low rank representation. CMC: Comput. Mater. Contin. **56**(1), 91–105 (2018)
16. Yan, L., Ling, H., Zou, F., Liu, C.: Iterated local search optimized hashing for image copy detection. Multimed. Tools Appl. **74**(21), 9729–9746 (2015)
17. Liu, J., Ling, H., Yan, L., Ou, X.: Feature fusion based hashing for large scale image copy detection. Int. J. Comput. Intell. Syst. **8**(4), 725–734 (2015)
18. Zhou, Z., Sun, X., Wang, Y., Fu, Z., Shi, Y.-Q.: Combination of SIFT feature and convex region-based global context feature for image copy detection. In: Shi, Y.-Q., Kim, H.J., Pérez-González, F., Yang, C.-N. (eds.) IWDW 2014. LNCS, vol. 9023, pp. 60–71. Springer, Cham (2015). https://doi.org/10.1007/978-3-319-19321-2_5
19. Lin, S.D., Yang, L.S.O.: An effective content-based copy detection scheme for image authentication. In: International Conference on Machine Learning and Cybernetics, pp. 321–325 (2014)
20. Heikkilä, M., Pietikäinen, M., Schmid, C.: Description of interest regions with center-symmetric local binary patterns. In: Kalra, P.K., Peleg, S. (eds.) ICVGIP 2006. LNCS, vol. 4338, pp. 58–69. Springer, Heidelberg (2006). https://doi.org/10.1007/11949619_6

21. Tang, Z., Zhang, X., Li, X., Zhang, S.: Robust image hashing with ring partition and invariant vector distance. IEEE Trans. Inf. Forensics Secur. **11**(1), 200–214 (2015)
22. Zhao, Y., Wang, S., Zhang, X., Yao, H.: Robust hashing for image authentication using Zernike moments and local features. IEEE Trans. Inf. Forensics Secur. **8**(1), 55–63 (2013)
23. Test Image. http://wang.ist.psu.edu/docs/related/. Accessed 21 Mar 2018
24. Müller, H., Müller, W., Squire, D.M., Marchand-Maillet, S., Pun, T.: Performance evaluation in content-based image retrieval: overview and proposals. Pattern Recogn. Lett. **22**(5), 593–601 (2001)

KM³SVM: A Efficient Min-Max Modular Support Vector Machine Based on Clustering

Xiyuan Zheng[1], Xiaonan Fang[2], Yanyan Tan[3], Lili Meng[3],
and Huaxiang Zhang[3(✉)]

[1] Shandong Women's University, Jinan, China
306732399@qq.com
[2] Shandong Management University, Jinan, China
[3] Shandong Normal University, Jinan, China
huaxzhang@163.com

Abstract. In recent years, more and more scholars have begun to study the problem of multi-label learning. In this paper, we propose a multi-label learning method called KM³SVM based on Clustering idea. First, for each label, KM³SVM method selects positive samples and negative samples, then uses clustering method to gain a number of training subsets. By using these relatively smaller and more balanced training subsets, we can get a group of classifiers. Given an unseen sample, we can obtain a series of outputs and combine them by two simple principles. Experimental results on two datasets demonstrate the superiority of the proposed method KM³SVM over several state-of-the-art multi-label learning algorithms.

Keywords: Multi-label learning · Min-Max Modular · Clustering · SVM

1 Introduction

In traditional machine learning, each instance is associated with one semantic label. However, one object of real-world usually inheres multiple semantic labels simultaneously. For example, a document on Napoleon may be associated with several predefined concepts such as war and French history simultaneously; an image showing ship in the sea belongs to several annotated words such as ship and sea simultaneously; in bioinformatics, one gene is associated with several functional categories such as Energy and Cell Rescue. Apparently, traditional machine learning can not describe such scenario, so multi-label learning is attracting a growing body of research. For multi-label learning framework, each instance may belong to multiple semantic labels. Multi-label learning has been used to text categorization [1–3], image annotation [4], scene classification [5,8], bioinformatics [6,7], web page classification [9,10], etc.

© Springer Nature Switzerland AG 2019
X. Sun et al. (Eds.): ICAIS 2019, LNCS 11634, pp. 467–475, 2019.
https://doi.org/10.1007/978-3-030-24271-8_42

In many classification problems, there is often a severe imbalance of data sets, and multi-label learning can be more serious. One of the most common strategies for multiple label learning problems is to turn them into two or more binary classification problems. Training data is often uneven, as positive samples come from one species and negative samples from multiple species. Aiming at the unbalanced problem of multi-label learning, some solutions are proposed. Lu et al. put forward a Min-Max modular support vector machine (M^3SVM) by using part-versus-part decomposition strategy. The imbalanced training data is divided into a series of relative balance of binary classification problems [11]. Decomposition strategy is of great importance for M^3SVM. Chen et al. used two new decomposition strategies to modify the (M^3SVM): PCA hyperplane decomposition and the same cluster decomposition [3]. These decomposition strategies in paper [3,11] usually break the distribution characteristics of original training data In order to keep all subsets of the same size. In this paper, we put forward a new method of multi-label learning called KM^3SVM to avoid this problem.

The rest of this paper is organized as follows. In Sect. 2 we briefly review Min-Max Modular Classifiers and K-means clustering algorithm. Section 3 describes the KM^3SVM method. Then we report experimental results in Sect. 4 and give the conclusion in Sect. 5.

2   Related Work

2.1   Min-Max Modular Classifiers

Paper [12] proposed the Min-Max Modular Classifiers. Suppose we have a binary classification problem. Let $S = X^+ \cup X^- X^+$ denote all positive samples and X^- denote all negative samples. In the training stage, according to the decomposition constant K^+ and K^- determined in advance, the original training set is decomposed into K^+ and K^- subsets. They have approximately equal number of samples and mutually disjoint. The training set needs to be divided equally to ensure the load balance of the processors when the sub-classifiers are trained in parallel. During the test phase, test samples are submitted to all sub-classifiers, and each self-classifier gives their classification results. Then using the min-max combination principle, the class label of that unknown sample can be determined at last.

2.2   Clustering

K-means clustering algorithm is one of the most widely used algorithms in clustering analysis because it can efficiently deal with large data sets. First, we specify k initial clustering centers and each sample is assigned to one of k disjoint clusters according to the principle of minimum distance. Second, the centers of k clusters are computed repeatedly and the category of each sample is adjusted at the same time. The iterative calculation will be stopped when the sum of the squares of the distance of each sample to its cluster center is minimized.

2.3 SVM

SVM [16,17] is a supervised learning algorithm used to solve binary classification problems. At present, it is widely used in many aspects [18–21]. Its basic idea is to find the best separation hyperplane in the feature space to maximize the positive and negative sample spacing in the training set.

3 KM³SVM

Given a multi-label classification problem. Let $S = \{(x_1, Y_1), (x_2, Y_2), \ldots, (x_n, Y_n)\}$ denote the training sample set. Let x_i be an instance and Y_i are the possible class labels associated with instance x_i. Let $y_{ij} = 1$ denote that instance x_i belongs to the class label y_j and 0 otherwise. By using one-versus-rest strategy, the multi-label classification problem can be divided into K binary-classification problems. In the training phase, for each class label y_j, the positive set O^j and negative set N^j are denoted as:

$$O^j = \{(x_i, Y_i) \in S, y_j \in Y_i\}$$
$$U^j = \{(x_i, Y_i) \in S, y_j \notin Y_i\}$$

That is, the set O^j consist of the training samples in S with the label y_j and the set U^j consist of the training samples in S without the label y_j. Let M_+^j be the number of samples in the set O^j and M_-^j be the number of samples in the set U^j.

Then the original multi-label classification problem was transformed into K binary-classification problems each of which can be dealt with binary classification methods. Each of binary-classification problems may be highly imbalanced because the set O^j consist of samples from one class while the set U^j consist of samples from K-1 classes especially when K value is big. The basic idea to overcome this question in paper [3] is that the set O^j and U^j are divided into a lot of smaller subset respectively and the number of samples in each positive subset is equal to the number in negative subset. The numbers of subsets are denoted by m_+^j and m_-^j respectively. Obviously, m_-^j is much bigger than m_+^j. We run k-means clustering algorithm respectively on O^j and U^j, with positive samples divided into m_+^j clusters and negative samples divided into m_-^j clusters. One positive cluster and one negative cluster constitute a training subset. Each of subset is denoted by O_n^j or U_n^j respectively. Now, the original problem is divided into $m_+^j * m_-^j$ relatively smaller and more balanced subproblems. Each subproblem can train one SVM classifier and $m_+^j * m_-^j$ classifiers can be obtained. Given an unseen sample, we can have $m_+^j * m_-^j$ outputs. Integrating them by Min-Max combination principles, we can get the label of this unseen sample.

The specific descriptions of our approach are presented in the following Table 1:

Table 1. Pseudo-code of KM^{3}SVM

$Y = KM^3SVM(k, q, t)$

Input:

S: the multi-label training data set $\{(x_i, Y_i)|1 \le i \le n\}(x_i \in X, Y_i \subseteq Y, X = \Re^d,$
$Y_i = \{y_{i1}, y_{i2}, \ldots y_{ij} \ldots y_{iQ}\})$

k: the number of clustering

q: the binary classifier

t: the new testing sample $(t \in X)$

Process:

(1) **for** j=1 to Q **do**

(2) form O^j and U^j from S;

(3) perform clustering algorithm on O^j and U^j respectively and we can get
many clustering cluster of positive samples and negative samples;

(4) a number of new training subsets are obtained, each of them consists of one subset
of O^j and one subset of U^j; denoted by $D_{l_i}^j$;

(5) induce a group of classifiers by D^j;

(6) **end for**

Classification:

Given a new instance t;

(7) **for** j=1 to Q **do**

(8) a number of outputs is given by the existing base classifiers ;

(9) combine these outputs by Min-Max combination principles (10) **end for**

Output:

Y: the set of possible labels of $t(t \in X)$

4 Experiment and Analysis

4.1 Evaluation Criteria and Data Sets

In this paper, we evaluate the effectiveness of KM^{3}SVM by five popular evaluation criteria [14], i.e., Hamming loss, One-error, Coverage, Ranking loss and Average precision on two data sets. For the first four evaluation criteria, the smaller their value the better the performance of algorithm evaluated. For Average precision, the greater its value the better the performance of algorithm evaluated.

4.2 Evaluation Criteria

In this paper, we use the following evaluation criteria [14] to estimate our multi-label learning algorithm:

(1) Hamming loss

The criterion is used to estimate the fraction of misclassified instance-label pairs, i.e., an instance not associated with the label is marked or an instance associated with the label is not marked. Its values range from 0 to 1. The performance of the algorithm evaluated is flawless when its value equals to 0; the smaller its value, the better the performance of algorithm evaluated.

$$coverage = \frac{1}{t} \sum_{i=1}^{t} |h(x_i) \Delta Y_i| \tag{1}$$

(2) One-error

The criterion is used to estimate the fraction of that the top-ranked label is not belong to the label set of the instance. Its values range from 0 to 1. The performance of algorithm evaluated is flawless when its value equals to 0; the smaller its value, the better the performance of algorithm evaluated.

$$one - error = \frac{1}{t} \sum_{i=1}^{t} \left[[argmax_{l_k \in Y} f_k(x_i)] \notin Y_i \right] \tag{2}$$

(3) Coverage

The criterion is used to estimate the average depth of labels in order to find out all the labels of the sample. The smaller its value the better the performance of algorithm evaluated.

$$coverage = \frac{1}{q} \left(\frac{1}{t} \sum_{i=1}^{t} \max_{l_k \in Y_i} rank(x_i, l_k) - 1 \right) \tag{3}$$

(4) Ranking loss

The criterion is used to estimate the average fraction of reversely ordered label pairs, i.e. an irrelevant label is ranked higher than a relevant label. Its values range from 0 to 1. The performance of algorithm evaluated is flawless when its value equals to 0; the smaller its value, the better the performance of algorithm evaluated.

$$rloss = \frac{1}{t} \sum_{i=1}^{t} \frac{|\{(l_k, l_j)| f_k(x_i) \le f_j(x_i), (l_k, l_j) \in Y_i \times \bar{Y}_i\}|}{|Y_i \bar{Y}_i|} \tag{4}$$

(5) Average precision

The criterion is used to calculate the average score of labels which were ranked higher than a particular label. Its values range from 0 to 1, when the value equals to 0, the performance of algorithm evaluated is worst. The greater its value the better the performance of algorithm evaluated.

$$avgprec = \frac{1}{t} \sum_{i=1}^{t} \frac{1}{|Y_i|} \sum_{l_k \in Y_i} \frac{|R(x_i, l_k)|}{rank(x_i, l_k)}, where \tag{5}$$

$$R(x_i, l_k) = l_j | rank(x_i, l_j) \le rank(x_i, l_k), l_j \in Y_i$$

4.3 Data Sets

We use two classic multi-label data sets to perform our algorithm. These two multi-label data sets are widely used to verify the proposed multi-label learning method. The first data set is studied in the literature [5], i.e., *image* data set. It contains 2000 samples and each of which is represented by a 294 dimensional feature vector. Each instance can be attached to five class labels, i.e., desert, sunset, trees, mountains and sea. The second data set is studied in the literature [15], i.e., *scenes* data set. It contains 2407 samples and each of which is also represented by a 294 dimensional feature vector. Each instance can belong to six class labels, i.e., beach, sunset, Fall foliage, mountains, Urban and Field.

4.4 Experimental Results

In order to evaluate the effectiveness of our method, we compare it with other seven approaches on the above two data sets in this section.

Data Set *Image*. A 5-cross validation method is performed on data set *image* and the best performance on each evaluation metric is emphasized in bold face. We firstly compare our method with RM^3SVM, HM^3SVM and EM^3SVM which are the classic version of M^3SVM. The results shown in Table 2 indicate that our method is obviously the best compared with the existing M^3SVM algorithms on *image*. Especially in terms of One-error and Average precision, there are significantly improvement.

Table 2. The experiment results of each comparing algorithm on the data set *image*.

Evaluation criterion	Algorithms			
	KM^3SVM	RM^3SVM	HM^3SVM	EM^3SVM
Hamming loss	**0.2123**	0.2191	0.2262	0.2349
One-error	**0.2687**	0.2838	0.3012	0.3253
Coverage	**1.0167**	1.1171	1.1310	1.1560
Ranking loss	**0.1691**	0.1781	0.1887	0.2026
Ave-precision	**0.8020**	0.7882	0.7733	0.7673

The best experiment results of each comparing algorithm on *image* are shown in Table 3 and the best performance on each evaluation metric is emphasized in bold face. From Table 3, we can find that, compared with BR and ECC, our method is the best one in all evaluation criteria. Compared with CLR and RAKEL, our method performs the best in most of the evaluation criteria.

Data Set *Scenes*. A 5-cross validation method is also performed on data set *scenes* and the best performance on each evaluation metric is emphasized in bold face. We firstly compare our method with RM^3SVM, HM^3SVM and EM^3SVM

Table 3. The experiment results of each comparing algorithm on the data set *image*.

Evaluation criterion	Algorithms				
	KM³SVM	BR	CLR	ECC	RAKEL
Hamming loss	0.2123	0.1851	0.1862	0.2182	**0.1734**
One-error	**0.2687**	0.4063	0.3285	0.3750	0.3121
Coverage	1.0167	1.4391	**0.9330**	1.1390	1.0500
Ranking loss	**0.1691**	0.2852	0.1712	0.2329	0.1968
Ave-precision	**0.8020**	0.7092	0.7895	0.7393	0.7886

which are the classic version of M³SVM. The results shown in Table 4 indicate that our method is obviously the best compared with the above three algorithms on *scenes*. Especially in terms of One-error and Average precision, there are significantly improvement.

Table 4. The experiment results of each comparing algorithm on the data set *scenes*.

Evaluation criterion	Algorithms			
	KM³SVM	RM³SVM	HM³SVM	EM³SVM
Hamming loss	**0.1225**	0.1351	0.1366	0.1533
One-error	**0.2053**	0.2287	0.3019	0.3259
Coverage	**0.0829**	0.0938	0.1057	0.1139
Ranking loss	**0.0826**	0.1023	0.1158	0.1223
Ave-precision	**0.8656**	0.8531	0.8335	0.8277

The best experiment results of each comparing algorithm on *scenes* are shown in Table 5 and the best performance on each evaluation metric is emphasized in bold face. From Table 5, we can find that, compared with BR, CLR and RAKEL, our method is the best one in all evaluation criteria. Compared with ECC, our method performs the best in most of the evaluation criteria.

Table 5. The experiment results of each comparing algorithm on the data set *scenes*.

Evaluation criterion	Algorithms				
	KM³SVM	BR	CLR	ECC	RAKEL
Hamming loss	0.1225	0.1113	0.1126	**0.0963**	0.0964
One-error	**0.2308**	0.3483	0.2559	0.2467	0.2469
Coverage	**0.0829**	0.1584	0.0833	0.0844	0.1043
Ranking loss	**0.0826**	0.1716	0.0834	0.0853	0.1073
Ave-precision	**0.8656**	0.7717	0.8560	0.8535	0.8433

5   Conclusion

A novel multi-label learning algorithm named KM³SVM is proposed in this paper. The proposed algorithm uses the Clustering idea to decompose the positive samples of each class label and select negative samples. Then M³ network is used to deal with the imbalance multi-label classification problem. From the experimental results, it can be easily to find that our algorithm is effective to address the imbalance multi-label classification problem.

References

1. Schapire, R.E., Singer, Y.: BoosTexter: a boosting-based system for text categorization. Mach. Learn. **39**(2–3), 135–168 (2000)
2. Yu, K., Yu, S., Tresp, V.: Multi-label informed latent semantic indexing. In: Proceedings of the 28th Annual International ACM SIGIR Conference on Research and Development in Information Retrieval, pp. 258–265. ACM (2005)
3. Chen, K., Lu, B.L., Kwok, J.T.: Efficient classification of multi-label and imbalanced data using min-max modular classifiers. In: International Joint Conference on Neural Networks, IJCNN 2006, pp. 1770–1775. IEEE (2006)
4. Kang, F., Jin, R., Sukthankar, R.: Correlated label propagation with application to multi-label learning. In: 2006 IEEE Computer Society Conference on Computer Vision and Pattern Recognition, vol. 2, pp. 1719–1726. IEEE (2006)
5. Zhang, M.L., Zhou, Z.H.: ML-KNN: a lazy learning approach to multi-label learning. Pattern Recogn. **40**(7), 2038–2048 (2007)
6. Barutcuoglu, Z., Schapire, R.E., Troyanskaya, O.G.: Hierarchical multi-label prediction of gene function. Bioinformatics **22**(7), 830–836 (2006)
7. Pavlidis, P., Grundy, W.N.: Combining microarray expression data and phylogenetic profiles to learn gene functional categories using support vector machines (2000)
8. Murthy, V.S.V.S., et al.: Application of hierarchical and K-means techniques in content based image retrieval. Int. J. Eng. Sci. Technol. **2**(5), 749–755 (2010)
9. Ma, J.: Based on the Fourier transform and the wavelet transformation of the digital image processing. In: 2012 International Conference on Computer Science and Information Processing (CSIP), pp. 1232–1234. IEEE (2012)
10. Kazawa, H., Izumitani, T., Taira, H., et al.: Maximal margin labeling for multitopic text categorization. In: Advances in Neural Information Processing Systems, pp. 649–656 (2004)
11. Liu, F.Y., Wu, K., Zhao, H., et al.: Fast text categorization with min-max modular support vector machines. In: Proceedings of 2005 IEEE International Joint Conference on Neural Networks, IJCNN 2005, vol. 1, pp. 570–575. IEEE (2005)
12. Lu, B.L., Ito, M.: Task decomposition and module combination based on class relations: a modular neural network for pattern classification. IEEE Trans. Neural Netw. **10**(5), 1244–1256 (1999)
13. Breiman, L.: Bagging predictors. Mach. Learn. **24**(2), 123–140 (1996)
14. Zhang, M., Zhou, Z.: A review on multi-label learning algorithms. IEEE Trans. Knowl. Data Eng. **26**, 1819–1837 (2013)
15. Boutell, M.R., Luo, J., Shen, X., et al.: Learning multi-label scene classification. Pattern Recogn. **37**(9), 1757–1771 (2004)

16. Boser, B., Guyon, I., Vapnik, V.: A training algorithm for optimal margin classifiers. In: Proceedings of the Fifth Annual Workshop on Computational Learning Theory, pp. 144–152. ACM, Pittsburgh (1992)
17. Vapnik, V.: The Nature of Statistical Learning Theory. Springer, New-York (1995). https://doi.org/10.1007/978-1-4757-2440-0
18. Shi, J., Zhang, Z., Li, Y., Wang, R., Shi, H., Li, X.: New method for computer identification through electromagnetic radiation. CMC: Comput. Mater. Continua **57**(1), 69–80 (2018)
19. Wang, B., et al.: Research on hybrid model of garlic short-term price forecasting based on big data. CMC: Comput. Mater. Continua **57**(2), 283–296 (2018)
20. Yuan, C., Li, X., Wu, Q.M.J., Li, J., Sun, X.: Fingerprint Liveness detection from different fingerprint materials using convolutional neural network and principal component analysis. CMC: Comput. Mater. Continua **53**(3), 357–371 (2017)
21. Gurusamy, R., Subramaniam, V.: A machine learning approach for MRI brain tumor classification. CMC: Comput. Mater. Continua **53**(2), 91–108 (2017)

An Image Forensic Method for AI Inpainting Using Faster R-CNN

Xinyi Wang, He Wang$^{(\boxtimes)}$, and Shaozhang Niu

Beijing Key Lab of Intelligent Telecommunication Software and Multimedia,
Beijing University of Posts and Telecommunications, Beijing, China
xawangxy@163.com, {fiphoenix, szniu}@bupt.edu.cn

Abstract. With the introduction of AI technology in the field of image inpainting, it makes up for the shortcomings of traditional inpainting methods. Since this technology can achieve object removal without obvious traces by learning visual semantics informations and performs better in complex environment, it brings great challenges to the existing image forensics work. So far, there are few detection methods for AI image inpainting forgery. In order to fill the gap in this field, this paper proposes a deep learning-based detection method. Considering Faster R-CNN model has demonstrated good performance on detecting semantic objects over a range of scales, we migrate it to the forensic field for image inpainting forgery. It turns out that Faster R-CNN model can capture inconsistencies features between the inpainted region and the authentic region. Therefore, this can further enrich the application range of digital image forensics algorithms. We construct a large-scale AI image inpainting dataset based on ImageNet dataset. The experimental results on this dataset demonstrate that our proposed approach achieves good performance.

Keywords: Image forensics · AI image inpainting · Faster R-CNN

1 Introduction

With the rapid development of the Internet and the popularity of digital image acquisition devices, the number of digital images has been rapidly increasing. At the same time, due to the popularity of processing and editing image software, the editing or tampering of digital images has lowered the threshold, if there is an individual or Institutions deliberately or even maliciously distribute fake images. These fake images not only fail to reflect objective reality, may even cause deception to the public. Therefore, how to identify the authenticity of digital images has become a key issue that needs to be solved urgently.

In order to solve this problem, many scholars began to study digital image forensics technology. At present, there are various forensic algorithms for specific image tampering techniques, such as double JPEG compression [1], median filtering [2], copy-move and splice [3]. However, there are few forensic studies on traditional image inpainting. Moreover, there has been no forensics research on AI image inpainting.

In the past few years, image inpainting has made great progress and is now playing an important role in contents correction and image restoration. However, it can also be

© Springer Nature Switzerland AG 2019
X. Sun et al. (Eds.): ICAIS 2019, LNCS 11634, pp. 476–487, 2019.
https://doi.org/10.1007/978-3-030-24271-8_43

a useful tool for object removal. Figure 1 is an example of forgery using image inpainting techniques, where (a) is the authentic image and (b) is the inpainted image. Image inpainting is an emerging image processing algorithm in recent years, there are some representative works. Criminisi et al. [4] proposed a patching method based on image block copy and paste. This scheme uses block-based sampling process to fill texture and structure information. The paper [5] established a spatial change image inpainting method and analyzed the basic model of image inpainting. The above two methods used the traditional methods on image inpainting. Traditional methods of graphic and visual research are mainly based on mathematical and physical methods, these approaches are still not fast enough for real-time applications and cannot make semantically aware patch selections.

(a) The authentic image   (b) The inpainted image

Fig. 1. The example of image tamper by image inpainting.

With the remarkable effects of deep learning in the field of vision in recent years, more and more graphic researchers have begun to look to the use of deep learning for image inpainting. The image inpainting with AI technology has a qualitative development in terms of effect and speed. In the paper [6], they presented an unsupervised visual feature learning algorithm driven by context-based pixel prediction. By analogy with auto-encoders, they proposed The Context Encoders – a convolutional neural network trained to generate the contents of an arbitrary image region conditioned on its surroundings. In the paper [7], they proposed a new deep generative model-based approach which can not only synthesize novel image structures but also explicitly utilize surrounding image features as references during network training to make better predictions.

At present, the representative work of the research on traditional image inpainting detection is Wu et al. [8] first proposed an image forensics algorithm for sample synthesis inpainting, which is the tamper detection for the paper [4]. They used the zero connectivity feature to screen out the suspicious parts (similar image block pairs), and then used the fuzzy membership degree between similar blocks to identify the inpainted block. However, this method required artificially selected regions, and the false alarm rate was high. Then Liang et al. [9] presented an efficient forgery detection algorithm for object removal by exemplar-based inpainting, which integrated central pixel mapping (CPM), greatest zero-connectivity component labeling (GZCL) and fragment splicing detection (FSD). Although the program speeded up the detection, the false alarm rate was also high. So far, there has been no forensics methods on AI image inpainting.

As deep learning is widely used in the image field, such as image segmentation, image fusion, image classification, etc. For example, in semantic segmentation, deep learning models [10–12] exhibit good performance by learning hierachical features of different objects in an image. In object detection, Ren et al. [13] introduced a Region Proposal Network (RPN) that shared full-image convolutional features with the detection network. They merged RPN and Fast R-CNN into a single network, which is called Faster R-CNN that simultaneously predicted object bounds and objectness scores at each position. Recent efforts in detecting manipulations exploit deep learning based model in [14–17]. These include detection of generic manipulations [14, 15], splicing [16], resampling [17]. Here we propose a new detection method for AI image inpainting forgery using Faster R-CNN model [13] and perform end-to-end training. Due to Faster RCNN model has demonstrate good performance on detecting semantic objects. RPN can propose the regions that may contain objects of interest, so we use RPN here for image inpainting manipulation detection. For distinguish inpainted regions from authentic regions, we utilize convolutional features to capture clues like visual inconsistencies at inpainted boundaries and contrast effect between inpainted regions and authentic regions.

The main contributions of this paper are:

1. providing the concept of confrontation between artificial intelligence, which is a method based on deep learning to detect AI image inpainting forgery.
2. the current datasets of tampered images do not contain the type that images inpainted by AI technology, so we lack data to train a deep network. To overcome this, we create an AI inpainting dataset based on ImageNet using the AI inpainting method [6, 7].
3. applying the Faster R-CNN model to detect and locate the AI inpainting regions.

2   The Principle of AI Image Inpainting

Since there are many deep learning-based image inpainting method. Our proposed forensic method is mainly for two classic deep learning inpainting papers [6, 7]. The paper [6] (published in CVPR 2016) is a very classic image inpainting article based on CNN and GAN, many papers published later, such as [18, 19], are based on this article. The paper [7] (published in CVPR 2018), which is one of the state-of-art deep learning inpainting papers, introducing attention mechanism. This method can not only synthesize novel image structures but also explicitly utilize surrounding image features as references during network training to make better predictions.

In the paper [6], they used deep learning techniques to infer missing images with surrounding image information through a learning algorithm based on unsupervised visual features driven by contextual pixel prediction. The Network framework (shown in Fig. 2) was consisted of an encoder capturing the context of an image into a compact latent feature representation and a decoder which used that representation to produce the missing image content. The main idea was to combine the Encoder-Decoder network structure and GAN (Generative Adversarial Networks). The Encoder-Decoder stage was used to learn the image features and generate the prediction map corresponding to the image to be repaired. The GAN part was used to judge the prediction map from the training set and the prediction set. The possibility that when the generated prediction graph was consistent with the content of GroundTruth on the image content, and the GAN discriminator cannot judge whether the prediction graph is from the training set or the prediction set, the network model parameters are considered to be in an optimal state.

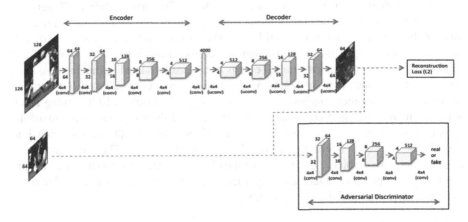

Fig. 2. The framework of the paper [6].

In the paper [7], they presented a unified feed-forward generative network with a novel contextual attention layer for image inpainting. The network consists of two stages. The first stage was a simple dilated convolutional network trained with reconstruction loss to rough out the missing contents. The contextual attention was integrated in the second stage. The core idea of contextual attention is to use the features of known patches as convolutional filters to process the generated patches. The model is a feedforward, fully convolutional neural network which can process images with multiple holes at arbitrary locations and with variable sizes during the test time.

Due to the characteristics of the Inpainting methods in paper [6, 7], the inpainting tamper dataset we have built so far is based on these two methods.

3 Proposed Method

We propose a novel forensic method for AI image inpainting forgery using Faster R-CNN model [13]. Faster R-CNN can be regarded as a model combining RPN and Fast R-CNN, which greatly improves the object detection speed based on Fast R-CNN [20], Faster R-CNN further proposes an RPN network that shares the convolutional layer with the detection network. The network has almost no additional overhead when generating the suggestion window. RPN is a full-convolution network that can simultaneously predict the position boundary of each object and the score of the belonging category and it is trained end-to-end to generate a high quality suggestion window. We use RPN here for image inpainting forgery detection. For distinguish inpainted regions from authentic regions, we utilize convolutional features to capture clues like visual inconsistencies at inpainted boundaries and contrast effect between inpainted regions and authentic regions.

The structure of our proposed method based on the Faster R-CNN model is shown in Fig. 3. The input are images inpainted from authentic images trained with the AI inpainting method [6, 7]. It consists of four modules. The first module is ZF network layer, this layer extracts the convolutional feature map on the original input image as input to the subsequent RPN and ROI layers. The second module is RPN network, this layer generates a suggestion window with the convolution feature map as input, and determines whether the anchor frame belongs to the positive label or the negative label through softmax, then uses the bounding box regression to correct the anchor frame to obtain an accurate object suggestion window. The third module is ROI pooling layer, which combines the input convolution feature map and the suggestion window of the RPN output, and extracts the candidate feature window after synthesis, and sends it to the subsequent fully connected layer to judge the object category. The fourth module is the classifier, it determines the category of the object according to the candidate feature window of the previous stage, and performs a bounding box regression to obtain the final precise position of the detection frame.

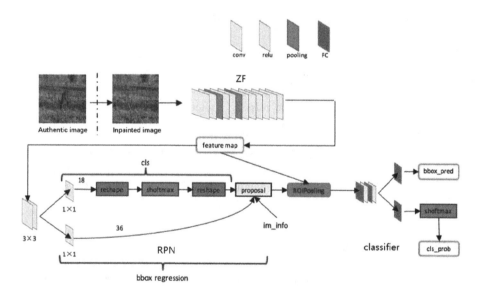

Fig. 3. The structure of our proposed method based on the Faster R-CNN model

3.1   Region Proposal Networks

RPN (Region Proposal Networks) can take any image as input, and output a set of object rectangle suggestion boxes, and the score corresponding to each suggestion box. The RPN model is constructed using a full convolution network. The ultimate goal is to share the calculation with the Fast R-CNN object detection network. The RPN network takes the convolution feature map as input, and runs a sliding window on the graph. Each sliding window maps to a lower-dimensional feature, which is sent to the two fully connected sibling layers - the regression layer and the category classify layer. Since the network runs as a sliding window, the fully connected layer is shared across all spatial locations. The architecture is implemented using an n × n convolutional layer, followed by two sibling layer-one regression layers and a convolutional layer of the classify layer 1 × 1.

3.2 Loss Function

The process of training the RPN, each anchor frame is assigned a binary tag, and the two types of tags are a positive tag and a negative tag, respectively. The positive label is assigned to the anchor box with the IOU area overlapping the Ground-truth bounding box greater than 0.7, the negative label is assigned to the anchor box with the IOU area overlapping the Ground-truth bounding box of less than 0.3. Finally, all non-positive anchor frames are defined as negative tags, because non-active anchor frames do not contribute to the training target.

Based on the above definition, the objective function is minimized according to the multitasking loss in Fast R-CNN, and the loss function is defined as (3–17):

$$L(\{s_i\}, \{t_i\}) = \frac{1}{N_{cls}} \sum_i L_{cls}(s_i, s_i^*) + \lambda \frac{1}{N_{reg}} \sum_i s_i^* L_{reg}(t_i, t_i^*) \qquad (1)$$

Above, i is the index of an anchor in a mini-batch and s_i is the predicted probability of anchor i being an object. The ground-truth label s_i^* is 1 if the anchor is positive, and is 0 if the anchor is negative. t_i is a vector representing the 4 parameterized coordinates of the predicted bounding box, and t_i^* is that of the ground-truth box associated with a positive anchor. The classification loss L_{cls} is log loss over two classes (object vs. not object). For the regression loss, we use $L_{reg}(t_i, t_i^*) = R(t_i - t_i^*)$ where R is the robust loss function (smooth L$_1$). The term $s_i^* L_{reg}$ means the regression loss is activated only for positive anchors ($s_i^* = 1$) and is disabled otherwise ($s_i^* = 0$). The outputs of the cls and reg layers consist of $\{s_i\}$ and $\{t_i\}$ respectively.

For bounding box regression, parameterization of four coordinates is used:

$$\begin{aligned}
t_x &= (x - x_a)/w_a, & t_y &= (y - y_a)/h_a, \\
t_w &= log(w/w_a), & t_h &= log(h/h_a), \\
t_x^* &= (x^* - x_a)/w_a, & t_y^* &= (y^* - y_a)/h_a, \\
t_w^* &= log(w^*/w_a), & t_h^* &= log(h^*/h_a)
\end{aligned} \qquad (2)$$

Where x, y, w, and h represent the center coordinates of the box and its width and height. The variable x, x_a and x^* are used for the prediction box, the anchor box, and the Ground-truth bounding box, respectively, and the definitions of y, w and h are the same as x.

3.3 Implementation Detail

The proposed network is trained end-to-end. Three anchor scales with size from 4^2, 8^2 to 16^2 are used, and the aspect ratios are 1:2, 1:1 and 2:1. The feature size after RoI pooling is $7 \times 7 \times 1024$. The batch size of RPN proposal is 20 for training and 300 for testing.

4 Experiments

In this paper, the experiment is conducted in Ubuntu 14.04, the operating environment is Intel (R) Core (TM) CPU@ 4.20 GHz i7-7700K, GeForce GTX 1080Ti, 32 GB memory PC machine.

4.1 Data Preparation

The current image manipulation datasets do not contain the type that images inpainted by AI technology, so we lack data to train a deep network. To overcome this, we create an AI inpainting dataset which contain 33000 images based on ImageNet using the AI inpainting method [6, 7]. The reasons for choosing these two deep learning-based inpainting methods have been explained in the second part. We will release this dataset for research use. Since our dataset contain two types of inpainted images, the process of preparing the data are as follows:

For the Dataset Obtained Based on Method [6] (Examples are shown in Fig. 4). We randomly selected 3000 images from ImageNet 2007, and then unified the size into 128×128 pixels. The removed regions we select is central region - the central square patch in the image. The input to a context encoder is an image with one regions "dropped out"; i.e., set to zero, assuming zero-centered inputs. Then we use the pre-trained model from the method [6] to restore those images. Finally, we get 3000 pairs of original images and corresponding inpainted images.

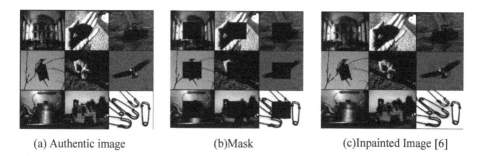

(a) Authentic image   (b)Mask   (c)Inpainted Image [6]

Fig. 4. The examples of the dataset obtained based on method [6]. (a) The authentic image (128×128 pixels). (b) Mask: images with the center region removed. (c) Inpainted images: image inpainting results based on the method [6].

For the Dataset Obtained Based on Method [7] (Examples are shown in Fig. 5). We randomly selected 3000 images from ImageNet 2007, and unified the size to 256 × 256 pixels. Make 10 masks by Photoshop and label the coordinates of the largest outer rectangle of the mask, then randomly combine them with 3000 images. At last, we use the pre-trained model from the method [7] to restore those images. Finally, we get 30000 pairs of original images and corresponding inpainted images.

 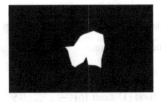 

    (a) Authentic image   (b) Mask (Ground-truth)   (c)Inpainted Image [7]

Fig. 5. The example of the dataset obtained based on method [7]. (a) The authentic image (256 × 256 pixels). (b) The mask of tampered image. (c) Inpainted image: Image inpainting results based on the method [7].

4.2 Training and Testing Model

Since there is no standard AI image inpainting dataset. We demonstrate the proposed method on our 33k inpainting dataset. The training (70%) and testing set (30%) is split to ensure the same background and tampered object do not appear in both training and testing set. The loss of RPN network in our model (the size of anchor scales is 8^2) is shown in Fig. 6. We train our model end-to-end on inpainting dataset and the ResNet 101 used in Faster R-CNN is pre-trained on ImageNet. The output of our model is bounding boxes with confidence scores indicating whether the detected regions have been inpainted or not.

We use Average Precision (AP) for evaluation. The size of anchor scales we choose are 4^2, 8^2 and 16^2. Considering the size of the training and test set images in the experiment, we selected 8^2 as the final anchor scales size.

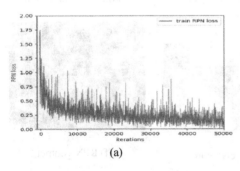 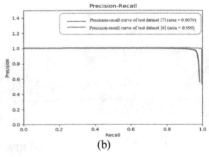

        (a)   (b)

Fig. 6. Results of training and testing our model. (a) The figure of RPN network training loss. (The size of anchor scale is 82). (b) The precision-recall of testing on our different test set. (Test set generated by inpainting methods [6, 7], respectively)

In the Table 1, we can see the Average Precision (AP) of the proposed method on inpainting dataset (generated by inpainting methods [6, 7]). It can be determined that the proposed algorithm can distinguish between authentic images and inpainting images, and can achieve an accuracy of more than 90% for detecting and locating the inpainting image. Different size of anchor scale have little effect on AP, due to the dataset, we find that when 8^2 is selected to the size of anchor scale, the inpainted region is positioned closer to the Ground-truth. So we choose the size of the anchor ruler to be 8^2.

Table 1. The Average Precision of our proposed method on different inpainting dataset

AP (our method on different dataset)		The size of anchor scales		
		4^2	8^2	16^2
Inpainting method	Dataset [6]	–	0.999	–
	Dataset [7]	0.9060	0.9079	0.9087

Figure 7 is a visualized image extracted at a portion of the network layer when the inpainting image is detected using the trained Faster R-CNN network. We can see that for the inpainting image, Faster R-CNN can extract the inconsistencies of the inpainted region. Conversely, it can be proved that for the image region inpainted by AI, there are features that are inconsistent with the authentic region. Human eyes sometimes not

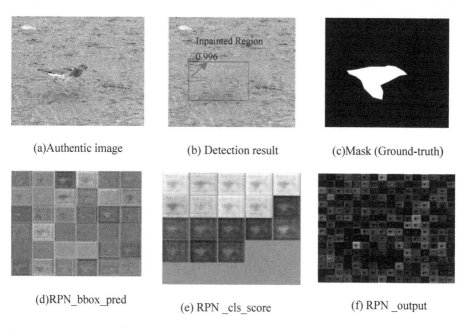

(a)Authentic image   (b) Detection result   (c)Mask (Ground-truth)

(d)RPN_bbox_pred   (e) RPN _cls_score   (f) RPN _output

Fig. 7. The visualization of image feature in our model. (a) is the authentic image (256 × 256 pixels), (b) is the detection result for the image (a), (c) is the mask of tampered image. (d), (e) and (f) are the visualized images of the bounding box, classifier and output layers in the RPN network of image (b), respectively.

easily recognize these inconsistent, but the deep learning network can find them through a large number of samples as can be seen from the following figure. When the model obtain the differences in features, the inpainted region will be detected and located.

4.3 AI Inpainting Detection and Localization

We evaluate AI Inpainting detection using our test dataset and another 10000 images from ImageNet that contain both untampered and inpainted images.

To include some authentic regions in Region of Interest (RoI) for better comparison, we slightly enlarge the default bounding boxes by 10 pixels during training so that the network can learn the inconsistency between inpainted and authentic regions. The output of our model is bounding boxes with confidence scores indicating whether the detected regions have been inpainted or not. In Fig. 8, we show multiple inpainted regions using the method of the paper [7], and Fig. 9 shows the tamper example using the method of the paper [6] (Fig. 10).

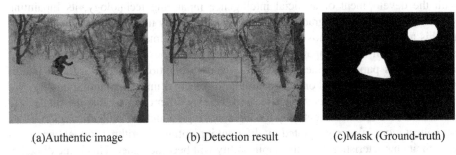

(a)Authentic image   (b) Detection result   (c)Mask (Ground-truth)

Fig. 8. The example of multiple inpainted regions using the method [7].

(a)Authentic image   (b) Detection result   (c)Mask

Fig. 9. The example of inpainted regions using the method [6].

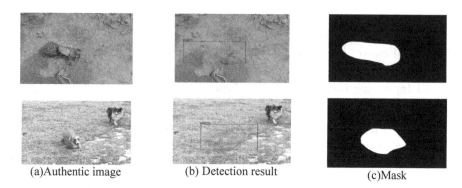

(a)Authentic image   (b) Detection result   (c)Mask

Fig. 10. More examples of detecting and locating inpainted image.

5 Conclusion

With the development of artificial intelligence inpainting technology, its Inpainting efficiency and quality are gradually improved, and finally non-professionals can easily use this technology to remove objects and tamper with image content. Therefore, the tamper detection for AI inpainting has gradually become a research topic worthy of attention. This paper provides the concept of confrontation between artificial intelligence, a new method based on deep learning to detect AI image inpainting forgery. We apply the Faser R-CNN network here, and the experiment proves that the model can capture the inconsistencies between the inpainted region and the authentic region. If we can collect more images generated by different inpainting algorithms and let our model learn their characteristics, then the applicability will become wider. This is the direction of our efforts in the future.

Acknowledgements. This work was supported by National Natural Science Foundation of China (No. 61370195, U1536121).

References

1. Taimori, A., Razzazi, F., Behrad, A., Ahmadi, A., Babaie-Zadeh, M.: A novel forensic image analysis tool for discovering double JPEG compression clues. Multimed. Tools Appl. **76**(6), 1–35 (2017)
2. Kang, H.R.: Median filtering detection using variation of neighboring line pairs for image forensic. In: IEEE International Conference on Consumer Electronics, Berlin, vol. 25, pp. 103–107 (2016)
3. Li, J., Yang, F., Lu, W., Sun, W.: Keypoint-based copy-move detection scheme by adopting MSCRs and improved feature matching. Multimed. Tools Appl. **76**, 20483–20497 (2016)
4. Criminisi, A., Perez, P., Toyama, K.: Region filling and object removal by exemplar-based image inpainting. IEEE Trans. Image Process. **13**(9), 1200–1212 (2004)
5. Zhou, C., Wang, Z., Liu, S., Astronautics, S.O.: Method of image restoration directly based on spatial varied point spread function. Acta Opt. Sin. **37**(1), 110–121 (2017)

6. Pathak, D., Krahenbuhl, P, Donahue, J., Darrell, T., Efros, A.A.: Context encoders: feature learning by inpainting. In: Computer Vision and Pattern Recognition, CVPR, pp. 2536–2544 (2016)
7. Yu, J., Lin, Z., Yang, J., Shen, X., Lu, X., Huang, T.S.: Generative image inpainting with contextual attention. arXiv:1801.07892 (2018)
8. Wu, Q., Sun, S.J., Zhu, W., Li, G.H., Tu, D.: Detection of digital doctoring in exemplar-based inpainted images. In: Proceedings of IEEE International Conference on Machine Learning and Cybernetics, vol. 3, pp. 1222–1226 (2008)
9. Liang, Z., Yang, G., Ding, X., Li, L.: An efficient forgery detection algorithm for object removal by exemplar-based image inpainting. J. Vis. Commun. Image Represent. 30(C), 75–85 (2015)
10. Meng, R., Rice, S.G., Wang, J., Sun, X.: A fusion steganographic algorithm based on faster R-CNN. CMC: Comput. Mater. Contin. 55(1), 001–016 (2018)
11. Li, C., Jiang, Y., Cheslyar, M.: Embedding image through generated intermediate medium using deep convolutional generative adversarial network. CMC: Comput. Mater. Contin. 56(2), 313–324 (2018)
12. Badrinarayanan, V., Kendall, A., Cipolla, R.: SegNet: a deep convolutional encoder-decoder architecture for image segmentation. IEEE Trans. Pattern Anal. Mach. Intell. 39(12), 2481–2495 (2017)
13. Ren, S., He, K., Girshick, R., Sun, J.: Faster R-CNN: towards real-time object detection with region proposal networks. IEEE Trans. Pattern Anal. Mach. Intell. 39(6), 1137–1149 (2017)
14. Bayar, B., Stamm, M.C.: A deep learning approach to universal image manipulation detection using a new convolutional layer. In: Proceedings of the 4th ACM Workshop on Information Hiding and Multimedia Security, pp. 5–10 (2016)
15. Bayar, B., Stamm, M.C.: Design principles of convolutional neural networks for multimedia forensics. Electron. Imaging 2017(7), 77–86 (2017)
16. Rao, Y., Ni, J.: A deep learning approach to detection of splicing and copy-move forgeries in images. In: 2016 IEEE International Workshop on Information Forensics and Security (WIFS), pp. 1–6. IEEE (2016)
17. Bayar, B., Stamm, M.C.: On the robustness of constrained convolutional neural networks to JPEG post-compression for image resampling detection. In: IEEE International Conference on Acoustics, Speech and Signal Processing, pp. 2152–2156 (2017)
18. Gao, R., Grauman, K.: On-demand learning for deep image restoration. In: IEEE International Conference on Computer Vision, pp. 1095–1104 (2017)
19. Yang, C., et al.: High-resolution image inpainting using multi-scale neural patch synthesis. In: IEEE Conference on Computer Vision and Pattern Recognition (CVPR), Honolulu, HI, pp. 4076–4084 (2017)
20. Girshick, R.: Fast R-CNN. In: IEEE International Conference on Computer Vision, pp. 1440–1448 (2015)

Kernel Generalized Canonical Correlation and a New Feature Fusion Strategy

Lina Wei$^{(\boxtimes)}$, Quansen Sun, and Xizhan Gao

Nanjing University of Science and Technology, Nanjing, China
Lina.wei@etu.emse.fr

Abstract. When processing face images, we usually use the data analysis tools to find the underlying relations in data. As an extraction method based on two groups of features, Canonical Correlation Analysis (CCA) can better reveal the inner relations between two variates. Recently, CCA has been widely used in multiple feature fusion and extraction and it has gained a series of achievements. The basic idea of CCA is: firstly, establish correlation criterion function between two groups of features; then extract the correlation feature of each data; finally, obtain the combined correlation feature, which is used in image classification. In practice, we can also add the category information of training samples by improving the discriminant criterion function. Furthermore, by exploiting corresponding kernel function, the original data can also be projected into higher dimensional spaces to reduce the gaps between the heterogeneous spaces. In this paper, we focus on the Generalized CCA(GCCA) and Kernel CCA(KCCA) and then introduce the idea of kernel GCCA(KGCCA). We solve the problem by Lagrangian multiplier method and we also propose a new feature fusion strategy (FFS). Finally, experiments on Yale and ORL face datasets demonstrate the performance of our proposed method KGCCA and the new FFS.

Keywords: Feature fusion · Generalized canonical correlation analysis · Kernel

1 Generalized Canonical Correlation Analysis

1.1 Introduction

Canonical Correlation Analysis (CCA) [1], Multiple Linear Regression (MLR) [2], Partial Least Squares Analysis [3] are commonly used multivariate statistical method for studying the relationship between two sets of data. Among them, MLR is the most widely used and has been successfully applied in many fields. PLS regression analysis is a new multivariate data processing method, which has become one of the important multi-feature fusion technologies [4]. Since CCA is based on the correlation between two sets and multiple sets of data, it is generally referred to as correlation projection analysis. In the past ten years, CCA has been gradually applied in the fields of pattern recognition, computer vision and signal processing, and has achieved good development results [5].

In the field of pattern recognition, Sun et al. [6] used CCA to first extract low-dimensional typical correlation components from two sets of variables, and then solved the relevant discrimination vector set under a given fusion strategy. In order to make up

© Springer Nature Switzerland AG 2019
X. Sun et al. (Eds.): ICAIS 2019, LNCS 11634, pp. 488–500, 2019.
https://doi.org/10.1007/978-3-030-24271-8_44

for the shortcomings of CCA as an unsupervised learning method, Sun et al. [7] introduced guidance for supervisory information and further used the generalized CCA (GCCA) method to include intra-class information. By minimizing the constraints of intra-class scatter matrix, this method greatly reduces the dispersion of samples within the class, thus improving the discriminating ability when the feature dimension is low. Similarly, they proposed discriminative CCA (DCCA) [8]. However, due to the limitation of the categories number, the maximum feature dimension extracted by DCCA may cause the problem of insufficient number of projection axes, which reduces the application range of the algorithm to some extent. Based on the idea of LDA, Kim et al. [9] used the linear feature extraction to compress the subspace dimension of image set, and proposed Discriminant-analysis of Canonical Correlation (DCC) and applied it to the image set. In the classification, the method achieves a satisfactory classification effect in practical applications.

Inspired by the kernel method, Sun et al. [10] proposed kernel DCCA (Kernelized DCCA, KDCCA). Subsequently, Peng et al. [11] proposed local discriminative CCA (LDCCA) based on the idea of localization, and successfully applied in face and handwritten digital image recognition. Although LPCCA can find nonlinear structures between data, it is difficult to obtain better recognition performance in pattern classification due to its lack of supervised information. As to feature selection, Liu et al. [12] used the fused gist feature as data descriptor for rare bird sparse recognition. Recently, with the development of deep learning, a Deep Generalized CCA(DGCCA) [13] has been proposed to learn non-linear transformations of arbitrary multiple-view data so that the final transformations are maximally informative of each other. Furthermore, semi-supervised deep learning methods [14] are also proposed to solve the classification problems.

1.2 Basic Theory of Generalized Canonical Correlation Analysis

The basic idea of GCCA [7] is to add the category information of training samples to it by improving the discriminant criterion function. Let A and B be the feature set of the pattern sample space Ω, the pattern sample satisfying $\zeta \in \Omega \in R^n$, and its corresponding feature vector $x \in A \in R^p$, $y \in B \in R^q$, respectively. Let S_{Wx} and S_{Wy} represent the inter-class scatter matrices of sample spaces A and B, respectively, then

$$S_{Wx} = \sum_{i=1}^{c} p(\omega_i) \left[\sum_{j=1}^{l_i} \frac{1}{l_i} \left(x_{ij} - m_i^x \right) \left(x_{ij} - m_i^x \right)^T \right]$$

$$S_{Wy} = \sum_{i=1}^{c} p(\omega_i) \left[\sum_{j=1}^{l_i} \frac{1}{l_i} \left(y_{ij} - m_i^y \right) \left(y_{ij} - m_i^y \right)^T \right]$$

where $x_{ij} \in A$, $y_{ij} \in B$ represent respectively the j-th data of the i-th training sample, $p(\omega_i)$ is the prior probability of class I, l_i is the number of training samples in class i. m_i^x, m_i^y are the mean vectors of the training sample class i. L_{xy} represents the inter-class covariance matrix of class A and B. We have

$$L_{xy}^T = L_{yx}, r = rank\left(L_{xy}\right)$$

$$L_{xy} = \frac{1}{n}\sum_{i=1}^{n}(x_i - m^x)(y_i - m^y)^T$$

where $x_i \in A$, $y_i \in B$, m^x, m^y represents the mean vector of the training sample space. Assuming that S_{Wx}, S_{Wy} is a positive-definite matrix, we establish a criterion function as follows:

$$J_g(\xi, \eta) = \frac{\xi^T L_{xy}\eta}{\left(\xi^T S_{Wx}\xi \cdot \eta^T S_{Wy}\eta\right)^{1/2}} \qquad (1)$$

The criterion function (1) is called the generalized canonical correlation criterion. The vector that maximizes the criterion function is called the projection direction. The physical meaning is that when the projected samples minimize the distribution between classes, the two sets of feature vectors have the greatest correlation.

The focus of GCCA is to find a pair of single directions ξ_k, η_k, so that

$$\{\xi_k, \eta_k\} = arg \max_{|\xi|=|\eta|=1} J_g(\xi, \eta), k = 1, 2, \cdots, r$$

which meets the following constraints

$$\xi_k^T S_{Wx}\xi_i = \eta_k^T S_{Wy}\eta_i = 0, 1 \leq i \leq k \qquad (2)$$

Through the above method, we can obtain two sets of projection vectors, which are called generalized canonical projection vectors (GCPV), and the features extracted by this method are called generalized canonical correlation discriminant features (GCCDF).

1.3   Solution of GCPV

Here, we will discuss the solution to obtain GCPV [15].

In order to guarantee the universality of the method, we assume

$$\xi^T S_{Wx}\xi = \eta^T S_{Wy}\eta = 1 \qquad (3)$$

The problem is therefore transformed into a problem of finding a set of generalized representative projection vectors A such that the criterion function (1) takes the maximum value under the constraint condition (3). Through the Lagrange multiplier method, the problem is further translated into two general problems:

$$L_{xy}S_{Wy}^{-1}L_{yx}\xi = \lambda^2 S_{Wx}\xi \qquad (4)$$

$$L_{yx}S_{Wx}^{-1}L_{xy}\eta = \lambda^2 S_{Wy}\eta \qquad (5)$$

So we can get the following Theorem 1:

Theorem 1. Based on the generalized canonical criterion function (1), the generalized canonical projection vector (GCPV) is the d pair of eigenvectors corresponding to the d large non-zero eigenvalues under Eqs. (4) and (5), and these generalized canonical typical projection vector must satisfy:

$$\begin{cases} \xi_i^T S_{Wx}\xi_j = \eta_i^T S_{Wy}\eta_j = 0 \\ \xi_i^T L_{xy}\eta_j = \lambda_i \delta_{ij} \end{cases} \quad (i,j = 1,2,\cdots,d)$$

where

$$\delta_{ij} = \begin{cases} 1, i = j \\ 0, i \neq j \end{cases}$$

Then we can get the corollary:

Corollary. If all the eigenvalues of (4) and (5), satisfy that

$$\lambda_1^2 > \lambda_2^2 > \cdots > \lambda_r^2 > \lambda_{r+1}^2 = \cdots = \lambda_p^2 = 0 (p \leq q)$$

and that the generalized canonical criterion function satisfy

$$J_g(\xi_i, \eta_i) = \lambda_i (i = 1, 2, \cdots, p)$$

Theorem 2. The number of genralised canonical projection vectors does not exceed $r, r = rank(S_{xy})$. These d pairs of generalized canonical projection vectors may contain eigenvectors satisfying Eq. (2) and consist of eigenvectors corresponding to the first d maximum eigenvalues of the generalized feature Eqs. (4) and (5).

2 The Kernel Generalized Canonical Correlation Analysis and Its Implementation

2.1 The Kernel Generalized Canonical Correlation Analysis

Now, we'll apply the kernel method [16, 17] to GCCA, which is called KGCCA. KGCCA first transforms two sets of data into a high-dimensional feature space using nonlinear mapping, and then performs GCCA in these two spaces. Again, assume that the two sets of raw data are $X = (x_1, x_2, \cdots, x_n) \in R^{n \times p}$ and $Y = (y, y_2, \cdots, y_n) \in R^{n \times q}$ respectively. Where n is the number of samples, and p and q represent the dimensions of the two sets of data, respectively. X and Y are mapped to the high dimensional feature spaces F_x and F_y by two non-linear mappings $\phi : x \rightarrow \phi(x) \in F_x$ and $\psi : y \rightarrow \psi(y) \in F_y$. In feature spaces F_x, F_y, two sets of raw data can be represented as $\phi(X) = (\phi(x_1), \phi(x_2), \cdots, \phi(x_n))$ and $\psi(Y) = (\psi(y_1), \psi(y_2), \cdots, \psi(y_n))$. KGCCA looks for a pair of projection directions α_ϕ and β_ψ in spaces F_x and F_y, so that there is maximum correlation between projections $\alpha_\phi^T \phi(X)$ and $\beta_\psi^T \psi(Y)$. The solution vectors α_ϕ and β_ψ of KGCCA can be expressed as a linear combination of two sets of samples, i.e.:

$$\alpha_\phi = \sum_{i=1}^n \alpha_i \phi(x_i) = \phi(X)\alpha$$

$$\beta_\psi = \sum_{i=1}^n \beta_i \psi(y_i) = \psi(Y)\beta$$

We define:

$$K_{Xx} = \phi(X)^T \phi(x) = [k(x_1, x), \cdots, k(x_n, x)]^T \in R^{n \times 1}$$

$$K_{Yy} = \psi(Y)^T \psi(y) = [k(y_1, y), \cdots, k(y_n, y)]^T \in R^{n \times 1}$$

so that:

$$\begin{aligned} cov(\alpha^T K_{Xx}, \beta^T K_{Yy}) &= E\{[\alpha^T K_{Xx} - E(\alpha^T K_{Xx})][\beta^T K_{Yy} - E(\beta^T K_{Yy})]\} \\ &= \alpha^T \{[K_{Xx} - E(K_{Xx})][K_{Yy} - E(K_{Yy})]\}\beta \end{aligned} \quad (6)$$

Let

$$\mu_{K_{Xx}} = E(K_{Xx}) = \sum_{i=1}^n K_{Xx_i}$$

$$\mu_{K_{Yy}} = E(K_{Yy}) = \sum_{i=1}^n K_{Yy_i}$$

and

$$\widetilde{K_{Xx}} = K_{Xx} - \mu_{K_{Xx}}$$

$$\widetilde{K_{Yy}} = K_{Yy} - \mu_{K_{Yy}}$$

then Eq. (6) can be expressed as:

$$cov(\alpha^T K_{Xx}, \beta^T K_{Yy}) = \alpha^T E\left(\widetilde{K_{Xx}}, \sim \widetilde{K_{Yy}}\right)\beta$$

Additionally, we have:

$$E(\tilde{K}_{Xx} \cdot \tilde{K}_{Yy}) = \frac{1}{n}\sum_{i=1}^n \tilde{K}_{Xx_i}\tilde{K}_{Yy_i}^T = \frac{1}{n}[\tilde{K}_{Xx_1}, \cdots, \tilde{K}_{Xx_n}][\tilde{K}_{Yy_1}, \cdots, \tilde{K}_{Yy_n}]^T$$

Let

$$K_X = \left[\tilde{K}_{Xx_1}, \cdots, \tilde{K}_{Xx_n} \right] \in R^{n \times n}$$

$$K_Y = \left[\tilde{K}_{Yy_1}, \cdots, \tilde{K}_{Yy_n} \right] \in R^{n \times n}$$

We'll have

$$cov\left(\alpha^T K_{Xx}, \beta^T K_{Yy} \right) = \frac{1}{n} \alpha^T K_X K_Y^T \beta$$

On the other hand, we perform the same deduction from the constraints

$$\alpha_\phi^T S_{Wx}^\phi \alpha$$
$$= \alpha^T \phi(X) S_{Wx}^\phi \phi^T(X) \alpha$$
$$= \alpha^T \phi(X) \left[\sum_{i=1}^c \sum_{j=1}^{l_i} \left(\phi(x_j) - m_i^\phi \right) \left(\phi(x_j) - m_i^\phi \right)^T \right] \phi^T(X) \alpha$$
$$= \alpha^T \sum_{i=1}^c \sum_{j=1}^{l_i} \left[\phi(X) \left(\phi(x_j) - m_i^\phi \right) \right] \left(\phi(x_j) - m_i^\phi \right)^T \phi^T(X) \alpha$$
$$= \alpha^T \sum_{i=1}^c \sum_{j=1}^{l_i} \left[\left(\phi(X)\phi(x_j) - \phi(X)m_i^\phi \right) \left(\phi^T(x_j)\phi^T(X) - \left(m_i^\phi \right)^T \phi^T(X) \right) \right] \alpha$$

Note $K_{Xx_j} = \phi(X)\phi(x_j)$, $K_{Xm_i} = \phi(X)m_i$, then

$$\alpha_\phi^T S_{Wx}^\phi \alpha = \alpha^T \sum_{i=1}^c \sum_{j=1}^{l_i} \left[\left(K_{Xx_j} - K_{Xm_i} \right) \left(K_{Xx_j} - K_{Xm_i} \right)^T \right] \alpha$$

The same can be obtained that

$$\beta_\phi^T S_{Wy}^\psi \beta = \beta^T \sum_{i=1}^c \sum_{j=1}^{l_i} \left[\left(K_{Yy_j} - K_{Ym_i} \right) \left(K_{Yy_j} - K_{Ym_i} \right)^T \right] \beta$$

So, the optimized model of KGCCA is as follows:

$$max J_k \left(\alpha_\phi, \beta_\psi \right) = \alpha_\phi^T C_{XY} \beta_\psi$$
$$s.t. \alpha_\phi^T S_{Wx}^\phi \alpha_\phi = \beta_\phi^T S_{Wy}^\psi \beta_\psi = 1$$

where

$$C_{XY} = \frac{1}{n} K_X K_Y$$
$$S_{Wx}^\phi = \sum_{i=1}^c p(\omega_i) \left[\sum_{j=1}^{l_i} \left[\left(K_{Xx_j} - K_{Xm_i} \right) \left(K_{Xx_j} - K_{Xm_i} \right)^T \right] \right]$$
$$S_{Wy}^\psi = \sum_{i=1}^c p(\omega_i) \left[\sum_{j=1}^{l_i} \left[\left(K_{Yy_j} - K_{Ym_i} \right) \left(K_{Yy_j} - K_{Ym_i} \right)^T \right] \right]$$

2.2 The Solution to the Generalized Canonical Correlation Analysis of Kernel

Combined with the solution of generalized canonical correlation analysis in 1.2, the problem is further generalized into the following two problems by the Lagrangian multiplier method:

$$C_{XY} \left(S_{Wy}^{\psi} \right)^{-1} C_{YX} \alpha = \lambda^2 S_{Wx}^{\phi} \alpha$$

$$C_{YX} \left(S_{Wx}^{\phi} \right)^{-1} C_{XY} \beta = \lambda^2 S_{Wy}^{\psi} \beta$$

2.3 Feature Fusion Strategies

Let x, y be the original feature vector and x^*, y^* be the transformed feature vector after KGCCA. Then the following features can be used to do classification.

$$Z_1 = \begin{pmatrix} x^* \\ y^* \end{pmatrix} \tag{7}$$

$$Z_2 = x^* + y^* \tag{8}$$

$$Z_3 = (x^*, y^*) \tag{9}$$

The transformations (7), (8) and (9) are called Feature Fusion Strategy1(FFS1), Feature Fusion Strategy2(FFS2) and Feature Fusion Strategy3(FFS3) [6]. Based on these strategies, we now propose a new feature fusion strategy, which is called FFS4:

$$Z_4 = \mu x^* + (1 - \mu) y^*$$

where μ is a weight to balance each new feature. In the experiments, we can improve the classification accuracy by optimizing μ.

3 Experiment Analysis

3.1 Image Pre-processing and K Nearest Neighbor Classifier

The image recognition is a high-dimension and small-sample problem. It's difficult to find enough training samples to ensure that the covariance matrix of the two vectors is non-singular. The Principal Component Analysis [18] is proposed to firstly reduce the sample dimension and then apply the CCA to the transformed sample space.

The classifier used in our experiment is k nearest neighbor classifier. Suppose that we have c patterns $w_1, w_2, \ldots, w_c$ and the total sample number is $n = n_1 + n_2 + \ldots + n_c$, where n_i is the sample number of class i. Each sample correspond to a feature matrix of dimension $d \times 2$. Now we define the distance between two features $M_i = \left[z_1^{(i)}, z_2^{(i)}\right]$ and $M_j = \left[z_1^{(j)}, z_2^{(j)}\right]$ is:

$$d\left(M_i, M_j\right) = \sum_{k=1}^{2} \left\|z_k^{(i)} - z_k^{(j)}\right\|_2$$

where $\|\cdot\|_2$ is Euclidean distance between two vectors. Suppose that we have the samples $\xi_1, \xi_2, \ldots, \xi_n$ and their feature matrix are $M_1, M_2, \ldots, M_n$. For any sample ξ and its feature matrix M, if $d(M, m_l) = \min_j d(M, M_j)$ and $M_l \in \omega_k(\zeta_l \in \omega_k)$ then $M \in w_k(\xi \in w_k)$.

3.2 Experiment on the ORL Face Dataset

ORL face dataset consists of 40 images, each of which has 10 different images of facial expressions (such as open/close eyes) and facial details (such as wearing glasses/not wearing glasses). These images are taken under the background of uniform gray level. The human upright and frontal postures have 20% tilt and rotation, and the face scale also has 10% changes. All images are gray-scale and the size is homogenized to 112 * 92. A part of the ORL image is shown in Fig. 1.

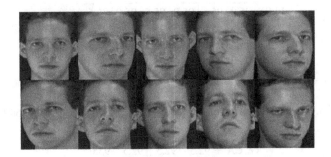

Fig. 1. Examples of images in ORL dataset

In the experiment, we used the first five images of each person as training samples, and the remaining five images as testing samples. Therefore, the total number of training samples and test samples is 200. Firstly, we use the original image as the first feature space, and then perform a biorthogonal wavelet transform on the original image to obtain the second training sample space. Then, we apply the GCCA and KGCCA methods to generate the canonical correlation features. The canonical correlation feature matrices of face images are extracted by FFS1, FFS2, FFS3 and FFS4. Finally, the nearest classifier is used for classification.

The classification results are shown in Tables 1 and 2. Table 3 gives the optimal recognition rate of CCA and KCCA on the ORL and the corresponding number of projection axes d. At the same time, in order to compare the CCA and KCCA algorithms, Fig. 2 shows the relation between the number of features and classification accuracy under FFS4.

Table 1. Classification accuracy (%) of GCCA on ORL under different FFS

d	40	50	60	70	80	90	100
FFS1	91.0	91.5	92.5	92.0	92.0	92.0	92.5
FFS2	91.5	92.0	92.5	92.5	92.5	92.0	92.5
FFS3	91.0	92.0	92.5	92.5	92.5	92.0	92.5
FFS4	92.0	92.5	93.0	92.5	92.5	92.0	92.5
d	110	120	130	140	150	160	
FFS1	92.0	92.0	92.0	92.5	92.0	92.0	
FFS2	92.0	92.0	92.0	92.5	92.0	92.0	
FFS3	92.0	92.0	92.0	92.5	92.0	92.0	
FFS4	92.0	92.0	92.0	92.5	92.0	92.0	

Table 2. Classification accuracy (%) of KGCCA on ORL under different FFS

d	40	50	60	70	80	90	100
FFS1	95.0	95.0	95.0	95.5	95.5	95.5	95.5
FFS2	95.5	95.5	95.0	95.5	95.5	95.5	95.0
FFS3	95.0	94.5	95.5	95.5	95.5	95.5	95.5
FFS4	95.5	95.5	95.5	96.0	96.0	96.0	96.0
d	110	120	130	140	150	160	
FFS1	95.0	95.5	95.0	95.5	95.0	95.5	
FFS2	95.5	95.0	95.5	95.0	95.5	95.5	
FFS3	95.5	95.0	95.0	95.5	95.0	95.5	
FFS4	96.0	95.5	96.0	95.5	96.0	96.0	

Table 3. Highest classification accuracy (%) of GCCA and KGCCA on ORL

	FFS1	FFS2	FFS3	FFS4
GCCA	92.5	92.5	92.5	93.0
KGCCA	95.5	95.5	95.5	96.0

We can see from the results shown in the above tables and curves that GCCA and KGCCA yield accurate recognition results, and the recognition rate tends to be stable. The curve in Fig. 2 shows that KGCCA is better than GCCA in terms of recognition rate, and this superiority is more obvious in higher dimension. This is because KGCCA maps the original data into high-dimensional space and then performs GCCA processing to convert the nonlinear data problem into a high-dimensional linear problem, which enhances the stability of the algorithm. By applying the kernel method to GCCA, the KGCCA algorithm undoubtedly has a higher recognition rate. The results in the table shows that the recognition rate is about 3% higher than GCCA. From the tables above, we can also conclude that the recognition rate of KGCCA under FFS4 is higher than those on FFS1, FFS2 and FFS3, which prove that our new FFS is more informative. We note here that μ is 0.7 and 0.3 in experiments of GCCA and KGCCA respectively.

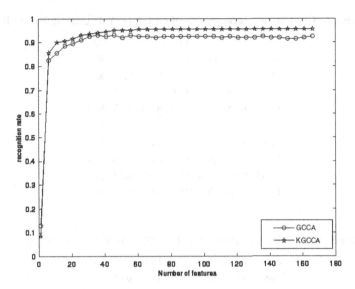

Fig. 2. Comparison of classification accuracy of GCCA and KGCCA on ORL under FFS4

3.3 Experiment on the Yale Dataset

The Yale face dataset is composed of 15 images and 11 images per person. The image size is 120 * 91, and there are 256 gray levels on each pixel. These images are different in visual angle, expression and illumination. Some images are incomplete. Examples of the image in Yale dataset are shown in Fig. 3.

In this experiment, we use the principal component analysis to extract the first feature space and then apply the wavelet transformation to generate the second feature space. The classification results using the features obtained by GCCA and KGCCA are shown in Tables 4 and 5. Table 6 shows the optimal recognition rate of GCCA and KGCCA and the number of corresponding projection axis d. At the same time, in order to compare the GCCA and KGCCA algorithms, Fig. 4 shows the relation between the number of features and classification accuracy under FFS4.

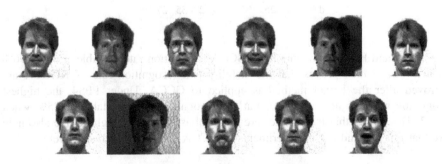

Fig. 3. Example of image in Yale dataset

Table 4. Classification accuracy (%) of GCCA on Yale under different FFS

d	13	15	17	19	21	23
FFS1	84.0	84.0	83.3	82.0	82.7	83.3
FFS2	81.3	81.3	81.3	81.3	82.7	82.7
FFS3	81.3	81.3	80.0	81.3	82.7	82.7
FFS4	81.3	82.7	80.0	81.3	82.7	84.0
d	25	27	29	31	33	35
FFS1	84.7	85.3	83.3	84.0	84.7	84.7
FFS2	82.7	84.0	85.3	84.0	84.0	84.0
FFS3	84.0	84.0	85.3	85.3	84.3	84.3
FFS4	84.0	85.3	85.3	85.3	85.3	85.3

Table 5. Classification accuracy (%) of KGCCA on Yale under different FFS

d	13	15	17	19	21	23
FFS1	89.3	89.3	89.3	89.3	89.3	89.3
FFS2	88.0	88.0	88.0	89.3	89.3	89.3
FFS3	88.0	88.0	88.0	89.3	89.3	89.3
FFS4	88.0	88.0	88.0	89.3	89.3	89.3
d	25	27	29	31	33	35
FFS1	90.7	90.0	90.0	90.0	90.0	90.0
FFS2	89.3	90.7	92.7	90.7	90.7	90.7
FFS3	89.3	90.7	92.7	90.7	90.7	90.7
FFS4	89.3	90.7	92.7	90.7	90.7	90.7

Table 6. Highest classification accuracy (%) of GCCA and KGCCA on Yale

	FFS1	FFS2	FFS3	FFS4
GCCA	85.3	85.3	85.3	85.3
d	27	29	29/31	27–35
KGCCA	90.7	90.7	90.7	90.7
d	25	27–35	27–35	27–35

Table 5 and Fig. 4 show that the KGCCA recognition rate is stable at about 90% when $d \geq 27$, which proves that the stability and recognition rate of KGCCA are improved after the kernel method is applied to GCCA. Under FFS4, the highest recognition rate has not improved, but the recognition rate is stable at 85% when $d \geq 27$. This shows that the features are more robust with the weight μ. We also note here that μ is 0.7 and 0.3 in experiments of GCCA and KGCCA respectively.

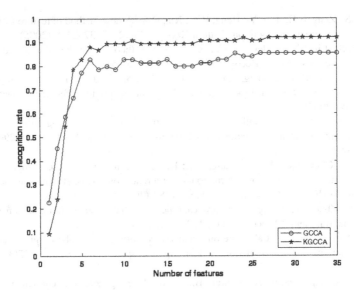

Fig. 4. Comparison of classification accuracy of GCCA and KGCCA on Yale under FFS4

4 Conclusion

In this paper, we first introduced the generalized canonical correlation analysis and then applied the kernel method to it through mathematical deduction. We then proposed a new feature fusion strategy based on three existed ones. The experiments on ORL and Yale face datasets proved that the kernel generalized canonical correlation analysis proposed in this paper has a good performance in terms of recognition rate and stability.

Acknowledgement. This research is supported by the National Science Foundation of China (Grant No. 61673220).

References

1. Abdi, H., Guillemot, V., Eslami, A., et al.: Canonical correlation analysis. In: Encyclopedia of Social Network Analysis and Mining, pp. 1–16 (2017)
2. Olive, D.J.: Multiple linear regression. In: Olive, D.J. (ed.) Linear Regression, pp. 17–83. Springer, Cham (2017). https://doi.org/10.1007/978-3-319-55252-1_2
3. Sarstedt, M., Ringle, C.M., Hair, J.F.: Partial least squares structural equation modeling. In: Homburg, C., Klarmann, M., Vomberg, A. (eds.) Handbook of market Research, pp. 1–40. Springer, Cham (2017). https://doi.org/10.1007/978-3-319-05542-8_15-1
4. Liang, H., Ju, T., Chao, L., et al.: Pattern recognition for partial discharge based on multi-feature fusion technology. High Volt. Eng. 41(3), 947–955 (2015)
5. Yuan, Y.H., Sun, Q.S., Ge, H.W.: Fractional-order embedding canonical correlation analysis and its applications to multi-view dimensionality reduction and recognition. Pattern Recogn. 47(3), 1411–1424 (2014)

6. Sun, Q.S., Zeng, S.G., Liu, Y., Heng, P.A., Xia, D.S.: A new method of feature fusion and its application in image recognition. Pattern Recogn. **38**(12), 2437–2448 (2005)
7. Sun, Q.-S., Liu, Z.-D., Heng, P.-A., Xia, D.-S.: A theorem on the generalized canonical projective vectors. Pattern Recogn. **38**(3), 449–452 (2005)
8. Sun, T.K., Chen, S.C., Yang, J.Y., Shi, P.F.: A supervised combined feature extraction method for recognition. In: Proceedings of IEEE International Conference on Data Mining, Pisa, Italy (2008)
9. Kim, T.-K., Kittler, J., Cipolla, R.: Discriminative learning and recognition of image set classes using canonical correlations. IEEE Trans. Pattern Anal. Mach. Intell. **29**(6), 1005–1018 (2007)
10. Sun, T.K., Chen, S.C., Jin, Z., Yang, J.Y.: Kernelized discriminative canonical correlation analysis. In: Proceedings of International conference on Wavelet Analysis and Pattern Recognition (ICWAPR), Beijing, pp. 1283–1287 (2007)
11. Peng, Y., Zhao, D., Zhang, J.: A new canonical correlation analysis algorithm with local discrimination. Neural Process. Lett. **31**, 1–15 (2010)
12. Liu, J., Sun, N., Li, X., et al.: Rare bird sparse recognition via part-based gist feature fusion and regularized intraclass dictionary learning. Comput. Mater. Contin. **55**(3), 435–446 (2018)
13. Benton, A., Khayrallah, H., Gujral, B., et al.: Deep generalized canonical correlation analysis. arXiv preprint arXiv:1702.02519 (2017)
14. Tu, Y., Lin, Y., Wang, J., et al.: Semi-supervised learning with generative adversarial networks on digital signal modulation classification. Comput. Mater. Contin. **55**(2), 243–254 (2018)
15. Sun, Q.-S., Heng, P.-A., Jin, Z., Xia, D.-S.: Face recognition based on generalized canonical correlation analysis. In: Huang, D.-S., Zhang, X.-P., Huang, G.-B. (eds.) ICIC 2005. LNCS, vol. 3645, pp. 958–967. Springer, Heidelberg (2005). https://doi.org/10.1007/11538356_99
16. Yamada, M., Pezeshki, A., Azimi-Sadjadi, M.R.: Relation between kernel CCA and kernel FDA. In: Proceedings of International Joint Conference on Neural Networks, pp. 226–231 (2005)
17. Lisanti, G., Masi, I., Del Bimbo, A.: Matching people across camera views using kernel canonical correlation analysis. In: Proceedings of the International Conference on Distributed Smart Cameras, p. 10. ACM (2014)
18. Lu, H.P., Plataniotis, K.N., Venetsanopoulos, A.N.: Uncorrelated multilinear principal component analysis for unsupervised multilinear subspace learning. IEEE Trans. Neural Netw. **20**(11), 1820–1836 (2009)

Multiple Obstacle Detection for Assistance Driver System Using Deep Neural Networks

Yuhua Fan[1]([📧])[iD], Luping Zhou[2], Liya Fan[1], and Jing Yang[1]

[1] School of Mathematical Sciences, Liaocheng University, Liaocheng, China
angelfyh@gmail.com
[2] School of Electrical and Information Engineering, University of Sydney, Sydney, Australia

Abstract. Multiple obstacle detection is a challenging problem and has many important applications including video tracking, intelligence surveillance, robot navigation and autonomous driving. In existing methods, individual obstacle's detection and contextual visual patterns are modeled separately and interactions from obstacles and their surroundings are mostly considered in a symmetric way, which we argue is not an optimal strategy. To tackle these difficulties, in this paper, we propose a deep convolutional networks for solving the online multiple obstacles detection problem. The method consists of deep visual information extraction and visual pattern learning. They are modeled as deep Convolution Neural Networks, which are able to learn discriminative visual features for obstacle detection and model inter-object relations in an asymmetric way and give the orientation extraction for the moving obstacles. The deep learning framework is trained in an end-to-end manner for better adapting the influences of visual information as well as inter-object relations and orientation information. Extensive experimental comparisons with state-of-the-arts as well as detailed component analysis of the proposed method on the benchmarks demonstrate the effectiveness of our proposed framework.

Keywords: Multiple obstacle detection · Deep network · Driver assistance system

1 Introduction

Almost half of traffic accidents were reported on interurban roads more and more in recent years. Moreover, most of them occurred in roads due to the carelessness of driver for the complex and different level of dangerousness. Or the other

---

Supported by the PhD Research startup Foundation of Liaocheng University (No. 318051654) and A Project of Shandong Province Higher Educational Science and Technology Program (No. KJ2018BAN109).

X. Sun et al. (Eds.): ICAIS 2019, LNCS 11634, pp. 501–513, 2019.
https://doi.org/10.1007/978-3-030-24271-8_45

hand, people need more reliable and safe assistance driver system to decrease the transport costs. The warning presented by Advanced Driver Assistance Systems (ADAS) are utilized to help drivers, poorly designed warnings may distract the driver, thus making driving less safe [1]. Examples of ADAS are lane departure warning systems and forward collision avoidance systems [2,3]. The aim of the current research was to address the problem of real-time automatic obstacle detection system using sensor fusion architecture based on computer vision and laser scanner technologies [4]. By defining the traffic area and new strategy in obstacle extraction from U-disparity, vision information was used to conduct the multiple obstacle detection and tracking [5]. Detection and recognition of mixed traffic for driver assistance system [6].

Multiple obstacle detection has been playing an important role in the road safety for ADAS. In the context of ADAS, the purpose of obstacle detection can monitor the dynamic situation of one or more obstacles. Hence, the ADAS can provide essential warnings for decision making and can help to avoid the potential collisions. This paper presents an approach for multiple obstacle detection using deeply neural networks to monitor the potential collision avoidance systems. We first extract multi-channel Harris space-time interest points (STIPS) information using Gaussian smoothing kernel and compute the depth cues. And then we encode visual features using multi-scale deeply described scheme to detect obstacles better. Note that we also consider the multi-scale correlogram to express the spatial co-occurrences of features. And then we learn and detect the multiple obstacles efficiently to improve the safety and efficiency while on the road by using the fully connect deep neural networks, the multiple obstacles are detected effectively. The pipeline of the presented paper is showing in Fig. 1.

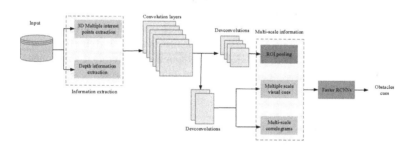

Fig. 1. The flowchart of the proposed method.

2   Related Works

One of the most important parts of environment perception is the detection of obstacles in the surrounding of the vehicle. Moving obstacles have potentially higher risks of collision than stationary obstacles in traffic. Therefore, it is meaningful to detect moving obstacles by sensors equipped on a car for drive assistance applications. To achieve that, several sensors like radars, LiDARs and cameras are installed in autonomous vehicles. The produced sensor data is fused to a general representation of the surrounding. The dynamic occupancy grid map approach of Nuss et al. [7] is used while three goals are achieved. First, the approach of Nuss et al. [8] to distinguish between moving and non-moving obstacles is improved by using Fully Convolutional Neural Networks to create a class prediction for each grid cell. For this purpose, the network is initialized with public pre-trained network models and the training is executed with a semi-automatic generated dataset.

A general problem of developing machine learning approaches like Neural Networks is the number of labeled data, which can always be increased. According to the technique of deep learning, more and more research works based on vision information extraction and machine learning occur for ADAS [9–11]. The proposed framework combines a novel deep learning approach with the use of multiple sources of local patterns and depth information to yield robust on-road vehicle and pedestrian detection, recognition, and tracking. Based on robust obstacle detection to identify obstacles appearing along the road that are likely to be vehicles and pedestrians, an efficient adaptive U-V disparity algorithm can be implemented to improve the efficiency of detection. Second, the results from the obstacle detection stage are input into a novel vehicle and pedestrian recognition system based on a deep learning model that processes multiple sources of depth information and local patterns. Finally, the results from the recognition stage are used to track detected objects in the next frame by means of a proposed tracking and validation model. Another system based on histograms of oriented gradients and cascade classifiers for specific obstacle detection is proposed by Sachine Sharma et al. [12]. This method considered the interior roads connecting villages and towns have been instrumental in multiple animal-vehicle collisions. Though these efforts can reduce the number of collisions, lack of practical applications have impeded any major breakthrough for the real complex road ADAS in the real-time navigation.

In this paper, we first use the Convolutional Neural Networks trained on colored images, which is another kind of input as used. For this reason, several parameters of the Fully Convolutional Neural Networks like the network structure, different combination of inputs and the weights of labels are optimized. We can first obtain the multi-scale information from vision and pattern cues. Then the second goal is to provide more accurate information for each detected obstacle. For the moving obstacles, we want to know their orientation extraction based on the Convolutional Neural Network to improve the reliability for the whole system. Extensive experiments on datasets can demonstrate that the proposed method can detect multiple obstacles efficiently.

3   Multiple Obstacle Detection

3.1   Spatial-Temporal Feature Extraction

3D Harris Corner Detection. To obtain the vision information effectively, we aim to extract the multi-channel Harris space-time interest points information using 3D Harris corner detection method. Similar to the spatial domain [13], we also consider the spatio-temporal feature extraction firstly. The spatio-temporal second-moment matrix, which is a 3-by-3 matrix composed of first order spatial and temporal derivatives averaged using a Gaussian weighting function $g(:, \sigma_i^2, \tau_i^2)$ can be defined as follows [14]:

$$\mu = g(:, \sigma_i^2, \tau_i^2) * \begin{pmatrix} L_x^2 & L_xL_y & L_xL_t \\ L_xL_y & L_y^2 & L_yL_t \\ L_xL_t & L_yL_t & L_t^2 \end{pmatrix}, \tag{1}$$

where the integration scales σ_i^2 and τ_i^2 can be related to the local scales σ_l^2 and τ_l^2 according to $\sigma_i^2 = s\sigma_l^2$ and $\tau_i^2 = s\tau_l^2$. Then the first-order derivatives are defined as:

$$\begin{aligned} L_x(:, \sigma_l^2, \tau_l^2) &= \partial_x(g * f), \\ L_y(:, \sigma_l^2, \tau_l^2) &= \partial_y(g * f), \\ L_y(:, \sigma_l^2, \tau_l^2) &= \partial_t(g * f), \end{aligned} \tag{2}$$

To detect interest points, we search for regions in f having significant eigenvalues $\lambda_1, \lambda_2, \lambda_3$ of μ. With extending the traditional Harris corner function, we can define the spatial domain into the spatio-temporal domain by combining the determinant the trace of μ as follows:

$$\begin{aligned} H &= det(\mu) - k \cdot trace\mu^3 \\ &= \lambda_1\lambda_2\lambda_3 - k(\lambda_1 + \lambda_2 + \lambda_3)^3. \end{aligned} \tag{3}$$

Note that the positive local maxima of H is corresponding to the points which may own high values of λ_1, λ_2, and λ_3. Here $\lambda_1 \leq \lambda_2 \leq \lambda_3$. Then the ratios $\alpha = \lambda_2 \backslash \lambda_1$ and $\beta = \lambda_3 \backslash \lambda_1$ can be defined and re-written as follows:

$$H = \lambda_1^3(\alpha\beta - k(1 - \alpha + \beta)^3). \tag{4}$$

Multi-channel Harris STIPS. Based on the local maxima of Harris energy function, multi-channel formulation of the structure tensor has been developed to express more information for detection tasks [15,16]. To improve the performance of multiple obstacle detection, we also integrate the multiple channel in the spatio-temporal structure tensor as [15].

Let $V = (V^1, V^2, \cdots, V^{n_c})^T$ denote the multi-channel volume that consisting of n_c channels. According to the base of 3D Harris function, j-th channel $V^j = g(:, \sigma_o, \mu_o) \times f(\cdot)^j$, $g(:, \cdot, \cdot)$ is the 3D Gaussian kernel with equal scales along the spatial dimensions, σ_o and μ_o are the spatial and temporal observation scales respectively. And $f^j : \mathbb{R}^3 \to \mathbb{R}$ is the function of the channel j. Then multi-channel spatio-temporal structure tensor [15] can be defined as follows:

$$\mu = g(:, \sigma_i, \tau_i) * \begin{pmatrix} V_x \cdot V_x & V_x \cdot V_y & V_x \cdot V_t \\ V_y \cdot V_x & V_y \cdot V_y & V_y \cdot V_t \\ V_t \cdot V_x & V_t \cdot V_y & V_t \cdot V_t \end{pmatrix}, \tag{5}$$

where σ_i and τ_i denote the spatial and temporal integration scale respectively. Considering the effective of Gabor filter for the feature extraction, we also use the Gabor STIP detector along the temporal axis. For the energy function of multiple channels is also positive by formulation, no conflicting will be considered for channels:

$$R = \sum_{j=1}^{n_c} (g(:, \sigma_o) * h_{ev}(:, \tau_o * V^j)^2) + (g(:, \sigma_o) * h_{od}(:, \tau_o) * V^j)^2, \tag{6}$$

where $g(:, \cdot)$ is the Gaussian smoothing kernel in spatial domain. The Gabor filter pair $\{h_{ev}(:, \cdot), h_{od}(:, \cdot)\}$ is used to measure the periodicity of the observed information along the temporal dimension.

3.2 Multi-scale Deeply Described Visual Information Encoding

The original concept of CNN was biologically inspired by "neocognitron" [17], a hierarchical network with invariance to image translations. The CNN framework is consisting with layers, and the first few stages are composed of convolutional layers and pooling layers.

In this work, the deeply described visual information are computed on the output of a single convolutional layer of the CNN, such as the last convolutional layer. Note that the input images need not be rescaled to a specific size for the non-required computation of fully connected layers. Thus, we can extract the dense convolutional features at different scales and pooled them in STIPs. Specifically, we construct multi-scale dense convolutional features with S scales by subsampling original images and extracting single-scale convolutional features. Then a visual vocabulary containing K entries was formed by a pooling method such as k-means [18] using a random subset of features at all scales from the training set (Fig. 2).

Multi-scale Information Extraction Using CNNs. Let $X = [X^1, X^2, \cdots, X^S]^T$ be a set of descriptors obtained through STIPs representation in an N-dimensional feature space at S different scales. Then the single-scale dense convolution descriptors X^S can be defined as follows:

$$X^S = [x_1^S, x_2^S, \cdots, x_{M_S}^S]^T \in \mathbb{R}^{m_S \times N}, s = \{1, \cdots, S\}, \tag{7}$$

where x_m^s is the m-th descriptor and M_S is the number of the descriptors at scale s. Assume the dictionary D has K training atoms $\{d_k\}_{k=1,2,\cdots,K}$, each of which

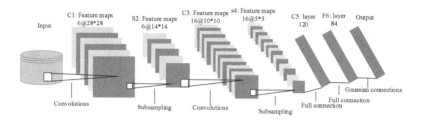

Fig. 2. Structure of convolutional neural networks trained to describe visual information.

is an N-dimensional vector. Then the dictionary can be formed by collecting all the multi-scale descriptors X from the training set. By applying a pooling strategy, we can encode the local descriptors using a subset of features. The multi-scale coefficient matrix V and single-scale coefficient matrix V^S is defined just like [19].

To detect the multiple obstacles effectively, multi-scale correlogram can be considered to express the spatial co-occurrences of features, encoding both distinctive local features and their spatial relationship features. And this will be more robust to the basic geometric transformations and occlusions.

During the procedure of the algorithm, labels for different class will be assigned as a forground/background at different scales. Assume the number of such labels is K. Let $\prod$ be a kernel (or the image mask), and $\prod_r$ be the r-th kernel. Then the number of occurrences of visual cues labeled l_p and l_q at scale s with the kernel $\prod_r$ can be defined as $h^S(\prod_r, l_p, l_q)(l_p \in \{1, \cdots, K\}, l_q \in \{1, \cdots, K\}, r \in \{1, \cdots, T\}, s \in \{1, \cdots, K\})$. Then, a correlogram at scale s (a $K \times K \times T$ matrix) $C(I)$ can be extracted from the value of $h^S(\prod_r, l_p, l_q)$.

During the learning stage, visual information will be learned by k-means scheme, while each descriptor can be given a label with a corresponding entry index in the matrix. Then a maximum map strategy can be used to assign the index of maximum non-zero entry in the coefficient matrix to the label, for the visual cues pooling method. Thus, the single-scale coefficient matrix $V^s \in R^{M_s \times K}$ using K-means can be represented as follows:

$$V^S = [v_1^S, v_2^S, \cdots, v_{M_S}^S]^T \in \mathbb{R}^{M_S \times K} \quad s.t. |v_m^S| = 1, v_{m_i}^S \in \{0, 1\}, \qquad (8)$$

where $v_{m_i}^S$ is the matrix element of m-th row and i-th column of V^S. Then the spatial co-occurrences of a pair of deeply described visual cues are easily exploited using the labels of descriptors. According to the multi-scale deeply described visual information, we can obtain the correlograms at each scale separately and integrate them into a large set just like [19] to improve the average precision of multiple obstacles detection.

Incoming information cannot be interpreted separately, but all cues need to be processed as complex data for the expression of important features. For each neuron x_{ij} on each layer l, compute the sum from the previous layer $l-1$

multiplied by its weight. Note that the local pair of points in foreground will signed by a larger weight to distinct its importance for detecting the obstacles.

3.3 Multiple Obstacle Detection Using Multiple Cues

The main problem is with the first two types of the data - visual information and depth cues. For the amount of image data form the practical traffic scenes, both types of data need to decrease the number of calculations. So we take only one frame every one seconds. After the multi-scale deeply described visual information encoding based on 3D interest points extraction, another CNN system will be trained to detect the obstacles effectively. To improve the performance of multiple obstacle detection, we aim to detect the obstacles fast and efficiently. We use the framework of the state-of-the-art object detection network as [20] based on the multiple information.

Weighted Matrix. For the dynamic scenes, the number of static pixels should obtain much more information than other dynamic pixels. That can cause problems with the back-propagation strategy to a higher affinity to the static class. For this purpose, weighted matrix C is introduced in the following cost function $J(\theta)$ of the multinomial logistic loss as:

$$J(\theta) = -[\sum_{i=1}^{m} \sum_{k=1}^{K} C^{(y^i)} 1\{y^{(i)} = k\} log P(y(i) = k | x^{(i)}; \theta)], \tag{9}$$

where C contains a weight for each labeled class $C = [c^{(1)}, c^{(2)}, \cdots, c^{(K)}]$.

Orientation Extraction. Orientation angle extraction from images is usually applied in the field of head pose estimation [22]. There, the orientation is often split in different bins and a classifier is trained for each separate bin. After that a linear regression over the bins can be calculated. These approaches restrict the capability of machine learning algorithms, especially if they are able to directly regress a continuous orientation range. This periodicity causes that gradient descent approaches (like in the training step of CNNs) cannot be used. Beyer et al. [21] introduced the Biternion representation, which is based on quaternions. There, the orientation q is represented as following:

$$q = (cos\phi, sin\phi). \tag{10}$$

Then the difference is that the machine learning method can regress sine and cosine variables in range of -1 and 1. And two regressions can be recombined to an angle θ with $\theta = arctan\frac{sin\phi}{cos\phi}$. Then the CNN can create a pixel-wise prediction for the DOG. This segmentation should improve a cluster and tracking algorithm as to provide more information to the multiple obstacle detection algorithm, the orientation of the object should be extracted. The orientation in this context is represented by the moving direction. To extract the moving direction of the obstacle, the output of the pixel-wise classification is used to create the clusters of dynamic objects. Based on this information, a means of the velocities $\bar{v}$ in x and y direction can be calculated, which can be used to extract the angel ϕ of the clusters with the following equation. The Fig. 3 is showing the illumination of the orientation extraction. Note that the pre-trained network structure is not changed, besides the last layers, which are transfered from fully connected to fully convolutional layers.

$$\phi = arctan(\frac{\bar{v}_y}{\bar{v}_x}). \tag{11}$$

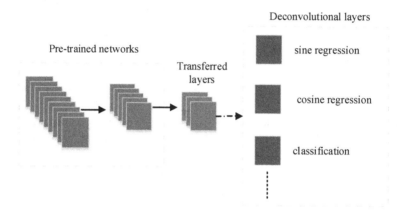

Fig. 3. Adaption of CNNs for orientation extraction: two more output maps at the deconvolutional layer are introducted for the regression of sine and cosine regression.

3.4   Implementation

Note that the base network is built on the 16-layer VGG net [23]. We initialize the parameters by sampling weights from the VGG-16 network pretrained on the training set. And some modifications according to our multiple obstacle detection task are as follows:

– Feature map will be computed to deal with extra-small obstacles by using multi-scale cues. In particular, 2x bilinear subsampling layer before feeding the last convolutions feature map to the last faster RCNN.
– To obtain the optimal pooling operation in the network, we use the 4x subsampling procedure to keep the distinctive information.
– For the faster RCNN framework, we use multi-scale ROI pooling cues and multi-scale visual information and correlograms to obtain the high performance of the whole detection framework.

4   Experiment

4.1   Dataset

The proposed detection method has been evaluated on different sequences of KITTI dataset [24]. The dataset consists of 7 481 images for training and 7 518 images for testing respectively. And it involves several traffic images, such as street, country side, high way and so on. To obtain more distinctive performance, we also extract the depth information using the method of non-parametric sampling just like [25].

We compare the proposed method with the popular multi-view 3D networks (MV3D) [26]. The relative experimental set for generating 3D candidate boxes and the deep fusion scheme to combine the region-wise features from multi-views are the same as the original paper. Another method used to compare with our method is the model using multimodal redundant warnings from the existing advanced assistance systems [27]. For an efficiency of the experiments, we also use the same method with the reference.

Table 1. Comparison of different methods for multiple obstacle detection: Average Precision (%) on KITTI validation set.

Method	IoU = 0.25			IoU = 0.5			IoU = 0.7		
	Easy	Moderate	Hard	Easy	Moderate	Hard	Easy	Moderate	Hard
[27]	92.31	85.22	85.64	95.40	87.36	87.36	70.02	61.17	55.13
MV3D [26]	96.51	88.79	89.1	96.1	89.11	88.23	71.22	62.01	56.41
Our method	97.01	89.23	90.31	97.24	90.03	89.61	73.56	64.02	58.01

Table 2. Comparison of different methods for obstacle localization performance: Average Precision (%) on KITTI validation set.

Method	IoU = 0.5			IoU = 0.7		
	Easy	Moderate	Hard	Easy	Moderate	Hard
[27]	95.61	88.17	88.91	86.33	77.23	76.10
MV3D [26]	96.30	90.01	88.71	86.60	78.0	76.65
Our method	97.01	91.32	89.35	88.0	79.2	78.51

4.2   Experiment and Analysis

We focus our experiments on the car category as KITTI [24] provides enough car instances for our deep network based approach. Following the KITTI setting, we also split the training data into training set and validation set and do evaluation on three difficulty regimes: easy, moderate and hard as [26,28].

Table 3. The ablation study of multiple scale features: performance are evaluated on KITTI validation set.

Data	IoU = 0.5			IoU = 0.7		
	Easy	Moderate	Hard	Easy	Moderate	Hard
RGB	73.65	68.91	62.31	77.3	71.72	64.55
MSV	79.83	77.21	75.34	80.3	79.6	71.21
MSC+MSV	85.72	83.6	80.3	85.41	82.34	81.2
MSDDVI	97.2	90.12	89.24	96.56	89.05	88.73

Table 4. Comparison of different methods: performance are evaluated on KITTI test set.

Method	IoU = 0.25			IoU = 0.5			IoU = 0.7		
	Easy	Moderate	Hard	Easy	Moderate	Hard	Easy	Moderate	Hard
[27]	88.63	88.04	87.61	95.34	83.21	87.19	93.65	86.91	77.89
MV3D [26]	96.01	89.13	88.30	96.41	84.38	88.68	95.02	87.61	79.89
Our method	96.67	90.21	88.97	97.10	95.6	89.31	96.01	88.32	80.13

Multiple Obstacle Detection. For the overlap of two obstacles, we use different IoU threshold value of 0.25, 0.5 and 0.7 for the multiple obstacle detection evaluation. Table 1 reports the statistical results for different obstacle detection. We can see that the proposed method can outperform other two excellent models for the detection of multiple obstacle on the testing set.

The presented strategy obtains about 1.5% and 5.1% higher when using IoU of 0.25, achieving 97% in the easy setting. With the criteria of IoU = 0.5 and IoU = 0.7, our method still achieve higher average precision on three different data respectively even on the hard setting. Experienced find that the multiple scale visual information can express the distinctive feature cues at different scales. However, the depth cues from the data set will provide more reliable evidence for mitigating the false alarm.

Multiple Obstacle Localization. For multiple obstacle detection problem, we also consider the information of localization for obstacles. We also use different IoU threshold of 0.5 and 0.7 for localization evaluation. Table 2 shows the average precision on KITTI validation set. As expected, our methods performs better than other two approaches. For the hard setting, our method outperforms two approaches by 0.6% and 0.8% respectively under IoU threshold of 0.5. When using IoU=0.7 as the criteria, the performance of our method is even larger, achieving about 2% higher average precision across three different settings than other two methods.

Ablation Studies. For the contributions of the features for the multiple obstacles detection in the proposed method, we experiment with different combination of the visual cues: RGB image (RGB), multiple scale visual information (MSV), multi- scale correlogram with MSV (MSC+MSV), and multi-scale deeply described visual information (MSDDVI). To formulate the distinct of the multiple features, we use the same layer VGG deep learning framework [23] to conduct the multiple obstacle detection. As shown in Table 3, the more distinctive features will bring more better detection results on the same dataset. With using spatial-temporal information, we can see that the average precision owning a more impressing detection results. The Table 4 has summarized the comparison of three different multiple obstacle detection strategies on KITTI validation set. And the experiments also show a better performance in comparison to an orientation extraction directly over the velocity information of the dynamic occupancy grid map [7].

5 Conclusion

In this paper, we propose a multiple obstacle detection framework for assistance driver system using deep neural networks to improve the road safety. Firstly, the multi-channel Harris STIPS and depth information be extracted. Then multi-scale information extraction using CNNs to encode the details to distinguish the potential obstacles. By using the popular fully connect deep neural networks, the multiple obstacles are detected effectively. Some extensive experimental results on KITTI dataset show that the proposed method can outperform other two popular methods with higher average precision under three different settings for multiple obstacle detection.

References

1. Biondi, F., Strayer, D.L., Rossi, R., Gastaldi, M., Mulatti, C.: Advanced driver assistance systems: using multimodal redundant warnings to enhance road safety. Appl. Ergon. **58**, 238–244 (2017)
2. Mahajan, R.N., Patil, A.: Lane departure warning system. Int. J. Eng. Tech. Res. **3**(1), 120–3 (2015)
3. Wei, H., Jia, Z., Chen, Y., Cao, X., Du, W.: Vision-based road lane and obstacle detection for ADAS and supervisory control of intelligent vehicles. In: Proceedings of the International Conference on Power Transmissions, pp. 717–724 (2016)
4. Sharma, S., Shah, D.: Real-time automatic obstacle detection and alert system for driver assistance on Indian roads. Int. J. Veh. Auton. Syst. **13**(3), 189–202 (2017)
5. Wang, B., Florez, S.A., Frémont, V.: Multiple obstacle detection and tracking using stereo vision: application and analysis. In: Proceedings of 13th International Conference on Control Automation Robotics and Vision (ICARCV), pp. 1074–1079 (2014)
6. Meshram, P., Wankhede, S.S.: Detection and recognition of mixed traffic for driver assistance system. Int. J. Eng. Res. Gen. Sci. **2**, 201–206 (2014)
7. Nuss, D., Yuan, T., Krehl, G., Stuebler, M., Reuter, S., Dietmayer, K.C.J.: Fusion of laser and radar sensor data with a sequential Monte Carlo Bayesian occupancy filter. In: Proceedings of IEEE Intelligent Vehicles Symposium (IV), pp. 1074–1081 (2015)

8. Nuss, D., et al.: A random finite set approach for dynamic occupancy grid maps with real-time application. ArXiv e-prints (2016)

9. Nguyen, V.D., Van Nguyen, H., Tran, D.T., Lee, S.J., Jeon, J.W.: Learning framework for robust obstacle detection, recognition, and tracking. IEEE Trans. Intell. Transp. Syst. **18**, 1633–1645 (2016). https://doi.org/10.1109/TITS.2016.2614818

10. Tu, Y., Lin, Y., Wang, J., Kim, J.: Semi-supervised learning with generative adversarial networks on digital signal modulation classification. Comput. Mater. Contin. **55**(2), 243–254 (2018)

11. Zeng, D., Dai, Y., Li, F., Sherratt, R.S., Wang, J.: Adversarial learning for distant supervised relation extraction. Comput. Mater. Contin. **55**(1), 121–136 (2018)

12. Sharma, S., Shah, D.: Real-time automatic obstacle detection and alert system for driver assistance on Indian roads. Int. J. Veh. Auton. Syst. **13**(3), 189 (2017)

13. Laptev, I.: On space-time interest points. Int. J. Comput. Vis. **64**(2–3), 107–23 (2005)

14. Wong, S.F., Cipolla, R.: Extracting spatio temporal interest points using global information. In: Proceedings of IEEE 11th International Conference on Computer Vision (ICCV), pp. 1–8 (2007)

15. Everts, I., Van Gemert, J.C., Gevers, T.: Evaluation of color spatio-temporal interest points for human action recogtion. IEEE Trans. Image Process. **23**(4), 1569–1580 (2014)

16. van de Weijer, J., Gevers, T., Smeulders, A.W.M.: Robust photometric invariant features from the colour tensor. IEEE Trans. Image Process. **15**, 118–127 (2006)

17. Fukushima, K., Miyake, S.: Neocognitron: a self-organizing neural network model for a mechanism of visual pattern recognition. In: Amari, S., Arbib, M.A. (eds.) Competition and Cooperation in Neural Nets. LNBM, vol. 45, pp. 267–285. Springer, Heidelberg (1982). https://doi.org/10.1007/978-3-642-46466-9_18

18. Sivic, J., Zisserman, A.: Video Google: a text retrieval approach to object matching in videos. In: Proceedings of the IEEE International Conference on Computer Vision, pp. 1470–1477 (2003)

19. Qi, K., Yang, C., Guan, Q., Wu, H., Gong, J.: A multiscale deeply described correlatons-based model for land-use scene classification. Remote Sens. **9**(9), 917 (2017)

20. Ren, S., He, K., Girshick, R., Sun, J.: Faster R-CNN: towards real-time object detection with region proposal networks. In: Advances in Neural Information Processing Systems, pp. 91–99 (2015)

21. Beyer, L., Hermans, A., Leibe, B.: Biternion nets: continuous head pose regression from discrete training labels. In: Gall, J., Gehler, P., Leibe, B. (eds.) GCPR 2015. LNCS, vol. 9358, pp. 157–168. Springer, Cham (2015). https://doi.org/10.1007/978-3-319-24947-6_13

22. Chen C., Odobez, J.M.: We are not contortionists: coupled adaptive learning for head and body orientation estimation in surveillance video. In: Proceeding of the IEEE Conference on Computer Vision and Pattern Recognition (CVPR) (2012)

23. Lu, C., Krishna, R., Bernstein, M., Fei-Fei, L.: Visual relationship detection with language priors. In: Leibe, B., Matas, J., Sebe, N., Welling, M. (eds.) ECCV 2016. LNCS, vol. 9905, pp. 852–869. Springer, Cham (2016). https://doi.org/10.1007/978-3-319-46448-0_51

24. Geiger, A., Lenz, P., Stiller, C., Urtasun, R.: Vision meets robotics: the KITTI dataset. Int. J. Robot. Res. **32**(11), 1231–1237 (2013)

25. Karsch, K., Liu, C., Kang, S.B.: Depth transfer: depth extraction from videos using nonparametric sampling. In: Hassner, T., Liu, C. (eds.) Dense Image Correspondences for Computer Vision, pp. 173–205. Springer, Cham (2016). https://doi.org/10.1007/978-3-319-23048-1_9

26. Chen, X., Ma, H., Wan, J., Li, B., Xia, T.: Multi-view 3D object detection network for autonomous driving. In: Proceedings of IEEE Conference on Computer Vision and Pattern Recognition (CVPR), pp. 3–11 (2017)

27. Biondi, F., Strayer, D.L., Rossi, R., Gastaldi, M., Mulatti, C.: Advanced driver assistance systems: using multimodal redundant warnings to enhance road safety. Appl. Ergon. 1(58), 238–44 (2017)

28. Chen, X., et al.: 3D object proposals for accurate object class detection. In: Advances in Neural Information Processing Systems, pp. 424–432 (2015)

Encryption and Cybersecurity

CABAC: A Content-Driven Attribute-Based Access Control Model for Big Data

Ke Ma[1] and Geng Yang[1,2(✉)]

[1] Nanjing University of Posts and Telecommunications, Nanjing 210023, China
marco1991@126.com, yangg@njupt.edu.cn
[2] Jiangsu Key Laboratory of Big Data Security and Intelligent Processing,
Nanjing 210023, China

Abstract. In recent years, attribute-based access control (ABAC) models have been widely used in big data and cloud computing. However, with the growing importance of data content, using data content to assist authorization for access controls has become more common. In this paper, we propose a dynamic content-driven attribute-based access control model (CABAC) for large-scale unstructured data. CABAC is a fine-grained access control model that use two-layer authorization to balance efficiency and accuracy. The first-layer authorization uses attributes to grant users basic authority and the second-layer authorization uses data content to grant broader authority over "related" data. Experimental results show that CABAC has acceptable efficiency and it can expand the authority of users without reducing security.

Keywords: Attribute-based access control · Content-driven ·
Authorization · Fine-grained · Big data

1 Introduction

As a key technology to ensure safe data sharing, access control plays an important role in the era of big data. Traditional access control models include but are not limited to Discretionary Access Control (DAC), Mandatory Access Control (MAC) and Role-Based Access Control (RBAC). However, as unstructured data have become a vital part of big data, traditional access control techniques have not meet some demands of big data, and it is difficult to determine the internal relationships between the unstructured data. In some applications, it

Supported by the National Natural Science Foundation of China (61572263, 61502251, 61602263, 61872197), the Postgraduate Research & Practice Innovation Program of Jiangsu Province (KYCX18_0891), the Natural Science Foundation of Jiangsu Province (BK20161516, BK20160916), the Postdoctoral Science Foundation Project of China (2016M601859), the Natural Research Foundation of Nanjing University of Posts and Telecommunications (NY217119).

© Springer Nature Switzerland AG 2019
X. Sun et al. (Eds.): ICAIS 2019, LNCS 11634, pp. 517–529, 2019.
https://doi.org/10.1007/978-3-030-24271-8_46

is not enough to grant the user authority over *target data* (the object that the user tries to access) to the user, but it may also require granting the user the authority to access other objects related to *target data.*

Different from traditional access control models, Attribute-Based Access Control (ABAC) can use a variety of parameters (attributes) to describe the relevant subject, object, environment and operations, while using a more comprehensive, accurate, and flexible description [7]. However, although we can directly use ABAC to tag attributes for unstructured data and use the attributes to grant corresponding authority to users, it is difficult for us to extract efficient attributes from unstructured data and to find "related" objects. Therefore, in the era of big data, it is not enough that we use basic attributes to explicitly identify accessible objects for each role/user, but it is also necessary to use data content to assist in the control of access. To further motivate our research, we provide the following example:

Example. In a medical research institute, a researcher named Alice requests the authority to access a report to carry out her research. In some cases, the requested research report may not be enough by itself, and Alice may have to request other similar or related reports to accomplish her work. If Alice searches for all the related reports and requests for them one by one, it will be too labor-intensive. Therefore, after Alice gets the authority to access the target research report, we also need to automatically grant her the authority to access similar or related reports to guarantee security.

There are two main requirements to grant Alice suitable authority: (i) computing the semantic relevance between the target report and other reports to obtain a list of related reports, and (ii) guaranteeing the security of all the authorized reports. To meet these demands, in this paper, we propose a content-driven attribute-based access control model CABAC. CABAC is a dynamic access control model that uses a 2-layer authorization mechanism to balance the efficiency and the accuracy of granting access. At the first layer, it can use attributes to evaluate whether to grant users the authority to access a target data object quickly. At the second layer, it can use the content of the data to grant broader authority to access other "related data" to users.

We made two main contributions in this paper: (i) We proposed a dynamic content-driven attribute-based access control model, which is a fine-grained access control model that uses both attributes and data content to execute authorizations; and (ii) We designed a 2-layer authorization mechanism, which realizes a balance between the efficiency and accuracy of authorization.

The remainder of this paper is organized as follows. Related works are presented in Sect. 2. The proposed access control model CABAC will be presented in Sect. 3, followed by its authorization policies in the Sect. 4. Section 5 shows the experimental results and analysis of CABAC. Section 6 concludes the paper and proposes future works of CABAC.

2   Related Work

It is necessary to enforce access control policies based on the content of data. Beginning with the content-based authorization mechanism [1] proposed in 2002, researchers have proposed various access control policies based on different types of content, including context content [12], text content in database [18], social network data [3,10], eXtensible Markup Languages (XML) [15], electronic data [16,17], content-centric network [8,9], and MapReduce systems [13,14]. However, their definition of "content" is quite different from ours, except for CBAC [18]. CBAC is a fine-grained content-based access control model (accurate to the file level for each user) that has two main components: initial authorization and content-based authorization. In the initial authorization module, each user is given access to a small set of data objects, denoted as the base set. The base set could be selected in the following ways. (i) It can be identified with attribute-based rules; for example, a doctor's base set can include his or her patients' medical treatment records. (ii) Data owners or administrators can assign several data objects to the user as his or her base set. (iii) Users can request items into the base set and ask the administrator to approve the items. In the authorization phase of CBAC, different access levels can be authorized for each user according to the relevance of the content in different data objects in the system and each user's base set.

However, CBAC aims for "safe" scenarios, which must work with basic privileges, that is to say that the users must be authenticated with basic trust. As in the above Example, CBAC can only grant authority to Alice when all the reports in the medical research institute are accessible to her. If the basic privileges are more than what Alice is allowed, it might be very risky to use CBAC without any other limits. Therefore, if there is an efficient method to guarantee the basic trust of users, it will be much easier to use the basic idea of CBAC for authorization.

Attribute-based access control (ABAC) defines an access control paradigm whereby access rights are granted to users by using policies that combine attributes, which can be used to specify the basic privileges of users. In recent years, many attribute-based access control models for different applications have been proposed. Aimed at solving the problems of attribute revocation and policy updating, *Liu et al.* proposed a dynamic access control scheme for cloud storage systems [6]. To protect the privacy of the users in e-commerce, *Li et al.* enforced fine-grained access control on logistical data [5]. By combining the role-based access control RBAC, *Qi et al.* proposed a fine-grained RABAC (RBAC + ABAC) model, which has also improved the flexibility of existing RABAC models [11]. Based on the enforcement of the Separation of Duty (SoD) constraint, *Jha et al.* introduced the problem of SoD specification, verification, and enforcement in ABAC and provided a methodology for solving it [4].

Aluvalu et al. combined the concept of risk with ABAC and proposed a risk-aware attribute-based access control model RA-ABAC for cloud computing [2]. RA-ABAC is a dynamic model that combines risk computation with attributes used for access control. In the RA-ABAC model, attributes are divided into two classes: *primary attributes* and *normal attributes*. An access request will be granted only when the number of attributes satisfying the access policy defined by the data owner is greater than the number of attributes not satisfying the policy and the *primary attributes* = *true*. However, very few of the existing ABAC models uses data content to assist authorizations, which is of great significance for fine-grained access controls.

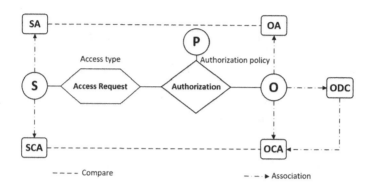

Fig. 1. CABAC model structure

3   CABAC Model

We will present the whole CABAC model in this section followed by its authorization policies in the next section. Figure 1 shows the structure of the CABAC model. The core components of this model are: subjects (S), objects (O), subject attributes (SA), subject content attributes (SCA), object attributes (OA), object data content attributes (ODC), object content attributes (OCA), permissions (P), access request, access type, and authorization policies.

An **attribute** is a function that returns a specific value from an entity (such as a subject). In the CABAC system, a **subject** denotes a user who uses the system and tries to get access authority, which is associated with a finite set of **subject attributes** whose values are assigned by security administrators. These attributes are the basic attributes of subjects, such as name, age, location, and roles. Meanwhile, each subject is also associated with a finite set of **subject content attributes**, which is closely related to the current duty of the subject (user). For example, a network engineer could be assigned an SCA set of {*computer science, software, network*}, and if his current work is using cloud computing to produce services, the attributes of *cloud computing* should also be added into his SCA set. **Objects** are resources that need to be protected, which are also associated with a finite set of **object attributes**. In CABAC, an object could be a file, a table, or other content-rich data, and the **object data content** is also an important component for granting access authority to users. Each object is also associated with a set of **object content attributes** according to its data content.

Access request (ar) indicates "who" wants to access "what", which can be specified as a 3-tuple {*subject, object, access type*}. One ar is initiated by subject to request for different authority of target objects. The third element **access type** $\in \{0, 1\}$ represents the category of access. Access type $= 0$ shows that the user (access subject) only requests for the authority to access the target data (access object), and access type $= 1$ indicates that the user requests for broader access authority based on his or her target data.

Permissions are privileges of accessible objects for subjects, which is divided into two parts in CABAC. The first part is the privilege of the target object for one subject in an access request. The second part is the privilege of other objects that have "similar" or "related" content with the target object. Permissions enable a subject to access object(s) in a particular mode, such as read. The definition of permissions is dependent on the real applications.

According to the two different access types, we design a **2-layer authorization policy** in CABAC. For each access request, the first layer of authorization grants the authority to access the target data based on the attribute values of the subject and the target object (CABAC attribute authorization). The second layer grants the authority to access a set of "content-related" objects based on both attribute values and data content (CABAC content authorization).

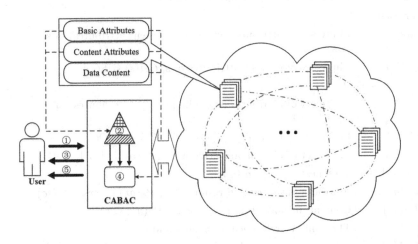

Fig. 2. Basic Frame of CABAC

Figure 2 shows the basic framework of CABAC. In CABAC, the content of each data will be stored and the data will be tagged with basic attributes (e.g., location, role) and content attributes (keywords of the data). The whole process of executing CABAC can be described as follows:

① a user sends an access request to the CABAC system for the authority to access target data (and "related" data);

② CABAC uses the attributes of the user (subject) and target data (object) to carry out attribute authorization;

③ CABAC sends the attribute authorization result to the user;

④ if CABAC grants the authority to access target data to the user in the above steps and the user requests for the authority of other "similar" or "related" data, CABAC will use both the attributes and data content to grant the user access;

⑤ CABAC sends the content authorization result to the user.

In CABAC, we use a 2-layer authorization structure (② & ④) to grant different authorities to users, which is the most concerning part of CABAC model. The authorization policies will be introduced in Sect. 4.

Table 1. Notations of CABAC

Notation	Definition
S	Finite set of existing subjects
O	Finite set of existing objects
SA	Finite set of subject attributes (excluding content attributes)
OA	Finite set of object attributes (excluding content attributes)
SCA	Finite set of subject content attributes
OCA	Finite set of object content attributes
for each $s \in S$:	
$A(s)$	Finite set of attributes (excluding content attributes) of s, $A(s) \subseteq SA$
$CA(s)$	Finite set of content attributes of s, $CA(s) \subseteq SCA$
for each $o \in O$:	
$A(o)$	Finite set of attributes (excluding content attributes) of o, $A(o) \subseteq OA$
$CA(o)$	Finite set of content attributes of s, $CA(o) \subseteq OCA$
$A_{pr}(o)$	Finite set of o's primary attributes, $A_{pr}(o) \subseteq A(o) \bigcup CA(o)$
for each access request $ar = \{s, o, 0/1\}$:	
$P_A(ar)$	Attribute authorization result of ar, $P_A(ar) \in \{true, false\}$
$P_C(ar)$	Content authorization result of ar, $P_C(ar) \subseteq O$
$CR(s, o)$	The Content relevance between s and o
$SIM_C(s, o)$	Whether s has sufficient content relevance with o, $SIM_C \in \{true, false\}$

4   CABAC Authorization Policies

In this section, we will introduce the CABAC authorization policies from these three aspects: (i) the total CABAC 2-layer authorization; (ii) CABAC attribute authorization policy; and (3) CABAC content authorization policy. Notations used in CABAC are given in Table 1.

4.1 CABAC 2-Layer Authorization

The goal of CABAC is to use the content of data and its attributes to evaluate each access requests from users and grant them corresponding authorities. When a user sends an access request to the CABAC system, it will use the attributes (including content attributes) to determine whether to grant him or her the authority to access the target data (the first layer). Then, if the authority to access the target data is granted and the user requests other similar or related data, CABAC will use the content of data to determine and grant authorization (the second layer).

Layer 1:

Attribute Authorization: The system uses attributes of both the user and the target data to grant the authority to access the target data to the user. It also evaluates *content similarity* between the user and the target data, which is one important index for deciding whether to enforce content authorization.

Layer 2:

Content Authorization: If the user requests for "broader" authority (authority to access data that is relevant to the target data) and *content similarity* reaches a given threshold, the system will evaluates the basic privileges for each data (excluding target data) for the user. If the user has basic privileges for one piece of data and the data has content relevance to the target data, the authority to access these data will be granted to the user.

When the system receives an access request $ar = \{s,\ o,\ access\ type\}$, $P_A(ar)$ (the attribute authorization result of ar) will be computed by algorithm $Authorization_A(ar)$, then the authority to access the target data will be granted; if the $access\ type = 1$ and $P_A(ar) = true$, algorithm $Authorization_C(ar)$ will compute the content authorization result of ar, then the authority of similar and related data will also be granted. Algorithm $Authorization_A(ar)$ will be introduced in CABAC Attribute Authorization Policy (Sect. 4.2) and Algorithm $Authorization_C(ar)$ will be introduced in CABAC Content Authorization Policy (Sect. 4.3).

4.2 CABAC Attribute Authorization Policy

The goal of CABAC Attribute Authorization Policy is to use attributes of the user (subject) and the target data (object) to determine whether to grant the user corresponding authority. To use different kinds of attributes explicitly, we propose a 3-level structure of authorization. Figure 3 shows the 3-level structure: primary attributes, content attributes and other attributes.

At the top of the structure are the **primary attributes**, which have a decisive effect on the authorization. When a data owner uploads data to the system, he should tag the basic attributes and the content attributes. The owner also

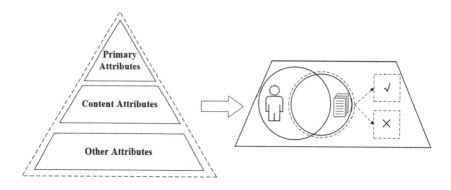

Fig. 3. 3-Level Structure of Attribute Authorization

needs to indicate which attributes are primary attributes. It is necessary for one user to have the corresponding primary attributes to get the authority to access authority of the data. For example, if the data owner sets the primary attributes of one file to {*department id = 1, location = company*}, a staff member of *department 1* will not get the authority when he tries to access the file *at home*.

In the middle of the structure are **content attributes**, which generally appears in the form of keywords. Before sending access requests, each user should be assigned with a set of keywords according to indicate his current work. The content relevance $CR(s, o)$ between subject s and data object o can be computed as Formula (1):

$$CR(s,o) = \frac{|CA(s) \bigcap CA(o)|}{|CA(o)|} \tag{1}$$

To evaluate whether the user (subject s) is sufficiently content relevant to the target data (object o), a relevance threshold $T_r(o)$ will be set for each object. The value of $T_r(o)$ can be set according to the real application environment, which is determined by the security level of o and we suggest that $T_r(o)$ should be no less than 0.5. $SIM_C(s, o)$ will be computed by Formula (2):

$$SIM_C(s,o) = \begin{cases} true, & CR(s,o) \geq T_r(o) \\ false, & CR(s,o) < T_r(o) \end{cases} \tag{2}$$

Note that $SIM_C(s, o)$ can be one *primary* attribute or *common* attribute, which depends on the data owner's settings. However, only if $SIM_C(s, o) = true$, content authorization can be enforced.

At the bottom of the structure are **other attributes** (*common attributes*), which have no special effect, but all the attributes will be calculated for granting or denying the access request according to algorithm *Authorization$_A$(ar)*:

Algorithm 1: $Authorization_A(ar : AR)$

Input: $ar = \{s, o, access\ type\}$, $T_a(o)$
Output: $P_A(ar)$

1 set $P_A(ar) = true$;
2 compute $CR(s, o)$ and $SIM_C(s, o)$;
3 **if** $A_{pr}(o) \bigcap A(s) \neq A_{pr}(o)$ **then**
4 $\quad|\quad P_A(ar) = false$;
5 **end**
6 **if** $P_A(ar) = true$ and $|A(s) \bigcap A(o)| < T_a(o)^{\text{a}}$ **then**
7 $\quad|\quad P_A(ar) = false$;
8 **end**

---

[a]Minimum number of satisfied attributes necessary to grant authority to access object o.

If $P_A(ar) = true$, CABAC will grant s the authority to access o. Based on the above premise, if $access\ type = 1$ and $SIM_C(s, o) = true$, CABAC will enforce content authorization.

4.3 CABAC Content Authorization Policy

In some cases, users not only request the access authority to access the target data but may also want to get the authority to access other related or similar data. However, the "similarity" is often semantic, and it could be difficult for us to use several keywords to find "semantic similarity" for large-scale unstructured data.

Illustrated by the example of unstructured text data, CABAC first uses Natural Language Processing (NLP) algorithms to preprocess the data content. Then, CABAC Content Authorization is enforced to grant the authority of "similar" and "related" data. In this section, we will use the TF-IDF algorithm to preprocess the data and compute content similarity; however, please note that the TF-IDF algorithm is not the only choice of NLP algorithm that can be used in CABAC, and all suitable NLP algorithms would be useful.

At the beginning of the TF-IDF algorithm, several terms will be chosen. Afterwards each object will be denoted as a vector, in which every element denotes the weight of one term. The weight of term t in one object o can be indicated as Formula (3):

$$w_{t,o} = tf_{t,o} \times idf_t = tf_{t,o} \times \frac{N}{df_t} \tag{3}$$

where $tf_{t,o}$ is the frequency of term t in object o, and df_t is the number of objects that contain term t. For each object o, the data content will be represented as a TF-IDF vector $v(o) = [v_1,\ v_2,\ v_3,\ ...v_d]$, where d is the dimension of each vector V, which is also the amount of all terms. We use $SIM(o_i, o_j)$ to indicate the content similarity between object o_i and object o_j:

$$SIM(o_i, o_j) = \frac{V_{o_i} \cdot V_{o_j}}{|V_{o_i}|\,|V_{o_j}|} \tag{4}$$

The pretreatment will be enforced only once, and the processed vectors will be used in content authorization to grant the authority to access related data according to algorithm $Authorization_C(ar)$. For each access request $ar = \{s, o, access\ type\}$, only when (i)$P_A(ar) = true$, (ii) $access\ type = 1$, and (iii) $SIM_C(s, o) = true$, $Authorization_C(ar)$ can be enforced as Algorithm 2:

CABAC will use the result of $P_C(ar)$ to grant corresponding authority to s.

Algorithm 2: $Authorization_C(ar : AR)$

Input: $ar = \{s, o, access\ type\}$, O
Output: $P_C(ar)$
1 set $P_C(ar) = \emptyset$;
2 **foreach** $o_i \in O$ **do**
3   **if** $A_{pr}(o_i) \bigcap A(s) = A_{pr}(o_i)$ and $|A(s) \bigcap A(o_i)| \geq T_a(o_i)$ **then**
4   **if** $SIM(o_i, o) \geq T_{SIM}$[a] **then**
5   add o_i into $P_C(ar)$;
6   **end**
7   **end**
8 **end**

---

[a]Threshold of similarity, if the similarity of content of the two objects reaches T_{SIM}, CABAC will determine that they are "related".

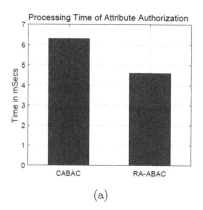 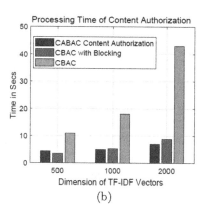

(a)   (b)

Fig. 4. Results of Access Risk (Comparison of Processing Time)

5   Experimental Results and Analysis

In this section, we use an NSF research award data set[1] to evaluate the efficiency of CABAC. The data set consists more than 120,000 abstracts of NSF awards for

---

[1] NSF research award data set: http://archive.ics.uci.edu/ml/datasets/NSF+Research +Award+Abstracts+1990-2003.

basic research, which have content-rich information. We choose 127,000 abstracts from the data set and use Porter Stemmer to extract the stems of each words for the abstracts. Then, we choose 500, 1000, 2000 meaningful stems and use TF-IDF algorithm to map the abstracts to 500-, 1000-, 2000-dimension vectors respectively. Then, we use the annotation method of *Tagme* to extract keywords for each abstract. Afterwards, we gather all the keywords and choose the most 100 frequent keywords as a keyword library. For each abstract, we choose the 6 most relevant keywords from a keyword library as its content attributes (if the number of these keywords is less than 6 for one abstract, we will add other keywords from the abstract). We set the relevance threshold $T_r(o) = 0.5$ and the threshold of similarity $T_{SIM} = 0.5$ for each abstract. We also simulate 30 attributes (excluding content attributes) for the attributes of users and data objects (abstracts). For each abstract, we choose 5–10 attributes (the value of T_a is half the number of attributes) from the 30 attributes, and for each user, we choose 10 attributes from the 30.

We compare the efficiency of the attribute authorization of CABAC with that of RA-ABAC, and compare the efficiency of the content authorization of CABAC with that of CBAC (the blocking method and basic CBAC) [18]. Figure 4 shows the experimental results of processing one access request.

Figure 4(a) shows the processing time of attribute authorization with CABAC and RA-ABAC (for one access request $ar = \{s,o,access\ type\}$, s has 10 attributes and o has 5–10 primary attributes). Since CABAC needs to compare content attributes of both the user and the target data, the speed of CABAC attribute authorization is lower than that of RA-ABAC. However, for one access request, the total processing time of CABAC attribute authorization is less than 7 ms, which is acceptable and can also meet the demand of fast authorization. Figure 4(b) shows the processing time of attribute authorization with CABAC and CBAC. *CBAC with blocking* uses a clustering algorithm to reduce the amount of processing data, and the two CBAC methods can be found in [18]. The results show that the processing time of CABAC content authorization is consistent with that of *CBAC with blocking*. For 127000 vectors of 500-, 1000-, and 2000-dimension, CABAC needs 4.4 s, 4.9 s, 7.1 s, respectively, to process them.

CABAC uses 2-layer authorization to grant two kinds of authority to users. The first-layer authorization is very fast (less than 7 ms for each request), and the second-layer authorization takes slightly longer. Since users are more concerned about the speed of the first layer of the authorization (target data) under normal circumstances, when a user uses CABAC, he or she will get his or her authority to access target data quickly and will get the authority to access related data later. Therefore, the efficiency of CABAC is acceptable and the authorization is a balance between efficiency and accuracy.

6   Conclusion

In this paper, we proposed a dynamic content-driven attribute based access control model (CABAC), which uses a two-layer authorization structure to grant suitable authority to users. In the first layer of authorization, CABAC uses the idea of ABAC to grant authority to access target data to a user within a short time period. In the second layer of authorization, CABAC grants broader authority to access "related" data based on data content without reducing security. CABAC can achieve a balance between efficiency and accuracy.

References

1. Adam, N.R., Atluri, V., Bertino, E., Ferrari, E.: A content-based authorization model for digital libraries. IEEE Trans. Knowl. Data Eng. **14**(2), 296–315 (2002)
2. Aluvalu, R.K., Muddana, L.: A dynamic attribute-based risk aware access control model (DA-RAAC) for cloud computing. In: IEEE International Conference on Computational Intelligence and Computing Research, pp. 1–5 (2016)
3. Jadliwala, M., Maiti, A., Namboodiri, V.: Social puzzles: context-based access control in online social networks. In: IEEE/IFIP International Conference on Dependable Systems and Networks, pp. 299–310 (2014)
4. Jha, S., Sural, S., Atluri, V., Vaidya, J.: Specification and verification of separation of duty constraints in attribute based access control. IEEE Trans. Inf. Forensics Secur. **13**(4), 897–911 (2018)
5. Li, T., Rui, Y.: Priexpress: privacy-preserving express delivery with fine-grained attribute-based access control. In: Communications and Network Security, pp. 333–341 (2017)
6. Liu, Z., Jiang, Z.L., Wang, X., Yiu, S.M., Zhang, C., Zhao, X.: Dynamic attribute-based access control in cloud storage systems. In: Trustcom/BigDataSE/ISPA, pp. 129–137 (2017)
7. Luo, X., Wang, W., Luo, W.: The retrospect and prospect of access control technology. Netinfo Secur. **12**, 19–27 (2016)
8. Mannes, E., Maziero, C., Lassance, L., Borges, F.: Optimized access control enforcement over encrypted content in information-centric networks. In: Computers and Communication, pp. 924–929 (2015)
9. Nagai, S., Kaida, T., Mizuno, O.: The group data access control method in content centric network, pp. 1–3 (2015)
10. Paradesi, S., Liccardi, I., Kagal, L., Pato, J.: A semantic framework for content-based access controls. In: International Conference on Social Computing, pp. 624–629 (2013)
11. Qi, H., Luo, X., Di, X., Li, J., Yang, H., Jiang, Z.: Access control model based on role and attribute and its implementation. In: International Conference on Cyber-Enabled Distributed Computing and Knowledge Discovery, pp. 66–71 (2017)
12. Rubart, J.: Context-based access control. In: Symposia on Metainformatics, p. 13 (2005)
13. Ulusoy, H., Colombo, P., Ferrari, E., Kantarcioglu, M., Pattuk, E.: GuardMR: fine-grained security policy enforcement for MapReduce systems. In: Proceedings of the 10th ACM Symposium on Information, Computer and Communications Security, pp. 285–296. ACM (2015)
14. Ulusoy, H., Kantarcioglu, M., Pattuk, E., Hamlen, K.: Vigiles: fine-grained access control for MapReduce systems. In: 2014 IEEE International Congress on Big Data (BigData Congress), pp. 40–47. IEEE (2014)
15. Wang, M., Wang, J., Guo, L., Harn, L.: Inverted XML access control model based on ontology semantic dependency. CMC: Comput. Mater. Continua **55**(3), 465–482 (2018)

16. Wu, M.Y., Chen, Y.W., Ke, C.K.: Design and implementation of a context and role-based access control model for digital content. In: IET International Conference on Frontier Computing, Theory, Technologies and Applications, pp. 253–257 (2010)
17. Wu, M.Y., Zhuo, Z.X.: Digital content access control for end-users. In: International Conference on Software Intelligence Technologies and Applications and International Conference on Frontiers of Internet of Things, pp. 39–42 (2014)
18. Zeng, W., Yang, Y., Luo, B.: Content-based access control: use data content to assist access control for large-scale content-centric databases. In: IEEE International Conference on Big Data, pp. 701–710 (2014)

Calculation of Network Security Index Based on Convolution Neural Networks

Hang Yang[1], Yan Jia[1], Wei-Hong Han[3], Yuan-Ping Nie[2],
Shu-Dong Li[3(✉)], and Xiao-Juan Zhao[1(✉)]

[1] School of Computer Science, National University of Defense Technology,
Changsha 410073, China
zhaoxiaojuan18@nudt.edu.cn
[2] Beijing Institute of System Engineering, Beijing 100101, China
[3] Cyberspace Institute of Advanced Technology, Guangzhou University,
Guangzhou 510006, China

Abstract. The Network Security Index System is an important means for network security situation assessment (NSSA). Through index selection, system construction and numerical calculation, it helps network managers obtain macro perspectives on networks. However, the traditional situation assessment methods based on an index system have always had some defects, such as excessive reliance on manual intervention, high deviation, and limited scope of application. Based on summing up the existing research results, this paper combines the advantages of adaptability, effective feature extraction and complexity reduction of convolutional neural networks (CNN). By constructing the convolutional kernels which are suitable for the characteristics of an index system we extract the potential correlation features; by using a pooling technique we shrink the model scale quickly and highlight the main features; by utilizing the deep network structure of multiple hidden layers, we implement a method of calculating network security indexes based on CNNs. Finally, the feasibility and effectiveness of this method are verified by experiments and comparisons.

Keywords: Network security · Index system · Convolutional neural networks · Feature extraction

1 Introduction

With the popularization of computer networks, network security has become more and more important. The "Stuxnet" worm which infiltrated the Iranian nuclear facilities, the Ukrainian power grid incident, the Dyn incident that caused the America Internet disconnection [1], the Eternal Blue incident, and the Petya extortion virus [2] security

Foundation Items: Funded by NSFC (No. U1636215), the national key research and development program [2016YFB0800303], NSFC: 61672020, Project funded by China Postdoctoral Science Foundation (2013M542560, 2015T81129), A Project of Shandong Province Higher Educational Science and Technology Program (No. J16LN61), Hunan Provincial Key R & D program (2018 GK2056).

© Springer Nature Switzerland AG 2019
X. Sun et al. (Eds.): ICAIS 2019, LNCS 11634, pp. 530–540, 2019.
https://doi.org/10.1007/978-3-030-24271-8_47

incident have warned us of the dynamic changes and complex diversities of network attacks. For network managers and information decision-makers, it is important to understand the real-time status of networks, to make timely and overall insight into network attacks that seem to be scattered and irrelevant but are actually related to each other closely. The traditional intrusion detection system (IDS), network firewalls, the intrusion prevention system (IPS) and other security devices are oriented to a single host and the local network environment [3], and each management function unit is in an independent working state, and the information data lacks interactivity. Thus, it is difficult to construct an information fusion mechanism to judge the network situation through a macroscopic point of view. Therefore, the whole of the following series of processes, such as extracting the abnormal information from massive network data for efficient analysis, quantifying the network situation within a unit time window, and assessing or prejudging the situation in order to help managers to make accurate decisions, is called situation awareness [4], which has become a key research topic at present.

In general, situation awareness is divided into three parts: situation factor extraction, situation understanding and situation prediction [5]. As the indispensable part, situation understanding has the core which is the situation quantification assessment technology, and it can be roughly divided into an evaluation method based on mathematics, an evaluation method based on probability statistics, and an evaluation method based on rule inference.

Finding the factors that affect situation, distinguishing the extent to which these factors affect the overall situation, and constructing a complete, scientific and computable indicator system is a typical mathematical model assessment method:

First, preprocess the original information such as software and hardware configurations, network traffic, security events, user behaviors, etc., convert the information into standardized forms, and integrate in a multi-source way the massive and heterogeneous data with differences in time and space [6].

Secondly, use an efficient and reasonable calculation model combined with the experience of network security experts, perform a correlation analysis from a macro perspective, and find the weight of each impact factor on the global network to synthesize the scattered individual information into an organic entirety. And then, raise the observational perspective from concreteness to abstractness, from locality to globality, and finally form a series of comprehensive indexes that summarize the overall network situation.

2 Related Work

Many domestic and foreign experts and scholars are committed to studying network security situation assessment techniques based on index systems.

Hariri et al. [7] proposed a vulnerability monitoring model based on the agent architecture for large-scale networks, provided new ways to measure the impact of faults and attacks, and evaluated and analyzed the impact of network attacks and failures on network system security based on network performance metrics.

Aiming at the basic principles and characteristics of WebService, Wang [8] established assessment indexes based on the perspective of attack threats, and used a fuzzy comprehensive evaluation method to evaluate the effectiveness of network attacks and network failures.

Aiming at the weaknesses of vulnerability analysis in traditional index systems, Refence [9], which is based on general vulnerability assessment systems, combined an algorithm for optimal vulnerability score weight combination search with an algorithm for information entropy weight selection, and did some improvement.

The above literatures conducted safety assessment from the perspective of threat or vulnerability, which is a good complement and enhancement to the index evaluation system, but still lacks multi-dimensional perspectives and is difficult to meet the needs of different priorities.

Chen [10] et al. implemented a LAN-oriented security index system based on the IDS sampling data and network bandwidths, proposed a local-to-global hierarchical model for the quantitative assessment of security threat situation, and put forth a quantitative calculation method.

Refence [11] started from the campus LAN, constructed a network security evaluation index system through the extension analytic hierarchy process, and used the system to verify the user group samples in the campus network.

Jia et al. [12] analyzed the wireless LAN, divided the network evaluation objective into three macro-attribute dimensions of confidentiality, integrity and availability, and further refined it into the index layer of specific expression to quantify the overall network situation.

Zhang [13] adopted a way of combining the group analytic hierarchy process with the entropy weight method to establish a multi-factor second-level evaluation model, and further constructed an index system and its weight calculation method more objectively to make the evaluation results more accurate.

The above-mentioned scholars constructed index system models adopting a first-global-then-local method, used the analytic hierarchy process and other weight assignment methods to comprehensively evaluate the security situations of local area networks, and obtained a good verification of practical applications, but the application scenario has been restricted. For index selection and system construction of more complex regional networks, and backbone networks, the portability is insufficient.

In the afore-mentioned traditional index system construction and assessment calculation methods, the weight assignment of each basic indicator relies on manual operations, and the values are relatively fuzzy, so sometimes the deviations are large [14]. In addition, the network data are complex and variable. Similar network incidents often occur in different time and space. The degree of impact on globality may be greatly different. Therefore, the static initial weights cannot be used to define dynamic network environments. Considering the flow pattern of network security data, it is necessary to construct a nonlinear system with real-timeness, adaptiveness and self-organizability. This system should include an online index weight learning mechanism, which combines the continuously updated network flow data for iteration, and forms a complete index system that can effectively assess the security situation of networks.

According to the above requirements, let the network security experts conduct an empirical evaluation on a certain scale of network security indexes in advance, which means manual labeling, and then obtain a vector set, which is composed of comprehensive indexes corresponding to the basic indexes, as an actual output result. Through the self-learning function of the deep learning model to learn and optimize the known samples, we can fit the experience of network security experts to construct an index calculation function, and carry out comprehensive index evaluation for different network scenarios and security incidents.

3 Convolutional Neural Networks

At present, many scholars have combined traditional neural networks with index calculations to evaluate network security, and have achieved good results. However, there is a prominent problem. When the fully connected structure of neural networks processes data with a large input scale, because the number of hidden layer nodes and the dimension of input data increase exponentially, in addition to the offset value corresponding to each intermediate node, the node weight parameters will be too many [15]. This problem will be more obvious when the number of hidden layers increases. Therefore, when dealing with high-dimensional data such as the network security index data, computational complexity is an unavoidable problem.

CNN, as a typical deep learning model, evolves from traditional neural network models and is widely used in image recognition, target detection, speech recognition, text processing, etc. with good results and effect [16, 17]. Convolutional neural networks have the characteristics of weight sharing. Convolution and pooling operations can effectively reduce the computational complexity of high-dimensional data. Weight sharing on the feature map also facilitates parallel computing, which is also conducive to improving the working efficiency of the model. In addition, pooling is also reflected in the summary statistical characteristics, which can show better results of the problem of preventing over-fitting. As shown in Fig. 1, the model performs an inner product on the convolution kernel represented by the light color and the training data matrix in the convolution operation, and generates a feature map by a certain step movement. The output of the convolution layer is used as the input of the pooling layer. Then a similar pooled kernel is calculated to reduce the computational complexity. Thus, the model is constructed by a combination of multiple convolutions and pooling operations.

Using the above operating characteristics of convolutional neural networks, we can efficiently calculate the fitting expert evaluation results by mining the correlation between eigenvalues and mining the nonlinear mapping relationships between input and output feature vectors.

And in general, network-generated data is divided into two types: bulk data and streaming data. While the data oriented by the network security situation domain has the characteristics of real-timeness and time sequence, and is a typical fluid format data. If just the information at a specific time interval is analyzed, the effect will certainly be limited. The analysis model should have the ability of online learning, that is, it can iteratively process the stream data generated in a real-time way, and continually update and optimize its learning function. And this requirement conforms to the characteristics of Convolutional Neural Networks, which is suitable for the analysis of network security data of large-scale fluidity.

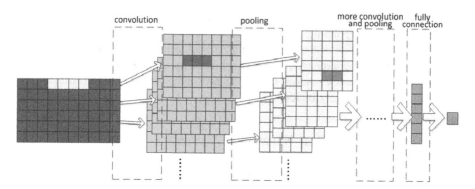

Fig. 1. Convolution neural network model structure for index system

4   Model Design

4.1   Construction of an Index System

We learn from the analytic hierarchy process [18] by using a tree-like hierarchical structure to construct an index system according to the principle from globality to locality and from abstractness to concreteness.

First of all, in order to facilitate the conceptual division of network security situation, considering the composition, boundaries, capacity, internal and external threats of the entire network, we define the first-level indexes of network situation as three dimensions: foundation, vulnerability and threat. It is the process of decomposing the final goal into individual criteria. Secondly, we further decompose the above three dimensions until the sub-goals of the lowest level are obtained. For better representation and calculation, we adopt a three-level index architecture, and refine the third level into 28 specific index features. Finally, we determine the measurement of each index and choose a reasonable way to standardize the data.

4.2   Construction of the Model Structure

(1) Input. As mentioned above, according to the design of an index system, we will need to analyze the network security data of flow format, to carry out the corresponding standardized processing in order to construct the form of multidimensional vector of equal length, and then to form these data into data set D = {d1, d2, ... , dn}, as the input of the model.

(2) Convolution. In Fig. 1, the first layer of the convolution operation extracts the features of the input data through the 1D convolution kernel window sliding of 1 * n, and the convolutions of the other deeper layers are similar to this operation. So, aiming at the input data x, we can define the convolutional calculation of the σ-th feature map Feature map-σ on the m-th layer Layer-m as:

$$c_\sigma^m(x) = f\left(\sum W^{(m,\sigma)} p_i^{(m-1)} + b^{(m,\sigma)}\right), \quad \sigma = 1, 2, \ldots, n \tag{1}$$

$c_\sigma^m(x)$ represents the output of feature extraction to the feature of the upper layer by the convolution kernel σ of the m-th layer. $w^{(m,\sigma)}$ represents the weight parameter of the convolution kernel σ of the m-th layer. $p_i^{(m-1)}$ represents the i-th feature map of the m-1-th layer. $b^{(m,\sigma)}$ is an offset value. $f(\cdot)$ is an activation function, and the Relu function is adopted here.

(3) Pooling. For each convolutional feature map, we apply the maximum pooling layer in the 1D form for down sampling

$$s_\sigma^m(x) = \max \cdot pooling\left(c_\sigma^{m-1}\right) + b^{(m,\sigma)} \tag{2}$$

Using the pooling operation is mainly to quickly shrink the network scale, to highlight the summary statistical features better, to reduce the noise interference, and to effectively overcome over-fitting.

(4) Output. The output is Pre = {pr1, pr2, ... , prn}, and the input index is converted into a predicted value by function calculation.

(5) Calculation. The model adopts the back propagation algorithm to calculate the weight. For the Layer-m, the calculation weight of the i-th input feature and the j-th feature of its output are updated to:

$$\Delta w_{ij} = \alpha \delta_j P_i \tag{3}$$

If Layer-m is the last layer, δ_j in the above formula is:

$$\delta_j = (T - C_j) d'(P_i) \tag{4}$$

Where $d'(p)$ is a function derivation. And if Layer-m is not the last layer, δ_j in (3) is:

$$\delta_j = d'(P_i) \sum_{k=1}^{N_{m+1}} w_{jk} \tag{5}$$

Where k is the k-th output of the m + 1 layer, j represents the j-th output of layer m. Therefore, the training process can be constructed as shown in Table 1:

4.3 Setting of Model Parameters

Considering the learning efficiency and the total amount of calculation, by using a smaller convolution kernel, we can construct a relatively deep model, which seems to be more complicated, but the effect will be better than a traditional shallow neural network that has more connections. We construct a 5-layer hidden layer part. The first 3 layers and the last 2 layers are convoluted by 1 * 4 and 1 * 3 convolution kernels respectively. The key parameters are shown in Table 2.

Table 1. Weight training update rule

1	**while**
2	**do** Input signal forward propagation
3	Calculate the error between the expected value and the target value.
4	**if** E converges
5	**end all**
6	**else** Update the weight w' of the last layer using Equation 3)
7	**do** Propel E back to the next layer and use 3) to update w
8	**while** Did not reach the first input layer

Table 2. Initial setting of model parameters

Parameters	Setting
Convolution kernel size	1@2@3@: 1*4, 4@5@: 1*3
Number of convolution kernels	64 * 5
Step of convolution kernel sliding	1
Pooling method	Max
Pooling window size	1*2
Sliding step of Pooling window	2
Activation function	Relu
Dropout	0.5
Fully connected layer neurons	100
Parameter solving algorithm	Rmsprop
Loss function	Mean_Squared_Error

5   Experimental Procedure

5.1   Experiment Data

Due to the lack of public data sets, this experiment deploys 367 virtual network nodes in a simulated network environment, sets up such lightweight intrusion detection terminals as Snort and NTOP, sets 19 DDoS attacks and 383 sniffing attacks within one week of the network time, uses 4138 historical simulation data which was manually labeled as data set, and preprocesses according to the 28 specific indexes of the designed index system. We take 3518 of them as the training set, 620 as the test set, and each set of indexes is comprehensively scored by network security experts based on experience, and the data magnitude is unified by a standard normalization method. The training set is used to learn how to fit the empirical mechanism of expert scoring. And finally, a more reasonable non-linear function is generated.

5.2   Experiment Results

We input the preprocessed experimental training data into the CNN model. Through multiple training, the function can realize the effect of learning manual evaluation of self-training. As shown in Fig. 2, the function model calculation results after self-learning are compared with the labeled expected values. The results can achieve a good fit.

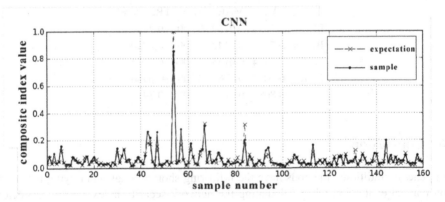

Fig. 2. Calculation results of CNN model

During the training process, as shown in Fig. 3, the function error converged optimally after the 39th iteration, thereby automatically stopped the iterative convergence.

In order to understand the calculation effect of the model more objectively in this paper, we put the experimental data into Linear Regression (LR), Back Propagation Neural Network (BPNN), Multi-layer Perceptron (MLP) and Kernel ridge Regression (KRR), comparing with the calculation result of CNN. We use such four evaluation

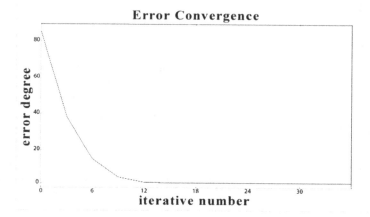

Fig. 3. CNN error convergence

indexes as Explained Variance Score (EVS), Mean Absolute Error (MAE), Mean Squared Error (MSE) and R2 Score to evaluate the performance of regression equations in order to compare with such models. We can see that the R2 Score of CNN is not optimal, but the other indexes perform better (Table 3).

Table 3. Comparison of regression evaluation indexes

	EVS	MAE	MSE	R2 score
LR	0.7325	0.0169	0.0007	0.7321
BPNN	0.7920	0.0142	0.0005	0.7920
MLP	0.7594	0.0155	0.0006	0.7567
KRR	0.7092	0.0167	0.0007	0.6986
CNN	0.8011	0.0137	0.0005	0.7913

6   Conclusion

In general, traditional methods have the following shortcomings: (1) relying too much on manual evaluation when calculating the network security index system; (2) determining the index weight with ambiguity; (3) sometimes the fluctuation of the set value is large; (4) adaptability is insufficient in the face of different network spaces and different attention factors. As for these shortcomings, we propose a network security index calculation method based on convolutional neural networks in this paper. We use the convolutional layers for local detection and depth extraction, and apply the pooling layers to quickly shrink the network scale and highlight the summary features. By the deep network structure with multiple hidden layers, we realize the process of fitting the expert experience to evaluate comprehensive indexes. And the adaptive characteristics such as online learning are available. Through experimental comparisons, the calculation results are obviously better than other models. However, there are still some flaws such as limited scale of experimental data, and the relatively old construction method for the index system. In addition, this convolutional neural network model lacks optimal parameter argumentation, which is our future direction of improvement and research.

References

1. Bin, W.: Progress and challenges of intelligent surveillance industry security. J. Inf. Secur. Res. **3**(3), 277–280 (2017). (in Chinese)
2. Scaife, N., Carter, H., Traynor, P., et al.: CryptoLock (and drop it): stopping ransomware attacks on user data. In: IEEE International Conference on Distributed Computing Systems. IEEE Computer Society, pp. 303–312 (2016)
3. Li, L.: The design of network security situation awareness system and the implementation of key module. Beijing University of Posts and Telecommunications (2015)
4. Tianfield, H.: Cyber security situational awareness. In: IEEE International Conference on Internet of Things, pp. 782–787. IEEE (2017)
5. Xi, R., Yun, X., Jin, S., Zhang, Y.: A survey of network security situational awareness. J. Comput. Appl. **32**(1), 1–4 (2012). (in Chinese)
6. Shen, Z., Ronghual, S., Yin, Z.: Visual fusion and analysis for multivariate heterogeneous network security data. J. Comput. Appl. **35**(5), 1379–1384 (2015). (in Chinese)
7. Hariri, S., Qu, G., Dharmagadda, T., et al.: Impact analysis of faults and attacks in large-scale networks. IEEE Secur. Priv. **99**(5), 49–54 (2003)
8. Wang, S.: Research on effect evaluation technology of network attack oriented web service. Shenyang Ligong University (2016). (in Chinese)
9. Zhou, C., Li, W., Mo, X., Li, Q.: An assessment method of network security vulnerability. J. Jiangsu Univ. (Nat. Sci. Ed.) **38**(1), 68–77 (2017)
10. Chen, X.-Z., Zheng, Q.-H., Guan, X.-H., Lin, C.G.: Quantitative hierarchical threat evaluation model for network security. J. Jiangsu Univ. (Nat. Sci. Ed.) **17**(4), 885–897 (2006). (in Chinese)
11. Shou, Z.-Q., Tao, J.-P., Zhou, J., Deng, L.: Study of campus network security evaluation index system based on extension analytic hierarchy process. J. Comput. **33**(11), 1643–1647 (2010). (in Chinese)
12. Jia, W.: Research and implementation of WLAN attack effect evaluation. Beijing University of Posts and Telecommunications (2015). (in Chinese)
13. Zhang, Y., Yang, Q.: Research on mobile internet security situation assessment based on fuzzy analytic hierarchy process. Comput. Eng. Appl. **52**(24), 107–111 (2016). (In Chinese)
14. Jia, Y., Wang, X., Han, W., et al.: YHSSAS: large-scale network oriented security situational awareness system. Comput. Sci. **38**(2), 4–8 (2011). (in Chinese)
15. O'Shea, K., Nash, R.: An introduction to convolutional neural networks. arXiv preprint arXiv:1511.08458 (2015)
16. Sainath, T.N., Kingsbury, B., Saon, G., et al.: Deep convolutional neural networks for large-scale speech tasks. Neural Netw. Off. J. Int. Neural Netw. Soc. **64**, 39–48 (2015)
17. LeCun, Y., Kavukcuoglu, K., Farabet, C.: Convolutional networks and applications in vision. In: Proceedings of 2010 IEEE International Symposium on Circuits and Systems (ISCAS), pp. 253–256. IEEE (2010)
18. Zhang, J.: Research on key technologies of network security assessment. National University of Defense Technology (2013). (in Chinese)

19. Tian, Z., Wang, Y., Sun, Y., Qiu, J.: Location privacy challenges in mobile edge computing: classification and exploration. IEEE Network (2019)
20. Tian, Z., et al.: Real time lateral movement detection based on evidence reasoning network for edge computing environment. IEEE Trans. Ind. Inform. (2019)
21. Tian, Z., Shen, S., Shi, W., Du, X., Guizani, M., Xiang, Y.: A data-driven model for future internet route decision modeling. Future Gener. Comput. Syst. **95**, 212–220 (2019). https://doi.org/10.1016/j.future.2018.12.054
22. Tian, Z., Cui, L.A., Su, S., Yin, X., Yin, L., Cui, X.: A real-time correlation of host-level events in cyber range service for smart campus. IEEE Access **6**, 35355–35364 (2018). https://doi.org/10.1109/ACCESS.2018.2846590
23. Tan, Q., Gao, Y., Shi, J., Wang, X., Fang, B., Tian, Z.H.: Towards a comprehensive insight into the eclipse attacks of tor hidden services. IEEE Internet Things J. (2018). https://doi.org/10.1109/jiot.2018.2846624
24. Xiao, Y., Rayi, V., Sun, B., Du, X., Hu, F., Galloway, M.: A survey of key management schemes in wireless sensor networks. J. Comput. Commun. **30**(11–12), 2314–2341 (2007)
25. Du, X., Xiao, Y., Guizani, M., Chen, H.H.: An effective key management scheme for heterogeneous sensor networks. Ad Hoc Netw. **5**(1), 24–34 (2007)
26. Xiao, Y., Du, X., Zhang, J., Guizani, S.: Internet Protocol Television (IPTV): the Killer application for the next generation Internet. IEEE Commun. Mag. **45**(11), 126–134 (2007)
27. Du, X., Chen, H.H.: Security in wireless sensor networks. IEEE Wirel. Commun. Mag. **15**(4), 60–66 (2008)
28. Du, X., Guizani, M., Xiao, Y., Chen, H.H.: Transactions papers, a routing-driven elliptic curve cryptography based key management scheme for heterogeneous sensor networks. IEEE Trans. Wirel. Commun. **8**(3), 1223–1229 (2009)
29. Hou, M., Wei, R., Wang, T., Cheng, Y., Qian, B.: Reliable medical recommendation based on privacy-preserving collaborative filtering. CMC **56**(1), 137–149 (2018)
30. Zhang, H., Yi, Y., Wang, J., Cao, N., Duan, Q.: Network security situation awareness framework based on threat intelligence. CMC-Comput. Mater. Continua **56**(3), 381–399 (2018)

A Method to Defense APT Based on Dynamic ID Transformation

Delei Nie[1], Hong Yu[2(✉)], Xiaobin Lu[2], and Chao Cui[1]

[1] Information Technology Innovation Center of Tianjin Binhai New Area,
Tianjin, China
[2] China National Digital Switching System Engineering and Technological
R&D Center, Zhengzhou, Henan, China
yh@ndsc.com.cn

Abstract. This paper focuses on the security protection of intranets in schools, government agencies, data centers and industrial control information systems, studies the dynamic randomization principle on the network side based on the path hopping and address hoping strategies, and proposes a network ID (including TCP session, port, IP address, MAC address and so on) transition method based on network threat intention. By exploring network threat intention, a system dynamic transition decision-making mechanism is formed to implement the dynamic and uncertain structure of network information system. Thus, the active security defense of network information system can be realized based on existing hardware and software environment with vulnerabilities and backdoors. The experimental results show that this method can effectively enhance the security of network information system.

Keywords: Dynamic ID transformation · APT defense ·
Dynamic randomization · Vulnerabilities and backdoors

1 Introduction

Intranet state concealment can effectively prevent intruders from sniffing and scanning the Intranet, APT attacks on specific terminals, and man-in-the-middle attacks with nodes in the Intranet as springboards. By dynamically mapping specific Intranet terminals/user IDs to virtual addresses and dynamically changing network paths, it can hide the Intranet users and topologies, and protect the Intranet terminals.

Network layer IP address is the basis of locating and communicating on the network. The persistent and static IP addresses of network hosts provide convenience for attackers to scan and attack continuously. After each device accesses the network, get configured or dynamically obtains the IP address, it can access other IP network hosts or devices. At the same time it can be accessed by other IP network hosts or devices, too. Because of this openness and continuous online presence of users, many security threats are introduced. First, whether or not the user host needs to access resources on the network, it will remain online so that it can be accessed by other user hosts. This provides conditions for the attacker to scan and infiltrate. Secondly, the IP address of a host is invariable or unchanged for a period of time. Once the attacker obtains the traffic

© Springer Nature Switzerland AG 2019
X. Sun et al. (Eds.): ICAIS 2019, LNCS 11634, pp. 541–550, 2019.
https://doi.org/10.1007/978-3-030-24271-8_48

between the hosts through bypassing or middleman method, the users' communication content can be continuously obtained. Finally, there is no isolation method between hosts in the same LAN. Either no communication between the two hosts or any communication between the two hosts. So that once a host is controlled by an attacker, it is easy to carry out further intranet penetration attacks based on the controlled host.

In a static network architecture, single network packet transmission path makes the communication parties more vulnerable to man-in-the-middle attacks. Routing protocol aims to find an optimal transmission path for both sides in the current network environment. Without node failure or dramatic changes in network traffic, the transmission path of network packets is usually unchanged. Once the switch is attacked and controlled, the attacker can use the switch to act as a middleman, making the communication parties on both sides of the transmission path, which passes through the switch, continue to be threatened by man-in-the-middle attack.

2 Related Research

The main idea of dynamic network defense is to constantly change the network basic properties, including host address.[1–3], port, network protocol [4], network topology, adding new dynamic layer [5], and so on. MTD has already been preliminarily implemented in Software-defined Network (SDN) [6], with IP address randomized hopping mechanism[1] and data stream path randomized hopping mechanism designed [7]. The idea of randomization in MTD is based on that changing addresses may decrease the attack success rate and increase the attacker's effort for infiltration.

Early APOD (Applications That Participate in Their Own Defense) [8] strategies used tunnel mutation techniques based on random addresses and random ports to disguise the identity of the terminal host to avoid network detection. But this strategy is not transparent, because the process of IP mutation requires the cooperation of the client and server. DyNAT [9] provides transparent IP mutations by translating IP addresses before packets enter the core network to avoid middleman detection, but this approach does little to protect against scanning that relies on probe replies to discover the terminal host. Jafarian and others designed an IP address randomization hopping mechanism [1]. Through mathematical analysis, formalized IP address transformation rate constraints, IP address pool range constraints, range uncertainty constraints, then used Yices SMT algorithm [10] to obtain the best hopping in a limited number of IP addresses to reduce the probability of being successfully attacked. Experimental results show that IP address hopping can invalidate 99% of the external and internal scans of the network and protect 90% of the network hosts from unknown worms.

The new way to improve the network security is employing flexible SDN architecture [12–15]. In [16] the authors use an algorithm to assign free addresses to host so that it can update its virtual addresses. And the DNS is responsible for updating name to virtual address mappings. OpenFlow programs flows and address translations according to the address change schedule. In [17], an IPv6 address update scheme is proposed by the authors and the implementation is given. In [18], the authors propose changing routes that connect a source and a destination. In this article, the authors describe a random route mutation scheme, which can be formulated according to MTD requirements, and optimized according to MTD costs. Experiments show that the most effective route generated can work without affecting any ongoing traffic or violating security integrity. However, the path selection strategies in these protocols are deterministic. In other words, if the attacker knows the path selection algorithm, the path chosen by the defender can be derived. Route randomization hopping is the key to multi-path security protocols. For example, the multi-path algorithm in literature [19] randomly generates multiple paths for wireless sensor networks. This randomly generated multi-path routing protocol can effectively defend against black hole attacks. Jafarian et al. [7] adopted the multi-path and random dynamic configuration method in their designed data stream path randomization (RRM) scheme.

3 Dynamic ID Transformation Strategy

By applying the dynamic idea of mimetic defense to IP address and packet transmission path in network layer, the IP address of IP packet can be transformed actively during transmission and the transmission path can be dynamically selected according to certain strategies without affecting (or affecting only a little bit of) the normal function and performance of the network. It can enhance network defense capabilities.

Through active transformation of network IP addresses, network shows external or internal uncertainty or dynamics. On one hand, it can shorten the effective time window for network attackers to carry out attacks, thus increase the difficulty of scanning and exploring vulnerabilities; on the other hand, it makes the attackers unable to continuously track and attack the host according to its network IP address. It is impossible to accumulate knowledge acquired in the previous stage, thereby breaking the advantage of attackers.

By dynamically changing the packet transmission path, even if the attackers succeed in controlling the traditional switching nodes on the transmission path, they still cannot obtain the continuous data packets between the two parties of the communication. In other words, it is impossible to obtain effective communication information and the ability to resist attacks of the network is improved.

Therefore, through the above two ways, the stability and effectiveness of the attack chain are shaken to some extent.

Dynamic variable IP addresses can be learned from the idea of Network Address Translation (NAT). NAT first appeared in order to temporarily solve the shortage of IP addresses. NAT technology maps IP addresses from one address domain to another, thus completing the conversion between internal private addresses and public addresses, and realizing the communication between the internal host and the public network. NAT technology allows different private addresses to be mapped to the same public address, which implements network address multiplexing and reduces the allocation of public addresses. When an outbound packet passes through a NAT device, NAT converts the address in the packet to hide the IP address of the internal host. In addition, a NAT device also acts as a firewall to block the packets sent by the external hosts, so that the external hosts cannot actively access the internal host, strengthening the security of the internal network.

544   D. Nie et al.

On the basis of NAT technology, we carried out an innovative design. Traditional IP virtualization is based on the host, each intranet host is assigned with a corresponding virtual address. While dynamic user ID transformation technology is based on session/data flow, aiming at each packet. Each data stream is assigned with a corresponding virtual ID, that is, sessions initiated by different ports on the same host are assigned with different virtual ID addresses. Traditional IP virtualization is not transparent to intranet hosts, while dynamic ID transformation technology is transparent to them. The hosts will not sense any impact brought by ID virtualization. Terminal/user IDs can be dynamically composed of IP addresses, MAC addresses, service port numbers, application protocol types and other network data keywords.

Dynamic ID transformation structure includes a virtual ID data flow status detection module and a virtual ID address switching module, as shown in Fig. 1. In addition, dynamic ID transformation technology can be combined with the traditional anomaly traffic analysis technology to detect the intent of network attackers, and based on which to make corresponding dynamic transformations.

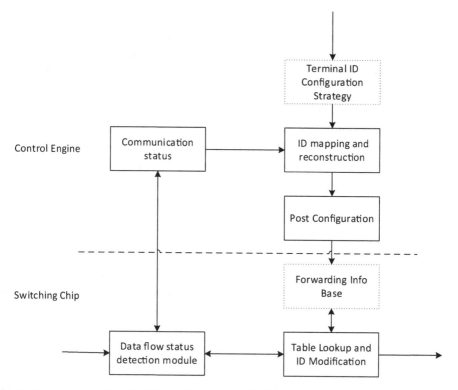

Fig. 1. Implement of dynamic ID transformation technology. Incoming packets are monitored and their IDs are modified when necessary. The control engine formulates virtualization strategy according to the information from the status detection module, maps IDs and posts the configuration. The switching chip modifies the IDs and forward the packets.

The randomization of the transmission path can be reflected in the configuration strategy of the routing table. Switches support dynamic routing changes using different strategies (timing, flow-oriented dynamic transformation, etc.). Network administrators can configure the transmission according to the system strategy, thus completing the dynamic routing of the entire network.

4   Dynamic ID Transformation Process

4.1   Data Flow Status Detection Module

The main function of the data flow status detection module is to detect the status of the data flow, including the virtualization ID configuration of each data flow through the switch, and report to the control engine about the status in order to provide reference for the decision-making of ID virtualization strategy.

The data flow status detection module consists of a message analysis and detection module and a flow status cache module. The packet analysis and detection module is responsible for analyzing incoming data flows and detecting incoming packets, determining the active status of the virtual IDs and buffering them (Fig. 2).

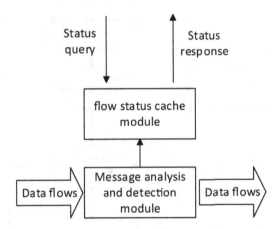

Fig. 2. Data flow status detection module is consisted of two sub-modules, message analysis and detection module and flow status cache module. Data flow comes in, gets processed by analysis and detection module and is passed on to the next module. Analysis and detection module extracts data flow status, and the cache module stores the information in the cache in a unified format and waits the control engine to query.

On the other hand, the flow status cache module is responsible for storing the received message status information in a unified format. And it's also responsible for handling the queries of the control engine. Whenever it receives a query for the status of certain data flow, it looks up its table, finds the corresponding information and send it back to the control engine. Based on what's sent back, the control engine determines whether or not to configure virtualization on a data flow. The virtualization configuration operation is only performed when the control engine determines that the status of a data stream is available for ID virtualization.

4.2 ID Transformation Module

Dynamic ID transformation technology implements the allocation of virtual ID addresses based on the sessions/data flows, so it is necessary to manage all virtual IDs according to the data flow status, make clear the virtual ID status (occupied, idle), handle the allocation and recovery of virtual IDs, and modify IDs for packets of different data flows. These functions are implemented by ID transformation module.

ID transformation module is partly deployed in the control engine and partly in the switching chip. The part in the control engine is called virtual ID management unit and it is for generation and management of virtual IDs. And the part in the switching chip is called virtual ID modification unit and it is for packet ID transformation between virtual IDs and actual IDs (Fig. 3).

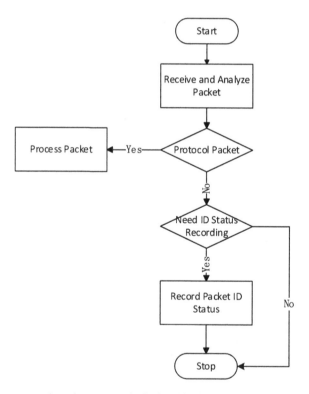

Fig. 3. Data flow status detection process is depicted in the picture above. Basically, if a packet is protocol packet, it does not need to be virtualized and goes straightly to the control engine and gets processed. If not, the module decides whether it needs ID status recording or not, and then process it accordingly.

The Processing at the Control Engine End. Virtual ID management unit is deployed in the control engine, the main task is to generate and manage the virtual IDs. It receives data flow status information from data flow status detection module, and combines these information with virtualization strategy, which can be preset by system administer or produced according to environmental variables, to generate virtual IDs. Algorithm is used to ensure that the newly generated IDs are not the same as any ID that is currently in use. And it's in charge of the allocation of virtual IDs. The unit is in constant ware of virtual IDs' status. Once it finds out a virtual ID turned idle (happens when one communication is terminated and the corresponding data flow is ended), it will reclaim the virtual ID for further use. This unit also sets a timing device for each data flow to mark packet time out.

By posting configuration table, this unit updates virtual ID information to switching chip. It can happen once in a certain amount of time or whenever the switching chip requires.

The Processing at the Switching Chip End. Virtual ID transformation unit is deployed in the switching chip. After processed by data flow status detection module, the packet is sent to this unit. The unit receives the packet and its status information, then looks up the forwarding table and modifies the ID of the packet. Then it transfers the processed packet to the forwarding engine for forwarding.

The Virtual ID transformation unit looks up the table, finds the corresponding entry, and modifies the ID address in the original message according to the content of the entry. For packets without hidden ID settings, there is no need to process and they are forwarded directly.

5 Experiment and Verification

The experiment simulates apt attacks and covers most links of the attack chain. The comparison objects are a network with dynamic ID defense on and a network with dynamic ID defense off, as shown in Fig. 4. The target host runs the Windows XP operating system based on the Intel i5 processor.

The designed test case covers all phases of the attack chain and contains a total of 14 tests, as shown in Table 1.

In the scanning and detecting phase, we use Zenmap and other scanning tools and remote security evaluation system of the NSFOCUS to perform multiple scans and detections. Finding out how much information these tools can help us get out of the target host, we can determine the effectiveness of our method.

In the vulnerability mining phase, we use Vuzzer automatic vulnerability mining tool to scan the host. Under the premise that there are directory browsing vulnerabilities in the system, we try to use this vulnerability to get the website directory, and intercepts and modifies the packets to induce access errors, and try to obtain the background information of the system through the displayed error information. Through the tests above, we evaluate the defense effect of dynamic ID transformation technology in vulnerability mining phase.

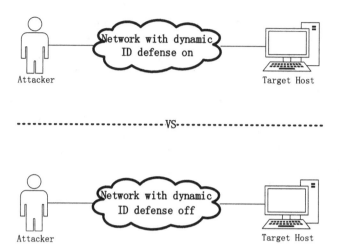

Fig. 4. Experiment environment contains two comparison objects, one network with dynamic ID defense on and one network with dynamic ID defense off.

Table 1. Test cases.

Attack phase	Test case	Defense ON	Defense OFF
Scanning and detecting	1. Zenmap scanning	Failed	Succeeded
	2. NSFOCUS remote security evaluation system scanning	Failed	Succeeded
Vulnerability mining	3. Vuzzer automatic vulnerability mining	Failed	Succeeded
	4. Access error induction	Failed	Succeeded
Attack implantation	5. 08_067_netapi exploit	Failed	Succeeded
	6. SAM exploit	Failed	Succeeded
	7. Upgrade program exploit	Failed	Succeeded
	8. Netspy trojan exploit	Failed	Succeeded
	9. Nethief trojan exploit	Failed	Succeeded
	10. Embed backdoor	Failed	Succeeded
	11. Explorer.exe virus infection	Failed	Succeeded
	12. Sql injection	Failed	Succeeded
	13. Host downtime	Failed	Succeeded
Attack maintenance	14. Preset a backdoor that has successfully attacked and re-trigger it	Failed	Succeeded
In total	14	0 success	14 success

In the phase of attack implantation, attack implantation processes such as vulnerability exploitation, Trojan horse implantation, virus infection, SQL injection and so on are simulated. The vulnerabilities/backdoors used in these process are known vulnerabilities in the system or deliberately created and then placed in the system. In particular, the Windows operating system retained 08_067_netapi vulnerability, SAM database vulnerability, and upgrade vulnerability during the tests to simulate unknown vulnerabilities to the defender. Also, we embed backdoors to simulate unknown backdoors to the defender. Through the tests above, the defense capability of the dynamic ID transformation technology against attacks using both the known and unknown vulnerabilities and backdoors is evaluated.

In the attack maintenance phase, a backdoor is embedded and the result of the attack is deliberately modified to make the first attack succeed. Then the backdoor is used again to verify the attack result. Through this test, the defense effect of the dynamic ID transformation on the attack maintenance phase is verified. In addition, a system local downtime test is performed to evaluate the technology's capability of handling exceptions other than attacks.

The tests above mostly adopt a method of artificial preset vulnerabilities and backdoors to ensure the directness and destructiveness of the attacks. The attacks affect every phase of the attack chain and use various types of techniques. Thus our experiment can evaluate the defense capabilities of dynamic ID translation to the maximum extent possible.

The test results show that the dynamic ID transformation can fully achieve the purpose of defense against attacks. Specifically, in the scanning and detecting phase, the technology can transform the fingerprint information of the system, showing uncertainty; in the vulnerability mining phase, the emergence of vulnerabilities is uncertain, increasing the difficulty of vulnerability exploitation; in the attack implantation phase, whether it is for known or unknown vulnerabilities and backdoors, the technology shows effectiveness; In the stage of attack maintenance, the technology can continuously resist attacks using unknown backdoors.

In conclusion: Dynamic ID transformation technology successfully resists every test attack shown in Table 1 and it has very strong network defense capability.

References

1. Jafarian, J.H., Al-Shaer, E., Duan, Q.: Spatiotemporal address mutation for proactive cyber agility against sophisticated attackers. In: First ACM Workshop on Moving Target Defense, MTD 2014 (2014)
2. Antonatos, S., Akritidis, P., Markatos, E.P., et al.: Defending against Hitlist worms using network address space randomization. Comput. Netw. **51**(12), 3471–3490 (2007)
3. Al-Shaer, E.: Toward network configuration randomization for moving target defense. In: Jajodia, S., Ghosh, A., Swarup, V., Wang, C., Wang, X. (eds.) Moving Target Defense. Advances in Information Security, vol. 54, pp. 153–159. Springer, New York (2011). https://doi.org/10.1007/978-1-4614-0977-9_9
4. Rowe, J., Levitt, K.N., Demi, T., et al.: Artificial diversity as maneuvers in a control theoretic moving target defense. In: National Symposium on Moving Target Research (2012)
5. Kewley, D., Fink, R., Lowry, J., et al.: Dynamic approaches to thwart adversary intelligence gathering. In: Proceedings of DARPA Information Survivability Conference & Exposition II, DISCEX 2001, pp. 176–185. IEEE (2001)

6. Nadeau, T.D., Gray, K.: SDN: Software Defined Networks. O'REILLY Media Inc., USA (2013)

7. Jafarian, J.H., Al-Shaer, E., Duan, Q.: Formal approach for route agility against persistent attackers. In: Crampton, J., Jajodia, S., Mayes, K. (eds.) ESORICS 2013. LNCS, vol. 8134, pp. 237–254. Springer, Heidelberg (2013). https://doi.org/10.1007/978-3-642-40203-6_14

8. Atighetchi, M., Pal, P., Webber, F., et al.: Adaptive use of network-centric mechanisms in cyber-defense. In: Second IEEE International Symposium on Network Computing and Applications, NCA 2003, pp. 179–188. IEEE (2003)

9. Kewley, D., Fink, R., Lowry, J., et al.: Dynamic approaches to thwart adversary intelligence gathering. In: DARPA Information Survivability Conference & Exposition II, DISCEX 2001, pp. 176–185. IEEE (2001)

10. Bjørner, N., de Moura, L.: Z310: applications, enablers, challenges and directions. In: CFV 2009 (2009)

11. Wan, M., Yao, J., Jing, Y., Jin, X.: Event-based anomaly detection for non-public industrial communication protocols in SDN-based control systems. CMC: Comput. Mater. Continua **55**(3), 447–463 (2018)

12. Kampanakis, P., Perros, H., Beyene, T.: SDN-based solutions for moving target defense network protection. In: World of Wireless, Mobile and Multimedia Networks, pp. 1–6. IEEE (2014)

13. Macfarland, D.C., Shue, C.A.: The SDN shuffle: creating a moving-target defense using host-based software-defined networking. In: ACM Workshop on Moving Target Defense, pp. 37–41. ACM (2015)

14. Chowdhary, A., Pisharodym, S., Huangm, D.: SDN based scalable MTD solution in cloud network. In: ACM Workshop on Moving Target Defense, pp. 27–36. ACM (2016)

15. Lei, C., Ma, D.H., Zhang, H.Q.: Optimal strategy selection for moving target defense based on Markov game. IEEE Access **PP**(99), 1 (2017)

16. Jafarian, J.H., Al-Shaer, E., Duan, Q.: Openflow random host mutation: transparent moving target defense using software defined networking. In: Proceedings of the First Workshop on Hot Topics in Software Defined Network, HotSDN 2012, pp. 127–132. ACM (2012)

17. Dunlop, M., Groat, S., Marchany, R., Tront, J.: Implementing an IPv6 moving target defense on a live network. In: National Symposium on Moving Target Research, June 2012

18. Al-Shaer, E., Jafarian, J.: On the random route mutation moving target defense. In: National Symposium on Moving Target Research, June 2012

19. Shu, T., Krunz, M., Liu, S.: Secure data collection in wireless sensor networks using randomized dispersive routes. IEEE Trans. Mob. Comput. **9**(7), 941–954 (2010)

20. Xiong, L., Shi, Y.: On the privacy-preserving outsourcing scheme of reversible data hiding over encrypted image data in cloud computing. CMC: Comput. Mater. Continua **55**(3), 523–539 (2018)

Emergency Analysis Based on Affective Computing in Universities Forum

Lu Zhang[1,2], Xu Wu[1,2,3(✉)], Xiaqing Xie[1,2], Jin Xu[1,2],
and Tianle Zhang[4]

[1] Key Laboratory of Trustworthy Distributed Computing and Service,
Ministry of Education, Beijing 100876, China
1049978082@qq.com, {wux,xiexiaqing}@bupt.edu.cn
[2] School of Cyberspace Security, BUPT, Beijing 100876, China
[3] Beijing University of Posts and Telecommunications Library,
Beijing 100876, China
[4] Cyberspace Institute of Advanced Technology, Guangzhou University,
Guangzhou 510006, China
tlezhang@sohu.com

Abstract. Emergency analysis for social networking sites have gained increased attention. In order to detect emergencies in University Forums, we present an emergency analysis method based on affective computing. The method detects the emergency and calculates the scores in real-time based on affective computing and the University Public Opinion Ontology (UPO_Ontology) established manually. The method is evaluated on two test datasets. The results show that the UPO_Ontology and affective computing greatly improved the accuracy, recall and F-measure. The method proposed in this paper meets the requirement of real-time detection. What's more, It gain of 1.24% in F-measure over the "event-specific detection" proposed by Laylavi et al. and outperforms emergency detect using contextual semantics by nearly 7.1% in F-measure. The analysis of the emergencies in University Forums will help Universities deal with emergencies more effectively and provide students with better service.

Keywords: Emergency detection · University BBS · Affective computing

1 Introduction

University emergency is an individual or group behavior occur in a short time which endanger students' health and safety. Nowadays, more and more emergencies happen in Universities. It is difficult for the current emergency detection system to obtain university information and deal with it. The University forum is developed and managed by university teachers and students, it become an important channel for University students to express their emotions. Therefore, the University Forum can be an important data source for detection emergencies in Universities.

At present, most of the researches on event detection are for Twitter, micro-blog and the other large social networking sites [1–3]. But there is lacking of relevant

© Springer Nature Switzerland AG 2019
X. Sun et al. (Eds.): ICAIS 2019, LNCS 11634, pp. 551–563, 2019.
https://doi.org/10.1007/978-3-030-24271-8_49

research on Universities. On the one hand, the detection of emergencies helps Universities pay attention to the students' living conditions and mental state. On the other hand, it helps Universities deal with emergencies effectively, maintain harmony and stability on campus [4]. So it is necessary to detect Emergencies in University forums.

2 Related Work

2.1 Emergency Detection Technology

Conventional emergency detection techniques for network communities include text clustering and Feature-Pivot Techniques [1]. According to the characteristics of Twitter, Weng et al. proposed Event Detection with Clustering of Wavelet-based Signals to detect emergencies [5]. Yin et al. detects key words and extracts context awareness information using Natural Language Processing and Data Miningtowadrs twitter message during natural disasters [6]. The real-time flow event monitoring problem for Twitter has also been summarized a lot [3, 7–9]. Popescu et al. proposed an event detection method that specifies a specific person or event over a period of time, while introducing a regression machine learning model to detect events that cause mass disputes from the Twitter data stream [10, 11].

2.2 Text Affective Computing

The contents published in University forums have strong emotional guidance and it is colloquial. It is necessary to apply Affective Computing to the emergency detection in University Forums. Picard, a professor at the MIT Media Lab in the United States, proposed the word "affective computing" and defined it as a calculation of emotions [12–14]. The main task of affective computing is emotion recognition and polarity monitoring. Chikersal et al. enhanced supervised learning system for polarity classification by leveraging on linguistic rules and sentic computing resources [15, 16] (Fig. 1).

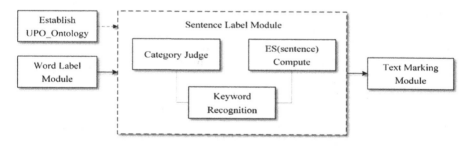

Fig. 1. Components of the affective computing model

2.3　Summary

Text information in university forums consists of two forms: fact and opinion [17].

2.4　Establishment of University Public Opinion Ontology (UPO_Ontology)

In order to find out the emergencies in Universities accurately, we traced the historical emergencies data of colleges and Universities for a long time, and summarizes the common types of emergencies in Universities, used the co-occurrence analysis technique [19]. Table 1 describes five types of emergencies.

Table 1. The five categories of emergencies.

Category	Description	Example
Group Emergencies (GPE)	Events Involving University students expressed their dissatisfaction by processions, rallies, protests etc.	Student & parade Playground & protest
University Management Emergencies (SME)	Events Involving University Improper management such as enrollment, fees, logistics, security	Leadership & academic corruption Canteen & liver
University Leadership Emergencies (LDE)	Events Involving bad behavior of University Leadership or teachers	Leadership & academic corruption Tutor & deduction of wages
University Students Emergencies (STE)	Events Involving rights and health of students	Student & cheating Graduate & unemployed
University Injury and Death Emergencies (DTE)	Events Involving Death, injury, casualties etc.	Student & suicide, Postgraduate & death

2.5　Word Label Module

It is necessary to preprocess the words which are basic unit of the text before dealing with the text. Operations include clauses, word segmentation, lexical markings, mark vocabulary dependencies.

(1) Clauses and word segmentation: according to the habit of Chinese, a text will be divided into sentences by punctuation such as {. ? ! ～ 。! ? ;}. Then, we use the word segmentation tool in Language Technology Platform (LTP) to segment sentences into individual words [20].
(2) Vocabulary marking model: the dependency relations between vocabulary is the basis of the affective computing of the text. The attributes of words are needed to be marked. The key words tagging model: WordFlags includeds six elements: pos, relationship, Roles, Entities, is predicate or not, is marked or not. The meaningful

words in a sentence are labeled by WordFlags. Table 2 explains the meaning of elements and how to get them (Fig. 2).

WordFlags = {pos, relationship, Roles, Entities, IsPredicate, IsMarked}

Table 2. The meaning and acquisition method of elements in WordFlags

Field	Description	Label content
Pos	Part-of-speech of words	Verb, noun, adjective
Relationship	Dependency relations between language components	Subject-verb (SBV), verb-object (VOB), attribute (ATT), adverbial (ADV), complement (CMP)
Roles	Semantic role labeling	Agent (A0), Patient (A1), Location (LOC)
Entities	Named entity recognition	Persons (Name), locations (place), organizations (organization)
IsPredicate	Is predicate or not	Is predicate (true), Is not predicate (false)
IsMarked	Marked by UPO_Ontology and named entity recognition	Is Marked (true), Is not Marked (false)

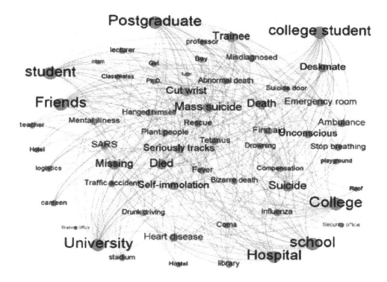

Fig. 2. The meta-event diagram of DTE

2.6 Sentence Label Module

The text is composed of sentences, words in sentences and sentence dependency relation bring emotion to sentence, sentence label module is based on the result of word label module. In this module, key words in sentence will be marked, the location of the key words in the dependency relationship are considered to calculate the emergency category and emergencies score (ES). The sentence label module (SentFlags) is defined as follows:

SentFlags = {Category, Emergency score}

(1) Category: The categories of a emergency that are defined in UPO_Ontology. Category includes Group Emergencies (GPE), University Management Emergencies (SME), University Leadership Emergencies (LDE), University Students Emergencies (STE), University Injury and Death Emergencies (DTE) and New Emergencies witch are not defined in UPO_Ontology.
(2) Emergency score (ES): The score of emergency, identify the sensitive keywords in sentences.

The following chapters will cover the category judge formula and the emergency score calculate model.

2.6.1 Emergency Category Judgment

UPO_Ontology includes five categories emergencies, each category includes three kinds of the thesaurus: person (UPO_PER), location (UPO_LOC), event (UPO_EVT). Because most of the words has the exclusive characteristics, the co-occurrence of person, location and event is important. Take a classification as an example, we define that if person belong to the category UPO_PER or location belong to the category UPO_LOC appears in the sentence and the events belong to the category UPO_ EVT appears in the sentence at the same time, this sentence is likely to belong to the emergency. However, determine category just by whether the words appear in the sentence will lead to misjudgment. In this paper, we use LTP Semantic Role Labeling method to main roles in sentence: Agent (A0), Patient (A1), Location (LOC) and predicate. We will determine the category according to the semantic role where keyword appears.

Through historical data analysis, "event" will appear in A0 or A1 as adjectives or appear in the predicate as verbs. "People" appear mostly in A0 or A1, and "place" will only appear in the LOC. Formula (1) is the emergency category judgment the formula, which achieve the purpose that identify the emergency category through person + event or location + event. The formula considered the position of the keyword in the sentence, it will reduce the probability of misjudgment.

$$\{(A0 \, or \, A1) \in UPO\_PER(cg) \, or \, LOC \in$$
$$UPO\_LOC(cg)\} \, and \, (A0 \, or \, A1 \, or \, Predicate) \in UPO\_EVT(cg) \rightarrow \qquad (1)$$
$$Category \in cg \quad Where \, cg \in \{GPE, LDE, SME, LTE, DTE\}$$

2.6.2 Emergency Keywords Recognition

Emergency keywords is important to Emergency score (ES) calculation, at the same time, recognize the emergency keywords will complete the word label module's "IsMarked" element. Using the results of word label module, on the one hand, we use the formula (1) to tag words which belongs to UPO_Ontology, and make "IsMarked" is assigned to "true". Figure 3 shows the emergency keywords recognition process.

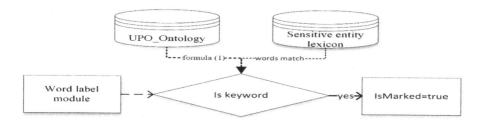

Fig. 3. The emergency keywords recognition process

2.6.3 Emergency Score (ES) Calculation

Dependency parsing holds that the predicate is the core of the whole sentence which dominates the other elements, Subject, predicate and object are the backbone of a sentence. subject-verb (SBV) and verb-object (VOB) can provide information about modifying relations in sentences. In general, we think that the subject and object are marked are nouns, predicates are verbs or adjectives, but the marked predicates are verbs.

In this paper, we obtain the SBV and VOB dependencies of sentences, the score of the key words are calculated and transferred to the predicate ES (predicate) in the sentence. The predicate's score will be passed to the sentence finally. Formula (2) shows the transfer process of emergency score calculation

$$ES(sentence) = ES(predicate) \xleftarrow{transfer\ polartity} ES(\text{SBV}) + ES(\text{VOB}) \quad (2)$$

Algorithm process:

(1) Get the SBV and VOB in sentences, get words' WordFlags in Word label module, calculate POI (word) using UPO_Ontology, Sensitive entity lexicon, Emotion Thesaurus and Polar Thesaurus, executive (2).

(2) Determine that the word is marked as a keyword or not, if not execute (3), else execute (4).

(3) Transfer the words score to the predicate, $ES(predicate) = ES(word)$

(4) Judge the pos of the word, if it is noun execute (5), otherwise execute (6)

(5) The word is noun, the modifier relation is usually ATT, the score of qualifier $ES(adj)$ is calculated using Emotion Thesaurus and Polar Thesaurus, Transfer the score to the word, $ES(predicate) = ES(word) + ES(adj)$, execute (9)

(6) The word is verb, so it is predicate, if it has relationship ADV, execute (7) get $ES_1(predicate)$, else if it has relationship CMP, execute (8) get $ES_2(predicate)$, then add the result together and Transfer the score to the word, $ES(predicate) = ES_1(predicate) + ES_2(predicate)$, execute (9)

(7) If the modifier is emphasizer, $ES_1(predicate) = 2 * ES(word)$, if the modifier is negative, $ES_1(predicate) = -1/2 * ES(word)$. The pos of the modifier is judged by emphatic thesaurus and negative thesaurus.

(8) Transfer the words score to the predicate, $ES_2(\text{predicate}) = 1.5ES(word)$. The pos of the word is judged by using Emotion Thesaurus and Polar Thesaurus.

(9) Transfer the score to the sentence, $ES(\text{sentence}) = ES(\text{predicate})$

Figure 4 shows the flow Emergency score(ES) calculation Algorithm process.

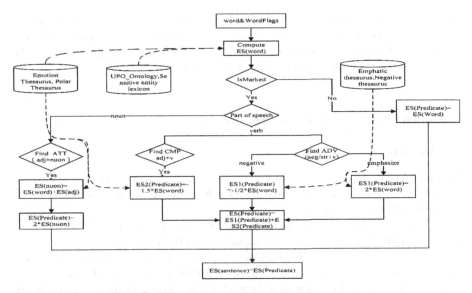

Fig. 4. Emergency score (ES) calculation algorithm process

2.7 The Text Marking Module

The sentence label module (SentFlags) has been obtained through the above process. Based on the SentFlags of sentence, The text marking module (TextFlags) is defined as follows:

TextFlags = {Text Category, Text Emergency score, Text Emergency level}

In TextFlags, the emergency category of text, emergency score of text and the emergency level of the text will be calculated.

(1) Text Category: the emergency category of text, according to the formula (1), sentences in a text maybe have different emergency category. The five categories in the UPO_Ontology are scored according to suddenness and importance. As shown in Formula (3), each emergency category is assigned to different score. While sentences in a text have different emergency category, the category with highest score will be choosed to be the category of the text.

$$\text{EventScores}\begin{cases} score(GPE) = score(DTE) = 3 \\ score(LDE) = score(STE) = 2 \\ score(SME) = 1 \\ others = 0.5 \end{cases} \quad (3)$$

(2) Text Emergency score: sentences in a text maybe have different emergency score: ES (sentence). Assuming that the text consist of N sentences, the text's emergency score is defined in formula (4).

$$ES(\text{text}) = \sum_{i=1}^{n} score(category(sentence_i)) * ES(sentence_i) \qquad (4)$$

(3) Text Emergency level: The cumulative operation will leads to great difference, so normalization processing is needed in ES (text). Nonlinear regression method is a reasonable method to solve the problem of large data difference, we use the formula $y = 1/(1 + e^{\wedge}(-x))$ to convert the result into (0, 1).

3   Datasets and Experiment Settings

3.1   Datasets

The experimental data source is from Chinese University Forums (University BBS). The University BBS is an important platform for students which has big influence among the national universities.

To avoid the error results caused by a single data set, we get the 3000 text from both a and BYR BBS and TDRD BBS respectively as two test datasets. The BYR BBS is an information platform of Beijing University of Post and Telecommunication and The TDRD BBS is an information platform of Renmin University of China. At the same time, The two test datasets (test dataset1 and test dataset2) are labeled manually for emergencies. Table 3 show the detail of the two test datasets. Test dataset1 contains 450 emergencies texts and 2550 texts without emergencies, Test dataset2 contains 438 emergencies texts and 2562 texts without emergencies.

Table 3. The detail of the two test datasets

Test dataset	All texts	Texts with emergencies	Texts without emergencies
Test dataset 1	**3000**	**450**	**2550**
Test dataset 2	3000	438	2562

3.2   Thesaurus Establishment

This paper takes National Taiwan University Sentiment Dictionary (NTUSD) and HowNet as emotional lexicon and polarity lexicon [21], and collects sensitive name, sensitive place and sensitive institutional as sensitive entity lexicon. The thesaurus are applied in emergency keywords recognition and emergency score calculation. And we assign the vocabulary scores in the lexicons manually. It includes positive emotional lexicon, negative emotional lexicon, positive polarity lexicon, negative polarity thesaurus, negative sensitive thesaurus, sensitive entity thesaurus, emphasis thesaurus and negative thesaurus.

3.3 Experiment Platform and Pre-processing

The experiment is based on the real-time flow data processing framework "SparkStreaming", The spark cluster is built to realize the distributed parallel processing and the processing effects near the real time are guaranteed [22–24]. LTP (Language Technology Platform) [20] is used for Word Segmentation, Part-of-speech Tagging, Dependency Parsing, Semantic Role Labeling and Named Entity Recognition and so on.

4   Experimental and Analysis

4.1   Emergency Detection Using Different Method

Dictionary is the basic for event detection [25]. On the basis of using only sensitive thesaurus to detect emergencies, UPO_Ontology and Affective Computing proposed in this paper are added gradually to judge whether our method can bring better results on detecting emergencies. Four experiments were applied on the two test datasets:

(1)   Emergency detection using only sensitive dictionary
(2)   Emergency detection using only UPO_Ontology
(3)   Emergency detection using UPO_Ontology and Polarity transfer algorithm
(4)   Emergency detection using UPO_Ontology and Affective Computing

Table 4 shows the results obtained by using different methods for emergency detection in two test datasets. The F-measure is an important indicator of performance evaluation. It's the Harmonic mean of accuracy and recall. The accuracy of the model is shown in the range of 0 to 1, where 1 is the best result [26].

Table 4. The results obtained by using different methods for emergency detection

| Methods ↓ | Test datasets → | Test dataset 1 | | | Test dataset 2 | | |
	Measure →	P\%	R\%	F\%	P\%	R\%	F\%
Using only sensitive dictionary		40.75	38.22	39.44	43.01	40.64	41.79
Using only UPO_Ontology		44.93	**67.08**	53.81	46.55	**66.21**	54.67
Using UPO_Ontology & Polarity transfer algorithm		**64.94**	61.33	63.08	**61.14**	58.90	60.00
Using UPO_Ontology & affective computing		78.94	76.67	**77.79**	80.04	73.29	**76.52**

Method 1: Emergency detection using only sensitive dictionary method just use sensitive thesaurus which include sensitive place names, sensitive organization names and negative words to match sensitive text words. The method detect emergencies by the sum of sensitive words number and a negative words number. Poor results were obtained in Method 1 with F values of 39.44% for test dataset1 and 41.79% for test dataset2. Method 2: Emergency detection using only UPO_Ontology method replace

sensitive thesaurus in Method 1 with UPO_Ontology, it can be found that the recall has been greatly improved by comparing with the result of method 1. It shows that UPO_Ontology plays an important role in the analysis of emergencies in the field of University emergencies detection. Method 3 shows that the Polarity transfer algorithm improves the accuracy, however, due to lacking of affective semantic judgment, the recall has been reduced because some sentiment of the text has been misjudged. Method 4: Emergency detection using UPO_Ontology & Affective Computing is the method proposed in this paper, affective computing rules are added in Method 3. It can be seen the F-measure of Method 4 is 77.79% for test dataset1 and 76.52% for test dataset2. It's obviously that the accuracy, recall and F value of the method proposed by us in emergency detection has achieved a good result.

4.2 Method Comparison with the Other Papers

Because the emergency detection technology proposed in this paper mainly relies on two techniques: affective computing and emergency detection, so we test the accuracy from the two aspects. The method proposed by this paper are compared with other methods in similar papers to compare it's accuracy. Laylavi et al. introduced a novel method for detecting event-specific in twitter [26].

We compared our mehods with "SentiCircle" and the affective computing in our method was replaced with contextual semantics computing in "SentiCircle". The method proposed in our paper gain of 1.88% in accuracy and 1.24% in F-measure over the "event-specific detection" proposed by Laylavi et al. What's more, It outperforms emergency detect using contextual semantics by nearly 6.92% in accuracy and 7.1% in F-measure.

4.3 Runtime Analysis

The real-time nature of the text in the Network has aroused researchers' widespread interest [3, 26]. TopicSketch which are proposed by Xie et al. can handle billions of Twitter a day on one machine, almost the same number as Twitter's daily tweets [27]. At present, the field of real-time data processing mainly solves two types of problems:

(1) Limit the processing of a job to a "second level".
(2) Achieve approximate real-time query mechanism and processing mechanism through continuously optimize.

Different from the batch framework, streaming processing needs to take into account the characteristics of real-time data:transient, sudden, random and so on [28]. In the Runtime analysis experiment, we get 50, 000 data using web crawlers from the university forum in real time, to calculate the processing speed. The data stream of text is 28 rates per second, and per-text latency of 0.76 ± 0.46 s. As shown in Table 5, although the result is not better than Real-time detection method for twitter:ReDites, but it can reach the "second level" and satisfies the requirement for real-time processing.

Table 5. Runtime analysis of ReDites for twitter and the proposed method

	Data stream	Delay time
ReDites for twitter	50/s	0.6 ± 0.55 s
The proposed method	28/s	0.76 ± 0.46 s

5 Discussion and Future Work

Experimental results show that the UPO_Ontology and affective computing improved the accuracy of emergency detection. In addition, the method proposed by this article is compared with the "specific event detection" technology:TopicSketch and Contextual Semantics, and the results show that there is a certain increase in accuracy, recall and F-measure. The processing speed also achieves near real-time processing effect. It meets the timeliness requirement of emergency detection well.

However the method proposed by this paper depends on the construction of the UPO_Ontology and the emotion dictionary, expansion of UPO_Ontology and emotional dictionary manually takes more manpower. It is worthy to extended UPO_Ontology automatically while emergencies are discovered.

Acknowledgements. This work is supported by the National Key Research and Development Plan (Grant No. 2017YFC0820603), BUPT's Informatization Innovative Application Project, "privacy protection and data release on Campus big data", and the Project of Chinese Society of Academic degrees and graduate education (2017Y0502).

References

1. Atefeh, F., Khreich, W.: A survey of techniques for event detection in twitter. Comput. Intell. **31**(1), 132–164 (2015)
2. Zhang, X., Chen, X., Chen, Y., et al.: Event detection and popularity prediction in microblogging. Neurocomputing **149**, 1469–1480 (2015)
3. Hasan, M., Orgun, M.A., Schwitter, R.: A survey on real-time event detection from the Twitter data stream. J. Inf. Sci. (2017). https://doi.org/10.1177/0165551517698564
4. Kiritchenko, S., Zhu, X., Mohammad, S.M.: Sentiment analysis of short informal texts. J. Artif. Intell. Res. **50**, 723–762 (2014)
5. Weng, J., Lee, B.S.: Event detection in twitter. ICWSM **11**, 401–408 (2011)
6. Yin, J., Karimi, S., Lampert, A., et al.: Using social media to enhance emergency situation awareness. In: Twenty-Fourth International Joint Conference on Artificial Intelligence (2015)
7. Aston, N., Munson, T., Liddle, J., et al.: Sentiment analysis on the social networks using stream algorithms. J. Data Anal. Inf. Process. **2**, 60 (2014)
8. Hasan, M., Orgun, M.A., Schwitter, R.: TwitterNews+: a framework for real time event detection from the twitter data stream. In: Spiro, E., Ahn, Y.-Y. (eds.) SocInfo 2016. LNCS, vol. 10046, pp. 224–239. Springer, Cham (2016). https://doi.org/10.1007/978-3-319-47880-7_14

9. Wan, M., Yao, J., Jing, Y., Jin, X.: Event-based anomaly detection for non-public industrial communication protocols in SDN-based control systems. CMC: Comput. Mater. Continua **55**(3), 447–463 (2018)

10. Popescu, A.M., Pennacchiotti, M.: Detecting controversial events from twitter. In: Proceedings of the 19th ACM International Conference on Information and Knowledge Management, pp. 1873–1876. ACM (2010)

11. Paltoglou, G.: Sentiment-based event detection in Twitter. J. Assoc. Inf. Sci. Technol. **67**(7), 1576–1587 (2016)

12. Picard, R.W., Picard, R.: Affective Computing. MIT Press, Cambridge (1997)

13. Cambria, E.: Affective computing and sentiment analysis. IEEE Intell. Syst. **31**(2), 102–107 (2016)

14. Kolchyna, O., Souza, T.T.P., Treleaven, P., et al.: Twitter sentiment analysis: Lexicon method, machine learning method and their combination. arXiv preprint arXiv:1507.00955 (2015)

15. Chikersal, P., Poria, S., Cambria, E., Gelbukh, A., Siong, C.E.: Modelling public sentiment in twitter: using linguistic patterns to enhance supervised learning. In: Gelbukh, A. (ed.) CICLing 2015. LNCS, vol. 9042, pp. 49–65. Springer, Cham (2015). https://doi.org/10. 1007/978-3-319-18117-2_4

16. Wang, R., Shen, M., Li, Y., Gomes, S.: Multi-task joint sparse representation classification based on fisher discrimination dictionary learning. CMC: Comput. Mater. Continua **57**(1), 25–48 (2018)

17. Agarwal, B., Poria, S., Mittal, N., et al.: Concept-level sentiment analysis with dependency-based semantic parsing: a novel approach. Cogn. Comput. **7**(4), 487–499 (2015)

18. Di Caro, L., Grella, M.: Sentiment analysis via dependency parsing. Comput. Stand. Interfaces **35**(5), 442–453 (2013)

19. Saif, H., He, Y., Fernandez, M., et al.: Contextual semantics for sentiment analysis of Twitter. Inf. Process. Manag. **52**(1), 5–19 (2016)

20. Che, W., Li, Z., Liu, T.: LTP: a Chinese language technology platform. In: Proceedings of the 23rd International Conference on Computational Linguistics: Demonstrations. Association for Computational Linguistics, pp. 13–16 (2010)

21. Peng, H., Cambria, E., Hussain, A.: A review of sentiment analysis research in chinese language. Cogn. Comput. **9**, 423–435 (2017)

22. Cai, N., Wei, S., Wang, F., et al.: A survey on stream distributed computing. In: 2015 8th International Conference on Intelligent Networks and Intelligent Systems (ICINIS), pp. 94–97. IEEE (2015)

23. Liao, X., Gao, Z., Ji, W., et al.: An enforcement of real time scheduling in Spark Streaming. In: 2015 Sixth International Green Computing Conference and Sustainable Computing Conference (IGSC), pp. 1–6. IEEE (2015)

24. Chintapalli, S., Dagit, D., Evans, B., et al.: Benchmarking streaming computation engines: storm, flink and spark streaming. In: 2016 IEEE International Parallel and Distributed Processing Symposium Workshops, pp. 1789–1792. IEEE (2016)

25. Cipolla, E., Vella, F.: Data dictionary extraction for robust emergency detection. In: De Pietro, G., Gallo, L., Howlett, R.J., Jain, L.C. (eds.) Intelligent Interactive Multimedia Systems and Services 2016. SIST, vol. 55, pp. 25–37. Springer, Cham (2016). https://doi. org/10.1007/978-3-319-39345-2_3

26. Laylavi, F., Rajabifard, A., Kalantari, M.: Event relatedness assessment of Twitter messages for emergency response. Inf. Process. Manag. **53**(1), 266–280 (2017)
27. Xie, W., Zhu, F., Jiang, J., et al.: Topicsketch: real-time bursty topic detection from twitter. IEEE Trans. Knowl. Data Eng. **28**(8), 2216–2229 (2016)
28. Raheja, V., Chopra, N.: System and method for real time text streaming: U. S. Patent 9, 535, 891[P], 3 January 2017

Network Attack and Defense Effectiveness Evaluation Based on Dematel Method

Liang Liu[1], Cheng Huang[1(✉)], Yong Fang[1], and Zhenxue Wang[2]

[1] College of Cybersecurity, Sichuan University, Chengdu 610207, China
opcodesec@gmail.com
[2] College of Electronics and Information, Sichuan University,
Chengdu 610065, China

Abstract. Taking the strategy combination of attack and defense as the basic parameter, Dematel method (decision test and experiment evaluation method) is introduced to analyze the causal relationship between attack strategies and defense strategies by constructing the matrix of "expertise". The method is used to calculate the effect of attack and defense strategies, compare the direct and indirect impact towards to target network system, thus achieve the purpose of assessing the overall impact of the offensive and defensive strategies on the target network system. Aiming at the attack and defense game theory based on Web service of a target network system, the attacker has four attack strategies: such as malicious code attack, denial of service attack. Defender has three defensive strategies: such as Web services security strategy defense, code reconstruction defense. The experimental results showed network defense in the network offensive and defensive system is the recipient of influence rather than those who are always in a passive position, cyber attacks are those who influence. Denial-of-service attacks are mainly those who affect the impact of the ability to resist other effects strong, the result is very important to study Web services-based network offensive and defensive game theory.

Keywords: Network attack and defense · Attack strategy · Defense strategy · "Expertise" matrix · Offensive and defensive effectiveness evaluation

1 Introduction

Cyber attack and network defense are the main forms of network warfare in information confrontation. The offensive and defensive effectiveness evaluation is not only an important part of the offensive and defensive game, but also a fundamental problem in the offensive and defensive game theory, which is worth to be study in-depth [1–3]. Whether it is cyber attack or network defense, the final result is related to the payment (payoff) function of both sides. However, the payment (payoff) function is not just a function to calculate the security risk of the target network system, but also a function to evaluate the strategy combination of both offense and defense sides [4–6]. Therefore, when constructing the offensive and defensive effectiveness evaluation model, it is necessary to consider the security risk change of target network system after offense or defense, and consider the impact of offensive and defensive strategy combination for

© Springer Nature Switzerland AG 2019
X. Sun et al. (Eds.): ICAIS 2019, LNCS 11634, pp. 564–575, 2019.
https://doi.org/10.1007/978-3-030-24271-8_50

target network system's overall performance. As for particular systems or specific field of research, researchers who uses decision test and experiment evaluation method must following:

a. Have ability to identify or classify the main concepts or the most influential factors in system or field.
b. All factors are put into a "direct impact" comparison matrix of paired combinations, and prioritize other factors in system by the influence level: level-0 to level-4 ("no impact" to "very high impact"). The matrix decomposition all the factors and their compared relation in system. It shows the level that each factor affects other factors in the system, and provides a clear selection order according to the influence level.
c. Describe the influence factors by causal diagram. The causal diagram shows the way each factor exerts pressure on other factors in system, and withstands the pressure from other factors in system, which includes the strength of each impact relationship.
d. Decision test and experiment evaluation method calculate the comprehensive effect of direct and indirect effect relation, then generates an overall impact score for all factors in the system. After that, it might put all the factors into a hierarchical architecture.

In this way, decision test and experiment evaluation method can provide decision makers with the effective way to achieve desired results. And it can help decision makers develop practical tactical plan and select superb strategic policy.

The paper will focus on the network offensive and defensive effectiveness evaluation related to the strategy combination. Dematel (Decision Making Trial and Evaluation Laboratory) method is a comprehensive scientific research method developed by Bottlelle Institute in 1970s. It is used to solve scientific, political, and economic issues involving multiple benefits that include a complex set of important factors. The method uses graph theory and matrix tools to analyse system factors, and analyze the logical relationship and direct influence relationship between the various factors in the system. The method calculate the influence level of each factor on other factors and from other factors, then calculate the centrality and cause value of each factor to judge the relationship between factors and make relationship strength assessment.

This paper takes the strategy combination of attack and defense as the basic parameter. Dematel method [7–10] is used to analyze the causal relationship between attack strategies and defense strategies by constructing the matrix of "expertise". The method is used to calculate the effect of attack and defense strategies, compare the direct and indirect impact towards to target network system, thus achieve the purpose of assessing the overall impact of the offensive and defensive strategies on the target network system.

2   Cyber Attack and Defense Strategies with Matrix of "Expertise"

Cyber attack and defense is a key technology in information countermeasure warfare. It includes cyber attack and defense confrontation system, network attack and network defense, etc. The cyber offensive and defensive effectiveness is determined by various factors, and two most important factors are: cyber attack strategy and cyber defense strategy. The purpose of using Dematel method to analyze the cyber offensive and defensive strategy including:

a. Understand the influence between factors
b. Demonstrate a system of factors by causal graph
c. Understand the controllability of the system
d. Have positive impact on the target cybersecurity system based on weakening the advantages of cyber attacks.
e. List the priority of cyber attack prevention strategies for decision makers.

There are three basic forms of cyber attacks, and of course, they can derivative many other forms.

(1) Confidentiality. It includes any unauthorized collection of information, such as undercover traffic analysis, in which an attacker can infer network communication content just by observing the way of communication. As for cyber attack and defense behavior based on Web application, the cyber attacks against confidentiality mainly include network sniffing, privilege elevation, etc [11, 12]. Cyber terrorism and cyber warfare are still be something that may happen in the future, but we have already lived in the "golden age of cyber spy". For example, the most famous case is the "Ghost Network", a network spy net spread across 103 countries, which aim at more than 1,000 victim computers related to diplomatic, political, economic and military information.

(2) Integrity. It refers to the unauthorized modification of information or information resources, such as databases. As for cyber attack and defense behavior based on Web application, the cyber attacks against integrity mainly include parameter modification, pattern pollution, and metadata spoofing [13–19]. Integrity attacks may destroying data for criminal, political or military purposes.

(3) Availability. Its goal is to prevent legitimate users from accessing the systems or data they need to perform tasks. This is often referred to denial of service attack (DOS attack), including a series of malware, network traffic, and physical attacks on computers, databases, and networks that connect them. As for cyber attack and defense behavior based on Web application, the cyber attacks against availability mainly include excessive payload, forced resolution, confusing attacks, etc.

As for three basic forms of web attack based on web applications, Literature [10] introduces several general defense strategies and measures. The most important viewpoint of literature is the Web services security strategy, which provides confidentiality, integrity, and authentication mechanisms for Web services. Besides, there are also defense strategies and measures such as pattern verification, pattern hardening, and code refactoring.

In the offensive and defensive game based on Web services around a target network system. Assume that the attacker's strategy set is $S_2 = [s_{21}, s_{22}, s_{23}, s_{24}]$, and the defense's strategy set is $S_1 = [s_{11}, s_{12}, s_{13}]$. Among the strategy sets, s_{21} represents sniffing attacks, privilege escalation attacks, etc; s_{22} represents parameter modification, pattern pollution, metadata spoofing, etc; s_{23} represents denial of service (Dos) attack; s_{24} represents malicious code attack; s_{11} represents Web service security defense strategy; s_{12} represents code reconstruction defense; s_{13} represents defense strategy such as mode verification and mode hardening.

The attack strategy and defense strategy constitute the Dematel method's influence matrix of "expertise". The matrix juxtaposes the cyber attack strategy and the cyber defense strategy according to the mutual influence level between the factors.

The affect worth of each single factor in the matrix affects the value based on the long-term work experience of relevant intelligence analysts and cyber offensive and defensive combat researchers. Literature [7] discusses the classification and quantification of offensive and defensive strategy, and divides the attack lethality (AL) and the defensive operational cost (OL) into three levels. In the matrix of "expertise", a factor's influence level for other factors can be referenced as follows: when the attack fatality or defensive operation cost is AL_1 or OL_1, the influence level can be selected as "none = 0" or "low = 1"; when the attack fatality or defensive operation cost is AL_2 or OL_2, the influence level can be selected as "medium = 2" or "high = 3"; when the attack fatality or defensive operation cost is AL_3 or OL_3, the influence level can be selected as "high = 3" or "very high = 4". The "expertise" matrix around a target network system based on the Web service offensive and defensive strategy is denoted as X, as shown in Table 1.

Table 1. The "expertise" matrix X based on dematel method.

	s_{21}	s_{22}	s_{23}	s_{24}	s_{11}	s_{12}	s_{13}	Direct impact
s_{21}	0	2	2	3	4	4	3	18
s_{22}	3	0	2	3	3	4	2	17
s_{23}	4	4	0	4	3	4	3	22
s_{24}	4	3	3	0	4	3	2	19
s_{11}	3	3	1	4	0	2	2	15
s_{12}	4	2	1	4	3	0	2	16
s_{13}	2	1	1	2	2	1	0	9
Affected level	20	15	10	20	19	18	14	

When conducting such research using Dematel method, researchers must be aware that while determining the impact values of different factors according to different target network systems, we must also consider the dynamic features of cyberspace, and various variables will change continuously with the passage of time.

As can be seen from Table 1, the matrix X is obviously controlled by the attack strategy, which means the attack strategy has more influence on the target network system than the defense strategy. The "direct impact" average value of cyber attack strategy is 19, and the "direct impact" average value of cyber defense strategy is 13.3. And in the "very high" influence level, the attack strategy has an overwhelming majority score compared to the defense strategy: 9 to 3. This result seems to meet people's actual senses. Nowadays, people usually feel that cyber attackers have a greater advantage than cyber defenders.

Table 2 lists the most affected factors in the matrix X by simply summing up the influence level scores of the individual factors, with the highest score being ranked first and the lowest score being ranked last. The table shows that the most influential factor in the attack and defense game based on Web services around a target network system is the ability of the attacker to maintain a denial of service attack, and the second influential factor is malicious code attack. In the defense strategy, the most effective defense against the target network system is code reconfiguration, followed by Web service security policy defense. And the least influential defense strategy is mode verification and mode hardening.

Table 2. Distinguish "direct influence" by factor.

	Factor	Direct impact
s_{23}	Denial of service attack (DOS attack)	22
s_{24}	Malicious code attack	19
s_{21}	Sniffing attack, privilege escalation attack	18
s_{22}	Parameter tampering, pattern pollution, metadata spoofing, etc.	17
s_{12}	Code reconfiguration defense	16
s_{11}	Web service security policy defense	15
s_{13}	Mode verification and mode hardening policy defense	9

Table 3 lists the most affected factors in the matrix X by simply summing up the influence level scores of the individual factors, with illustrating the susceptible of each factor from other factors in the matrix. The table shows that the highest and lowest ranking factors are cyber attack strategies. This seems to be a natural result. The highest ranking factor is mainly for the strategy of cyber confidentiality attacks, and the success of the attack is easily affected by other factors. The lowest ranking factor is the strategy for cyber availability, such as denial of service attack (DOS attack), and its strategy is relatively simple and has least affected by other factors.

This is unfortunate for the cyber defense strategy. Tables 2 and 3 show that the cyber attack strategy not only gets a higher direct impact score than the cyber defense strategy, but also has better resistant to external influences in general. In Table 3, the average score of the cyber defense strategy is 17, compared to the average cyber attack strategy score of 16.25. The denial of service attack is the most difficult to defend because it is less affected by other factors.

Table 3. Easily affected property ("Indirect influence").

	Factor	Direct impact
s_{21}	Sniffing attack, privilege escalation attack	20
s_{24}	Malicious code attack	20
s_{11}	Web service security policy defense	19
s_{12}	Code reconfiguration defense	18
s_{22}	Parameter tampering, pattern pollution, metadata spoofing, etc.	15
s_{13}	Mode verification and mode hardening policy defense	14
s_{23}	Denial of service attack (DOS attack)	10

3 Causal Diagram

The next step in the Dematel method analysis involves drawing a causal diagram, as shown in Fig. 1. Visualizing complex data can promote people's understanding. Various factors have become an interconnected system through causal diagram. The fewer parameters the system contains, the easier it is to be controlled and display by graphic. The matrix X is large, which has 7×7 (49) in size and has become a complex system. In order to fully demonstrate the role of causality diagrams and facilitate analysis, we only show the factors in the matrix X that have a "very high" influence level.

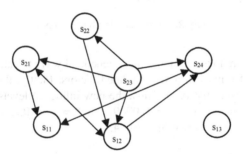

Fig. 1. Network attack and defense strategy: causal relationship.

In the Fig. 1, s_{23} (denial of service attack) is the most influential factor in matrix X. It has "very high" influence level for other four factors: s_{21} (sniffing attack, privilege escalation attack), s_{22} (parameter tampering, pattern pollution, metadata spoofing, etc.), s_{24} (malicious code attack), s_{12} (code reconfiguration defense). High direct influence. However, factor s_{13} (mode validation, mode hardening policy defense) does not affect any other factor of the "very high" level and is the least influential factor in matrix X.

The causal diagram reveals another major aspect of the interaction between factors in the system: although some factors have less influence, whether exert or suffer influence, these factors still have multiple important connections with other factors. In addition to s_{23}, the five factors (s_{21}, s_{22}, s_{24}, s_{12}, s_{11}) form a "very high" influence relationship with at least two other factors (including two), which makes them to play a very important role in the system. If the decision maker is able to take action to change the essential attributes of any factors, it will have a major impact on the whole system.

4   Calculate Direct and Indirect Effects

The causal diagram (Fig. 1) reveals that each factor not only has a direct impact on other factors in the system, but also has a indirect impact on other factors, and ultimately each factor in the system will have an impact on itself. The Fig. 2 describes the direct effects and indirect effects, which are dynamic and practical. As figure showed, the direct impact of s_{23} (denial of service attack) on s_{22} (parameter tampering, mode pollution, metadata spoofing, etc.) is 4 ("very high"). The direct impact of s_{22} on s_{21} (sniffing attack, privilege escalation attack, etc.) is 3 ("high"), and the indirect effect of s_{23} on s_{21} is 2 ("middle").

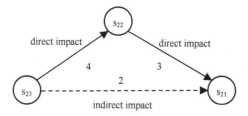

Fig. 2.   Direct and indirect effects.

Dematel method are the easiest and most beneficial ways to calculate the total point of direct and indirect impact in a set of related factors. Firstly, the matrix X is transformed into a normalized matrix D. Thus, the new influence levels are: "no = 0" = 0; "low = 1" = 0.455; "medium = 2" = 0.0909; "high = 3" = 0.1364; "very high = 4" = 0.1818. The matrix D is shown in Table 4.

Table 4.   Standardized matrix based on dematel method.

	s_{21}	s_{22}	s_{23}	s_{24}	s_{11}	s_{12}	s_{13}
s_{21}	0	0.0909	0.0909	0.1364	0.1818	0.1818	0.1364
s_{22}	0.1364	0	0.0909	0.1364	0.1364	0.1818	0.0909
s_{23}	0.1818	0.1818	0	0.1818	0.1364	0.1818	0.1364
s_{24}	0.1818	0.1364	0.1364	0	0.1818	0.1364	0.0909
s_{11}	0.1364	0.1364	0.0455	0.1818	0	0.0909	0.0909
s_{12}	0.1818	0.0909	0.0455	0.1818	0.1364	0	0.0909
s_{13}	0.0909	0.0455	0.0455	0.0909	0.0909	0.0455	0

Secondly, the matrix D is transformed into a "comprehensive impact" matrix T, where the association relation between T and D is determined by the Dematel formula:

$$T = D + D^2 + \ldots + D^n = (t_{ij})_{n*n} \tag{1}$$

In the formula, n is the number of factors, and n = 7 here. The direct impact level f_i and the indirect impact level e_j of the factors are respectively calculated by the following formula:

$$f_i = \sum_{j=1}^{n} t_{ij}, \ i = 1, 2, \ldots, n \tag{2}$$

$$e_j = \sum_{i=1}^{n} t_{ij}, \ j = 1, 2, \ldots, n \tag{3}$$

The matrix T is shown in Table 5. Indirect impact not only change the matrix, but also change our understanding of system essence. The indirect impact is the "feedback" influence, which allows each factor to effect other factors in the system, and ultimately each factor in the system will also have an impact on itself.

Table 5. "Comprehensive impact" matrix T.

	S_{21}	S_{22}	S_{23}	S_{24}	S_{11}	S_{12}	S_{13}	Direct impact
S_{21}	0.3509	0.3494	0.2697	0.4719	0.4958	0.4681	0.3703	2.7761
S_{22}	0.4621	0.2585	0.2662	0.4617	0.4517	0.4641	0.3262	2.6905
S_{23}	0.5862	0.4831	0.2336	0.5844	0.5390	0.5469	0.4280	3.4012
S_{24}	0.5356	0.4114	0.3250	0.3814	0.5258	0.4659	0.3563	3.0014
S_{11}	0.4235	0.3508	0.2130	0.4571	0.2978	0.3592	0.2995	2.4009
S_{12}	0.4773	0.3268	0.2216	0.4757	0.4363	0.2902	0.3132	2.5409
S_{13}	0.2695	0.1876	0.1463	0.2694	0.2661	0.2133	0.1347	1.4869
Indirect impact	3.1051	2.3676	1.6754	3.1016	3.0125	2.8077	2.2282	

5 Analyze the Comprehensive Impact

According to the direct and indirect impact calculated by Dematel method, Table 6 further reveals a more complete causal relationship based on the "comprehensive impact" of each factor in the system. The "comprehensive impact" is also the "centrality" of the factor, which is defined as the sum of the direct impact level (direct impact indicator) and the indirect impact level (indirect impact indicator). We mark it as c_i:

$$c_i = f_i + e_i, \quad i = 1, 2, \ldots, n \tag{4}$$

The combined calculation of direct and indirect "comprehensive impact" produces another ranking of all factors. The first five factors in Table 6 are same as those in Fig. 1, because they have the most influence (whether exert or suffer influence) with other factors. However, after increasing the indirect impact score, the order of factor rankings has changed according to the "comprehensive impact" ranking: s_{24} (malicious code attack) ranked first, and s_{23} (denial of service attack) that has the most direct impact ranked fifth; the original defense strategy s_{11} (Web service security policy defense), s_{12} (The code refactoring defense has been upgraded to the third and fourth places; only s_{13} (strategic verification, mode hardening and other strategic defenses) are still ranked last.

The final step of the Dematel method analysis is to subtract the indirect impact from the direct impact in Table 6, and draw the final standardized comprehensive impact indicator that is shown in Table 7.

Table 6. Initial comprehensive impact indicators.

Factor	Direct impact indicator	Indirect impact indicator	Comprehensive impact
s_{24}	3.0014	3.1016	6.1030
s_{21}	2.7761	3.1051	5.8812
s_{11}	2.4009	3.0125	5.4134
s_{12}	2.5409	2.8077	5.3486
s_{23}	3.4012	1.6754	5.0766
s_{22}	2.6905	2.3676	5.0581
s_{13}	1.4869	2.2282	3.7151

Table 7. Final comprehensive impact indicators.

	Dematel method analysis of comprehensive impact	Score
s_{23}	Denial of service attack (DOS attack)	1.7258
s_{22}	Parameter tampering, pattern pollution, metadata spoofing, etc.	0.3238
s_{24}	Malicious code attack	−0.1002
s_{12}	Code reconstruction defense	−0.2668
s_{21}	Sniffing attack, privilege escalation attack	−0.3290
s_{11}	Web service security policy defense	−0.6116
s_{13}	Mode verification and mode hardening policy defense	−0.7413

The number in the "score" column is also the "cause value", which is defined as the disparity between the direct impact (direct impact indicator) and the indirect impact (indirect impact indicator). We mark it as R_i:

$$R_i = f_i - e_i, \quad i = 1, 2, \ldots, n \tag{5}$$

After completing the final calculation, we found that the overall ranking of each factor is close to the initial direct impact ranking in Table 2. In fact, the ranking of the cyber defense strategy has not changed, as shown in Fig. 3.

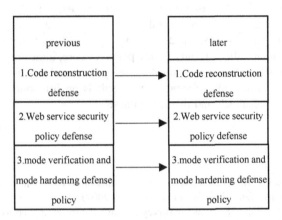

Fig. 3. Summary of network defense strategy.

It is noted that each cyber defense strategy has a negative score in the final indicator, which indicates that the network defense is suffer influence in the cyber attack and defense system rather than exert influence, and is always in a passive position.

The ranking changes of the cyber attack strategy are shown in Fig. 4. The malicious code attack strategy (s_{24}) is reduced from the second to the third; the sniffing attack and

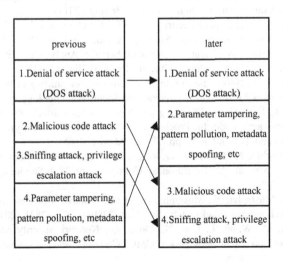

Fig. 4. Summary of network attack strategy.

privilege escalation attack strategy (s_{21}) are reduced from the third to the fourth; the attack strategies such as parameter tampering, pattern pollution, and metadata spoofing (s_{22}) are rose from the fourth to the second. The only constant is the denial of service attack (s_{23}), which always stays in the first place.

It is noted that the malicious code attack (s_{24}), the sniffing attack (s_{21}) and the privilege escalation attack (s_{21}) in the attack strategy also have negative points in the final indicator, indicating that they not only exert influence in the cyber attack and defense system, but also suffer more influence. The Dos attack (s_{23}) and parameter tampering, pattern pollution, metadata spoofing attacks (s_{22}) are not only ranked first and second in the final indicator, but also the positive score, indicating that they mainly exert influence in the cyber attack and defense system, and has a stronger ability to withstand influence from other factors. This result is an important discovery in the research of web-based attack and defense games.

References

1. Ming, X., Weidong, B., Yongjie, W., et al.: Introduction to the Evaluation of Cyber Attack Effects. National Defense Industry Press, Beijing (2007)
2. Roy, S., Ellis, C., Shiva, S., et al.: A survey of game theory as applied to network security. In: Hawaii International Conference on System Sciences, pp. 1–10. IEEE (2010)
3. Yuan, Z., Jianguo, H.: Network attack information support effectiveness evaluation method based on system entropy. J. PLA Univ. Sci. Technol. (Nat. Sci. Ed.) 15(2), 127–132 (2014)
4. Manshaei, M.H., Zhu, Q., Alpcan, T., et al.: Game theory meets network security and privacy. ACM Comput. Surv. (CSUR) 45(3), 25 (2013)
5. Liang, X., Xiao, Y.: Game theory for network security. IEEE Commun. Surv. Tutor. 15(1), 472–486 (2013)
6. Do, C.T., Tran, N.H., Hong, C., et al.: Game theory for cyber security and privacy. ACM Comput. Surv. (CSUR) 50(2), 30 (2017)
7. Zhenxue, W., Anming, Z., Yong, F., Xiaocong, O.: Information System Security Risk Estimation and Control Theory. Science Press, Beijing (2011)
8. Geers, K.: Strategic Cyberspace Security. CCD COE Publication, Estonia (2015)
9. Rongsheng, G.: Cyberspace Security Strategy. Aviation Industry Press, Beijing (2016)
10. Chuang, L., Yuanzhuo, W., Yang, W.: Network Security Analysis and Evaluation Based on Stochastic Game Model. Tsinghua University Press, Beijing (2011)
11. Tsai, C.L., Wu, T.H.: Information protection from network sniffing of bandwidths sharing. In: IEEE International Carnahan Conference on Security Technology, pp. 84–88 (2008)
12. Zhu, J., Chu, B., Lipford, H.: Detecting privilege escalation attacks through instrumenting web application source code. In: Proceedings of the 21st ACM on Symposium on Access Control Models and Technologies, pp. 73–80. ACM (2016)
13. Jensen, M., Gruschka, N., Herkenhoner, R., et al.: SOA and web services: new technologies, new standards – new attacks. In: European Conference on Web Services, pp. 35–44. IEEE (2007)
14. Kakavand, M., Mustapha, N., Mustapha, A., et al.: Towards a defense mechanism against REST-based web service attacks. Adv. Sci. Lett. 22(10), 2827–2831 (2016)
15. Zhang, H., Yi, Y., Wang, J., Cao, N., Duan, Q.: Network security situation awareness framework based on threat intelligence. CMC: Comput. Mater. Continua 56(3), 381–399 (2018)

16. Gruschka, N., Jensen, M., Dziuk, T.: Event-based application of WS-security policy on soap messages. In: ACM Workshop on Secure Web Services, pp. 1–8. ACM (2007)
17. Cheang, C.F., Wang, Y., Cai, Z., Xu, G.: Multi-VMs intrusion detection for cloud security using Dempster-Shafer theory. CMC: Comput. Mater. Continua **57**(2), 297–306 (2018)
18. Attacking and Defending Web Services (2004). http://forumsystems.com/papers/Attacking-and-Defending-WS.pdf
19. Williams, C., Mobasher, B., Burke, R., et al.: Detection of obfuscated attacks in collaborative recommender systems. In: Proceedings of the ECAI 2006 Workshop on Recommender Systems, p. 94 (2006)

Web Application-Layer DDoS Attack Detection Based on Generalized Jaccard Similarity and Information Entropy

Bo Li, Minghui Gao$^{(\boxtimes)}$, Li Ma, Ye Liang, and Guifeng Chen

NARI Group Corporation (State Grid Electronic Power Research Institute),
Nanjing, China
{libo5,gaominghui,mali,liangye,
chenguifeng}@sgepri.sgcc.com.cn

Abstract. With the rapid growth of the number of Web services, the application-layer DDoS attack problem has become increasingly serious. User behavior in the application-layer is often closely related to DDoS attacks, and the abnormal behavior of users can be analyzed to identify and discover DDoS attacks at an early stage. Firstly, the feature vectors describing user behavior are extracted by using information entropy, then the deviation degree between the feature vectors describing normal user behavior and current user behavior can be described by calculating the generalized Jaccard similarity of the feature vectors. If the deviation degree exceeds the threshold we set, it is determined that the current user behavior is abnormal. Based on the above detection process, we construct an application-layer DDoS attack detection system based on user behavior anomaly detection. Besides, we test the function and performance of the system by using the actual data set on the network. The test results indicate that the system can describe user behavior well and detect DDoS attack effectively.

Keywords: DDoS attack detection · Application-layer · User behaviors · Generalized Jaccard similarity · Information entropy

1 Introduction

In the early days of the Internet, Distributed Denial of Service (DDoS) [1, 2] did not attract enough attention, but with the rapid development and expansion of the Internet [3, 4], a variety of network attacks with rapid development momentum have brought huge economic losses and security threats to all walks of life. DDoS attack is the most harmful, the most vulnerable to attack effects and the most difficult to defend, which has become one of the important threats to network security. Actually, DDoS attack evolves from traditional denial-of-service attacks. It sends a large number of attack packets to the victim by the attacker-controlled puppet machine, consuming the victim's processing, storage and network bandwidth resources, making the victim unable to provide services normally. In recent years, many famous websites, such as Facebook, Baidu, Flickr and so on, have encountered large-scale DDoS attacks. According to a network security survey by Arbor, DDoS attacks have grown rapidly in recent

© Springer Nature Switzerland AG 2019
X. Sun et al. (Eds.): ICAIS 2019, LNCS 11634, pp. 576–585, 2019.
https://doi.org/10.1007/978-3-030-24271-8_51

years, from 100 Gbps in 2010 to 800 Gbps [5] in 2016, and to a peak of 1.7 Tbps in early March 2018 for Github's DDoS attacks, bringing DDoS attacks into the "T-bit attack era".

DDoS attack detection and defense has been a hot topic in the field of network security. Among foreign researchers, Lemon et al. proposed the SYN Cache detection strategy and proposed the SYN Cookies algorithm to detect SYN flooding attacks [6]; Udaya et al. proposed ISP collaboration methods to resist DDoS attacks through routing arbitration in multiple ISPs [7]; Based on the well-defined rules and conditions, Limwiwatkul could detect DDoS attack signals by analyzing the header of TCP packets [8]. Wang et al. realized the identification of illegal data packets by using the characteristic of constant hops in the transmission routing [9]; Li et al. modified the basic probabilistic edge sampling FMS scheme by IP tracking packet marking technology [10]. Nevertheless, most of the methods above are confined to the TCP/IP layer, which is suitable for traditional network-oriented DDoS attacks, but not enough for application-level DDoS attacks.

Intrusion detection is the discovery of intrusion behavior. By collecting and analyzing the information of some key points in the network or computer system, we can find out whether there is any violation of security policies and signs of attack in the network or system. Intrusion detection system (IDS) is a combination of hardware and software security system which can discover intrusion behavior by establishing corresponding security assistant measures according to a certain security strategy. At present, the mainstream network intrusion detection technology can be divided into misuse detection and anomaly detection technology [11]. Misuse detection first establishes a feature library of known attack patterns, and then matches the system behavior with the information in the feature library. If consistent information is found, it indicates that there is an attack in the system; Anomaly detection is the main direction of the current intrusion detection system, which was first proposed by Denning [12]. It first establishes the normal operation model, then calculates the deviation degree between the user or network behavior and the normal behavior to judge the intrusion behavior.

Applying anomaly-based intrusion detection technology to Web application-layer DDoS attack detection can provide an active defense means for Web servers, and even resist unknown types of attacks. However, the related research at domestic and abroad mainly focuses on TCP/IP layer, and the detection of application-layer DDoS is insufficient. This paper presents an application-layer DDoS detection system based on user behavior analysis, which provides a new idea and scheme for application-layer DDoS detection.

2   Detection Process

In DDoS attack detection of Web application-layer, compared with normal users, the attack traffic sent by the attacker usually has the following characteristics: (1) from the server side, the switching frequency of attacker's browsing behavior is much higher than that of normal users; (2) the request sequence of attack traffic is different from that of normal users, which includes the differences in content and order. Based on the above considerations, the following two observations are used to describe the browsing behavior of the user: (1) the sequence of objects which user requests to the server; (2) the time interval of the adjacent HTTP requests arriving at the server.

The anomaly detection system based on user behavior mainly includes two processes: one is the training process, which makes the system run for a period of time in the normal environment, and extracts the characteristics of normal user behavior using the idea of information entropy, then gets the feature vector of normal behavior and establishes the detection model of normal behavior; the other is the detection process. When the system establishes the normal behavior model, it collects the current behavior data, and also extracts the behavior characteristics using the information entropy idea to obtain the current behavior feature vector. The generalized Jaccard similarity coefficients are calculated to compare the current behavior characteristics with the normal behavior characteristics, and the generalized Jaccard similarity coefficients are used to judge whether an abnormality has occurred. If the current behavior is normal, in order to ensure the real-time and accuracy of the normal behavior model, the normal behavior feature vector should be updated; if the current behavior is abnormal, then the abnormal processing will be carried out to generate an alarm.

To sum up, the anomaly detection system architecture proposed in this paper mainly includes three stages:

(1) Data preprocessing stage: read the log file, extract typical features, and preprocess the typical features (i.e. the HTTP request sequence in the log file, the HTTP request time interval, etc.) to accord with the input of the trainin 3.3 g module;
(2) Training phase: analyze user behavior characteristics, extract normal user behavior patterns, and form normal user behavior feature vectors;
(3) Detection phase: extract the current behavior characteristics and obtain the current behavior feature vector. The behavioral characteristics of the current data are compared with the normal behavior characteristics, if it is determined to be normal, the normal behavior feature vector is updated, otherwise, the exception is handled.

3 System Design

First, the data in the log file is read, and the typical data which can represent the user's behavior is extracted. Then the data is preprocessed to accord with the input of the training module. The training system can obtain the behavior characteristics of the normal users through training the preprocessed data. When a new data (i.e. user behavior) arrives, the detection system extracts the features of the current behavior to be detected, compares them with the previous normal behavior characteristics and handles the anomalies if there are anomalies.

In the data preprocessing stage, the log files are read to extract the typical features which can describe the behavior of users, and then these features are processed to make them accord with the input of the training stage. During the training stage, the normal behavior data after preprocessing are collected and extracted by the method of information entropy. It forms the feature vector of normal user behavior to describe the normal behavior pattern of the user.

In the detection phase, the newly added data in the log file is collected as the detection data. The detection data also needs to be preprocessed to obtain the feature vectors of the detected data, and the feature vectors of the detected behavior are compared with those of the normal behavior to determine whether the current behavior is abnormal. If the deviation between them exceeds a certain threshold, it is considered abnormal, and the exception processing is performed; if the deviation is within the normal range, the behavior is considered normal, and the detected behavior is added to the feature vector of the normal behavior to update the normal behavior. Exception handling will show an exception in the current server and will display the current Jaccard similarity coefficient.

3.1 Data Preprocessing

Data preprocessing module includes data collection submodule and data preprocessing submodule.

(1) Data collection submodule

Data collection requires collection and reading of log file. For Apache web server, log files include the access log file (i.e. *access.log*) and the error log file (i.e. *error.log*). Since the access behavior of Web users is mainly in access.log, this paper selects access.log as the input of data collection. In addition, since many requests in the log file are not actively initiated by the user, for example, GET requests for images or animations (jpg, gif) on the web page. So it is necessary to filter out the user's click behavior from the log file. Therefore, in the data collection stage, in addition to reading the access log file, the data in the access log file is also filtered.

(2) Preprocessing submodule

The preprocessing submodule is mainly used to process the original user data (data in the log file) obtained by the data collection submodule so as to accord with the input of the training module. For Apache log files, some feature fields cannot be directly used as input to the training module and need to be processed to accord with the input of the training module. For example, the date and time fields in the log file are recorded in the form of: day/month/year: hour:minute:second, such as 30/Apr/1998: 22:00:04, which requires format conversion. In addition, since the time field is only accurate to the second, but more than one hundred requests can be generated in one second when DDoS occurs. Therefore, in order to calculate the adjacent time interval, data processing is needed.

3.2 Data Training

The main function of the data training module is to train the preprocessed data to form a feature vector describing the user behavior.

Set the feature vector of the normal user behavior is $x = (x_1, x_2, \ldots x_i, \ldots, x_n)$. Wherein, n is the number of fields to be detected, $x_1, x_2, \ldots, x_i, \ldots, x_n$ is the information entropy of the n fields to be detected. Therefore, the main task of the training stage is to obtain the information entropy x_i of each field to be detected.

The k-th data stream in the log file is defined as $flow_k$, and the number of data streams generated in time t is defined as N. Then the data stream $flow\_all$ generated during the normal running time t of the system can be expressed as:

$$flow\_all = \{flow_1, flow_2, \ldots, flow_k, \ldots, flow_N\} \tag{1}$$

Let $P(flow_j^i)$ be the value of the i-th field to be detected on the j-th data stream, and p_j^i indicates its probability distribution, then

$$p_j^i = \frac{P(flow_j^i)}{P(flow\_all_i)} \tag{2}$$

$$P(flow\_all_i) = \sum_{j=1}^{N} P(flow_j^i) \tag{3}$$

$$x_i = -\sum_{j=1}^{N} p_j^i \log p_j^i \tag{4}$$

From this, we can get the feature vector of normal users as $x = (x_1, x_2, \ldots, x_i, \ldots, x_n)$.

3.3 Anomaly Detection

The exception handling module mainly includes anomaly detecting submodule and exception handling submodule.

(1) Anomaly detection submodule
In the data training stage, the feature vector of the normal user is formed. In the anomaly detection stage, the detected data stream is processed first, and the method is the same as the training stage of the normal data stream. Finally, the feature vector $y = (y_1, y_2, \ldots y_i, \ldots y_n)$ of the detected data is formed. Then the feature vector of the detected data is compared with that of the normal user behavior using the generalized Jaccard similarity, and the compared result $Sim(x, y)$ is used as a basis for judging whether the current behavior is abnormal or not. The formula for comparison is as follows:

$$Sim(x, y) = \frac{x * y}{|x|^2 + |y|^2 - x * y} \tag{5}$$

When $Sim(x, y)$ is closer to 1, the more similar x and y are, i.e. the closer the current behavior is to normal behavior. If and only if when $x = y$, $Sim(x, y) = 1$, which means x is completely similar to y. Therefore, the selection of the threshold r has a great influence on the accuracy of the detection system. Too high threshold setting may produce a lot of false alarms, and too low threshold setting will reduce the success rate of detection, then many false negatives may occur.

If the current behavior is detected as normal, that is, $Sim(x, y)$ is greater than or equal to a given threshold, the current normal behavior feature vector is updated to ensure that the normal behavior feature vector is real-time and dynamic, so as to better detect possible attacks. Let the updated normal behavior feature vector be $x_{new} = (x_{new\_1}, x_{new\_2}, \ldots, x_{new\_i}, \ldots, x_{new\_n})$. Since updating the normal behavior only needs the previous normal behavior feature vector x and the current behavior feature vector y, the entropy value x_{new_i} of the updated field i only needs to calculate the average of x_i and y_i, ie:

$$x_{new\_i} = \frac{x_i + y_i}{2} \tag{6}$$

(2) Exception handling module

If an abnormality is detected, that is, $Sim(x, y)$ is less than a given threshold, then exception handling is performed. The exception handling module will pop up an alarm to prompt the system administrator an exception and display the current $Sim(x, y)$. The system administrator takes corresponding measures according to the alarm.

4 Experimental Analysis

4.1 Parameter

The relevant parameters used in this paper are as follows:

True Positive (TP) and True Negative (TN) both represent correct predictions, that is, the predicted category matches the actual category; False Positive (FP) represents the predicted category as yes while the true category is no, False Negative (FN) means that the prediction category is no while the actual category is yes. When a normal behavior is judged to be abnormal, the false alarm rate increases; when an abnormal behavior is judged to be normal, the false negative rate increases; when an abnormal behavior is detected, the detection rate increases. The result is perfect when the diagonal of the matrix is all zero.

For binary classification problems, there are the following criteria:

Definition 1. The True Positive Rate (TPR) equals TP divided by the total number of true categories of yes (TP + FN).

$$TPR = \frac{TP}{TP + FN} \tag{7}$$

Definition 2. The True Negative Rate (TNR) equals TN divided by the total number of true categories of no (FP + TN).

$$TNR = \frac{TN}{FP + TN} \tag{8}$$

Definition 3. The False Positive Rate (FPR) equals FP divided by the total number of true categories of no (FP + TN).

$$FPR = \frac{FP}{FP + TN} \qquad (9)$$

Definition 4. The False Negative Rate (FNR) equals FN divided by the total number of true categories of yes (TP + FN).

$$FNR = \frac{FN}{TP + FN} \qquad (10)$$

In this paper, ROC curve and AUC are used to evaluate the performance of the system.

Receiver Operating Characteristic (ROC) curve is a graphical method that shows a tradeoff between the true positive rate and the false positive rate. In the ROC curve, the x-axis is the false positive rate and the y-axis is the true positive rate. The point in the top left corner of the ROC curve represents a 100% detection rate and a 0% false positive rate. Therefore, the closer the ROC curve is to the top left corner, the better the performance of the anomaly detection system and the higher the accuracy of the detection.

Area under the Curve (AUC) is a method of evaluating the average performance of the model. The closer AUC is to 1, the more perfect the model and the better the performance; if AUC is 0.5, the model is completely random guessed.

4.2 Test Data

The experimental data used in this paper are mainly from the actual Web server access log data set of FIFA WorldCup 1998 [44]. The data set records more than 1 billion user requests accepted by servers during the World Cup from April 30, 1998 to July 26, 1998. Some of the data are selected for data training and testing.

Since a Web page contains multiple embedded elements and page links, when a user clicks on a Web page, it triggers the browser to automatically make a series of HTTP requests to the server. Therefore, when analyzing the server logs, we need to filter out the records of user clicking behavior. Then select typical fields that describe user behavior from the filtered records, and extract typical fields to form the original data of training and detection. In this data set, the typical fields extracted are "time" and "number of bytes transferred", that is, the feature vector of user behavior is a two-dimensional feature vector.

4.3 Experimental Results

The experiment selects 9676 HTTP request object sequences from server logs as training data and 3000 HTTP request object sequences as test data. In order to verify the system's ability to detect DDoS attacks, DDoSIM uses random IP addresses to establish 15 TCP connections with the server and sends valid HTTP requests to simulate HTTP Flood attacks; Use the tool SlowHTTPTest to establish a connection with the server every 100 s at a speed of 20 s and a content length of 8000, simulate a slow connection attack. For Flash Crowd, this paper selects some logs of the 1998 World Cup semi-finals as Flash Crowd data.

Figure 1 shows the distribution of the number of requests per minute between July 5th and July 14th, as shown in Fig. 1. It can be seen from the image that the number of requests during the non-significant match day is relatively average, and the number of requests that the server has to process is about 250/s, and the attack rate of each host can reach 100/s when the DDoS is launched. During the semi-final competition, the number of requests per minute of users increased sharply, about 20 times the normal number, which is equivalent to the occurrence of Flash Crowd. Therefore, the above experiment has a certain detection effect, and can simulate the actual scene of DDoS attacks to a certain extent.

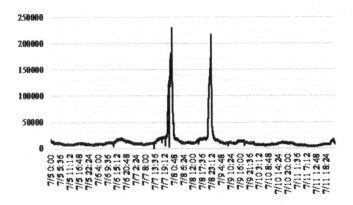

Fig. 1. World Cup user request distribution.

We select 200 sets of data for each attack and perform similarity calculations. The results are shown in Fig. 2.

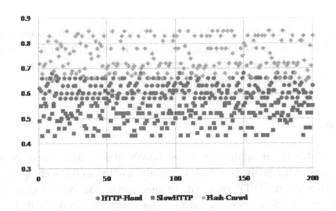

Fig. 2. Similarity for various attacks.

As can be seen from Fig. 2, the similarity value $Sim(x, y)$ also differs when different attacks occur, as shown in Table 1.

Table 1. Comparison of similarity.

Attack type	Similarity (min)	Similarity (max)
HTTP flood	0.56	0.68
Slow connection attack	0.43	0.66
Flash crowd	0.65	0.85

As can be seen from Table 1, in this experimental environment, the system can effectively identify Flash Crowd, Slow connection attack and HTTP Flood. The system sets the decision threshold to 0.85, which effectively distinguishes normal behavior from abnormal behavior.

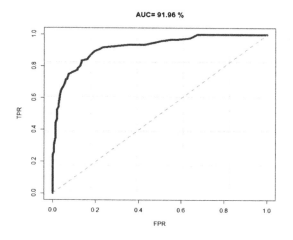

Fig. 3. ROC curve of anomaly detection system.

At that time, the ROC curve of the anomaly detection system is shown in Fig. 3. It can be seen that the curve at this time is closer to the top left corner, and the area of AUC accounts for 91.96% of the total area, indicating that the system has a high accuracy in detecting abnormal behavior.

5 Conclusion

This paper constructs an application-layer DDoS attack anomaly detection system based on user behavior analysis, which is mainly applied to the web application-layer DDoS attack based on HTTP protocol. In this paper, the typical characteristics of application-layer DDoS attacks are selected for behavior analysis, that is, the time interval of the adjacent HTTP request arriving at the server and the sequence of objects requested by the user to the server. Since some fields cannot be directly used as input to the training module, they need to be preprocessed. In the training stage, the information entropy of the fields is calculated by the relevant data of the normal user to obtain the feature vector of the normal user behavior. In the detection phase, the generalized Jaccard similarity coefficient is used to describe the difference between normal behavior and current behavior. First, the feature vector of the current behavior is calculated, and then the generalized Jaccard similarity coefficient is calculated and compared with the threshold. If the calculated coefficient value is less than the threshold, the current behavior is considered abnormal. To evaluate the effectiveness of the system, the system was tested using the real data set of FIFA World Cup 1998. The experimental results show that the system can effectively distinguish between normal user browsing behavior and abnormal behavior, and can distinguish various attack scenarios such as HTTP Flood, Slow connection attack, and Flash Crowd.

References

1. Somani, G., Gaur, M.S., Sanghi, D., Conti, M., Buyya, R.: DDoS attacks in cloud computing: issues, taxonomy, and future directions. Comput. Commun. **107**(10), 30–48 (2017)
2. Somani, G., Gaur, M.S., Sanghi, D., Conti, M.: DDoS attacks in cloud computing: collateral damage to non-targets. Comput. Netw. **109**, 157–171 (2016)
3. Cheang, C.F., Wang, Y.Q., Cai, Z.P., Xu, G.: Multi-VMs intrusion detection for cloud security using Dempster-Shafer Theory. CMC: Comput. Mater. Continua **57**(2), 297–306 (2018)
4. Xu, J., Jiang, Z.H., Wang, A.D., Wang, C., Zhou, F.C.: Dynamic proofs of retrievability based on partitioning-based square root oblivious RAM. CMC: Comput. Mater. Continua **57**(3), 589–602 (2018)
5. Network Infrastructure Security Report. https://www.netscout.com/report/
6. Lemon, J.: Resisting SYN flood DDoS attacks with a SYM cache. In: Proceedings of the BSD Conference, pp. 89–98. ACM (2002)
7. Tupakula, U.K., Harajan, V.V.: Counteracting DDoS attacks in multiple ISP domain using routing arbiter architecture. In: Proceedings of the 11th IEEE International Conference on Networks, pp. 155–460. IEEE (2003)
8. Limwiwatkul, L., Rungsawangr, A.: Distributed denial of service detection using TCP/IP header and traffic measurement analysis. In: International Symposium on Communications and Information Technology, vol. 1, pp. 605–610. IEEE (2004)
9. Wang, H., Zhang, D., Shin, K.: Detecting SYN flooding attacks. In: Twenty-First Annual Joint Conference of the IEEE Computer and Communications Societies, vol. 3, pp. 1530–1539. IEEE (2002)
10. Li, D.-Q., Su, P.-R., Feng, D.G.: Notes on packet marking for IP traceback. J. Softw. **15**(2), 250–258 (2004)
11. Zhou, L., Yu, X., Wei, Z.: Optimized detection algorithm for network intrusion based on the glowworm swarm algorithm. J. Jilin Univ. (Inf. Sci. Ed.) **33**(3), 338–343 (2015)
12. Zheng, H., Wu, Z.: User's abnormal behavior detection model. Comput. Syst. Appl. **18**(8), 190–192 (2009)

Ultra-broad Bandpass Filter Based on Composite Right-Left Handed Transmission Line Model

Yinghua Zhang[1,2](✉) ⓘ, Lei Wang[1] ⓘ, Jian Liu[1], Yunfeng Peng[1], Jiapeng Pu[2], and Guozhong Sun[2]

[1] School of Computer and Communication Engineering, University of Science and Technology Beijing, Beijing 100083, People's Republic of China
82774807@qq.com, ustb_wl16@163.com, {liujian,pengyf}@ustb.edu.cn
[2] Dawning Information Industry Co., Ltd., Beijing 100193, People's Republic of China
{zhangyh,pujp,sungzh}@sugon.com

Abstract. An equivalent circuit model based on composite right-left handed transmission line is investigated in this paper. The dispersion relation of the equivalent circuit model is derived and a zero order resonator is designed using one-dimensional composite right-left handed transmission line model. Compared with traditional filters, the ultra-broad bandpass filter can achieve any specified impedance matching bandwidth with proper adjustment. Simulation results show that the filter has perfect spectral characteristic, which can be introduced to the application of frequency selective network of oscillator. Finally we use electromagnetic simulation software to design corresponding circuit and further validate the performance of the filter.

Keywords: Ultra-broad · Composite right-left handed · Transmission line · Resonator

1 Introduction

In 1968, the Soviet scientist Veselago analyzed the electromagnetic properties of isotropic homogeneous medium theoretically, in which both permittivity and magnetic permeability effects, such as the inverse Snell effect, the inverse Doppler effect, the inverse Qilun Markov radiation, negative light pressure phenomena and so on [1]. In 2001, Itoh scholar put forward the concept of composite right-left handed transmission line [2]. He reconstructed a circuit structure to realize the theory and made the experiment of the left features. Caloz also put forward the concept of composite right-left handed transmission line [3–6]. His work

This work is supported by Intelligent Manufacturing Standardization Program of Ministry of Industry and Information Technology (No. 2016ZXFB01001), and also supported by National Key R&D Program of China (2017YFB1001600).

© Springer Nature Switzerland AG 2019
X. Sun et al. (Eds.): ICAIS 2019, LNCS 11634, pp. 586–595, 2019.
https://doi.org/10.1007/978-3-030-24271-8_52

showed that the composite right-left handed transmission line performs the left hand characteristics at low frequency, and performs the right hand characteristics at high frequency. So it is possible to develop a new high-performance device to explore its border frequency characteristics [7]. Many microwave components based on the structure of composite right-left handed transmission line are investigated by researchers [8–10,12,15–17]. In [13], the author designed a wide-band bandpass filter using composite right/left-handed transmission line structure. Liu and Wen designed a kind of high-temperature superconducting composite right/left-handed Resonator [14,18,19].

In this paper, a zero order resonator is designed using the one-dimensional composite right-left handed transmission line. The resonator can be applied widely with less restriction. An ultra-broad bandpass filter is designed based on simplified composite right-left handed transmission line model. The center frequency of the filter is 5.225 GHz, and the bandwidth ranges from 3.8 GHz to 7.65 GHz. So the frequency can be easily adjusted to adapt many application scenes.

2 Basic Theory of Composite Right-Left Handed Transmission Line Model

Figure 1 shows an equivalent circuit model of composite right-left handed transmission line. The differential length is expressed as Δx. L_R, L_L, C_R, C_L are the inductance and capacitance of the circuit.

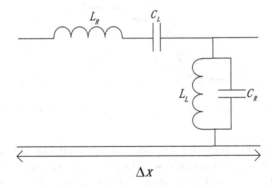

Fig. 1. Equivalent model based of composite right-left handed transmission line

The impedance and admittance of an element model:

$$Z = j\left(\omega L_R - \frac{1}{\omega C_L}\right) = j\frac{(\omega/\omega_{se})^2 - 1}{\omega C_L} \tag{1}$$

$$Y = j\left(\omega C_R - \frac{1}{\omega L_L}\right) = j\frac{(\omega/\omega_{sh})^2 - 1}{\omega L_L} \tag{2}$$

The definition of the resonator's frequency:

$$\omega_{se} = \frac{1}{\sqrt{L_R C_L}} \tag{3}$$

$$\omega_{sh} = \frac{1}{\sqrt{L_L C_R}} \tag{4}$$

Based on the theory of transmission line, the propagation constant of composite right-left handed transmission line can be written as:

$$\gamma = j\beta = \sqrt{Z(\omega) Y(\omega)} \tag{5}$$

Thus the dispersion relation of composite right-left handed transmission line is expressed as:

$$\beta_{CRLH} = S(\omega) \sqrt{\omega^2 L_R C_R + \frac{1}{\omega^2 L_L C_L} - \left(\frac{L_R}{L_L} + \frac{C_R}{C_L} \right)} \tag{6}$$

Among which

$$S(\omega) = \left(-1, \omega \le \min \left(\frac{1}{\sqrt{L_R C_L}}, \frac{1}{\sqrt{C_R L_L}} \right) + 1, \omega \ge \max \left(\frac{1}{\sqrt{L_R C_L}}, \frac{1}{\sqrt{C_R L_L}} \right) \right) \tag{7}$$

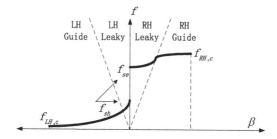

Fig. 2. The dispersion curves of composite right-left handed transmission line model

The relationship between the propagation constant and the frequency of the composite right-left handed transmission line is nonlinear, which is different from the traditional LH curve and RH curve. This characteristic can help design high or low order harmonic resonator depending on applications.

As shown in Fig. 2, the dispersion curves of the dispersion diagram are divided by the four frequency points. f_{se} is the resonant frequency of the cascade element in the circuit. f_{gh} is the resonant frequency of the parallel element in the circuit. The low cut-off frequency of the left hand curve is $f_{LH,C}$. The high-end cut-off frequency of the right hand curve is $f_{RH,C}$.

$$\left(f_{LH,C} = \frac{1}{4\pi\sqrt{L_L C_L}} f_{RH,C} = \frac{1}{4\pi\sqrt{L_R C_R}} f_{SH} = \frac{1}{2\pi\sqrt{L_L C_R}} f_{SE} = \frac{1}{2\pi\sqrt{L_R C_L}} \right) \tag{8}$$

$$\left(Z_L = \sqrt{\frac{L_L}{C_L}} Z_R = \sqrt{\frac{L_R}{C_R}} \right) \tag{9}$$

Both the left hand characteristic impedance and the right hand characteristic impedance Z_L decide the size of f_{se} and f_{gh}. $Z_L < Z_R$, $f_{se} < f_{gh}$; $Z_L > Z_R$, $f_{se} > f_{gh}$; $Z_L = Z_R$, $f_{se} = f_{gh}$. The cut-off area between f_{se} and f_{gh} disappears and the resonator based on composite right-left handed transmission line enters into a balancing state.

3 Design of Resonator Based on Composite and Right-Handed Transmission Line

In Fig. 3, the microstrip resonator is constructed of one-dimensional composite right-left handed transmission line units. Here we use two parameters, series C and parallel L to design a new type of resonant circuit. The value of C is set as 3, and both the gap width and cross width are set as 0.2 mm. The cross length is set as 1.6 mm. The parallel L is made up of short wires with a width of 0.5 mm. The height of the short wires is set as 5.25 mm. The substrate material is Rogers 4350B. Dielectric constant is set as 3.66 and the thickness of substrate is set as 0.51 mm.

Fig. 3. A new type of resonant circuit based on the method of composite right-left handed transmission line.

The simulation results of resonator unit is shown in Fig. 4. As for the S11 curve, it is clear to see that the zero order harmonic produced by the resonator is 5.8 GHz.

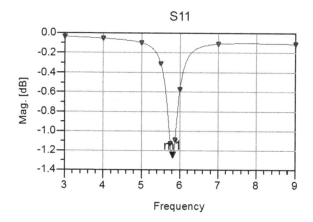

Fig. 4. The simulation results of resonator.

Simulation results show that S11 has a good frequency selective characteristic, and the central frequency locates at 5.8 GHz. Also the length of the resonator made up of right hand transmission line is 0.3 mm. However, the length of the microstrip resonator that is made up of one-dimensional composite right-left handed transmission line units is much shorter. This suggests that the new resonator is much more minimized. In other words, the circuit can be applied to application scenarios such as frequency selective network of oscillator.

4   Application of Composite and Right-Handed Transmission Line in the Design of Filters

By using the broad band characteristics of composite right-left handed transmission line, a new type of filter is designed.

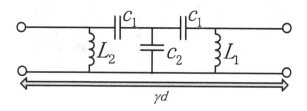

Fig. 5. The capacitive circuit of composite right-left handed transmission line.

In Fig. 5, we use C_1 and C_2 to represent serial capacitor and shunt capacitance. L_1 and L_2 denote the two parallel inductances in the circuit. The circuit has a symmetrical structure. So no matter seen from the left side or the right side, the serial capacitor C_1, C_2 and the ratio of L_1/L_2 construct the simplified structure of the basic right-left handed transmission line unit. The shunt capacitance C_2 here is essential and contributes to the capacitive characteristic of the circuit. Commonly we use clustered capacitors and inductances to combine a network, which embodies specific frequency selective characteristic. The length of guided electromagnetic wave is defined as l_g and the length d is limited with the condition of $d < 1_g/5$. The following formula expresses the dispersion relations and the characteristic impedance of composite right-left handed transmission line [11].

$$\gamma(\omega) = \frac{1}{d}\cos^{-1}(A) \tag{10}$$

$$Z_B(\omega) = B/\sqrt{A^2 - 1} \tag{11}$$

Z_B denotes the characteristic impedance of the normalized impedance of the port Z_0. ω is the frequency. Suppose the transferring function of capacitive composite right-left handed transmission line to be A and B. So that the specific expression can be written as:

$$A = \frac{\omega^2 C_1^2 L_2 + \omega^2 C_1 C_2 L_2 + 2C_1 - C_2}{\omega^2 C_1^2 L_2} \tag{12}$$

$$B = \frac{j\omega C_2 + 2C_1}{j\omega C_1^2} \tag{13}$$

Assuming that $\gamma = \alpha + j\beta$, α denotes the attenuation constant and β denotes the phase shift constant. According to formula (10), the constraint condition of transmission function is $|A| \leq 1$. When $\alpha = 0$, the size of βd range is $(0, \pi)$. The following formula is conversion formula of formula (10):

$$\beta d = \cos^{-1}(A) \tag{14}$$

According to model (12) and model (13), when $\beta d = 0$, we can get the following formula.

$$\omega = \omega_1 = \sqrt{\frac{2C_1 + C_2}{L_2 C_1 C_2}} \tag{15}$$

However, when $\beta d = \pi$,

$$\omega = \omega_2 = \frac{1}{\sqrt{C_1 L_2}} \tag{16}$$

The upper and lower cut-off frequency of composite right-left handed transmission line is written as ω_1 and ω_2. while $\alpha \neq 0$, $\beta = 0$,

$$ad = \cosh^{-1}|A| \tag{17}$$

The center frequency is written as

$$\omega_0 = \frac{\omega_1 + \omega_2}{2} \tag{18}$$

Figures 6 and 7 show typical phase shift, attenuation and impedance characteristics of capacitive composite right-left handed transmission line model. Parameters are set as follows, $Z_0 = 50\,\Omega$, $C_1 = 1.8\,\mathrm{pF}$, $C_2 = 1.1\,\mathrm{pF}$, $L_1 = L_2 = 1\,\mathrm{nH}$. In Fig. 6, the spectrum from $3.8\,\mathrm{GHz}$ to $7.65\,\mathrm{GHz}$ constructs the pass band range of electromagnetic wave propagation. Attenuation constant is 0 in the pass band, and the phase shift constant is a real number. Outside the spectrum of $3.8\,\mathrm{GHz}$–$7.65\,\mathrm{GHz}$ is the stop band of electromagnetic wave propagation. Figure 7, shows the impedance and frequency characteristic of block filter. We can easily set the value of inductance and capacitance to change the frequency characteristic of the band pass filter or block filter.

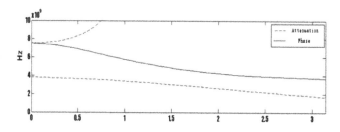

Fig. 6. Characteristics of phase shift and attenuation characteristics

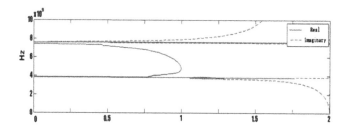

Fig. 7. Block impedance characteristics

In the paper, we use the software ADS to help the simulation of electromagnetic unit circuit. The circuit design is shown in Fig. 8.

Finally, simulation results is shown in Fig. 9. The bandwidth increases with the increase of capacitance C_1 and C_2, while the frequency ω_1 and ω_2 decrease. Also the transmission loss should catch much attention as it would increase with the increase of capacitance C_3 in the circuit. There are three important points

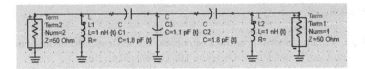

Fig. 8. The circuit diagram of lumped parameter

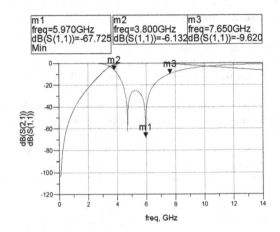

Fig. 9. The circuit diagram of lumped parameter

denoting as m_1, m_2 and m_3 in the spectrum. The central frequency on m_1 is 5.97 GHz with an attenuation of -67.725 dB, and the pass band from m_2 to m_3 exhibits a good spectrum characteristic, which can be used to design ultra-broad bandpass filters.

5 Conclusions

In this paper, we firstly introduces the theory of composite right-left handed transmission line and its features. In the frequency-selection circuit of microwave oscillator, resonator is proved to be one of the most important parts. The theory of composite right-left handed transmission line has achieved extensive attention because of its unique frequency characteristic. Based on the method of one-dimensional composite right-left handed transmission line, the zero order resonators is designed. A new ultra-broad bandpass filter is designed subsequently. The filter can be easily adjusted to realize any specified impedance matching bandwidth. Compared with theoretical method of filter design, simulation results prove that the new type structure of the band-pass filter can be easily adjusted to realize any ultra-broad bandpass filters.

References

1. Veselago, V.: The electrodynamics of substances with simultaneously negative values of ε and μ. Soviet Phys. Uspekhi **10**(4), 509–514 (1968)
2. Forooraghi, K., Atlasbaf, Z.: A wideband uniplanar polarization independent left-handed metamaterial. IEEE Antennas Wirel. Propag. Lett. **10**, 524–527 (2011)
3. Caloz, C., Itoh, T.: Application of the transmission line theory of left-handed (LH) materials to the realization of a microstrip LH Line. In: IEEE International Symposium on Antennas & Propagation, TX, San Antonio, pp. 412–415 (2002)
4. Caloz, C., Okabe, H.: Transmission line approach of left-handed (LH) materials. In: USNC/URSI National Radio Science Meeting, pp. 39–41 (2002)
5. Caloz, C., Lin-Hsiang, I.: Characteristics and potential applications of nonlinear left-handed transmission lines. Microwave Opt. Technol. Lett. **40**(6), 471–473 (2004)
6. Yang, T., Chi, P.: Folded substrate integrated waveguide based composite right/left-handed transmission line and its application to partial-plane filters. IEEE Trans. Microwave Theory Tech. **61**(2), 789–799 (2013)
7. Zhou, C., Zhang, X.: Design of UWB filter with steep rejection slope based on fractal-shaped Composite Right/Left Handed Transmission Line. In: Cross Strait Quad-Regional Radio Science and Wireless Technology Conference (CSQRWC), pp. 451–454, 21–25 (2013)
8. Mao, S., Wu, M.: A novel 3-dB directional coupler with Broadband width and compact sizeusing composite right/left-handed coplanar waveguides. IEEE Microwave Wirel. Compon. Lett. **17**(5), 331–333 (2007)
9. Lin, X., Ma, H.: Design and analysis of super-wide bandpass filters using a novel compact meta-structure. IEEE Trans. Microwave Theory Technol. **55**(4), 747–753 (2007)
10. Wang, W., Liu, C.: A novel power divider based on dual-composite right/left handed transmission line. J. Electromagn. Waves Appl. **23**, 1178–1180 (2009)
11. Pozar, D.M.: Microwave Engineering, pp. 319–325 (2006)
12. George, B., Bhuvana, N.: Compact band pass filter using triangular open loop resonator. In: Progress in Electromagnetics Research Symposium, pp. 757–760 (2017)
13. Liu, H., Wen, P.: High-temperature superconducting composite right/left-handed resonator. IEEE Trans. Appl. Supercond. **26**(3), 1–4 (2016). https://doi.org/10.1109/TASC.2016.251713
14. Ren, B., Liu, H.: Design of wide-band bandpass filter using composite right/left-handed transmission line structure. Active Passive Electron. Compon. **2016**, 1 (2016)
15. Liu, C., Chu, Q.: An UWB filter using a novel coplanar-waveguide-based composite right/left-handed transmission line structure. In: Microwave Conference, APMC 2009, Asia Pacific, 7–10 December 2009, pp. 953–955 (2009)
16. Gil, M., Bonache, J.: Composite right/left-handed metamaterial transmission lines based on complementary split-rings resonators and their applications to very wideband and compact filter design. IEEE Trans. Microwave Theory Tech. **55**(6), 1296–1304 (2007)
17. Roshan, G., Jin, C.: Dual bandpass filter using MIM based Composite Right/Left handed Transmission Line. In: 2011 8th International Conference on Information, Communications & Signal Processing (ICICS), 13–16 December 2011, pp. 1–4 (2011)

18. Kumar, P., Srinivas, J.: Three phase composite cylinder assemblage model for analyzing the elastic behavior of MWCNT-reinforced polymers. CMC: Comput. Mater. Continua **54**(1), 001–020 (2018)
19. Li, C., Li, C.: Lower bound limit analysis of anisotropic soils. CMC: Comput. Mater. Continua **54**(1), 021–041 (2018)

An Automatic Identification Algorithm for Encrypted Anti-counterfeiting Tag Based on DWT-DCT and Chen's Chaos

Qianning Dai[1], Jingbing Li[1,2(✉)], Uzair Aslam Bhatti[1], Jieren Cheng[1],
and Xiaobo Bai[3]

[1] College of Information Science and Technology, Hainan University,
Haikou 570228, China
dqn0526@163.com, Jingbingli2008@hotmail.com,
uzairslambhatti@hotmail.com,
cjr22@163.com

[2] State Key Laboratory of Marine Resource Utilization in the South China Sea,
Hainan University, Haikou 570228, China

[3] Hainan College of Software Technology, Qionghai 57400, Hainan, China
baixiaobols@163.com

Abstract. The production, distribution, and consumption of counterfeit goods have been increasing at an alarming rate around the world. In order to resist the bad influence of fake and inferior products, an automatic encryption algorithm for anti-counterfeiting tags based on DWT-DCT and Chen's chaos is proposed in this paper. Chen's chaos is used to encrypt anti-counterfeiting tags on the basis of anti-counterfeiting technology in the algorithm, and the feature vectors are extracted from the encrypted tags by DWT-DCT. Then we set up the corresponding feature vector database. The normalized correlation coefficient (NC) is used to realize the automatic identification of encrypted anti-counterfeit tags. The experimental results show that the algorithm has a good robustness to common and geometrical attacks and has a larger key space to resist attacks such as brute-force attack and other deciphering methods. The results of our experiments indicate that the proposed algorithm is satisfactory in term of the higher security and extraordinary speed as compared to the existing algorithms.

Keywords: Automatic identification · DWT-DCT · Feature extraction ·
Chaos encryption · Anti-counterfeiting

1 Introduction

With the rapid development of the market economy, fake and inferior products have become rampant and seriously infringe the rights and interests of consumers. Therefore, in order to resist fake and inferior products a lot of research has been done in the past 20 years, anti-counterfeiting technology has developed rapidly. At present, the most widely used Quick Response code [1–3] and barcode anti-counterfeiting methods can realize automatic identification fast, but it is easy to copy and imitate because of its surface printing. However, the research hotspot in the field of anti-counterfeiting at

© Springer Nature Switzerland AG 2019
X. Sun et al. (Eds.): ICAIS 2019, LNCS 11634, pp. 596–608, 2019.
https://doi.org/10.1007/978-3-030-24271-8_53

present – RFID anti-counterfeiting technology [4–6] are difficult to apply to the market due to its high cost. In view of the existing problems of anti-counterfeiting technology, some engineers have proposed a new anti-counterfeiting technology–authentic anti-counterfeiting technology [7].

Authentic work anti-counterfeiting is a new anti-counterfeiting technology which makes use of special textpatterns. Each word in the selected phrase is rotated at random angles and then carved randomly according to the text to form a unique text pattern. This kind of unique character design tag made randomly is used for anti-counterfeiting [8].

In this paper, the anti-counterfeiting tags are encrypted and stored in the cloud on the basis of authentic work anti-counterfeiting. Experiments show that the security performance of encrypted anti-counterfeiting tags is improved without loss of robustness [9]. Compared with the low-dimensional chaotic system which has the defect of small secret keyspace and low security [10, 11], the high dimensional chaotic image encryption algorithm proposed in this paper has higher complexity, randomness, and unpredictability, and able to resist attacks such as brute attack and other deciphering methods better.

2 The Fundamental Theory

2.1 Logistic Map

The logistic map is one of the most famous chaotic maps, which is a simple dynamic nonlinear regression with chaotic behavior. Even small changes in the initial value can cause significant differences in the output sequence [10–12], and it has statistical properties similar to white noise. Its mathematical definition can be expressed as follows:

$$x_{k+1} = \mu x_k(1 - x_k) \tag{1}$$

where $0 \le \mu \le 4$ and $xk \in (0, 1)$ are the system variable and parameter respectively, and k is the number of iteration. Logistic Map system works under haotic condition when $3.569945 \le \mu \le 4$. It can be seen that a small difference in initial conditions would lead to a significant difference of chaotic sequences. These statistical characteristics are the same as white noise, so the above sequence is an ideal secret key sequence. In this paper, we set $\mu = 4$, and the chaotic sequences are generated by different initial values.

2.2 Chen's Chaotic System

In 2002, Lü et al. connected the Lorenz system and Chen's system with a new three-dimensional chaotic system [13], calling it a unified chaotic system. Its mathematical definition can be expressed as follows:

$$\begin{cases} \dot{x} = (25a + 10)(y - x), \\ \dot{y} = (28 - 35a)x - xz + (29a - 1)y, \\ \dot{z} = xy - (8 + a)z/3 \end{cases} \tag{2}$$

Where $(x, y, z) \in R^3$ is the state of the system, and the system parameter $a \in [0, 1]$. The unified system has the characteristic of regional chaos. When $a \in [0, 0.8]$ the system belongs to the generalized Lorenz system; when $a = 0.8$ the system belongs to the generalized Liu system; when $a \in [0.8, 1]$ the system belongs to the generalized Chen's system [14]. Here we take $a = 1$ to construct the encryption key of the image with the chaotic sequence generated by the generalized Chen's system. Chen's chaotic system is very similar to Lorenz chaotic system, but it is not topological equivalent to Lorenz chaotic system, which is a new system with more complex dynamic characteristics than Lorenz chaotic system [15]. Here we take x(0) = 0, y(0) = 1, z(0) = 0 as the initial value; integration time step h = 0.001 [16]. The fourth-order Runge-Kutta method is used to solve the differential Eq. (2) to obtain the trajectory curve of the system phase space. As shown in Fig. 1, it can be seen that the phase space trajectory of Chen's chaotic system is composed of many discrete points, which indicates that the system has complex chaotic characteristics.

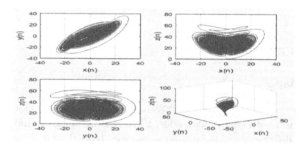

Fig. 1. Chaotic behavior of Chen's system: $x(n), y(n), z(n)$ are the Chen's chaotic sequences.

2.3   The Discrete Wavelet Transform (DWT)

The wavelet transform is a time-frequency transform, which can be used for multiresolution analysis. It is aimed to use the wavelet function to decompose the signal. The discrete wavelet transform is obtained by discretization of scale and shift of basic wavelet. Define the wavelet function $\psi_{a,b}(t)$ as the base, and the wavelet transform of $f \in L^2(R)$ by is defined as:

$$W_{f(a,b)} = \int_R f(t)\bar{\psi}_{a,b}(t)dt \quad k \in Z \tag{3}$$

Where the wavelet function $\psi_{a,b}(t)$ is obtained by translating and scaling the same base ψ.

$$\psi_{a,b}(t) = |a|^{-1/2}\psi((t-b)/a) \quad a, b \in R, a \neq 0 \tag{4}$$

Where ψ is called the base wavelet, a is the dilation factor, b is the translation factor. Mallat wavelet algorithm decomposition formula is as follows:

$$c_{j+1,k} = \sum_{n=Z} c_{j,n} \bar{h}_{n-2k} \quad k \in R \tag{5}$$

$$d_{j+1,k} = \sum_{n=Z} c_{j,n} \bar{g}_{n-2k} \quad k \in Z \tag{6}$$

Mallat wavelet algorithm reconstruction formula is as follows:

$$c_{j,k} = \sum_{n=Z} c_{j+1,n} h_{n-2k} + \sum_{n=Z} d_{j+1,n} g_{n-2k} \quad k \in Z \tag{7}$$

After one-level wavelet decomposition is performed on the image, a low-frequency subgraph and three high-frequency subgraphs can be obtained.

2.4 The Discrete Cosine Transform (DCT)

The discrete cosine transform (DCT) is similar to the Fourier transform. The discrete cosine transform takes only the real part of the Fourier transform. Discrete cosine transform has a very important property–energy concentration characteristics: After discrete cosine transform of the image, the energy is concentrated in the low-frequency part of the spectrogram. When applied to an M × N size image or matrix, the 2D-Discrete Cosine Transform (DCT) is as follows:

$$F(u,v) = c(u)c(v) \sum_{x=0}^{M-1} \sum_{y=0}^{N-1} f(x,y) \cos\frac{\pi(2x+1)u}{2M} \cos\frac{\pi(2y+1)v}{2N} \tag{8}$$

$$u = 0, 1, \cdots, M-1; v = 0, 1, \cdots, N-1;$$

In the formula:

$$c(u) = \begin{cases} \sqrt{1/M} & u = 0 \\ \sqrt{2/M} & u = 1, 2, \cdots, M-1 \end{cases}$$

$$c(v) = \begin{cases} \sqrt{1/N} & v = 0 \\ \sqrt{2/N} & v = 1, 2, \cdots, N-1 \end{cases}$$

Where M × N is the anti-counterfeiting image size, $f(x,y)$ correspond to the value of the anti-counterfeiting image at the point (x,y) and $F(u,v)$ is the DCT coefficient at the point (u,v) in the frequency. The Formula shows that the sign of the DCT coefficient is related to the phrase of the component.

3 The Algorithm

In this paper, an authentic work anti-counterfeiting tag is selected as the original anti-counterfeiting tag. It is written as $F = \{F(i,j)|F(i,j) \in [0,255]; 1 \le i \le M, 1 \le i \le N\}$, where $F(i,j)$ represents the pixel grayscale value of the original authentic work anti-counterfeiting tag. The specific algorithm is as follows. The algorithm process is shown in Fig. 2.

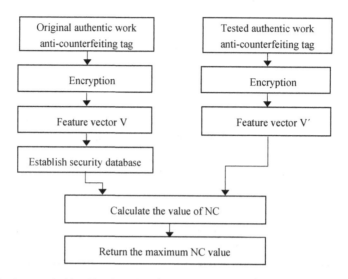

Fig. 2. Automatic identification of encryption security tag based on transform domain.

3.1 Establishing an Encrypted Anti-counterfeiting Tag Feature Database

Original Authentic Work Anti-counterfeiting Tag Encryption. The encryption algorithm flow is shown in Fig. 3.

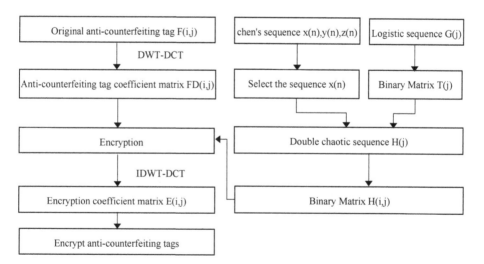

Fig. 3. Original anti-counterfeit tag encryption process.

The anti-counterfeiting tag is encrypted as follows:

Step 1: The DWT transform is performed on the anti-counterfeiting tag to obtain f_A, f_B, f_C, f_D subband wavelet coefficients.

$$\{f_A, f_B, f_C, f_D\} = DWT2(F(i,j)) \tag{9}$$

Step 2: The DCT transform is performed on wavelet subband coefficients f_A, f_B, f_C, f_D to obtain DCT coefficients $FD(i,j)$.

$$FD(i,j) = DCT2(f_A, f_B, f_C, f_D) \tag{10}$$

Step 3: Generate chaotic sequence $G(j)$ from the initial value by using Logistic map, and binarize it to get $T(j)$, from the initial $x(0), y(0), z(0)$, Chen's chaotic real-valued sequence $x(n), y(n), z(n)$ is generated by the Runge-Kutta fourth-order method. Selecting one of Chen's chaos sequences such as $x(n)$ and performing point multiplication with $T(j)$ to obtain a double chaotic sequence $H(j)$.

Step 4: Construct a binary sequence. According to the chaotic sequence $H(j)$, a threshold function $sng(x)$ is set to obtain a sequence of binary symbols, and a binary matrix $H(i,j)$ is formed according to the size of the anti-counterfeiting tag, where $1 \leq i \leq M, 1 \leq j \leq N$.

$$sng(H(j)) = \begin{cases} 1 & H(j) \geq 0.5 \\ -1 & H(j) < 0.5 \end{cases} \tag{11}$$

Step 5: Multiply the coefficient matrix with the binaries matrix to obtain $D(i,j)$.

$$D(i,j) = FD(i,j). * H(i,j) \tag{12}$$

Step 6: Perform inverse DCT transformation on $D(i,j)$ to obtain an encrypted anti-counterfeit tag $ED'(i,j)$ and obtain an encrypted sub band wavelet coefficient sequence matrix after reconstruction.

$$ED'(i,j) = IDCT\ 2(D(i,j)) \tag{13}$$

Step 7: Perform IDWT transformation on $ED'(i,j)$ to obtain an encrypted anti-counterfeiting tag.

$$E(i,j) = IDWT2(ED'(i,j)) \tag{14}$$

Figure 4 shows 8 different authentic work anti-counterfeiting tags, and Fig. 5 shows the corresponding encrypted anti-counterfeiting tags. The original image of the encrypted image is invisible to the naked eye, so it is of no value to others after the leak. In this way, the security and reliability of anti-counterfeiting tags are improved.

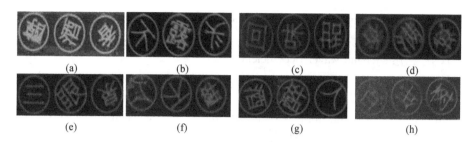

Fig. 4. 8 different anti-counterfeit tags.

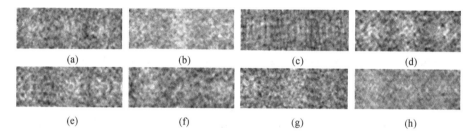

Fig. 5. 8 corresponding encrypted anti-counterfeit tags.

Key Sensitivity and KeySpace. The initial values of the chaotic system used for decryption are: $x'(0) = x(0) + 10^{-8}$, $y'(0) = y(0)$ and $z'(0) = z(0)$.. Only $x'(0)$ differs by 10^{-8} from the value $x(0)$ used for encryption, the decryption results are shown in the figure below. As you can see, the subtle differences in the key make it undecipherable. The sensitivity test results to $y(0)$ and $z(0)$ indicate that when $y(0)$ and $z(0)$ change 10^{-8} respectively, they cannot be decrypted. The above results show that the algorithm is highly sensitive to keys. If the initial value of the chaotic system is the initial key, represented by a double-precision real number that is accurate to 9 decimal places, so the key space is $10^9 \times 10^9 \times 10^9 = 10^{27} \approx 2^{90}$ which equivalents to a 90-bit long keyspace. It means that extending the key space of 90 bits long on the basis of one-dimensional chaos. Therefore, the password system is strong enough to resist attacks such as brute-force attack and other deciphering methods.

Fig. 6. When $x(0)$ error is 1×10^{-8}: (a) original anti-counterfeiting tag; (b) decrypted tag.

Extract the Feature Vector of the Encrypted Anti-counterfeiting Tag. First, we carry out the first level DWT transform of the original anti-counterfeiting tag to obtain

Table 1. Change of DWT-DCT low-frequency coefficients under different attacks to encrypted tag.

Image processing	PSNR (dB)	C1	C2	C3	C4	C5	C6	C7	C8	Sequence of coefficient signs	NC
Encrypted original image	90.19	164.09	−2.68	−0.09	0.42	0.79	−0.67	−14.13	−0.11	10011000	1.00
Gaussian noise (5%)	13.23	163.62	−2.26	−1.09	0.10	1.16	−1.18	−13.87	0.31	10011001	0.84
JPEG compression (5%)	24.28	163.72	−3.10	−0.08	0.42	1.37	−0.79	−14.58	−0.11	10011000	0.75
Median filter [3 × 3] (10 times)	26.95	162.58	−3.00	−0.72	0.17	0.18	−0.78	−14.69	−0.20	10011000	0.85
Zoom (×2.0)		325.95	−5.25	−0.22	1.00	1.88	−0.62	−28.12	−1.03	10011000	0.85
Zoom (×0.5)		83.16	−1.50	−0.08	0.05	0.15	−0.69	−7.16	0.29	10011001	0.97
Translation (2%, left)	18.32	161.91	0.81	−3.36	4.06	−2.29	4.59	−16.85	0.43	11010101	0.71
Translation (2%, down)	19.26	156.70	−2.65	−0.30	0.42	0.72	−0.67	−13.39	−0.21	10011000	0.78
Shearing (3%, Y direction)		162.27	−2.67	−0.12	0.45	0.82	−0.75	−13.80	−0.07	10011000	0.85
Shearing (2%, X direction)		162.71	−2.90	0.25	0.06	1.38	−2.23	−13.86	1.47	10111001	0.82

four subgraphs. Second, we take the low-frequency subgraph for global DCT transform. Then the low intermediate frequency coefficient is extracted after transformation. "one" is used to represent the positive coefficients, and "zero" is used to represent the negative coefficients. Thus, we can obtain a series of binary logic sequences based on the DWT-DCT transformed coefficient symbols. We take this binary logical sequence as the feature vector of the authentic anti-counterfeiting tag. In order to verify the robustness of the feature vector extracted by this method. We selected eight number of DWT-DCT to transform low intermediate frequency coefficients (C1, C2, ..., C8), which is shown in the third column to the tenth column of Table 1. The corresponding binary logical sequence is shown in column eleven of Table 1. We can see the normalized correlation coefficient (NC) of the feature vectors obtained under various types of attacks is relatively large with that of the feature vectors of the original encrypted tag from column twelve in table one. In conclusion, we can think that DWT-DCT transform after the coefficient symbol sequence can be used as tag's feature [17, 18].

Table 2. Correlation coefficients of feature vector of different encrypted tags.

	V1	V2	V3	V4	V5	V6	V7	V8
V1	1.00	0.03	−0.08	0.16	0.14	0.18	0.28	0.06
V2	0.03	1.00	0.20	0.13	0.42	−0.23	0.25	0.09
V3	−0.08	0.20	1.00	0.01	0.08	−0.02	−0.19	0.10
V4	0.16	0.13	−0.01	1.00	0.02	0.04	0.25	−0.03
V5	0.14	0.42	0.08	0.02	1.00	0.08	0.03	0.07
V6	0.18	−0.23	−0.02	0.04	0.08	1.00	−0.22	0.19
V7	0.28	0.25	−0.19	0.25	0.03	−0.22	1.00	−0.09
V8	0.06	0.09	0.10	−0.03	0.07	0.19	−0.09	1.00

The DWT-DCT coefficient unit is 1.0e+002, and the correlation coefficient is 64 bit.

From Table 2, it is not hard to find that the correlation coefficient is 1, only when the encrypted anti-counterfeiting tag is compared with their own, which is smaller when the encrypted tag is compared with other tags. Those with a minimum of −0.23 and a maximum of 0.42 are generally less than 0.5. The more similar the tag is, the greater the correlation coefficient is, and vice versa. Therefore, it can be seen that it is feasible to select the low medium frequency coefficient as the feature vector of the encrypted anti-counterfeiting tag.

3.2   Automatic Identification of Encrypted Anti-counterfeiting Tags

An anti-counterfeiting tag $F'(i,j)$ is selected to be tested, which perform the same encryption processing and feature extraction as the steps described in the previous section, and we get the feature vector $V'(j)$ to be measured. Then calculate the peak signal-to-noise ratio (PSNR) and the normalized correlation coefficient (NC). The PSNR reflects the quality of the anti-counterfeit tag image after being attacked. The higher the PSNR value, the better the image quality. The NC value reflects the similarity between the two graphs. The larger the NC value, the higher the similarity between the two graphs.

$$PSNR = 10 \lg \left[\frac{MN \ \max\limits_{i,j} \left(I_{(i,j)}\right)^2}{\sum_i \sum_j \left(I_{(i,j)} - I'_{(i,j)}\right)} \right] \tag{15}$$

$$NC = \frac{V(i) \times V'(j)}{V^2(j)} \tag{16}$$

Where $I(i,j)$ is the pixel value of each image, $\Gamma(i,j)$ is the average pixel value of the image and M and N are the rows and columns of the texture image. Finally, determine whether NC value is greater than 0.5. If the NC value is greater than 0.5, the detected maximum NC value and his corresponding tag are returned to the consumer. If the NC value is less than 0.5, a message is returned to the consumer: the product is false.

4 Simulation and Analysis

In the MATLAB R2016a simulation platform, we selected an encrypted anti-counterfeiting tag to perform a common attack and geometric attack simulation experiments. Select 1000 sets of independent pseudo-random binary logic sequences (values 1 or 0) with a length of 32 bits. Among these 1000 sets of data, one set (this article uses the 500th set of data) is selected as the embedded feature vector. The original encrypted anti-counterfeit tag is shown in Fig. 6 who is denoted as $F(i,j)$, $1 \leq i \leq 220, 1 \leq j \leq 76$. The corresponding DWT-DCT coefficient matrix is denoted as $FD(i,j)$. Considering the complexity and speed of the algorithm, we select the low intermediate frequency $4 \times 8 = 32$ coefficients for symbolic operations to obtain the feature vector V(j).

In the simulation results, the PSNR value is used to measure the quality of the anti-counterfeit tag to be tested, and the NC value is used to evaluate whether the image to be tested is the original encryption anti-counterfeiting tag. We set the determination threshold of the NC value to 0.5. If the NC value is greater than or equal to 0.5, we consider that the encryption anti-counterfeiting tag under test is the original encryption anti-counterfeiting tag. If the NC value is less than 0.5, it is determined that the encrypted anti-counterfeiting tag to be tested is not the original encrypted anti-counterfeiting tag. We can see from Tables 3, 4, 5 and 6, compared with the original anti-counterfeiting tags, the security performance of the encrypted anti-counterfeiting tags is improved without loss of robustness. The NC values between the 1000 available pseudo morph sequences and the extracted feature vector is achieved by using DWT-DCT and symbolic operation.

4.1 Gaussian Attack

Gaussian noise intensity coefficient is measured the added noise interference size in the encrypted anti-counterfeiting tag. Under the Gaussian attack, the corresponding NC valuels is shown in the Table 3. NC1 corresponds to the NC value of the encrypted image, while NC2 corresponds to the NC value of the original image. We still can extract the encrypted anti-counterfeiting image at this situation. Table 3 shows that the algorithm can resist Gaussian attack.

Table 3. The PSNR and NC values under Gaussian noise.

Noise intensity/%	1	2	3	5	10	15
PSNR/dB	19.95	16.88	15.11	13.23	10.9	9.89
NC1	0.89	0.87	0.90	0.84	0.75	0.62
NC2	0.88	0.82	0.82	0.87	0.65	0.68

4.2 JPEG Compression Attack

The percentage of the compression quality is examined the impact after JPEG compression for the encrypted anti-counterfeiting tag. Under the Gaussian attack, the corresponding NC valuels is shown in the Table 4. NC1 corresponds to the NC value of the encrypted image, while NC2 corresponds to the NC value of the original image. The encrypted anti-counterfeiting image can still be accurate to extract. Table 4 shows that the algorithm can resist JPEG compression attack.

Table 4. PSNR and NC values under JPEG compression attack.

Compression quality/%	2	5	10	20	30	40
PSNR/dB	21.50	24.28	27.33	29.83	31.05	31.65
NC1	0.79	0.75	0.85	1.00	1.00	0.90
NC2	0.75	0.75	0.93	1.00	1.00	0.82

4.3 Scaling Attack

Under the Gaussian attack, the corresponding NC valuels is shown in the Table 3. NC1 corresponds to the NC value of the encrypted image, while NC2 corresponds to the NC value of the original image. We still can extract the encrypted anti-counterfeiting image accurately. Table 5 shows that the algorithm can resist scaling attack.

Table 5. The PSNR and NC values under scaling attack.

Percentage	0.2	0.5	0.8	1.1	1.5	2.0
NC1	0.55	0.97	0.87	0.87	0.85	0.85
NC2	0.88	1.00	1.00	0.94	1.00	1.00

4.4 Shearing Attack

The encrypted anti-counterfeiting tag is sheared from the Y-axis direction. Under the Gaussian attack, the corresponding NC valuels is shown in the Table 3. NC1 corresponds to the NC value of the encrypted image, while NC2 corresponds to the NC value of the original image. The encrypted anti-counterfeiting image can still be accurate to extract. Table 6 shows that the algorithm can resist shearing attack.

Table 6. The PSNR and NC values under shearing attack.

Parameter/°	1	3	5	6	7	8
NC1	0.97	0.85	0.69	0.69	0.69	0.59
NC2	1.00	0.85	0.59	0.56	0.56	0.46

5 Conclusion

In order to improve the security performance of the anti-counterfeiting tag, the paper presents an automatic identification algorithm based on DWT-DCT and Chen's chaos for anti-counterfeit tags. The feature vector is extracted by a DWT-DCT transform from the encrypted authentic work anti-counterfeiting tags. The identification of anti-counterfeiting tags is completed by calculating the normalized correlation coefficient (NC). Experiments show that the algorithm has the good robustness to common attack and geometric attack and larger keyspace against powerful attacks. Compared with the original anti-counterfeiting tags, the security performance of the encrypted anti-counterfeiting tags is improved without loss of robustness. It has high security and simple operation. This algorithm only requires the use of the Internet and the ordinary photo-taking function to realize the identification of encrypted tags, which is convenient and fast, and it is an identification method adapted to large data [19].

Acknowledgments. This work is supported by the Key Research Project of Hainan Province [ZDYF2018129], and by the National Natural Science Foundation of China [61762033] and the Natural Science Foundation of Hainan [20166227, 617048, 2018CXTD333] and the Key Innovation and Entrepreneurship Project of Hainan University [Hdcxcyxm201711].

References

1. Wang, W.W.: Research and application of commodity anti-counterfeiting system based on mobile QR code technology. Beijing University of Posts and Telecommunications (2012)
2. Liu, S.Y.: Anti-counterfeit system based on mobile phone QR code and fingerprint. In: Intelligent Human-Machine Systems and Cybernetics (IHMSC), pp. 236–240 (2010)
3. Sun, A.D., Sun, Y., Liu, C.X.: The QR-code reorganization in illegible snapshots taken by mobile phones. In: Fifth International Conference on Computational Science and Applications (ICCSA), pp. 532–538 (2007)
4. Choi, S.H., Yang, B., Cheung, H.H., et al.: RFID tag data processing in manufacturing for track-and-trace anti-counterfeiting. Comput. Ind. **68**, 148–161 (2015)
5. Yan, B., Huang, G.W., et al.: Application of RFID and internet of things in monitoring and anti-counterfeiting for products. In: Business and Information Management (ISBIM), pp. 392–395 (2008)
6. Chen, C.L., Chen, Y.Y., Shih, T.-F., et.al.: An RFID authentication and anti-counterfeit transaction Protocol. In: Computer, Consumer and Control (IS3C), pp. 419–422 (2012)
7. Zhang, Y.: Research on the automatic identification algorithm of genuine and anti-counterfeiting tags. Hainan University (2017)
8. Li, F.: Text security, bar code combination identification structure and methods, China, 2012101185260 [P] (2012)
9. Zhang, Y., Li, J.B.: An automatic identification authentic work anti-counterfeiting algorithm based on DWT-DCT. Int. J. Secur. Appl. **10**, 135–144 (2016)
10. Liao, X.F.: Analysis and improvement of image encryption algorithm based on Logistic chaotic system. Softw. Guide **16**(5), 39–41 (2017)
11. Rostami, M.J., Shahba, A., Saryazdi, S., et al.: A novel parallel image encryption with chaotic windows based on logistic map. Comput. Electr. Eng. **62**, 348–400 (2017)

12. Sabery K, M., Yaghoobi, M.: A new approach for image encryption using chaotic logistic map. In: Proceedings of 2008 International Conference of the IEEE on Advanced Computer Theory and Engineering, pp. 585–590 (2008)
13. Lü, J.H., Chen, G.R., Zhang, S.C.: The compound structure of a new chaotic attractor. Chaos, Solitons Fractals **14**(5), 669–672 (2002)
14. Liu, C.X., Liu, T., Liu, L., et al.: A new chaotic attractor. Chaos, Solitons Fractals **22**(5), 1031–1038 (2004)
15. Lü, J.H., Lu, A., Chen, S.H.: Chaos Time Series Analysis and Its Application. Wuhan University Press, Wuhan (2002)
16. Zhu, C.X., Chen, Z.G., et al.: A new image encryption algorithm based on generalized Chen's chaotic system. J. Cent. S. Univ. (Nat. Sci. Ed.) **37**, 1142–1148 (2006)
17. Cheng, J.R., Xu, R.M., Tang, X.Y., et al.: An abnormal network flow feature sequence prediction approach for DDoS attacks detection in big data environment. Comput. Mater. Contin. **55**(1), 95–119 (2018)
18. Cheng, J.R., Zhou, J.H., Liu, Q., Tang, X.Y., Guo, Y.X.: A DDoS detection method for socially aware networking based on forecasting fusion feature sequence. Comput. J. **61**(7), 959–970 (2018). https://doi.org/10.1093/comjnl/bxy025
19. Cui, J.H., Zhang, Y.Y., Cai, Z.P., et al.: Securing display path for security-sensitive applications on mobile devices. CMC: Comput. Mater. Contin. **55**(1), 017–035 (2018)

Security Analysis and Improvement of Elliptic Curve Digital Signature Scheme

Yamin Li[(⊠)] and Ping Zhang

School of Mathematics and Statistics, Henan University of Science
and Technology, Luoyang 471023, China
2390043823@qq.com, zhangping76@126.com

Abstract. In digital signature, the digital signature based on elliptic curve cryptosystem has higher security. Elliptic curve cryptography (ECC) is the transfer of discrete logarithmic cryptography to elliptic curve. Compared with other cryptosystems, elliptic curve cryptography has the advantages of short key, small storage space, narrow bandwidth and high security. This paper focuses on the security of elliptic curve digital signature scheme. By analyzing the signature scheme of Zhang Qingsheng et al., we find that this scheme has the risk of replacing messages to forge the signature. In view of this risk, this paper proposes an improved scheme based on elliptic curve discrete logarithm problem. Furthermore, in this paper, we analyze the security of our improved scheme against the random number attack, the unknown plaintext and ciphertext attack and the replacement messages forged signature attack.

Keywords: Digital signature · Elliptic curve · Random number attack · Random number attack

1 Introduction

With the continuous development and popularization of the network, computer viruses, hackers, electronic crimes and electronic eavesdropping incidents emerge one after another, causing great hidden dangers to people's life. They have caused great potential problems to people's lives. Therefore, it is necessary to strengthen network security awareness, minimize security vulnerabilities and minimize the loss caused by network security [1].

Digital signature is one of the research hotspots in the field of network security. Digital signature mechanism is one of the means to guarantee the network information security, which widely used in cloud environment [2]. It can solve the problem of signature forgery, repudiation, impersonation and tampering [3]. Digital signature has important applications in the realization of identity authentication, data integrity, nonrepudiation and other functions. For simulating the manual signature or seal of daily life in the network environment, digital signature was designed. With elliptic curve cryptosystem (ECC) based security scheme, the security level of the digital signature will be increased [4]. The elliptic curve cryptosystem is the transfer of discrete logarithm over the elliptic curve. It is a kind of cryptosystem, which is obtained by the finite group of elliptic curves on the finite field instead of the finite cyclic group

© Springer Nature Switzerland AG 2019
X. Sun et al. (Eds.): ICAIS 2019, LNCS 11634, pp. 609–617, 2019.
https://doi.org/10.1007/978-3-030-24271-8_54

based on the discrete logarithm problem cryptosystem. Its security is based on the difficulty of solving the elliptic curve discrete logarithm problem (ECDLP). Therefore, strictly speaking, it is not a new cryptosystem. It is only an elliptic curve version of the existing cryptosystem. The history of the elliptic curve cryptosystem is not very long. However, because of the outstanding advantages of the elliptic curve cryptosystem, it has gained great attention and widely spread in the cryptography.

In 2008, Zhang and others improved the modular multiplication operation, and proposed a new elliptic curve digital signature scheme [5]. In the same year, Pan [6] proposed a new digital signature scheme based on elliptic curve, which has no model inverse operation. This improvement greatly improves the efficiency of the signature. Yang and others [7] also proposed an improved elliptic curve digital signature scheme, which can effectively resist birthday attacks and improve the security of digital signature. In 2009, Wu and others [8] improved the elliptic curve digital signature algorithm, and the improved algorithm needed no inverse operation. Compared with the traditional algorithm, it has a smaller time complexity. In 2011, Chen and others improved the ECDSA algorithm, and proposed a new elliptic curve digital signature scheme [9]. In 2014, Yan and others [10] designed a fast segmented scalar multiplication algorithm. The application of the algorithm improved the efficiency of the ECDSA scheme. In 2015, Huiyan and others [11] designed a digital signature scheme with forward security, which effectively reduced the loss of key disclosure. In 2016, Zhou [12] designed an elliptic curve digital signature scheme with message recovery function. The scheme not only can resist forgery signature attacks, but also has forward security. In 2017, Han et al. proposed a method to verify the integrity of election data [13]. This method is based on SM2 elliptic curve public key cryptography algorithm and improved SM3 cryptography hash algorithm. In the same year, Li et al. [14] improved an elliptic curve digital signature scheme because of its serious security vulnerabilities. Based on elliptic curve cryptography, Zhang et al. [15] proposed a new ring signature scheme based on ECC concealed identity. In 2018, Li [16] constructed an identity-based multi-party simultaneous signature scheme on ECC.

This paper mainly studies the algorithm of Zhang et al. [5], and finds that this algorithm has the risk of replacing messages to forge the signature. This paper analyzes the reasons and puts forward a new improvement scheme.

2   The Description of the Algorithm of Zhang Qingsheng et al.

2.1   Parameter Selection

We select the security parameters $D = (p, F_p, a, b, G, n, h)$ firstly. We enter the size p of the finite field, and then the system randomly generates a secure elliptic curve $E : y^2 = x^3 + ax + b \pmod{p}$ on the F_p. We look for a base point G on the elliptic curve, and G can't be changed arbitrarily. We select a prime number $n > 2^{160}$ and $n > 4\sqrt{p}$, $nG = O$, $h = \frac{\#E(F_p)}{n}$ ($h \ll n$). $SHA - 1$ is a secure hash function. We select the private key $d \in [1, n-1]$ and Compute the public key $Q = dG$. If $Y = O$, reselect the private key. We open $D = (p, F_p, a, b, G, n, h)$, Q, $SHA - 1$ and keep d secret.

2.2   Signature Generation

The signer A uses the above parameters to sign the message m. A does the following:

(1) Select a random or pseudorandom integer $k \in [1, n-1]$.
(2) Compute $kG = (x_1, y_1), r = x_1 \bmod n$.
(3) Compute $e = SHA - 1(m)$.
(4) Compute $s = (er)^{-1}(k+d) \bmod n$.
(5) The signature for the message m is (r, s).

2.3   Signature Verification

Verifier B verifies that (r, s) is the signature of A for message m. B does the following:

(1) Verify $r, s \in [1, n-1]$. if not, return and reject the signature.
(2) Compute $e = SHA - 1(m)$.
(3) Compute $w = (er)s \bmod n$, $(er)s = (k+d) \bmod n$.
(4) Compute $wG - Q = (x_2, y_2)$.
(5) Compute $v = x_2 \bmod n$.
(6) Accept the signature if and only if $v = r$.

2.4   Security Analysis

In the signature equation $s = (er)^{-1}(k+d) \bmod n$ of this algorithm, the signature forgery can be achieved by replacing the original message m with another message m'. The reasons are as follows: Since s, e and r are known, $(k+d) \bmod n$ can be obtained from $s = (er)^{-1}(k+d) \bmod n$. $s' = (e'r)^{-1}(k+d) \bmod n$ can be Computed by calculating $e' = SHA - 1(m')$. Thus a forged signature (r, s') is obtained.

In addition, there is such an error in the fast signature equation $s = k - 1 - rd \bmod n$ of Gao [1].

3   A New Elliptic Curve Digital Signature Scheme

3.1   Parameter Selection

First we select the security parameters $D = (p, F_p, a, b, G, n, h)$. We enter the size p of the finite field, and then the system randomly generates a secure elliptic curve E : $y^2 = x^3 + ax + b \pmod{p}$ on the F_p. We look for a base point G on the elliptic curve, and G can't be changed arbitrarily. We select a prime number $n > 2^{160}$ and $n > 4\sqrt{p}$, $nG = O$, $h = \frac{\#E(F_p)}{n}$ $(h \ll n)$. $SHA - 1$ is a secure hash function, and O denotes a point at infinity. We open $D = (p, F_p, a, b, G, n, h)$, $SHA - 1$.

3.2 Key Generation

(1) Select a random or pseudorandom integer $x \in [1, n-1]$.
(2) Compute $Y = xG$, $Z = x^{-1}G$. if $Y = O$ or $Z = O$, go to step (1).
(3) The public key is (Y, Z), the private key is x.
(4) Make public key (Y, Z) is open and private key x is confidential.

3.3 Signature Generation

The signer A uses the above parameters to sign the message m. A does the following:

(1) Select a random or pseudorandom integer $k \in [1, n-1]$.
(2) Compute $R = kG = (x_1, y_1)$, $r = x_1 \bmod n$, if $r = 0$, go to step (1).
(3) Compute $e = H(m)$.
(4) Compute $s = x^{-2}(xke - re^2) \bmod n$ (For the x^{-2}, we can improve the signature speed by preprocessing). If $s = 0$, go to step (1).
(5) The signature for the message m is (r, s).

3.4 Signature Verification

Verifier B verifies that (r, s) is the signature of A for message m. B does the following:

(1) Verify r, s in $[1, n-1]$. if not, return and reject the signature.
(2) Compute $e = H(m)$.
(3) Compute $w = e^{-1}$, $u_1 = ws \bmod n$ and $u_2 = re \bmod n$.
(4) Compute $X = u_1 Y + u_2 Z = (x_2, y_2)$.
(5) if $X = O$, reject the signature.
(6) Compute $v = x_2 \bmod n$.
(7) accept the signature if and only if $v = r$.

3.5 Correctness Proof of the Scheme

If $v = r$, then

$$R = u_1 Y + u_2 Z = (se^{-1})Y + reZ \tag{1}$$

That is

$$kG = xse^{-1}G + x^{-1}reG \tag{2}$$

Then we can divide it by G:

$$k = (xse^{-1}) + x^{-1}re \bmod n \tag{3}$$

Through the formula transformation, we can get:

$$s = kx^{-1}e - x^{-2}re^2 \bmod n \tag{4}$$

On the right side of the equal sign, we extract the common factor x^{-2} to get:

$$s = x^{-2}(xke - re^2) \bmod n \tag{5}$$

4 Security Analysis

Digital signatures mainly face the following threats [17]:

- An attacker obtains the signer's private key by attacking a random number or other attacks.
- The attacker forges the signature without the signer's private key and has some control over the data which be signed.
- The attacker falsifies the signature without the signer's private key, but does not have any control over the data which be signed.

The ideal signature protocol should have good resistance to all the above threats.

4.1 Prevent Random Number Attack

The ECDSA scheme cannot resist random number attack. Many people have mentioned that it is not possible to use the same random number (The probability is very small) when different messages are signed with the same signature scheme [17], because once the random number is the same, the private key can be solved by a two order linear equation group, which causes the key leak. If the same random number is used when using the ECDSA scheme to sign different messages, then the $k = (s_2 - s_1)^{-1}(e_2 - e_1) \bmod n$ can be solved according to the equation group $\begin{cases} s_1 k = e_1 + xr \bmod n \\ s_2 k = e_2 + xr \bmod n \end{cases}$, and then the private key $x = r^{-1}(s_1 k - e_1) \bmod n$ is solved. In fact, some schemes are not safe against the extension of this attack method even if every time use different random Numbers. For example, let $u = xe + s \bmod n$, where x is the private key, s is the signature result, and e is the hash function of the signed message or the signed message. Then the value of u in the interval $[0, n-1]$ is random. The attacker only needs to compute $eY + sG$. If $e_1 Y + s_1 G = e_2 Y + s_2 G \bmod n$ is established in the signature to the message m_1 and m_2, then $u_1 = u_2 \bmod n$ can be deduced. Therefore, $e_1 x + s_1 = e_2 x + s_2 \bmod n$ is true, so that we get the private key $x = (e_1 - e_2)^{-1}(s_2 - s_1) \bmod n$.

The improved scheme can resist random number attack. If only two times the same random number is used when using the improved scheme to sign a signature, since $\begin{cases} s_1 = x^{-1}ke_1 - x^{-2}re_1^2 \bmod n \\ s_2 = x^{-1}ke_2 - x^{-2}re_2^2 \bmod n \end{cases}$ is a quadratic system of equations, the square root of the modular n needs to be computed in order to solve for x, whereas The method of factor decomposition can only be used to compute the n-square root problem. However, the factorization of large numbers is a difficult mathematical problem. In addition, it is impossible to solve the improved scheme through the promotion of the above attack method. It is necessary to compute whether a random variable with different signature will take the same value when cracking the improvement scheme. This probability is so small that the amount of calculation is very large, and it is more difficult than to compute the discrete logarithm directly. Suppose the probability that u values on interval $[0, n-1]$ is uniformly distributed, according to the conclusion of the birthday attack [18], when the probability of $u_1 = u_2$ in a time different messages is 0.5, $a \approx 1.17 sqrt(n)$ is established, which is a very large number. Without the direct eY and sG values, the computational difficulty is very large. Therefore, the improvement scheme can prevent the attack against random numbers.

4.2   Unknown Plaintext and Ciphertext Attack [19]

(1) It is impossible for an attacker to solve x directly by $Y = xG$, because it needs to solve the mathematical problem of the discrete logarithm on the elliptic curve.
(2) It is impossible for an attacker to forge the signature (s', r') of m' by verification equation $kG = xse^{-1}G + x^{-1}reG$, because the attacker needs to determine r'(or s') before solving s'(or r'). It is necessary to solve the mathematical problem of the discrete logarithm on the elliptic curve.

4.3   Anti-replacement Messages Forged Signature Attack Analysis

Because the signature equation involves e^2 term, so it is impossible for an attacker to replace e in $s = x^{-2}(xke - re^2) \bmod n$ into e' through add, subtract, multiply and divide operations. In addition, it is difficult to guarantee $r' = x \bmod n$ (where $k'G = (x, y)$) while replacing.

The security analysis of the improved scheme shows that the security of the improved scheme is higher than that of the ECDSA scheme. Compared with the algorithm of Zhang Qingsheng et al., the improved scheme involves e and e^2, which greatly increasing its resistance to alternative message attacks. In addition, the improved scheme involves x and x^2, which reduces the risk of the private key being cracked by the same random number attack.

5   Efficiency Analysis

Assuming that the data size of the modular multiplication operation is n, we analyze from the angle of arithmetic operation, the complexity of one doubling operation is $O(n^2)$, the complexity of one model inverse operation is $O(9n^2)$ (equivalent to 9 times the doubling operation), the complexity of one modular multiplication is $O(n^2 \log_2 n)$ [20]. We compared the computation of the improved scheme, the computation of the Zhang Qingsheng and others schemes, and the computation the ECDSA scheme.

MM denotes modular multiplication operation, MI denotes model inverse operation, and kP denotes $P + P + \cdots + P$(with k summands). The results are shown in Table 1.

Table 1. Efficiency comparison of ECDSA, Zhang and Improvement

Scheme	Key Generation			Signature			Verification			Length
	MM	MI	kP	MM	MI	kP	MM	MI	kP	
ECDSA	0	0	1	2	1	1	2	1	2	$2|n|$
Zhang	0	0	1	2	1	1	2	0	1	$2|n|$
Improvement	0	1	2	6	1	1	2	1	2	$2|n|$

The chart shows that the total computation of ECDSA is $N_1 = O[(4 \log_2 n + 22)n^2]$, the total computation of the scheme of Zhang Qingsheng et al. is $N_2 = O[(4 \log_2 n + 12)n^2]$, the total computation of Improvement scheme is $N_3 = O[(8 \log_2 n + 32)n^2]$. The three complexity graphs are shown in Fig. 1.

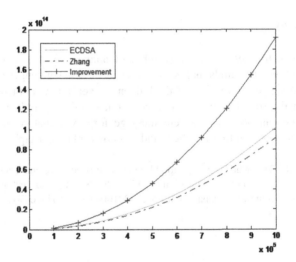

Fig. 1. Comparison of three signature complexities

In order to test the efficiency of signature, we use MATLAB programming to simulate the signature algorithm. Hardware environment: CPU is 2.2G, memory is 4G. Parameter set $(p, a, b, G, n, h, k) = (211, 1, 1, (53, 233), 233, 1, 50)$. Software environment: MATLAB 7.0. We use these three schemes to sign the same file, which takes time as shown in Table 2.

It can be seen from the above table that the three schemes have the same signature length. Although the time spent on the improved scheme is longer than that on Zhang and others in the signature verification phase, but its signature verification efficiency is

Table 2. Comparison of running time between three signature algorithms (unit: second)

Scheme	Public Keys Generation	Signature	Verification
ECDSA	0.007072	0.103254	0.110437
Zhang	0.008064	0.104372	0.003960
Iprovement	0.043791	0.155588	0.109231

not less than the ECDSA scheme. The main operations to affect the complexity are modular multiplication and inverse operation. Improvement scheme has a model inverse operation on the public key generation than the other two schemes, but this can improve the speed by preprocessing. In addition, in the signature generation stage, although improvement scheme has 4 modular multiplication operations than either Zhang Qingsheng et al. schemes or ECDSA schemes, the improved scheme not only prevents message forgery signature attacks, but also prevents random number attacks. In general, the improvement scheme enhances security and sacrifices speed appropriately. Therefore, this scheme is suitable for applications that require high security but do not pay attention to efficiency.

6 Conclusions

Firstly, this paper focuses on the research and analysis of the scheme of Zhang Qingsheng and others, and finds that the scheme has the hidden danger of replacing the messages forged signature. In view of the hidden danger, a new improvement scheme is proposed and the security analysis is carried out in this paper. It is found that the improved scheme can not only prevent message forgery signature attacks, but also prevent attacks against random numbers and unknown plaintext cipher text attack.

Acknowledgement. This work was supported by the grant of Science and Technology Projects of Henan Provincial Department of Education (17A520006), Science and Technology Projects of Henan Science and Technology Department (162102210047, 162102310474).

References

1. Gao, W., Zhang, G., Wang, X.: An improved elliptic curve digital signature algorithm. J. Nat. Sci. Heilongjiang Univ. **26**(06), 775–780 (2009)
2. Wu, F., Zhang, X., Yao, W., et al.: An advanced quantum-resistant signature scheme for cloud based on eisenstein ring. CMC: Comput. Mater. Contin. **56**(1), 19–34 (2018)
3. Ren, Z.G., Zhai, D.: Selection of security elliptic curve in finite field GF(q). Inf. Electron. Eng. **7**(05), 493–496 (2009)
4. Gopinath, V., Bhuvaneswaran, R.S.: Design of ECC based secured cloud storage mechanism for transaction rich applications. CMC: Comput. Mater. Contin. **57**(2), 341–352 (2018)
5. Zhang, Q., Guo, B., Xu, S., et al.: Fast elliptic curve signature verification algorithm. Comput. Eng. Des. **29**(17), 4425–4427 (2008)

6. Pan, X.: A new digital signature scheme based on elliptic curve. Appl. Comput. Syst. **17**(1), 35–37 (2008)
7. Yang, Q., Xin, X., Ji, W.: Digital signature and proxy digital signature based on elliptic curve. Comput. Eng. **34**(23), 147–149 (2008)
8. Wu, M., Liu, R., Zhang, F.: An improved algorithm for elliptic curve digital signature based on wireless LAN. Commun. Technol. **42**(04), 108–110 (2009)
9. Chen, L., You, L.: Optimization and design of elliptic curve digital signature algorithm. Electron. Dev. **34**(1), 89–93 (2011)
10. Yan, L., Lu, C.: An elliptic curve digital signature scheme based on fast scalar multiplication algorithm. Electron. Sci. Technol. **27**(4), 23–26 (2014)
11. Huiyan, C., Yong, Y., Zongjie, W., et al.: A forward secure digital signature based on elliptic curve. Telecommun. Sci. **31**(10), 99–102 (2015)
12. Zhou, K.: Analysis and improvement of an elliptic curve message recovery digital signature scheme. J. Northwest Normal Univ. (Nat. Sci. Ed.) **52**(4), 38–40 (2016)
13. Han, J., Cui, Z.: Data consistency verification method for election system. J. Comput. Appl. **37**(S2), 52–56 (2017)
14. Li, J., Miao, X.: Analysis and improvement of forward-secure digital signature scheme. J. Jilin Univ. (Inf. Sci. Ed.) **35**(6), 608–611 (2017)
15. Zhang, W., Gao, D., Li, Y.: Hidden identity ring signature scheme using ECC. Comput. Eng. Appl. **53**(23), 88–90 (2017)
16. Li, Y.: Simple analysis of ID-based multi-party simultaneous signature scheme on ECC. Kexue yu Xinxihua (2), 35–36 (2018)
17. Qin, X., Xin, Y., Lu, G.: Design and implementation of digital signature system based on elliptic curve. Comput. Eng. Appl. **39**(28), 151–155 (2003)
18. Li, X., Zhao, H., Wang, J., et al.: Improvement of ElGamal digital signature algorithm based on adding a random number. J. Northeast. Univ. (Nat. Sci. Ed.) **31**(08), 1102–1104, 1112 (2010)
19. Zhang, X.: Digital Signature Principle and Technology, p. 95. Mechanical Industry Press, Beijing (2004)
20. Han, Y., Yang, X., Hu, J., et al.: Improved ECDSA signature algorithm. Comput. Sci. **30**(10 Supplement), 377–378 (2003)

Risk Taking Behavior in Crowdsourcing Adoption: The Case of Witkey

Jie Jian[1($\boxtimes$)], Xiaoming Yu[1], and Yufei Yuan[2]

[1] Chongqing University of Posts and Telecommunications,
Nan'an District, Chongqing, People's Republic of China
jianjie@cqupt.edu.cn
[2] DeGroote School of Business, McMaster University, Hamilton, Canada

Abstract. Purpose: Crowdsourcing is a process of obtaining needed services, ideas, or products by soliciting contributions from a large group of people, and especially from an online community, rather than from traditional employees or suppliers. It has been popular in E-business supply chain management This paper studies the risk raking behavior in crowd sourcing adoption and tries to find out how the perceived risks of contract-issuing party would influence their consumption behavior. We constructs a theoretical model for perceived risk of contract-issuing party to characterize how perceived risk of contract-issuing party serves the E-commerce transactions and the antecedents of the perceived risk, taking Witkey as a case. The model comprises four concepts of perceived risk, namely perceived financial risk, perceived time risk, perceived services risk, perceived psychosocial risk, which influence the transaction online. We posit the hypothesis that factors of website, such as authenticity, convenience and safety, are assumed to decrease the perceived risk of contract-issuing party, which accordingly influence crowdsoucing adoption.

Methodology: The paper tests the hypothesis with the questionnaires on the interaction of Witkey and contract-issuing party. 325 questionnaire responses were collected from contract-issuing party and Witkeys and employees of the Witkey website. Questionnaire response validation and reliability were tested and structural equation modelling was used to analyze the data.

Findings: The results show that most of the hypotheses were supported. Specifically, adopting intention was negatively affected by contract-issuing part's perceived risks had significant effects on satisfaction. Both website authenticity and website convenience had significant negative impact on the four dimensions of contract-issuing part's perceived risks. Website security had significant negative impact on three of contract-issuing part's perceived risks (perceived financial risk, perceived time risk and perceived services risk) while only website authenticity was found to have no significant relation to contract-issuing part's perceived psychosocial risk.

Contribution: On the theoretical side, our study extended the perceived risk research on the contract-issuing parts in Witkey mode, i.e. this study added website factors as pre-factors of the contract-issuing part's perceived risk, and explored the dimensions of contract-issuing part's perceived risk. It fills a gap in the contract-issuing part perceived risk theory under Witkey mode, and laying a solid foundation for further in-depth study. From a practical perspective, the results of our study provide implications for Witkey websites which want to improve their service quality and enhance their competitive advantage. It is

© Springer Nature Switzerland AG 2019
X. Sun et al. (Eds.): ICAIS 2019, LNCS 11634, pp. 618–631, 2019.
https://doi.org/10.1007/978-3-030-24271-8_55

necessary to promote techniques to protect contract-issuing part's personal information, improve the payment system, and simplify the payment process with signs to remind users, which can decrease contract-issuing part's perceived risks.

Keywords: Witkey mode · Contract-issuing party · Perceived risk

1 Introduction

Crowdsourcing is the process of obtaining needed services, ideas, or content by soliciting contributions from a large group of people, and especially from an online community, rather than from traditional employees or suppliers. It combines the efforts of numerous self-identified volunteers or part-time workers, through using crowd-based outsourcing to apply to specific requests. The word "crowdsourcing" was coined in 2006 (Howe 2006), now there are some common categories of crowdsourcing that can be used effectively in the commercial world, such as crowdvoting, crowdfunding, microwork, creative crowdsourcing, wisdom of the crowd, and inducement prize contests (Howe 2008). At the same time, a wide range of activities crowdsourcing websites had been applied, for example, zhubajie.com is the biggest crowdsourcing website with more than 9 million users in the world. LinkedIn.com has become the biggest competitor to headhunters, InnoCentive.com helped Procter & Gamble increase the proportion of the innovation outside from the original 15% to 50%, while the R&D's capabilities increased by 60%. Wikipedia.org average monthly page views reached 19 billion times. IstockPhoto.com made many professional photographers feel the threat of unemployment. Aaron Koblin used Mechanical Turk to collect 10,000 drawings of sheep from contributors around the world. Additionally, 100 million drivers are using INRIX, which collects users' driving times to provide better GPS routing and real-time traffic updates. Crowdsourcing has attracted great attention from both practitioners and scholars over the years (Zhao and Zhu 2012).

2 Literature Review and Hypotheses

2.1 The Structure of Witkey Site

The main research directions for IS scholars are from three perspectives—the Witkey (provider or crowd), platform (Intermediation platform), and contract-issuing party (assigner), which is shown in Fig. 1 (Zhao and Zhu 2012).

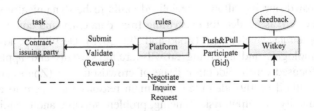

Fig. 1. Composition of Witkey site

Witkey

Witkey is referred to as individuals or members of communities forming the crowd. They respond to the task and attempt to submit their solutions as feedbacks. The extant literature mainly focuses on the motivation and behavior of participant. The motivation to participate in a no-for-profit or business-oriented crowdsourcing contest have some differences (Zhao and Zhu 2012). Some researchers and practitioners think the financial incentives are the important motivation in a business-oriented crowdsourcing contest (Brabham 2010; Prpić et al. 2015; Gefen et al. 2016; Zogaj et al. 2014). Some think that intrinsic motivation (e.g. psychological, cognitive, emotional, social aspects) is the motivation to participate in a no-business crowdsourcing contest (Nov 2011; Raddick 2010; Ke and Zhang 2009, 2010; Poetz and Schreier 2012; Daren and Brabham 2012; Zheng et al. 2011).

Platform

Platform is an intermediation system building a link between the contract-issuing party and Witkey, which serves as a crowdsourcing enabler and has some parameters as the rules for the whole lifecycle of crowdsourcing, such as the skill-set, certification level, due date, expected outcomes, and payments for the winners (not a necessity). Platform responds to the platform component, including the incentive mechanism design of interface, system, and platform, and some other related technology issues. Some researchers define and explore the characteristics of crowdsourcing models and yield implications for the design of crowdsourcing systems directly (Doan et al. 2011; Huberman et al. 2009; Stewart et al. 2009, 2010; Horton and Chilton 2010; Feng et al. 2017; Allahbakhsh et al. 2013). Other researchers integrate the idea of crowdsourcing into the design of collective intelligence systems, such as IT-based ideas competition systems (Vreede et al. 2013; Mao et al. 2017; Zhao and Zhu 2014; Zogaj et al. 2014; Briscoe et al. 2016).

Contract-Issuing Party

Contract-issuing party refers to the organizations directly benefiting from the crowd input. The party initiates the process of crowdsourcing and have a task as the main appendant. Contract-issuing party can provide richer content and better solutions in a creative and cost-effective way from a diverse crowd than what may be possible within an organizational unit or function. Contract-issuing party's perspective responds to the assigner component, including some relevant activities, such as adoption, implementation and governance (Bonabeau 2009; Jain 2010; Djelassi and Decoopman 2013; Lukyanenko et al. 2014), and evaluation of crowdsourcing cases and projects (Keen 2007; Hsueh et al. 2009; Poetz and Schreier 2009; Wiggins and Crowston 2011; Seltzer and Mahmoudi 2013).

Crowdsourcing adoption is the first step of a crowdsourcing process. Enterprise adoption of crowdsourcing allows specialized skills to be dynamically sourced from anyone or anywhere as needed for everything from data entry and coding to advanced analytics and product development (Zhao and Zhu 2012). Despite the advancement of Web 2.0 technologies and emerging crowdsourcing systems and applications, few studies have focused on the adoption issue of crowdsourcing (Zhao and Zhu 2012). Schenk and Guittard (2009) identified four main reasons for a firm to adopt crowdsourcing, i.e. quality of output, risk reducing, problem solving, and organizational core competences. Maiolini and Naggi (2010) focused on the relation between SMEs and crowdsourcing. They indicated that crowdsourcing allows SMEs to build up new competences that normally cannot be implemented or developed due to scarcity of expertise and available investments (Zhao and Zhu 2012).

The existing literature lacks of research on the enablers and barriers to acceptance and effective use of crowdsourcing. Some potential factors influencing crowdsourcing adoption are worth further examining. Hence we take Chinese crowdsourcing Witkey website for example, to search the main factors affecting the crowdsourcing adoption from the risk taking behavior perspective. This research focus on three aspects: (1) exploring dimensions of risk taking behavior in crowdsourcing adoption, and constructing the structural equation model by the perceived risk factors of website; (2) identifying the impact of each dimension of the site on each dimension of the perceived risk and the impact of perceived risk on crowdsourcing adoption wishes with empirical analysis; (3) providing appropriate management recommendations for third-party trading crowdsourcing websites.

2.2 Perceived Risk

Perceived risk to some extent influences consumers' purchasing decisions (Chi et al. 2016). When consumers make changes, delay or cancel the purchase, decisions may be caused by a higher perceived risk (Cunningham et al. 2013). Thus, perceived risk has been an important variable in empirical studies in consumer behavior research field (Zhang and Gu 2015). Perceived risk was first proposed to be an expected loss, and the perceived risk was composed of four dimensions. Time risk would arise when consumers spend time replacing or repairing the goods that they are not satisfied with; dangerous risk may be caused by defected products; self-esteem loss risk is a feeling of embarrassment the consumers would have when they bought products; money risk happens when consumers buy the products that are not satisfied with and need to pay extra money (Hendrix 2015). Peter and Tarpey (1975) proposed a perceived risk model with six dimensions, which includes financial risk, social risk, functional risk, psychological risk, physical risk and time risk in studying the consumer perceived risk of choosing the brand of cars in 1975. In domestic studies, Miao (2007) categorized perceived risk of the consumers into economic risk, functional risk, social risk, time risk, physical risk, psychological risk, privacy risk and service risk in online-shopping environment. From the researches above, we conclude that consumers would feel different risks in different situations.

While studying the risk perception of the service products, Mitchen and Greatorex creatively used six-dimensional model to measure the perceived risk in service products, which was used to measure the perceived risk of the physical products. The six dimensions were then reduced to four dimensions. They incorporated psychological and social risk into psychosocial risk and removed functional risk which is not suitable for measuring perceived risk in service. They considered that using perceived risk model to explain the purchasing behavior of service products was more convincing than physical products, and the respondents' perceived risk of service products was higher too. As the literature lack studies of contract-issuing party's perceived risk, and contract-issuing party can be regarded as consumer to some extent while their purchase intention can be regard as an adopting intention, we employ Mitchen and Greatorex's dimensions as the bases of this study.

2.3 Website

The biggest worry the consumers have when shopping online is the fear of being cheated by suppliers, privacy being disclosed, etc. (Chen and Chang 2012). Network security-aware control, perceived privacy control, perceived honesty and perceived ability affect the consumer's perception of risk (Sheau-Fen et al. 2012). When consumers shop online, they attach great importance to the security of website payment system and credibility of business reputation (Einwiller 1996). Website security, the environment of online shopping market and the technical level of online shopping platform are important factors to reduce consumer perception risk (Miyazaki and Fernandez 2013). The website factors have an important impact on consumers' perceived risk.

Website Authenticity

Website authenticity is the credibility of the information content on Witkey website. Hong (2015) believes that the trust expectation is one of the important sources of consumers' perceived risk. Website locates on the simulated environment of the Internet, and consumers can only make judgments based on the content of the website, which makes consumers who do network transactions seek to the authenticity of the content. Michell and Boustani (1999) presented that on the cognitive stage in consumer transactions, since there is no way to touch and feel the real products, the perceived risk would rise constantly. When consumers take the initiative to start looking for information and gain more useful information, risk levels begin to decline. The consumers on Witkey site pay much attention to the authenticity of the site content. The results of interviews with senior buyers showed that, when asked "What criteria do they judge by to choose Witkey", the answer were more concentrated on "the ability level of Witkey (credit rating), historical evaluation of buyers, nearly three months of income of Witkey, the completed transactions of Witkey, service description, forum" and many other dimensions of judgment, in which the most important criterion was the ability level of Witkey. Many consumers only trade with high level ability Witkey, because they generally believe that trading with these Witkey has the lowest risk, which shows that the authenticity of the Witkey site has a significant impact on consumer's perceived risk. This means the higher authenticity of the site, the lower risk the consumers perceive. Therefore, we proposed the following hypothesis:

H1:   Website authenticity and each dimension of contract-issuing part's perceived risk on Witkey website have negative correlation.

H1a: Website authenticity and contract-issuing part's perceived financial risk on Witkey website are negatively correlated.

H1b: Website authenticity and contract-issuing part's perceived time risk on Witkey website are negatively correlated.

H1c: Website authenticity and contract-issuing part's perceived services risk on Witkey website are negatively correlated.

H1d: Website authenticity and contract-issuing part's perceived psychosocial risk on Witkey website are negatively correlated.

Website Convenience

Website convenience is the level of convenient and efficiency during the entire transaction the users feel on the Witkey sites. In the view of the entire transaction process on Witkey site, from the contract-issuing party entering the website to searching related information, to communicating after established links with Witkey, and to paying for the services to Witkey, the convenience of the Website has an impact on every aspect of the transaction. Staelin (1994) reported that the bad mood contract-issuing party generated on the site was mainly due to the architecture of the site and navigation problems caused by speed, and these problems will increase contract-issuing party's time (convenience) risk. Gu and Xie (2013) found that competitive firms' strategies to facilitate fit revelation critically depend on the product qualities they offer. Accordingly, we propose the following hypothesis:

H2:   Website convenience and each dimension of contract-issuing part's perceived risk on Witkey website have negative correlation.

H2a: Website convenience and contract-issuing part's perceived financial risk on Witkey website are negatively correlated.

H2b: Website convenience and contract-issuing part's perceived time risk on Witkey website are negatively correlated.

H2c: Website convenience and contract-issuing part's perceived services risk on Witkey website are negatively correlated.

H2d: Website convenience and contract-issuing part's perceived psychosocial risk on Witkey website are negatively correlated.

Website Security

The biggest problem the users are concerned with the network transactions is the security of transactions. The interviews with contract-issuing party on the Witkey websites show that 80% of the people treat the website security as their conditions precedent when they choose to trade on the websites. What worries them most is personal information or credit card information disclosure by the sites. Zendehdel and Paim (2013) found that there are three factors for explaining attitude and intention towards online shopping, which are privacy, security and subjective norm. The results show that if students worry about whether their information due to the process of online shopping will be used for other purposes, it will reduce their purchase attitude. Ein-willer (1996) find that users are worried about the security of site trading systems and the accuracy of business reputation, and the most obvious is the security of the site trading systems when they shop online. Anthony (2001) believe that privacy and safety risks are the main risks affecting consumers online shopping in B2C e-commerce. If the sites use appropriate techniques to effectively prevent hackers stealing personal privacy information, users will reduce the perceived risk and think that the site is safe to have a transaction. Accordingly, we propose hypothesis as follows:

H3:   Website security and each dimension of contract-issuing part's perceived risk on Witkey website have negative correlation.

    H3a: Website security and contract-issuing part's perceived financial risk on Witkey website are negatively correlated.

    H3b: Website security and contract-issuing part's perceived time risk on Witkey website are negatively correlated.

    H3c: Website security and contract-issuing part's perceived services risk on Witkey website are negatively correlated.

    H3d: Website security and contract-issuing part's perceived psychosocial risk on Witkey website are negatively correlated.

2.4   Adopting Intention

Fishbein and Ajzen (1975) presented that willingness is the subjective probability of individuals engaged in specific behaviors. Adopting intention in this article is the subjective probability of contract-issuing party on Witkey website to make decisions on purchase and adopting the services. He demonstrated that perceived risk and adopting intention have a negative relationship, that is, if the product has a higher perceived risk, the users' adopting intention will be relatively lower. And this relationship in non-store shopping (such as telephone shopping, mail order, catalog shopping, online shopping, etc.) has a higher perceived risk than physical shopping (Cox 1964; Lascu and Zinkhan 1999). Many studies (Lascu and Zinkhan 1999; Forsythe and Shi 2003) pointed out that the perceived risk is the biggest obstacle of non-store shopping willingness. The Witkey mode is a kind of online shopping, and we thereby propose the following assumptions:

H4:   All dimensions of contract-issuing part's perceived risk on Witkey website and the contract-issuing part's purchasing intention have negative correlation.

    H4a: Contract-issuing part's perceived financial risk on Witkey website and the contract-issuing part's purchasing intention are negatively correlated.

    H4b: Contract-issuing part's perceived time risk on Witkey website and the contract-issuing part's purchasing intention are negatively correlated.

    H4c: Contract-issuing part's perceived services risk on Witkey website and the contract-issuing part's purchasing intention are negatively correlated.

    H4d: Contract-issuing part's perceived psychosocial risk on Witkey website and the contract-issuing part's purchasing intention are negatively correlated.

    Based on the literature reviews, we have proposed our research model as illustrated in Fig. 2. We propose that website authenticity, website convenience and website security would negatively enhance the contract-issuing part's perceived risk, which include four dimensions: perceived financial risk, perceived time risk, perceived services risk and perceived psychosocial risk. We then hypothesize that contract-issuing part's perceived risk is negatively related to pursuit intention.

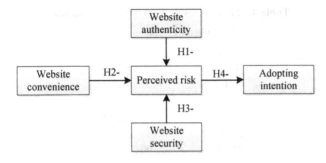

Fig. 2. Research model

3 Methodology

3.1 Measurement Development

To ensure the validity of the scale, we adapted most of the items from previous researches. As there is no scale to directly measure contract-issuing parts perceived risk in context of the Witkey, we designed the items to measure website factors by Miao (2007), and designed the items to measure dimensions of perceived risk by Mitchell and Greatorex (1999). All items were measured using five-point Likert scales ranging from strongly disagree to strongly agree. We then distributed the questionnaires to several researchers and users of Witkey websites for pilot test and made further revisions based on their feedback. Finally, we collected 325 responses and adjusted our scales to do the study.

3.2 Data Collection

Questionnaires were divided into two forms: written questionnaire and a network questionnaire. 70 written questionnaires were distributed to employees of Witkey websites, which accounts for 20% of the total questionnaires. 280 network questionnaires were distributed to users on Witkey websites, including: www.zhubajie.com, www.epweike.com and www.680.com, by offering a reward, which accounts for 80% of the total questionnaires. After scrutinizing the responses, we removed surveys that proved invalid responses. As a result, we collected 325(92.8%) valid responses. The sample consisted of 190 males (58.3%) and 135 females (41.7%) whose ages above 20. Most of the participants hold bachelor's degree (72.4%), while 22.7% hold master's degree, 1.8% have doctoral degree. Of the participants' parents' educational levels, 47. 3% hold bachelor's degrees and 33.2% have attained graduate degrees. The respondents' profile is presented in Table 1.

Table 1. Frequencies of participant characteristics

Characteristics	N	%
Gender		
Male	190	58.30%
Female	135	41.70%
Age		
21–25	41	12.60%
26–30	140	43.20%
31–40	99	30.50%
>40		13.7%
Education		
High school	10	3.10%
College	235	72.4%
Graduate school	74	22.7%
Net age		
<4	20	6.10%
5–8	108	33.40%
>8	197	60.50%

3.3   Data Analysis

Using structural equation modeling (SEM), we first examined our measurement model and then tested the structural model by employing SPSS 17.0 and AMOS17.0.

Measurement Model Test

We fist conducted T-test to test the items discrimination. The results showed that, except Q12 and Q25, the remaining 29 items passed test, and they were suitable for subsequent analysis. We then conducted reliability and validity tests for the measurement model and summarized the scale properties in Table 2. All Cronbach's alpha values were above the 0.80 threshold, indicating that the scales had high reliability (Nunnally 1978). The results of confirmatory factor analysis revealed that the standardized loading of items was mostly above 0.7. The average variance extracted (AVE) for every construct was above 0.6, which means that the scales had good convergent validity (Baggozi 1988). Table 3 presents the correlation matrix and the square roots of the AVEs and the square roots of the AVEs are the diagonal elements, which are all greater than their corresponding correlation coefficients with the constructs. This suggests that the scales have good discriminant validity.

Structural Model Test

We tested our structural model and summarized the results with AMOS coefficients in Fig. 3. As expected, adopting intention was negatively affected by contract-issuing part's perceived risk. Thus, H4 was supported. The four dimensions of perceived interactivity (perceived financial risk, perceived time risk, perceived services risk and perceived psychosocial risk) had significant effects on satisfaction. Thus, H4a— H4D were supported. Both website authenticity and website convenience had significant

Table 2. Scale properties

Factor	Item	Standardized loading	Cronbach's alpha	Composite reliability	AVE
Website authenticity	Q1	0.793	0.830	0.751	0.6586
	Q2	0.803			
	Q3	0.838			
Website convenience	Q4	0.796	0.840	0.758	0.6644
	Q5	0.852			
	Q6	0.769			
Website security	Q7	0.747	0.886	0.818	0.6241
	Q8	0.797			
	Q9	0.824			
Financial risk	Q10	0.844	0.886	0.750	0.6855
	Q11	0.874			
	Q13	0.808			
	Q14	0.783			
Time risk	Q15	0.794	0.902	0.774	0.6579
	Q16	0.804			
	Q17	0.831			
	Q18	0.815			
Services risk	Q19	0.812	0.891	0.754	0.6779
	Q20	0.831			
	Q21	0.857			
	Q22	0.792			
Psychosocial risk	Q23	0.804	0.863	0.709	0.6797
	Q24	0.810			
	Q26	0.841			
	Q27	0.842			
Adopting intention	Q28	0.807	0.884	0.743	0.6622
	Q29	0.790			
	Q30	0.847			
	Q31	0.810			

negatively impact on the four dimensions of contract-issuing part's perceived risk. Thus H1—H1d and H2—H2d were all supported. Website security had significant negatively on three of contract-issuing part's perceived risk— perceived financial risk, perceived time risk and perceived services risk. Thus, H3a—H3c were supported, while H3 and H3d were rejected.

Table 3. Correlation coefficient matrix and square roots of AVEs (shown as diagonal elements)

	F1	F2	F3	F4	F5	F6	F7	F8
F1	.811							
F2	.356	.815						
F3	.328	.385	.790					
F4	−.311	−.309	−.381	.827				
F5	−.317	−.421	−.509	.386	.811			
F6	−.314	−.319	−.431	.213	.389	.823		
F7	−.251	−.249	−.146	.091	.238	.169	.824	
F8	.301	.344	.447	−.248	−.391	−.367	−.272	.813

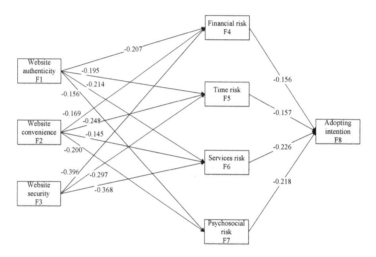

Fig. 3. Model testing result

4 Discussion

This study examined how website factors weakened contract-issuing part's perceived risk, and how such contract-issuing part's perceived risk further influenced their adopting intention. We investigated the contract-issuing part's perceived risk that contained four dimensions: perceived financial risk, perceived time risk, perceived services risk and perceived psychosocial risk. The results indicate that the four dimensions of consumes' perceived risk are significantly affected by website authenticity and website convenience, while only three dimensions are significantly affected by website security. As expected, contract-issuing part's purchasing intention is negatively influenced by four dimensions of contract-issuing part's perceived risk towards Witkey mode, which confirms the importance of perceived risk in continuing information technology use. Perceived risk explained a great portion of adopting intention, and among the three website factors, only website authenticity was found to have no significant relation to contract-issuing part's perceived psychosocial risk.

Similar to previous research conducted on website factors (Cheung 1999; Einwiller 1996), our results showed that website factors will lead to positive outcomes, such as decreased contract-issuing part's perceived risk. However, we found that the dimensions of website have different effects on every dimension of perceived risk. In contract-issuing part's financial risk, time risk and services risk, website security was found to be the strongest predictor. This is consistent with the conclusions of previous research that security is an important factor affecting the acceptance of systems (Einwiller 1996). It also as the same to the result of contract-issuing part's interviews of Witkey website, 80% of the users thought the security is the most important factor to choose the website when they have trade online. They are concerned about that their personal information and credit card password would be leaked. However in contract-issuing part's psychosocial risk, website convenience is the stronger predictor instead of security. Website security was found to insignificantly effect on contract-issuing part's psychosocial risk towards Witkey mode. It is because that our definition of psychological risk is anxiety or other emotions which rise from poor quality of service, which did not meet contract-issuing part's expectations. So the website convenience became more effective to reduce the contract-issuing part's perceived psychology risk (Richard Staelin 1994). In addition to security and convenience, the website authenticity would also affect contract-issuing part's perceived risk. When the Witkey websites provide real and effective information to contract-issuing parts, the contract-issuing parts would trust the sites more, thus reducing the perceived risk.

All of the dimensions of contract-issuing part's perceived risk were significantly impacted by adopting intention. Service was significantly affected by adopting intention, which is consistent with the findings from previous research. However, the effects of financial and time risk on purchasing intention were much weaker while services and psychosocial are much stronger. This might be due to more contract-issuing parts seek for psychological feelings rather than economic benefits on Witkey websites.

5 Conclusion

5.1 Limitations

There are some limitations for this research. Fistly, this study uses website factors as the pre-factors of contract-issuing part's perceived risk, but there might be some other factors in real life such as Wiktey factors and contract-issuing part individual factors, which influence the contract-issuing part's perceived risk in varying degrees. Secondly, the scale designed mainly were from classical scales combined with the characteristic of Witkey websites. Due to the different situations, there will be some deviations. Lastly, this study collected questionnaires responses mainly by Witkey website, and would have some distortion. So in the future research, we could try to get first-hand data from contract-issuing parts and Witkeys to ensure more effectiveness.

5.2 Implications

On the theoretical side, based on previous research that focused on buyer in trade, our study extended the perceived risk research on the contract-issuing parts in Witkey mode. Thus our study added website factors as pre-factors of the contract-issuing part's perceived risk, and explored the dimensions of contract-issuing part's perceived risk. Bauer (1960) firstly introduced the concept of perceived risk to contract-issuing part behavior field, and then, more scholars did extensive and deep research in perceived risk. But the birth of the Internet has changed the traditional shopping channels, so research of the contract-issuing part's perceived risk in network environment is necessary. Many scholars studied the dimensions of perceived risk under different application environments. However, there are rarely researchers exploring the contract-issuing part's perceived risk in trade of servicing products. This study discussed the impact of perceived risk under Witkey website and each dimension of perceived risks. Therefore, this study fills the gap in the contract-issuing part perceived risk theory under Witkey mode, and laying a solid foundation for further in-depth study.

From a practical perspective, the results of our study provide implications for Witkey websites which want to improve their service quality and enhance their competitive advantage. First, contract-issuing parts' feeling of being authentic and reliable of the website is very important. Witkey websites require constructing a complete qualification. By ways of a third-party certification and other multi-dimensional objective and accurate evaluation of qualifications, Witkey websites can provide as much information as possible to enhance the authenticity of the information on the website, thus reducing the perceived risk of the contract-issuing parts.

Next, optimizing the website experience and improving site convenience can attract more users. Using simple icons instead of obscure text can improve contract-issuing part's understanding of the contents of the interface in the shortest time; using a unified element, color, style to facilitate contract-issuing parts quickly locate and search. Collecting contract-issuing part's questions that are frequently asked can aid to establish helping section. The website service phone should would help solve the problems contract-issuing parts might encounter.

Finally, it is necessary to promote techniques protecting contract-issuing part's personal information. Upgrading website password protection with multiple warning measures can improve the payment system, and reducing the payment process with signs to remind users, can decrease contract-issuing part's perceived risk.

References

Allahbakhsh, M., Benatallah, B., Ignjatovic, A., et al.: Quality control in crowdsourcing systems: issues and directions. IEEE Internet Comput. 17(2), 76–81 (2013)

Brabham, D.C.: Moving the crowd at threadless: motivations for participation in a crowdsourcing application. Inf. Commun. Soc. 13(8), 1122–1145 (2010)

Chi, Y.S., Kang, M.Y., Han, K.S., et al.: A study on the discontinuance intention on O2O commerce: with a focus on the mediating effects of perceived risk and user resistance. Int. J. u- and e-Service 9(2), 207–218 (2016)

Djelassi, S., Decoopman, I.: Customers' participation in product development through crowdsourcing: issues and implications. Ind. Mark. Manag. **42**(5), 683–692 (2013)

Fishbein, M., Ajzen, I.: Belief, Attitude, Intention, and Behavior: An Introduction to Theory and Research. Addison-Wesley, Reading (1975)

Hendrix, F.G.: The total cost of manufacturing … money, time and risk. Manuf. Eng. **154**(3), 17–18 (2015)

Howe, J.: Crowdsourcing. Crown Publishing Group, New York (2008)

Nunnally, J.C.: Psychometric Theory. McGraw-Hill, New York (1978)

Lascu, D.N., Zinkhan, G.: Consumer conformity: review and application for marketing theory and practice. J. Mark. Theory Pract. **3**, 1–12 (1999)

Li, D., et al.: Modelling the roles of cewebrity trust and platform trust in consumers propensity of live-streaming an extended TAM method. Comput. Mater. Continua **55**(1), 137 (2018)

Jing, M., Zhou, Y., Wang, F.: Empirical study on shopping perceived risk. J. Syst. Manag. **16**(2), 164–169 (2007)

Peter, J.P., Tarpey, L.X.: A comparative analysis of three-consumer decision strategies. J. Consum. Res. **2**(1), 29–37 (1975)

Staelin, R.: A model of perceived risk and intended risk-handling activity. J. Consum. Res. **21**, 119–134 (1994)

Sheau-Fen, Y., Sun-May, L., Yu-Ghee, W.: Store brand proneness: effects of perceived risks, quality and familiarity. Australas. Mark. J. **20**(1), 48–58 (2012)

Wang, T., Wu, T., Ashrafzadeh, A.H., He, J.: Crowdsourcing-based framework for teaching quality evaluation and feedback using linguistic 2-tuple. CMC: Comput. Mater. Continua **57**(1), 81–96 (2018)

Wiggins, A., Crowston, K.: From conservation to crowdsourcing: a typology of citizen science. In: Proceedings of the Forty-fourth Hawaii International Conference on System Science (HICSS-44) (2011)

Zheng, H.C., Li, D.H., Hou, W.H.: Task design, motivation, and participation in crowdsourcing contests. Int. J. Electron. Commer. **15**(4), 57–88 (2011)

Anomaly Detection in Wireless Sensor Networks Based on KNN

Lingren Wang[1], Jingbing Li[1,2]([⊠]), Uzair Aslam Bhatti[1],
and Yanlin Liu[1]

[1] College of Information Science and Technology, Hainan University,
Haikou 570228, China
lingren_good@163.com, Jingbingli2008@hotmail.com,
duzairslambhatti@hotmail.com, yanlinliu567@163.com
[2] State Key Laboratory of Marine Resource Utilization in the South China Sea,
Hainan University, Haikou 570228, China

Abstract. In recent years use of a Wireless Sensor Network (WSN) has become a leading area of research in various applications. Because of WSN limitation of its own features that low ability of calculation, small volume of storage, resource constrain, bad communicational environment of wireless, which lead to WSN be besieged by imminent security problems, the abnormal detection in WSN is vary important at this time. We focus on the quality of data, and aim at the characteristics of wireless sensor network node data with time and spatial similarity, and the current research on anomaly analysis. We use the classification to detect outliers. This paper presents a method of detecting the proximity of distance based on distance, which is the main reason for the study of the anomalous value of the network. The KNN (K-Nearest Neighbor) algorithm is used to analyze and detect the data to achieve the purpose of data anomaly detection in WSN. The algorithm of outlier detection is based on the design and achieve of QualNet simulation platform. It is effective and accurate to evaluate and test. The simulation results show the effectiveness of the proposed KNN algorithm.

Keywords: WSN · KNN algorithm · Anomaly detection · QualNet

1 Introduction

The development of technology is intensifying, and smart sensors are widely used because of their low price, multi-function, simple and flexible deployment [1]. Compared with traditional wireless networks, wireless sensor networks do not require infrastructure, low node price, strong anti-interference, and network topology. Flexibility and other advantages, so the research on wireless sensor networks has become a hot spot for scholars and experts in many fields. As a kind of sensing technology that always exists around us like air, wireless sensor network has begun to penetrate into all aspects of our lives and successfully applied to all walks of life, such as industry, agriculture, smart medical, smart home, transportation, disaster monitoring, military, and transportation [2]. Wireless sensor network is developing rapidly in the promising

© Springer Nature Switzerland AG 2019
X. Sun et al. (Eds.): ICAIS 2019, LNCS 11634, pp. 632–643, 2019.
https://doi.org/10.1007/978-3-030-24271-8_56

era, and its universal application has exposed many urgent practical problems. Those problems that should be due to its own application scenarios and limitations will greatly reduce the network performance and efficiency, as well as the security issues of WSN about which we are more concerned in this paper. Although the research and development of security issue are late, its importance cannot be ignored, which concerns the timely and correct processing of data information and the normal operation of the whole network. In general, there are two main types of information security technologies, both defense and detection. The former is to intercept malicious intrusions, but cannot fully guarantee the security of the network, especially after the sensor nodes are captured, the original application will be lost [3]. In order to better cope with and solve the security problems of wireless sensor networks, we urgently need to be able to extract reliable information in massive time series data, because low-quality raw data largely limits the accuracy of analytical data and decision making. Sexual, real-time outlier detection methods can cope with sensor data quality problems, and achieve the purpose of improving and ensuring network security. The use of outlier detection in the WSN will improve node data detection, improve network efficiency, and maintain network security. Therefore, it is necessary to develop an appropriate outlier detection system.

2 Research on Outlier Detection of WSN

2.1 Wireless Sensor Network

A large number of sensor nodes deployment is our first impression of WSN, and also is an important part of the WSN, the sensor nodes usually with perception, calculation, storage, and the function of wireless communication, the many nodes randomly placed in the area of the need to be monitored, they will perceive and collect all kinds of parameter information, and through the sink node transmission to the server [2]. The construction of the sensor node is divided into four modules, which are data acquisition module, data processing module, wireless communication module, and energy supply module [3]. The data collection module includes AC/DC conversion and data collection, in which the content of data collection is generally the sensing collection of interested event parameters, such as humidity, temperature, and voltage used in the experiment below [2, 3]. The data processing module has processor and memory, which is mainly responsible for node control, including positioning, routing selection, time synchronization, task scheduling, energy management, and data processing. The main task of the wireless communication module is to exchange node information [2–4]. WSN is Ad-hoc self-organizing network in the application in sensor technology, its purpose is data exchange between sensory information, in order to reach normal observation and real-time processing of the monitoring area, interested in within the scope of the whole network coverage and useful thing to respond or record, after processing the perceived information will get more specific and accurate information, will transmit information to the observer [4]. The WSN structure normally contains sensor nodes, Sink nodes, Internet or satellite networks, task management nodes, and observers.

2.2 Overview of Outliers

Outlier detection has also been understood as a deviation, outliers are deviating from the expected values or normal observation, the earliest Hawkins defines a data set of outliers as [5] abnormal points is deviating from the other sample observations, it deviates from the level is so great that that let people suspect it is caused by other mechanisms. Outliers detection can be considered to find interesting and helpful information from a large number of complex and changeable data, which is one of the basic tasks of data mining. In wireless sensor networks, the number of nodes is huge, and the amount of original data is massive and low-quality. There are many reasons for such abnormal data in some databases, such as some special data, incomplete data or noise data. The occurrence is affected by many factors, including human factors, nodes or other equipment failures [6], but the actual event is the actual response when the event of interest occurs, which contains more important information, such as in environmental monitoring. In many applications, such as forest risk prevention and disease diagnosis and detection, outliers are the main targets of such data analysis. In WSN, the anomaly detection of time series data will be conducive to the prediction and analysis of the sequence, so as to realize real-time and effective decision-making and make situational cognition. We can classify WSN into two categories by purpose, namely event monitoring network and space-time sampling network [7]. In the event monitoring network, when the monitored event property changes dramatically, a large number of outliers will be generated. At this point, the detected data will be regarded as an indicator of the occurrence of interesting events, which makes the sensor producing the abnormal value traceable. In the spatiotemporal sampling network, data will be collected at a fixed time interval. Its fundamental purpose is to monitor and record the changes of attribute phenomena, which requires real-time abnormal value monitoring method to guarantee the quality of sensor data, so as to realize timely data analysis, evaluation, and development of appropriate solutions.

2.3 Correlation of Data

In data processing, it is usually necessary to consider the similarity between data or the similarity between the signal and its own historical data after a certain delay, which is used to test the function of signal detection and feature recognition. The correlation of data is an important information to study these contents and also an important basis for our study of data anomalies. The data collected by the sensor is a set of temporal data with temporal correlation, that is, temporal correlation and spatial correlation.

Time correlation can be understood in this way. The information collected by nodes in WSN shows the consistency of a certain rule in the moments before and after, which is usually reflected by function relation [8]. In WSN, the nodes are collecting and forwarding data periodically. In a short period of time, the data values received at the first moment are generally very similar to those received at the second moment.

Spatial similarity can be understood as follows: in those places that are artificially monitored, sensor nodes close to each other in physical coordinates have highly consistent characteristics of perception and information sent. If the monitored content is mutated, then the nodes can jointly perceive the response [9]. Generally, nodes are arranged in a highly dense way in the monitored place. Only in this way can the spatial connection of data be closer and more correlated.

2.4   The Anomaly Detection Algorithm

In this research and discussion, in order to be able to simply and effectively complete the detection of outliers in WSN, we use KNN algorithm as it is very simple machine learning algorithm and developed based on the approach of neighboring points. A data classification method [9, 10] KNN has been adhering to the characteristics of excellent robustness, smoothness and simple implementation method in the process of classification, and has become the direction for experts and scholars to devote their enthusiasm and energy. Its features can be summarized as the following two main points [11]: Firstly, the distance between samples is calculated based on the entire feature values of the samples, which can reduce the adverse effects caused by the poor selection of category features and minimize the error term in the classification process. Secondly, when KNN conducts classification judgment in data set, the hypothesis of basic data will not be used as the judgment basis, and it can survive in various situations.

2.5   KNN Algorithm Model and Analysis

The main idea of KNN classification algorithm is to search for K neighbors in the feature space, make statistics and classification of neighbor categories [12]. Assumption of data classification in advance, the data is divided into normal and abnormal value, set the maximum initial distance Dmas, the distance dist is the same class and are density maximum distance of two nodes in the biggest category, compared with one kind of recent node, if the maximum initial distance represents the node does not belong to this class, this article namely was identified as outliers. The distance between the unknown sample point and all nodes is calculated. All dist nodes are sorted from small to large. The nodes of the first K dist are selected(note: under the premise of dist < Dmas, unknown points may belong to the type already output). The algorithm flow chart is shown in Fig. 1.

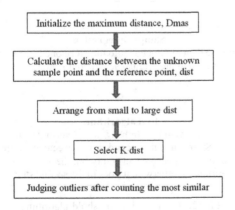

Fig. 1. The flow chart of the KNN algorithm.

We choose Euclidean distance as the calculation standard for calculating point to point and use it as the basis to evaluate whether the two reference points are consistent within the requirements. X = (x1, x2, x3, ..., Xn) and Y = (y1, y2, y3, ..., N) represents the data of two samples, N is the number of feature attributes of the sample.

$$d(x,y) = \sqrt{\sum_{i=1}^{n} (xi - yi)^2} \tag{1}$$

X = (x1, x2, x3, ..., Xn) and Y = (y1, y2, y3, ..., N) represents the data of two samples, N is the number of feature attributes of the sample [13]. When KNN nearest neighbor algorithm is applied to the detection of sequential data, it can achieve the purpose of simple and convenient detection of outliers. The KNN algorithm is roughly composed of two parts:

(1) Traversal and sorting of data, selecting K most suitable data;
(2) Statistical results and classification.

In the analysis of the computational complexity of the time series data algorithm, we discuss and pre-classify the data through the hypothesis, that is, before the KNN is used, the historical sample point information is observed and divided into abnormal parts and non-abnormal parts [14]. The amount of data used in this paper is much smaller than the amount of data compared to cloud data. When a large amount of data needs to be detected, we can use the compression proximity algorithm corresponding to the KNN algorithm [12, 13]. Two memories are defined here, one for the empty set to store the data to be generated, and the other for the original sample set. The algorithm flow chart is shown in Fig. 2.

For neighbor selection is the key to the KNN algorithm, the K value set is accurate algorithm is the key step, we from the two methods of feasibility analysis and cross-

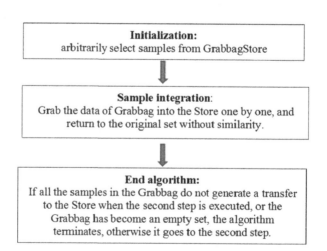

Fig. 2. Compression threshold algorithm.

validation (experience), select the experience analysis method to select set of K, which is at the beginning of the K to a smaller value, KNN algorithm through constant inspection outlier analysis of error rate, until the test when the lowest rates to get the optimal values of K.

3   Simulation Analysis and Results

3.1   Detection Design

(See Table 1).

Table 1. Detection processes.

Processes	Interpretation
Step1	Arranging nodes and getting initial data
Step2	Based on the collected data and the actual experience of real events, we will use the eigenvalues of the data to classify the normal value categories and outlier categories
Step3	Suppose the K value is a small value
Step4	Initialization (maximum distance Dmax between two nodes in the same class)
Step5	Calculating the distance dist of the unknown data from each sample
Step6	Sort, sort all dists from small to large
Step7	Select the K samples with the smallest distance
Step8	Count the sample categories and classify the unknown data into the largest number
Step9	Calculate the eigenvalues of the unknown sample and the class\other class, namely d, and d′. When d < Dmax and d′ > Dmax, the classification decision of the algorithm is reasonable, otherwise the data is removed from the class and put into another one type
Step10	All the unknown data required to be detected are all detected. If the positive detection rate is the highest and the highest, K is the optimal value; if the false detection rate is higher than the normal value, the K value is set poorly, and the process returns to step 3

3.2   QualNet Network Simulation Tool

QualNet is developed by Scalable Networks Technologies of the United States and is mainly used to analyze behavioral research and performance statistics of wireless mobile communication networks [15]. It has a large number of protocol library models, supports dedicated networks (WiFi, WiMAX, WSN, cellular, etc.), can be a semi-physical simulation, and powerful 3D visualization, QualNet simulation software in simulation speed, accuracy, robustness, and flexibility Better than other network simulation software [16]. The main advantages of QualNet: covering many preset models, protocols and algorithms to help with learning; the speed, efficiency, and accuracy of operation can be ensured by efficient scheduling, parallel algorithms, and high fidelity modeling;

as part of a real network, Add to the network test, directly used for semi-physical simulation; parallel distributed simulation, robust, fast, and high precision [16, 17].

3.3 Simulation Process

For the KNN algorithm used in this article, the QualNet has the operation flow to the source code as shown in Fig. 3.

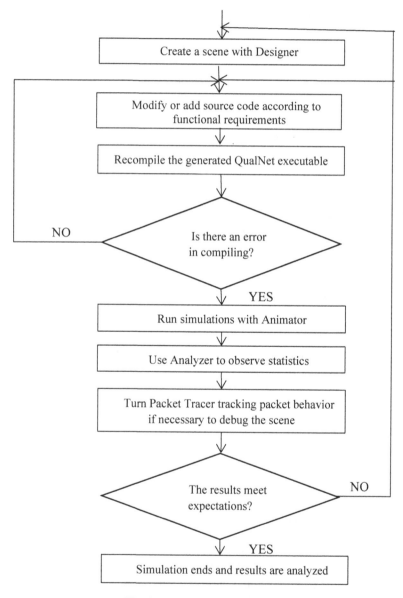

Fig. 3. Simulation on QualNet.

For the use of QualNet, there is a process that has no operation on the source code. The difference between the two is based on the implemented functions. Whether there is a change to the QualNet framework code. Because the functions expected by KNN are beyond the existing functions of QualNet, it is necessary to modify the source code to embed the appropriate algorithm, recompile and generate the executable program available for the available software [15]; compile correctly, that is, run the simulation scenario.

3.4   Constructing a Simulation Environment

In order to evaluate the performance of this algorithm, this paper simulates the application of a WSN monitoring environment on the QualNet simulation platform (see Table 2). The QualNet simulation runs on an Intel(R) Core(TM) i5-4210u, 2.4 GHz, 8 GB memory (RAM) PC [15]. We will randomly distribute 50 sensor nodes and place the base station at the local dot, where 10% of the nodes are randomly designated as abnormal attack nodes, as shown in Fig. 4. We set the MAC layer and routing protocol of all devices to IEEE802.11 and AODV; the total running time of the simulation is set to 1000 s; the source of the perceptual data we use is shown in Fig. 5, Intel Berkeley Research Laboratory (Intel Berkeley Research) Lab, IBRL) Data information collected by 54 sensors deployed from February 28 to April 5, 2004. Sensor nodes send three types of perceptual data attribute values to the base station every 10 s: humidity, temperature, and voltage. As shown in Fig. 6(a) and (b), we present 1000 data as data graphs (temperature and humidity) [17] (Table 3).

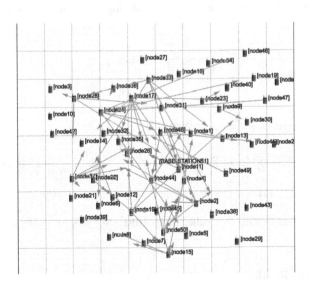

Fig. 4. QualNet simulation scene graph.

Table 2. Simulation scenario configuration parameters.

Parameters	Value
Simulation time	1000
Area size	100 m × 100 m
Total number of nodes	50
Total number of malicious nodes	5
MAC protocol	IEEE802.11
Routing protocol	AODV
business type	CBR
Perceptual data type (attribute)	Humidity, temperature and voltage
Data transmission time	10 s

Fig. 5. Schematic diagram of sensor deployment in IBRL network.

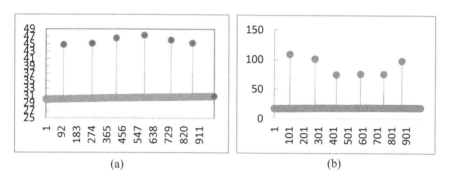

(a)   (b)

Fig. 6. (a) 1000 Temperature data collected by IBRL. (b) 1000 Humidity data collected by IBRL.

3.5   Simulation Results

In order to verify the classification effect and outlier detection ability of KNN algorithm, this paper simulates the wireless transmission scene of the sensor, and repeats the experiment in this scenario and takes the middle 5 experimental data as the final experimental result. The experimental results are shown in Table 4. Accuracy rate and false rate are used as evaluation indexes in this paper.

Table 3. The meaning of TN, TP, FN, FP.

Symbol	Meaning
TN	Normal samples are identified as normal quantity
TP	Abnormal samples are identified as normal quantity
FN	Normal samples are identified as abnormal quantity
FP	Abnormal samples are identified as abnormal quantity

Table 4. Test experimental data sheet.

	CR (%)	FR (%)	Time (s)
Test 1	99.718054	8.598081	0.025403
Test 2	99.555888	10.213108	0.024732
Test 3	97.901297	11.013625	0.024723
Test 4	99.444264	12.352397	0.025280
Test 5	99.299324	9.673040	0.024745

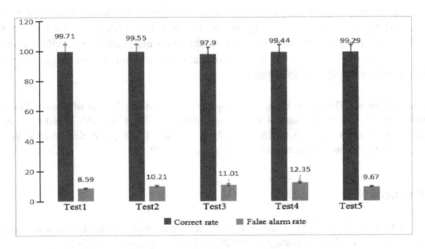

Fig. 7. Utility value of KNN algorithm for abnormal data detection.

Correct Rate:

$$CR = \frac{TP + TN}{TP + TN + FP + FN} \tag{2}$$

False Rate:

$$FR = \frac{FN}{TN + TP + FP + FN} \tag{3}$$

The experimental results show (see Fig. 7) that the KNN algorithm has a good detection effect on the abnormal data in the WSN, and can maintain a high detection accuracy rate, and also ensures a low false positive rate. The main reason is that the distribution of detection features of normal events is more concentrated and significantly different from other anomalies.

4 Conclusion

The research on the abnormal data of wireless sensors has been rapidly developed in recent years. The research content covers many aspects, and many of them are in the theoretical research stage [3]. A large part of the problems must be combined with the real situation in life. In-depth discussion, summarization of learning and continuous practical experimentation. Due to the limited time and space, this paper proves that the KNN classification algorithm used in this paper can achieve good detection rate and relatively low error by theoretical analysis of outlier detection of wireless sensor networks and verification of the feasibility of KNN algorithm. In this paper, the compressed proximity algorithm is used to reduce the original massive data. We also considered the method of clustering to find the center of gravity of the sample and directly determine the distance between the unknown sample and the samples. In order to achieve the reduction of the amount of data and the amount of calculation, the selection of the K value is facilitated.

Acknowledgment. This work is supported by the Key Research Project of Hainan Province [ZDYF2018129], and by the Natural Science Foundation of China [61762033] and the Natural Science Foundation of Hainan [20166227,617048, 2018CXTD333], the Key Innovation and Entrepreneurship Project of Hainan University [Hdcxcyxm201711].

References

1. Branch, J., Szymanski, B., Giannella, C., et al.: In-network outlier detection in wireless sensor networks. In: Proceedings of the IEEE ICDCS, pp. 384–391 (2006)
2. Madeti, S.R., Singh, S.N.: Modeling of PV system based on experimental data for fault detection using kNN method. J. Solar Energy **173**, 139–151 (2018)
3. Baragona, R., Battaglia, F., Cucina, D.: Empirical likelihood for outlier detection and estimation in autoregressive time series. J. Time **37**, 315–336 (2015)
4. Zhang, Y., Meratnia, N., Havinga, P.J.M.: Distributed online outlier detection in wireless sensor networks using ellipsoidal support vector machine. Ad Hoc Netw. **11**, 1062–1074 (2013)
5. Cheng, J., Zhou, J., Liu, Q., Tang, X., Guo, Y.: A DDoS detection method for socially aware networking based on forecasting fusion feature sequence. Comput. J. **61**, 959–970 (2018). https://doi.org/10.1093/comjnl/bxy025

6. Zhang, X., Liu, Y., Luo, B., Pan, L.: Computational power of tissue P systems for generating control languages. Inf. Sci. **278**, 285–297 (2014)
7. Cheng, J., Xu, R., Tang, X., Sheng, V.S., Cai, C.: An abnormal network flow feature sequence prediction approach for DDoS attacks detection in big data environment. Comput. Mater. Continua **55**(1), 095–119 (2018)
8. Zhang, G., Li, F.: Application of the KNN algorithm based on KD tree in intelligent transportation system. In: 2014 IEEE 5th International Conference on Software Engineering and Service Science (2014)
9. Hawkins, D.: Identification of Outliers. Chapman and Hall, London (1980)
10. Guo, Y.: Centipeda minima (Ebushicao) extract inhibits PI3K-Akt-mTOR signaling in nasopharyngeal carcinoma CNE-1 cells. Chin. Med. **10**, 26 (2015)
11. Hu, X., Zhu, F.: Metadata web classifiers using KNN and porter. In: 2013 International Conference on Education and Educational Research (2013)
12. Wang, Q., Wang, S., Meng, Z.: Applying an intrusion detection algorithm to wireless sensor networks. In: Second International Workshop on Knowledge Discovery and Data Mining. IEEE Computer Society (2009)
13. He, Z., Zhu, H., Yu, F.: A vehicle detection algorithm based on wireless magnetic sensor networks. In: 2014 4th IEEE International Conference on Information Science and Technology (2014)
14. Wei, Z., Zhigang, L.: Network modeling and simulation based on QualNet. In: The 15th Information Theory Academic Annual Meeting of the Chinese Institute of Electronics and the 1st National Network Coding Academic Annual Meeting. National Defense Industry Press (2008)
15. Balasundaram, A., Rajesh, L., Bagan, K.B.: A study on fourth generation wireless network using QualNet simulator. In: SCIEI 2015 Paris Conference.th. Madras Institute of Technology, Anna University, Paris (2015)
16. Liu, M., Qiao, H., Lan, J.: Research on communication network simulation based on QualNet. Electron. Des. Eng. (10), 33–136 (2014)
17. Xu, C., Ni, S.Z., Shao, H.G.: Energy balanced self-adaptive intelligent water drops routing algorithm. In: Proceedings of the 2014 International Conference on Future Information Engineering and Manufacturing Science (2014)

Comparison of the Legal Principle Foundation of Chinese and American Secret Information Access Control Technique

LongJuan Wang[1($\boxtimes$)] and FangMing Tang[2]

[1] College of Information Science and Technology, Hainan University, Haikou, HaiNan, China
juanywong@126.com
[2] Institute of Computer Application, Academy of Engineering Physics, Mianyang, SiChuan, China

Abstract. This paper firstly put forward the concept of secrecy legal principle foundation for information security and Secrecy Techniques. Secondly, the variance of the secret information access control technique between China and American was analyzed using contrast analysis. Thirdly, analysis of American sensitive compartmented information based on the lattice which was not suitable in China was given. Finally, according to the limitations of China control scheme in access scope, the suggestions for establishing secret information access control mechanism and model with China legal principle foundation is put forward.

Keywords: Information security · Secrecy · Legal principle foundation · SCI · Secret level label · Secret marking · Access scope · Access control · Mechanism

1 Introduction

State secrets are valuable resources of the state and are monopolized and held by the state. At the same time, state secrets have extremely distinct and strong national political attributes and legal nature. It is a common practice around the world to regulate and manage secrets by law [1].

Secret information system with the characters of a large number of secret information, high-degree of secret information and easily divulging is the most important state secret container under the condition of information technology. Information security and security control technology which is the fundamental mission to protect state secrets in the secret information system is an important means and tool to protect the national secret security according to the requirements of national laws and regulations. Those technologies must embody the will of the country, follow the legal provisions, and implement the requirements of the laws and regulations. National will and legal provisions are the highest criteria, the most fundamental demand source and driving force of information security and confidentiality control technology.

The concept and classification of state secrets, the system of secret laws and regulations, the state secret governance system and the system mechanism of secret

© Springer Nature Switzerland AG 2019
X. Sun et al. (Eds.): ICAIS 2019, LNCS 11634, pp. 644–657, 2019.
https://doi.org/10.1007/978-3-030-24271-8_57

management, and the requirements for the subject of secret not only constitute the legal principle foundation, of the state secret governance in a country, but also the legal principle foundation of secret management and control technology in information security domain.

Based on American secret legal principle foundation unique requirement background, application background and corresponding security label, the American multilevel security [2–4], BLP model [5–7], BIBA model [7, 8], access control model based on lattice and so on [9, 10] basically solve the access control and sharing problems of SCI secret information in the American information system and had considerable importance from the significance and theoretical values in China. It is very limited to apply those technologies to sharing control of secret information in China secret information systems because of the secret laws and regulations and the secret management mechanisms in American which are totally different.

The information flow control and access control in the secret information system have different control requirements with the general information system and other national information systems. The system must follow the China legal principle foundation meet the command of secret laws and regulations of China and the standard of classification protection.

In order to carry out the requirements of classification protection, implement precision control, avoid expanding the scope of access and clog the divulgement danger, it is necessary to design an access control mechanism adapted to China's secret legal principle foundation. This mechanism also follows the Chinese conditions, China legal principle foundation and obey the Chinese security law, standard specification and secret management mechanism.

2 The Concept of "State Secret" in American

2.1 The Classification of State Secret in American

State secrets are matters or information that are related to the security and interests of the state and need to be protected. From the state's interests, the governments of all countries will protect the information as secret information which will bring damage to the security and interests of the state. The United States has never formed a unified concept of state secrets. There are many forms of state secrets in the United States, which can be roughly divided into three parts [1].

The state secrets of the United States can be divided into three major categories: national security information, atomic energy information, special contact scheme and sensitive compartmented information SCI. The national security information is the information that needs to be protected as a secret from national defense and diplomacy. This kind of secret fall into three categories: most confidential, classified and confidential. The atomic energy information is the information about the development and application of atomic energy in the nuclear industry: restriction usage information and prior restriction usage information. Special contact scheme and sensitive compartmented information SCI (SCI) are mainly information obtained by intelligence agencies through information collection, which is generally determined by the United States

Secretary of state, the defence secretary, the Minister of Energy and the director of the Central Intelligence Agency. This kind of secret shall take more strict measures to protect because of three-level dense protection that is hard to protect it [1, 11].

2.2 Particularity of American SCI

In order to collect all kinds of information, the United States has established the most complex, the largest and most advanced intelligence system in the world, involving seven independent agencies and 16 departments. The Office of the Director of National Intelligence is responsible for coordinating the work of the various agencies and implementing the national intelligence program particular the national signal intelligence strategy (see Fig. 1) [12].

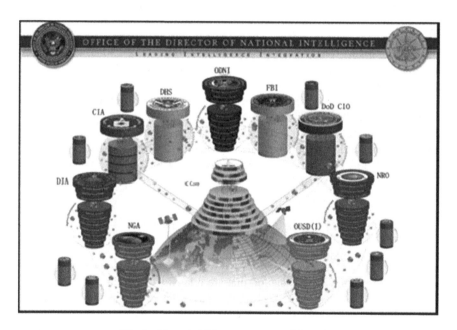

Fig. 1. Huge intelligence agency of America

After "911", the Intelligence Unit was integrated and the IC (Intelligence Community) was established to collect and analyze information about the construction of international relations and national security actions. The US-oriented Intelligence Community involves four major international Intelligence Community organizations, including 5 eye Intelligence Community (Second Club), 14 eye Intelligence Community (SSEUR), 28 state Intelligence Community (NATO), and 33 state Intelligence Community (third club), and 48 countries or regions (each country with one 3 letter word as the code name) (see Fig. 2) [12].

The ways and sources of information acquisition by American intelligence agencies can be divided into 5 major categories: human intelligence (HUMINT), signal intelligence

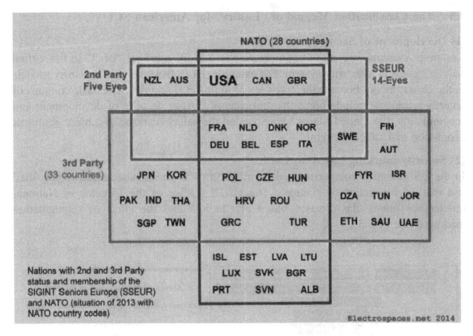

Fig. 2. American-led international intelligence alliance

(SIGINT), image information intelligence (IMINT), measurement and feature information intelligence (MASINT) and open source intelligence (OSINT). The SIGINT can be divided into communication information (COMINT) and weapon test data information (TELINT) and electronic radiation intelligence (ILINT) [13–16].

These intelligence agencies acquire astronomical intelligence information by using the world's largest institutions and state-of-the-art technologies at all times. It is said that only the CIA has more than 850 thousand employees, obtain 1 billion 700 million intelligence every day [12].

The sensitive compartmented information (SCI) in the national secret of the United States which unlike other types of state secrets, has extremely distinctive features: a very wide way of sources, a huge amount of information, a wide range of surfaces, high sensitivity, and a very complex sharing of demand and control.

National secret information and state secret information of atomic energy in the United States are usually used only in the domestic-related business areas. However, SCI information must share between large-scale international agencies, and sometimes it needs to share for non-intelligence departments. The United States not only needs to acquire information obtained by other allied countries but also to control intelligence and to share information in its hands (highly selective), thus some information cannot be shared at all. Therefore, safe and reliable information sharing is the goal that pursued by the intelligence agencies of the United States [12].

Such an amazing amount of, diverse and complex of sharing information, a classification of information to classify, effective management, control and information sharing is an important issue. To this end, the United States has set up specialized agencies to research and daily manage how to classify and identify this intelligence information.

2.3   The Classification Method of "Lattice" for American SCI

(1) Development of Security marking

Computer systems, it is a common practice to add the attribute "label" to the virtual host and guest in a security system. For example, BLP, Biba and other security models as the classic theory become the core idea of multi-level security. The basic contents of security markings include hierarchy and category. After decades of development and accumulation, the United States has expanded the safety marking to a more abundant expression that called Marking.

(2) Security marking based on Lattice

In the US, sensitive compartmented information (SCI) in its state secrets is classified and marked by means of "lattice". The ONDI (Office of the Director of National Intelligence) gives classification based on "lattice" and the effect of segmentation markings (see Fig. 3).

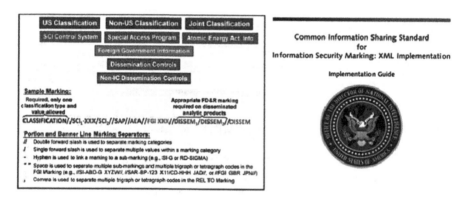

Fig. 3. The format of the US SCI's "Lattice" compartment

The "lattice" marked method is stricter and stricter than the requirements of level-classification information. It includes level and classification, and also authorization.

The meaning of Lattice is to classify secret information like a grid. According to public documents, Lattice is currently known as the two levels classification system: "secret class + // + /", SCI is divided into two classes, the main class and the subclass. The "lattice" classification: "double slash //, single slash /, hyphen-, space and comma" to separate information from control information, the format:

CLASSIFICATION//SCI₁-XXX/SCI₂//SAP//AEA//FGI   XXX//DISSEM₁/DISSEM₃//DISSEM//DI

Among them:

CLASSIFICATION: secret classification marking, one of the US secret classification, non-American secret classification and joint secret classification. This item is a must. Followed by // behind is the main class, / behind is a subclass classification under the main class.

Classification method based on the "lattice" and the function and usage of the division marking, can see from Fig. 4. The "lattice" marking consists of 9 parts:

(1) US Classification: most confidential, classified, confidential and non-confidential.
(2) Non-US Classification: use by other countries and international organizations.
(3) Joint Classification: information secret level that is shared or formulated by many countries.
(4) SCI Control System: specification guides the sensitive information set by each program established by the Central Intelligence Agency's core executive.
(5) Special Access Program.
(6) Foreign Government Information: controlled documents of the United States controlled by Chinese foreign governments.
(7) Dissemination Controls: a set of markings that can be used to identify the dissemination of information which can be released or restricted.
(8) Non-ICs Dissemination Controls: a set of markings used by departments outside the intelligence service.
(9) Document Description: include decryption date or artificial description, such as decryption conditions.

3 The Concept of "State Secret" in China

3.1 Basic Definition

(1) State Secrets
Article 2 of the Law of the People's Republic of China on Keeping Confidentiality of State Secrets defines state secret:

State secrets shall be matters that have a vital bearing on state security and national interests and, as specified by legal procedure, are entrusted to a limited number of people for a given period of time.

(2) Categories of State Secrets
Article 9 the following matters involving the security and interests of the state, which may damage the state's security and interests in the political, economic, national defense, foreign affairs and other fields after the disclosure, shall be determined as state secrets:

(1) secrets concerning major policy decisions on state affairs;
(2) secrets in the building of national defence and in the activities of the armed forces;
(3) secrets in diplomatic activities and in activities related to foreign countries as well as secrets to be maintained as commitments to foreign countries;
(4) secrets in national economic and social development;
(5) secrets concerning science and technology;
(6) secrets concerning activities for safeguarding state security and the investigation of criminal offences;
(7) other matters that are classified as state secrets by the state secret-guarding department.

Secrets of political parties that conform with the provisions of Article 2 of this Law shall be state secrets.

Article 10. State secrets shall fall into three categories: most confidential, classified and confidential.

3.2 Legal Provisions of Access Scope

Article 16 of the Law of the People's Republic of China on Keeping Confidentiality of State Secrets defines: the access scope of a state secret shall be minimized according to the work needs.

The access scope of a state secret shall be limited to a specific person. If not, shall be limited to Authority unit, then limited to the person by Authority unit.

If work desired, those who are not in the scope of state secrets shall be approved by the person in charge of the Authority unit.

The above basic definitions and the provisions of the secrecy law shows that the protection of state secrets is obviously different from the protection of general secrets. In order to avoid expanding the access scope, it is necessary to ensure that the state secret shall be limited to the people within the access scope. Expanding the access scope and person who beyond the access scope learn the information will lead to the divulge dangers. Therefore, access scope is a key element of protecting state secrets [17, 18].

4 Comparative Analysis of the Differences Between Chinese and American Confidential Management Mechanisms

China and America have relatively large differences in terms of the confidentiality regulation system, the concept and classification of national secrets, the national secret management system, the confidentiality management system, and the requirements for confidentiality (see Table 1).

Table 1. Comparison of differences between China and America

No.	Comparative items	Nationality	
		America	China
1	Laws of Confidential Management	There is no complete legal system for the protection of national secrets. Seen in fragmented laws (such as the Espionage Act, the Information Disclosure Act, the Atomic Energy Act, etc.), presidential decrees (especially Presidential Decree 13526), multi-level safety-related standards and models	Law of the People's Republic of China on the Protection of National Secrets, Regulations on the Implementation of the Law of the People's Republic of China on the Protection of National Secrets, Information Security Classified Protection, and classified protection-related regulations and standards

(*continued*)

Table 1. (*continued*)

No.	Comparative items	Nationality	
		America	China
2	Principles of Confidential Management	The principle is information disclosure The exception is information confidentiality Emphasis on information disclosure	The secrecy work implements the principle of active prevention, highlighting key points, and administering according to law, which not only ensures the security of national secrets but facilitates the rational use of information resources. It is conducive to information sharing and utilization with emphasis on the premise of ensuring the security of national secrets
3	Broad and Strict	Varies during different periods, related to the president	Keep stable and consistent
4	Definition of National Secrets	There is no unified definition of national secrets. Generally, it can be divided into three categories: 1. National Security Information 2. Atomic energy information 3. Sensitive Compartmented Information (SCI)	The Law of Secrecy clearly stipulates that national secrets are matters that concern national security and interests and are limited known to a certain range of personnel within a certain period of time according to legal procedures
5	Definition of National Secrets	The three categories of national secret information are different. Four levels: 1. National security information: top secret, secret, confidential, non-confidential 2. SCI information: four levels + classification	three levels of classification + knowledge range + period Three levels are top secret, secret, confidential Non-confidential information can be divided into internal information and public information
6	Marking of National Secrets	The confidentiality points should be marked in the documents involving national secrets, and those	Confidential documents are marked as a whole, rather than labeled with specific confidentiality points

(*continued*)

Table 1. (*continued*)

No.	Comparative items	Nationality	
		America	China
		without marking are not national secrets	
7	Secret-Level Setting Management System	Secret-Level Setting Officer	Secret-Level Setting Decider + Secret-Level Setting Procedure
8	Decryption	The period, duration and conditions of confidentiality set by the Secret-Level Setting Officer. The National Decryption Center provides automatic decryption review, system decryption review and discretionary decryption review, as well as decryption application and active decryption	Articles 15 and 19 of The Law of Secrecy stipulate the conditions and time for decryption, as well as self-decryption and pre-decryption. The confidentiality period, confidentiality duration, confidentiality conditions and active decryption shall be prescribed by the Secret-Level Setting Authority or its superior authority
9	Civics Responsibility	Ordinary citizens and institutions shall not be liable for confidentiality	All national organs, armed forces, political parties, social organizations, enterprises, institutions and citizens have the obligation and responsibility to keep secret
10	The Scope of Knowledge Determination & The Regulations of Secret-Related Personnel Knowledgement	For SCI, the "lattice" classification method is adapted to classify and mark information and is also used to implement classification and authorization for those who know it. In the same "lattice" category, high-level personnel is allowed to know the lower-level secrets	National secrets shall be prescribed to be known by a certain range of personnel. The range of personnel shall be limited by means of "work needs and authorization", in other words, national secrets shall be limited known by the specific personnel according to the needs of the work; if it is not limited to specific personnel, it shall be limited to a certain institution or department, and the certain institution or department shall designate specific personnel

(*continued*)

Table 1. (*continued*)

No.	Comparative items	Nationality	
		America	China
11	Information System Security Management	Multi-level Security	Information System Classified Protection (Regulation) Confidential Information System Cascade Protection (Regulation)
12	Adaptive Access Control Mechanism	Lattice-based access control mechanism can basically solve the problem	It may be more desirable to have an access control mechanism based on both the level of confidentiality and the rules of knowledge access

5 Conclusions of Basic Analysis

From the comparison above, we can draw the following basic analysis conclusions:

5.1 Problems in the Multi-level Security Model

Multi-Level Security (MLS) has been proposed by reference [2–4] for more than 40 years, but the current MLS technology, systems and solutions are far from being available. In reference [2, 5, 6], the current information security measures, whether from the perspective of the implementation effect or the formal proof, are considered to be "low security" and cannot meet the need to ensure information security. MLS can handle various security-level information, it allows users of different security levels to access the corresponding information and ensure the security of the information under the premise of controlling the knowledge scope (need to know), preventing the unauthorized users from intentionally or unintentionally accessing. But there are still three types of problems that have not been resolved:

(1) Information release issues from high-security domains to low-security domains. MLS inherits the limitations of the BLP model, which users with high-security levels share the low safety-level information to users with low-security levels is difficult.

(2) Convert channel problem. Reference [19] pointed out that any two-way communication cannot give a formal proof of convert channel elimination. MLS must address the issue of confidentiality when transmitting low safety-level information from high-security domains to low-security domains, at least to prove that there is no convert channel or convert channel has been eliminated when enforcing mandatory access control.

(3) Bypass problem. WikiLeaks is an example, and bypassing, which is usually caused by a hypothetical error, is more harmful than hidden channels. It is very difficult to find the bypass problem, and it is also hard to correct the bypass problem as well as avoid it.

The basic security strategy of the classic multi-level security BLP (Bell-LaPadula) model [5, 6, 20] is the basic principle of current confidential computer security design (including network, information system), which is summarized as "preventing high safety-level information flows to low-security domains" (Information Flow Policy). It is difficult to achieve the goal of multi-level security by relying solely on the BLP model because except the secret level, it has to fulfill another basic security property— the scope that knowledge is known. The general principle of information security and confidentiality [9, 10] includes the "Least Privilege", "Need to Know" and other similar principles. The BLP model does not reflect authorization and access based on the scope that knowledge is known.

The central topic of the security model is always confidential and integrity. The BLP model proposed by Bell and LaPadula [5, 6] mainly solves the control of object confidentiality and prevents information from flowing from high-security level to low-security level, but it lacks integrity control, and cannot effectively limit the converted channel. On the contrary, the Biba model [8] focuses on protecting the integrity of information but lacks confidentiality control. It is difficult to reconcile both for a long time. An important reason for the limitations of the various models mentioned above is that there is no harmonization of confidentiality and integrity on a theoretical basis [21].

The United States uses the Lattice-based method to classify and identify/mark information. The Lattice method is stricter than information classification. It has both grading and classification, and it also implies authorization. DE Denning, Ravi S. Sandhu's Lattice-Based Access Control Models (Lattice Model) [9, 10] introduced the concept of SCI Lattice Security Compartment, which is a formal model of "Safety Level+ the Scope That Knowledge is Known", extending the multi-level security model to the "Multilateral Secure" model. The Lattice model has been promoted and applied in the multi-level security fields in the US and Western countries. This "lattice" authorization is based on a mechanism that simultaneously marks a "Lattice" to information and authorizes personnel the same "Lattice". It is a "total order" permission that allows those who know the high-level information to know low-level information. The "partial order" license is actually the decomposition and refinement of the "total order" license, and it is still "total order" in essence; it does not fully satisfy the actual needs of Chinese information security legal basis and the access control of the secret-involved information cascade protection system.

5.2   Inadaptation of Lattice-Based Method Used in Knowledge Access Control in China

The core idea and mechanism of American "Lattice" classification is classifying and authorizing SCI according to the US law and legal basis. For information, "Lattice" is a classification and identification method; for personnel, it is a license.

(1) SCI is a kind of special information that needs to be shared with domestic and foreign intelligence agencies. The scope of its knowledge is based on the Lattice-based knowledge licensing and restriction system. It is essentially a kind of licensing mechanism that "is based on information classification (sub-classes are partitioned under the general category), categorizes information and knowers, and grants a license to the class". Under this mechanism, it basically allows the high-safety class to know the low-safety information. In conclusion, the total order permission between different levels holds.

(2) The determination of the scope of China's state secrets is a kind of licensing mechanism based on the need for work and authorization, limited to people. There is a big difference between the US SCI's scope that knowledge to be known. Without job requirement, the high-safety class may not be allowed to know the same-level information of other work domains, or even low-level information. Only if the knowledge is required and authorized (i.e., enters the scope of acknowledgement). In this mechanism, the total-order license between US SCI levels does not necessarily hold. In China, we must follow Chinese secrecy laws and regulations, Chinese secrecy legal principles, and determine the knowledge scope according to Chinese laws.

(3) There are huge differences between American SCI management and national secret control methods of China in terms of control limit, demand background, distribution objects and legal basis. Models and methods such as Lattice, BLP, BIBA, and MLS are suitable for the United States, while they are not suitable for Chinese national conditions, and cannot effectively protect the security of national secrets in China, and may even lead to other hidden dangers.

(4) China must explore the access control mechanism of classified information systems accorded with national legal provisions and legal basis. According to laws, regulations and confidentiality standards related to China's classified protection, cascade protection, this mechanism shall be suitable for access control mechanisms based on both flow rules and knowledge access rules.

5.3 The Network Security Control Model Accord with the Legal Principle Foundation of Chinese

The author puts forward a network security control model accord with the legal principle foundation of Chinese to ensure the security protection of confidential information (see Fig. 4).

In order to ensure the confidentiality of secret information, prevention must be carried out. Authorized personnel can access and control confidential information through authentication, authorization, access control and audit technology. The operation of secret information can be traceable and auditable. For any entity carrying secret information on the network, including carriers, platforms, networks and applications, insert security, I/O security, access security and transmission security are guaranteed.

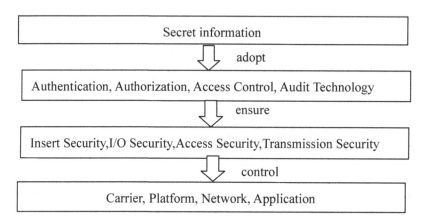

Fig. 4. The network security control model accord with the legal principle foundation of Chinese

6   Conclusion

Information security and confidentiality technologies with the fundamental mission of protecting national secrets in classified information systems must follow the legal basis of China. In order to fully implement the requirements of the classified protection, it is necessary to provide the control environment, control conditions and control basis for accurate access control of confidential information and establish a confidential information access control mechanism and model in accordance with the legal basis of China.

The realization of the precise access control mechanism of secret information not only requires a profound understanding and cognition of the core attributes of secret information, such as the secret level, the access scope, the time limit for secret, and the principle of secret when work is based on scientific secret-level setting, but also needed for the access control mechanism and model to be based on the legal basis of China and the theoretical basis, underlying support with secret-level of various entities, scientific description and expression, effective control mechanism and environmental support with information exchange control system and application system. In engineering implementation, the corresponding expression models and algorithms are also needed.

Acknowledgement. The research was supported by Hainan Provincial Natural Science Foundation (Grant No. 617079).

References

1. The Overview of Foreign Confidentiality Legislation (2009). http://lanxicy.com/read/3933d3c8fdee354b219ee9d6.html
2. Muller, E., Grant, T., Poll, E.: Multi Level Security, 3 1/2 decades later (13th ICCRTS:C2 for Complex Endeavaors)

3. Bell, D.E., LaPadula, L.J.: Secure computer systems: a mathematical model, M74- 244. The MITRE Corporation (1973)
4. Bell, D.E., LaPadula, L.J.: Secure computer system: unified exposition and multics interpretation. The Mitre Corp. (1976)
5. Bell, D.E.: Looking Back at the Bell-La Padula Model Reston VA, 20191, 7 December 2005
6. Bell, D.E.: Looking back at the Bell-LaPadula model. In: ACSAC, pp 337–351. IEEE Computer Society, 7 December 2005
7. Sun, D., Wang, Y., Mao, R.: Standards and implements of foreign electronic documents marking technology. Confidentiality Sci. Technol. (01), 49 (2010)
8. Biba, K.J.: Integrity considerations for secure computer system, ESD-76- 372. PSAF Electronic System Division, Hanscom Air Force Base, Bedford (1977)
9. Denning, D.E.: A lattice model of secure information flow. Commun. ACM **19**(5), 236–243 (1976)
10. Sandhu, R.S.: Lattice-based access control models. Computer **26**(11), 9–19 (1993)
11. Zhong, J.: Special Contact Project – Special Types of the US Secret Management Confidentiality, no. 03 (2015)
12. Mei, M., Tianfu, B.: How Does the US Use the "Safety Marking" to Achieve Confidential Information Sharing. http://www.360doc.com/content/17/0330/13/40745881_641388699. shtml
13. Tianfu, B.: The Threat of the US Signal Intelligence Strategy. http://zhuanlan.51cto.com/art/ 201706/541657.htm
14. Wang, H.: Important military information resources measurement and characteristic signal information. Modern Mil. (07) (2003)
15. Zhang, M.: Measurement feature information and signal subtle feature analysis. Air Force Equipment Res. **4**(004) (2001)
16. Jin, Y.: The US National intelligence agency and its activities. Foreign Mil. Inf. Warfare (04) (2010)
17. Zhou, Q., et al.: Steganography using reversible texture synthesis based on seeded region growing and LSB. CMC: Comput. Mater. Continua **55**(1), 151–163 (2018)
18. Qu, Z., Zhu, T., Wang, J., Wang, X.: A novel quantum stegonagraphy based on brown states. CMC: Comput. Mater. Continua **56**(1), 47–59 (2018)
19. Qing, S.: Covert channel analysis of high security level security operating system. J. Softw. **15**(12), 1837–1849 (2004)
20. Anderson, R., Ning, Q.: Information Security Engineering, 2nd edn, pp. 173–185, 197–200. Tsinghua University Press (2012)
21. Zhou, Z., Liu, Y., Shen, C.: A new unified security strategy for confidentiality and integrity. Comput. Eng. Appl. (34) (2007)

Author Index

Printed in the United States
By Bookmasters